AI-Driven Network Security and Privacy

AI-Driven Network Security and Privacy

Guest Editors

Yu-an Tan
Qikun Zhang
Yuanzhang Li
Xiao Yu

MDPI

Basel • Beijing • Wuhan • Barcelona • Belgrade • Novi Sad • Cluj • Manchester

Guest Editors
Yu-an Tan
School of Cyberspace Science and Technology
Beijing Institute of Technology
Beijing
China

Qikun Zhang
School of Computer and Communication Engineering
Zhengzhou University of Light Industry
Zhengzhou
China

Yuanzhang Li
School of Computer Science and Technology
Beijing Institute of Technology
Beijing
China

Xiao Yu
School of Computer Science and Technology
Shandong University of Technology
Zibo
China

Editorial Office
MDPI AG
Grosspeteranlage 5
4052 Basel, Switzerland

This is a reprint of the Special Issue, published open access by the journal *Electronics* (ISSN 2079-9292), freely accessible at: www.mdpi.com/journal/electronics/special_issues/8914CEJ0XD.

For citation purposes, cite each article independently as indicated on the article page online and using the guide below:

Lastname, A.A.; Lastname, B.B. Article Title. *Journal Name* **Year**, *Volume Number*, Page Range.

ISBN 978-3-7258-3116-6 (Hbk)
ISBN 978-3-7258-3115-9 (PDF)
https://doi.org/10.3390/books978-3-7258-3115-9

Contents

About the Editors vii

Preface ix

Yu-an Tan, Qikun Zhang, Yuanzhang Li and Xiao Yu
AI-Driven Network Security and Privacy
Reprinted from: *Electronics* **2024**, *13*, 2311, https://doi.org/10.3390/electronics13122311 . . . . . **1**

Wenjie Guo, Jingfeng Xue, Wenheng Meng, Weijie Han, Zishu Liu and Yong Wang et al.
MalOSDF: An Opcode Slice-Based Malware Detection Framework Using Active and Ensemble Learning
Reprinted from: *Electronics* **2024**, *13*, 359, https://doi.org/10.3390/electronics13020359 . . . . . . **9**

Zengyu Cai, Hongyu Du, Haoqi Wang, Jianwei Zhang, Yajie Si and Pengrong Li
One-Dimensional Convolutional Wasserstein Generative Adversarial Network Based Intrusion Detection Method for Industrial Control Systems
Reprinted from: *Electronics* **2023**, *12*, 4653, https://doi.org/10.3390/electronics12224653 . . . . . **28**

Jian Lyu, Jingfeng Xue, Weijie Han, Qian Zhang and Yufen Zhu
A Streamlined Framework of Metamorphic Malware Classification via Sampling and Parallel Processing
Reprinted from: *Electronics* **2023**, *12*, 4427, https://doi.org/10.3390/electronics12214427 . . . . . **45**

Yuanping Nie, Shuangshuang Liu, Cheng Qian, Congyi Deng, Xiang Li and Zhi Wang et al.
Multimodel Collaboration to Combat Malicious Domain Fluxing
Reprinted from: *Electronics* **2023**, *12*, 4121, https://doi.org/10.3390/electronics12194121 . . . . . **72**

Gangqiang Duan and Shuai Li
Verifiable and Searchable Symmetric Encryption Scheme Based on the Public Key Cryptosystem
Reprinted from: *Electronics* **2023**, *12*, 3965, https://doi.org/10.3390/electronics12183965 . . . . . **96**

Jiazheng Sun, Li Chen, Chenxiao Xia, Da Zhang, Rong Huang and Zhi Qiu et al.
CANARY: An Adversarial Robustness Evaluation Platform for Deep Learning Models on Image Classification
Reprinted from: *Electronics* **2023**, *12*, 3665, https://doi.org/10.3390/electronics12173665 . . . . . **121**

Shuo Zhang, Fangyu Shen, Yaping Liu, Zhikai Yang and Xinyu Lv
A Novel Traffic Obfuscation Technology for Smart Home
Reprinted from: *Electronics* **2023**, *12*, 3477, https://doi.org/10.3390/electronics12163477 . . . . . **164**

Ga Xiang, Chen Shi and Yangsen Zhang
An APT Event Extraction Method Based on BERT-BiGRU-CRF for APT Attack Detection
Reprinted from: *Electronics* **2023**, *12*, 3349, https://doi.org/10.3390/electronics12153349 . . . . . **188**

Yuzhao Liu, Wan Li, Li Tan, Xiaokai Huang, Hongtao Zhang and Xujie Jiang
DB-YOLOv5: A UAV Object Detection Model Based on Dual Backbone Network for Security Surveillance
Reprinted from: *Electronics* **2023**, *12*, 3296, https://doi.org/10.3390/electronics12153296 . . . . . **203**

Zengyu Cai, Yajie Si, Jianwei Zhang, Liang Zhu, Pengrong Li and Yuan Feng
Industrial Internet Intrusion Detection Based on Res-CNN-SRU
Reprinted from: *Electronics* **2023**, *12*, 3267, https://doi.org/10.3390/electronics12153267 . . . . . **218**

Jingyu Liu, Xiaoqin Fan, Youxi Wu, Yong Zheng and Lu Liu
HoaKV: High-Performance KV Store Based on the Hot-Awareness in Mixed Workloads
Reprinted from: *Electronics* **2023**, *12*, 3227, https://doi.org/10.3390/electronics12153227 . . . . . **235**

Lujuan Deng, Tiantian Yin, Zuhe Li and Qingxia Ge
Sentiment Analysis of Comment Data Based on BERT-ETextCNN-ELSTM
Reprinted from: *Electronics* **2023**, *12*, 2910, https://doi.org/10.3390/electronics12132910 . . . . . **252**

Shaohan Wu, Jingfeng Xue, Yong Wang and Zixiao Kong
Black-Box Evasion Attack Method Based on Confidence Score of Benign Samples
Reprinted from: *Electronics* **2023**, *12*, 2346, https://doi.org/10.3390/electronics12112346 . . . . . **269**

Yi Sun, Jun Zheng, Lingjuan Lyn, Hanyu Zhao, Jiaxing Li and Yunteng Tan et al.
The Same Name Is Not Always the Same: Correlating and Tracing Forgery Methods across Various Deepfake Datasets
Reprinted from: *Electronics* **2023**, *12*, 2353, https://doi.org/10.3390/electronics12112353 . . . . . **286**

Xiaojin Fan, Mengmeng Liao, Lei Chen and Jingjing Hu
Few-Shot Learning for Multi-POSE Face Recognition via Hypergraph De-Deflection and Multi-Task Collaborative Optimization
Reprinted from: *Electronics* **2023**, *12*, 2248, https://doi.org/10.3390/electronics12102248 . . . . . **301**

Lu Liu, Zixuan Xu, Daqing He, Dequan Yang and Hongchen Guo
Local Pixel Attack Based on Sensitive Pixel Location for Remote Sensing Images
Reprinted from: *Electronics* **2023**, *12*, 1987, https://doi.org/10.3390/electronics12091987 . . . . . **325**

Li Tan, Xiaokai Huang, Xinyue Lv, Xujie Jiang and He Liu
Strong Interference UAV Motion Target Tracking Based on Target Consistency Algorithm
Reprinted from: *Electronics* **2023**, *12*, 1773, https://doi.org/10.3390/electronics12081773 . . . . . **344**

Zixiao Kong, Jingfeng Xue, Zhenyan Liu, Yong Wang and Weijie Han
MalDBA: Detection for Query-Based Malware Black-Box Adversarial Attacks
Reprinted from: *Electronics* **2023**, *12*, 1751, https://doi.org/10.3390/electronics12071751 . . . . . **364**

Minghui Li, Jingfeng Xue, Yong Wang, Rui Ma and Wei Huo
NACDA: Naming-Based Access Control and Decentralized Authorization for Secure Many-to-Many Data Sharing
Reprinted from: *Electronics* **2023**, *12*, 1651, https://doi.org/10.3390/electronics12071651 . . . . . **377**

Qikun Zhang, Yuzhi Zhang, Yanling Shao, Mengqi Liu, Jianyong Li and Junling Yuan et al.
Boosting Adversarial Attacks with Nadam Optimizer
Reprinted from: *Electronics* **2023**, *12*, 1464, https://doi.org/10.3390/electronics12061464 . . . . . **396**

Jing Li, Kaixi Wang and Xiaozhu Jia
A Coverless Audio Steganography Based on Generative Adversarial Networks
Reprinted from: *Electronics* **2023**, *12*, 1253, https://doi.org/10.3390/electronics12051253 . . . . . **412**

Shengang Hao, Li Zhang, Kefan Qiu and Zheng Zhang
Conditional Generative Adversarial Network for Monocular Image Depth Map Prediction
Reprinted from: *Electronics* **2023**, *12*, 1189, https://doi.org/10.3390/electronics12051189 . . . . . **434**

Jonghoo Han and Wooguil Pak
High Performance Network Intrusion Detection System Using Two-Stage LSTM and Incremental Created Hybrid Features
Reprinted from: *Electronics* **2023**, *12*, 956, https://doi.org/10.3390/electronics12040956 . . . . . . **452**

About the Editors

Yu-an Tan

Yu-an Tan received his BEng degree in Computer Software in 1991 and his PhD in Computer Science in 2003. He has over 30 years of teaching and research experience and has been a professor at the Beijing Institute of Technology since 2010. He is a senior member of the China Computer Federation. He has contributed to 100+ peer-reviewed journal papers and conference papers, including five papers in the top 1% of Essential Science Indicators. He has received over 20 research funds from the National Natural Science Foundation of China, the National Key Research and Development Program of China, etc. His research areas include artificial intelligence security, cybersecurity, and storage sub-systems.

Qikun Zhang

Qikun Zhang received his BEng degree in Computer Science in 2004 and his PhD in Computer Science in 2013. He has more than 11 years of teaching and research experience and has been a professor at the Zhengzhou University of Light Industry since 2022. He is a member of the China Artificial Intelligence Federation. He has contributed to 50+ peer-reviewed journal papers and conference papers. He has received over 10 research funds from the National Natural Science Foundation of China, the National Key Research and Development Program of China, etc. His research areas include information security, cryptographic protocol, and artificial intelligence security.

Yuanzhang Li

Yuanzhang Li received his BS degree, MS degree, and PhD degree in computer science and technology in 2001, 2004, and 2015 from the Beijing Institute of Technology. He is a senior member of the China Computer Federation. He has contributed to 60+ peer-reviewed journal papers and conference papers. Now, he is an associate professor at the Beijing Institute of Technology. His main research interests focus on AI security and information security.

Xiao Yu

Xiao Yu received his BEng degree in Computer Science and Technology in 2003 and his PhD in Computer Science in 2018. He has more than 20 years of teaching and research experience and has been an associate professor at the Shandong University of Technology since 2019. He is a member of the China Computer Federation. He has contributed to 10+ peer-reviewed journal papers and conference papers. He has received research funds from the National Natural Science Foundation of China, the National Key Research and Development Program of China, etc. His research areas include artificial intelligence security, cybersecurity, and storage sub-systems.

Preface

In recent years, new information technologies and their applications, such as big data, blockchain, and artificial intelligence, have developed very rapidly. At the same time, the application of these new information technologies faces severe challenges in data security, communication security, and privacy protection, such as network attacks, data destruction, the disclosure of private information, etc., which seriously affect the promotion and application of new information technologies. To ensure the security of new information technologies in scenarios such as smart life, smart cities, smart networks, etc., and promote and enhance the development of network security, this Special Issue, named "AI-Driven Network Security and Privacy", is organized. In this Special Issue, new-generation network attacks and defense technology, new secure cryptographic algorithms, data security and privacy protection technology, network and communication security protocol, security analysis, and the evaluation of new application scenarios are discussed. It provides a platform to discuss, exchange insights, and share experiences among researchers, industry specialists, and application developers.

Yu-an Tan, Qikun Zhang, Yuanzhang Li, and Xiao Yu
Guest Editors

electronics

MDPI

Editorial

AI-Driven Network Security and Privacy

Yu-an Tan [1], Qikun Zhang [2,*], Yuanzhang Li [3] and Xiao Yu [4]

1 School of Cyberspace Science and Technology, Beijing Institute of Technology, Beijing 100081, China; tan2008@bit.edu.cn
2 School of Computer and Communication Engineering, Zhengzhou University of Light Industry, Zhengzhou 450002, China
3 School of Computer Science and Technology, Beijing Institute of Technology, Beijing 100081, China; popular@bit.edu.cn
4 School of Computer Science and Technology, Shandong University of Technology, Zibo 255049, China; yuxiao@sdut.edu.cn
* Correspondence: qkzhang@zzuli.edu.cn

1. Introduction

While creating unprecedented opportunities, artificial intelligence is also accompanied by unprecedented risks. Although artificial intelligence has many advantages in network security, it also faces some challenges in the fields of data security, communication security, and privacy protection, including in terms of network attacks, data destruction, and disclosure of private information, which seriously affect the promotion and application of new information technologies. Ensuring that they are implemented securely in scenarios such as smart life, smart cities, and smart networks, as well as promoting and enhancing the development of network security are the goals of this Special Issue of *Electronics*, entitled "AI-Driven Network Security and Privacy".

2. The Present Issue

This Special Issue focuses on new-generation network attack and defense technology, new secure cryptographic algorithms, data security and privacy protection technology, network and communication security protocols, and security analysis, while also evaluating their new application scenarios. In our call for papers, we sought to provide a platform for researchers, industry specialists, and application developers to discuss the most pressing issues in the field, exchange insights, and share experiences. We collected a large number of research results, and through strict and careful selection, 23 papers were selected for publication. We have excerpted and collated the main findings of these articles, which are described below.

Wenjie Guo et al. introduce the opcode slice-based Malware Detection Framework Using Active and Ensemble Learning (MalOSDF) framework, designed to address the need for efficient and rapid feature extraction from malware samples and develop a resilient malware detection engine capable of identifying unknown malware types (contribution 1). Specifically, their work presents an opcode slice-based feature engineering method and a Semi-supervised Ensemble Active Learning (SSEAL) malware detection algorithm. The opcode slice-based feature engineering method conducts semantic aggregation, effectively reducing feature dimensionality. Simultaneously, malicious samples are embedded with semantic information to resolve the issue of sparse features and dimensionality explosion associated with the one-hot encoding of all opcodes. The MalOSDF malware detection method employs the principles of semi-supervised learning and utilizes active learning and ensemble learning techniques. This approach enhances the quality of knowledge extraction and learning for model training while addressing the limitations of classical machine learning models in detecting unknown categories of malware and their vulnerability to noisy data.

Citation: Tan, Y.-a.; Zhang, Q.; Li, Y.; Yu, X. AI-Driven Network Security and Privacy. *Electronics* **2024**, *13*, 2311. https://doi.org/10.3390/electronics13122311

Received: 5 June 2024
Accepted: 6 June 2024
Published: 13 June 2024

Zengyu Cai et al. propose an intrusion detection method for industrial control systems based on a one-dimensional convolutional Wasserstein generative adversarial network (1D CWGAN) (contribution 2). The 1D CWGAN is a network attack sample generation method that combines a 1D convolution neural network (CNN) and a Wasserstein generative adversarial network (WGAN). Firstly, the problem of low industrial control system (ICS) intrusion detection accuracy caused by a few types of attack samples is analyzed. This method balances the number of various attack samples in the dataset in terms of data enhancement to improve detection accuracy. According to the temporal characteristics of network traffic, the algorithm uses 1D convolution and 1D transposed convolution to construct the modeling framework of network traffic data of two competing networks and uses gradient penalty instead of weight cutting in the WGAN to generate virtual samples similar to real samples.

Jian Lyu et al. present a streamlined and efficient framework of malware family classification (MalSEF) (contribution 3) which leverages sampling and parallel processing to efficiently and effectively classify a vast number of metamorphic malware variants. The proposed parallel processing strategy is employed to reduce processing times and ameliorate processing efficiency for feature extraction and feature matrix generation from the entire dataset. By constructing the above lightweight feature set and applying the parallel processing strategy, the time overhead required for classifying large amounts of malware can be efficiently reduced. Finally, the strategy evaluates MalSEF on the Microsoft Kaggle malware dataset and achieves a promising classification accuracy. In addition, the processing time overhead can apparently be reduced compared with the serial processing mode. To this end, the strategy first attenuates the complexity of feature engineering by extracting a small portion of representative samples from the entire dataset and establishing a simple feature vector based on opcode sequences; then, it generates the feature matrix and conducts the classification task in parallel with collaboration utilizing multiple cores and a proactive recommendation scheme. At last, its practicality is strengthened to cope with the large volume of diversified malware variants based on common computing platforms.

Yuanping Nie et al. combined the analysis of artificial features and advanced neural network features to detect Domain Generation Algorithm (DGA) domain names (contribution 4). A total of 34 artificial features related to string structure, language characteristics, and distribution statistics were extracted. Deep neural networks were used to actively mine high-level features of domain name characters. Then, the DGA domain name was detected by combining traditional machine learning methods and deep learning methods. In terms of the multi-model decision-making mechanism, a method based on statistical learning was proposed to provide a fair comparison standard for heterogeneous models and produce decision results with a certain level of confidence through voting. When the prediction labels of all models lacked sufficient confidence, confidence and credibility were considered to comprehensively evaluate the prediction quality of the model, and the prediction result with the highest quality was selected as the final decision result.

Gangqiang Duan et al. propose a verifiable dynamic encryption scheme (v-PADSSE) based on the public key cryptosystem (contribution 6). In order to achieve efficient and correct data updating, the scheme designs verification information (VI) for each keyword and constructs a verification list (VL) to store it. When dynamic update operations are performed on the cloud data, it is easy to quickly update the security index through obtaining the latest verification information in the VL. The paper explores the use of the public key cryptosystem in a dynamic searchable symmetric encryption (DSSE) scheme to verify the correctness and integrity of the result returned by the cloud server and to manage the encryption key effectively and securely.

Jiazheng Sun et al. present the design, implementation, and evaluation of Canary, a platform that aims to answer this question (contribution 6). Canary uses a common scoring framework that includes four dimensions with twenty-six (sub) metrics for evaluation. First, Canary generates and selects valid adversarial examples and collects metrics data through a series of tests. Then, it uses a two-way evaluation strategy to guide the data organization and finally integrates all the data to give scores for model robustness and attack effectiveness. The paper is the first to use Item Response Theory (IRT) in this process to ensure that all the metrics can be fairly calculated into a score that can visually measure the platform's capability. In order to fully demonstrate the effectiveness of Canary, the authors conduct large-scale testing of 15 representative models trained on the ImageNet dataset using 12 white-box attacks and 12 black-box attacks and come up with a series of interesting in-depth findings, further illustrating the capabilities and strengths of Canary as a benchmarking platform. The paper provides an open-source framework for model robustness evaluation, allowing researchers to perform comprehensive and rapid evaluations of models or attack/defense algorithms, thus inspiring further improvements and greatly benefiting future work.

The subsequent contribution to this Special Issue focuses on privacy protection based on traffic obfuscation technology (contribution 7), which is used to obscure the true traffic of smart home devices to prevent malicious traffic listeners from analyzing user privacy information based on traffic characteristics. The paper proposes an enhanced smart home traffic obfuscation method called SHTObfuscator (smart home traffic obfuscator) based on the virtual user technology concept and introduces a virtual user behavior construction method based on logical integrity. By injecting the traffic fingerprints of different device activities into the real traffic environment of smart homes as obfuscating traffic, attackers cannot distinguish between the working status of real devices and the user behavior privacy strategies introduced by the system, effectively reducing the effect of traffic classification attack models. The protection level can be manually or automatically adjusted, achieving a balance between privacy protection and bandwidth overhead.

A novel approach for extracting Advanced Persistent Threat (APT) attack events from web texts is proposed in paper (contribution 8). First, an APT event schema is proposed based on analyzing APT attack stages. Event schemas differ from field to field. For APT events, the correct schema must be defined in order to extract effective information. Secondly, an APT event dataset in Chinese is constructed to train models. Among the many existing event datasets, there is no APT event dataset. Therefore, it is necessary to construct a corresponding dataset to train extraction models. Finally, an APT event extraction method based on the BERT-BiGRU-CRF model is proposed. This offers numerous advantages which are helpful for solving the issues of insufficient attack sample data and low detection accuracy.

Yuzhao Liu et al. propose a dual-backbone network detection method (DB-YOLOv5) for an object detection model that is suitable for unmanned aerial vehicles (UAVs), aiming at the problem of excessively small targets UAV (contribution 9). The model adopts a composite backbone network which connects multiple identical backbone networks in a composite manner and fuses their high-level and low-level features, thus expanding the network's receptive field of. A bidirectional feature pyramid network structure is also introduced in the feature extraction stage and can fuse multi-scale features conveniently, quickly, and effectively to improve the detection accuracy of small-scale targets. The spatial pyramid attention mechanism is used in the output stage and can maintain the feature representation and spatial location information of the target, further strengthening the model's ability to identify and locate small targets. Finally, EIoU_loss is used to further optimize the bounding box of the small-scale target to improve the bounding box problem in small target detection.

A depth feature extraction method for high dimensional network traffic is proposed in paper (contribution 10). The method can extract local features without losing time features and add residual connections, which not only alleviates the problem of gradient disappearance but also improves the convergence speed of the network. It is combined with a parallel algorithm for simplified recurrent unit (SRU) abnormal traffic detection. Compared with the traditional long short-term memory (LSTM) model, the SRU model has the advantages of high computational efficiency, fast training, strong sequence modeling ability, low memory utilization rate, and the ability to train the accuracy of the model faster.

At the same time, the training time required for this method is also greatly shortened, and it can perform efficient intrusion detection on the industrial Internet.

Jingyu Liu et al. propose a dynamic adjustment technology for hot and cold data to achieve high scalability in large key–value (KV) stores (contribution 11). Specifically, they perform timely adjustments to data classification and change the store management method according to the heat of real-time data changes. They introduce a hybrid index method to improve I/O performance and reduce memory overhead. They also implement fine-grained partial KV separation, distinguishing between small and large KV pairs in cold data management to reduce the I/O overhead caused by frequent value movement due to the compression operation of large KV pairs in the log-structured merge-tree. In order to improve reading, writing, and scanning performance, they also propose a dynamic value grouping method to effectively manage large KV pairs.

Lujuan Deng et al. propose a BERT-ETextCNN-ELSTM (bidirectional encoder representations from transformers–enhanced convolution neural network–enhanced long short-term memory) model for sentiment analysis (contribution 12). The model takes text after word embedding and BERT encoder processing and feeds it to an optimized convolutional neural network (CNN) layer for convolution operations in order to extract local features of the text. Features from the CNN layer are then fed into the LSTM layer for time-series modeling to capture long-term dependencies in the text. It uses pretrained models and optimized hybrid (combinatorial, fusion) neural networks for sentiment analysis to effectively address the problem of ignoring contextual semantics in traditional sentiment analysis methods and to better extract semantic information from the corresponding words to achieve an effective sentiment classification of text.

Yi Sun et al. employ a number of models to extract forgery features from various deepfake datasets and utilize the K-means clustering method to identify datasets with similar feature values (contribution 13). They analyze feature values using the Calinski–Harabasz Index method. Their findings reveal that datasets with the same or similar labels in different deepfake datasets exhibit different forgery features. To solve this problem, the authors propose the KCE system, which combines multiple deepfake datasets according to feature similarity, and point out that the forgery category labels in the deepfake dataset lack objectivity. The KCE system is a deepfake dataset similarity evaluation index system that provides a measure of the similarity between different datasets. Its implementation lays the foundation for subsequent researchers, allowing them to use these datasets comprehensively. The authors' experiments confirm that when the forgery method of the deepfake dataset is unknown, the model can achieve better generalization performance by training on datasets that are merged based on closer feature distances.

Shaohan Wu et al. propose a black-box evasion attack method based on the confidence score of benign samples (contribution 14). The method extracts sequence fragments called benign payload from benign samples based on detection results and uses an RNN generative model to learn the benign features embedded in these sequences. Then, it uses the end of the original malicious sample as input to generate an adversarial perturbation that reduces the malicious probability of the sample and appends it to the end of the sample to generate an adversarial sample. According to different adversarial scenarios, the authors propose two different generation strategies, which are the one-time generation method and the iterative generation method.

Xiaojin Fan et al. propose a few-shot, multi-pose face recognition method based on hypergraph de-deflection and multi-task collaborative optimization (HDMCO) (contribution 15). In HDMCO, the hypergraph is embedded in a non-negative image decomposition to obtain images without pose deflection. Furthermore, a feature-encoding method is proposed by considering the importance of samples and combining support vector data description, triangle coding, etc. This feature-encoding method is used to extract features from pose-free images. Finally, multi-tasks such as feature extraction and feature recognition are jointly optimized to obtain a solution closer to the optimal global solution.

Lu Liu et al. take adversarial examples from remote sensing image recognition as their research object and systematically study vanishing attacks against a remote sensing image object detection model (contribution 16). To solve the problem of difficult attack implementation on remote sensing image object detection, they propose an adversarial attack adaptation method based on interpolation scaling and patch perturbation stacking. Their method is an adaptation of classical attack algorithms. A hot restart perturbation update strategy is proposed, and the joint attack of the first and second stages of the two-stage remote sensing object detection model is achieved through the design of the attack loss function. To solve the problem of the excessively high modification cost of global pixel attack, a local pixel attack algorithm based on sensitive pixel location is proposed. By searching for the location of sensitive pixels and constructing a mask of the attack area, a good local pixel attack effect is achieved.

To address the problem of inaccurate target tracking results in aerial unmanned aerial vehicle (UAV) videos due to complex backgrounds, a high density of small-scale targets, and mutual occlusion between targets, Li Tan et al. propose a strong interference motion target tracking method based on the target consistency algorithm for UAVs (contribution 17). An interframe fusion method is introduced in the model to correct its tracking trajectory of the target by fusing the current frame with previous frames. The method successfully updates the model's tracking trajectory by combining the tracking results from the previous frames and learning them again. The model introduces a trajectory confidence mechanism which defines the tracked trajectory's confidence level according to its duration and then corrects and updates the trajectory in multiple directions to ensure the accuracy of the tracking results. It also optimizes the objective function using the alternating direction method of multipliers (ADMM) algorithm and solves the function by iteration to obtain the optimal tracking trajectory.

Zixiao Kong et al. propose a MalDBA (detection for query-based malware black-box adversarial attacks) method for experiments on the VirusShare dataset (contribution 18). MalDBA defends against query-based malware black-box attacks, helping analysts effectively detect the existence of adversarial attacks. It also can be run on ordinary personal workstations and does not require high-performance hardware resources, so it meets the needs of ordinary researchers who deal with a large number of malicious codes. A stateful detection method for black-box adversarial attacks is proposed. Most of the previous detection methods for adversarial examples (AEs) are stateless, and the method introduced by the authors can precisely carry out a supplementary defense. Existing stateful detection methods for malware black-box attacks are based on the feature space level, while the new method is based on the complete malicious file.

In (contribution 19) a naming-based access control model is proposed. The model is based on identity-based encryption with wildcard key derivation (WKD-IBE), which ensures data confidentiality and integrity as well as fine-grained access control for many-to-many communications in named data networks (NDNs). To effectively and securely share resources, the paper introduce a decentralized authorization mechanism which allows data subjects to manage the data and access policies. Furthermore, this mechanism grants permissions in a transparent and auditable manner.

Qikun Zhang et al. propose a Nadam iterative fast gradient method (NAI-FGM), which combines an improved Nadam optimizer with gradient-based iterative attacks (contribution 20). Specifically, they introduce the look-ahead momentum vector and the adaptive learning rate component based on the Momentum Iterative Fast Gradient Sign Method (MI-FGSM). The look-ahead momentum vector is dedicated to making the loss function converge faster and get rid of the poor local maximum. Additionally, the adaptive learning rate component is used to help the adversarial example to converge to a better extreme point by obtaining adaptive update directions according to the current parameters. Furthermore, they also carry out different input transformations to further enhance the attack performance before using NAI-FGM for attack. Finally, they consider attacking the ensemble model. Extensive experiments show that the NAI-FGM has stronger transferability and black-box attack capability than advanced momentum-based iterative attacks.

Jing Li et al. propose a coverless audio-steganography model to conceal secret audio (contribution 21). In this method, the stego-audio is directly synthesized by their model, which is based on the WaveGAN framework. An extractor reconstructs the secret audio and contains resolution blocks to learn the different resolution features. The method does not perform any modification to an existing or generated cover. It is the first directly generated stego-audio concealment method. The authors prove that it is difficult for current steganalysis methods to detect the existence of the secret stego-audio generated by their method because there is no cover audio. The Mean Opinion Score (MOS) metric indicates that the generated stego-audio has high audio quality. Spectrum diagrams in different forms are used to show that the extractor can reconstruct the secret audio successfully on hearing it, which guarantees complete semantic transmission.

Shengang Hao et al. propose and implement an optimized monocular image depth estimation algorithm based on conditional generative adversarial networks (contribution 22). The goal is to overcome the limitations of insufficient data diversity training and overly blurred depth estimation contours in current monocular image depth estimation algorithms based on generative adversarial networks. The proposed algorithm employs an enhanced conditional generative adversarial network model with a generator that adopts a network structure similar to UNet and a novel feature upsampling module. The discriminator uses a multi-layer patchGAN conditional discriminator and incorporates the original depth map as input to effectively utilize prior knowledge. The loss function combines the least squares loss function. Compared to traditional depth estimation algorithms, the proposed optimization algorithm can effectively restore image contour information and enhance the visualization capability of depth prediction maps. The experimental results demonstrate that the method can expedite the convergence of the model on NYU-V2 and Make3D datasets and generate predicted depth maps that contain more details and clearer object contours.

Jonghoo Han et al. propose a novel intrusion detection system (NIDS) that requires low memory storage space and exhibits high detection performance without detection delay (contribution 22). The proposed method directly inputs the received packet data to the classifier without collecting them and stores the output through them. When the next session packet is received, the previously stored output and received new packet are input back to the classifier. Therefore, partial classification is performed every time a packet is received. Further, whenever a new session packet is received, several state values for the session are updated, and a feature set of the machine learning (ML) model is finally created using these values. In addition, instead of using all packets for each session, intrusion detection is performed before session termination because only some packets are used at the beginning of the session, as in the conventional method. The proposed method does not need to store packets for the current session and uses only some packets, as in conventional methods, but achieves very high detection performance.

3. Future Directions

The future of AI-driven network security and privacy is expected to follow several key directions, as outlined by the collection of research articles in this Special Issue. These directions are as follows:

- Secure data sharing: through consensus calculation, the secure exchange of multi-party keys can be completed, leading to the secure sharing of multi-party-encrypted data;
- Privacy protection: through machine learning and model training, the purposes of data classification and identification can be achieved without providing local datasets for training, so as to protect local privacy data from being leaked;
- Threat detection and prevention: by learning and analyzing massive amounts of data, AI can quickly identify potential attacks and provide early warning;

- Intrusion detection and prevention: through deep learning and analysis of network traffic, AI can detect unusual network behavior and react quickly;
- Identification and protection of malicious code: through learning and analyzing malicious code samples, artificial intelligence can automatically extract features and build corresponding models, so as to achieve the accurate identification and effective protection of malicious code;
- Automated attack defense: artificial intelligence can automatically detect and identify abnormal patterns in network traffic to determine whether there is a potential attack behavior in real time;
- Threat intelligence: AI can also be used to gather and analyze cyber threat intelligence. Through large amounts of network traffic data, AI is able to identify the behavior patterns of attackers, which can help predict future attack trends and strategies;
- Automated response and repair: when an attack is detected, AI can quickly isolate the affected system and prevent further spread of the attack. At the same time, AI can also automatically find and repair security vulnerabilities in the system, improving its overall security.

Author Contributions: Conceptualization and formal analysis, Y.-a.T.; Selection and arrangement of study excerpts, Q.Z.; review and editing, Y.L.; supervision, X.Y. All authors have read and agreed to the published version of the manuscript.

Funding: This work was partially supported by the Collaborative Innovation Project of Zhengzhou (No. 2021ZDPY0206).

Data Availability Statement: Not applicable.

Acknowledgments: We would like to thank all the researchers who submitted their papers to this Special Issue. We congratulate the authors of the published papers and thank them for sharing their excellent results through our platform. Our appreciation also goes to the reviewers who carefully, responsibly, and fairly selected excellent papers for this Special Issue and provided valuable review comments for the authors. We acknowledge the Editorial Board of *Electronics* for granting us the opportunity of being this Special Issue's Guest Editors. Lastly, we are grateful to the *Electronics* Editorial Office staff for their strict supervision and responsible management to ensure the timely publication of this Special Issue.

Conflicts of Interest: The authors declare no conflicts of interest.

List of Contributions:

1. Guo, W.; Xue, J.; Meng, W.; Han, W.; Liu, Z.; Wang, Y.; Li, Z. MalOSDF: An Opcode Slice-Based Malware Detection Framework Using Active and Ensemble Learning. *Electronics* **2024**, *13*, 359. https://doi.org/10.3390/electronics13020359.
2. Cai, Z.; Du, H.; Wang, H.; Zhang, J.; Si, Y.; Li, P. One-Dimensional Convolutional Wasserstein Generative Adversarial Network Based Intrusion Detection Method for Industrial Control Systems. *Electronics* **2023**, *12*, 4653. https://doi.org/10.3390/electronics12224653.
3. Lyu, J.; Xue, J.; Han, W.; Zhang, Q.; Zhu, Y. A Streamlined Framework of Metamorphic Malware Classification via Sampling and Parallel Processing. *Electronics* **2023**, *12*, 4427. https://doi.org/10.3390/electronics12214427.
4. Nie, Y.; Liu, S.; Qian, C.; Deng, C.; Li, X.; Wang, Z.; Kuang, X. Multimodel Collaboration to Combat Malicious Domain Fluxing. *Electronics* **2023**, *12*, 4121. https://doi.org/10.3390/electronics12194121.
5. Duan, G.; Li, S. Verifiable and Searchable Symmetric Encryption Scheme Based on the Public Key Cryptosystem. *Electronics* **2023**, *12*, 3965. https://doi.org/10.3390/electronics12183965.
6. Sun, J.; Chen, L.; Xia, C.; Zhang, D.; Huang, R.; Qiu, Z.; Xiong, W.; Zheng, J.; Tan, Y.A. CANARY: An Adversarial Robustness Evaluation Platform for Deep Learning Models on Image Classification. *Electronics* **2023**, *12*, 3665. https://doi.org/10.3390/electronics12173665.
7. Zhang, S.; Shen, F.; Liu, Y.; Yang, Z.; Lv, X. A Novel Traffic Obfuscation Technology for Smart Home. *Electronics* **2023**, *12*, 3477. https://doi.org/10.3390/electronics12163477.
8. Xiang, G.; Shi, C.; Zhang, Y. An APT Event Extraction Method Based on BERT-BiGRU-CRF for APT Attack Detection. *Electronics* **2023**, *12*, 3349. https://doi.org/10.3390/electronics12153349.

9. Liu, Y.; Li, W.; Tan, L.; Huang, X.; Zhang, H.; Jiang, X. DB-YOLOv5: A UAV Object Detection Model Based on Dual Backbone Network for Security Surveillance. *Electronics* **2023**, *12*, 3296. https://doi.org/10.3390/electronics12153296.
10. Cai, Z.; Si, Y.; Zhang, J.; Zhu, L.; Li, P.; Feng, Y. Industrial Internet Intrusion Detection Based on Res-CNN-SRU. *Electronics* **2023**, *12*, 3267. https://doi.org/10.3390/electronics12153267.
11. Liu, J.; Fan, X.; Wu, Y.; Zheng, Y.; Liu, L. HoaKV: High-Performance KV Store Based on the Hot-Awareness in Mixed Workloads. *Electronics* **2023**, *12*, 3227. https://doi.org/10.3390/electronics12153227.
12. Deng, L.; Yin, T.; Li, Z.; Ge, Q. Sentiment Analysis of Comment Data Based on BERT-ETextCNN-ELSTM. *Electronics* **2023**, *12*, 2910. https://doi.org/10.3390/electronics12132910.
13. Sun, Y.; Zheng, J.; Lyn, L.; Zhao, H.; Li, J.; Tan, Y.; Liu, X.; Li, Y. The Same Name Is Not Always the Same: Correlating and Tracing Forgery Methods across Various Deepfake Datasets. *Electronics* **2023**, *12*, 2353. https://doi.org/10.3390/electronics12112353.
14. Wu, S.; Xue, J.; Wang, Y.; Kong, Z. Black-Box Evasion Attack Method Based on Confidence Score of Benign Samples. *Electronics* **2023**, *12*, 2346. https://doi.org/10.3390/electronics12112346.
15. Fan, X.; Liao, M.; Chen, L.; Hu, J. Few-Shot Learning for Multi-POSE Face Recognition via Hypergraph De-Deflection and Multi-Task Collaborative Optimization. *Electronics* **2023**, *12*, 2248. https://doi.org/10.3390/electronics12102248.
16. Liu, L.; Xu, Z.; He, D.; Yang, D.; Guo, H. Local Pixel Attack Based on Sensitive Pixel Location for Remote Sensing Images. *Electronics* **2023**, *12*, 1987. https://doi.org/10.3390/electronics12091987.
17. Tan, L.; Huang, X.; Lv, X.; Jiang, X.; Liu, H. Strong Interference UAV Motion Target Tracking Based on Target Consistency Algorithm. *Electronics* **2023**, *12*, 1773. https://doi.org/10.3390/electronics12081773.
18. Kong, Z.; Xue, J.; Liu, Z.; Wang, Y.; Han, W. MalDBA: Detection for Query-Based Malware Black-Box Adversarial Attacks. *Electronics* **2023**, *12*, 1751. https://doi.org/10.3390/electronics12071751.
19. Li, M.; Xue, J.; Wang, Y.; Ma, R.; Huo, W. NACDA: Naming-Based Access Control and Decentralized Authorization for Secure Many-to-Many Data Sharing. *Electronics* **2023**, *12*, 1651. https://doi.org/10.3390/electronics12071651.
20. Zhang, Q.; Zhang, Y.; Shao, Y.; Liu, M.; Li, J.; Yuan, J.; Wang, R. Boosting Adversarial Attacks with Nadam Optimizer. *Electronics* **2023**, *12*, 1464. https://doi.org/10.3390/electronics12061464.
21. Li, J.; Wang, K.; Jia, X. A Coverless Audio Steganography Based on Generative Adversarial Networks. *Electronics* **2023**, *12*, 1253. https://doi.org/10.3390/electronics12051253.
22. Hao, S.; Zhang, L.; Qiu, K.; Zhang, Z. Conditional Generative Adversarial Network for Monocular Image Depth Map Prediction. *Electronics* **2023**, *12*, 1189. https://doi.org/10.3390/electronics12051189.
23. Han, J.; Pak, W. High Performance Network Intrusion Detection System Using Two-Stage LSTM and Incremental Created Hybrid Features. *Electronics* **2023**, *12*, 956. https://doi.org/10.3390/electronics12040956.

electronics

MDPI

Article

MalOSDF: An Opcode Slice-Based Malware Detection Framework Using Active and Ensemble Learning

Wenjie Guo [1], Jingfeng Xue [1], Wenheng Meng [1], Weijie Han [2], Zishu Liu [1], Yong Wang [1] and Zhongjun Li [1,*]

1 School of Computer Science and Technology, Beijing Institute of Technology, Beijing 100081, China; 3120215536@bit.edu.cn (W.G.); xuejf@bit.edu.cn (J.X.); 3220221066@bit.edu.cn (W.M.); wangyong@bit.edu.cn (Y.W.)
2 School of Space Information, Space Engineering University, Beijing 101416, China
* Correspondence: leezj@bit.edu.cn

Abstract: The evolution of malware poses significant challenges to the security of cyberspace. Machine learning-based approaches have demonstrated significant potential in the field of malware detection. However, such methods are partially limited, such as having tremendous feature space, data inequality, and high cost of labeling. In response to these aforementioned bottlenecks, this paper presents an Opcode Slice-Based Malware Detection Framework Using Active and Ensemble Learning (MalOSDF). Inspired by traditional code slicing technology, this paper proposes a feature engineering method based on opcode slice for malware detection to better capture malware characteristics. To address the challenges of high expert costs and unbalanced sample distribution, this paper proposes the SSEAL (Semi-supervised Ensemble Active Learning) algorithm. Specifically, the semi-supervised learning module reduces data labeling costs, the active learning module enables knowledge mining from informative samples, and the ensemble learning module ensures model reliability. Furthermore, five experiments are conducted using the Kaggle dataset and DataWhale to validate the proposed framework. The experimental results demonstrate that our method effectively represents malware features. Additionally, SSEAL achieves its intended goal by training the model with only 13.4% of available data.

Keywords: malware classification; opcode slice; active learning; ensemble learning

check for updates

Citation: Guo, W.; Xue, J.; Meng, W.; Han, W.; Liu, Z.; Wang, Y.; Li, Z. MalOSDF: An Opcode Slice-Based Malware Detection Framework Using Active and Ensemble Learning. *Electronics* **2024**, *13*, 359. https://doi.org/10.3390/electronics13020359

Academic Editor: Aryya Gangopadhyay

Received: 10 December 2023
Revised: 11 January 2024
Accepted: 12 January 2024
Published: 15 January 2024

1. Introduction

In an era of unprecedented expansion in the digital landscape's gray areas, the proliferation of numerous threats has reached an alarming scale. According to Kaspersky, there has been a 20% increase in detected malware attack attempts, surpassing 74.2 million incidents in 2022 compared to 61.7 million in the previous year. By 2025, it is projected that the total volume of human-generated data will reach a staggering 175 ZB [1]. This surge in data and evolving digital threats underscores the growing significance of network security. The relentless pace of malware evolution, characterized by the continuous emergence of new versions and families, poses a formidable challenge for cybersecurity professionals.

Malware not only adapts to its environment but also enhances its anti-detection capabilities through advanced techniques such as obfuscation, encryption, and shell usage, thereby posing significant challenges for cybersecurity. Traditional methods, including classic virus signature databases and heuristic scanning, have encountered limitations due to their inability to effectively combat malware while exhibiting high false-positive rates. As a result, these methods have struggled to cope with the current state of network security. The evolving threat landscape has prompted the emergence of machine learning as a critical tool in malware detection [2]. Machine learning techniques have proven their ability to analyze known malware samples, extract discriminative features, and accurately classify these samples [3,4].

The essence of effective malware detection lies in feature engineering [5]. Feature engineering aims to extract the intrinsic attributes that are most likely to be used to distinguish malicious software from benign software in PE files, and then generate corresponding digital features for representation. Feature engineering generally includes the analysis, definition, extraction and other steps of features. With accurate feature selection, the detection engine can capture the deep and unique features of malicious software, providing strong support for subsequent malicious code detection. Features typically encompass both static and dynamic attributes. In the real physical world, initiating the dynamic analysis of unknown software can be challenging, rendering static analysis the most immediate and expeditious method for initial assessment. Moreover, from an efficiency perspective, static features remain the industry's preferred choice for detection [6]. While existing static structures such as Data Flow Graphs (DGs) [7], Control Flow Graphs (CFGs) [8], and Function Call Graphs (CGs) [9] can encompass a substantial amount of semantic information, they suffer from significant space consumption. Furthermore, even minor alterations in the source code can result in substantial variations in the extracted graph features [10]. Therefore, the extraction of features from opcodes remains the most common and efficient approach [11].

Machine learning-based methods not only require a large amount of computing resources to train models but also have high data requirements [12]. The distribution of benign and malware samples in the real world exhibits significant imbalances. Simultaneously, the rapid evolution of potential and unknown samples occurs at an extraordinary pace. Despite the existence of platforms such as VirusShare, which provides an extensive repository of malware samples, machine learning-based models for malware code detection may still result in false negatives when they fail to adequately learn the characteristics of malware samples. On the classic Win32 Platform, disassembling malware generates more than 800 different instructions, where there is significant semantic duplication and redundancy among them. Therefore, generating features solely based on all assembly instructions is not the most efficient method. Features corresponding to invalid instructions and redundant instructions can reduce detection efficiency and even lead to overfitting problems. Some existing methods [13] have performed feature selection during feature engineering to reduce dimensionality. However, this practice may result in the loss of some semantic information that could affect the accuracy of the detection results.

Additionally, current malware detection engines [14] demonstrate effective performance in detecting known sample types. However, they face challenges when dealing with emerging families and unknown types of malware. Moreover, the high cost associated with human judgment needs to be considered. Therefore, the current research focus lies in designing a detection model that can accurately operate with minimal known labeled samples. This model should possess the capability to withstand label scarcity and the unequal distribution of types. This challenge limits the effectiveness of existing methods, necessitating the exploration of solutions to overcome this bottleneck.

Why is the opcode slice defined by this work? Firstly, the concept of slicing, referred to as program slicing, was initially proposed by Mark D. Weiser in the 1980s for debugging and modifying source code [15]. With technological advancements, the scope of slicing has gradually expanded from static to dynamic analysis and from forward to backward traversal [16], encompassing a single process to multiple processes and non-distributed to distributed programs. Application scenarios also include software debugging, testing, maintenance, reconstruction, and security purposes [17]. Additionally, classic objects for slicing include data streams, information flows, and dependency graphs [18], which involve handling control flows, composite data types, and pointers. The ability to identify the behavioral points of malware, such as data transfers, process comparisons, flow control, program control, loop control, and other operations, offers malware analysts a clearer understanding of the intent behind the malware. On the other hand, detection engines primarily focus on feature engineering that can extract and quantify the critical behavioral points of each malware.

Despite extensive research on malware detection techniques based on semantic information, researchers continue to face several challenging issues:

- Existing deep learning methods based on opcodes demand embedding all instructions, which can be time consuming. Moreover, the extensive variety of opcodes, some of which lack meaningful semantic information, can protract model construction.
- Malware evolves at a rapid pace, making it challenging to obtain accurate labels for the latest, real-world malware samples. The central research concern revolves around employing a minimal set of labeled samples for effective detection—a pivotal issue for practical engineering applications.
- Current detection engines unavoidably grapple with false positives and false negatives when confronted with previously unknown types of malware. These challenges are intrinsically linked to human expert analysis and judgment. Consequently, it is imperative to consider the associated costs of manual detection.

This paper introduces the MalOSDF framework designed to address the need for efficient and rapid feature extraction from malware samples and develop a resilient malware detection engine capable of identifying unknown malware types. Specifically, this work presents an opcode slice-based feature engineering method and Semi-supervised Ensemble Active Learning (SSEAL) malware detection algorithm. The opcode slice-based feature engineering method conducts semantic aggregation, effectively reducing feature dimensionality. Simultaneously, malicious samples are embedded with semantic information to resolve the issue of sparse features and dimensionality explosion associated with the one-hot encoding of all opcodes [19]. The MalOSDF malware detection method employs the principles of semi-supervised learning, and utilizes active learning and ensemble learning techniques. This approach enhances the quality of knowledge extraction and learning for model training while addressing the limitations of classical machine learning models in detecting unknown categories of malware and their vulnerability to noisy data.

The contributions of this article include the following points:

- In this paper, the opcode slice-based feature engineering method is proposed to reduce dimensions efficiently.
- This work presents the SSEAL approach, which effectively addresses the limitations of having extensive dataset requirements and encourages a more comprehensive exploration of sample knowledge.
- This paper uses the Kaggle dataset for experiments and evaluates the effectiveness of the proposed framework.

The rest of the paper is organized as follows. Section 2 surveys the related work in the field of malware detection. Section 3 describes the framework of MalOSDF. Section 4 evaluates its performance and compares it with similar studies. Section 5 discusses this work. Section 6 concludes our findings in the paper.

2. Related Work

Malware detection can be considered a classic feature engineering process, which includes feature definition, feature extraction, and feature detection [20]. Malware detection methods can be categorized into syntax-based and semantic-based approaches. The semantic-based approach provides stable support for interpretability.

MalInsight [21] is proposed by profiling malware from three aspects, which are the basic structure, low-level behavior, and high-level behavior. And the importance of the three aspects is evaluated and sorted, quantitatively demonstrating that these aspects have the same effects with the optimal feature set. Han et al. proposed MalDAE [22], which correlates and fuses dynamic and static API sequences into one hybrid sequence based on semantics mapping and constructs the hybrid feature vector space. MalDAE gives an understandable explanation for common types of malware and provides predictive support for understanding and resisting malware. Inspired by this method, this work believes that we can focus on selecting opcode with strong maliciousness for slicing.

Huang et al. [23] proposed EAODroid, an approach based on the enhanced API order for Android malware detection, which learns the similarity of system APIs from a large number of API sequences and groups similar APIs into clusters. The extracted API clusters are further used to enhance the original API calls executed by an app to characterize the behaviors and perform classification. The method of clustering similar APIs provides us with inspiration, that is, we can define corresponding slices for similar opcode.

The issue of feature redundancy is addressed by Kong et al. [24] through the utilization of mutual information-based feature selection techniques. This approach effectively reduces over 900 features to 64 dimensions while incorporating sample row and size characteristics, thereby achieving efficient feature detection. However, extensive feature selection based on mutual information consumes a substantial amount of time. Our intuition is to directly extract features from a semantic perspective, which can offer a more rapid and potentially even more interpretable alternative. Therefore, this paper endeavors to define feature slices from a semantic standpoint as the basis for subsequent feature engineering.

In the feature detection phase, machine learning has been widely adopted by numerous scholars as the primary technical approach due to its powerful data mining capabilities [25]. The field of machine learning encompasses various subfields, including supervised learning, unsupervised learning, semi-supervised learning, and reinforcement learning. Both supervised and unsupervised learning require labeled data for model training.

The conventional approach in existing semi-supervised machine learning methods typically involves assigning pseudo-labels to unlabeled data that closely resemble the distribution of existing labeled data. However, this practice may lead to potential model detection failures when confronted with unknown samples. The acquisition of malicious samples varies across different scenarios, resulting in imbalances within the sample distribution. Addressing this challenge is crucial during the model training process, prompting researchers to contemplate effective strategies for training models using an unbalanced and limited amount of malware samples.

Renato et al. [26] proposed an iterative data preprocessing method capable of increasing the separation between clusters. Unlike other methods, it iteratively favors more meaningful features. Wang et al. proposed SIMPLE [27], a few-shot malware classification approach that utilizes a multi-prototype modeling technique to generate multiple prototypes for each malware family, thereby enhancing its generalization capacity based on observations derived from dynamic analysis of API call sequences. Gao et al. proposed MaliCage, a packed malware family classification framework based on DNN and GAN. MaliCage consists of three core modules: a packer detector, a malware classifier, and a packer generative adversarial network (GAN). This method effectively overcomes the bottleneck caused by an insufficient sample size.

Numerous scholars have conducted research in the realm of the cost-effective acquisition of labeled data, employing technical and mathematical methods. This domain is referred to as active learning, which involves human intervention in the labeling process during the training of detection models. Annotated samples contain knowledge that is more amenable to exploration, thereby enhancing the model's capabilities.

The paper argues that samples which can be easily misclassified by existing detection engines actually contain more information that is helpful for improving the accuracy of the detector. In other words, these challenging-to-categorize samples may possess crucial features. If these features can be correctly identified and utilized, they have the potential to enhance the performance of the detector. The work presented in [28] focuses on the anomaly detection domain and introduces an active learning-based approach. The crucial aspect of this study lies in the fact that data points located at the classification boundaries of detection engines are likely to possess a wealth of untapped information, particularly when making determinations about unknown samples. In machine learning models that require extensive training data, accurately labeling these data points holds paramount importance for enhancing the model's detection performance. Consequently, active learning becomes exceptionally vital in such scenarios.

3. Methdology

To tackle the above challenges, this section provides an overview of the MalOSDF framework. Specifically, this paper presents a comprehensive assembly slicing approach to characterize malicious behavior and proposes a feature engineering method for the efficient embedding and optimal utilization of semantic information. Additionally, this section outlines the SSEAL detection algorithm that considers the real-world expert costs associated with addressing threats posed by rapidly malware evolving.

3.1. MalOSDF Overall Architecture

This work introduces a malware detection framework based on opcode slice as depicted in Figure 1. It consists of two main components: the feature engineering method and the SSEAL algorithm. In this section, we provide a brief description for each step as follows:

1. Disassembly: Decompiling binary code.
2. Feature Definition: Based on the semantic analysis of assembly instructions, we customarily define malware opcode slice. Assembly program slicing refers to the statements or expressions in assembly programs that affect specified variables within the sample, leading to the creation of a mapping dictionary.
3. Feature Engineering: Data preprocessing is performed on the samples, and based on predefined opcode slice types, opcode slice sequences are extracted from the assembly programs of malware.
4. Generating Feature Matrices: The statistical features are calculated for each malware sample based on the opcode slice sequences. Specifically, this method counts the occurrences of each slice and N-gram statistically, thereby generating the feature matrix of the set of malware samples.
5. Malware Detection: Using the proposed SSEAL algorithm, a classifier is trained based on the feature vectors of malware samples.

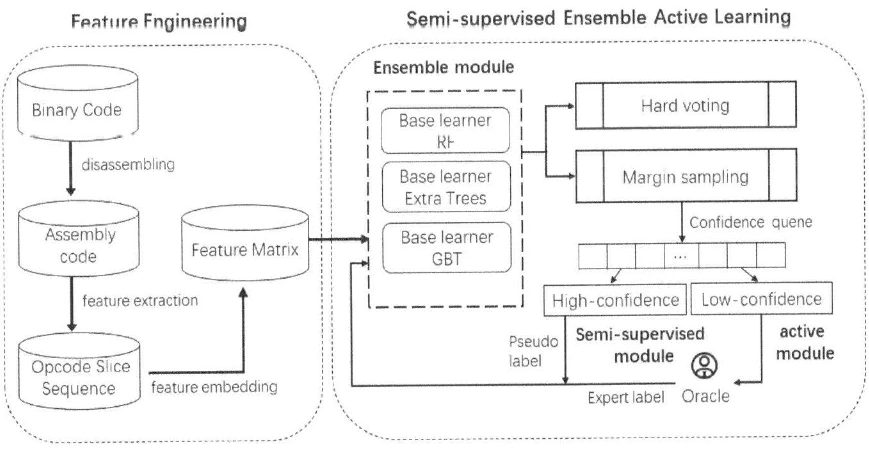

Figure 1. MalOSDF overall architecture.

The classifier utilized for malware detection consists of two key modules, which will be introduced in Section 3.3 in detail. For the Ensemble Learning Module, ensemble classifiers are generated through a hard voting mechanism, including Random Forest (RF), Extra Trees (ET), and Gradient Boosting Trees (GBT). And the Semi-Supervised Active Learning Sample Sampling Module handles the semi-supervised active learning process.

This paper addresses the challenge of managing a large number of features in traditional machine learning-based malware detection. This work proposes a method based on opcode slice construction for generating static features of malware. This approach not only conserves significant computational resources but also reduces the time required for malware detection, thereby providing a robust foundation for efficient detection.

Furthermore, this framework introduces a Semi-supervised Ensemble Active Learning algorithm that not only enhances the efficiency of training multi-class models but also reduces the training time, mitigates the impact of noisy data, tackles the issue of imbalanced sample distribution, and equips the system with the capability to identify unknown family samples of malware.

3.2. Feature Engineering

From the above analysis, this section proposes an opcode slice-based feature engineering method. Specifically, we give the definition of opcode slices and describe the method of features embedding.

3.2.1. Opcode Slice Definition

After disassembling the malware binary file, the assembly instruction is obtained. An assembly instruction generally consists of two parts: the operation code and the operation number. Building upon classical instructions that encompass data transfer, arithmetic operations, logical operations, string operations, program control, input–output operations, processor control, privilege instructions, and system function call instructions, this invention leverages the distinctive semantics of opcode in malware assembly instructions. Furthermore, we explore the inclusion of additional semantic information from the operands associated with opcodes, such as pointers, variable values, function addresses, and memory details, to enhance the feature engineering process.

Specifically, after extracting all the opcodes and operands, we first normalize and standardize the operands according to the method [29] shown in Table 1. (1) Immediate numbers are divided into function call, jump address, reference, and default classes based on their purpose. Calling functions are further classified as standard library function calls, recursive calls, internal calls (within the same file), and external calls (in different files). Jump addresses represent jumps between basic blocks within a function. References distinguish between string references, static variable references (in the program's global data area or static data area), and data references (in the program's data segment or stack). Other immediate numbers are not differentiated. (2) Registers are classified into the following categories: The flag registers, such as control registers, debugging registers, floating-point registers and segment registers, are classified into one class. In the special purpose register, the stack pointer register, base register and instruction pointer register are grouped into one class. Except for the aforementioned registers, all others are classified as general-purpose registers and further differentiated based on the number of bytes they can hold (such as 1 byte, 2 bytes, 4 bytes, 8 bytes, etc). (3) Pointers are divided into direct addressing and indirect addressing based on their addressing method. Direct addressing is further categorized into pointers less than 8 bytes in size and pointers greater than 8 bytes in size. Indirect addressing is divided into string pointers and other pointers according to their pointing object class. The second step is to sort the importance of operation instructions based on TF-IDF (term frequency–inverse document frequency) statistical analysis. Then, semantic analysis is performed on opcodes with a TF-IDF value greater than 1 to obtain the opcode slices. Our work customizes the corresponding opcode slices for frequently occurring opcodes within malware by categorizing 157 commonly appearing assembly instructions into 35 distinct opcode slices as shown in the Table 2.

Table 1. Normalization rules for instruction operands: immediate, register and pointer [29].

Operand	Categories	Normalized Form
Immediate	function call jump address reference default	libc[funcname], self, innerfunc, externfunc jmpdst dispstr, dispbss, dispdata immval
Register	size stack/base/instruction special purpose	reg[1 | 2 | 4 | 8] [s | b | i]p[1 | 2 | 4 | 8] reg[cr | dr | st], reg[c | d | e | f | s]s
Pointer	direct indirect	memptr [base + index×scale + dispstr]

Table 2. Opcode slice definition.

Slice Label	Opcode Contained	Slice Label	Opcode Contained
Data_Transfer	mov, movsx, movzx	Arithmetic_Div	div, idiv
Data_Swap	xchg, xlat, bswap	Logical_Operation	and, or, not, xor
Stack_Operation	push, pop, pusha, pushad, popa, popad	Test	test
Address_Transmission	lea, lds, lss, les, lfs, lgs	Bit_Test	bt, bts, btr, btc
Flag_Transfer_Ah	lahf, sahf	Bit_Scan	bsf, bsr
Flag_Transfer_Stack	pushf, pushfd, popf, popfd	Shift_Operation	shl, shr, sal, sar, rol, ror, rcl, rcr, shld, shrd
Type_Conversions	cbw, cwd, cwde, cdq, bswap	Unconditional_Tran	jmp
String_Operation	movs, movsb, movsw, movsd	Conditional_Tran	jz, jnz, je, jne, js, jns, jo, jno, jp, jpe, jnp, jpo, jc, jnc, jb, jnb, jae, jnae, jl, jnge, jnl, jge, jle, jng, jnle, jg, ja, jnbe, jna, jbe
String_Storage	stos, stosb, stosw, stosd	Conditional_Transfer	jcxz, jecxz
String_Reads	lods, lodsb, lodsw, lodsd	Loop_Control	loop, loopz, loope, loopnz, loopne
String_Comparison	cmps, cmpsb, cmpsw, cmpsd	Call	call
String_Scan	scas, scasb, scasw, scasd	Return	ret
Arithmetic_Add	add, adc, inc	Interrupt	int, iret
Arithmetic_Sub	sub, sbb, dec	Repeat	rep, repe, repz, repne, repnz, irp, irpc
Arithmetic_Neg	neg	Basic_Input_Output	in, out
Compare	cmp	String_Input_Output	ins, ins, insb, insw, insd, outs, outsb, outsb, outsw, outsd
Arithmetic_Mul	mul, imul	Flag	clc, cmc, stc, cld, stc, cli, sti
Processor	nop, hlt, wait	Privilege	sgdt, lsi, invd

3.2.2. The Process of Feature Engineering

Regarding the section on assembly program feature representation, after obtaining the opcode slices, our method computes their statistical features. This involves calculating the N-gram statistical features based on the opcode slices for each malware sample. These features serve as the feature vectors for the assembly program training samples. The specific workflow is shown in Figure 2:

1. Malware samples' disassembled opcodes are sequentially read, and opcode slices are extracted based on predefined opcode slice definitions, ignoring undefined opcodes.
2. The occurrences of opcode slice N-grams are counted and sorted for N = 1, 2, 3.
3. The top-k opcode slices N-grams are selected as features.
4. The N-gram statistical features are computed for each assembly sample, forming individual sample feature vectors.
5. A feature matrix is constructed for the code sample dataset.

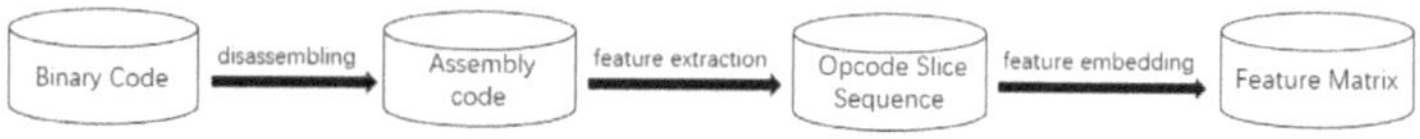

Figure 2. The process of feature engineering.

For example, we can use $s_1 \sim s_m$ to mark assembler training samples.

Define the top-k opcode slice n-gram as follows: $S_i, i \in (1\ n)$. Given the assembler sample s_p of a malware, count the number of Si occurrences as $N_{p,i}$. Then, the feature vector of sample s_p is defined as Equation (1), where $label_p$ is the label of the assembler sample $malware_p$:

$$\vec{F}_{pj} = \{\ N_{p,1} \quad \cdots \quad N_{p,i} \quad \cdots \quad N_{p,n} \quad label_p\ \} \tag{1}$$

Defining the feature matrix as a collection of feature vectors, then the feature matrix for p assembly program samples is shown as Equation (2):

$$FM = \begin{Bmatrix} N_{1,1} & \cdots & N_{1,i} & \cdots & N_{1,n} & label_1 \\ N_{p,1} & \cdots & N_{p,i} & \cdots & N_{p,n} & label_p \\ N_{m,1} & \cdots & N_{m,i} & \cdots & N_{m,n} & label_m \end{Bmatrix} \tag{2}$$

The various dimensions (columns) of N in the figure above represent the frequency of corresponding slice types. Subsequently, we can use the feature matrix FM derived from the assembly program samples to train the subsequent detection engine.

3.3. *Semi-supervised Ensemble Active Learning*

One of the challenges that semi-supervised learning algorithms need to address is the introduction of a significant amount of noisy samples during the training process, which can hinder the model from learning the correct information. SSEAL alleviates the issue of noisy samples by employing a collaborative training algorithm for multiple classifiers, which is an ensemble learning approach.

Active learning methods enable a more efficient identification of samples that contain valuable information within the dataset. Expert queries also equip the model with the capability to detect unknown samples. It is important to note that, for the purpose of analysis, we assume that all labels provided by experts are reliable.

This algorithm includes the following modules in sequence.

1. Ensemble Learning Module
   The integrated learning module includes multiple base learners. In this method, three base learners are designed, namely RF, Extra Trees, and GBT. Each sample is inputted to different base learners to obtain the probabilities of the test samples belonging to different categories. Simultaneously, the detection results of each base learner are outputted, and the final results of the test samples are obtained by hard voting from the three base learners.
   Let us delve deeper into the three base learners involved. Each of these base learners possesses unique characteristics and operating mechanisms, collectively forming the framework of our integrated learning module (Figure 3).

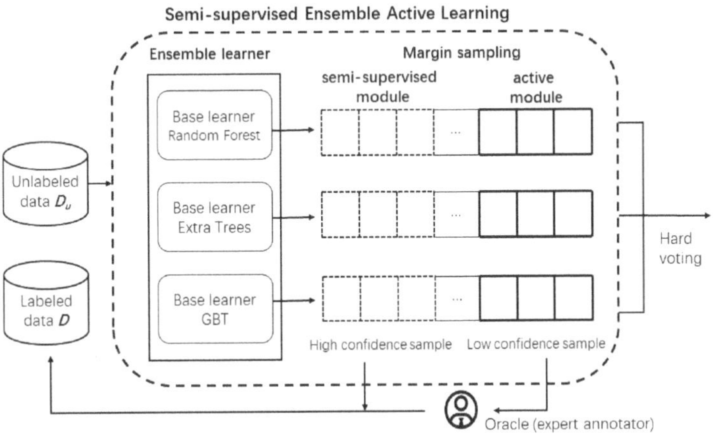

Figure 3. The process of feature engineering.

Random Forest (RF): Random Forest is an ensemble learning method that operates by constructing a multitude of decision trees at training time and outputting the class that is the mode of the classes (classification) or mean prediction (regression) of the individual trees. It enhances the performance of a single decision tree by introducing randomness in the feature selection and bootstrap sampling, thereby improving robustness and generalization.

Extra Trees (ET): Extra Trees, or Extremely Randomized Trees, is another ensemble learning method that builds multiple decision trees and combines their predictions. Similar to Random Forest, it introduces randomness in the feature selection process, but Extra Trees takes it a step further by using random thresholds for each feature rather than searching for the best split points. This additional randomness can lead to increased diversity among the trees and potentially better generalization.

Gradient Boosting Trees (GBT): Gradient Boosting is an ensemble technique where weak learners (typically shallow decision trees) are combined to create a strong learner. GBT builds trees sequentially, with each tree correcting the errors made by the previous ones. It minimizes a loss function by adding weak learners, which allows it to capture complex relationships in the data and achieve high predictive accuracy. Gradient Boosting Trees are particularly effective in handling diverse and non-linear patterns in the data.

2. Semi-supervised active learning module

The integrated learning module calculates the detection confidence value for each sample by determining the probability that it belongs to different categories as output by the three classifiers. Samples with high and low confidence levels are marked according to preset screening criteria, which will be described in detail below. The active learning component transfers low-confidence samples to an expert marker, who inputs labeled codes into the tagged dataset. In the semi-supervised learning part, firstly, count the maximum value Num_max of different types of samples in the labeled sample set. Then obtain the corresponding pseudo tags for these high-confidence samples and calculate the difference Num_aug between this category and Num_max. Finally, select the high-confidence samples with the maximum Num_aug from this category to add them to the labeled dataset.

Uncertainty sampling involves the extraction of samples that are challenging for the model to distinguish, which are then provided for expert annotation. These hard-to-distinguish samples contain valuable knowledge that can significantly enhance algorithmic detection. The key here is quantifying the model's difficulty in differentiation. Classic approaches include least confident, margin sampling, and entropy methods. Margin sampling selects samples that are almost equally likely to be classified into two categories, meaning the difference in the model's probabilities for these data points is minimal. Specifically, margin sampling chooses samples with the smallest difference between the highest and second-highest predicted probabilities. In the context of multi-class malware detection in this paper, margin sampling is found to be more effective for model training.

The newly added dataset with tags needs to be removed from the original test set, which is the unlabeled set. Then, it should be re-entered into Module 1 to update the model until reaching the specified number of iterations or when the overall tag ratio reaches the threshold. At that point, the loop stops, and we obtain the final training model and classification results.

The overall algorithm is shown in Algorithm 1.

Algorithm 1: Semi-supervised Ensemble Active Learning (SSEAL).

Input: unlabeled data D_u, labeled data D, classifiers *RF,Extra Trees and GBT*, confidence threshold θ.
Output: trained models *RF,Extra Trees,GBT*.

// *Ensemble learning*
foreach x_i *in* D_u **do**
    $prob_{rf} \leftarrow RF(x_i)$
    $prob_{et} \leftarrow ExtraTrees(x_i)$
    $prob_{gbt} \leftarrow GBT(x_i)$
end
pseudo label $pl_i \leftarrow$ vote$(prob_{rf}, prob_{et}, prob_{gbt})$
// *Semi-supervised active sampling*
foreach x_i *in* D_u **do**
    $conf_rf \leftarrow RF(x_i)$
    $conf_et \leftarrow ExtraTrees(x_i)$
    $conf_gbt \leftarrow GBT(x_i)$
    if *conf*<θ **then**
        // *Active learning*
        get expert label el_i
        add <x_i, el_i> to data *Temp*
        add data *Temp* to labeled data D
        remove data *Temp* from unlabeled data D_u
    else
        // *Semi-supervised Learning*
        $num_{max} \leftarrow max(num_{(class_1)}, num_{(class_2)}, \ldots, num_{(class_n)})$
        if $num(pl_i) < num_{max}$ **then**
            add <x_i, pl_i> to data *Temp*
            add data *Temp* to labeled data D
            remove data *Temp* from unlabeled data D_u
        else
        end
    end
end

In particular, each base learner outputs the probability of classification results for each sample. Then, the edge sampling margin sampling is carried out to calculate the probability difference between the largest and second categories. It is called reliability, shown in the following formula:

$$Conf_x = margin(x) = P_{y_1} - P_{y_2} \tag{3}$$

The classifier has a low confidence in the sample, which indicates that the sample contains more mining knowledge and is more useful for model training. Then, we select M samples with a mining value in turn as shown in the following formula:

$$x_M^* = \operatorname{argmin}_x(P_\theta(\hat{y}_1 \mid x) - P_\theta(\hat{y}_2 \mid x)) \tag{4}$$

The algorithm utilizes the pool-based active learning method. Pool-based active learning allows for labeling by experts, enabling the algorithm framework to identify unknown samples. Specifically, the tested sample queues are sorted from high to low to obtain a confidence queue. Experts are then contacted to manually label samples with low confidence levels. Samples with higher reliability can be used to enrich and balance datasets. The classification results of all classifiers are unified, that is, the confidence level is high, and pseudo tags are directly added. After the newly obtained pseudo-label sample is selected, it is initially qualified to be added to the training set. However, the sample selection strategy also needs to consider the sample equilibrium situation. This algorithm sets that if the malware sample type already occupies the largest distribution, it will not be added to the training set.

The above measures make the training dataset of the model balanced and enable the model to obtain the ability to resist noise data.

4. Experiment and Analysis

In this section, we provide details about the experiments conducted to evaluate the proposed method for disassembling binary code and its application in malware detection. We start by introducing the dataset used in the experiments and then proceed to discuss the experimental setup.

4.1. Dataset

To disassemble binary code, this work employs IDA Pro 6.4 for the disassembly of binary source files. This paper uses Microsoft's Kaggle dataset [30] and Intel's DataWhale dataset for experiments. The distribution of various types in the dataset is shown in the following Table 3.

Table 3. Distribution of samples in experimental dataset Kaggle.

Family	Kaggle	DataWhale
1 (Ramnit)	1541	385
2 (Lollipop)	2478	598
3 (Kelihos_ver3)	2942	784
4 (Vundo)	475	6641
5 (Simda)	42	5676
6 (Tracur)	751	7563
7 (Kelihos_ver1)	398	7560
8 (Obfuscator.ACY)	1228	11,368
9 (Gatak)	1013	9425
Total	10,868	50,000

4.2. Experiment Setup

4.2.1. Experimental Environment

The runtime environment of the experiment is (1) Intel(R) Core(TM) i7-10870H CPU @ 2.20 GHz, 16 GB memory, (2) Ubuntu 18.04 (64 bit).

4.2.2. Experimental Design

In order to verify the effectiveness of the proposed method, we designed experiments to verify the effectiveness of the proposed feature engineering and SSEAL. Specifically, the following five types of experiments are designed in this paper. Reducing the cost of data labeling is one of the core focuses of our research. Therefore, out of a total of over 10,000 samples, we select only 100 labeled samples as initial data. The model obtains 50 semi-supervised learning samples and 50 active learning samples, respectively, in each iteration as supplements to the training set.

(1) To demonstrate that feature engineering can effectively reflect the characteristics of different malicious code families, we compare the performance of traditional machine learning methods using features of varying dimensions.
(2) To verify that SSEAL is more robust than a single classifier, we compare SSEAL with a single classifier. This work observes an accuracy trend of SSEAL and single classifiers as the number of iterations increases. The single classifiers includes Random Forest, GBT and Extra Trees. There is no difference in the sampling strategy between SSEAL and base classifiers except that the base classifier only uses its own queue to filter low-confidence samples and high-confidence samples.
(3) To verify the effect of SSEAL under different dimensional features, we compare SSEAL algorithms in different N-gram dimensions.
(4) To verify the ability of SSEAL to detect unknown malicious samples, this paper observes its performance on unknown malware that was not included in the initial labeled dataset.
(5) To verify the ability of SSEAL to detect unbalanced malware datasets, this study compared the performance of SSEAL with different numbers of labeled samples for the initial training. We set 50, 100, and 200 samples in the initial labeled sample set, and each experiment performed 20 iterations with 50 samples queried in each iteration to evaluate the performance of SSEAL by observing the accuracy of the model in each iteration.

4.3. Results and Analysis

4.3.1. Comparison of Machine Learning Methods Across Varying Feature Dimensions

In order to evaluate the feature engineering method proposed in this paper, this paper adopts classifiers such as Random Forest, decision tree, nearest neighbor classification and extreme gradient lifting tree to carry out the experiments. The results of the classification detection based on traditional classifiers are shown in Table 4.

Table 4. Detection results of traditional classifiers.

		Random Forest	Decision Tree	KNN	XGBoost
Kaggle	Accuracy	97.93%	96.23%	96.04%	97.38%
	precision	97.38%	94.32%	95.93%	95.19%
	Recall	93.12%	91.52%	91.39%	91.43%
	F1 score	97.59%	92.52%	92.96%	92.69%
DataWhale	Accuracy	98.11%	97.28%	96.19%	97.13%
	precision	97.70%	94.81%	93.06%	92.74%
	Recall	94.34%	94.06%	90.58%	91.55%
	F1 score	95.36%	94.02%	91.39%	92.38%

As shown in Table 4, the accuracy of using the Random Forest classification algorithm is relatively higher, and the experimental results show that 97.93% accuracy can be obtained based on 37-dimensional feature vectors.

Further, in order to prove whether this feature engineering method has space for further optimization, this paper further selects top-k (k = 37, 21, 15) dimension slice features for classification according to the occurrence frequency of these features. The experimental results are shown in Table 5.

Table 5. Classification results of different dimension of opcode slice features.

Feature Dimension	Metric	Random Forest	Decision Tree	KNN	XGBoost
N = 37	Accuracy	97.93%	96.23%	96.04%	97.38%
	Precision	97.38%	94.32%	95.93%	95.19%
	Recall	93.12%	91.52%	91.39%	91.43%
	F1 Score	94.59%	92.52%	92.96%	92.69%
N = 21	Accuracy	97.79%	96.55%	96.04%	97.33%
	Precision	97.22%	95.77%	95.93%	96.62%
	Recall	93.07%	91.84%	91.39%	91.27%
	F1 Score	94.47%	93.10%	92.96%	92.89%
N = 15	Accuracy	97.47%	95.63%	96.14%	97.06%
	Precision	97.03%	92.42%	96.03%	96.40%
	Recall	92.81%	91.02%	91.47%	92.49%
	F1 Score	94.25%	91.47%	93.04%	93.77%

The experimental results demonstrate that the Random Forest algorithm still achieves higher detection rates, and the impact is not significantly reduced when reducing the slice dimension. The accuracy rate reaches 97.79% when selecting 21-dimensional slice features and 97.47% when selecting 15-dimensional slice features.

This experiment proves that by only selecting key opcode slice features with richer semantics, the desired classification effect can be achieved.

It can be observed that the feature engineering designed in this paper yields superior results compared to other methods, as it saves time for feature preprocessing and training while also reducing the space complexity.

4.3.2. Comparison between SSEAL and Single Classifiers

In this experiment, SSEAL is compared with single classifiers with the BSS strategy to show the impact of ensemble classifiers. Figure 4 shows that the accuracy of SSEAL is higher than other single classifiers. When the iteration rounds 20 times, the accuracy of the approaches gradually becomes stable, and the accuracy of SSEAL is slightly higher than the other approaches; when the iteration round is less than 20, SSEAL has better performance than the other approaches in most iterations.

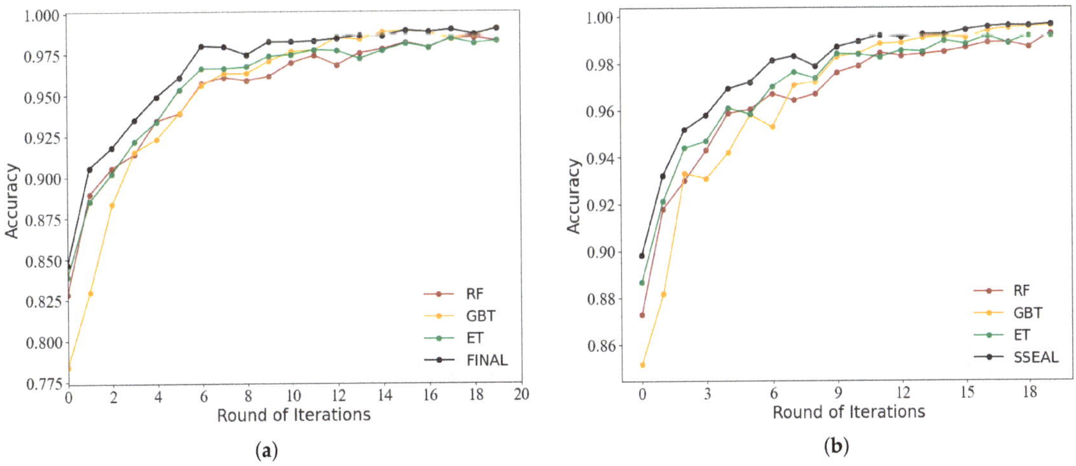

Figure 4. Comparison between SSEAL and single classifier. (**a**) Kaggle, (**b**) DataWhale.

Our advantage is that we use a small part of the data. The total sample size is 10,212, but our initial data size is 100, and after 20 iterations, we use a total of 1098 samples, which accounts for 1098/8169 = 13.4% of the unlabeled data, and our work still achieves over 99 percent accuracy.

4.3.3. Comparison of SSEAL Algorithms in Different Feature Dimensions

In this experiment, we compared the effect of SSEAL algorithm using different feature dimensions. Figure 5 shows the running results of the 956-dimensional feature (left) and the 4250-dimensional feature (right), which take 7 min 25 s and 13 min 54 s, respectively. Although the final accuracy of using the 956-dimensional characteristic matrix is slightly lower than the result of the 4250-dimensional one, it still reaches 98.9%. On the basis of maintaining high accuracy, the model with low feature dimension converges faster and takes less training time, showing excellent performance.

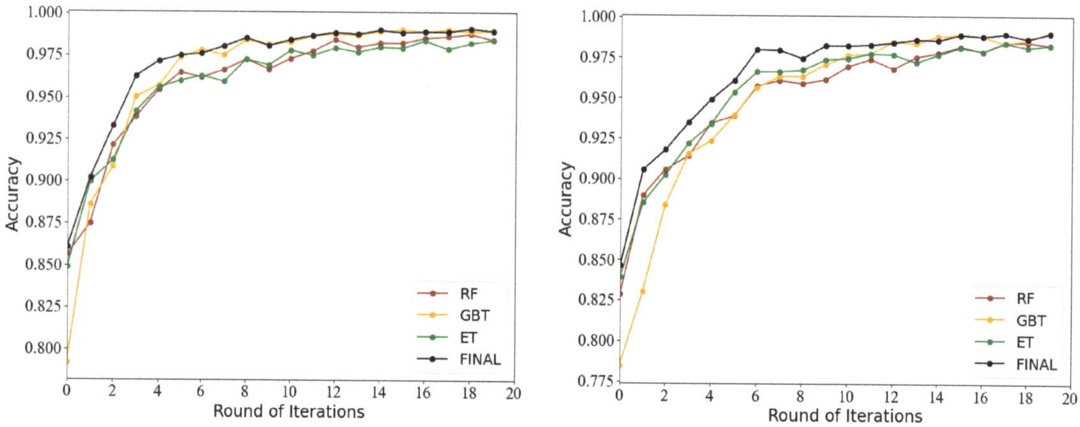

(a) (b)

Figure 5. Comparison of SSEAL algorithms in different feature dimensions. (**a**) 956-dimension, (**b**) 4250-dimension.

4.3.4. Evaluation of SSEAL to Detect Unknown Malware

In this experiment, the ability of SSEAL to detect unknown malware is evaluated. As shown in Figure 6, SSEAL can achieve a good detection effect on the samples with a relatively large proportion. The detected F1-score gradually converges to 1. For malware of the fourth and sixth categories, which have very few samples, SSEAL can quickly filter out these rare attack samples. The detection rate of the fifth category samples is completely undetected in the beginning, but it can be found in the sixth round. As the iterations increase, the detection ability of SSEAL for this malware improves rapidly.

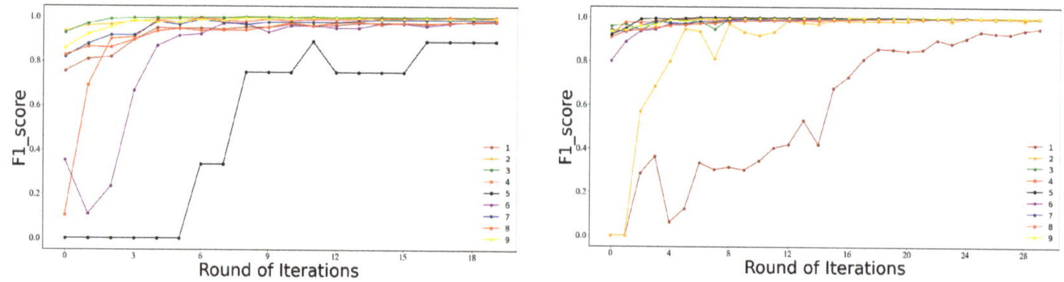

(a) (b)

Figure 6. F1 scores of nine families. (**a**) Kaggle, (**b**) DataWhale.

Figure 7 shows the distribution of different types of samples input to the model in each round after using the sample selection equalizer. It can be seen that the nine types of samples basically meet the equilibrium conditions and can provide a good training environment for the sample to resist noise data.

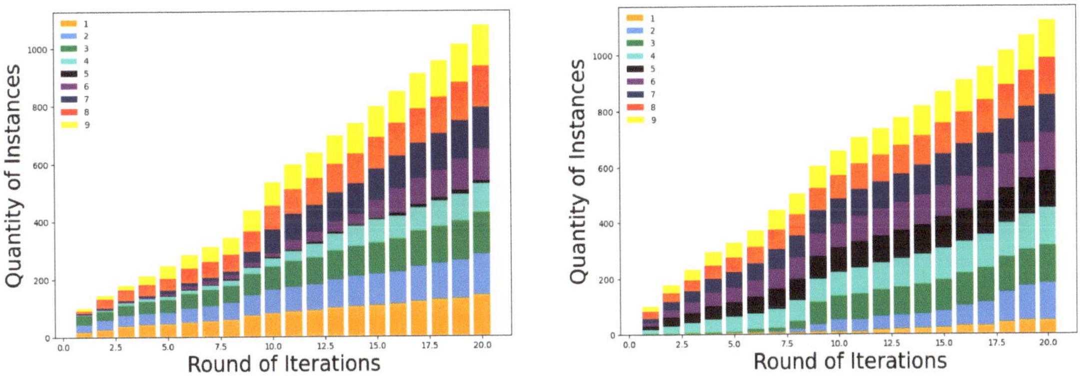

(**a**) (**b**)

Figure 7. Sample distribution of different categories. (**a**) Kaggle, (**b**) DataWhale.

4.3.5. Evaluation of SSEAL with Different Samples in Pre-Training

This experiment evaluates the influence of the pre-training dataset to SSEAL. This work pre-trains SSEAL with 20, 50, and 100 labeled samples, and records the accuracy of SSEAL in each iteration. As shown in Figure 8, the influence of the pre-training data to SSEAL is obvious. When there are fewer pre-training samples, the initial accuracy of SSEAL is lower.

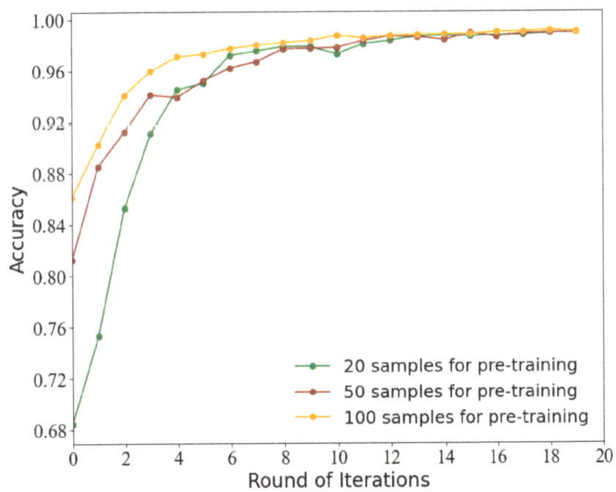

Figure 8. Accuracy of different pre-training sample sizes.

When the pre-training samples are 20, the initial accuracy of SSEAL is only below 70%, but when the pre-training samples are 100, the accuracy can reach 86%. As the number of iterations increases, the detection capability of SSEAL is rapidly improved, and the advantage of using more labeled samples in the pre-training is no longer reflected. After 14 iterations, the 20-sample pre-trained model catches up with the 100-sample pretrained model in terms of performance.

4.3.6. Comparison with Similar Studies

In this section, we compared our method with other studies using the same dataset or similar algorithms, from the aspects of accuracy, features, time consumption and occupied space. The comparison results are shown in Table 6, where "-" means unstated.

Table 6. Comparison with similar studies.

	This Work	**All Opcode**	**Ahmadi et al.** [31]	**Kong et al.** [24]	**Raff et al.** [32]	**Le et al.** [33]
Dataset	"Kaggle" from Microsoft Malware Classification Challenge					
Selected Feature	Opcode Slice	Opcode	Hex dump-based features + Features extracted from disassembled files	Mutual information method based Top-18 opcodes	Entire malware as embedded input	Entire malware as embedded input
Dimension of feature	35	737	1804	18	-	10,000
Classification accuracy (%)	97.93	98.80	99.77	98.60	97.80	98.20
Time consumption of feature engineering (s)	3059.41	5889.16	183,477	5907.27	-	-
Time consumption of model training (s)	-	-	-	-	32,087.4	6372
Time consumption of model classification (s)	2.38	24.92	15	7.76	804.65	214.32
Occupied space (KB)	1223	15,120	-	1043	-	-

In addition, [34] utilized ensemble learning and achieved high accuracy. However, this work extracted information from different sections of PE and converted it into images, and then used multiple CNN models as base classifiers, resulting in a longer training time than ours. In contrast to [35], this work builds four static feature comprehensive description PE files, including API and dll, which will consume more feature processing time. The proposed feature engineering method based on opcode slice in this paper achieves the optimal compromise between efficiency and classification accuracy. The length of the feature vector constructed by our method is 35, and the classification accuracy is 97.93%. On the one hand, although the classification accuracy is slightly lower than that of similar studies [24,33], it can meet the detection requirements. On the other hand, the feature processing time in this paper is the shortest [32,36], which means that this method can provide promising classification results under the condition of reducing the complexity of feature engineering.

Above all, the method proposed in this paper has a main advantage: our work can effectively reduce the time and space occupation of model training and classification while retaining high accuracy.

5. Discussion

As we reflect on the findings and implications of our proposed method, it is essential to recognize both its strengths and limitations. In this discussion, we address some of the key considerations related to the limitations, scalability, and ethical implications of our approach.

5.1. Limitations of Our Work

Not limited to the same malware family, functional similarities of opcode slice may also exist between benign samples and malicious samples, which will lead to the detection of false negatives. In addition, there are some cases where the training data are unbalanced due to the small sample size. For example, the Simda family in the Kaggle dataset is sensitive to the detection results due to its relatively small data, which leads to false positives.

Another limitation of our study is that the high-information samples are manually labeled, which is assumed to always be correct. However, experts may mislabel some samples in practical applications so that mislabeled high-information samples may be added into the labeled training set. In this context, a more sophisticated study should be conducted on how to avoid the impact of manually mislabeled samples on the detection model.

5.2. Scalability of Our Work

We think this method has good scalability in practical application. When implementing the framework in the real world, our opcode slicing method only needs to make a simple substitution based on semantic analysis, which can support the subsequent feature engineering. As for adaptability to evolving malware techniques, some malware will pack itself to escape the disassembly tool, which will destroy the foundation of the slicing operation, thus affecting the final detection result. Therefore, we need to detect whether the malware is packed first.

5.3. Ethical Implications and Considerations

Due to concerns related to data leakage, enterprises or individuals may be hesitant to provide raw samples, making it challenging for many research methods to be widely applied. The privacy protection issues associated with original or feature data of malicious code need to be addressed [37]. In response to this situation, the introduction of federated learning techniques [38] can be considered. This approach facilitates the training process without the need for users to transmit their training data models directly. As a result, the entire training procedure can be conducted without compromising the privacy of user data.

6. Conclusions and Future Work

Our work proposes an Opcode Slice-Based Malware Detection Framework Using Active and Ensemble Learning in order to address the rapid evolution of malicious code, the high cost of manual annotation, and the unbalanced distribution of different families. Specifically, it introduces a feature engineering method based on opcode slice and a SSEAL detection algorithm for malware classification. The experiments conducted in this paper are based on the Kaggle dataset and DataWhale. The feature engineering method utilizing opcode slice is proven effective in extracting behavioral characteristics from malware samples, laying the foundation for efficient classification. SSEAL has demonstrated its ability to reduce data labeling costs, extract more knowledge from samples, and exhibit higher reliability compared to single classifiers.

After conducting research in this paper, we have the intuition that further work can be conducted as follows: we will try to put forward a solution for the problem of insufficient datasets caused by sample imbalance. In addition, we will combine more semantic information, such as API, to improve the robustness of our system.

Author Contributions: Conceptualization, W.G. and W.H.; methodology, W.G. and W.M.; software, W.M.; validation, W.G.; formal analysis, W.M.; investigation, J.X., Y.W. and Z.L. (Zhongjun Li); data curation, Z.L. (Zishu Liu); writing—original draft preparation, W.G. and W.H.; writing—review and editing, W.M.; supervision, J.X.; project administration, J.X.; funding acquisition, J.X. All authors have read and agreed to the published version of the manuscript.

Funding: This work was supported by Major Scientific and Technological Innovation Projects of Shandong Province (2020CXGC010116) and the National Natural Science Foundation of China (No. 62172042).

Data Availability Statement: The data used to validate the outcomes of this investigation can be obtained by contacting the corresponding author.

Conflicts of Interest: The authors declare no conflict of interest.

References

1. Kaspersky Cyber Security Solutions for Home and Business | Kaspersky. Available online: https://usa.kaspersky.com/ (accessed on 10 November 2023).
2. Hu, Y.; Wang, S.; Li, W.; Peng, J.; Wu, Y.; Zou, D.; Jin, H. Interpreters for GNN-Based Vulnerability Detection: Are We There Yet? In Proceedings of the 32nd ACM SIGSOFT International Symposium on Software Testing and Analysis, Seattle, WA, USA, 18–20 July 2023; pp. 1407–1419.
3. Li, H.; Cheng, Z.; Wu, B.; Yuan, L.; Gao, C.; Yuan, W.; Luo, X. Black-box Adversarial Example Attack towards FCG Based Android Malware Detection under Incomplete Feature Information. *arXiv* **2023**, arXiv:2303.08509.
4. Hu, P.; Liang, R.; Cao, Y.; Chen, K.; Zhang, R. {AURC}: Detecting Errors in Program Code and Documentation. In Proceedings of the 32nd USENIX Security Symposium (USENIX Security 23), Anaheim, CA, USA, 9–11 August 2023; pp. 1415–1432.
5. Ye, Y.; Li, T.; Adjeroh, D.; Iyengar, S.S. A survey on malware detection using data mining techniques. *ACM Comput. Surv. (CSUR)* **2017**, *50*, 1–40. [CrossRef]
6. Chow, Y.W.; Schäfer, M.; Pradel, M. Beware of the unexpected: Bimodal taint analysis. *arXiv* **2023**, arXiv:2301.10545.
7. Gollapudi, R.T.; Yuksek, G.; Demicco, D.; Cole, M.; Kothari, G.; Kulkarni, R.; Zhang, X.; Ghose, K.; Prakash, A.; Umrigar, Z. Control flow and pointer integrity enforcement in a secure tagged architecture. In Proceedings of the 2023 IEEE Symposium on Security and Privacy (SP), San Francisco, CA, USA, 21–25 May 2023; pp. 2974–2989.
8. Wu, X.; Guo, W.; Yan, J.; Coskun, B.; Xing, X. From Grim Reality to Practical Solution: Malware Classification in Real-World Noise. In Proceedings of the 2023 IEEE Symposium on Security and Privacy (SP), San Francisco, CA, USA, 22–24 May 2023; pp. 2602–2619.
9. Yang, L.; Chen, Z.; Cortellazzi, J.; Pendlebury, F.; Tu, K.; Pierazzi, F.; Cavallaro, L.; Wang, G. Jigsaw puzzle: Selective backdoor attack to subvert malware classifiers. In Proceedings of the 2023 IEEE Symposium on Security and Privacy (SP), San Francisco, CA, USA, 21–25 May 2023; pp. 719–736.
10. Patrick-Evans, J.; Dannehl, M.; Kinder, J. XFL: Naming Functions in Binaries with Extreme Multi-label Learning. In Proceedings of the 2023 IEEE Symposium on Security and Privacy (SP), San Francisco, CA, USA, 21–25 May 2023; pp. 2375–2390.
11. Luo, Z.; Wang, P.; Wang, B.; Tang, Y.; Xie, W.; Zhou, X.; Liu, D.; Lu, K. VulHawk: Cross-architecture Vulnerability Detection with Entropy-based Binary Code Search. In Proceedings of the NDSS, San Diego, CA, USA, 27 February–3 March 2023.
12. Ucci, D.; Aniello, L.; Baldoni, R. Survey of machine learning techniques for malware analysis. *Comput. Secur.* **2019**, *81*, 123–147. [CrossRef]
13. Cui, L.; Cui, J.; Ji, Y.; Hao, Z.; Li, L.; Ding, Z. API2Vec: Learning Representations of API Sequences for Malware Detection. In Proceedings of the 32nd ACM SIGSOFT International Symposium on Software Testing and Analysis, Seattle, WA, USA, 18–20 July 2023; pp. 261–273.
14. Lucas, K.; Pai, S.; Lin, W.; Bauer, L.; Reiter, M.K.; Sharif, M. Adversarial Training for {Raw-Binary} Malware Classifiers. In Proceedings of the 32nd USENIX Security Symposium (USENIX Security 23), Anaheim, CA, USA, 9–11 August 2023; pp. 1163–1180.
15. Weiser, M. Programmers use slices when debugging. *Commun. ACM* **1982**, *25*, 446–452. [CrossRef]
16. Horwitz, S.; Reps, T.; Binkley, D. Interprocedural slicing using dependence graphs. *ACM Trans. Program. Lang. Syst. (TOPLAS)* **1990**, *12*, 26–60. [CrossRef]
17. Xu, B.; Qian, J.; Zhang, X.; Wu, Z.; Chen, L. A brief survey of program slicing. *ACM SIGSOFT Softw. Eng. Notes* **2005**, *30*, 1–36. [CrossRef]
18. Ottenstein, K.J.; Ottenstein, L.M. The program dependence graph in a software development environment. *ACM Sigplan Not.* **1984**, *19*, 177–184. [CrossRef]
19. Lee, Y.; Kwon, H.; Choi, S.H.; Lim, S.H.; Baek, S.H.; Park, K.W. Instruction2vec: Efficient Preprocessor of Assembly Code to Detect Software Weakness with CNN. *Appl. Sci.* **2019**, *9*, 4086. [CrossRef]
20. Haq, I.U.; Caballero, J. A Survey of Binary Code Similarity. *ACM Comput. Surv.* **2021**, *54*, 1–38. [CrossRef]
21. Han, W.; Xue, J.; Wang, Y.; Liu, Z.; Kong, Z. MalInsight: A systematic profiling based malware detection framework. *J. Netw. Comput. Appl.* **2019**, *125*, 236–250. [CrossRef]
22. Han, W.; Xue, J.; Wang, Y.; Huang, L.; Kong, Z.; Mao, L. MalDAE: Detecting and explaining malware based on correlation and fusion of static and dynamic characteristics. *Comput. Secur.* **2019**, *83*, 208–233. [CrossRef]
23. Huang, L.; Xue, J.; Wang, Y.; Qu, D.; Chen, J.; Zhang, N.; Zhang, L. EAODroid: Android Malware Detection Based on Enhanced API Order. *Chin. J. Electron.* **2023**, *32*, 1169. [CrossRef]
24. Kong, Z.; Xue, J.; Wang, Y.; Zhang, Q.; Han, W.; Zhu, Y. MalFSM: Feature Subset Selection Method for Malware Family Classification. *Chin. J. Electron.* **2023**, *32*, 26–38. [CrossRef]
25. Alrabaee, S. A stratified approach to function fingerprinting in program binaries using diverse features. *Expert Syst. Appl.* **2022**, *193*, 116384. [CrossRef]
26. Cordeiro de Amorim, R.; Lopez Ruiz, C.D. Identifying meaningful clusters in malware data. *Expert Syst. Appl.* **2021**, *177*, 114971. [CrossRef]
27. Wang, P.; Tang, Z.; Wang, J. A novel few-shot malware classification approach for unknown family recognition with multi-prototype modeling. *Comput. Secur.* **2021**, *106*, 102273. [CrossRef]

28. Niu, Z.; Guo, W.; Xue, J.; Wang, Y.; Kong, Z.; Huang, L. A novel anomaly detection approach based on ensemble semi-supervised active learning (ADESSA). *Comput. Secur.* **2023**, *129*, 103190. [CrossRef]
29. Koo, H.; Park, S.; Choi, D.; Kim, T. Semantic-aware binary code representation with bert. *arXiv* **2021**, arXiv:2106.05478.
30. Panconesi, A.; Marian; Cukiersk, W.; WWW BIG-Cup Committee. Microsoft Malware Classification Challenge (BIG 2015). *Kaggle*. 2015. Available online: https://kaggle.com/competitions/malware-classification (accessed on 10 November 2023).
31. Ahmadi, M.; Ulyanov, D.; Semenov, S.; Trofimov, M.; Giacinto, G. Novel feature extraction, selection and fusion for effective malware family classification. In Proceedings of the Sixth ACM Conference on Data and Application Security and Privacy, New Orleans, LA, USA, 9–11 March 2016; pp. 183–194.
32. Raff, E.; Nicholas, C. Malware classification and class imbalance via stochastic hashed lzjd. In Proceedings of the 10th ACM Workshop on Artificial Intelligence and Security, Dallas, TX, USA, 3 November 2017; pp. 111–120.
33. Le, Q.; Boydell, O.; Mac Namee, B.; Scanlon, M. Deep learning at the shallow end: Malware classification for non-domain experts. *Digit. Investig.* **2018**, *26*, S118–S126. [CrossRef]
34. Niu, W.; Cao, R.; Zhang, X.; Ding, K.; Zhang, K.; Li, T. OpCode-level function call graph based android malware classification using deep learning. *Sensors* **2020**, *20*, 3645. [CrossRef]
35. Soni, H.; Kishore, P.; Mohapatra, D.P. Opcode and API based machine learning framework for malware classification. In Proceedings of the 2022 2nd International Conference on Intelligent Technologies (CONIT), Hubli, India, 24–26 June 2022; pp. 1–7.
36. Santos, I.; Brezo, F.; Ugarte-Pedrero, X.; Bringas, P.G. Opcode sequences as representation of executables for data-mining-based unknown malware detection. *Inf. Sci.* **2013**, *231*, 64–82. [CrossRef]
37. Dara, S.; Zargar, S.T.; Muralidhara, V.N. Towards privacy preserving threat intelligence. *J. Inf. Secur. Appl.* **2018**, *38*, 28–39. [CrossRef]
38. Lyu, L.; Yu, H.; Ma, X.; Chen, C.; Sun, L.; Zhao, J.; Yang, Q.; Philip, S.Y. Privacy and robustness in federated learning: Attacks and defenses. *IEEE Trans. Neural Netw. Learn. Syst.* **2022**. [CrossRef] [PubMed]

electronics

MDPI

Article

One-Dimensional Convolutional Wasserstein Generative Adversarial Network Based Intrusion Detection Method for Industrial Control Systems

Zengyu Cai [1], Hongyu Du [2], Haoqi Wang [3], Jianwei Zhang [4,*], Yajie Si [1] and Pengrong Li [1]

1 School of Computer and Communication Engineering, Zhengzhou University of Light Industry, Zhengzhou 450001, China; czy@zzuli.edu.cn (Z.C.); 332107020571@email.zzuli.edu.cn (Y.S.); 332207030629@email.zzuli.edu.cn (P.L.)
2 School of Informatics, Xiamen University, Xiamen 361005, China; duhongyu@stu.xmu.edu.cn
3 School of Mechanical and Electrical Engineering, Zhengzhou University of Light Industry, Zhengzhou 430002, China; haoqiwang0218@zzuli.edu.cn
4 School of Software Engineering, Zhengzhou University of Light Industry, Zhengzhou 450003, China
* Correspondence: ing@zzuli.edu.cn

Abstract: The imbalance between normal and attack samples in the industrial control systems (ICSs) network environment leads to the low recognition rate of the intrusion detection model for a few abnormal samples when classifying. Since traditional machine learning methods can no longer meet the needs of increasingly complex networks, many researchers use deep learning to replace traditional machine learning methods. However, when a large amount of unbalanced data is used for training, the detection performance of deep learning decreases significantly. This paper proposes an intrusion detection method for industrial control systems based on a 1D CWGAN. The 1D CWGAN is a network attack sample generation method that combines 1D CNN and WGAN. Firstly, the problem of low ICS intrusion detection accuracy caused by a few types of attack samples is analyzed. This method balances the number of various attack samples in the data set from the aspect of data enhancement to improve detection accuracy. According to the temporal characteristics of network traffic, the algorithm uses 1D convolution and 1D transposed convolution to construct the modeling framework of network traffic data of two competing networks and uses gradient penalty instead of weight cutting in the Wasserstein Generative Adversarial Network (WGAN) to generate virtual samples similar to real samples. After a large number of data sets are used for verification, the experimental results show that the method improves the classification performance of the CNN and BiSRU. For the CNN, after data balancing, the accuracy rate is increased by 0.75%, and the accuracy, recall rate and F1 are improved. Compared with the BiSRU without data processing, the accuracy of the s1D CWGAN-BiSRU is increased by 1.34%, and the accuracy, recall and F1 are increased by 7.2%, 3.46% and 5.29%.

Keywords: intrusion detection; industrial control systems; Wasserstein generative adversarial network

check for updates

Citation: Cai, Z.; Du, H.; Wang, H.; Zhang, J.; Si, Y.; Li, P. One-Dimensional Convolutional Wasserstein Generative Adversarial Network Based Intrusion Detection Method for Industrial Control Systems. *Electronics* **2023**, *12*, 4653. https://doi.org/10.3390/electronics12224653

Academic Editor: Hamid Reza Karimi

Received: 13 October 2023
Revised: 13 November 2023
Accepted: 13 November 2023
Published: 15 November 2023

1. Introduction

The traditional industrial control system (ICS) is in a physical environment completely isolated from the external network, and its operating system requires a dedicated communication protocol [1]. Most existing ICSs, such as building energy management systems (EMSs), had only physical threats in the past. With the continuous integration of information technology (IT) and ICSs, the integration process of industrialization and informatization is accelerating, and potential ICS network security problems are gradually exposed. ICSs are now usually connected to a communication network, so they can be accessed remotely. The inherent connectivity in these services makes such systems face network security risks. And this expands the attack surface, including the possibility of complex cyber attacks, which may adversely affect ICS operations, resulting in service outages, equipment damage, security issues and related financial impacts.

Intrusion detection can take the initiative to monitor network traffic and host equipment and find and prevent network attacks. In the ICS network environment, the imbalance between normal samples and attack samples leads to a low recognition rate of intrusion detection models for a small number of abnormal samples in the classification. The industrial control intrusion detection model pays special attention to the detection success rate of abnormal samples. With the development of artificial intelligence technology, machine learning is more and more widely used in ICS intrusion detection. Although the traditional machine learning method is simple and the training time is short, the detection accuracy is relatively low. In addition, complex data preprocessing and artificial feature extraction are required before processing these industrial control data, which requires rich experience and a lot of practice. The deep learning method can avoid complex data preprocessing and identify attack-type data with high precision [2–5].

Researchers [6] have demonstrated that deep learning algorithms are more accurate than traditional machine learning algorithms. However, when a large amount of unbalanced data is used for training, the detection performance of deep learning decreases significantly. The imbalance of traffic data of ICSs is the main factor, and generative adversarial networks (GANs) have become a research hotspot for enhancing a few types of data. However, GANs have the problems of unstable training, disappearing gradient and mode collapse. In view of the shortcomings of GANs, WGANs make the training of the model more stable and reduce the occurrence of mode collapse by introducing the Wasserstein distance. At the same time, WGANs can generate more samples by optimizing the Wasserstein distance. In general, WGANs are improved on the basis of GANs, which improve the stability of training and the diversity of generated samples and alleviate the problem of gradient disappearance.

Aiming at the imbalance of ICS traffic data, this paper proposes a network attack sample generation method, 1D CWGAN, which integrates 1D CNN and WGAN. The algorithm uses 1D convolution and 1D transposed convolution to construct two competitive network traffic data modeling frameworks and uses gradient penalty instead of weight pruning in the WGAN to improve the stability of model training. Finally, a convolutional neural network (CNN) and bidirectional simple recurrent unit (BiSRU) are used to verify the 1D CWGAN model on the enhanced data set.

2. Related Work

In this section, we introduce related work, including intrusion detection methods based on machine learning and deep learning ICSs.

2.1. Intrusion Detection Method Based on Machine Learning

There are many classical machine learning methods, including support vector machine (SVM) [7], decision tree [8] and naive Bayes [9]. Anton et al. [10] used SVM to detect seven different classes of attacks in the gas pipeline of the standard industrial data set. Although a high accuracy rate was achieved, the precision rate was low. Al-Asiri et al. [11] used the gas pipeline of the standard industrial data set to verify the effectiveness of the decision tree classifier for various features in the SCADA system using an IDS with a single network metric and physical metric. Khan et al. [12] used the original features from the gas pipeline data set to formulate a new set of features for attack detection using naive Bayes in supervised learning mode. Tian et al. [13] proposed a method that combines machine learning optimized by a swarm intelligence algorithm and deep learning. They used a stack autoencoder to reduce the dimension of data feature and then combined SVM and an artificial bee colony algorithm to perform an intrusion detection experiment. Although machine-learning-based methods have achieved good results in recent years, they can only perform shallow learning and cannot accurately identify network attacks in ICSs [14].

For example, SVM instead leads to a decrease in accuracy when the number of samples increases, naive Bayes methods do not handle data with correlated attributes well and decision tree has poor generalization capabilities [15,16].

2.2. Intrusion Detection Method Based on Deep Learning

With the increasing computing power of computers, deep learning methods are rapidly emerging in various fields, especially in image detection and speech recognition [17]. At the same time, this has led many scholars in the direction of industrial Internet security to apply deep learning to intrusion detection of ICSs. Yang et al. [18] proposed a CNN for intrusion detection systems (IDSs). Liu et al. [19] proposed a hybrid method of deep learning and population intelligence optimization algorithms. They used a CNN for feature extraction and anomaly recognition; then, the features extracted by the CNN model were invoked as input to the algorithm to construct a normal state process transfer model. RNNs are widely used as temporal deep learning models for intrusion detection of ICSs. The IDSs provide an effective method of abnormal traffic detection. Yin Let al. [20] proposed an IDS based on the RNN-IDS algorithm. The method was validated using the NSL_KDD data set, and the results showed that it outperformed traditional machine learning methods. LSTM is a variant of SimpleRNN, and it alleviates the problem of gradient vanishing and gradient explosion of SimpleRNN to a certain extent. Roy et al. [21] proposed an Internet of Things (IoT) intrusion detection method based on a bidirectional long short-term memory recurrent neural network (BLSTM RNN) to improve the problem of insufficient SimpleRNN temporal storage capacity. Sokolov et al. [22] used GRU for experiments on intrusion detection in the gas pipeline data set and investigated the applicability of the method in various aspects of intrusion detection of ICSs. In 2018, Lei et al. proposed an SRU model [23]. The model used a simpler structure to solve the sequence dependence problem in previous LSTM and GRU models, further alleviating the problem of RNN gradient vanishing and gradient explosion and enabling parallel computation. SRU has been successfully applied in the field of classification and conversational systems.

Researchers have proved that deep learning algorithms are more accurate than traditional machine learning algorithms. However, when training with a large amount of imbalanced data, the detection performance of deep learning decreases significantly. The imbalance of ICS traffic data is the main factor, and GANs have become a research hotspot for enhancing several types of data. However, GANs have problems such as unstable training, gradient disappearance and model collapse. This paper proposes an ICS traffic data detection model based on a CNN and BiSRU. The CNN can effectively extract the spatial features of traffic data, and the BiSRU can effectively learn the forward and backward time series features of ICSs. At the same time, one-dimensional convolution and one-dimensional transposed convolution are used to establish discriminator D and generator G, which is conducive to the establishment of the network model and the better simulation of data distribution of the ICS network traffic. The WGAN with gradient penalty (GP) can effectively solve the problem of model collapse during training. This study has conducted sufficient experiments on multiple data sets to verify our proposed method.

3. ICS Intrusion Detection Method Based on 1D CWGAN

In this paper, 1D convolution and 1D transposed convolution are used to build discriminator D and generator G, which is conducive to the network model to better simulate the data distribution of the ICS network traffic. The WGAN with gradient penalty (GP) can effectively solve the problem of model collapse during training. The detection models of the ICS traffic data based on a CNN and BiSRU are proposed, respectively.

3.1. Overview of GAN

A GAN is a powerful neural network for unsupervised learning, first developed and introduced in 2014. A GAN is a system composed of two competing neural network models that compete with each other and can analyze, capture and replicate changes in the data set [24]. In a GAN, there is a generator and a discriminator. The generator generates false data samples and tries to deceive the discriminator. On the other hand, the discriminator attempts to distinguish between true and false samples. Both the generator and the discriminator are neural networks. The generator network needs to continuously optimize the data generated by itself so that the discriminator network cannot judge. The discriminator network also needs to optimize itself to make its judgment more accurate. The relationship between the two forms a confrontation, so it is called a confrontation network. They compete with each other in the training phase and repeat these steps. In this process, the generator and discriminator become better and better in their respective work after each game.

3.1.1. Generator

The generator G is responsible for learning the real distribution of the sample. The function of the generator is similar to that of the autoencoder. The random vector z is sampled from the prior distribution, and the generated sample G (z) is obtained by generating the network parameterized distribution. From the input and output level, the function of the generator is to convert the hidden vector z into the sample vector x through the neural network.

3.1.2. Discriminator

The discriminator is similar to the ordinary binary classification network. It accepts the data set of the input sample x, including the samples sampled from the real data distribution, and also includes the false samples sampled from the generated network, which together form the discriminator training data set [25]. The discriminator output is the probability P belonging to the real sample, the labels of all real samples are labeled as true, and the samples generated by all generators are labeled as false.

3.1.3. Network Training

The training process is a process of the generator and discriminator game. The generator generates false data and then inputs both the generated false data and the true data into the discriminator, which determines what is true and what is false. The discriminator must have a large error for the first time, and then the discriminator is optimized according to the error. As the discriminator level increases, it is difficult to deceive the discriminator again with the data generated by the generator, so the optimization of the generator continues. As the generator level increases, in turn, it continues to train the discriminator, so that the cycle is repeated until Nash equilibrium is reached.

The training of the GAN first trains D and then trains G in the first round. It is not necessary to wait for all of the D training to start training G, because the training of D also requires the output value of G in the previous round as the input. In the first stage, only discriminant model D is involved. The sample in the training set is used as the input of D, and a certain value between 0 and 1 is output. The larger the value, the greater the possibility that the sample is real data. In this process, we hope that D can make the output value close to 1 as much as possible. In the second stage, both the discriminant model D and the generation model G are involved. First, the noise z is input into G, G learns the probability distribution from the real data set and generates false samples, and then inputs the false samples into the discriminant model D. This time, D will enter the value 0 as much as possible. Therefore, in this process, the discriminant model D is equivalent to a binary classifier, and the data are either classified as 1 or 0. The result of the last two model games is that G can generate false data G (z). However, it is difficult for D to determine whether the data generated by G are true, that is, D (G (z)) = 0.5.

3.2. Data Enhancement Method Based on 1D CWGAN

In order to solve the problem of unbalanced data set samples caused by the small number of attack samples, this chapter proposes a 1D CWGAN algorithm to generate virtual samples to balance the number of samples in various data sets. Aiming at the temporal characteristics of network traffic, the algorithm uses 1D convolution and 1D transposed convolution to construct two network traffic data modeling frameworks of competitive networks and uses the gradient penalty in the WGAN instead of weight clipping to improve the stability of model training. Finally, a CNN and BiSRU are used to verify the 1D CWGAN model of the enhanced data set. The ICS intrusion detection data enhancement model based on 1D CWGAN is shown in Figure 1.

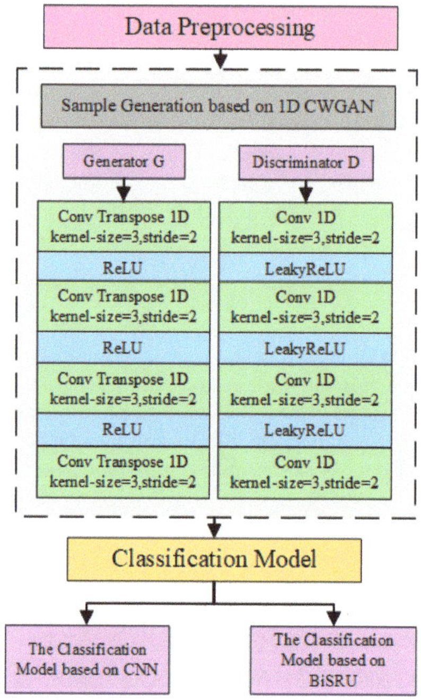

Figure 1. Schematic diagram of the 1D-CWGAN-based intrusion detection model framework.

3.3. *Description of Intrusion Detection Algorithm Based on 1D CWGAN*

Using the generative adversarial network to learn the data distribution of the ICS network traffic data, a virtual sample similar to the real sample is generated. The confrontation process needs to train the generator G and the discriminator D at the same time. For serial data like the network traffic of ICSs, this paper uses 1D convolution and 1D transposed convolution to construct a modeling framework for network traffic data for two competing networks. The generator model generates synthetic data examples with similar distribution to the real sample data by random Gaussian noise; the discriminator model is used to distinguish whether the generated synthetic data are real or not. In the process of the game between the two models, the generator model generates samples to deceive the discriminator model as much as possible, and the discriminator model avoids this deception as much as possible. Finally, generator G and discriminator D will be in Nash equilibrium. The objective function is written in the form of a minimum–maximum game:

$$\min_{D}\max_{G} V(D, G) = E_{x\sim p_r}[\log D(x)] + E_{z\sim p_g}[\log(1 - D(G(z)))] \quad (1)$$

where x is the real data, p_r is the probability distribution of the real data, z is the input noise of the generator, p_g is the distribution of the generated data G(z) and D(x) is the output of the discriminator network. The objective function in (1) is essentially to minimize the

Jensen–Shannon (JS) dispersion between the real data distribution and the virtual data distribution under the premise that the discriminator D is optimal.

Arjovsky et al. [26] theoretically analyzed that the JS dispersion is not suitable for measuring the distance between disjoint parts of the distribution and used the Wasserstein distance to measure the distance between the generated distribution and the real data distribution, providing meaningful gradient information to solve the problem of instability of GAN training data and model collapse. Although the training stability of the WGAN is further enhanced than that of the original GAN, the WGAN uses Lipschitz weight pruning to limit the parameters of the discriminator model to a certain range during training, which makes the network parameters tend to be unreasonable extreme values and weakens the fitting ability of the neural network. When the pruning range approaches the limit, it also re-causes the phenomenon of gradient explosion. Therefore, this paper introduces the gradient penalty (GP) term, which improves the Lipschitz continuity constraint and uses the gradient penalty instead of weight clipping in the WGAN to improve the stability of model training. The loss function of the 1D CGAN with the introduction of the GP term is shown in Equation (2):

$$L = E_{G(z)\sim P_g}[D(G(z))] - E_{x\sim P_r}[D(x)] + \varphi E_{\hat{x}\sim P_{\hat{x}}}\left[(\|\nabla_{\hat{x}}D(\hat{x})\|_2 - 1)^2\right] \quad (2)$$

where φ is the gradient penalty coefficient and $P_{\hat{x}}$ is the random sample between the real data x and the random noise z. $\nabla_{\hat{x}}D(\hat{x})$ represents the gradient of discriminator D. The first two terms of the loss function are the original discriminator D loss, and the latter is the introduced GP.

The specific steps of the algorithm are as follows:

Step 1: Separate different types of attack data and generate corresponding virtual samples through the following steps.

Step 2: Generate the random sample set. The random noise z is used as the input layer of the generation network, denoted as $\{z_1, z_2, \cdots, z_n\}$, where z_n is a random number. The generator network generates close to real dummy samples by capturing the probability distribution of the network traffic data of ICSs during the training process. The simulation of the generated attack samples is very low at this time.

Step 3: Train discriminator D. Fix the generator G, network traffic data of the ICSs and the set of fake attack samples generated from the G as the input of the D. $-E_{G(z)\sim P_g}D(G(z))$ and Equation (2) are used to establish the loss functions of the G and D, respectively, as the reference standard for the adversarial training of the G and D. The objective function value of the D is denoted as L.

Step 4: Train generator G. The further training of generator G is to be trained through the G–D concatenation. After step 2, the D has a certain discriminative ability. The purpose of training G is to generate a false sample that D cannot discriminate between true and false. The set of false attack samples generated after step 1 with a similar distribution of network traffic data of ICSs is used as the input layer of D.

Step 5: Alternate training. If the objective function value or the specified number of cycles does not reach the threshold, step 2 and step 3 are cycled to alternate training for D and G. The gradient update using an Adam optimizer optimizes the D loss value L.

Step 6: Generate data. The final output generates data for the generator G model, solves the data set imbalance problem and reconstructs the data set.

A CNN and BiSRU were used to validate the 1D CWGAN model against the data set after enhancement. Our CNN network stacks two convolutional layers before the pooling layer. By stacking the convolutional layers, the activation function relu is sandwiched between the convolutional layers. The stacking of nonlinear functions increases the non-linear expressiveness of the activation function, which enables it to learn well the spatial feature information of the ICSs' complex high-dimensional network traffic data. Due to the efficiency of the SRU, it is used to replace LSTM and GRU, but it can only extract sequence features in a single direction and does not fully consider the influence before and after features of network traffic of ICSs. In this paper, we use the BiSRU for feature extraction of long-distance dependence information of network traffic in both positive and negative directions, and finally, through the intrusion detection, the results are finally output by softmax.

4. Experiment

4.1. Data Set

In this paper, a large number of data sets are used to verify the proposed data augmentation method. They are the gas pipeline industrial data set proposed by Mississippi State University in 2014 and the TON_IoT (UNSW-IoT20) data set collected from a real large-scale network of the University of New South Wales and the Australian Defence College in 2020. It includes network data sets, Linux data sets and Windows data sets.

In 2014, Mississippi State University provided the gas pipeline standard industrial data set. In recent years, it has been widely used in simulation experiments of ICS intrusion detection. The system was collected from a set of natural gas pipeline systems based on Modbus tcp, and its structure is similar to the data acquisition and monitoring control system in the real production environment. The gas pipeline data set contains normal data and seven types of attack data. See Table 1 for details.

Table 1. Description of data sets.

Attack Type	Describe	Number
Normal	Normal (0)	61,156
Naïve malicious response injection	NMRI (1)	2763
Complex malicious response injection	CMRI (2)	15,466
Malicious state command injection	MSCI (3)	782
Malicious parameter command injection	MPCI (4)	7637
Malicious function code injection	MFCI (5)	573
Denial of service	DOS (6)	1837
Reconnaissance	Recon (7)	6805

TON_IoT includes Linux operating system data, Windows operating system logs and IoT network traffic. TON_IoT is represented in CSV format.

TON_IoT network data set: The network TON_IoT data set contains 44 attributes, and each data point has a label classified as normal or attack. Table 2 shows the statistical data of network data samples in the TON_IoT data set.

Table 2. Statistical records of TON_IoT network data sets.

Attack Type	Normal	DoS	Ransomware	Password	Scanning
Number	300,000	20,000	20,000	20,000	20,000
Attack type	Injection	DDoS	backdoor	XSS	mitm
Number	20,000	20,000	20,000	20,000	1043

TON_IoT Linux data set: The Linux data set is divided into three categories: disk, memory and process. The first CSV file contains the properties of normal behavior and attack disk usage. The second CSV file is related to memory activity and contains 11 attributes, a tag column marked as normal or attacked and an attack type column containing attack types. The last file belongs to the process in the Linux operating system. Table 3 shows the statistics recorded on the TON_IoT Linux process data set.

Table 3. Statistical records of TON_IoT Linux process data sets.

Attack Type	Normal	DoS	Password	Scanning
Number	100,000	10,000	10,000	10,000
Attack type	Injection	DDoS	XSS	mitm
Number	10,000	10,000	10,000	112

4.2. Data Preprocessing

The data preprocessing stage mainly includes low variance filtering, normalization and single-hot coding. In the preprocessing stage, the above method is used to remove irrelevant data, which provides more effective data for the detection of subsequent algorithms.

4.2.1. Gas Pipeline Industrial Data Set

The data set is complex and variable, with many eigenvalues, but not every eigenvalue is well distinguished, that is, it has a very low variance. Such eigenvalues have no analytical value, so we chose to remove them directly. For example, if a feature in a column accounts for 95% of the instance value of all input samples, it can be considered not very useful. If 100% is 1, then this feature is meaningless. Nine feature columns with the smallest variance were selected, and finally a data set with 17-dimensional effective eigenvalues was obtained.

The classifier cannot directly process the unordered discrete features of the gas pipeline data set. Using one-hot coding, a mapping table was established for discrete feature data to make it ordered and continuous. The data set has eight classification results, as shown in Equation (3), including Normal (0), NMRI (1), CMRI (2), MSCI (3), MPCI (4), MFCI (5), DOS (6) and Recon (7). They can be encoded as (1, 0, 0, 0, 0, 0, 0, 0), (0, 1, 0, 0, 0, 0, 0, 0), (0, 0, 1, 0, 0, 0, 0, 0), (0, 0, 0, 1, 0, 0, 0, 0), (0, 0, 0, 0, 1, 0, 0, 0), (0, 0, 0, 0, 0, 1, 0, 0), (01, 0, 0, 0, 0, 0, 1, 0) and (0, 0, 0, 0, 0, 0, 0, 1).

$$One-hot\ encoding = \begin{cases} (1,\ 0,\ 0,\ 0,\ 0,\ 0,\ 0,\ 0), & if\ the\ result\ is\ Normal(0). \\ (0,\ 1,\ 0,\ 0,\ 0,\ 0,\ 0,\ 0), & if\ the\ result\ is\ NMRI(1). \\ (0,\ 0,\ 1,\ 0,\ 0,\ 0,\ 0,\ 0), & if\ the\ result\ is\ CMRI(2). \\ (0,\ 0,\ 0,\ 1,\ 0,\ 0,\ 0,\ 0), & if\ the\ result\ is\ MSCI(3). \\ (0,\ 0,\ 0,\ 0,\ 1,\ 0,\ 0,\ 0), & if\ the\ result\ is\ MPCI(4). \\ (0,\ 0,\ 0,\ 0,\ 0,\ 1,\ 0,\ 0), & if\ the\ result\ is\ MFCI(5). \\ (0,\ 0,\ 0,\ 0,\ 0,\ 0,\ 1,\ 0), & if\ the\ result\ is\ DOS(6). \\ (0,\ 0,\ 0,\ 0,\ 0,\ 0,\ 0,\ 1), & if\ the\ result\ is\ Recon(7). \end{cases} \quad (3)$$

4.2.2. TON_IoT (UNSW-IoT20) Data Set

In the ToN_IoT data set, missing values must be filled and attributes that lead to overfitting must be deleted.

1. Missing value filling. Missing values are common in ToN_IoT, and these missing values must be handled appropriately. In the proposed model, the imputation of missing values is replaced by the most frequent value in each feature containing missing data.
2. Delete the attributes that cause overfitting. Multiple attributes such as timestamp, IP address, source port and target port in the data set are deleted because they may cause overfitting.

4.3. Evaluation Indicators of Intrusion Detection

Intrusion detection has different indicators to evaluate the results obtained. Among these metrics, the most commonly used are accuracy, precision, recall and F1. A common way to present these concepts is the cross-list between the class predicted by the model and the actual class. This table is called the confusion matrix. The confusion matrix is a 2D matrix used to visualize the prediction of the classification model of the test label data set. Table 4 shows the confusion matrix. True negative (TN) indicates the number of benign samples correctly classified as benign, true positive (TP) indicates the number of malicious samples misclassified as malicious, false negative (FN) indicates the number of benign samples misclassified as malicious and false positive (FP) indicates the number of malicious samples misclassified as benign.

$$\text{Accuracy} = \frac{\text{TN} + \text{TP}}{\text{TP} + \text{FP} + \text{TN} + \text{TP}} \tag{4}$$

Table 4. Confusion matrix.

	Predictive Value = 1	Predictive Value = 0
True value = 1	TP	FN
True value = 0	FP	TN

The precision, also known as the precision rate, aims to predict how many of the positive results are correct, that is, how many are true positive, as shown in Formula (5).

$$\text{Precision} = \frac{\text{TP}}{\text{TP} + \text{FP}} \tag{5}$$

Recall, also known as the recall rate, aims to find out how many of the samples that are actually positive are predicted to be positive, that is, how many predictions are correct for all the actual categories that are positive, as shown in Formula (6).

$$\text{Recall} = \frac{\text{TP}}{\text{FN} + \text{TP}} \tag{6}$$

Precision and the recall index sometimes appear to be contradictory, so they need to be evaluated. The most common method for this is F1. F1 is an evaluation index that can reflect both the accuracy and recall rate, as shown in Formula (7). F1 combines the results of precision and recall rate. When F1 is higher, it can show that the test method is more effective.

$$\text{F1} = \frac{2\text{TP}}{2\text{TP} + \text{FP} + \text{FN}} \tag{7}$$

4.4. Analysis of Experimental Results

In this paper, all experiments were implemented in Python 3.6 and Keras 2.10.0. The experiments were performed on a machine with Intel Core i7-9700H CPU, NVIDIA GeForce GTX745 GPU.

4.4.1. Verify the Gas Pipeline Data Set

This section first verifies the gas pipeline data set released by Mississippi State University in 2014, and the detailed information of the gas pipeline data set is described in the previous section. Firstly, the virtual samples of two minority classes MSCI and MFCI in the gas pipeline data set are generated, so that the amount of data of different classes in the training set is balanced. The specific number of generated samples is shown in Table 5. In order to evaluate the performance of the 1D CWGAN, experiments were carried out using 10,000 samples from the gas pipeline data set sample, of which 1250 samples were of all types. The ratio of training set to test set is 8:2.

Table 5. The number of samples generated by the training set.

Attack Types	Normal	NMRI	CMRI	MSCI	MPCI	MFCI	DOS	Recon
Number of original samples	61,156	2763	15,466	782	7637	573	1837	6805
Number of samples generated	0	0	0	468	0	677	0	0
Total	61,156	2763	15,466	1250	7637	1250	1837	6805

In order to verify the superiority of the data enhancement method based on the 1D CWGAN in the gas pipeline data set, a CNN and BiSRU were selected as the experimental baseline methods. Previous studies used the traditional data replicator GAN method to deal with unbalanced data, and this study used the 1D CWGAN method to generate minority samples. In order to further illustrate the superiority of the performance of the model in this paper, the original training set, the GAN enhanced data set and the 1D CWGAN enhanced data set were sent to the CNN classifier and the BiSRU classifier for testing.

It can be seen from the analysis of the data in Table 6 that although the CNN and BiSRU have achieved high accuracy on the gas pipeline data set, the F1 score is low, and the F1 score is improved after using the GAN algorithm to generate a small number of samples. It shows that the CNN and BiSRU methods cannot handle class-imbalanced data well alone. The 1D CWGAN unbalanced sample generation method proposed in this study significantly improves the classification performance of the CNN and BiSRU. For the CNN, after data balancing, the accuracy rate is increased by 0.75%, and the accuracy, recall rate and F1 are improved. Compared with the BiSRU without data processing, the accuracy of the 1D CWGAN-BiSRU is increased by 1.34%, and the accuracy, recall and F1 are increased by 7.2%, 3.46% and 5.29%, respectively. In contrast, the data augmentation method proposed in this paper obtains the highest F1 score on each classifier, showing better performance than the GAN.

Table 6. Performance of different algorithms.

Method	Accuracy (%)	Precision (%)	Recall (%)	F1(%)
CNN [27]	97.58	90.42	89.97	90.30
BiSRU [14]	97.66	90.78	90.44	90.61
GAN-CNN	97.85	91.11	92.67	91.90
GAN-BiSRU	98.01	93.34	93.08	93.21
1D CWGAN-CNN	98.33	93.34	93.08	93.19
1D CWGAN-BiSRU	99.00	97.90	93.90	95.90

The experiment compares the classification performance of the model directly using CNN classification without data enhancement with the GAN-CNN model based on GAN data enhancement and the 1D CWGAN-CNN model based on 1D CWGAN data enhancement. It can be seen that the 1D CWGAN-CNN model has better performance than the single CNN model and the GAN-CNN model after data enhancement. As shown in Figure 2, accuracy is the ratio of well-classified data to total data, so the accuracy of all categories is significantly improved. In particular, after the data augmentation of MSCI and MFCI minority classes, the performance of a few attack classes is the same as that of normal classes. As shown in Figure 3, the same verification with the BiSRU model also shows that the data augmentation method proposed in this study understands more about the characteristics of a few attacks.

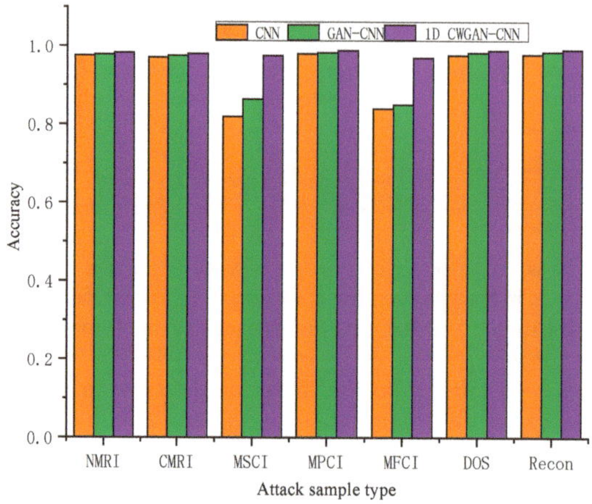

Figure 2. Comparison of attack sample recognition accuracy based on CNN model.

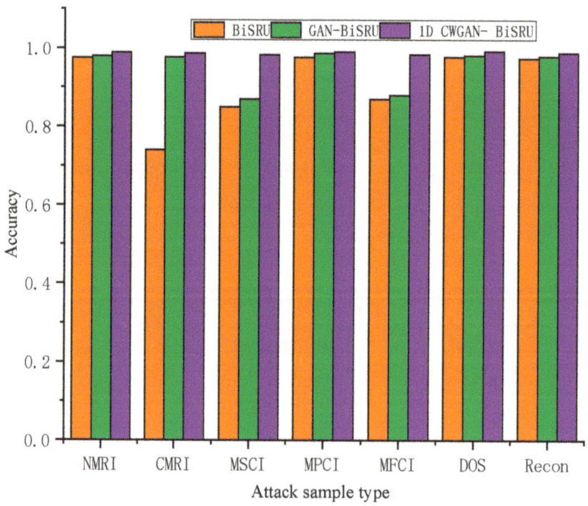

Figure 3. Comparison of attack sample recognition accuracy based on BiSRU model.

4.4.2. Verify the TON_IoT Network Data Set

This section next verifies the TON_IoT (UNSW-IoT20) network data set jointly published by the University of New South Wales and the Australian Defence College. The details of the network data set are described in the previous section. First, a small number of mitm samples in the network data set are generated to balance the amount of data in different categories in the training set. The specific number of generated samples is shown in Table 7. In order to evaluate the performance of the 1D CWGAN, the experiment used 20,000 samples in the TON_IoT data set, of which 2000 samples were of all types. The ratio of training set to test set is 8:2.

Table 7. The number of samples generated by the training set.

Attack Types	Normal	Scanning	Injection	DDoS	Mitm
Number of original samples	300,000	20,000	20,000	20,000	1043
Number of samples generated	0	0	0	0	957
Total	300,000	20,000	20,000	20,000	20,000
Attack Types	Ransomware	DOS	XSS	Password	Backdoor
Number of original samples	20,000	20,000	20,000	20,000	20,000
Number of samples generated	0	0	677	0	0
Total	20,000	20,000	20,000	20,000	20,000

In order to verify the superiority of the data enhancement method based on the 1D CWGAN in the TON_IoT (UNSW-IoT20) network data set, a CNN and BiSRU were selected as the experimental baseline methods. Previous studies used the traditional data replicator GAN method to generate minority samples, and this study used the 1D CWGAN method to generate minority samples. In order to further illustrate the superiority of the performance of the model in this paper, the original training set, the GAN enhanced data set and the 1D CWGAN enhanced data set were sent to the CNN classifier and the BiSRU classifier for testing.

The analysis of the data in Table 8 shows that although the CNN and BiSRU have achieved high accuracy on the TON_IoT network data set, the F1 score is low, and the F1 score is improved after using the GAN algorithm to generate a small number of samples. It shows that the CNN and BiSRU methods cannot handle class-imbalanced data well alone. The 1D CWGAN unbalanced sample generation method proposed in this study significantly improves the classification performance of the CNN and BiSRU. For the CNN, after data balancing, the accuracy rate is increased by 4.63%, and the accuracy, recall rate and F1 are improved. Compared with the BiSRU without data processing, the accuracy of the 1D CWGAN-BiSRU is increased by 5.28%. In contrast, the data augmentation method proposed in this paper obtains the highest F1 score on each classifier, showing better performance than the GAN.

Table 8. Performance of different algorithms.

Method	Accuracy (%)	Precision (%)	Recall (%)	F1 (%)
CNN [27]	92.76	84.42	84.66	84.54
BiSRU [14]	92.84	84.78	84.54	84.66
GAN-CNN	94.89	87.14	87.74	87.44
GAN-BiSRU	95.76	88.34	88.21	88.27
1D CWGAN-CNN	97.39	90.34	90.45	90.39
1D CWGAN-BiSRU	98.12	92.90	91.54	92.21

The experiment also compares the classification performance of the model that directly uses CNN classification without data enhancement with the GAN-CNN model based on GAN data enhancement and the 1D CWGAN-CNN model based on 1D CWGAN data enhancement. It can be seen that the performance of the 1D CWGAN-CNN model is better than that of the single CNN model and the GAN-CNN model after data enhancement. As shown in Figure 4, accuracy is the ratio of well-classified data to total data, so the accuracy of all categories is significantly improved. In particular, after data augmentation of the mitm minority class, the performance of the minority attack class is the same as that of the normal class. As shown in Figure 5, the same verification with the BiSRU model also shows that the data augmentation method proposed in this study understands more about the characteristics of a few attacks.

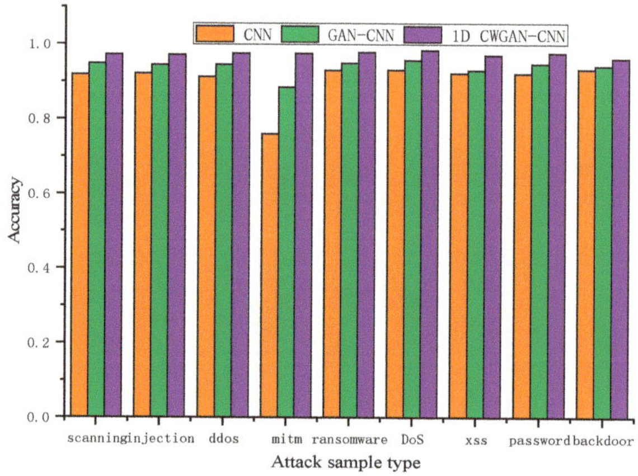

Figure 4. Comparison of attack sample recognition accuracy based on CNN model.

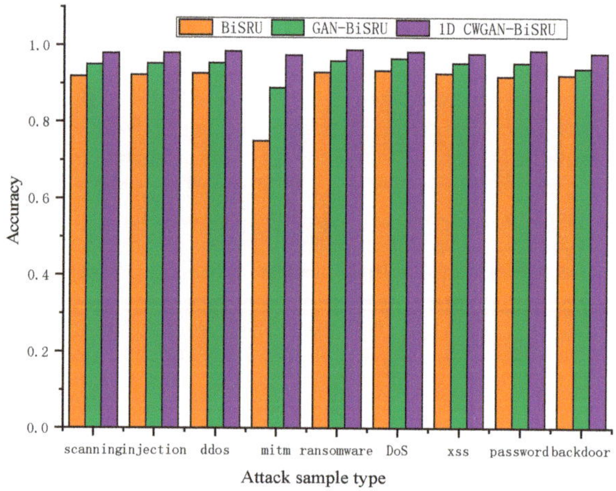

Figure 5. Comparison of attack sample recognition accuracy based on BiSRU model.

4.4.3. Verify the TON_IoT Linux Process Data Set

This section next verifies the TON_IoT (UNSW-IoT20) Linux process data set jointly released by the University of New South Wales and the Australian National Defense College. Firstly, a small number of mitm samples in the Linux process data set are generated, so that the amount of data in different categories in the training set is balanced. The specific number of generated samples is shown in Table 9. In order to evaluate the performance of 1D CWGAN, experiments were performed using 10,000 samples from the TON_IoT (UNSW-IoT20) Linux process data set sample, of which all kinds of samples were 1250. The ratio of training set to test set is 8:2.

Table 9. The number of samples generated by the training set.

Attack Types	Normal	Scanning	Injection	DDoS
Number of original samples	60,112	10,000	10,000	10,000
Attack Types	Mitm	DOS	XSS	Password
Number of original samples	112	10,000	10,000	10,000

In order to verify the superiority of the data enhancement method based on 1D CWGAN in the TON_IoT (UNSW-IoT20) Linux process data set. CNN and BiSRU were also selected as the experimental baseline methods. Previous studies used the traditional data replicator GAN method to generate minority samples, and this study used the 1D CWGAN method to generate minority samples. In order to further illustrate the superiority of the performance of the model in this paper, the original training set, the GAN enhanced data set and the 1D CWGAN enhanced data set are sent to the CNN classifier and the BiSRU classifier for testing.

It can be seen from the analysis of the data in Table 10 that although CNN and BiSRU have achieved high accuracy on the Linux process data set, the F1 score is low, and the F1 score is improved after using the GAN algorithm to generate a few samples. It shows that the CNN and BiSRU methods cannot handle class-imbalanced data well alone. The 1D CWGAN unbalanced sample generation method proposed in this study significantly improves the classification performance of CNN and BiSRU. For CNN, after data balancing, the accuracy rate is increased by 4.66%, and the accuracy, recall rate and F1 are improved. Compared with BiSRU without data processing, the accuracy of 1D CWGAN-BiSRU is improved by 4.33%. In contrast, the data augmentation method proposed in this paper obtains the highest F1 score on each classifier, showing better performance than GAN.

Table 10. Performance of different algorithms.

Method	Accuracy (%)	Precision (%)	Recall (%)	F1 (%)
CNN [27]	92.54	84.22	83.14	83.68
BiSRU [14]	92.87	84.54	84.18	84.98
GAN-CNN	94.65	87.87	87.54	87.70
GAN-BiSRU	95.54	88.01	88.21	88.11
1D CWGAN-CNN	97.78	90.54	90.41	90.47
1D CWGAN-BiSRU	97.20	92.45	91.76	92.10

The experiment also compares the classification performance of the model that directly uses CNN classification without data enhancement with the GAN-CNN model based on GAN data enhancement and the 1D CWGAN-CNN model based on 1D CWGAN data enhancement. It can be seen that the 1D CWGAN-CNN model has better performance than the single CNN model and the GAN-CNN model after data enhancement. As shown in Figure 6, accuracy is the ratio of well-classified data to total data, so the accuracy of all categories is significantly improved. In particular, after data augmentation of the mitm minority class, the performance of the minority attack class is the same as that of the normal class. As shown in Figure 7, the same verification with the BiSRU model also shows that the data augmentation method proposed in this study understands more about the characteristics of a few attacks.

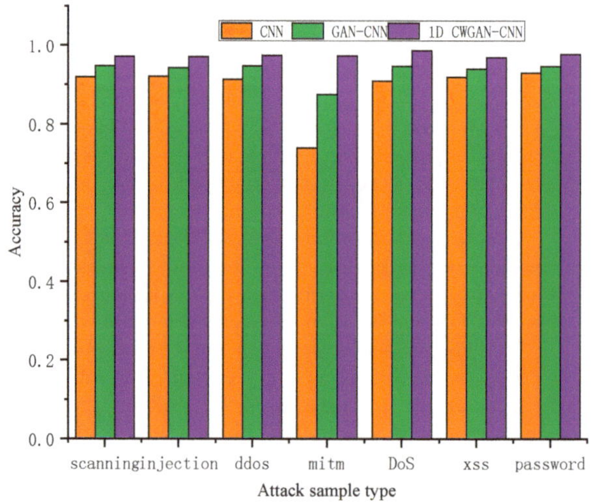

Figure 6. Comparison of attack sample recognition accuracy based on CNN model.

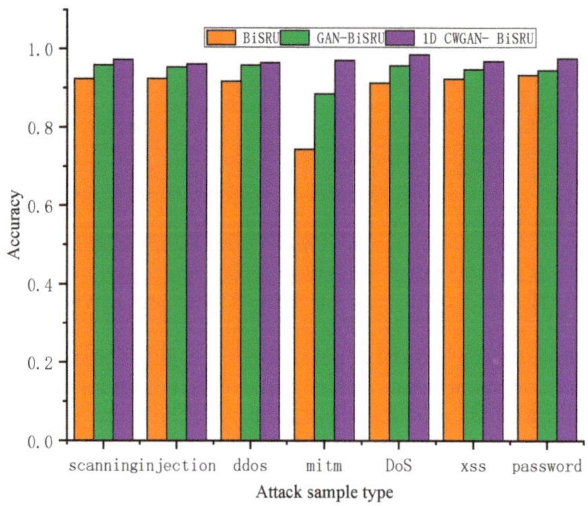

Figure 7. Comparison of attack sample recognition accuracy based on BiSRU model.

5. Conclusions

Aiming at the existing problems in the research topic of industrial control network intrusion detection, this paper proposes a network traffic data enhancement model based on a 1D CWGAN, which solves the problem of unbalanced traffic data categories in the field of ICS network intrusion detection. A generator and discriminator based on the 1D CWGAN model are constructed by using a 1D CNN and a 1D transposed CNN, and a WGAN neural network with a GP term is used to expand network traffic data samples. The verification experiment was carried out on a large number of industrial data sets. The experimental results show that the ICS intrusion detection model based on the 1D CWGAN has achieved good results. Although this method has potential applications in industrial control system intrusion detection, it also has some shortcomings. First, like any other generation model, this method can introduce noise into the data set, so additional processing will be needed to mitigate the effects of noise in future work. In addition, in order to find the best hyperparameter configuration, it is often necessary to conduct multiple trials and adjustments, which also increases the training time. In future research, we will carry out more in-depth theoretical research to optimize the algorithm and hardware, speed up its training and convergence process, and improve the computational efficiency of the model to meet the real-time requirements of industrial control systems. In addition, interpretive artificial intelligence techniques, such as interpretable machine learning models or visualization tools, can be introduced to improve the interpretability of methods.

Author Contributions: Conceptualization, Z.C. and H.D.; methodology, Z.C. and H.D.; validation, H.W. and J.Z.; data curation, Y.S. and P.L. All authors have read and agreed to the published version of the manuscript.

Funding: This research was funded by the National Natural Science Foundation of China (No. 62072416), the Key Research and Development Special Project of Henan Province (221111210500), and the Key Technologies R&D Program of Henan Province (232102211053, 222102210170, 222102210322).

Data Availability Statement: Data are contained within the article.

Conflicts of Interest: The authors declare no conflict of interest.

References

1. Altunay, H.C.; Albayrak, Z.; Özalp, A.N.; Çakmak, M. Analysis of Anomaly Detection Approaches Performed Through Deep Learning Methods in SCADA Systems. In Proceedings of the 2021 3rd International Congress on Human-Computer Interaction, Optimization and Robotic Applications (HORA), Ankara, Turkey, 11–13 June 2021; pp. 1–6.
2. Balla, A.; Habaebi, M.H.; Elsheikh, E.A.; Islam, M.R.; Suliman, F.M. The Effect of Dataset Imbalance on the Performance of SCADA Intrusion Detection Systems. *Sensors* **2023**, *23*, 758. [CrossRef] [PubMed]
3. Dusan, N.; Zivana, J. CNN based Method for the Development of Cyber-Attacks Detection Algorithms in Industrial Control Systems. *Comput. Secur.* **2022**, *114*, 102585.
4. Qian, J.; Du, X.; Chen, B.; Qu, B.; Zeng, K.; Liu, J. Cyber-Physical Integrated Intrusion Detection Scheme in SCADA System of Process Manufacturing Industry. *IEEE Access* **2020**, *8*, 147471–147481. [CrossRef]
5. Shen, C.; Liu, C.; Tan, H.; Wang, Z.; Xu, D.; Su, X. Hybrid-Augmented Device Fingerprinting for Intrusion Detection in Industrial Control System Networks. *IEEE Wirel. Commun.* **2018**, *25*, 26–31. [CrossRef]
6. Jamoos, M.; Mora, A.M.; AlKhanafseh, M.; Surakhi, O. A New Data-Balancing Approach Based on Generative Adversarial Network for Network Intrusion Detection System. *Electronics* **2023**, *12*, 2851. [CrossRef]
7. Reddy, R.R.; Ramadevi, Y.; Sunitha, K.V.N. Effective discriminant function for intrusion detection using SVM. In Proceedings of the International Conference on Advances in Computing, Communications and Informatics (ICACCI), Jaipur, India, 21–24 September 2016; pp. 1148–1153.
8. Moon, D.; Im, H.; Kim, I.; Park, J.H. DTB-IDS: An intrusion detection system based on decision tree using behavior analysis for preventing APT attacks. *J. Supercomput.* **2017**, *73*, 2881–2895. [CrossRef]
9. Mughal, M.O.; Kim, S. Signal classification and jamming detection in wide-band radios using Nave Bayes classifier. *IEEE Commun. Lett.* **2018**, *22*, 1398–1401. [CrossRef]
10. Anton, S.D.D.; Sinha, S.; Schotten, H.D. Anomaly-based intrusion detection in industrial data with SVM and Random Forests. In Proceedings of the 27th International Conference on Software, Telecommunications and Computer Networks (SOFTCOM), Split, Croatia, 19–21 September 2019; pp. 465–470.
11. Al-Asiri, M.; El-Alfy, E.-S.M. On Using Physical Based Intrusion Detection in SCADA Systems. *Procedia Comput. Sci.* **2020**, *170*, 34–42. [CrossRef]
12. Khan, A.A.Z.; Serpen, G. Misuse intrusion detection using machine learning for Gas Pipeline SCADA networks. In Proceedings of the International Conference on Security and Management (SAM), Las Vegas, NV, USA, 29 July–1 August 2019; pp. 84–90.
13. Tian, Q.; Li, J.; Liu, H. A Method for Guaranteeing Wireless Communication Based on a Combination of Deep and Shallow Learning. *IEEE Access* **2019**, *7*, 38688–38695. [CrossRef]
14. Ding, P.; Li, J.; Wen, M.; Wang, L.; Li, H. Efficient BiSRU Combined with Feature Dimensionality Reduction for Abnormal Traffic Detection. *IEEE Access* **2020**, *8*, 164414–164427. [CrossRef]
15. Mubarak, S.; Habaebi, M.H.; Islam, M.R.; Balla, A.; Tahir, M.; Elsheikh, A.; Suliman, F.M. Industrial Datasets with ICS Testbed and Attack Detection Using Machine Learning Techniques. *Intell. Autom. Soft Comput.* **2022**, *31*, 1345–1360. [CrossRef]
16. Mubarak, S.; Habaebi, M.H.; Islam, M.R.; Rahman FD, A.; Tahir, M. Anomaly Detection in ICS Datasets with Machine Learning Algorithms. *Comput. Syst. Sci. Eng.* **2021**, *37*, 014384. [CrossRef]
17. Liao, X.; Li, K.; Zhu, X.; Liu, K.J.R. Robust Detection of Image Operator Chain with Two-Stream Convolutional Neural Network. *IEEE J. Sel. Top. Signal Process.* **2020**, *14*, 955–968. [CrossRef]
18. Yang, H.; Cheng, L.; Chuah, M. Deep-learning-based network intrusion detection for SCADA Systems. In Proceedings of the IEEE Conference on Communications and Network Security (CNS), Washington, DC, USA, 10–12 June 2019; pp. 1–7.

19. Liu, J.; Yin, L.; Hu, Y.; Lv, S.; Sun, L. A novel intrusion detection algorithm for industrial control systems based on CNN and process state transition. In Proceedings of the 37th International Performance Computing and Communications Conference (IPCCC), Orlando, FL, USA, 17–19 November 2018; pp. 1–8.
20. Yin, C.; Zhu, Y.; Fei, J.; He, X. A deep learning approach for intrusion detection using recurrent neural network. *IEEE Access* **2017**, *5*, 21954–21961. [CrossRef]
21. Roy, B.; Cheung, H. A deep learning approach for intrusion detection in internet of things using bi-directional long short-term memory recurrent neural network. In Proceedings of the 28th International Telecommunication Networks and Applications Conference (ITNAC), Sydney, NSW, Australia, 21–23 November 2018; pp. 57–62.
22. Sokolov, A.N.; Alabugin, S.K.; Pyatnitsky, I.A. Traffic modeling by recurrent neural networks for intrusion detection in industrial control systems. In Proceedings of the International Conference on Industrial Engineering, Applications and Manufacturing (ICIEAM), Sochi, Russia, 25–29 March 2019; pp. 1–5.
23. Lei, T.; Zhang, Y.; Wang, S.I.; Dai, H.; Artzi, Y. Simple recurrent units for highly parallelizable recurrence. In Proceedings of the Conference on Empirical Methods in Natural Language Processing (EMNLP), Brussels, Belgium, 31 October–4 November 2018; pp. 4470–4481.
24. Alotaibi, A.; Rassam, M.A. Enhancing the Sustainability of Deep-Learning-Based Network Intrusion Detection Classifiers against Adversarial Attacks. *Sustainability* **2023**, *15*, 9801. [CrossRef]
25. Mari, A.G.; Zinca, D.; Dobrota, V. Development of a Machine-Learning Intrusion Detection System and Testing of Its Performance Using a Generative Adversarial Network. *Sensors* **2023**, *23*, 1315. [CrossRef] [PubMed]
26. Du, P.H.; Nguyen, H.N. APELID: Enhancing real-time intrusion detection with augmented WGAN and parallel ensemble learning. *Comput. Secur.* **2024**, *136*, 103567.
27. Ling, J.; Zhu, Z.H.; Luo, Y.; Wang, H. An intrusion detection method for industrial control systems based on bidirectional simple recurrent unit. *Comput. Electr. Eng.* **2021**, *91*, 107049. [CrossRef]

electronics

Article

A Streamlined Framework of Metamorphic Malware Classification via Sampling and Parallel Processing

Jian Lyu [1], Jingfeng Xue [1], Weijie Han [2], Qian Zhang [1,*] and Yufen Zhu [2]

1 School of Computer Science and Technology, Beijing Institute of Technology, Beijing 100081, China; 3120195531@bit.edu.cn (J.L.); xuejf@bit.edu.cn (J.X.)
2 School of Space Information, Space Engineering University, Beijing 101416, China; 3120185536@bit.edu.cn (W.H.); 3120205525@bit.edu.cn (Y.Z.)
* Correspondence: zhangqian16@bit.edu.cn

Abstract: Nowadays, malware remains a significant threat to the current cyberspace. More seriously, malware authors frequently use metamorphic techniques to create numerous variants, which throws malware researchers a heavy burden. Being able to classify these metamorphic malware samples into their corresponding families could accelerate the malware analysis task efficiently. Based on our comprehensive analysis, these variants are usually implemented by making changes to their assembly instruction sequences to a certain extent. Motivated by this finding, we present a streamlined and efficient framework of malware family classification named MalSEF, which leverages sampling and parallel processing to efficiently and effectively classify the vast number of metamorphic malware variants. At first, it attenuates the complexity of feature engineering by extracting a small portion of representative samples from the entire dataset and establishing a simple feature vector based on the Opcode sequences; then, it generates the feature matrix and conducts the classification task in parallel with collaboration utilizing multiple cores and a proactive recommendation scheme. At last, its practicality is strengthened to cope with the large volume of diversified malware variants based on common computing platforms. Our comprehensive experiments conducted on the Kaggle malware dataset demonstrate that MalSEF achieves a classification accuracy of up to 98.53% and reduces time overhead by 37.60% compared to the serial processing procedure.

Keywords: malware classification; malware family; parallel processing; microsoft kaggle malware dataset

Citation: Lyu, J.; Xue, J.; Han, W.; Zhang, Q.; Zhu, Y. A Streamlined Framework of Metamorphic Malware Classification via Sampling and Parallel Processing. *Electronics* **2023**, *12*, 4427. https://doi.org/10.3390/electronics12214427

Academic Editor: Aryya Gangopadhyay

Received: 15 September 2023
Revised: 15 October 2023
Accepted: 24 October 2023
Published: 27 October 2023

1. Introduction

In the digital age, networks became a prime target for many attackers. Malware is a prevailing weapon for attackers to launch network attacks and became a major challenge to cyberspace worldwide. In spite of the fact that anti-malware researchers put considerable efforts into the analysis task, it is still not ideal to curb malware attacks. Especially with high returns earned by malware, a consistent surge was found in malware attacks and obfuscated variants [1]. These variants are usually produced by modifying their binary codes or assembly instructions based on obfuscation techniques. Through the obfuscation process, the malware samples can change their structural characteristics and evade detection while preserving malicious functions [2]. The AV-TEST Institute reported that more than 350,000 fresh malware samples are discovered every day [3]. The proliferation of malware variants created a significant challenge for anti-malware analysis. To tackle the malware challenges, a significant amount of previous work was devoted to malware detection [4]. However, it is still a challenging issue to tackle with the obfuscated malware variants detection.

Motivated by the above-mentioned challenge, this paper focuses on the issues of malware variants classification aiming at accurately and effectively classifying the sheer number of variants into their families. Because it is a time-consuming workload to cope with the large quantities of malware samples, the first issue we need to consider is to simplify the feature engineering phrase.

To extract features from malware, two traditional methods are often used: static analysis and dynamic analysis [5]. Behavioral information of malware is derived from a malware sample without actual execution in static analysis. On the contrary, a malware program needs to be run actually in dynamic analysis mode. Compared with dynamic analysis, static analysis can achieve high accuracy and efficiency due to being free from the overhead of execution cost [6]. Among the features extracted from static analysis, Opcode sequences garnered significant interest from malware researchers and are widely used in anti-malware analysis, which is because assembly instructions can reveal program behavior characteristics [7,8]. In order to accelerate the classification of a huge amount of malware, we decided to conduct static analysis and extract features from the assembly instructions. In addition to simplifying feature engineering, another strategy that we take into account is to employ parallel processing techniques to accelerate the classification of these massive malware variants by utilizing our ordinary computing platforms.

To this end, a light and parallel classification framework named MalSEF (a streamlined and efficient framework for detecting metamorphic malware families) is proposed in this paper. MalSEF mainly consists of four modules: sampling, feature extraction, feature matrix generation in parallel, and classification in parallel. MalSEF is implemented as follows. Firstly, select a small proportion of samples and construct a subset from the entire dataset according to a validated sampling criterion. Secondly, extract the Opcode sequence from the sampled subset to represent the entire dataset. Then, because the metamorphic technique is usually applied at the assembly instruction layer of malware, we analyze the behavioral characteristics based on the Opcode sequence, select the ranked Top-N Opcodes in frequency, and build a simple feature vector taking the frequency of Opcode as the eigenvalue to construct feature matrix in parallel for the initial dataset, based on the simple feature vector. The proposed parallel processing strategy is employed to reduce processing time and ameliorate processing efficiency for feature extraction and feature matrix generation from the entire dataset. By constructing the above lightweight feature set and applying the parallel processing strategy, the time overhead required for classifying large amounts of malware can be efficiently reduced. Finally, we evaluate MalSEF on the Microsoft Kaggle malware dataset and achieve promising classification accuracy. In addition, the processing time overhead can be reduced apparently compared with the serial processing mode. In conclusion, the following contributions are made in this paper:

(1) We suggest to extract a small proportion of samples from the entire dataset according to the selection criteria and construct a simple and efficient feature vector from the assembly (ASM) files that can reflect the original dataset. The final evaluations prove that the lightweight eigenvector can not only attenuate the complexity of feature engineering, but also satisfy classification requirements.

(2) We propose a parallel processing approach with commonly available hardware resources that utilizes collaboration of multi-core and active recommendation. The parallel strategy can run on the popular personal computer without high-performance hardware resources, and open the door for analysts to leverage general computers to tackle tough tasks due to the large volume of malware.

(3) We conduct systematic assessments using the Microsoft Kaggle malware dataset. The classification accuracy can reach up to 98.53%. The parallel processing technique results in a 37.60% reduction in the processing time compared with the conventional serial process mode. MalSEF can deliver a similar performance to the first winner of the challenge competition with the feature space effectively simplified, outperforming the existing algorithms in terms of simplicity and efficiency.

The remainder of the paper is organized as follows: Section 2 provides background information and summarizes related research; Section 3 describes the inspiration and framework of MalSEF; Section 4 presents the detailed implementation of MalSEF; Section 5 details the experiments and evaluations conducted on MalSEF; and the paper is concluded in Section 6.

2. Overview of Related Studies

A brief introduction of the necessary background knowledge and an overview of related research are provided in this section.

2.1. Background

2.1.1. Metamorphic Techniques

The purpose of metamorphism is to change its structure of the malware and generate new features at time of propagation, so as to avoid traditional feature-based detection [9]. Metamorphic techniques are quite widely used; some obfuscating method adopted in adversarial attacks [10] and backdoor attacks [11] can also be seen as metamorphism in a broader view, where metamorphism is usually implemented through resize and imperceptible perturbations [12]. As for malware, the metamorphic technique is usually applied in the assembly instruction layer, i.e., Opcode. The popular metamorphic methods include instruction reordering, dead/trash instruction insertion, and substitution [13]. The metamorphic technique is mainly applied at the assembly instruction level, which lies in the scope of this study (since the Kaggle dataset includes both assembly and binary formats of malware [14]). Below, we provide a brief overview of the common ways in which malware can be deformed.

(1) Instruction reordering

Instruction reordering involves division of code into segments, permutation of these segments, and inserting branch instructions as necessary to maintain the initial functionality. This code manipulation is extremely effective in modifying the initial signature and may also be effective against structure inspection techniques, such as detecting the change in entropy [15].

Instruction reordering can be realized in two ways. One way to accomplish instruction reordering is to randomize the sequence of instructions and remain the original control flow by inserting unconditional branches or jumps. As shown in Figure 1, the malware variant 'BKXtxeYlLsprabEWIQhn' in the Kaggle dataset employs this method to generate new variants. The other way is to swap independent instructions. Similar to compiling instructions, different compilers will generate different compilation instructions. The difference is that the goal of swapping instructions is to randomize the instruction stream.

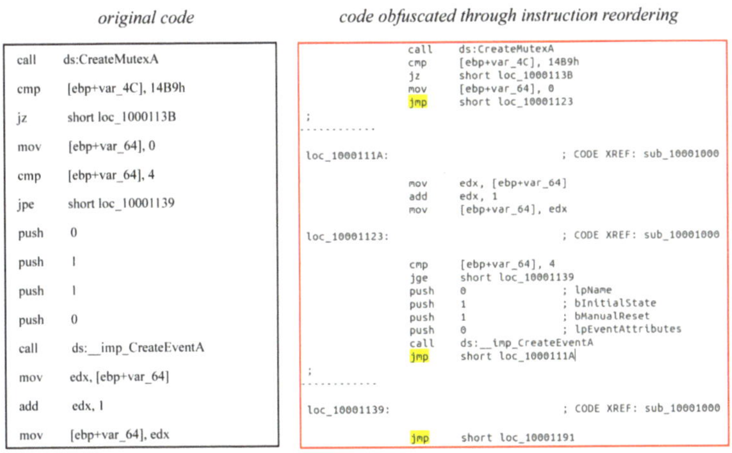

Figure 1. Example of metamorphism through instruction reordering.

This kind of metamorphism may interfere with the manual analysis process. However, many automatic analysis approaches that rely on intermediate representations, such as control flow diagrams or program dependency diagrams [16], can effectively overcome it because they are less sensitive to the unwanted changes in the control flow.

(2) Trash code or dead code insertion

Trash instructions are "not do anything" instructions that are executed without any impact on program functionality. Trash/dead instruction insertion adds code to a program without changing the program's original behavior. The simplest example is to insert a series of 'nop' instructions into a program. As shown in Figure 2, the malware variant 'i5u2KDJ9t0OyAdokafj7' in the Kaggle dataset employs this method to obfuscate and generate new variants.

original code

```
push    ebp
mov     ebp, esp
push    ebx
sub     esp, 24h
lea     ebx, [ebp+var_8]
mov [esp+28h+hwinsta], offset sub_401000
call    sub_403833
sub     esp, 4
call    sub_40274B
```

code obfuscated through dead code insertion

```
                nop
                nop

loc_402314:                                     ; CODE XREF: .text:00402C5E↑j
                nop
                nop
                nop
                nop
                nop
                nop
                nop
                nop
                nop
                nop
                nop
                push    ebp
                mov     ebp, esp
                push    ebx                     ; uType
                sub     esp, 24h
                lea     ebx, [ebp+var_8]
                mov     [esp+28h+hwinsta], offset sub_401000 ; hwinsta
                call    sub_403833
                sub     esp, 4
                call    sub_40274B
```

Figure 2. Example of metamorphism through dead code insertion.

Trash/dead instruction inserts are frequently used by malicious personnel to influence the detection based on features, and as for bypassing statistical detection, these metamorphic techniques are particularly effective.

(3) Instruction substitution

Instruction substitution means equivalent instruction replacement, which uses an equivalent instruction sequence dictionary to replace one instruction sequence with another.

The example of instruction substitution is illustrated in Figure 3. Because this modification relies on equivalent instruction knowledge, it makes the most serious obstacle to automatic analysis. The Intel Architecture 32-bit instruction set is abundant enough to perform the same operation in numerous ways. In addition, the IA-32 instruction set has some structural inconsistencies, such as a memory-based stack, which may be accessed by specialized instructions as a memory address. Operations of standard memory can also be accessed as a memory address, which makes the assembly language of IA-32 provide rich means for instruction replacement.

This kind of metamorphism is an effective way to evade feature-based detection and statistics-based detection. To tackle this form of obfuscation, an equivalent instruction sequence dictionary, which needs to be similar to the one used in generating the equivalent instruction, must be maintained for the analysis tool. This is not a fundamental way to tackle the instruction replacement problem, nevertheless, it is usually enough to handle usual situations.

original code

```
call    __EH_prolog3
pop     ebx
lea     ecx, [ebx+var_8]
push    ecx
push    eax
push    eax
sub     esp, 4
pop     ebx

add     ebx, 1Ch
```

code obfuscated through instruction substitution

```
call    __EH_prolog3
pop     ebx
lea     ecx, [ebx+var_8]
sub     esp, 03h


sub     esp, 4
add     [esp], 1Ch
mov     ebx, [esp]
inc     esp
```

Figure 3. Example of metamorphism through instruction substitution.

2.1.2. Methods for Malware Analysis

In the field of malware analysis, two fundamental tasks are malware detection and malware classification [17]. To find malicious samples from unknown programs is the target of malware detection, while to separate malware into corresponding families is the target of malware classification. Features of programs extracted in the detection stage can still be used in the classification process. Based on the different ways of program feature extracting, methods of malware detection and classification are put into two categories: static and dynamic.

Static analysis does not run the program actually. To understand the malicious nature of a program, researchers usually gather information from its PE header, PE body, and binary code. Alternatively, they can disassemble the binary code and extract Opcodes or other pertinent details from the assembly program to characterize it [18]. The static analysis technique is more efficient but must contend with packaging and obfuscation disturbances.

Dynamic analysis is an approach based on behavior that needs to run the program to capture its run time behavior characteristics. The main behavior characteristics of the dynamic analysis method include program API sequence and behavior interaction with OS during run time. In order to avoid damage to the terminal system caused by malware, a virtual environment is usually used while dynamic analysis is performed [19,20].

Additionally, combining static and dynamic analysis, there are also researchers that conducted hybrid analysis. During the hybrid analysis, static and dynamic features are derived separately, and then fused together to overcome the defects of static or dynamic analysis alone, so as to achieve a more comprehensive and accurate analysis of malware [21,22].

2.1.3. Parallel Processing Techniques

Parallel processing is a technique that allows for the execution of multiple tasks simultaneously by dividing a serial work process into multiple processes or threads [23–25]. Some common parallel processing methods are as follows:

(1) Task parallel: during a complete working process, if there are some independent modules executing in parallel, this parallel processing method is called task parallelism. As shown in Figure 4, in this data flow diagram, when module A and B execute in parallel, it is called task parallel.

(2) Pipeline parallel: when a series of connected modules (forming a complete working process) process independent data elements in parallel (these data elements are usually a time series or an independent subset of a certain dataset), this parallel processing method is called pipeline parallelism. As shown in Figure 4, when modules A, C, and D execute in parallel, it is called pipeline parallel.

(3) Data parallel: when a dataset can be divided into a number of subsets and these subsets can be processed simultaneously, this kind of parallel processing method is

called data parallelism. As shown in Figure 4, if module B reads data in parallel, it is called data parallel.

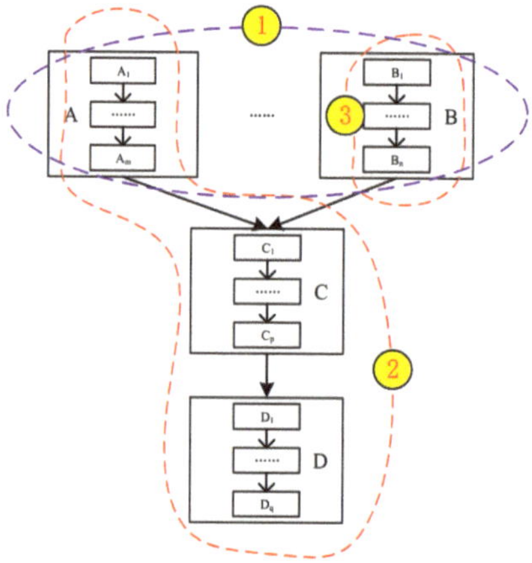

Figure 4. A data flow diagram.

2.2. Related Studies

Since the target of this research is malware family classification based on parallel processing technology, this section makes a brief summary of the relevant research work on malware family classification and malware analysis using parallel technologies.

In the process of malware classification, researchers usually extract different features to represent samples, and then select an automatic classifier to realize classification. For example, Bailey Michael et al. [26] proposed to describe malware behavior characteristics according to system state changes (such as file reading and writing, process creation, etc.). On this basis, malware is automatically classified into groups with similar behavior types in automatic mode, so as to handle the phenomenon of the sharp increase in malware scale and behavior difference. In addition, some researchers also proposed methods to analyze the binary code of malicious programs. Nataraj Lakshmanan et al. [27] applied the binary texture analysis method to analyze the malicious code and made a comprehensive comparison. The authors found that the binary texture analysis method not only achieves relatively high classification accuracy, but also surpasses the dynamic analysis by nearly 4000 times in speed. Furthermore, some of the current strategies can even be resisted by texture-based analysis.

In view of the sharp increase in the scale of malware variants, Ahmadi Mansour et al. [28] designed a novel classification strategy for malware family, utilizing the dataset of the Microsoft malware challenge as the research object. An innovative approach for feature set extraction and selection was devised to effectively characterize malware samples. According to the different characteristics of malicious code, the features were classified and weighted. This method can effectively address the challenge brought by the increasing variants of malware. To cope with the challenge of the increasing number of malware from an extensible perspective, Hu Xin et al. [29] proposed a machine learning framework that utilizes diverse content features (such as string, instruction sequence, section information, and other characteristics) and gathers intelligence information from external resources (such as anti-virus output). Several optimization methods were designed to further improve the performance of the classifier. Finally, an experiment was conducted on the Kaggle dataset of the Microsoft malware challenge to evaluate the performance of the propounded approach in processing malware datasets with a large scale. Considering that most malicious programs are variants created from existing malware, Lee Taejin et al. [30] presented a method for malware detection and classification in light of the local clustering coefficient. In this way, the classification reliability can be enhanced, the automatic selection and management of the malware family can be realized, and the large-scale malware can be classified efficiently.

Aiming at overcoming the limitations of current malware classification that requires domain knowledge, Raff Edward et al. [31] used a new representation named the SHWeL feature vector through expanding the concept of Lempel-Ziv Jaccard distance. The SHWeL vector improves the accuracy of LZJD, and its performance is better than the byte n-grams feature representation method, which can build an effective eigenvector input for classifier training and reasoning. In addition, Quan Le et al. [32] also presented a method of malware classification that does not require domain knowledge. This method converts a binary file into a one-dimensional representation and then constructs a deep learning network for automatic classification. The advantage of this method is that researchers do not need to extract features from malware, but only use the universal image scaling algorithm to convert a malware into a one-dimensional form of fixed size.

With the increase in the scale of malware, the analysis workload becomes more and more onerous. To ameliorate the efficiency of malware analysis, some researchers began to apply parallel and distributed processing technologies.

Junji NAKAZATO et al. [33] designed a new malware classification method to tackle the problems that existing methods are inadequate for achieving efficient and accurate classification. The authors initially conducted a dynamic analysis to automatically extract execution traces of malware, then employed their behavioral characteristics to classify them into distinct categories. In the process of obtaining behavior characteristics, the author adopted a parallel processing method to extract the API information of malware. Sheen Shina et al. [34] derived features of different categories from the executable file and applied them to the integrated classifier. The integration approach combined several separate pattern classifiers for better results. The problem was how to select classifiers of a minimum number and acquire the best results. This paper designed a compact integration technique using the harmony search method, which was derived from the music harmony-inspired algorithm. For malware detection, the simplified integrated classifier was used. For selecting the optimal subset of classifiers, multiple variegated classifiers were integrated into harmony and parallel search. Wang Xin et al. [35] used parallel machine learning and information fusion technology to achieve more effective detection. The author first extracted eight types of static features from the program and constructed two sets of features through feature selection; subsequently, a parallel machine learning model was employed to expedite the classification process. Finally, information fusion was achieved through probability analysis and Dempster–Shafer theory to complete the final detection.

Based on the above-introduced literature, the researchers made multi-aspect attempts at coping with the sharp increase in the scale of malware variants; nonetheless, there still exist apparent deficiencies as follows (as illustrated in Table 1):

(1) The feature vectors constructed by these methods can usually effectively represent the features of malware. However, when applying to analyze massive malware, the feature space will become too large and bring a heavy burden to analysts. For example, the feature vector proposed by [28] can achieve perfect classification accuracy; however, its feature vector is too large to be realized under the condition of ordinary computing resources.

(2) The parallel processing method above is usually applied to multiple classifiers for parallel detection. In essence, it is still a serial processing mode, and the parallel analysis target of massive samples is not achieved. When faced with a large scale of malware, it will inevitably affect the analysis efficiency.

Table 1. Pros and cons of similar approaches for malware family classification and parallel processing.

Related Work	Analysis Method	Dataset	Feature Set	Pros	Cons
Bailey et al. [26]	Dynamic analysis	Network security community and a part of the Arbor Malware Library	system state changes	Offer an innovative perspective on comprehending the connections between malware	The underlying shortcomings due to dynamic analysis
Nataraj Lakshmanan et al. [27]	Static analysis	Host-Rx dataset, Malhuer dataset and a VX Heavens dataset	binary texture feature	With comparable classification accuracy, faster than dynamic technique	Lack of the semantic analysis of the binary programs
Ahmadi Mansour et al. [28]	Static analysis	Microsoft Malware Challenge dataset	features extracted from hex dumps and decompiled files	High classification accuracy	Complicated feature matrix and high time consumption
Hu Xin et al. [29]	Static analysis	Microsoft Malware Challenge dataset	multifaceted content features and threat intelligence	High classification accuracy	The process of feature extraction will require a large amount of time
Lee Taejin et al. [30]	Dynamic analysis	Malware collected from a commercial environment	System call sequences	Good dependability on processing malware volume	May fail to yield an accurate result; high time consumption due to dynamic analysis
Raff Edward et al. [31]	Static analysis	Microsoft Kaggle dataset and Drebin dataset	SHWeL feature vector by extending Lempel-Ziv Jaccard Distance	Not require domain knowledge	High time consumption
Quan Le et al. [32]	Static analysis	Microsoft Kaggle dataset	One dimensional representation of the malware sample	Not require domain knowledge	Lack of the semantic analysis of the binary code due to the black-box feature of the deep learning model
Junji Nakazato et al. [33]	Dynamic analysis	Not clearly stated	Dynamic execution traces	Extract API calls in parallel thread	The parallel processing is not clearly stated
Sheen Shina et al. [34]	Hybrid analysis	Not clearly stated	PE features and API calls	Construct the at least as good as ensemble classifiers in parallel fashion	Not apply parallel technique into the analysis process
Wang Xin et al. [35]	Static analysis	Drebin and Android Malware Genome Project	Eight types of static features	Achieve higher detection accuracy	Not apply parallel technique into the analysis process

3. Overview of MalSEF

3.1. Motivation

The malware detection process typically consists of two main stages: feature extraction and detection/classification, which constitute a serial process [6]. Malware detection and malware classification are two distinct tasks. The former aims to determine whether an unknown sample is malicious, while the latter involves grouping detected malware into its most appropriate family. In the current cyberspace environment, we are witnessing a surge in malware families, coupled with a high number of variants within each family, posing a significant challenge to the anti-malware community [2].

Actually, the scale of malware volume is increasing mainly due to the widespread application of metamorphic technologies. The metamorphic malware will modify its code structurally while maintaining its functionality at time of propagation. How to cope with the large volume of metamorphic malware variants and group them into appropriate families became a crucial task for the security community. During the grouping process, the following challenges need to be addressed:

(1) The complexity of feature engineering may increase sharply due to the large scale of malware variants. The complexity is mainly derived from two aspects: (1) The feature set of the cutting-edge analysis methods is usually fairly complicated, because we often utilize APIs or Opcodes, or their combination (n-grams) as the feature vector to profile the malware. The number of API and Opcode on the Win32 platform is relatively large. (2) The increasing volume of malware variants will further aggravate the complexity, especially in the current massive malware environment.

(2) The efficiency of coping with the sheer number of malware samples cannot be guaranteed. The existing detection methods mainly include the training stage and detection stage. These two stages are separately implemented and the detection process is essentially a serial processing one. We may inevitably fail to tackle the challenge facing the environment of large-scale malware.

Driven by the above issues, we put forward the following ideas in this paper:

(1) How to establish a simple feature set for the large number of malware variants so as to alleviate the computation cost and deliver satisfactory classification performance simultaneously?

(2) How to efficiently handle numerous malware variants and classify them into their homologous families to ensure the efficiency of the classification process?

(3) How to implement the complicated task for analyzing a huge amount of malware on a simple personal computer, so as to enable ordinary researchers to accomplish the seemingly impossible task due to the conventional paradigm?

The answers to these questions were already provided in previous studies. Motivated by the above inspiration, we aim to propose a lightweight approach for ordinary researchers to perform heavy analysis tasks using common computing platforms.

3.2. Parallel Processing Model of Massive Malware Classification

Based on the principle of parallel processing technology, the procedures in malware detection that can be optimized by parallel processing include:

(1) In the training stage, the process of extracting features from the training set include "assembly commands of samples $\rightarrow$ extracting Opcode lists $\rightarrow$ counting the occurrences of every Opcode $\rightarrow$ generating feature vectors $\rightarrow$ generating feature matrices", which can be implemented in parallel mode.

(2) In the detection stage, the process performing on unknown samples include "assembly commands of samples $\rightarrow$ generating feature vectors $\rightarrow$ classification", which can be implemented in parallel mode.

By considering the above malware analysis process, we employ parallel processing techniques to compress the needed analysis time and boost the malware classification efficiency. According to the above discussion, the malware classification process in parallel is designed as displayed in Figure 5.

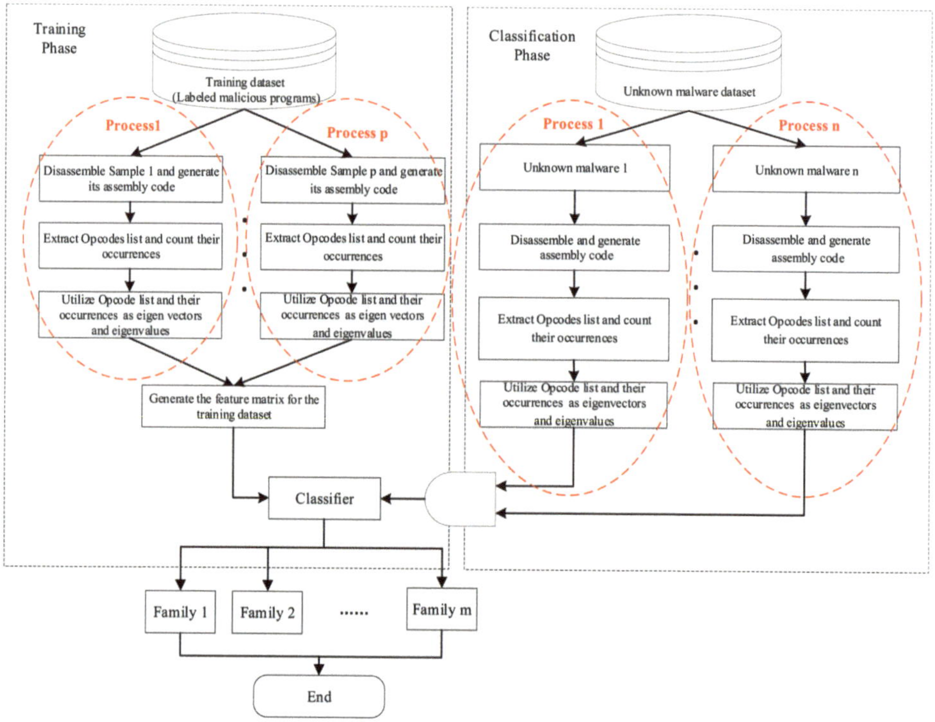

Figure 5. Parallel classification model of massive malware.

3.3. Overall Framework of MalSEF

MalSEF mainly includes four modules, namely, sampling of massive samples, feature extraction, feature vector generation, and classification, as shown in Figure 6.

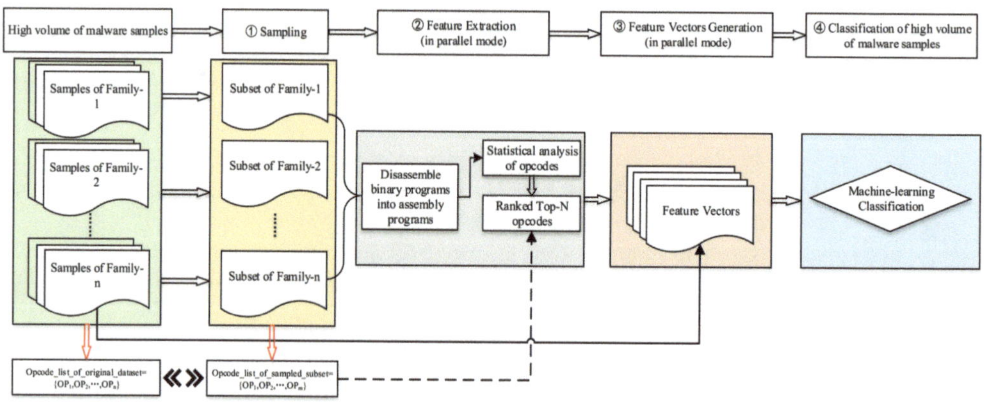

Figure 6. The framework of MalSEF.

(1) Sampling of massive samples

The task of this module is to construct sampled subsets that consist of a small part of samples randomly selected from each family of the massive samples collected, which will be used as the data source for feature extraction. The purpose of this module is to select features from subsets of samples to represent the original dataset rather than extract features directly from massive samples, so as to attenuate the complexity of the extraction of features. The subset size is determined on the criteria of selecting a smaller quantity of samples from the entire dataset and obtaining the same results that reflect the original dataset as previously as needed [36].

(2) Feature extraction

Because the malware program is often in the form of binary code, we have to firstly convert the binary malware programs into assembly programs. The most frequently used disassembling tool is IDA Pro. In our study, because the experiment dataset of this paper is released by Microsoft in Kaggle, which is in the form of the assembly instructions after disassembling, accordingly, features can be extracted statically from the assembly programs of malware samples. This module first counts the occurrences of every Opcode in the sample subsets and then ranks Opcodes according to their occurrence frequencies. Finally, the Top-N ranked Opcodes are selected as the feature vector (Top-N is set by researchers flexibly) and the number of occurrences of each Opcode is taken as its feature value.

(3) Feature matrix generation

After generating feature vectors in the previous module, the task of this module is to generate the feature matrix for the samples. According to the experimental method of cross-validation, we need to generate feature matrices for the samples in the training set and testing set, respectively. Among them, the training set is a labeled dataset, and the test set is an unlabeled dataset. Since the number of samples in the testing set is much larger than that in the training set, it requires more time to construct feature matrices for the testing set. To this end, we adopted a parallel processing approach to generate feature matrices for the testing set.

(4) Classification of massive malware samples

Having gotten the feature matrix as illustrated above, we can verify the result of MalSEF by cross-validation.

4. Detailed Implementations of MalSEF

This section describes the implementation of MalSEF in detail.

4.1. Sampling from the Massive Samples Set and Feature Extraction

4.1.1. Sampling from the Massive Sample Set

The aim of this module is to select a certain number of samples from each family to form a subset for each family. The size of each subset is determined by a sample size determination criterion. The required sample size is decided based on the following formula.

$$n_0 = \frac{z^2 \times p \times q}{d^2} \tag{1}$$

where: n_0 is expected sample size; z is standard normal deviation of expected confidence level; p is the assumed proportion of the target population with an estimated particular characteristic; $q = 1 - p$; and d is the degree of accuracy expected in estimated proportion. This is a theoretical formula that is used to determine the number of selected samples n_0 under a certain expected confidence level and certain marginal error, allowing n_0 to represent the overall samples in a statistical sense. It is based on the assumption that the samples follow a normal distribution, noting that the expected confidence level is determined by z (e.g., z = 1.96 for 95% confidence level), and the marginal error is determined by d (e.g., d = 0.01 for a margin of error of 1%). As for p, when z and d are given and the estimator p is not known, $p = 0.5$ can be used to yield the largest sample size, which is the p value we used in this research.

The formal description of the sampling process is as follows:

$$Set(S\begin{bmatrix} F_1(f_{11}, f_{12}, \cdots, f_{1N_1}) \\ \vdots \\ F_m(f_{11}, f_{12}, \cdots, f_{1N_m}) \end{bmatrix}) : Sampling :\rightarrow Subset(S'\begin{bmatrix} F_1\left(f_{11}, f_{12}, \cdots, f_{1N_1'}\right) \\ \vdots \\ F_m\left(f_{11}, f_{12}, \cdots, f_{1N_m'}\right) \end{bmatrix}) \quad (2)$$

where $N_1{}' \leq N_1, \cdots, N_m{}' \leq N_m$, and $S' \subseteq S$.

Description of the algorithm implementation of the sampling process is illustrated as Algorithm 1.

Algorithm 1: Sample a subset from the original dataset

```
//S represents the original dataset.
//ẑ represents the set of standard normal deviations for desired confidence level of original dataset.
//p̂ represents the set of assumed proportions in the target population of original dataset.
//d̂ represents the set of degrees of accuracy desired in the estimated proportion of the original dataset.
Input: the original malware dataset S, ẑ, p̂, d̂
Output: the sampled malware subset S'
trainLabels = readDataset() //read the original dataset
labels = getLabels(S) //read the labels of the original dataset
for i = 1 to labels do
    mids = trainLabels[trainLabels.Class == i] //get the samples of Class == i
    mids = mids.reset_index() //reset the index of the samples of Class == i
    n_i = (ẑ_i^2 × p̂_i × (1 − p̂_i)) / d̂_i^2 //calculate size of the subset for the ith original dataset
    for j=1 to n_i do
        rchoice = randit(0, n_i) //select digits from 1 to 100 randomly
        rids = mids [1, rchoice] //build the subset for the Class = i
    end for
    S'.append(rids) //append the subset of Class == i to S'
end for
return S'
```

4.1.2. Feature Extraction and Feature Vectors Construction

Opcode is a mnemonic of machine code, which is usually represented by assembly command [2]. Because this paper is based on a dataset released by Microsoft in Kaggle, which contains the assembly program of malware, we build the features of samples by extracting Opcodes from the assembly program. The procedure of extracting features using the sampled subset is as follows:

(1) Analyze samples in the subset one by one and extract Opcodes from each sample;
(2) Count the occurrences of each Opcode in the subset;
(3) Sort Opcodes based on their occurrences;
(4) Select Top-N Opcodes as the feature vector (the value of Top-N is set by the researchers flexibly).
(5) Construct the feature matrix by counting the occurrence numbers of each opcode in each set as the feature value for the feature element.

The description of the implementation process of feature extraction and feature vectors construction is illustrated as Algorithm 2.

Algorithm 2: Feature matrix construction

Input: assembly programs of the malware samples $P = \{p_1, p_2, p_3, \cdots, p_n\}$
Output: the feature matrix FM

for i=1 to Len(P) **do**
  //Append the opcodes of the analyzed program to the Opcode list
  $OpList \leftarrow Opcodes\ of\ p_i$
  //Build the opcode sequence of all the programs
  $\text{OpSeq}\left[\vec{\text{P}}\right] \leftarrow \text{OpListofp}_\text{i}$
  //Count the occurrence times of each Opcode
  $\text{OccSeq}\left[\vec{\text{P}}\right] \leftarrow \text{OpSeq}\left[\vec{\text{P}}\right]$
end for
//Sort the Opcode sequence based on occurrences
$\text{Sorted\_OpSeq}\left[\vec{\text{P}}\right] \leftarrow \text{OpSeq}\left[\vec{\text{P}}\right]\left(\text{Key} : \text{OccSeq}\left[\vec{\text{P}}\right]\right)$
//Select the ranked Top-N Opcodes as the feature vector and their occurrences as the feature values
$\text{FM} \leftarrow \text{Ranked}\left[\text{Sorted\_OpSeq}\left[\vec{\text{P}}\right]\right]$
return FM

4.2. Feature Extraction with Multi-Core Collaboration and Active Recommendation in Parallel

Parallel processing in the procedures of massive malware detection has the following characteristics:

(1) Within the two procedures of parallel processing described in Section 3.2, the relationship between tasks in each procedure is loosely coupled.
(2) In the two procedures of parallel processing described in Section 3.2, we should adopt the iteration method to tackle the distributed parallel tasks load in the practical processing.
(3) In the procedure of parallel processing, different tasks will inevitably lead to different running speeds because of the different performance of the running environment and different computational load. Thus, tasks should be adaptively distributed according to the practical performance of each running node.

Based on the characteristics of the above procedures of parallel processing, we consider using the idea of multi-core to build multiple task nodes to extract code features in parallel. According to the practical implementation of each task, we can actively assign processing tasks to better performance nodes or faster nodes, so as to achieve parallel feature extraction of massive malware.

To this end, we design a parallel processing method with collaboration among multi-cores and active recommendation. Figure 7 illustrates the procedure, and the comprehensive implementation process is as listed below:

(1) Construct the analysis sample queue based on the malware sample sets. The queue is illustrated as follows:

$$Queue_{sample} = \{sample_1, sample_2, \cdots, sample_n\}. \tag{3}$$

(2) Construct a multi-core resource pool based on the computing resource nodes, each of which serves as a processing core. The core pool is illustrated as follows:

$$Queue_{core} = \{core_1, core_2, \cdots, core_m\}. \tag{4}$$

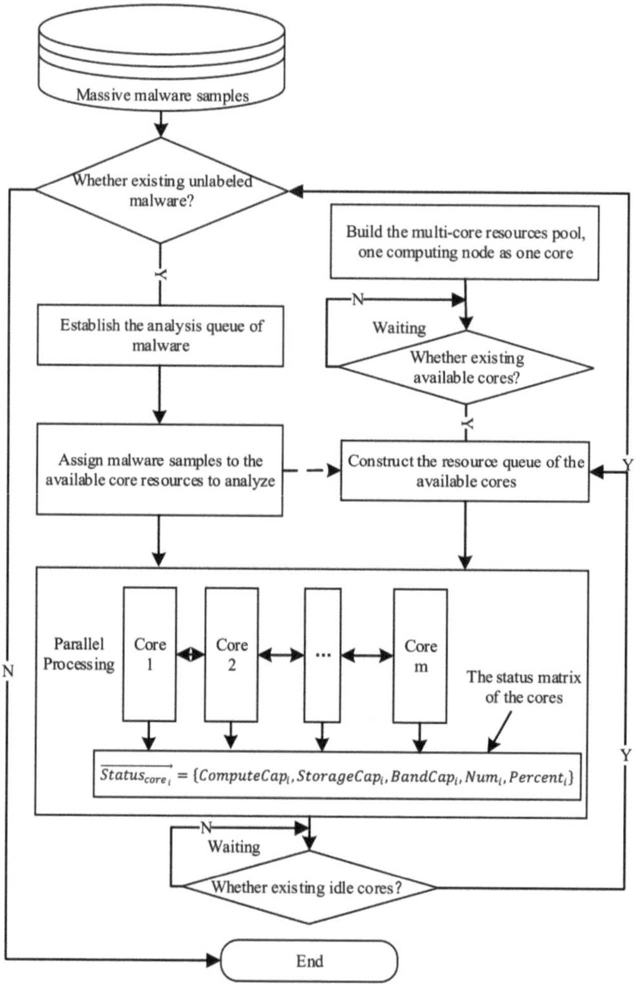

Figure 7. Feature extraction with multi-core collaboration and active recommendation in parallel.

(3) Query the current available resources in the resource pool and establish a queue of current available resources. The available resource queue is depicted as below:

$$Queue_{core'} = \{core_1, core_2, \cdots, core_{m'}\}(1 \leq m' \leq m). \quad (5)$$

(4) According to the currently available resource queue, the master node (the node that stores the sample sets) fetches m' samples from the sample sets and allocates them to the resource queue for processing.

(5) In the procedure of task parallel processing, each node monitors its own running state in real time, maintains and updates its own state vector in real time, and communicates the state vector information with each other. Based on the real-time interactive state vector information among the cores, the state vectors are combined to form a global state matrix within the cores.

The state vector describes the progress of current task processing, computational resource consumption, storage resource consumption, bandwidth resource consumption, and the number of tasks that were assigned in a node. The state vector is illustrated as follows:

$$\overrightarrow{Status_{core_i}} = \{ComputeCap_i, StorageCap_i, BandCap_i, Num_i, Percent_i\}. \quad (6)$$

The elements in the state vector are defined as follows:

(1) $ComputeCap_i$: computational resource consumption of node i;
(2) $StorageCap_i$: storage resource consumption of node i;
(3) $BandCap_i$: bandwidth resource consumption of node i;
(4) Num_i: the number of tasks assigned to node i;
(5) $Percent_i$: the progress of current task processing of node i.

In order to ensure a reasonable allocation of the subsequent tasks when combining the state vectors of each node to construct the state matrix, it is essential to rank the nodes based on their real-time status. Nodes with a lighter load are positioned higher, while those with a heavier load are placed lower.

To this end, after receiving the state vectors from other nodes, each node compares the values of each element in the state vector according to the importance order of "$Percent > ComputeCap > Num > StorageCap > BandCap$", and forms the final state matrix, which is described as follows:

$$[Status] = \begin{bmatrix} \overrightarrow{Status_{core_1}} \\ \cdots \\ \overrightarrow{Status_{core_{m'}}} \end{bmatrix} = \begin{bmatrix} ComputeCap_1 & StorageCap_1 & BandCap_1 & Num_1 & Percent_1 \\ \cdots & \cdots & \cdots & \cdots & \cdots \\ ComputeCap_{m'} & StorageCap_{m'} & BandCap_{m'} & Num_{m'} & Percent_{m'} \end{bmatrix}. \quad (7)$$

(6) The master node will continuously monitor the state matrix and sort the samples to be analyzed. Once a node finishes its task, it notifies the master node, which then assigns new samples to that node, allowing it to start a new processing task. By this way, our method realizes the real-time and active pushing of processing tasks.
(7) Run continuously until the samples are processed entirely according to the above scheme.

5. Evaluation

5.1. Experimental Configuration

Hardware: Lenovo ThinkStation, Intel® CoRE™ i7-6700U CPU@3.40GHz×8, 8 GB memory (Made by Lenovo in China).

Operating system: 64 bit Ubuntu 14.04.

5.1.1. Dataset

In the evaluation phase, we use the training dataset released by Microsoft in Kaggle, which includes 10,868 malicious samples. We carry out cross-validation on the training dataset directly because we could not obtain the labels of the testing samples. Each malware sample has a 20-character hash value as its ID. The dataset comprises nine distinct malware families, namely Ramnit (R), Lollipop (L), Kelihos ver3 (K3), Vundo (V), Simda (S), Tracur (T), Kelihos_ver1 (K1), Obfuscator.ACY (O), and Gatak (G). Each sample family is assigned a class label from 1 to 9. The training dataset is shown in Table 2, which illustrates the distribution of each malware family.

5.1.2. Classifier

During the malware classification stage, we use data mining techniques to automate the task. To evaluate the effectiveness of MalSEF, we apply four different classifiers for identifying malware, including decision tree (DT), random forest (RF), K-nearest neighbor (KNN), and extreme gradient boosting (XGB), which are commonly used in the fields of data mining, information security, and intrusion detection [37].

Table 2. Experimental dataset.

Family ID	Family Name	#
1	Ramnit (R)	1541
2	Lollipop (L)	2478
3	Kelihos ver3 (K3)	2942
4	Vundo (V)	475
5	Simda (S)	42
6	Tracur (T)	751
7	Kelihos_ver1 (K1)	398
8	Obfuscator.ACY (O)	1228
9	Gatak (G)	1013
Total		10,868

5.2. *Experimental Results and Discussion*

We evaluate MalSEF comprehensively through detailed experiments in this section. Firstly, we build Opcode lists from the original samples set and the sampled subset separately and evaluate the classification effect of the total sample set using different Top-N Opcode lists, which are selected to construct feature vectors. Secondly, we apply the parallel processing technology in the procedure of classification based on the origin sample set and sampled subset separately, and verify the effect of parallel classification. Finally, we compare MalSEF with similar studies comprehensively.

5.2.1. Classification Using Features Derived from the Original Set and the Sampled Subset

This section indirectly evaluates the effect of using a sampled subset to characterize the original dataset. Features are extracted from the original set and the sampled subset, respectively, and then we classify the Train dataset to evaluate its classification effect.

Composition of the Sampled Dataset—Subtrain

In the experimental stage, we first select a small part of samples from the whole experimental dataset to form the subset, which is used to construct feature vectors. Because the experimental dataset we applied in this research is the Train dataset from Microsoft in Kaggle, we named this subset as Subtrain. Subtrain consists of 803 samples with specific information as shown in Table 3.

Table 3. Subtrain: the sampled dataset from the Train dataset.

Family ID	Family Name	#
1	Ramnit (R)	95
2	Lollipop (L)	100
3	Kelihos ver3 (K3)	97
4	Vundo (V)	96
5	Simda (S)	39
6	Tracur (T)	92
7	Kelihos_ver1 (K1)	91
8	Obfuscator.ACY (O)	97
9	Gatak (G)	96
Total		803

Evaluation of the Classification Results Using Features Extracted from the Entire Train Dataset

By analyzing the dataset released by Microsoft in Kaggle, we find that there are 735 Opcodes in the Train dataset. To verify the impact of the 735 Opcodes on classification results, we rank them according to their occurrences and select Top-N Opcodes as the feature vector to verify the final classification effect.

We first select various Top-N Opcodes to generate feature vectors, followed by conducting 10-fold cross-validation experiments using random forest (RF), decision trees (DT), support vector machine (SVM), and extreme gradient boosting (XGBST) classifiers. We utilize the open-source Python library Scikit learn (version 1.0.2) and opt for the default values when it comes to setting the hyper parameters for various classification methods which makes it easier to ensure the generalization ability of MalSEF without intentional optimization. The classification outcomes are presented in Table 4.

Table 4. Evaluation of the classification results according to various Top-N Opcodes extracted from the Train dataset.

	RF	**DT**	**SVM**	**XGBST**	**Number of Feature Opcodes**
Accuracy	98.34%	97.06%	97.38%	98.16%	N = 735
Precision	97.93%	92.13%	97.17%	96.29%	
Recall	97.83%	94.92%	93.63%	97.57%	
F1 Score	97.77%	93.17%	95.02%	96.80%	
Accuracy	98.20%	97.52%	97.65%	98.21%	N = 400
Precision	97.62%	94.20%	90.58%	93.90%	
Recall	91.00%	90.31%	90.31%	89.69%	
F1 Score	92.67%	91.49%	90.35%	90.69%	
Accuracy	98.57%	97.52%	97.19%	98.39%	N = 300
Precision	98.26%	91.11%	89.18%	97.98%	
Recall	93.65%	90.20%	92.39%	95.69%	
F1 Score	95.34%	90.56%	90.29%	96.65%	
Accuracy	98.44%	97.15%	96.55%	98.30%	N = 200
Precision	97.97%	96.48%	87.77%	97.81%	
Recall	93.30%	90.82%	88.87%	93.16%	
F1 Score	94.85%	92.36%	88.08%	94.72%	

As can be seen from Table 4, results of classification are similar using different Top-N Opcodes. The classification effect of the RF classifier with different Top-N opcodes is as shown in Figure 8, where Train_N stands for Top-N Opcodes extracted from the Train dataset and the fold line at the top portrays the variation in accuracy when the selected number of opcodes is changed.

The results of this experiment demonstrate that selecting all Opcodes as feature vectors is not necessary to represent the characteristics of samples. Because there exists redundancy in the extracted Opcode lists, only a part of key Opcodes is needed to achieve the desired classification effect.

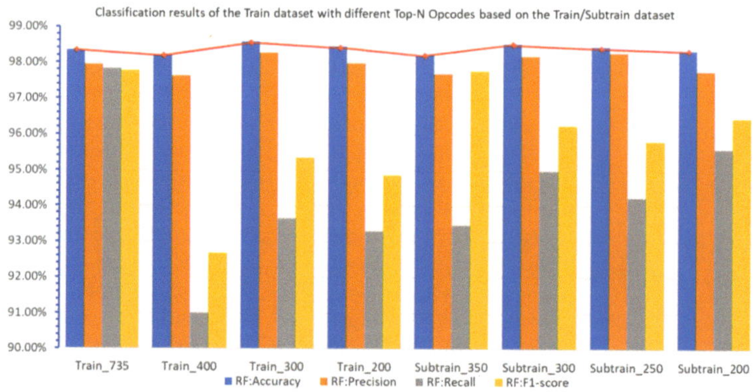

Figure 8. Comparison of the classification results of RF classifier with different Top-N Opcodes based on Train/Subtrain dataset.

Evaluation of the Classification Results Using Features Extracted from the Sampled Subtrain Dataset

In order to verify whether the sampled set Subtrain can comprehensively and effectively represent the features of the Train set, in this section, we use the sampled Subtrain set as a data source to count the occurrences of all Opcodes and sort them. Subsequently, various Top-N opcodes are chosen as the feature vector to create feature matrices for the original Train set. Finally, we carry out cross-validation experiments on the Train set to verify the validity of using the sampled subset to classify the original set.

There are 394 different Opcodes extracted from the Subtrain set, and we chose different Top-N Opcodes to classify the Train set separately. Outcomes of the experiment are presented in Table 5.

Table 5. Evaluation of the classification results according to various Top-N Opcodes extracted from the Subtrain dataset.

	RF	DT	SVM	XGBST	Number of Feature Opcodes
Accuracy	98.21%	97.24%	96.87%	98.39%	N = 350
Precision	97.69%	96.75%	91.61%	96.20%	
Recall	93.47%	89.73%	92.11%	93.67%	
F1 Score	95.01%	91.54%	91.71%	94.67%	
Accuracy	98.53%	97.38%	96.83%	97.98%	N = 300
Precision	98.18%	93.76%	92.16%	97.74%	
Recall	94.99%	90.53%	90.32%	91.43%	
F1 Score	96.25%	91.57%	90.98%	93.24%	
Accuracy	98.44%	97.29%	96.83%	98.34%	N = 250
Precision	98.27%	94.04%	93.44%	98.17%	
Recall	94.23%	91.09%	94.46%	95.87%	
F1 Score	95.81%	92.22%	93.81%	96.87%	
Accuracy	98.34%	97.06%	96.92%	98.11%	N = 200
Precision	97.76%	93.99%	94.11%	97.48%	
Recall	95.60%	94.09%	93.08%	94.10%	
F1 Score	96.45%	93.86%	93.36%	95.35%	

We compare the classification effects of RF classifier with different Top-N Opcodes, and the outcome is as follows, illustrated in Figure 8, where Subtrain_N stands for Top-N Opcodes extracted from the subTrain dataset and the fold line at the top portrays the variation in accuracy when the selected number of opcodes is changed. We can see that when 350, 300, 250, and 200 Opcodes are selected as the feature vector, the classification accuracy all exceed 98%, and the highest reaches up to 98.53%. We can draw the conclusion from this part of the experiments that the classification effect can meet our requirements when we use the Subtrain dataset to characterize the original Train dataset.

5.2.2. Experimental Results of Parallel Processing

This section is divided into stages of feature extraction, classifier training, and practical detection. We carry out cross-validation according to serial processing and parallel processing separately, and compare the experimental results of the two different processing modes.

Experimental Results of Parallel Processing of Train Dataset with Top-N Opcodes Extracted from Subtrain

Because the Subtrain is small, it takes only 3.86 s to extract the Opcode lists from the Subtrain subset. Then Top-N Opcodes are selected as the feature vectors to generate the feature matrix for the Train dataset, which is a time-consuming process. We use the parallel processing mode designed in Section 4.2 to realize the feature generation process. The effect of parallel processing with different parameters is shown in Table 6, where the first row, designated with a yellow background, is serial processing, and the most efficient parameter settings for parallel processing are indicated in red. We compare the experimental result of parallel processing visually and compare the optimal time performance of each parallel setting with different Top-N, as shown in Figure 9.

Table 6. Experimental result of the parallel generation of feature vectors with Top-N Opcodes extracted from Subtrain.

Num_of_Processes	Num_of_Files_ Per_Operation	Num_of_Files_ Per_Process	Time_Cost (s) N = 350	Time_Cost (s) N = 300	Time_Cost (s) N = 250	Time_Cost (s) N = 200
1	1	1	3144.43	3123.36	3094.76	2991.99
4	8	8/4 = 2	2015.38	2017.66	2011.31	2005.77
4	12	12/4 = 3	2001.01	2055.59	2009.72	1997.88
4	16	16/4 = 4	2006.25	2004.85	2005.57	2002.26
4	20	20/4 = 5	2015.54	2021.01	2013.73	2015.71
6	12	12/6 = 2	1903.09	1905.85	1899.42	1899.04
6	18	18/6 = 3	1910.87	1909.65	1906.55	1908.51
6	24	24/6 = 4	1901.23	1903.48	1899.35	1898.98
6	30	30/6 = 5	1916.27	1907.38	1912.05	1904.48
6	36	36/6 = 6	2054.21	1900.02	1908.02	1900.46
8	16	16/8 = 2	2134.08	1802.31	1804.88	1794.36
8	24	24/8 = 3	2234.32	1814.57	1811.59	1806.29
8	32	32/8 = 4	2163.13	1800.85	1805.47	1800.34
8	40	40/8 = 5	2141.56	1814.20	1810.56	1806.71
16	32	32/16 = 2	2441.05	1784.22	1786.66	1786.38
16	48	48/16 = 3	2452.15	1804.17	1785.43	1789.29
16	64	64/16 = 4	2234.93	1804.81	1780.26	1854.18
32	64	64/32 = 2	3798.22	3366.90	3362.39	3378.62
32	96	96/32 = 3	3716.72	3454.91	3457.42	3446.34

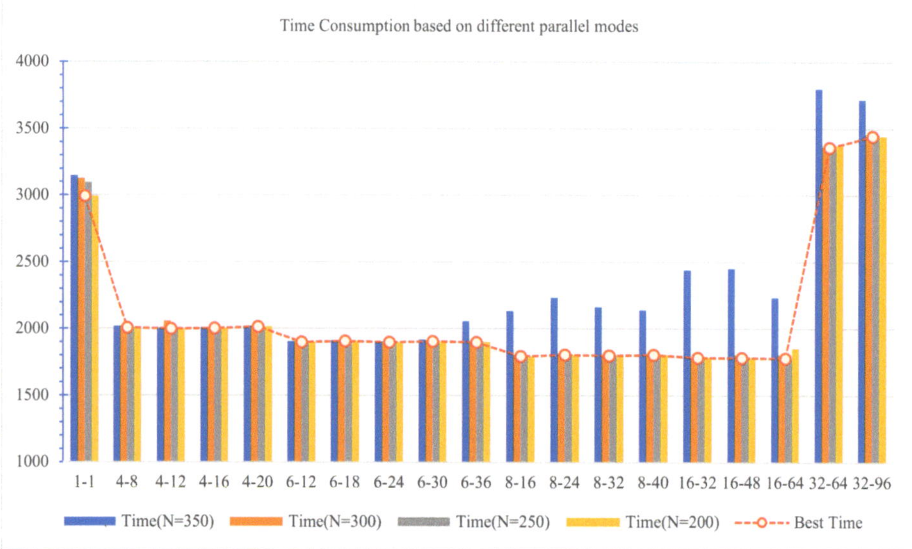

Figure 9. Comparison of time consumption based on different parallel modes.

The experimental outcomes allow us to draw the following conclusions:

(1) The smaller the Top-N that is selected, the less the processing time is, because the shorter feature vector will result in less processing workload and less time consumption.

(2) The time of parallel processing is the shortest when generating 16 processes and processing 32 samples each time, i.e., 2 samples are allocated to each process for analysis. This is because the personal PC workstation used in our experiment has eight cores. According to this setting, we can make the best use of computing resources and obtain the best results.

Experimental Results of Parallel Processing of Train dataset with Top-N Opcodes Extracted from Train

The workload will increase significantly if we extract Opcode lists directly from the Train dataset as a feature vector and then generate a feature matrix for the Train dataset. In this section, we extract feature vectors directly from the Train dataset and then carry out cross-validation. In the process of cross-validation, we extract Opcode lists from Train and construct a feature vector space for Train based on the extracted Opcode lists. Because of the large number of samples in Train dataset, these two steps are time-consuming. Therefore, we use parallel processing technology to implement these two processes, and the experimental result of parallel processing are shown in Tables 7 and 8, respectively.

Firstly, we utilized various parallel processing configurations to compile Opcode lists from the Train dataset. The findings are presented in Table 7, with the most effective parameter settings for parallel processing depicted in red, and another competitive setting depicted with a green background. A visual representation of the time-consuming comparison is illustrated in Figure 10.

Table 7. Experimental result of parallel extraction of Opcode lists from the Train dataset.

Num_of_Processes	Num_of_Files_ Per_Operation	Num_of_Files_ Per_Process	Time_Cost (s)
1	1	1	2714.30
4	8	8/4 = 2	2024.43
4	12	8/2 = 4	2006.35
4	16	10/2 = 5	1988.46
6	18	18/6 = 3	1906.77
6	24	24/6 = 4	1891.73
6	30	30/6 = 5	1890.48
6	36	36/6 = 6	1881.11
8	24	24/8 = 3	1798.20
8	32	32/8 = 4	1795.16
8	40	40/8 = 5	1798.95
16	32	32/16 = 2	1786.84
16	48	48/16 = 3	1784.62
16	64	64/16 = 4	1785.14
32	64	64/32 = 2	3377.65

Table 8. Experimental results of generating Opcode feature vectors based on parallel processing of the Train dataset.

Num_of_ Processes	Num_of_Files_ Per_Operation	Num_of_Files_ Per_Process	Time_Cost (s) N = 735	Time_Cost (s) N = 400	Time_Cost (s) N = 300	Time_Cost (s) N = 200
1	1	1	3629.03	3421.50	3094.94	2992.25
4	8	8/4 = 2	2095.58	2023.76	2018.67	2010.66
4	12	12/4 = 3	2074.93	2015.57	2000.30	2010.03
4	16	16/4 = 4	2066.56	2022.45	2016.49	2009.50
4	20	20/4 = 5	2037.21	2020.76	2038.26	2017.21
6	12	12/6 = 2	1923.39	1900.61	1903.36	1894.10
6	18	18/6 = 3	1965.54	1915.90	1911.74	1896.31
6	24	24/6 = 4	1970.55	1903.14	1899.78	1893.46
6	30	30/6 = 5	2063.14	1916.33	1910.19	1896.37
6	36	36/6 = 6	1926.12	1911.70	1898.43	1900.29
8	16	16/8 = 2	1822.72	2101.03	1800.09	1787.23
8	24	24/8 = 3	1964.03	2121.85	1809.51	1804.67
8	32	32/8 = 4	1995.37	2104.43	1792.06	1793.99
8	40	40/8 = 5	1971.58	2078.92	1811.06	1802.45
16	32	32/16 = 2	2843.86	2268.49	1782.34	1777.53
16	48	48/16 = 3	2500.37	2247.56	1775.79	1776.38
16	64	64/16 = 4	2418.35	2258.10	1771.14	1774.33
32	64	64/32 = 2	3805.67	3746.52	3360.62	3410.64
32	96	96/32 = 3	3812.21	3854.86	3461.20	3479.62

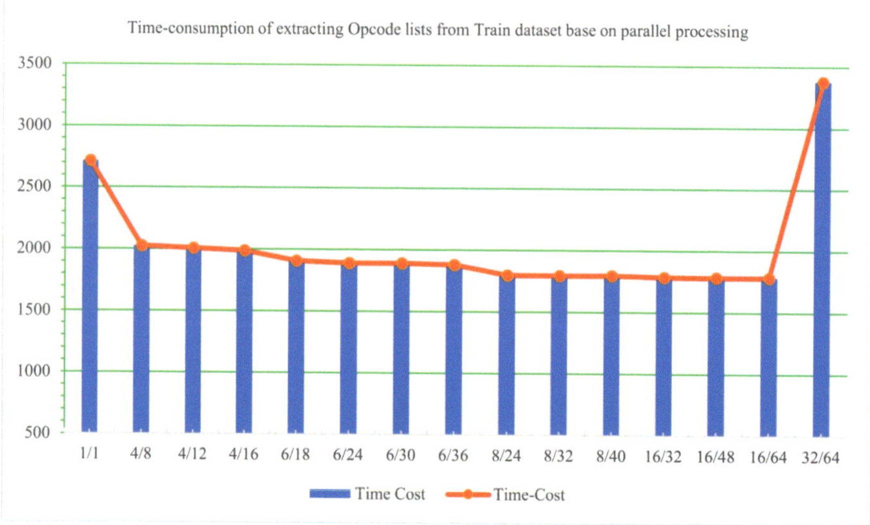

Figure 10. Time consumption of extracting Opcode lists from the Train dataset base on parallel processing.

On the basis of extracting Opcode lists from the Train dataset, the experimental results of generating feature vectors of the Train dataset based on parallel processing are shown in Table 8, with the most effective parameter settings depicted in red for each different N. The visual display of comparison of time consumption is shown in Figure 11.

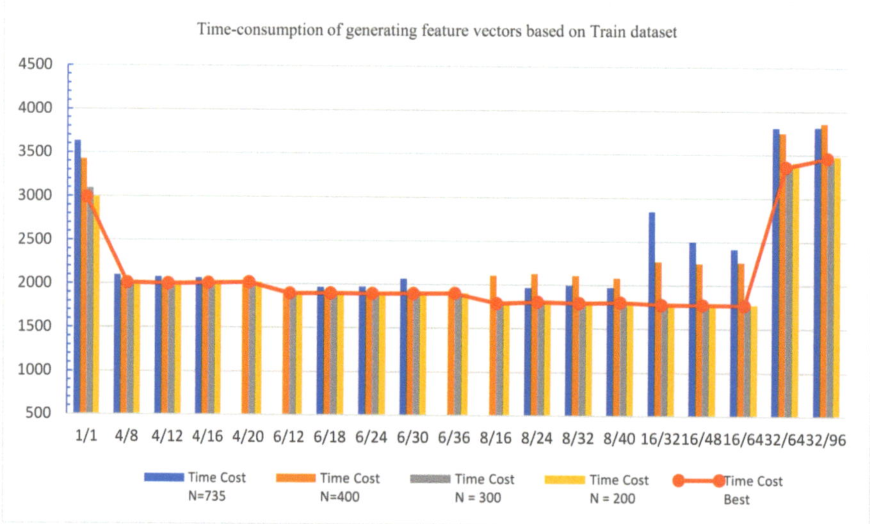

Figure 11. Time consumption of generating feature vectors based on the Train dataset.

Comparative Analysis of Overhead between Parallel Process and Serial Process

From the above experimental results of serial processing and parallel processing, we can draw the following conclusions:

(1) Parallel processing can effectively ameliorate processing efficiency

The serial processing procedures based on Train and Subtrain datasets include "extracting the feature vector from dataset → generating feature matrix for the training dataset → training classifier → practical classification". The two stages of "extracting the feature vector from dataset" and "generating feature matrix for the training dataset" are time-consuming in analyzing a massive sample set, and the application of parallel processing technology can effectively reduce the processing time.

As mentioned above, the time required to complete feature extraction and feature vector generation (Top-N = 200) based on the Subtrain subset with serial processing is 3.86 + 2991.99 = 2995.85 (s). In contrast, the optimal time consumption to complete the above process with parallel processing is 3.86 + 1786.38 = 1790.24 (s), which takes only 59.76% of the original one.

If feature extraction is based on the Train dataset, the time required to complete feature extraction and feature vector generation (Top-N = 200) is 2714.30 + 2992.25 = 5706.55 (s) with serial processing. By contrast, the optimal time consumption to complete the above process is 1784.62 + 1776.38 = 3561 (s) with parallel processing, which takes 62.4% of the original one. The parallel processing achieved promising results.

(2) Choosing the best parallel processing setting based on computing resource condition

Computing the resource platform has a fundamental impact on the parallel processing settings. As shown in the table, because our personal workstation platform has eight cores and the workload of analyzing a single malware sample is not large, the parallel processing effect is usually the best when generating 16 processes. That is to say, two processes are allocated to each core for the process, which can maximize the advantage of hardware resources. In addition, considering the allocation of computing resources on eight cores, we should not allocate too many samples to each process in parallel processing. We should ensure that each process is not overloaded to maximize the performance of each process.

5.2.3. Comparison with Similar Studies

To assess the performance of MalSEF, we compare it with related studies in terms of classification accuracy and time efficiency in this section. Since we utilize the dataset released by Microsoft in Kaggle, we select similar studies utilizing the same dataset for comparison. The four baseline models in Table 9 are classic methods that utilize the Kaggle dataset and hold significant influence, making them ideal candidates for comparison with MalSEF. The outcomes of the comparison are presented in Table 9.

In comparison to similar studies, MalSEF offers the following benefits:

(1) MalSEF strikes an optimal balance between the feature space and classification accuracy while sampling the feature vectors. When only 300 features are needed, MalSEF can achieve an accuracy of 98.53%. In contrast, the Ahmadi Mansour method [28] employed 1804 features, and the Hu Xin et al. method [29] required 2000 features, both more than six times the number of features in MalSEF. Their accuracy was only marginally higher than MalSEF by no more than 1.30%. Meanwhile, the time cost of MalSEF is significantly lower than other comparable methods. Although the classification accuracy of MalSEF may be slightly lower than the above-mentioned research, it still meets the requirements. Furthermore, when compared to other similar studies, MalSEF's feature vector is the most succinct and readily available, achieving promising classification results while minimizing the complexity of feature extraction.

Table 9. Comparison with analogous approaches.

	MalSEF	Ahmadi Mansour [28]	Hu Xin et al. [29]	Raff Edward et al. [31]	Quan Le et al. [32]
Dataset	The Microsoft Malware Classification Challenge dataset in Kaggle				
# Features	300	1804	2000	--	10,000
Feature Set	Top-N opcode list	features extracted from hex dumps + features extracted decompiled files	multifaceted content features + threat intelligence	Not clearly stated	One dimensional representation of the malware sample
Classification Accuracy	98.53%	99.77%	99.80%	97.80%	98.20%
Time cost (s)	1790.24	5656.00	2867.00	32,087.40	6372.00 (Train time for deep learning network)
Required hardware platform	Lenovo ThinkStation, Intel® Core™ i7-6700U CPU @3.40GHz × 8, 8 GB memory	A laptop with a quad-core processor (2 GHz), and 8 GB RAM	Not clearly stated	A workstation with an Intel Xeon E5-2650 CPU at 2.30 GHz, 128 GB of RAM, and 4 TB of SSD storage	A workstation with a 6 core i7-6850K Intel processor

Features means the number of Features.

(2) MalSEF really realized the parallel analysis of massive malware, which can effectively reduce the analysis time. Compared with the serial processing, the time efficiency is improved by 37.60%. Compared with similar research, the handing time required by MalSEF is the shortest. There may be concerns over whether the baselines could achieve better time efficiency if they use a smaller feature set. The aforementioned comparison of models is conducted under the terms of their respective required feature size. When only 300 features are used, MalSEF can achieve ideal detection results. However, if the size of the features in the baseline modes decreases, it is not confirmed whether their accuracy can remain. This raises a promising question for future research. It can also be observed that the time reduction is not especially significant when the feature size is decreased. This is because the dataset is not particularly large, and as the size of the dataset increases, the time efficiency of MalSEF will become more apparent.

(3) The performance of the hardware platform required by MalSEF is moderate, so ordinary researchers can earn the opportunity. As a consequence, it can be generalized in the field of popular network security and has good applicability.

(4) As for the similarities among variants of malware, MalSEF provides and verifies semantic explanations by extracting and mining Opcode information from malware samples, which compensates for the lack of semantic explanations in deep learning-based malware classification.

6. Conclusions

Considering the widespread use of metamorphic techniques by malware to evade detection, we conducted a comparative analysis of the similarities between malware variants. We found that variants are reproduced in the form of filling old wine in a new bottle actually, and there are manifest similarities between variants. To enhance the efficiency of malware analysis, accurately classifying these variants into their families is of theoretical and practical value. To achieve this goal, we proposed a new malware classification framework called MalSEF. MalSEF adopts a lightweight feature engineering framework by extracting a small part of the samples from the larger dataset to construct a sampled subset. Based on the sampled subset, it generates feature vectors to represent the original samples dataset, and then generates lightweight feature matrices, thereby reducing the workload of generating feature matrices from a large number of samples. Based on the above theory, our method uses multi-core parallel processing to analyze malware, thus making full use of the computing resources of the modern personal PC. Compared with the traditional serial processing, the time consumption is decreased and the analysis efficiency is promoted significantly. The key advantage of this paper is that MalSEF provides a practical and effective approach for analyzing and processing vast amounts of malware on personal computers. Going forward, we aim to explore the following areas: (1) Since cloud computing platforms are extensively utilized in the realm of network security, we can leverage these resources to conduct extensive parallel processing [38]; (2) utilizing Opcode to depict malware's features is a practical approach. By doing so, we can conduct a multi-dimensional malware analysis and utilize various features for a more comprehensive portrayal of malware [39]. (3) With the increasing frequency of APT attacks and the large-scale malware outbreaks in APT, how to apply parallel processing technology to detect APT attacks and take timely response measures is also a valuable research direction in the future [40,41].

Author Contributions: Conceptualization, W.H.; Methodology, J.L.; Software, W.H.; Validation, J.L.; Investigation, Q.Z.; Data curation, Y.Z.; Writing—original draft, W.H.; Writing—review & editing, J.L. and Q.Z.; Supervision, J.X.; Project administration, J.X.; Funding acquisition, J.X. All authors have read and agreed to the published version of the manuscript.

Funding: This research was funded by the National Natural Science Foundation of China (No. 62172042), the National Key Research & Development Program of China (2020YFB1712104), and the Major Scientific and Technological Innovation Projects of Shandong Province (2020CXGC010116).

Data Availability Statement: The data used to validate the outcomes of this investigation can be obtained by contacting the corresponding author.

Conflicts of Interest: There is no potential conflict of interest in the submission of this manuscript, and all authors have approved its publication.

References

1. Rezaei, T.; Manavi, F.; Hamzeh, A. A PE header-based method for malware detection using clustering and deep embedding techniques. *J. Inf. Secur. Appl.* **2021**, *60*, 102876. [CrossRef]
2. Darem, A.; Abawajy, J.; Makkar, A.; Alhashmi, A.; Alanazi, S. Visualization and deep-learning-based malware variant detection using OpCode-level features. *Future Gener. Comput. Syst.* **2021**, *125*, 314–323. [CrossRef]
3. Malware. Available online: https://www.av-test.org/en/statistics/malware/ (accessed on 7 July 2021).
4. Singh, J.; Singh, J. A survey on machine learning-based malware detection in executable files. *J. Syst. Archit.* **2021**, *112*, 101861. [CrossRef]
5. Botacin, M.; Ceschin, F.; Sun, R.; Oliveira, D.; Grégio, A. Challenges and pitfalls in malware research. *Comput. Secur.* **2021**, *106*, 102287. [CrossRef]
6. Han, W.; Xue, J.; Wang, Y.; Huang, L.; Kong, Z.; Mao, L. MalDAE: Detecting and explaining malware based on correlation and fusion of static and dynamic characteristics. *Comput. Secur.* **2019**, *83*, 208–233. [CrossRef]
7. Santos, I.; Brezo, F.; Ugarte-Pedrero, X.; Bringas, P.G. Opcode sequences as representation of executables for data-mining-based unknown malware detection. *Inf. Sci.* **2013**, *231*, 64–82. [CrossRef]
8. Tien, C.W.; Chen, S.W.; Ban, T.; Kuo, S.Y. Machine learning framework to analyze IoT malware using elf and opcode features. *Digit. Threat. Res. Pract.* **2020**, *1*, 5. [CrossRef]
9. Ling, Y.T.; Sani, N.F.M.; Abdullah, M.T.; Hamid, N.A.W.A. Structural features with nonnegative matrix factorization for metamorphic malware detection. *Comput. Secur.* **2021**, *104*, 102216. [CrossRef]
10. Zheng, J.; Zhang, Y.; Li, Y.; Wu, S.; Yu, X. Towards Evaluating the Robustness of Adversarial Attacks Against Image Scaling Transformation. *Chin. J. Electron.* **2023**, *32*, 151–158. [CrossRef]
11. Zhang, Q.; Ma, W.; Wang, Y.; Zhang, Y.; Shi, Z.; Li, Y. Backdoor attacks on image classification models in deep neural networks. *Chin. J. Electron.* **2022**, *31*, 199–212. [CrossRef]
12. Guo, F.; Zhao, Q.; Li, X.; Kuang, X.; Zhang, J.; Han, Y.; Tan, Y.A. Detecting adversarial examples via prediction difference for deep neural networks. *Inf. Sci.* **2019**, *501*, 182–192. [CrossRef]
13. Rudd, E.M.; Rozsa, A.; Günther, M.; Boult, T.E. A survey of stealth malware attacks, mitigation measures, and steps toward autonomous open world solutions. *IEEE Commun. Surv. Tutor.* **2016**, *19*, 1145–1172. [CrossRef]
14. Microsoft Malware Classification Challenge, Kaggle. Available online: https://www.kaggle.com/c/malware-classification (accessed on 27 October 2022).

15. Radkani, E.; Hashemi, S.; Keshavarz-Haddad, A.; Amir Haeri, M. An entropy-based distance measure for analyzing and detecting metamorphic malware. *Appl. Intell.* **2018**, *48*, 1536–1546. [CrossRef]
16. Yagemann, C.; Sultana, S.; Chen, L.; Lee, W. *Barnum*: Detecting document malware via control flow anomalies in hardware traces. In Proceedings of the Information Security: 22nd International Conference, ISC 2019, New York City, NY, USA, 16–18 September 2019; Proceedings 22. Springer International Publishing: Cham, Switzerland, 2019; pp. 341–359.
17. Ye, Y.; Li, T.; Adjeroh, D.; Iyengar, S.S. A survey on malware detection using data mining techniques. *ACM Comput. Surv. (CSUR)* **2017**, *50*, 1–40. [CrossRef]
18. Fan, Y.; Ye, Y.; Chen, L. Malicious sequential pattern mining for automatic malware detection. *Expert Syst. Appl.* **2016**, *52*, 16–25. [CrossRef]
19. Burnap, P.; French, R.; Turner, F.; Jones, K. Malware classification using self organising feature maps and machine activity data. *Comput. Secur.* **2018**, *73*, 399–410. [CrossRef]
20. Garcia, D.E.; DeCastro-Garcia, N. Optimal feature configuration for dynamic malware detection. *Comput. Secur.* **2021**, *105*, 102250. [CrossRef]
21. Han, W.; Xue, J.; Wang, Y.; Liu, Z.; Kong, Z. MalInsight: A systematic profiling based malware detection framework. *J. Netw. Comput. Appl.* **2019**, *125*, 236–250. [CrossRef]
22. Guerra-Manzanares, A.; Bahsi, H.; Nõmm, S. Kronodroid: Time-based hybrid-featured dataset for effective android malware detection and characterization. *Comput. Secur.* **2021**, *110*, 102399. [CrossRef]
23. Xin, Y.; Xie, Z.Q.; Yang, J. A load balance oriented cost efficient scheduling method for parallel tasks. *J. Netw. Comput. Appl.* **2017**, *81*, 37–46. [CrossRef]
24. Smilovich, D.; Radovitzky, R.; Dvorkin, E. A parallel staggered hydraulic fracture simulator incorporating fluid lag. *Comput. Methods Appl. Mech. Eng.* **2021**, *384*, 114003. [CrossRef]
25. Wang, K.; Li, X.; Gao, L.; Li, P.; Gupta, S.M. A genetic simulated annealing algorithm for parallel partial disassembly line balancing problem. *Appl. Soft Comput.* **2021**, *107*, 107404. [CrossRef]
26. Bailey, M.; Oberheide, J.; Andersen, J.; Mao, Z.M.; Jahanian, F.; Nazario, J. Automated classification and analysis of internet malware. In Proceedings of the Recent Advances in Intrusion Detection: 10th International Symposium, RAID 2007, Gold Goast, Australia, 5–7 September 2007; Proceedings 10. Springer: Berlin/Heidelberg, Germany, 2007; pp. 178–197.
27. Nataraj, L.; Yegneswaran, V.; Porras, P.; Zhang, J. A comparative assessment of malware classification using binary texture analysis and dynamic analysis. In Proceedings of the 4th ACM Workshop on Security and Artificial Intelligence, Chicago, IL, USA, 21 October 2011; pp. 21–30.
28. Ahmadi, M.; Ulyanov, D.; Semenov, S.; Trofimov, M.; Giacinto, G. Novel feature extraction, selection and fusion for effective malware family classification. In Proceedings of the Sixth ACM Conference on Data and Application Security and Privacy, New Orleans, LA, USA, 9–11 March 2016; pp. 183–194.
29. Hu, X.; Jang, J.; Wang, T.; Ashraf, Z.; Stoecklin, M.P.; Kirat, D. Scalable malware classification with multifaceted content features and threat intelligence. *IBM J. Res. Dev.* **2016**, *60*, 6:1–6:11. [CrossRef]
30. Lee, T.; Kwak, J. Effective and reliable malware group classification for a massive malware environment. *Int. J. Distrib. Sens. Netw.* **2016**, *12*, 4601847. [CrossRef]
31. Raff, E.; Nicholas, C. Malware classification and class imbalance via stochastic hashed lzjd. In Proceedings of the 10th ACM Workshop on Artificial Intelligence and Security, Dallas, TX, USA, 3 November 2017; pp. 111–120.
32. Le, Q.; Boydell, O.; Mac Namee, B.; Scanlon, M. Deep learning at the shallow end: Malware classification for non-domain experts. *Digit. Investig.* **2018**, *26*, S118–S126. [CrossRef]
33. Nakazato, J.; Song, J.; Eto, M.; Inoue, D.; Nakao, K. A novel malware clustering method using frequency of function call traces in parallel threads. *IEICE Trans. Inf. Syst.* **2011**, *94*, 2150–2158. [CrossRef]
34. Sheen, S.; Anitha, R.; Sirisha, P. Malware detection by pruning of parallel ensembles using harmony search. *Pattern Recognit. Lett.* **2013**, *34*, 1679–1686. [CrossRef]
35. Wang, X.; Zhang, D.; Su, X.; Li, W. Mlifdect: Android malware detection based on parallel machine learning and information fusion. *Secur. Commun. Netw.* **2017**, *2017*, 6451260. [CrossRef]
36. Kabir, E.; Hu, J.; Wang, H.; Zhuo, G. A novel statistical technique for intrusion detection systems. *Future Gener. Comput. Syst.* **2018**, *79*, 303–318. [CrossRef]
37. Abusitta, A.; Li, M.Q.; Fung, B.C. Malware classification and composition analysis: A survey of recent developments. *J. Inf. Secur. Appl.* **2021**, *59*, 102828. [CrossRef]
38. Mishra, P.; Verma, I.; Gupta, S. KVMInspector: KVM Based introspection approach to detect malware in cloud environment. *J. Inf. Secur. Appl.* **2020**, *51*, 102460. [CrossRef]
39. Wang, P.; Tang, Z.; Wang, J. A novel few-shot malware classification approach for unknown family recognition with multi-prototype modeling. *Comput. Secur.* **2021**, *106*, 102273. [CrossRef]

40. Han, W.; Xue, J.; Wang, Y.; Zhang, F.; Gao, X. APTMalInsight: Identify and cognize APT malware based on system call information and ontology knowledge framework. *Inf. Sci.* **2021**, *546*, 633–664. [CrossRef]
41. Liras, L.F.M.; de Soto, A.R.; Prada, M.A. Feature analysis for data-driven APT-related malware discrimination. *Comput. Secur.* **2021**, *104*, 102202. [CrossRef]

electronics

Article

Multimodel Collaboration to Combat Malicious Domain Fluxing

Yuanping Nie [1,†], Shuangshuang Liu [2,†], Cheng Qian [1,*], Congyi Deng [2], Xiang Li [1], Zhi Wang [2] and Xiaohui Kuang [1]

[1] National Key Laboratory of Science and Technology on Information System Security, Bejing 100085, China; yuanpingnie@nudt.edu.cn (Y.N.); ideal_work@163.com (X.L.); xiaohui-kuang@163.com (X.K.)
[2] DISSec, College of Cyber Science, Nankai University, Tianjin 300350, China; shuangliu0309@163.com (S.L.); dcy@nankai.edu.cn (C.D.); zwang@nankai.edu.cn (Z.W.)
* Correspondence: qiancheng@nudt.edu.cn
† These authors contributed equally to this work.

Abstract: This paper proposes a novel domain-generation-algorithm detection framework based on statistical learning that integrates the detection capabilities of multiple heterogeneous models. The framework includes both traditional machine learning methods based on artificial features and deep learning methods, comprehensively analyzing 34 artificial features and advanced features extracted from deep neural networks. Additionally, the framework evaluates the predictions of the base models based on the fit of the samples to each type of sample set and a predefined significance level. The predictions of the base models are statistically analyzed, and the final decision is made using strategies such as voting, confidence, and credibility. Experimental results demonstrate that the DGA detection framework based on statistical learning achieves a higher detection rate compared to the underlying base models, with accuracy, precision, recall, and F1 scores reaching 0.979, 0.977, 0.981, and 0.979, respectively. The framework also exhibits a stronger adaptability to unknown domains and a certain level of robustness against concept drift attacks.

Keywords: domain generation algorithms; machine learning; deep learning; statistical learning; heterogeneous models

Citation: Nie, Y.; Liu, S.; Qian, C.; Deng, C.; Li, X.; Wang, Z.; Kuang, X. Multimodel Collaboration to Combat Malicious Domain Fluxing. *Electronics* **2023**, *12*, 4121. https://doi.org/10.3390/electronics12194121

Academic Editor: Javid Taheri

Received: 9 September 2023
Revised: 26 September 2023
Accepted: 29 September 2023
Published: 2 October 2023

1. Introduction

With the rapid development of the Internet, the scale of hosts has increased significantly. The Domain Name System (DNS), as a fundamental element of the Internet, becomes more vital to Internet applications. The security of DNS has been a hot topic in the security research area. Obviously, malicious domain names are essential to many attack chains. Malicious domain names frequently appear in various cyberattacks, especially in botnets [1–6]. A botnet is a network of compromised computers, known as bots or zombies, that could be instructed by a controller on the Internet, a so-called bot master. Currently, botnets have become one of the most significant threats to the Internet. The bot masters employ botnets to send spam emails, host phishing web pages, execute DDoS attacks, mine cryptocurrency, and so on. The command and control (C&C) communication channel is vital to the botnet organization. In order to evade detection and blocking, many botnets use DNS to maintain C&C communication channels. Previous botnets used dynamic DNS and fast-flux DNS to communicate with C&C servers, but domain name blacklists can cut off these techniques effectively. To avoid blacklist detection and enhance self-survival ability, most botnets today, such as Conficker, Kraken, and Torpig, used domain generation algorithms (DGAs) [7–10] to create a candidate list of C&C server domains [11,12].

A DGA is a technique used by malware to generate a large number of randomly generated and variable malicious domain names. The working principle of a DGA involves generating a multitude of domains using a random seed and algorithm, allowing the malware to communicate with its command and control (C&C) servers without being easily detected or blocked by network security systems. This technology finds widespread application in modern malware and network attacks. The applications of DGAs include the persistence and covert dissemination of malware. Malware developers leverage DGA-generated random domain names to propagate malware by enticing users to click on malicious links, ads, or phishing emails, thereby infecting their systems. Some malicious software also employs DGA-generated domain names as the addresses for their control servers, enabling the theft of sensitive data or maintaining a dormant state. Additionally, DGAs are used for covert communication purposes [2,13,14], allowing malware to transmit data through generated domain names and evade traditional network monitoring and defense mechanisms.

A DGA uses random seeds to generate a large number of different domain names, but bot masters usually only register one or some domains in the candidate list and use registered domains to distribute their command. It would be increasingly difficult to block malicious domain names generated by DGAs only using blacklists and reverse engineering [15–18]. Fortunately, many researchers have applied learning techniques to detect malicious domains. Davuth et al. [19] used two-gram features to build an SVM model for malicious domain name classification. Vinayakumar et al. [20] employed a deep learning model based on DNS logs text to capture malicious domain names in scale traffic. Mowbray et al. [21] used a special string length distribution in a domain name lookup service to detect malicious domain names. Woodbridge et al. [22] introduced an LSTM network to detect DGA-generated domains without feature extracting. Schüppen et al. [23] trained classifiers on random forests and support vector machines utilizing structural features, linguistic features, and statistical features extracted from domain name sequences. The commonly used methods for DGA domain name detection are based on artificial features or deep learning methods, but most of the previous researchers have proposed methods to detect DGA domain names using a single framework, which leads to a single perspective of analyzing DGA domain names.

In order to solve the problem of a single analysis perspective of the DGA domain name classification algorithm, this paper proposes a multimodel collaborative domain name classification (malicious or benign) framework by integrating multiple underlying predictive models. The research motivation of this paper is as follows:

- Improve detection accuracy: A single detection model may not be able to cover all malicious behaviors and variants comprehensively. Therefore, utilizing multiple models for collaborative detection can enhance the accuracy of detection. Each model can emphasize different features or algorithms, thereby increasing the detection rate of malicious software and reducing false positives.
- Counteract the evolution of malicious software: Malicious software evolves rapidly, with new variants constantly emerging. By employing multiple detection models, the sensitivity to different variants of malicious software can be increased, enabling a timely detection and response to new threats.
- Compensate for the limitations of a single model: Each detection model has its own limitations. Some models may perform well in specific types of malicious behaviors while being less accurate in others. A collaborative detection with multiple models can compensate for these limitations by integrating and analyzing the results of multiple models, thereby improving overall detection performance.
- Enhance robustness and stability: A single model can be susceptible to false positives or false negatives, thereby impacting the robustness and stability of the entire system. Collaborative detection with multiple models can mitigate this issue by integrating and analyzing the detection results from multiple models, reducing the probability of false positives and false negatives and improving the system's robustness and stability.

For the above questions, the innovations of this paper are described below.

- This paper analyzes DGA domain names from multiple perspectives in terms of both artificial features and neural network advanced features. In this paper, 34 artificial features are extracted from three aspects, namely, string structure, language characteristics, and distribution statistics, and deep neural networks are used to actively mine the advanced features of domain name characters to detect DGA domain names through traditional machine learning methods and deep learning methods.
- A multimodel decision-making framework based on statistical learning is proposed. This statistical learning-based approach provides the same comparison criteria for heterogeneous models, determines the prediction labels based on the performance of the samples in each type of sample set as well as a predetermined level of significance, and produces decision results with a certain level of confidence through voting, If the prediction labels of all models do not have sufficient confidence, the combined confidence and credibility metric comprehensively evaluates the prediction quality of the models and selects the highest quality prediction as the final decision result.
- In this paper, we design and implement a DGA detection algorithm based on statistical learning. The detection algorithm takes domain name strings as the research object, uses four heterogeneous methods, XGBoost, B-RF, LSTM, and CNN, to detect DGA domain names, evaluates the prediction quality of these heterogeneous methods based on statistical learning, and generates the DGA detection results. The detection algorithm analyzes DGA domain names from multiple perspectives from the artificial features and high-level features unearthed by the neural network, improves the detection effect, and can effectively identify the elimination of invalid prediction results in the decision-making process, maximize the stability of the algorithm, and is a real-time, lightweight detection method.

The paper is organized as follows. In Section 2, we provide static feature extraction methods and dynamic feature extraction methods. In Section 3, we introduce the theoretical foundations of feature extraction. Section 4 provides a multimodel detection framework. Section 5 provides the description of the dataset, evaluation criteria, and comparative experiment results. Finally, the conclusion and future work are found in Section 6.

2. Related Work

In the work related to DGA domain characterization, researchers usually analyze the characteristics of DGA domains from different perspectives in order to propose effective detection methods. These methods can be categorized into static characterization methods, dynamic characterization methods, deep learning methods, and heterogeneous information network-based methods.

Static feature analysis methods refer to the parameters and rules used in domain name generation algorithms, such as seed value, domain length, character set, and so on. Researchers analyze these parameters and rules to identify DGA domain names and build corresponding classifiers or models. For example, some researchers have used machine learning methods such as support vector machines (SVM), random forests, and neural networks to identify DGA domain names. They rely on static features, such as character frequency, character position, and character type, to build classifiers and evaluate the accuracy and robustness of the classifiers through the performance of training and test sets. Among them, Yu et al. [24] proposed a character n-gram and sequence pattern-based approach that combined static features and sequence patterns to improve the recognition rate of DGA domain names. Yadav and Reddy et al. [25] used entropy-based features to detect algorithmically generated domain names, where the entropy was a measure of uncertainty of the characters in a domain name, with a higher value indicating that the domain name was more difficult to speculate about. This was a static feature based on the length of the domain name and the distribution of characters. Schüppen et al. [23] proposed a novel feature-based system for classifying nonexistent domain names, FANCI, which detected malware infections based on DGA by monitoring DNS traffic for nonexistent domain name (NXDomain) responses and used machine learning to extract twenty-one features from domain names for classification, including twelve structural features, seven linguistic features, and two statistical features, but the FANCI system did not support multiple classification tasks. Zhao et al. [26] proposed a DOLPHIN system that could detect DGA-based botnets by extracting effective phonetic features. DOLPHIN was the first method to introduce a phonetic method to detect AGD by classifying variable-length vowels and consonants. In addition, they proposed a new automaton matching method based on the AC algorithm to handle variable-length vowels and consonants, thus extracting features from domain names more accurately. However, the static feature detection methods have a limited effectiveness when dealing with new malicious domain names. The creators of malicious domain names can circumvent static signature detection methods by constantly changing the domain name structure and using new signatures.

Dynamic characterization methods refer to the behaviors and patterns of DGA domain names in actual use, such as temporal correlation, domain traffic distribution, and DNS query patterns. Researchers analyze these features to identify DGA domain names and propose corresponding detection methods. For example, some researchers [11,27] use temporal correlation features, such as the relationship between domain name generation time and DNS query time, to identify DGA domain names. Some other researchers use domain traffic distribution features, such as domain query frequency and query source, to identify DGA domains. For example, Kolias et al. [28] use DNS traffic analysis techniques to detect DGA-based botnets, where dynamic features include the query frequency, query source, and temporal correlation of DGA-generated domains. However, dynamic feature detection usually requires real-time monitoring and analysis of the dynamic behavior of domain names, which may result in a certain time delay. During this delay, the malicious domain may have caused harm to users or spread malicious content. In addition, dynamic feature detection usually requires the collection and analysis of users' network behavior data, which may involve personal privacy issues. Ensuring appropriate protection and privacy of user data is crucial.

In recent years, deep learning methods have also made significant progress in malicious domain name detection. In 2020, Zhao et al. [29] proposed a malicious domain name identification method integrated with effective DNS response features, which identified malicious domain names by using linguistic features and statistical features. Linguistic features were generated by a bidirectional long short-term memory (BiLSTM) neural network to generate vector representations from a sequence of domain name characters, and statistical features were composed of six manually designed statistics that made up a data structure representing a domain name. In addition, Zhao et al. [30] used models such as convolutional neural networks (CNNs) and long short-term memory networks (LSTMs) in order to rely on static features such as character frequencies and character positions to recognize DGA domain names. This study showed that the method had a high accuracy and robustness. At present, attack methods targeting deep neural networks are also beginning to appear [31,32]. In addition, in the process of detecting malicious domains using deep learning models, the number of legitimate domains far exceeds the number of malicious domains, leading to data imbalance issues. This may negatively impact the performance of the training model, making it more likely to misclassify malicious domains as legitimate.

In addition, some researchers have proposed heterogeneous information network-based approaches to improve the detection of malicious domains. These methods construct a heterogeneous information network model to simulate DNS scenarios by analyzing the characteristics of domains and the complex relationships between domains, clients, and IP addresses. For example, Sun et al. [33] proposed a malicious domain name detection method based on a heterogeneous graph convolutional network approach, which employed a metapath-based attention mechanism that could simultaneously process node features and graph structures in a heterogeneous information network. Detecting malicious domain names based on heterogeneous graph information networks has some difficulties in data acquisition and integration, and constructing heterogeneous graph information networks requires the collection and integration of many types of data, including domain names,

IP addresses, WHOIS information, and so on. Acquiring and integrating these data may require a lot of time and resources, and the issue of credibility and consistency of data sources needs to be addressed. In addition, building heterogeneous graphs requires considering the connectivity of different types of nodes and edges, as well as the attributes of nodes and edges. Determining the representation of nodes and edges with appropriate feature engineering is a challenging task. The number and weight of different types of nodes and edges may also have an impact on the performance of the model.

3. Feature Engineering

The object of this paper was the domain name string itself, so the feature extraction work focused on the domain name string and did not consider other information in the DNS data. Since most of the DGA generation algorithms operate on second-level domain names, in this paper, only second-level domain names (SLDs) and top-level domain names (TLDs) were considered [34–37]. In the following, domain name specifically refers to a string consisting of second-level domain names and top-level domain names. When the original domain name contained other labels, they were ignored and deleted, such as "bbs.at.worl.com", and only "worl.com" was selected as the domain name in this paper.

Inspired by papers [11,12,23], so far, we have collected 34 human-engineered string features; these features can be divided into three categories: structural features, linguistic features, and statistical features. The introduction of each feature and the details of the calculation process are given below:

1. Structural features: This paper extracted six structural features, which represent the characteristics of the domain name in the string structure. The specific information is shown in Table 1. We used $d1$ and $d2$ as examples to illustrate the specific values of these features, where d1 $=$ *baidu.com* is a well-known normal domain name, and $d2 = 159vthg1nqmpuyh6.viajes$ is a malicious domain name. For a better understanding, the fourth feature in Table 1 is introduced in detail below.
   (#4) tld_dga: It indicates whether the top-level domain name is frequently related to malicious activities. It is a Boolean value ('0' indicates that the top-level domain name is not related to malicious activities, "1" indicates related, and "0" indicates unrelated).
2. Linguistic features: This paper extracted a total of 15 linguistic features. This type of feature mainly focuses on the differences in language patterns between normal domain names and DGA domain names. It has a great effect on machine learning classifiers. Table 2 lists these features' information, and specific values for $d1$ and $d2$, where $d1 = baidu.com$, $d2 = geb3jnercfn28qeq.org$. Below is a detailed introduction to features #7, #11, #12, #14, #15, #16, and #18 in Table 2.
   - (#7) uni_domain: It indicates the number of unique characters in the secondary domain name, which is the number of characters that only appear once.
   - (#11) sym_sld: It refers to the ratio of the frequency of the three special symbols ".", "-", and "_" in a secondary domain name to the total length of the secondary domain name.
   - (#12) hex_sld: It refers to the ratio of the number of hexadecimal characters (0–9 and a–f) to the total length of the secondary domain name in the secondary domain name.
   - (#14) vow_sld: It refers to the ratio of vowel characters ("a", "e", "i", "o", "u") to the total length of the secondary domain name in the secondary domain name.
   - (#15) con_sld: It refers to the ratio of consonant characters ("b", "c", "d", "f", etc.) to the total length of a secondary domain name.
   - (#16) repeat_letter_sld: It refers to the ratio of the number of characters with a frequency greater than 1 in a secondary domain name to the total length of the secondary domain name.
   - (#18) cons_con_ratio_sld: It refers to the ratio of the total length of subsequences composed of continuous consonants in a secondary domain name to the total length of the secondary domain name.

- (#20) gib_value_sld: Using the Gibberish method to detect the readability of secondary domain name strings, this feature is a Boolean value, where "1" indicates the string is readable, and "0" indicates the string is unreadable and difficult to pronounce.
- (#21) hmm_log_prob_sld: This feature uses a hidden Markov model (HMM) to measure the readability of secondary domain names, thus distinguishing between normal and malicious domains. Due to the fact that normal domain names generally use combinations of common words or abbreviations of certain words to form domain names, this method selects common English words or abbreviations to construct an HMM model. In general, the HMM coefficient of normal domain names will be higher, greater than −100, while the HMM coefficient of DGA domain names is lower, less than −100, due to being randomly generated.

Table 1. Domain name structure characteristics table.

#	Feature	Note	*d*1	*d*2
1	domain_len	Length of SLD.TLD	9	23
2	sld_len	Length of secondary domain name	5	16
3	tld_len	Length of top domain name	3	6
4	tld_dga	Whether some malicious top-level domain names are included	0	1
5	tokens_sld	Number of tokens divided by "-"	0	0
6	flag_dig_tld	Does it start with a number?	0	1

Table 2. Domain name linguistic feature table.

#	Feature	Note	*d*1	*d*2
7	uni_domain	Number of unique characters in the domain name	8	13
8	uni_sld	Number of unique characters in the secondary domain name	5	12
9	uni_tld	Total number	3	3
10	digits_sld	Total number	0	3
11	sym_sld	Proportion of special characters	0.0	0.0
12	hex_sld	Ratio of hexadecimal characters	0.6	0.56
13	dig_sld	Number proportion	0.0	0.19
14	vow_sld	Proportion of vowel letters	0.6	0.19
15	con_sld	Proportion of consonant characters	0.4	0.63
16	repeat_letter_sld	Proportion of duplicate characters	0.0	0.19
17	rep_char_ratio_sld	Ratio of repeated characters to unique characters	0.0	0.25
18	cons_con_ratio_sld	Proportion of continuous consonants	0.0	0.38
19	cons_dig_ratio_sld	Proportion of consecutive numbers	0.0	0.13
20	gib_value_sld	Gib written detection	1	0
21	hmm_log_prob_sld	HMM written detection	0.0	−999

3. Statistical features: This paper extracted 13 statistical features that distinguish normal domain names from DGA domain names from the perspective of character distribution. The basic information of these features is summarized in Table 3, and we take $d1 = baidu.com$ and $d2 = geb3jnercfn28qeq.org$ as examples to illustrate the specific selection of these features' values. We provide a detailed introduction to features #22, #23, #25, #28, #31, #33, and #34 in Table 3.
    - (#22) entropy_sld: It represents the Shannon entropy value of the secondary domain name, which can measure the randomness of the secondary domain name. Generally, the randomness of a normal domain name is low, with the Shannon entropy being low. However, the randomness of the DGA domain name generated by the algorithm is high, and the corresponding entropy value is also high.
    - (#23) gram2_med_sld: It refers to the median frequency of the occurrence of binary (2-gram) character groups in the secondary domain name string. In

natural language, the distribution of n-gram character groups is uneven, so this feature can distinguish between normal domain names and DGA domain names from the perspective of the frequency of n-gram character groups.

- (#25) gram2_cmed_sld: This feature is also the median frequency of the occurrence of binary (2-gram) character groups. The difference from feature #23 is that before calculating the feature, it is necessary to copy the secondary domain name to construct a new string. Assuming "baidu" is the secondary domain name, we use "baidubaidu" to calculate the feature. Repetitive operations can increase the length of a string, which is beneficial for the calculation of n-grams, especially for shorter domain names. In addition, repetitive operations can also amplify the characteristics of the string and facilitate classification. Assuming the secondary domain name is "aaaa", repeating it to form "aaaaaaaa" will make the character string look even more abnormal.
- (#28) avg_gram2_rank_sld: This feature represents the average frequency of all 2-gram character groups in the secondary domain name.
- (#31) std_gram2_rank_sld: This feature represents the standard deviation of the frequency of all 2-gram character groups in the secondary domain name and can measure the degree of dispersion of these character groups.
- (#33) gni: It refers to the Gini value of characters in a secondary domain name, calculated as shown in formula 1. In the formula, n represents the number of unique characters in the secondary domain name (#8), and p_i represents the frequency of unique characters c_i appearing in the secondary domain name.

$$gni = 1 - \sum_{i=1}^{n} p_i^2, \tag{1}$$

- (#34) cer: It represents the classification of character errors in a secondary domain name, calculated as shown in Formula (2). p_i represents the frequency of the unique character c_i appearing in the secondary domain name.

$$cer = 1 - \max_{i=1 \cdots n} p_i. \tag{2}$$

Table 3. Statistical characteristic table.

#	Feature	Note	*d*1	*d*2
22	entropy_sld	Shannon entropy	2.32	3.45
23	gram2_med_sld	2-Gram median of metacharacter frequency	4.38	3.32
24	gram3_med_sld	3-Gram median of metacharacter frequency	3.17	1.56
25	gram2_cmed_sld	2-Gram median of metacharacter frequency	4.23	3.32
26	gram3_cmed_sld	3-Gram median of metacharacter frequency	3.17	1.49
27	avg_gram1_rank_sld	1-Gram average value of metacharacter frequency sorting	8.2	15.56
28	avg_gram2_rank_sld	2-Gram average value of metacharacter frequency sorting	130.17	588.88
29	avg_gram3_rank_sld	3-Gram average value of metacharacter frequency sorting	1783.4	7640.06
30	std_gram1_rank_sld	1-Gram standard deviation of metacharacter frequency sorting	5.19	11.55
31	std_gram2_rank_sld	2-Gram standard deviation of metacharacter frequency sorting	71.10	440.15
32	std_gram3_rank_sld	3-Gram standard deviation of metacharacter frequency sorting	1062.69	8081.53
33	gni	Gini value	0.8	0.90
34	cer	character classification error	0.8	0.81

4. Multimodel Detection

4.1. XGBoost Model Training

This paper used the XGBClassifier in the xgboost library to construct an XGBoost detection model and trained the XGBoost detection model offline using known DGA domain names and normal domain names. The XGBoost model contains numerous parameters. To achieve better detection results, this paper used loss as the judgment criterion and adjusted the six parameters nes, depth, child, ga, colsample, and lr using GridSearchCV and a 5-fold cross-validation, as shown in Table 4.

In Table 4, "nes" represents the possible values of the parameter "n_estimators", which refers to the number of base weak learners (base estimators) in the gradient boosting tree model. It represents the number of trees to be built during gradient boosting. "depth" represents the possible values of the parameter "max_depth", which refers to the maximum depth of each tree in the decision tree model. "child" represents the possible values of the parameter "min_child_weight", which refers to the lower limit of the minimum sample weight sum of each leaf node. "ga" represents the possible values of the parameter "gamma", which refers to the minimum loss function reduction required when performing tree splitting. "colsample" represents the possible values of the parameter "colsample_bytree", which refers to the proportion of features that each tree samples when building. It is used to control the proportion of features used by each tree to increase the diversity of the model. "lr" represents the possible values of the parameter "learning_rate", which refers to the contribution reduction factor of each tree, which controls the contribution of each tree to the final model.

Table 4. XGBoost parameter tuning process.

```
xgb = XGBClassifier(silent=True,objective='binary:logistic')
nes = [50, 100]
depth = [3, 5, 10]
child = [2, 4, 6]
ga = [2, 0.3, 0.5]
colsample = [0.6, 0.8, 1]
lr = [0.2, 0.1, 0.01]
gird_par = dict(n_estimators = nes, max_depth = depth, min_child_weight = child, gamma = ga,
colsample_bytree = colsample, learning_rate=lr)
clf = GridSearchCV(xgb, gird parameters, cv=5, n_jobs=-1, scoring='neg_log_loss')
clf.fit(x_train, y_train)
cv_result = pd.DataFrame.from_dict(clf.cv_results_)
best_param = clf.best_params
```

To determine the optimal parameter combination, we conducted a total of 324 experiments and employed the GridSearchCV algorithm, which performs a comprehensive search over the specified parameter grid using cross-validation. This algorithm trains the XGBoost classifier on the training data and evaluates its performance using the specified scoring metric. The parameter combination that achieved the highest performance score was selected as the optimal parameter set. After multiple experiments, we determined the optimal parameter combination for the XGBoost detection model, as shown in Table 5. XGBoost iterated 100 times and generated 100 decision trees during the training process. The maximum depth of each decision tree in the model was 10, the weighted sum of the minimum sample was 2, the minimum loss function value remained the default value of 0 when the decision tree node was split, and the loss value of the detection model was the lowest when the learning rate was set to 0.2.

Table 5. XGBoost optimal parameter table (loss = 0.0639).

Parameter	Value	Parameter	Value
n_ estimators	100	gamma	0
max_depth	10	colsample_bytree	0.6
min_child_weight	2	learning_rate	0.2

4.2. B-RF Model Training

B-RF (binary random forest) refers to the random forest used for binary tasks. This article used Sklearn's RandomForestClassifier to construct a B-RF detection model and trained the model offline using known DGA domain names and normal domain names. Similar to the XGBoost tuning process, B-RF also uses loss as the judgment criterion and searches for the optimal parameter combination through GridSearchCV and cross-validation, as shown in Table 6.

In Table 6, "brf" is an instantiation object of a RandomForestClassifier. "crit" represents the possible values of the parameter "criterion", which is an indicator or criterion used to measure the purity of a node. "feature" represents the possible values of the parameter "max_features", which is used to control the maximum number of features considered for each node when splitting.

Table 6. B-RF parameter tuning process.

```
brf = RandomForestClassifier(random_state=23, n_jobs=-1)
nest = [50, 100]
crit =['gini', 'entropy']
feature = [15, 20, 30]
gird _par = dict(n_estimators=nest, criterion=crit, max_feature=feature)
clf = GridSearchCV(brf, gird parameters,cv=5, n _jobs=-1, scoring='neg_log_loss')
clf.fit(x _train, y_train)
cv_result = pd.DataFrame.from_dict(clf.cv_results_)
best_param = clf.best_params
```

After multiple experiments, we obtained the optimal parameter combination as shown in Table 7. The final B-RF classifier in this paper contained 100 trees, which means that the weak classifier needed to iterate 100 times. Each classifier used a maximum of 15 feature subsets for training, and entropy was used as the judgment criterion for attribute segmentation.

Table 7. B-RF optimal parameter table (loss = 0.07382).

Parameter	Value
n_ estimators	100
max_feature	15
criterion	entropy

4.3. LSTM Model Training

The structure of the LSTM model used in this paper is shown in Figure 1, which includes an embedding layer, an LSTM layer, a dense layer, and an activation layer.

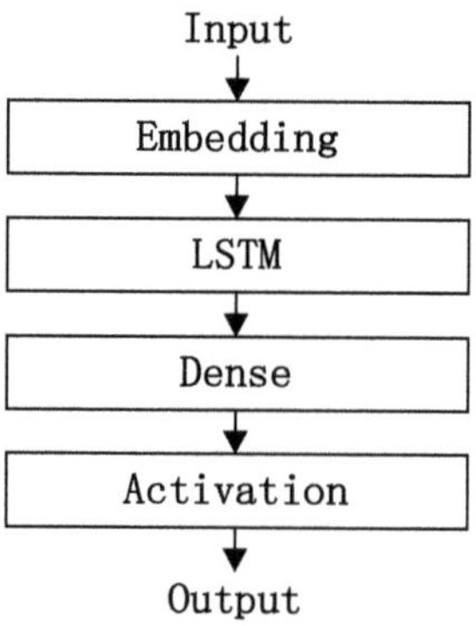

Figure 1. LSTM model architecture.

The embedding layer in Figure 1 maps the input sequence to a multidimensional feature space, forming an input matrix. The rows in the matrix represent the characters in the input sequence, and the list shows the dimensions of the feature space. The LSTM layer can implicitly extract advanced features from the sequence. The dense layer and activation layer complete the classification based on the extracted feature information and use the sigmoid function to compress the results to the range [0–1]. Finally, a prediction probability is output, representing the probability that the domain name belongs to a certain category. In this article, if the output probability is greater than or equal to 0.5, it indicates that the domain name is a DGA domain name, and vice versa, that it is a normal domain name.

This paper implemented an LSTM detection model based on the Keras framework, as shown in Table 8. In order to pursue better detection results, this paper used loss as a comparative indicator and a cross-validation to adjust the parameters in the LSTM layer. Table 9 is the optimal parameter table for the LSTM detection model, with a maximum length of 60 for the input string. The input string was converted into an index value vector and input into the embedding layer. In the embedding layer, each character was mapped to a 128-dimensional embedding vector. In the selection section of the optimizer, experiments have shown that the Adam optimizer [38] can achieve a better loss convergence compared to RMSProp [22].

Table 8. LSTM detect model code snippets.

```
model = Sequential()
model.add(Embedding(max_features,128, input_length=max_len))
model.add(LSTM(128))
model.add(Dropout(0.5))
model.add(Dense(1))
model.add(Activation('sigmoid'))
model.compile(loss='binary_crossentropy', optimizer='adam')
```

Table 9. LSTM optimal parameter table (loss = 0.0529).

Parameter	Value	Parameter	Value
bacth_ size	128	epoch	10
max_feature	40	dropout	0.5
max_len	60	learning_rate	0.001
optimizer	adam		

4.4. CNN Model Training

This paper used the open-source CNN detection model from reference [39] for DGA domain name detection, and the model structure is shown in Figure 2. The model code is shown in Table 10. The model uses the embedding layer to transform the input sequence into a distributed representation containing rich semantic information. The model adopts a parallel structure of multiple convolution layers, and the pooling operation is aimed at the entire domain name sequence, which makes the model only focus on whether there are patterns in the domain name but does not save its specific location information, so the model is robust to the insertion and deletion of characters, and subsequences that appear anywhere in the domain name sequence can be detected.

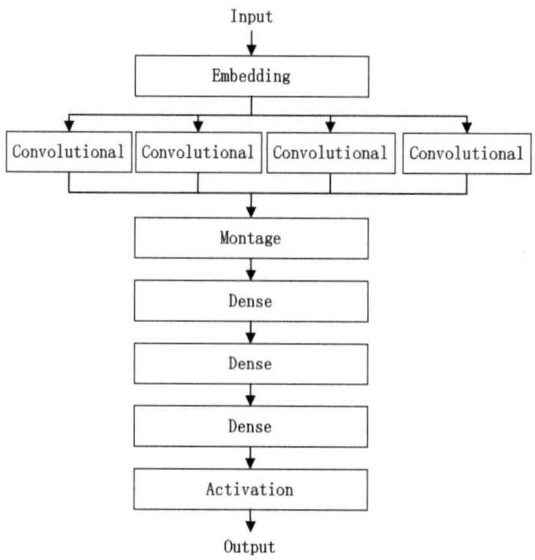

Figure 2. CNN model.

Table 10. CNN model code snippets.

```
def getconvmodel(self, kernel_size, filters):
model = Sequential()
model.add(Conv1D(filters=filters, input_shape=(128,128), kernel_size=kernel_size,
padding='same', activation='relu', strides=1))
model.add(Lambda(lambda x: k.sum(x, axis=1), output_shape=(filters,)))
model.add(Dropout(0.5))
return model
```

```
main_input = Input(shape=(self.max_len,), dtype='int32')
embedding = Embedding(input_dim=self.max_features, output_dim=128,
input_length=self.max_len)(main_input)
conv1 = self.getconvmodel(2,256)(embedding)
conv2 = self.getconvmodel(3,256)(embedding)
conv3 = self.getconvmodel(4,256)(embedding)
conv4 = self.getconvmodel(5,256)(embedding)
merged = Concatenate()([conv1, conv2, conv3, conv4])
middle = Dense(1024, activation='relu')(merged)
middle = Dropout(0.5)(middle)
middle= Dense( 1024, activation='relu')(middle)
middle = Dropout(0.5)(middle)
output = Dense(1, activation='sigmoid')(middle)
model = Model(inputs=main_input, outputs=output)
model.compile(loss='binary_crossentropy', optimizer='adam')
return model
```

Table 11 shows the optimal parameter information of the CNN detection model, with loss as the comparison indicator and parameter adjustment using cross-validation. The input sequence was transformed into a 128-dimensional embedding vector in the embedding layer, and then a one-dimensional convolutional layer was used to extract local features of character sequences at different levels. All layers in the model except the input layer used Relu (rectified linear unit) as the activation function, the Adam optimizer was selected, and the parameter of the dropout was set to 0.5 [40], which destroyed the complex collaborative adaptation in the network and prevented overfitting.

Table 11. CNN optimal parameter table (loss = 0.107).

Parameter	Value	Parameter	Value
bacth_ size	128	epoch	10
max_feature	40	dropout	0.5
max_len	60	learning_rate	0.001
optimizer	adam		

4.5. DGA Domain Name Detection Based on Statistical Learning

The main work of this section is to evaluate the prediction quality of the basic detection model based on the various basic detection models obtained in the previous text, using the conformal evaluator and significance evaluation. Based on the evaluation results, corresponding strategies are adopted to obtain the final label. Figure 3 is a multimodel decision flowchart based on statistical learning.

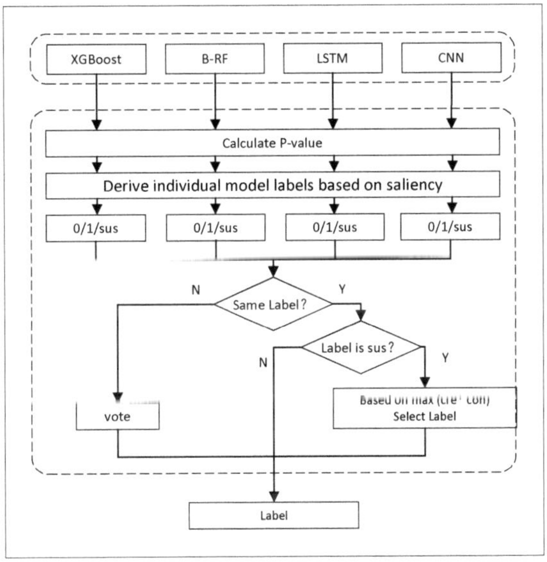

Figure 3. Multimodel decision flowchart based on statistical learning.

As shown in Figure 3, the decision-making mechanism can be divided into two parts: (1) determining the predictive labels of the basic model based on p-values and significance levels and (2) determining the final labels based on statistical analysis. Next, we elaborate on the implementation details of these two parts (In the figure, * represents product.).

4.5.1. Determining Basic Model Prediction Labels

When inputting a new test sample, the detection model first analyzes the sample using four basic models: XGBoost, B-RF, LSTM, and CNN. Each basic model outputs a probability score that represents the probability that the sample belongs to a certain class. Based on these probability scores, p^l, $l \in L$, and L representing all class labels of the sample in each class can be calculated. The following text provides a detailed explanation of the process of calculating the p-value.

For a binary classification task, $L = (0, 1)$, assuming M is the DGA domain name sample set with sample labels of 1, and G is the normal domain name sample set with sample labels of 0. Using M and G to train the basic model A, after training, model A outputs a probability score for each DGA sample in M, forming a DGA sample score set

$Score_M = \{\alpha_1, \alpha_2 \ldots \alpha_n\}$. Similarly, we generate a normal sample score set for the normal samples in $Score_G = \{\beta_1, \beta_2 \ldots \beta_n\}$. At this point, we input the sample point z^* to be tested, and model A outputs its probability score s^*. Then, the p^0 and p^1 values of the sample point z^* in model A are shown in Formulas (3) and (4).

$$\frac{p^0 = |\{i = 1, 2 \ldots, n|\beta_i \geq s^*\}|}{|n|}, \tag{3}$$

$$\frac{p^1 = |\{i = 1, 2 \ldots, n|\alpha_i \leq s^*\}|}{|n|}. \tag{4}$$

The range of probability scores is [0–1], and the larger the probability score, the more similar the sample is to the DGA sample. Therefore, the probability score of most samples in the normal domain name sample set G is closer to 0, and the smaller the value, the more normal the sample is. p^0 is equal to the proportion of samples in G with scores higher than s^*. This means that the larger the p^0, the more samples in G have scores higher than z^*, indicating that the fitting degree between z^* and G is better than most samples, and z^* and G have a higher similarity degree; for the malicious sample set, most samples have scores closer to 1, and the higher the probability score, the more malicious the samples are. Therefore, p^1 is equal to the proportion of samples in M with scores lower than s^*. The larger the p^1, the more similar z^* is to M.

After obtaining the p-value, we use significance ε (maximum error probability) to divide the prediction labels of the basic model into acceptable and unacceptable. If $max(p^0, p^1) = p^0$ and $p^0 \geq \varepsilon$, then it means that the basic model A has a probability of at least $1 - \varepsilon$. The confidence level assumes that the sample label is 0, which is acceptable, $Label_A = 0$. If $max(p^0, p^1) \leq \varepsilon$, the prediction quality of the basic model A for this sample is very low, exceeding the acceptable tolerance range. Therefore, the prediction result is rejected and marked as "suspicious", $Label_A = suspicious$. The specific process is shown in Algorithm 1.

Algorithm 1: Determine a single model label based on p-value and confidence level ε

Input: confidence level ε
p^0, p^1 of the sample
Output: $Label_{Model}$
1: if $p^0 > p^1$ and $p^0 > \varepsilon$
2: $Label_{Model} = 0$
3: else if $p^1 > p^0$ and $p^1 > \varepsilon$
4: $Label_{Model} = 1$
5: else if $max(p^0, p^1) < \varepsilon$
6: rejecting predicted outcomes
7: $Label_{Model} = suspicious$

Unlike determining prediction labels based on probability and static thresholds, this method determines classification labels based on the overall fit between the sample and the sample set and introduces a significance level in the detection results of the basic model, further subdividing the detection results, so that the output results of the basic model have a certain level of confidence and improve the reliability of the results.

4.5.2. Multimodel Collaborative Prediction Based on Statistical Learning

After obtaining the label results of the basic model through the above steps, a set of basic model labels can be obtained. Next, a statistical analysis is conducted on this label set, and the final result is determined according to the following strategies.

1. If the label results of all models are 1 or 0, it indicates that the decision results of all basic models are consistent and have a certain level of confidence in this result. Therefore, the label is directly output as the final result.
2. If the label results of all models are "suspicious", it indicates that the prediction quality of all models is lower than ε. In this case, it is necessary to calculate the confidence and credibility values of each model for the sample based on the *p*-value and comprehensively evaluate the prediction quality of the basic model from two perspectives. When the confidence and credibility are both large, it indicates that the sample points are similar to the predicted category and have significant differences from other categories, indicating that the basic model has a higher classification quality for z^*. Therefore, this article used the product (cre * con) method to select the model with the highest quality from these basic models and uses the prediction label of this model as the final result.
3. If the label results of all models are inconsistent, a vote is taken to determine the label ("suspicious" results are not included). If there is an equal number of votes, the final label is selected based on the combination of confidence and credibility.

In summary, in the multimodel collaborative decision-making section based on statistical learning, labels are determined based on the fitting degree between the samples and each type of sample set by calculating the *p*-value in the conditional evaluator, and a manually preset significance level ε is used to perform a secondary screening and partitioning on the prediction results of the basic model (0, 1, suspicious) and narrow the scope of suspicious results by statistically analyzing the set of basic model labels. When all models are unable to make predictions with a certain level of confidence, we evaluate the model results from the perspectives of confidence and credibility and make decisions. On the contrary, voting is used to obtain the final result. This decision-making method based on statistical learning provides the same comparison standard for heterogeneous methods, has wide applicability and good application prospects, and introduces significance and confidence levels in the decision-making process, making the prediction results more reliable.

5. Experimental Process and Results Analysis

This section is an experiment and validation of the DGA detection algorithm based on multiple models. This section first briefly introduces the experimental environment, experimental data, data preprocessing process, and evaluation indicators and then trains and tests the detection performance of the model using known sample data. The experimental environment used in this paper is shown in Table 12.

Table 12. Experimental environment table.

CPU	4 cores
Memory	8G
Operating system	Ubuntu 16.04 64 bit
Python version	3.6
Python library version	tensorflow2.2.0, keras2.4.3

5.1. Experimental Data and Data Preprocessing

5.1.1. Dataset

The dataset used in this experiment included DGA domain name data obtained by crawlers and Tranco_K26W-1m, as shown in Table 13.

Table 13. Experimental data table.

Dataset	Data Size
C_DGA	15,713,816
Tranco_K26W-1m	1,000,000

C_DGA: C_DGA is the latest published DGA domain name data obtained from multiple intelligence sources such as 360 and Bambenek using a crawler in this experiment. The C_DGA dataset includes DGA domain names published by various intelligence sources from 31 October 2019 to 17 May 2023. As of now, a total of 6,442,220 DGA domain names have been obtained. These domain names come from different DGA families. Taking 894,247 domain names obtained from 31 October 2019 as an example, they belong to 54 DGA families. Figure 4 shows the number of domain names in some of the DGA families.

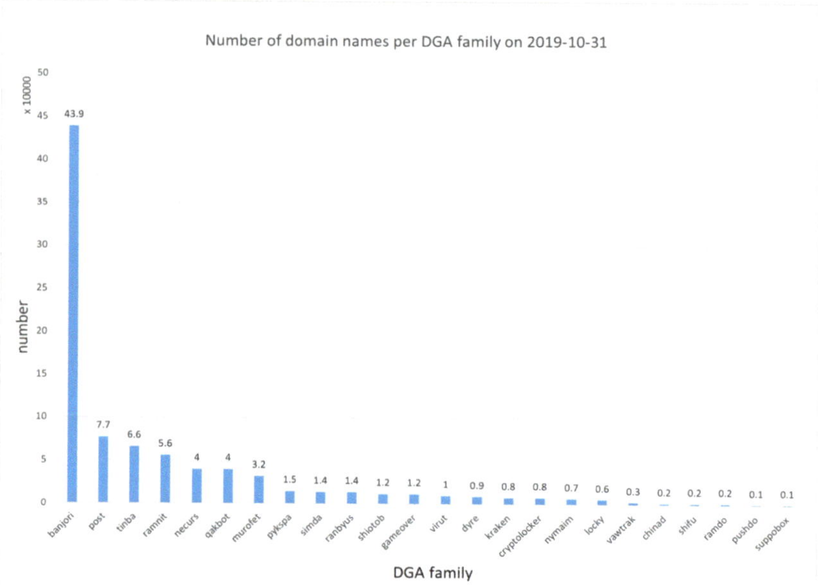

Figure 4. Number of domain names in partial DGA families (31 October 2019).

Tranco_K26W-1m dataset: Although Alexa is the most commonly used whitelist, the literature [41] demonstrates that Alexa is highly susceptible to manipulation and contamination, which may have an impact on experimental results. Therefore, this paper selected the Tranco_K26W-1m dataset as the normal sample dataset, which was proposed by Le Pochat [41] to be formed by aggregating three commonly used whitelists, Alexa, Cisco Umbrella, and Majestic. These whitelists generate website rankings based on website traffic and popularity and then use the top-ranked domain names as whitelist data. However, the three are generated by different companies, so there are very few data that truly overlap. Therefore, the Tranco_K26W-1m label generated by the aggregation operation is more accurate and has a higher credibility.

5.1.2. Data Preprocessing

For all domain name data, we followed the following rules for data cleaning:

1. Convert alphabetical characters in domain names to lowercase.

2. Remove all domain names starting with "*xn–*". Because a domain name starting with '*xn–*' is an Internationalized Domain Name (IDN), the DGA algorithm will not generate an IDN domain name.
3. Using "." as a separator, remove domain names with more than four segments.
4. Remove domain names from www.com and www.com.cn.
5. Remove duplicate data.

Because most of the domain names generated by the DGA algorithm only generate intermediate domain name strings, and a complete domain name is formed after adding a top-level domain name, this experiment focused more on the secondary domain name and top-level domain name. If the domain name sample also contained subdomains such as a third-level domain name, this part of the character string was ignored, such as www.google.com,where only google.com was retained.

The DGA domain name samples and benign domain name samples used in this experiment are shown in Table 14:

Table 14. Test sample information table.

DGA Domain Name Sample	Benign Sample
q4z1an1ca8icv1cl501sukun.biz	google.com
geb3jnercfn28qeq.org	facebook.com
1ihowds1u8fcu8kzuy549uytaj.com	windowsupdate.com
hpgkofoukqshvmt.info	yahoo.com

5.1.3. Evaluation Criteria

In the experiment, DGA domain names were defined as positive samples and normal domain names were defined as negative samples. The classification results of this experiment included the following four types, as shown in Table 15 in the confusion matrix.

1. TP (true positive): it refers to the cases where the model correctly identifies a domain name as malicious, and it is indeed malicious.
2. TN (true negative): it refers to the cases where the model correctly identifies a domain name as benign, and it is indeed benign.
3. FP (false positive): it refers to the cases where the model incorrectly identifies a domain name as malicious, whereas it is actually benign.
4. FN (false negative): it refers to the cases where the model incorrectly identifies a domain name as benign, whereas it is actually malicious.

Table 15. Confusion matrix table.

	Positive	Negative
True	TP (true positive)	TN (true negative)
False	FP (false positive)	FN (false negative)

This experiment was a dichotomous task with supervised learning. Therefore, accuracy, precision, recall, and F1 score were selected as evaluation criteria. Assuming that TP, TN, FP, and FN, respectively, represent the number of corresponding situations, the evaluation criteria are defined as follows:

1. *Accuracy* (ACC): represents the ratio of the number of correctly classified samples to the total number of samples.

$$ACC = \frac{(TP + TN)}{(TP + TN + FP + FN)}, \tag{5}$$

2. *Precision*: represents the ratio of the true number of positive samples to the number of positive samples in the classification results.

$$Precision = \frac{TP}{(TP + FP)}, \quad (6)$$

3. *Recall*: represents the proportion of correctly classified positive samples to all positive samples, $Recall = TPR$.

$$Recall = \frac{TP}{(TP + FN)}, \quad (7)$$

4. $F1$: Represents the harmonic mean of the accuracy rate and the recovery rate. When the $F1$ value is high, it means that both the accuracy rate and the recovery rate are high.

$$F1 = \frac{(2 * Precision * Recall)}{(Precision + Recall)}. \quad (8)$$

For classification tasks, the higher the accuracy, precision, recall, and F1 values, the better the classification effect.

5.2. Experimental Results and Analysis

Experiment on C_DGA random sampling, compared to Tranco_K26W-1m, was merged as experimental data, and the training and testing sets were divided into a fivefold cross-validation ratio of 8:2. The specific information is shown in Table 16.

Table 16. Training data and testing data size.

Dataset	Data Size
Training set	1,419,148
Testing set	354,788
Total	1,773,936

Using training data to train a statistical learning-based DGA detection model, the detection performance of the model was tested using test data and the four evaluation indicators mentioned above. The model was compared with multiple basic models, and the maximum fault tolerance rate was set to 0.01 in the experiment. The experimental results are shown in Table 17. The boldface represents the highest value detected.

Table 17. Table of experimental results for each model.

	Model Name	ACC	Precision	Recall	F1
1	B-RF	0.97551	0.96976	0.98063	0.97516
2	XGBoost	0.97554	0.96982	0.98062	0.97518
3	LSTM	0.97480	0.97066	0.979193	0.97490
4	CNN	0.96944	0.95212	**0.98859**	0.97001
5	B-RF + XGBoost	0.97498	0.97500	0.97496	0.97498
6	LSTM + CNN	0.97554	0.97613	0.97404	0.97833
7	B-RF + XGBoost + LSTM	0.97771	0.97498	0.98059	0.97778
8	B-RF + XGBoost + CNN	0.97768	0.97472	0.98081	0.97775
9	B-RF + LSTM + CNN	0.97791	0.97562	0.98032	0.97796
10	XGBoost + LSTM + CNN	0.97554	0.97661	0.97851	0.97756
11	XGBoost + B-RF + LSTM + CNN	**0.97908**	**0.97712**	0.98113	**0.97912**

The first four rows in Table 17 represent the accuracy of traditional basic models B-RF and XGBoost, which was 0.97551 and 0754, respectively, slightly better than the detection accuracy of deep learning models LSTM and CNN, which was 0.97480 and 0.96944. The F1 values of traditional basic models B-RF and XGBoost were 0.97516 and 0.97518, which were also better than the F1 values of deep learning models of 0.97490 and 0.97001. This may be due to the more comprehensive and high-quality features selected in this paper, which better fit the dataset used in this paper and improved the detection performance of the traditional machine learning model. At the same time, due to the shorter length of the domain name, it belonged to a short text. Therefore, the hidden features that deep learning models can mine were limited, resulting in slightly lower performance than B-RF and XGBoost.

The 5th to 11th rows in Table 17 show the detection results of various combination models based on statistical learning decisions, such as LSTM + CNN representing the detection model based on statistical learning combined with LSTM and CNN. Comparing lines 3, 4, and 6, it can be found that the LSTM + CNN model outperformed the basic models LSTM and CNN in terms of accuracy, precision, and F1 value, indicating that the former had a higher comprehensive detection ability. For rows 1, 2, and 5, the B-RF + XGBoost model did not improve on the original foundation. This is because both B-RF and XGBoost are ensemble learning methods, and in this article, they were analyzed and trained on the same feature set. The two were relatively similar. When using significance level to subdivide the detection results in decision-making, the addition of the subclass class caused more noise in the B-RF + XGBoost method, which affected the detection performance of the B-RF + XGBoost model.

In addition, according to rows 5, 6, 7, 8, 9, 10, and 11 in observation Table 17, these combined models were superior to the basic model in accuracy, precision, and F1 value, which indicated that the decision-making mechanism based on statistical learning could effectively improve the detection effect on the basis of a single model. The detection performance of B-RF + XGBoost + LSTM and B-RF + XGBoost + CNN in the table was better than that of B-RF + XGBoost, while the detection performance of B-RF + LSTM + CNN and XGBoost + LSTM + CNN was better than that of LSTM + CNN. This indicates that the more types of basic models included in the detection model, the better the detection performance. When both machine learning methods based on artificial features and deep learning methods were included, the detection performance was better than only including one type of method.

The 11th row in Table 17 is the DGA detection model proposed in this article, which includes two machine learning methods based on artificial features and two deep learning methods, achieving a balanced state. By comparing with other models, it can be concluded that the detection model proposed in this paper outperformed the basic model in terms of accuracy, precision, and F1 value and was also superior to other combination models. In terms of recall index, it was only lower than the CNN model, indicating that the DGA detection model based on statistical learning had a stronger detection ability compared to these models.

DGA domain names belonged to different DGA families, so we used 360netlab's DGA family domain name information to test the detection performance of the model for each family. During the experiment, one domain name of the DGA family was detected each time. As the test samples only contained positive samples, only accuracy was selected as the evaluation criterion. The experimental results are shown in Table 18, and the last column in the table represents the detection performance of the proposed model. From the table, it can be seen that the detection performance of the model on these DGA families was better than that of the basic model.

With the passage of time, DGAs are constantly evolving, and new DGA domain names appear every day, leading to the aging of DGA detection methods and a decrease in detection performance. Therefore, this paper used outdated data to train the detection model and tested the model's detection performance over time on new data in the coming year.

In the experiment, data from the C_DGA dataset from 31 October 2019 to 28 December 2019 were extracted as DGA domain name samples for the training set, and Tranco_K26W-1m was used as the normal domain name sample for the training set. The experimental results are shown in Figures 5–8. The blue curve represents the

B-RF detection model, the orange curve represents XGBoost, the green curve represents the LSTM detection model, the red curve represents the CNN detection model, and the purple curve represents the DGA detection model based on statistical learning in this paper.

Table 18. The detection accuracy of each model for each DGA family.

DGA Family	Number	B-RF	XGBoost	LSTM	CNN	Ours
bamital	104	0.98076	0.94230	1.00000	1.00000	1.00000
conficker	497	0.73440	0.74849	0.75653	0.72434	0.77464
cryptolocker	1000	0.98700	0.98700	0.99100	0.98600	0.99400
dyre	1000	1.00000	1.00000	1.00000	0.99700	1.00000
emotet	446,590	0.99153	0.99074	0.99527	0.99521	0.99543
feodo	263	1.00000	0.99661	1.00000	1.00000	1.00000
fobber-v1	299	1.00000	1.00000	1.00000	1.00000	1.00000
gameover	12,000	1.00000	1.00000	0.99983	0.99981	1.00000
necurs	8188	0.94589	0.94687	0.95994	0.95346	0.96433
nymaim	478	0.82383	0.82642	0.82642	0.78497	0.86139
padcrypt	168	0.97619	0.97619	0.97023	0.96428	0.98809
pykspa-v1	44,702	0.89168	0.89224	0.96470	0.96085	0.96492
pykspa-v2-fake	800	0.86875	0.88250	0.84750	0.84000	0.89375
pykspa-v2-real	198	0.69697	0.83333	0.86868	0.84848	0.87878
ranbyus	10,920	0.99340	0.99322	0.99505	0.99587	0.99688
rovnix	179,991	0.98386	0.88268	0.99660	0.99745	0.99860
virut	9740	0.74589	0.76324	0.75657	0.71899	0.78839

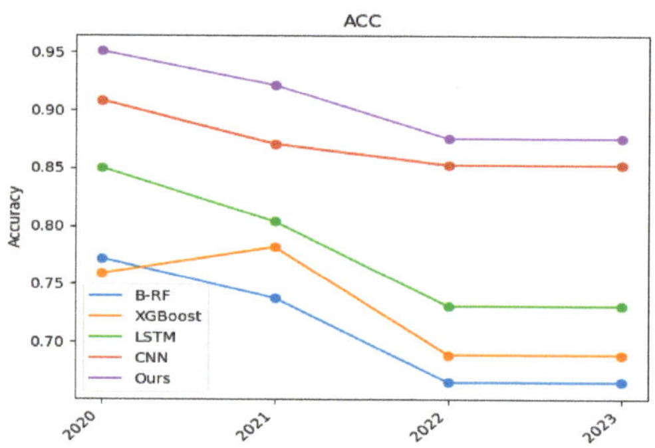

Figure 5. Accuracy versus time.

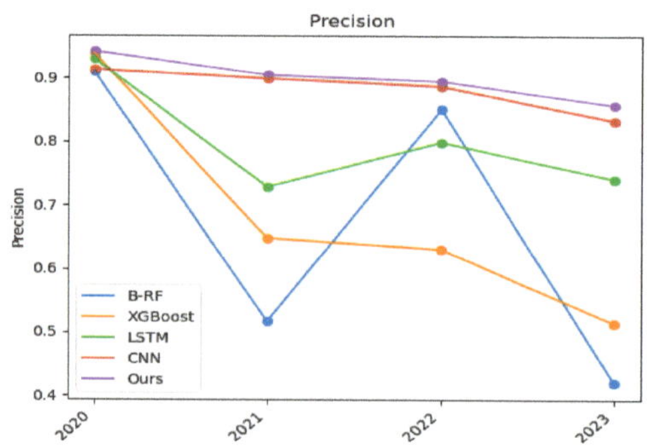

Figure 6. Precision versus time.

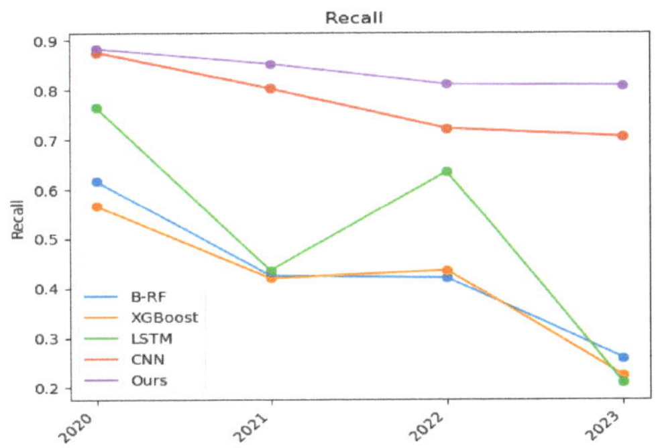

Figure 7. Recall versus time.

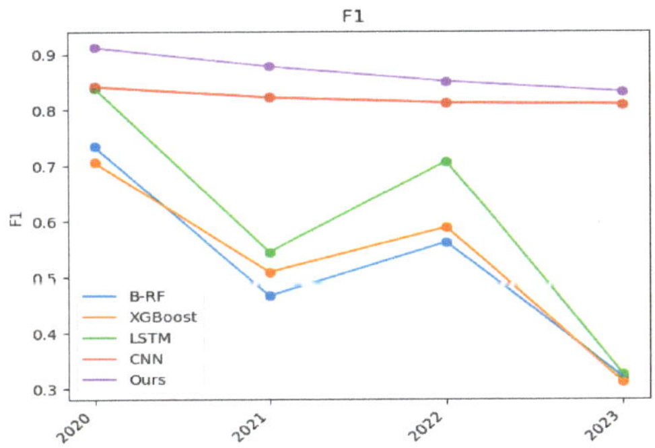

Figure 8. F1 versus time.

The accuracy of the four base models, as well as the detection model proposed in this paper at four time nodes are shown in Figure 5, from which it can be seen that the accuracy of the DGA detection model based on statistical learning is higher than that of the four base models, indicating that more samples were correctly categorized in the detection results of this model. Statistically based models show the highest accuracy among all models. This may be because the multimodel collaborative model combines the advantages of different models and improves the overall detection performance through ensemble learning. This result demonstrates the effectiveness and advantages of a model ensemble.

Figure 6 shows the variation of the precision rate of the base model and the statistical learning-based DGA detection model over four time nodes, from which it can be seen that the precision rate of the model detection decreases over time, which is caused by the degradation of the model. It can also be seen that the precision rate of CNN is significantly higher than that of other single-model detection but lower than that of statistically based multimodel detection. Thus, statistically based multimodel detection methods have a clear advantage.

Figure 7 demonstrates the variation of the recall of the base model and the statistical learning-based DGA detection model over the four time nodes. In terms of the single-model detection methods, the CNN model has a higher detection recall than the other three single-model detection methods. Due to the advantages of the CNN model in image processing and feature extraction, it can better capture and identify the characteristics of DGA attacks. These features include pattern recognition, frequency analysis, or other statistical features relevant to DGA attacks. However, it can be seen from the figure that the statistical learning-based DGA detection model has a higher recall than the CNN detection model at all time nodes. In summary, it can be seen that the statistical-based multimodel detection method has a higher recall than the other single-model detection methods.

Figure 8 demonstrates the variation of the F1 values of the base model and the statistical learning-based DGA detection model over the four time nodes, which is a combined assessment of precision and recall and responds to the comprehensive detection capability of the model. From the figure, it can be seen that the F1 value of the statistical learning-based DGA detection model is higher than the base model at all time nodes. Statistical learning-based DGA detection model may be better able to identify patterns, variants, and characteristics of DGA attacks, thereby improving the overall performance of the model. This indicates that the detection effect of the model is overall better than that of the base model.

In summary, when the detection model was trained with the outdated data and we tested the detection effect on the DGA domain name data for the next four years, the statistical learning-based DGA detection model outperformed the four base models in terms of accuracy, recall, and F1 value, which indicates that the detection model proposed in this paper possesses stronger comprehensive detection capability. When there were new DGA domain names that the model had not seen in the test data, the oscillation of the model on the four metrics was slightly lower than that of the other base models, which indicates that the detection model can effectively identify the internal aging models when making decisions based on statistical learning and eliminate the detection results of the less effective models according to various decision mechanisms, so that the overall detection effect of the whole model remains stable and has a certain degree of robustness.

5.3. Summary

This section validated the statistical learning-based DGA domain name detection algorithm proposed in the previous section through experiments. This section first utilized the C_DGA and Tranco_K26W-1m data to train and generate a statistical learning-based DGA detection model. Subsequently, the model's classification ability was tested on the test set. The experimental results showed that the model outperformed the base model in three indexes of accuracy, precision, and F1 value, reaching values of 0.97908, 0.97712, and 0.97912, respectively, and the recall rate was also only lower than that of the CNN model, reaching 0.98113, indicating that the model had a stronger comprehensive detection ability than the other models. By comparing the base model and other combined models, we learned that the multimodel collaborative decision-making based on statistical learning proposed in this paper could effectively improve the detection effect on the basis of a single model, and the detection effect was better when the model contained both the base model based on artificial features and the base model based on deep learning. Next, this section tested the detection effect of this detection model for each DGA family using the DGA domain family data from 360netlab, and the experiments showed that the detection accuracy of our model on multiple DGA families was higher than that of the base model. Finally, we used the old data in C_DGA to generate detection models and test the detection effectiveness of these models over time, and the experimental results showed that in the time range from 2020 to 2023, the accuracy, recall, and F1 values of the statistical learning-based DGA detection model were higher than those of the base model, the comprehensive detection ability was stronger, and for unknown families of domain names, the detection model had less oscillation than the base model and had a certain robustness.

6. Conclusions and Future Work

6.1. Conclusions

This paper combined the analysis of artificial features and advanced neural network features to detect DGA domain names. First, 34 artificial features were extracted from the perspectives of string structure, language characteristics, and distribution statistics.

Secondly, deep neural networks were used to actively mine high-level features of domain name characters. Then, the DGA domain name was detected by combining traditional machine learning methods and deep learning methods. In terms of the multimodel decision-making mechanism, a method based on statistical learning was proposed to provide a fair comparison standard for heterogeneous models and produce decision results with a certain level of confidence through voting. When the prediction labels of all models lacked sufficient confidence, confidence and credibility were considered to comprehensively evaluate the prediction quality of the model, and the prediction result with the highest quality was selected as the final decision result.

Finally, a DGA detection algorithm based on statistical learning was designed and implemented using four heterogeneous methods, XGBoost, B-RF, LSTM, and CNN, to detect DGA domain names and evaluate the prediction quality of these methods through statistical learning to generate DGA detection results. This algorithm analyzed DGA domain names from multiple angles. The experimental results of this model performed well, with accuracy, precision, recall, and F1 scores reaching 0.979, 0.977, 0.981, and 0.979. Our research was compared with previous studies and discussed with related studies. We found that our method outperformed the performance of a previously proposed single model, improved the detection effect based on a single method, and was able to effectively identify invalid prediction results, ensuring the stability of the algorithm. Overall, this algorithm is a real-time, lightweight DGA detection method with high accuracy and reliability.

6.2. Future Work

In this paper, a statistical learning-based DGA detection method was proposed, but due to the limited research time, there are still some problems that need further research and improvement:

1. The detection method proposed in this paper contains four heterogeneous methods, XGBoost, B-RF, LSTM, and CNN, and provides a unified comparison standard for these heterogeneous models using statistical learning, which has strong scalability and provides a new way of thinking for multimodel detection of DGA domain names, so more and better detection methods can be considered for integration into this algorithm in future research to further improve the detection capability of the algorithm.
2. In this paper, we studied the binary classification problem in DGA detection, and in future research, we can try to apply this detection algorithm to the DGA family multiclassification problem. By extending the algorithm to classify different DGA families, a more comprehensive understanding of the diverse nature of DGA domains can be achieved.
3. Incorporating explainability: In future research, it would be valuable to enhance the interpretability and explainability of the detection algorithm. By providing insights into the decision-making process of the model and the importance of different features, users can gain a better understanding of how the algorithm detects DGA domains.
4. Real-time detection: This study mainly focuses on offline detection of DGA domains. In future research, it would be beneficial to explore real-time detection methods that can effectively identify DGA domains in a timely manner. This would enable the algorithm to be deployed in dynamic environments, such as network security systems, where quick detection and response are crucial.
5. Robustness to adversarial attacks: Investigating the robustness of the detection algorithm against adversarial attacks would be an important direction for future research. Adversarial attacks aim to deceive the algorithm by introducing subtle modifications to the input data. Developing techniques to enhance the algorithm's resilience to such attacks would be valuable in practical applications.

Author Contributions: Methodology, S.L.; Validation, Z.W.; Formal analysis, Y.N. and C.D.; Investigation, C.Q.; Resources, X.K.; Writing—original draft, S.L.; Writing—review and editing, S.L.; Visualization, X.L. All authors have read and agreed to the published version of the manuscript.

Funding: This research received no external funding.

Data Availability Statement: The data can be shared upon request.

Conflicts of Interest: The authors declare no conflict of interest.

References

1. Wagan, A.A.; Li, Q.; Zaland, Z.; Marjan, S.; Bozdar, D.K.; Hussain, A.; Mirza, A.M.; Baryalai, M. A Unified Learning Approach for Malicious Domain Name Detection. *Axioms* **2023**, *12*, 458. [CrossRef]
2. Chen, S.; Lang, B.; Chen, Y.; Xie, C. Detection of Algorithmically Generated Malicious Domain Names with Feature Fusion of Meaningful Word Segmentation and N-Gram Sequences. *Appl. Sci.* **2023**, *13*, 4406. [CrossRef]
3. Wang, H.; Tang, Z.; Li, H.; Zhang, J.; Cai, C. DDOFM: Dynamic malicious domain detection method based on feature mining. *Comput. Secur.* **2023**, *130*, 103260. [CrossRef]
4. Abu Al-Haija, Q.; Alohaly, M.; Odeh, A. A Lightweight Double-Stage Scheme to Identify Malicious DNS over HTTPS Traffic Using a Hybrid Learning Approach. *Sensors* **2023**, *23*, 3489. [CrossRef]
5. Zhou, J.; Cui, H.; Li, X.; Yang, W.; Wu, X. A Novel Phishing Website Detection Model Based on LightGBM and Domain Name Features. *Symmetry* **2023**, *15*, 180. [CrossRef]
6. Liang, Y.; Cheng, Y.; Zhang, Z.; Chai, T.; Li, C. Illegal Domain Name Generation Algorithm Based on Character Similarity of Domain Name Structure. *Appl. Sci.* **2023**, *13*, 4061. [CrossRef]
7. Wei, L.; Wang, L.; Liu, F.; Qian, Z. Clustering Analysis of Wind Turbine Alarm Sequences Based on Domain Knowledge-Fused Word2vec. *Appl. Sci.* **2023**, *13*, 10114. [CrossRef]
8. Chaganti, R.; Suliman, W.; Ravi, V.; Dua, A. Deep learning approach for SDN-enabled intrusion detection system in IoT networks. *Information* **2023**, *14*, 41. [CrossRef]
9. Rahali, A.; Akhloufi, M.A. MalBERTv2: Code Aware BERT-Based Model for Malware Identification. *Big Data Cogn. Comput.* **2023**, *7*, 60. [CrossRef]
10. Zhai, Q.; Zhu, W.; Zhang, X.; Liu, C. Contrastive refinement for dense retrieval inference in the open-domain question answering task. *Future Internet* **2023**, *15*, 137. [CrossRef]
11. Antonakakis, M.; Perdisci, R.; Nadji, Y.; Vasiloglou, N.; Abu-Nimeh, S.; Lee, W.; Dagon, D. From Throw-Away Traffic to Bots: Detecting the Rise of DGA-Based Malware. In Proceedings of the 21st USENIX Security Symposium (USENIX Security 12), Bellevue, WA, USA, 8–10 August 2012; pp. 491–506.
12. Plohmann, D.; Yakdan, K.; Klatt, M.; Bader, J.; Gerhards-Padilla, E. A Comprehensive Measurement Study of Domain Generating Malware. In Proceedings of the 25th USENIX Security Symposium (USENIX Security 16), Austin, TX, USA, 10–12 August 2016; USENIX Association: Austin, TX, USA, 2016; pp. 263–278.
13. Al lelah, T.; Theodorakopoulos, G.; Reinecke, P.; Javed, A.; Anthi, E. Abuse of Cloud-Based and Public Legitimate Services as Command-and-Control (C&C) Infrastructure: A Systematic Literature Review. *J. Cybersecur. Priv.* **2023**, *3*, 558–590.
14. Sui, Z.; Shu, H.; Kang, F.; Huang, Y.; Huo, G. A Comprehensive Review of Tunnel Detection on Multilayer Protocols: From Traditional to Machine Learning Approaches. *Appl. Sci.* **2023**, *13*, 1974. [CrossRef]
15. Zhang, C.; Chen, Y.; Liu, W.; Zhang, M.; Lin, D. Linear Private Set Union from Multi-Query Reverse Private Membership Test. In Proceedings of the 32nd USENIX Security Symposium (USENIX Security 23), Anaheim, CA, USA, 9–11 August 2023; pp. 337–354.
16. Eltahlawy, A.M.; Aslan, H.K.; Abdallah, E.G.; Elsayed, M.S.; Jurcut, A.D.; Azer, M.A. A Survey on Parameters Affecting MANET Performance. *Electronics* **2023**, *12*, 1956. [CrossRef]
17. Ogundokun, R.O.; Arowolo, M.O.; Damaševičius, R.; Misra, S. Phishing Detection in Blockchain Transaction Networks Using Ensemble Learning. *Telecom* **2023**, *4*, 279–297. [CrossRef]
18. Bubukayr, M.; Frikha, M. Effective Techniques for Protecting the Privacy of Web Users. *Appl. Sci.* **2023**, *13*, 3191. [CrossRef]
19. Davuth, N.; Kim, S.R. Classification of malicious domain names using support vector machine and bi-gram method. *Int. J. Secur. Its Appl.* **2013**, *7*, 51–58.
20. Vinayakumar, R.; Soman, K.; Poornachandran, P.; Sachin Kumar, S. Evaluating deep learning approaches to characterize and classify the DGAs at scale. *J. Intell. Fuzzy Syst.* **2018**, *34*, 1265–1276. [CrossRef]
21. Mowbray, M.; Hagen, J. Finding domain-generation algorithms by looking at length distribution. In Proceedings of the 2014 IEEE International Symposium on Software Reliability Engineering Workshops, Naples, Italy, 3–6 November 2014; pp. 395–400.
22. Woodbridge, J.; Anderson, H.S.; Barford, P. Inferring domain generation algorithms with a Viterbi algorithm variant. In Proceedings of the 2016 ACM SIGSAC Conference on Computer and Communications Security, Vienna, Austria, 24–28 October 2016; pp. 1010–1021. [CrossRef]
23. Schüppen, S.; Teubert, D.; Herrmann, P.; Meyer, U. FANCI: Feature-based Automated NXDomain Classification and Intelligence. In Proceedings of the 27th USENIX Security Symposium (USENIX Security 18), Baltimore, MD, USA, 15–17 August 2018; USENIX Association: Baltimore, MD, USA, 2018; pp. 1165–1181.
24. Yu, S.; Wu, J.; Xiang, Y. A novel method for DGA domain name detection based on character n-gram and sequence pattern. *Secur. Commun. Netw.* **2017**, *2017*, 4176356. [CrossRef]
25. Yadav, S.; Reddy, A. Detecting algorithmically generated domain names with entropy-based features. In Proceedings of the 2013 ACM conference on Computer and Communications Security, Berlin, Germany, 4–8 November 2013; pp. 447–458. [CrossRef]

26. Zhao, D.; Li, H.; Sun, X.; Tang, Y. Detecting DGA-based botnets through effective phonics-based features. *Future Gener. Comput. Syst.* **2023**, *143*, 105–117. [CrossRef]
27. Bilge, L.; Balduzzi, M.; Kirda, E. Dissecting Android malware: Characterization and evolution. In Proceedings of the 2011 IEEE Symposium on Security and Privacy, Oakland, CA, USA, 22–25 May 2011; pp. 95–110. [CrossRef]
28. Kolias, C.; Kambourakis, G.; Stavrou, A.; Gritzalis, D. Detecting DGA-based botnets using DNS traffic analysis. *IEEE Trans. Dependable Secur. Comput.* **2016**, *13*, 218–231. [CrossRef]
29. Zhao, C.; Zhang, Y.; Wang, Y. A Feature Ensemble-based Approach to Malicious Domain Name Identification from Valid DNS Responses. In Proceedings of the 2020 International Joint Conference on Neural Networks (IJCNN), Glasgow, UK, 19–24 July 2020; pp. 1–7.
30. Zhao, N.; Jiang, M.; Zhang, X.; Liu, Y. Detection of DGA domains using deep learning. In Proceedings of the 2018 15th IEEE International Conference on Advanced Video and Signal Based Surveillance (AVSS), Auckland, New Zealand, 27–30 November 2018; pp. 1–6. [CrossRef]
31. Zhang, Q.; Ma, W.; Wang, Y.; Zhang, Y.; Shi, Z.; Li, Y. Backdoor attacks on image classification models in deep neural networks. *Chin. J. Electron.* **2022**, *31*, 199–212. [CrossRef]
32. Zheng, J.; Zhang, Y.; Li, Y.; Wu, S.; Yu, X. Towards Evaluating the Robustness of Adversarial Attacks Against Image Scaling Transformation. *Chin. J. Electron.* **2023**, *32*, 151–158. [CrossRef]
33. Sun, X.; Yang, J.; Wang, Z.; Liu, H. Hgdom: Heterogeneous graph convolutional networks for malicious domain detection. In Proceedings of the NOMS 2020-2020 IEEE/IFIP Network Operations and Management Symposium, Budapest, Hungary, 20–24 April 2020; pp. 1–9.
34. Li, C.; Xie, J.; Cheng, Y.; Zhang, Z.; Chen, J.; Wang, H.; Tao, H. Research on the Construction of High-Trust Root Zone File Based on Multi-Source Data Verification. *Electronics* **2023**, *12*, 2264. [CrossRef]
35. Li, X.; Lu, C.; Liu, B.; Zhang, Q.; Li, Z.; Duan, H.; Li, Q. The Maginot Line: Attacking the Boundary of {DNS} Caching Protection. In Proceedings of the 32nd USENIX Security Symposium (USENIX Security 23), Anaheim, CA, USA, 9–11 August 2023; pp. 3153–3170.
36. Ashiq, M.I.; Li, W.; Fiebig, T.; Chung, T. You've Got Report: Measurement and Security Implications of {DMARC} Reporting. In Proceedings of the 32nd USENIX Security Symposium (USENIX Security 23), Anaheim, CA, USA, 9–11 August 2023; pp. 4123–4137.
37. Xu, C.; Zhang, Y.; Shi, F.; Shan, H.; Guo, B.; Li, Y.; Xue, P. Measuring the Centrality of DNS Infrastructure in the Wild. *Appl. Sci.* **2023**, *13*, 5739. [CrossRef]
38. Glorot, X.; Bengio, Y. Understanding the difficulty of training deep feedforward neural networks. In Proceedings of the Thirteenth International Conference on Artificial Intelligence and Statistics, JMLR Workshop and Conference Proceedings, Sardinia, Italy, 13–15 May 2010; pp. 249–256.
39. Yu, B.; Gray, D.L.; Pan, J.; Cock, M.D.; Nascimento, A.C.A. Inline DGA Detection with Deep Networks. In Proceedings of the IEEE International Conference on Data Mining Workshops, Orleans, LA, USA, 18–21 November 2017.
40. Srivastava, N.; Hinton, G.; Krizhevsky, A.; Sutskever, I.; Salakhutdinov, R. Dropout: A simple way to prevent neural networks from overfitting. *J. Mach. Learn. Res.* **2014**, *15*, 1929–1958.
41. Pochat, V.L.; Van Goethem, T.; Tajalizadehkhoob, S.; Korczyński, M.; Joosen, W. Tranco: A research-oriented top sites ranking hardened against manipulation. *arXiv* **2018**, arXiv:1806.01156.

electronics

Article

Verifiable and Searchable Symmetric Encryption Scheme Based on the Public Key Cryptosystem

Gangqiang Duan and Shuai Li *

School of Information Engineering, Ningxia University, Yinchuan 750021, China; 12022131924@stu.nxu.edu.cn
* Correspondence: lis198707@gmail.com

Abstract: With the rapid development of Internet of Things technology and cloud computing technology, all industries need to outsource massive data to third-party clouds for storage in order to reduce storage and computing costs. Verifiable and dynamic searchable symmetric encryption is a very important cloud security technology, which supports the dynamic update of private data and allows users to perform search operations on the cloud server and verify the legitimacy of the returned results. Therefore, how to realize the dynamic search of encrypted cloud data and the effective verification of the results returned by the cloud server is a key problem to be solved. To solve this problem, we propose a verifiable dynamic encryption scheme (v-PADSSE) based on the public key cryptosystem. In order to achieve efficient and correct data updating, the scheme designs verification information (VI) for each keyword and constructs a verification list (VL) to store it. When dynamic update operations are performed on the cloud data, it is easy to quickly update the security index through obtaining the latest verification information in the VL. The safety and performance evaluation of the v-PADSSE scheme proved that the scheme is safe and effective.

Keywords: Internet of Things; cloud computing; verifiable; searchable; symmetric encryption; public key cryptosystem

check for updates

Citation: Duan, G.; Li, S. Verifiable and Searchable Symmetric Encryption Scheme Based on the Public Key Cryptosystem. *Electronics* **2023**, *12*, 3965. https://doi.org/10.3390/electronics12183965

Academic Editors: Yu-an Tan, Qikun Zhang, Yuanzhang Li and Xiao Yu

Received: 30 July 2023
Revised: 4 September 2023
Accepted: 7 September 2023
Published: 20 September 2023

1. Introduction

With the development of IoT technology, in order to achieve industrial informatization, more and more IoT devices are being connected, and the amount of data is becoming larger and larger. In order to save on storage and computing costs, enterprises choose to outsource massive amounts of data to cloud servers. However, while enjoying the convenience brought by the cloud, the security of the data has become crucial. To protect data privacy, sensitive private data need to be encrypted before being outsourced to the IoT cloud [1]. Song et al. [2] proposed searchable symmetric encryption (SSE). SSE is an encryption scheme that allows users to store encrypted data on a third-party cloud server and search the encrypted cloud data through the trapdoor generated by the keywords. However, most SSE schemes only consider keyword search operations on statically encrypted cloud data, which is inconsistent with the real-time and dynamic update requirements for enterprise data. Moreover, some studies have shown that conventional SSE schemes are vulnerable to leakage abuse attacks [3], file injection attacks [4], and technical attacks [5]. In order to realize the dynamic update (add, delete, or modify) operations of encrypted data stored on cloud servers, some SSE schemes supporting the dynamic update operations of private data have been proposed [6–9]. Kamara et al. [6] proposed an SSE scheme that supports dynamic data updating. The scheme realizes a sublinear search via extending an inverted index and uses a search array and delete array combined with other storage space to realize the dynamic update of the data. Subsequently, they proposed another method based on the keyword red–black tree index structure [7] to support parallel keyword search and parallel data insertion and deletion. Guo et al. [8] proposed a dynamic SSE scheme based on an inverted index. The scheme records the keyword position by the inverted index and realizes the data dynamics through updating the index. Xia et al. [9] proposed a dynamic keyword search scheme for encrypted cloud data based on the tree index structure that supports multi-keyword sorting.

The above DSSE schemes do not consider the correctness and integrity verification of the returned matching result of the cloud server. In practice, the cloud server may return un-updated or incorrect matching results to the user in order to save computing resources. Therefore, users need to verify the results returned by the cloud server to ensure the correctness and integrity of the returned results. Some schemes [10–12] use the timestamp function of the RSA accumulator to verify the search results, which generates accumulator bits for all files and indexes, which can be saved by the data owner. If the cloud server returns an un-updated result, the user can check it with the latest accumulator. The RSA accumulator [13] can synthesize a large number of data into a fixed-size value to achieve member authentication, which can effectively reduce communication overhead. The RSA accumulator is applied to the compressed prefix tree structure to realize both efficient retrieval and result verification. However, the RSA accumulator is based on asymmetric cryptosystems, and the computational costs and verification costs are high. Some research teams have proposed verifiable schemes based on message authentication code (MAC) [14–16], but in DSSE application scenarios, MAC cannot verify whether the results returned by the cloud server are the latest, that is, it cannot resist replay attacks [17]. Ge et al. [18] proposed a verifiable DSSE scheme based on cumulative authentication tags (AATs), which generates authentication tags for keywords and verifies the returned results through recording the number of global updates and the number of updates of a single file containing those keywords. Each update operation consumes only one label, which is highly efficient. However, the pseudo-random permutation and pseudo-random function are used in this scheme to replace and encrypt the keywords and global update times, which leads to key management problems. Relational authentication tags (RALs) [19] are used to verify the relationship of query keywords in documents, and audit certificates can be generated without exposing sensitive information. However, the program requires third-party auditors to be involved in the search process. Therefore, how to effectively verify the correctness and integrity of the returned results is an urgent problem to be solved.

According to the research on the above schemes, the verification of search results in most schemes is not comprehensive and also involves key management problems. Therefore, how to effectively verify the correctness and integrity of search results as well as the security management of encryption keys are the problems we should focus on and solve.

In this paper, we explore how to use the public key cryptosystem in the DSSE scheme to verify the correctness and integrity of the result returned by the cloud server and to manage the encryption key effectively and securely.

The contributions of this paper can be summarized as follows:

(1) In order to efficiently realize the index update and index lookup, we constructed a bitmap index to store the relationship between the keywords and encrypted files. A verification list (VL) was used to store the latest verification information of files containing keywords so that we can quickly obtain the latest verification information from the VL to perform the secure index update.

(2) In order to support the effective verification of dynamic data, we designed public-key-based cumulative verification information (VI), which is stored in the bitmap index. When the encrypted cloud data are dynamically updated, the verification information can be easily updated. In addition, the verification information contains the corresponding keywords' information, which makes the verification information of various keywords different. Moreover, replay attacks can be resisted by the VI, that is, through verifying whether the returned result is up to date.

(3) In order to achieve forward security, the scheme places the node information in the bitmap index to avoid statistical attacks. When we need to search or update private data,

the cloud server will return or change the whole column's data so that malicious cloud software cannot obtain the relationship of the keywords and index.

(4) Based on the above description, we design a verifiable DSSE scheme based on the public key cryptosystem. The security, verification efficiency, and updating efficiency of the scheme are analyzed and explored. The results show that the scheme is safe and effective.

Organization: The rest of the paper is organized as follows. We summarize the related work in Section 2. In Section 3, the formulas and algorithms involved in the scheme are defined, including model construction, design objectives, etc. In Section 4, we describe the construction of the scheme and the execution of the algorithm. The security analysis of the v-PADSSE scheme is given in Section 5. In Section 6, the implementation efficiency and updating efficiency of the program are analyzed and evaluated.

2. Related Work

With the development and application of the Internet of Things and cloud computing technology, many industries have chosen to outsource data to third-party clouds for storage. While cloud storage brings convenience to enterprises, it also brings new security challenges. Users cannot directly control the data stored in the cloud, so it is impossible to determine whether the data stored are complete and correct. To solve the problem of data verification, the research community has proposed some cloud storage verification schemes [20–22] to audit and verify data in the cloud. In addition, before uploading private data to the cloud for storage, users need to encrypt it to prevent it from being accessed directly by cloud providers. However, in this case, how users perform search operations on encrypted cloud data is also an important problem to be solved. To solve the above problems, the research community proposes searchable symmetric encryption (SSE), which allows users to perform search operations directly on the ciphertext. Compared with the searchable encryption scheme of the public key encryption system [23,24], the efficiency of the SSE scheme has received more attention from the industry.

Dynamic SSE. Searchable encryption can be divided into two categories: symmetric key encryption [25] and public key encryption [26]. Song et al. [2] first proposed a searchable encryption scheme that encrypts each keyword through constructing a special two-layer encryption structure. Some static SSE schemes, such as semantic search schemes [27] and ranked keyword search schemes [28,29], are also proposed. However, in practice, industrial data are dynamically updated in real time, and the static SSE scheme does not support the dynamic update of encrypted cloud data, so it cannot meet the requirements of cloud storage data encryption at this stage. In order to support the dynamic update of encrypted data, Kamara et al. [6] proposed a dynamic SSE scheme through constructing an extended inverted index to achieve sublinear search efficiency and CKA-2 security. Scheme [30] proposed a dynamic SSE scheme which allows data owners to store privacy files in a way that the cloud server does not know the number of files through constructing a blind storage system on the cloud server. Guo et al. [9] proposed a DSSE scheme based on the inverted index, which allows data users to search multiple phrases in a query request, and the scheme supports the ordering of search results. In recent years, a number of cloud-assisted schemes have been proposed for searchable encryption [31]. Scheme [32] utilized the searchable encryption technologies of keyword range search and multi-keyword search. Since the cloud is untrustworthy, scheme [32] used Bloom filters and message verification codes to classify health information, filter out fake data, and check data integrity. In order to verify whether the cloud faithfully performs the search operation, a multi-user verifiable searchable symmetric encryption is proposed in scheme [25]. Authorized users can search the data, verify the authenticity of the search results, and improve the accuracy of the search results. Since the access rights of authorized users are always valid, it is not secure. In order to automatically revoke a user's access, the time key was introduced in [33]. At the beginning of encryption, the key is encapsulated in ciphertext, which means that all users, including the data owner, are bound by the time period. Later, Yang et al. [34] proposed a conjunctional keyword search with the function of specifying testers and enabling timed proxy re-encryption. It utilizes a time server to generate time tokens for users. In addition, it implements time-controlled access revocation to prevent authorized users from accessing future EHRs. Scheme [35] proposed timed-release computational secret sharing and threshold encryption which used a time-release function instead of a time server to reduce overhead. Scheme [36] proposed 0-encoding and 1-encoding to generate the time key. However, the retrieval efficiency of this work is low. In order to improve search efficiency, scheme [37] with hidden data structures was proposed in the literature. The user expected to find more ciphertexts in one step. However, scheme [37] reduced the number of computation-intensive operations without searching for at least two matching ciphertexts in just one step. This work cannot meet the need for a quick search and prevent authorized users from accessing future data. While all of the above work enables cloud-based search, there is still a challenge: the cloud is not a fully trusted entity and can collude with other entities to gain access to users' private information.

Verifiable SSE. In practice, cloud servers are semi-trusted entities [38] that may return incorrect or un-updated results to the data user in order to save on computing overhead. Miao et al. [39] constructed the verifiable SE framework (VSEF), which can withstand internal KGA and achieve verifiable searchability. Wu et al. [40] proposed a new authentication data structure based on homomorphic encryption and showed how to apply it to verify the correctness and integrity of search results. However, the verification proof in their scheme is generated by the cloud server, which can forge the proof to pass the verification when the cloud server is seen as an adversary. To avoid this, Chai et al. [41] first proposed a verifiable keyword search scheme for encrypting cloud data, using hash functions to generate proof of document identity. Jiang et al. [14] proposed a verifiable multi-keyword ranked search scheme based on encrypted cloud data, which realized an efficient keyword search through constructing the special data structure QSet. Yang et al. [42] designed a forward-privacy VDSSE scheme with Bloom filters and message authentication codes to allow verification and support dynamic updates of outsourced data. Zhang et al. [43] proposed a verifiable data structure based on a multi-set hash function, which guarantees forward security and realizes effective verifiable data updates. Gao et al. [19] used relational authentication tags (RALs) to verify the relationship of the query keywords in the document, which can generate audit certificates without exposing sensitive information. However, the program requires third-party auditors to be involved in the search process. Merkle hash trees [44] are used to validate data elements in large databases. Through adding data elements to the leaf node of the tree, the tree structure is constructed layer by layer from the leaf node to the root node, and finally the unique root node is obtained. A change to any element in the data set will make the root node change. A Merkle Patricia tree is proposed in GSSE [45] to reduce the storage overhead of index structures in schemes based on Merkle hash trees. It reduces storage space through reducing the depth of the tree. However, in the above two scenarios, the proof provided by the cloud server to the DU is larger in scale, which brings more communication overhead. Chen et al. [46] extend the Merkle hash tree [47] to a searchable index tree to achieve efficient result verification, where search time grows sublinearly with the size of the data set, and verification is more efficient than the accumulator structure. In addition, verifiable DSSE has been implemented by schemes [45,48], but they either support a single keyword match search or use two rounds of communication in a single-user setup to achieve result verification. The RSA accumulator [13] can aggregate a large amount of data into a fixed value to achieve member verification, which can effectively reduce communication overhead. The RSA accumulator is applied to the compressed prefix tree structure to realize the combination of efficient retrieval and result verification. Schemes [10,12,13] all use an RSA accumulator to realize result verification for dynamic data. Most of the above VDSSE schemes are based on asymmetric key cryptography, and the results returned by the cloud server are verified using the public key signature.

Forward secure SSE. Forward privacy protection requires that update operations (insert or delete) performed by the data owner cannot be associated with previously performed search operations. Because the secret key is used for the deterministic encryption of private data in the DSSE scheme, it is easy for untrusted servers to obtain repeated queries and other information, which leads to information leakage (such as the number of keyword queries, etc.). If ORAM is introduced into the scheme, such problems will be avoided, but the communication cost and calculation cost are high, which causes the calculation and execution efficiency of DSSE to be exchanged through allowing some information to be leaked in actual use. However, such leaks are often attacked in different ways [49,50]. Bost et al. [51] proposed to use a one-way trapdoor replacement to eliminate the correlation between the latest trapdoor and the previous trapdoor, that is, the latest trapdoor can search all encrypted documents, but the previous trapdoor cannot match the latest encrypted document. Cao et al. [52] used the KNN method to construct the security index and trapdoor. This method is used to encode indexes and trapdoors so that even if the keyword is the same, the encoding is different. In this way, the cloud server can avoid obtaining the number of keyword queries and the association between keywords and encrypted data based on data user query operations, thereby protecting forward privacy. Li et al. [53] used partitioning and pointer hiding technology to partition the secure index and extracted sub-keywords according to the original keywords as the keywords of partition search, then encrypted and hid the index block, which only needed to save the index table header identification and encryption key locally. Since the search token information is calculated using subkeywords, it is difficult for subsequent query keywords to be directly associated with the newly added encrypted document.

3. Security Model and Related Definitions

3.1. Security Model

In the design scheme, there are four entities that need to be involved, namely: the data owner (DO), the data user (DU), the cloud server (CS), and the key distribution center (KGC). The system security architecture is shown in Figure 1.

- Data owner: This entity encrypts private files and secure indexes with a symmetric key and encrypts verification information with the data user's public key. After the encryption is finished, the ciphertext and index are uploaded to the cloud server. When the data owner wants to update the privacy data, the update token needs to be generated locally and then sent to the cloud server for data updating. Upon receiving the VI request from the data user, the data owner returns the number of files N and the total number of file updates V that contain the keyword w.

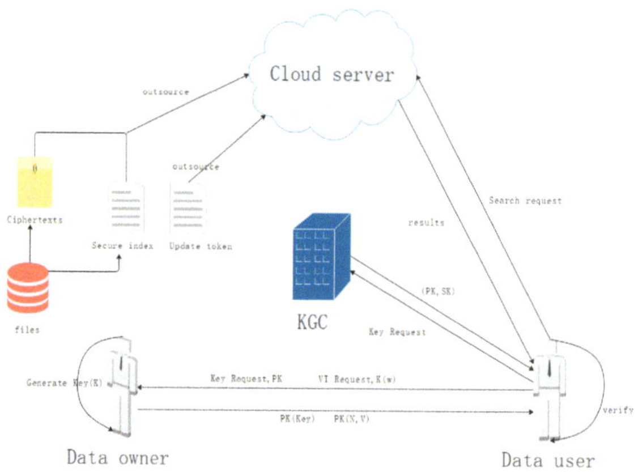

Figure 1. System security architecture.

- Data user: The entity shares the encrypted private key with the data owner. When he wants to perform a search operation containing keywords, he needs to generate a trapdoor locally, then send the trapdoor to the cloud server for searching, and apply to the data owner for the latest verification information of the keyword. The w of VI indicates the keyword for which the user wants to perform the search operation. Upon receiving the returned results from the cloud server, the correctness and integrity of the results are verified according to the verification information.

- Cloud server: This entity stores the ciphertext and security index information uploaded by the data owner. When it receives a search request, it performs the search operation on the security index and returns the corresponding matching results and verification information. When it receives an update request, it performs an update operation on the security index and the corresponding ciphertext.
- Key Distribution Center (KGC): This entity is primarily used to generate keys. Upon receiving a key request from the data user, the entity returns a key pair (PK, SK) to the corresponding user.

In the system model, both the data owner and data user must be trusted entities. The data owner honestly encrypts the private files and builds the secure index. The data user honestly generates trapdoors for the desired keywords and sends them to the cloud server. The cloud server is an untrusted entity that allows search operations to record the correspondence between search keywords and encrypted files, and it may return incorrect or un-updated results to the data user in order to save computing overhead. The key distribution center is a trusted entity that honestly generates the key pair requested by the data user and sends it to the requesting user.

3.2. Design Goals

Based on the above model architecture, to achieve a verifiable DSSE scheme, we design a scheme which needs to meet the following objectives:

- Support keyword search over the encrypted cloud data: The scheme needs to match all ciphertexts containing the corresponding keywords according to the search token and demonstrate high query efficiency.
- Support efficient dynamic data updates: The scheme needs to support the dynamic update of encrypted data and secure indexes, such as dynamic addition, dynamic deletion, and dynamic modification.
- Support search result verification: The scheme needs to support data users in efficiently verifying the correctness and integrity of the matching results returned by the cloud server, and the verification does not involve any complex operations.
- Privacy protection.: Due to the scheme being based on the public key cryptosystem, the public key cannot be used to encrypt private information directly. The private information is encrypted using the symmetric key, and the asymmetric key is used to encrypt the verification information. In addition, the scheme should hide the encrypted file containing information about keyword quantity and keyword search frequency.
- Replay attack resistance: To save on computing or storage overhead, the cloud server directly returns the un-updated results to the data user. The scheme should enable data users to verify the returned results to determine whether the returned results are up to date.

3.3. Algorithm Definition

The related algorithms in the v-PADSSE scheme we designed are KeyGen, PSKeyGen, IndexBuild, Building VL, GenToken, Search, Verify, Decrypt, UpdateToken, and Update. These algorithms are defined as follows:

- $K \leftarrow KeyGen(1^{\lambda_1})$. The data owner outputs the key (K) through using the secure random parameter λ_1 as the input.
- $(PK, SK) \leftarrow PSKeyGen(\lambda_2)$. The KGC outputs the key pair (PK,SK), using the secure random parameter λ_2 as input.

- $(I, C) \leftarrow IndexBuild(K, PK, F, W, N, V, v_i, flag)$. When building a secure index, encrypt the file F and the keywords W with K. Use the public key (PK) to encrypt the number of files (N) and the total number of updates (V) containing the keywords, the number of updates (v_i) per file, and the flag bit of whether the file contains the keyword ($flag$), where the random number generator function $rand()$ is used to generate random numbers ($randA$ for odd numbers, $randB$ for even numbers). If the file contains the keyword, the $flag$ is odd. If not, the $flag$ is an even number. Calculate the file F using the SHA-3 hash algorithm (later replaced with the symbol "H"), and finally, output security index I and ciphertext C.
- $T_w \leftarrow GenToken(K, w)$. The data user executes the trapdoor generation algorithm. Take key K and keyword w as inputs, and output trapdoor T_w.
- $(VI, C(w)) \leftarrow Search(T_w, I, C)$. The output is the verification information VI, matching ciphertext set $C(w)$. The VI contains the update times of the file (v_i) matching the trapdoor, the flag of whether the ciphertext contains the keyword, and the result $H(F)$ after hashing the plaintext file using T_w, I and C as input.
- $(Y, N) \leftarrow Verify(VI, SK, T_w, C(w))$. Output the result of verifying (Y or N) through using VI, $PK(N, V)$, SK, T_w, and $C(w)$ as inputs.
- $F(w) \leftarrow Decrypt(K, C(w))$. Take K and $C(w)$ as inputs, and output plaintext file F.
- $\tau \leftarrow UpdateToken(K, PK, F, \{w, flag\}, v_i)$. Update token information includes the update operation type, the newly updated file F, the document identifier F_{id}, the number of updates per file v_i, $H(F)$ (the hash result of F), the set of keywords w contained in the file, and $flag$. When the add operation is performed, the VL is matched according to the keyword set contained in file F, $V = V + 1$ and $N = N + 1$ are calculated in the matched node, and the document ID (F_{id}) and update number $v_i = 1$ of file F are added to the node. At this point, the update token contains the addition of F_{id}, v_i, the keyword set w_i contained in the file F, and $H(F)$. If F contains the keyword, $flag = randA$; otherwise, $randB$. When the delete operation is performed, the verification list VL is matched according to the keyword set contained in F; then, $N = N - 1$ and $V = V - v_i$ are calculated in the matched nodes, and F_id and its update times v_i in the nodes are deleted, so that $v_i = 0$ and $flag = randB$. When the modify operation is performed, the verification list VL is matched according to the keyword set contained in F. In the matching node, perform $V = V + 1$ and $v_i = v_i + 1$; N and $flag$ remain unchanged, and the new file is hashed to $H(F)$. After the above verification information is modified, the public key is used to encrypt this information except for $H(F)$.
- $(I', C') \leftarrow Update(\tau)$. The cloud server executes the update algorithm. Match according to F_id contained in τ, and replace the nodes' value in the column. According to the update token τ, The cloud server generates a new index item I' and ciphertext C'.

3.4. Security Definition

- Updated Reliability: A verifiable DSSE scheme first needs to ensure that the cloud server performs reliable update operations, that is, replay attack resistance. Since the cloud server is not trusted after it receives an update request from the data owner, it may not perform the corresponding update operation according to the update token content, that is, it will not update the security index and ciphertext collection. After receiving a search request from the data user, the un-updated data are returned to the data user, and the data user should verify that the returned results are up to date. If the opponent obtains the latest authentication information VI' and valid ciphertext $C(w)'$, and the forged information can pass the verification algorithm, the opponent wins.
- Verifiability: If the probability of the opponent successfully forging search results is negligible, the v-PADSSE scheme is considered verifiable. Due to the unreliability of the cloud server, it may return incorrect or incomplete results to the data user. Data users should be able to detect the improper behavior of the cloud server using verifi-

cation algorithms to ensure the correctness and integrity of the returned results. If the opponent obtained the latest verification information VI' and the valid ciphertext set $C(w)'$ and can forge the authentication information to pass the verification algorithm, the opponent wins.

4. v-PADSSE Scheme Construction and Algorithm Description

We have summarized some common symbols used in the design of the v-PADSSE scheme, as shown in Table 1.

Table 1. Common symbols and descriptions

Symbol	Description
N	the number of files containing keywords
n	the number of keywords
F	plaintext file set
W	keywords set
w_i	the i-th keyword in the keywords set
V	the total number of updates to the file containing keyword w
v_i	the number of updates to per file containing the keyword w_i
I	secure index
C	ciphertext set
T_w	the search trapdoor of keyword w
C(w)	ciphertext set containing keyword w
VI	verification information set
F(w)	plaintext file set containing keyword w
τ	update token
VL	verify list
I′	updated security index
C′	updated ciphertext set
docId	document identification
H	SHA-3 hash algorithm
flag	indicates whether the file contains the keyword
rand()	random number generation function
randA	odd numbers generated by rand()
randB	even numbers generated by rand()

4.1. *Overview of the v-PADSSE Scheme*

In order to solve the problem of correctness and integrity verification of the results returned by the cloud server, this paper designs a DSSE scheme based on public key verification (v-PADSSE). In this scheme, verification information is added to the security index and encrypted using the public key of the data user, so that the user can verify the returned results. Below, the construction of the v-PADSSE scheme is described in detail.

When constructing VI, the v-PADSSE scheme needs to include v_i, $flag$, and $H(F)$. The VI needs to be encrypted with the user's public key. Assume that the encryption function is $PK(VI)$. To prevent the cloud server from collecting statistics on the correlation between keywords and updated files, all index nodes in the column of the document representation of the updated file must be updated so that the update operation can hide the correlation between the ciphertext and the keywords. Therefore, the verification information $VI = PK(v_i) + PK(flag) + H(F)$. In addition, the data owner creates a verification list (VL) locally, which stores the latest verification information of each keyword, including the number of files containing keyword N, the total number of updates of files containing keyword V, the document identification of files containing keyword id, and its single set of file update times v_i so that the latest update token can be generated directly when the update operation is performed. For different update operations (such as modify, add, and delete), VI needs to be performed in different operations. VI is calculated as follows:

- Add new file F'.

When the data owner obtains the latest VI and performs the add operation, the number of updates of a single file is initialized to $v_i = 1$. If the newly added file F' contains the keyword w in the VL, the corresponding node in the VL needs to execute $N = N + 1$, $V = V + 1$, then add the document *id* of the new file F and the number of updates v_i to the node. If it does not, a new node needs to be added to the VL, where $N = 1$, $V = 1$, $v_i = 1$, and $VI = PK(v_i) + PK(flag = randA) + H(F')$.

- Modify file F to F'.

When file F needs to be updated to a new file F' (both F and F' contain the keyword w), the data owner updates VL with the latest verification information for the keyword w in the corresponding node and executes $V = V + 1$ and $v_i = v_i + 1$. $VI' = VI - pk(v_i) + PK(v_i + 1) - H(F) + H(F')$.

- Delete file F.

File F contains keyword w, and the data owner updates $N = N - 1$, $V = V - v_i$, and $v_i = 0$ in the VL in the node where keyword w resides. In this case, the latest verification information $VI' = VI - PK(N) + PK(N-1) - PK(v_i) + PK(v_i = 0) - PK(flag = randA) + PK(flag = randB)$. Additionally, the document *id* and v_i of file F are removed from the VL.

After the data owner performs different update operations, the corresponding update token τ is generated and sent to the cloud server, which updates the security index and ciphertext according to the update token information.

4.2. Secure Index Structure

In v-PADSSE, the data owner constructs the security index through using the bitmap index and constructs VL locally. The data owner generates the symmetric encryption key through executing the algorithm *KeyGen*, and the data user's key pair (PK, SK) is generated via KGC executing the *PSKeyGen* algorithm.

First, the data user publicly releases the public key, and the data owner, after obtaining the user's public key, uses the symmetric private key K to encrypt the privacy files and keywords and uses PK to encrypt the verification information corresponding to the keywords. When the security index is firstly constructed, the data owner needs to initialize VI through initializing N to the number of files containing the keyword w, $V = \sum_{i=1}^{n} v_i$, $v_i = 1$ $(1 \leq \mathrm{i} \leq \mathrm{N})$. When the security index is constructed, the column header contains the keyword w_i, and the row header contains the document ID $docId$. Middle node information includes v_i (the number of updates to the file containing the keyword w_i), $flag$ (indicating whether the document contains the keyword), and $H(F)$ (the result of the hash operation of the plaintext file). The security index structure is shown in Figure 2.

keyWord docId	id1	id2	id3	...
$K(w_1)$	$PK(v_1),PK(flag_{11}),H(F_1)$	$PK(v_2),PK(flag_{12}),H(F_2)$	$PK(v_3),PK(flag_{13}),H(F_3)$	...
$K(w_2)$	$PK(v_1),PK(flag_{21}),H(F_1)$	$PK(v_2),PK(flag_{22}),H(F_2)$	$PK(v_3),PK(flag_{23}),H(F_3)$	...
$K(w_3)$	$PK(v_1),PK(flag_{31}),H(F_1)$	$PK(v_2),PK(flag_{32}),H(F_2)$	$PK(v_3),PK(flag_{33}),H(F_3)$	...
$K(w_4)$	$PK(v_1),PK(flag_{41}),H(F_1)$	$PK(v_2),PK(flag_{42}),H(F_2)$	$PK(v_3),PK(flag_{43}),H(F_3)$	...
...	...	...	...	...

Figure 2. Security index structure.

The number of rows in the secure index is determined by the number of keywords, and each row is associated with a keyword. The number of column nodes is determined by the number of privacy files. When the data owner needs to perform an update operation, $\mathrm{PK}(v_i)$, $PK(flag)$, and $H(F)$ in all nodes in the whole column are modified according to the updated document identifier.

The data owner needs to obtain the latest verification information of the corresponding keyword when generating the update token. Therefore, VL is designed in the scheme and is owned by the data owner. The latest VI of keywords contained in each privacy file must be recorded in VL. When updating, the data owner modifies the VI in VL to ensure that the VL and VI in the security index are updated simultaneously. The structure of the VL is shown in Figure 3, where N indicates the number of files containing the keyword, V indicates the total number of updates to files containing the keyword, and $\{id, v_i\}$ indicates the set composed of the document identification of the file containing the keyword and the number of updates to the file.

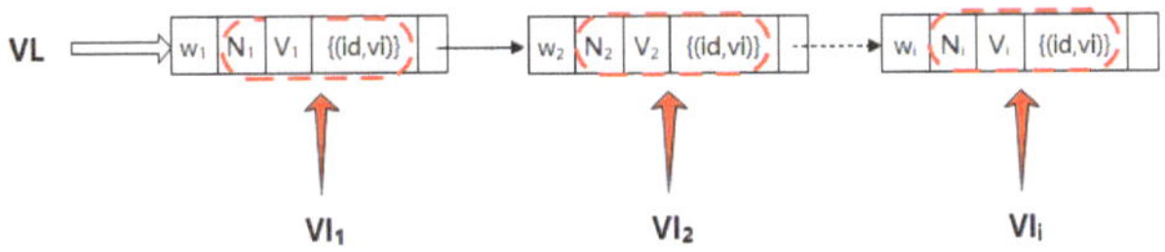

Figure 3. Structure of VL.

4.3. Algorithm Description

In this section, we give the execution steps of the core algorithm of the v-PADSSE scheme and explain the related functions in detail.

In v-PADSSE, the core algorithms involved are *IndexBuild* (Algorithm 1), *Building VL* (Algorithm 2), *GenToken*, *Search* (Algorithm 3), *Verify* (Algorithm 4), *UpdateToken* (Algorithm 5), and *Update* (Algorithm 6). The *IndexBuild* Algorithm 1 is used by the data owners to construct the secure index with bitmaps. Among them, the header node stores keyword and document identification, and the middle node stores keyword-related verification information. After constructing the secure index, data users upload the secure index and encrypted files to the cloud server. Data users use the *GenToken* algorithm to generate a trapdoor and send it to the cloud server. The cloud server executes the *Search* Algorithm 3, performs the matching query on the security index according to the trapdoor, and returns the matching results and verification information to the data user. After receiving the results, the user executes the *Verify* Algorithm 4 to verify the correctness and integrity of the results. If not verified, refuse. To update the privacy file, the data owner obtains the verification information related to the keyword contained in the file from VL, runs the *UpdateToken* Algorithm 5 to generate the corresponding update token, and sends it to the cloud server. The cloud server executes the *Update* Algorithm 6 based on the updated token information to update the security index and related ciphertext. Below, we will give a detailed explanation of the above core algorithm execution process.

- Initialization parameters:
  (1) Obtain the keyword set $\{w\}$ contained in the plaintext file and save it in the keyword set $W = \{w_1, w_2, \ldots, w_n\}$, where n is the number of keywords.
  (2) Obtain the number of files containing keyword w, $N = F(w).num$, the total number of updates to files containing keyword w, $V = N$, the set $\{id, v_i = 1\}$ consisting of the document ID and the number of updates per file, and whether the file contains the $flag$ of the keyword. $(PK(v[N]), PK(flag)) \leftarrow EncryptPK(v[N], flag)$ through using the public key.
  (3) Encrypt keyword w and plaintext file F using the symmetric key algorithm, compute $(Kw, C) \leftarrow EncryptK(w, F)$, and hash file F to obtain $H(F)$.
- Building secure index:

  For each privacy file, document identification $docId$ and keyword set $\{w_i\} \in W(1 \leq i \leq n)$ are used to construct the bitmap index. The functions and parameters required to construct the security index are described as follows:
  (1) Create the header node $BuildHeadNode(K_w, docId)$, where K_w is the keyword set after symmetric key K encryption, and $docId$ is the private file identification set.

(2) Create an intermediate node $BuildMiddleNode(K_w, docId, PK(v_i), PK(flag), H(F))$; K_w and $docId$ indicate where verification information is stored in the bitmap index, $PK(v_i)$ is the number of file updates containing the keyword w, and $PK(flag)$ indicates whether the privacy file corresponding to $docId$ contains keyword w. If yes, $flag = randA$; if no, $flag = randB$. $H(F)$ is the result of hashing the privacy file F.

The algorithm process is as follows:

Algorithm 1 $(I, C) \leftarrow IndexBuild(K, PK, F, W, N, V, v_i, flag)$

```
DO:
N=F.num();V=F.num();v[N]={1,1,...,1};
(K_w,C) ← EncryptK(w,F);
PK(v_i),PK(flag) ← EncryptPK(v_i,flag);
H(F) ← Hash(F);
// Assuming a total of n keywords and n privacy files, the following procedure is
   executed n * n times.
for i = 0; i < n; i++ do
    for j = 0; j < n; j++ do
        BuildHeadNode(K_w,docId);
        BuildMiddleNode(K_w,docId,PK(v_i),PK(flag),H(F));
    end for
end for
//The above process of creating head nodes and middle nodes together forms
   the bitmap index, and assigns the flag bit according to whether the keyword is
   contained in the privacy file, and generates the security index I.
//The data owner sends the generated security index I and ciphertext C to the
   cloud server.
Send to CS(I,C);
```

- Building verification list: VL

  The verification list is constructed and stored locally by the data owner. The VL is a single linked list, and the linked list node needs to contain the verification information of each keyword. The creation process is as follows.

  The VL header node does not store any information, only the address of the first keyword.

  $BuildHeadNode(*firstKeyWord)$:$*firstKeyWord$ indicates the address of the first keyword.

  $BuildListNode(w_i, N_i, V_i, \{id, v_i\}, *nextKeyWord)$. The middle node of the linked list stores the keyword w_i, the number of files N_i containing w_i, and the total number of updates to files V_i containing w_i. A set of the document identification of the privacy file containing w_i and the number of updates v_i to the file, and a pointer to the next keyword address $*nextKeyWord$ are also included.

Algorithm 2 Building VL

```
//Because there are n keywords, the creation of the intermediate index node
   needs to be executed n times.
for i = 0; i < n; i++ do
    BuildListNode(w_i,N_i,V_i,{id,v_i},*nextKeyWord);
end for
```

The Search algorithm process is as follows:

Algorithm 3 $(verifyInfo, C(w)) \leftarrow Search(T_w, I, C)$

DO:
//Data users execute trapdoor generation algorithm *GenToken*, use symmetric key K to encrypt keyword information, generate trapdoor T_w, and send it to the cloud server. It is also sent to the data owner through the channel to obtain the latest verification information of the keyword.
$T_w \leftarrow GenToken(K, w)$;
Send (T_w) to CS and DO;
CS:
if IndexSearch(T_w) = null **then**
  Then return null;
else
  //Obtain keyword verification information.
  verifyInfo = GetVerifyInfo(PK(v_i),PK(flag),H(F));
  C(w) = search(docId);
end if
//Return the search results and VI to the data user.
Return (verifyInfo,C(w));

The Verity algorithm process is as follows:

Algorithm 4 $(Y, N) \leftarrow Verify(verifyInfo, SK, T_w, C(w))$

DU:
//The user uses the private key SK to decrypt the verification information.
$(v_i, flag) \leftarrow DecSK(PK(v_i), PK(flag))$;
//Decrypt the latest verification information returned by the data owner.
$getNewVerifyInfo(T_w, PK(N_w), PK(V_w))$;
$DecSK(PK(N_w), PK(V_w))$;
//Check whether the keyword is contained in the privacy file according to the $flag$. If yes, proceed with the execution. If not, the privacy file will not be decrypted.
if flag% 2=0 **then**
  Delete;
  //The verification information returned by the data owner compares with that returned by the cloud server. If the verification information is correct, the ciphertext is accepted and decrypted. If not, the ciphertext is rejected.
else
  if $N_w = C(w)$. num and $V_w = \sum v_i$ and H(Decrypt(K,C(w)))=H(F) **then**
    Return Y;
  else
    return N;
  end if
end if

The UpdateToken algorithm process is as follows:

Algorithm 5 $\tau \leftarrow UpdateToken(K, PK, F, \{w, flag\}, v_i)$

DO:
Add:
//The data owner needs to add the privacy file F, he firstly obtains the keyword set $\{w\}$ and document identification $docIdF$ in F and then encrypts F and keyword $\{w\}$ with K, v_i is the number of updates corresponding to the privacy file.
$(\{K_w\}, C) \leftarrow EncryptK(\{w\}, F)$;

Algorithm 5 *Cont.*

//The VL is matched according to the keywords contained in F. If $\{w_i\}$ contained in F already exists, add ($docIdF$, 1) to the $\{id, v_i\}$ in the matched node, and do $N = N + 1$, $V = V + 1$ in this node. If not, add a new node $(w, N = 1, V = 1, \{docIdF, 1\})$ to VL.
//Assume there are k keywords in file F, it needs to be executed k times.
for $i = 0; i < k;$ i++ **do**
    if search(w_i) is true **then**
        N = N + 1;V = V + 1;
        Add(docIdF,1);
    else
        $BuildListNode(w_i, N_i = 1, V_i = 1, \{docIdF, 1\}, *nextKeyWord);$
    end if
end for
//The updated verification information is encrypted using public key PK, and generates the added token τ_{add}. If w is contained by the file F, the value of $flag$ is $randA$ in node $(w, docIdF)$, If not, the $flag$'s value is $randB$.
$PK(v_i), PK(flag) \leftarrow EncryptPK(v_i, flag);$
$H(F) \leftarrow Hash(F);$
$\tau_{add} = ("add", \{PK(v_i), PK(flag), H(F), K_w, docIdF\}, C);$
$Send(\tau)toCS;$
Delete:
//If the data owner needs to delete file F, he obtains the set of keyword $\{wi\}(1 \leq i \leq k)$ in file F and uses K to encrypt the keywords and the deleted file F. The document identification of the file F is $docIdF$.
$(\{K_w\}, C) \leftarrow EncryptK(\{w\}, F);$
//Search for $\{w_i\}$ in VL, and update N, V and the set $\{id, v_i\}$ in the corresponding node according to the keyword w_i. This procedure takes k times.
for $i = 0; i < k;$ i++ **do**
    if search(w) is true **then**
        N=N-1;V=V-v[docIdF];
        //Removes $\{docIdF, v\}$ from the document identification $\{id, vi\}$ set in matched node;
        Delete $\{docIdF, v\}$;
    else
        Return error;
    end if
end for
//The updated verification information is encrypted using the public key, and the deleted token τ_{del} is generated and sent to the cloud server.
$PK(v_i), PK(flag) \leftarrow EncryptPK(v_i = 0, flag = randB);$
$H(F) \leftarrow Hash(F);$
$\tau_{del} = ("delete", \{PK(v_i), PK(flag), H(F), K_w, docIdF\}, C);$
Send(τ) to CS;
Modify:
//If the data owner needs to modify the privacy file, he uses K to encrypt the modified file F and keywords contained in F.
$(\{K_w\}, C) \leftarrow EncryptK(\{w\}, F);$
//Update VI in VL according to the keywords contained in file F. After updating, the verification information is encrypted using the public key, and the modified token τ_{mod} is generated and sent to the cloud server.
//Since the modified file F contains k keywords $\{w_i\}(1 \leq i \leq k)$, the following procedure needs to be performed k times.

Algorithm 5 *Cont.*

for $i = 0; i < k;$ i++ **do**
  if search(w) is true **then**
    V=V+1;v[docIdF]=v[docIdF]+1;
  end if
end for
$PK(v[docIdF]) \leftarrow EncryptPK(v[docIdF]);$
$H(F) \leftarrow Hash(F);$
//During the modification, the $flag$ remains unchanged.
$\tau_{mod} = ("modify", \{PK(v[docIdF]), PK(flag), H(F), K_w, docIdF\}, C);$
Send(τ) to CS;

Algorithm 6 $(I', C') \leftarrow Update(\tau)$

CS:
//After receiving the updated token from the data owner, the cloud server performs operations on the security index I and ciphertext C according to the token.
if τ.operate = "add" **then**
  //Add a new column $docIdF$ to the bitmap index, or add a new row if the keyword contained in F does not exist in the bitmap index.
  BuildHeadNode(docIdF);
  //Assume there are n keywords in the bitmap index, that is, n rows, which need to be executed n times.
  for $i = 0; i < n;$ i++ **do**
    $BuildMiddleNode(K_w, docIdF, PK(v_i), PK(flag), H(F));$
  end for
  if K_{wi} does not exist in the bitmap index **then**
    $BuildHeadNode(K_{wi});$
    //Assume there are n document identifications in bitmap, the following procedure needs to be performed n times.
    for $i = 0; i < n;$ i++ **do**
      $BuildMiddleNode(K_w, id, PK(v_i), PK(flag), H(F));$
    end for
  end if
  addFile(C′);
else if τ.operate = "delete" **then**
  //Delete All nodes in the bitmap index if the value of column head node is $deleteId$.
  deleteColumn(deleteId);
  deleteFile(C′);
else if τ.operate = "modify" **then**
  //Assume there are n keywords in the bitmap index, all nodes need to be changed if the value of column head node is $modifyId$.
  for $i = 0; i < n;$ i++ **do**
    $ChangeNode(K_{wi}, modifyId, PK(v_i), PK(flag), H(F));$
  end for
  changeFile(C,C′);
end if

In conclusion, when the cloud server performs the update operation, the updated column needs to be modified. At this time, the existence of the $flag$ and the correct update of the $flag$ will not affect the verification result, even if the keyword w which is not contained in F changes. Moreover, since the update operation involves the change of an entire column in the secure index, it is also a good way to hide the correlation between the keywords and the updated file.

4.4. Comparison

In this section, we compare our scheme with $\Sigma o\phi o\varsigma$ [51], Ge's scheme [18], Gao's scheme [19], and Zhang's scheme [43]. All of those schemes can ensure the verifiability of search results. Assume there are n files and m keywords in total. For simplification, we assume that each search returns n files. We neglect the communication costs and only compare the computation overhead in different phases of these schemes. Table 2 shows the results of the comparison.

Table 2. Performance comparison.

Schemes	FS	Update	Search	Verify
$\Sigma o\phi o\varsigma$ [51]	✓	$O(mn)$	$O(m)$	
Zhang's scheme [43]	✓	$O(mn)$	$O(m)$	$O(n)$
Gao's scheme [19]	✓	$O(mn)$	$O(m)$	$O(n)$
Ge's scheme [18]	✓	$O(n)$	$O(m)$	$O(n)$
our scheme	✓	$O(n)$	$O(m)$	$O(n)$

As can be seen from Table 2, the efficiency of our scheme is close to Zhang's scheme [43], Gao's scheme [19], and Ge's scheme [18] in terms of search and verify operations. However, in the update process, our scheme and Ge's scheme [18] are better than others; the time complexity of the two schemes is O(n).

5. Security Analysis

In this section, we will analyze the security of the v-PADSSE scheme in two aspects: update reliability and verifiability.

5.1. Update Reliability Analysis

Due to the cloud server being unreliable in v-PADSSE, it may not update the security index and ciphertext after receiving the update request from the data owner in order to save computing or storage resources. We are going to prove that the Verify algorithm outputs "N" when the cloud server returns un-updated results.

Assume that the result returned by the cloud server is $(VI', C'(w))$, and the correct result and verification information is $(VI, C(w))$. The number of files containing the keyword w is N', and the total number of updates to files containing the keyword w is V'. In addition, the scheme proposes that when the data user performs a query, it will apply to the data owner for the latest verification information $PK(N)$, $PK(V)$ for the keyword. At this time, we will consider the following three scenarios to prove the reliability of the v-PADSSE.

(1) VI = VI', C(w) $\neq$ C'(w)

If the cloud server updates only the security index but not the ciphertext, the returned result is $(VI, C'(w))$.

$VI = \{PK(v_i), PK(flag), H(F)\}$;

$PK(V) = PK(\sum v[1, \ldots, N])$;

But the return verification information contains $H(F)$. At this time, we decrypt the return ciphertext $C'(w)$ to get F'. If you want to pass the verification, then $H(F) = H(F')$; that is, $F = F'$. If the plaintext is the same, the result $C(w) = C'(w)$ after encryption with the same key, which is inconsistent with the assumption that $C(w) \neq C'(w)$. The above calculation shows that if only the security index is updated without the ciphertext, the Verify Algorithm 4 cannot output 'Y' when the data user performs verification.

(2) VI $\neq$ VI', C(w) = C'(w)

In this case, the cloud server only updates the ciphertext but not the verification information in the security index.

$VI = \{PK(v_i), PK(flag), H(F)\}$;

$VI' = \{PK(v_i'), PK(flag'), H(F')\}$;

If we want the Verify Algorithm 4 to output 'Y', that means

$\{PK(v_i), PK(flag), H(F)\} = \{PK(v_i'), PK(flag'), H(F')\}$.

Since the verification information in the security index is not updated, if $PK(v_i) \neq PK(v_i')$ and the rest are equal, the total update times $V = \sum v[1, \ldots, N']$ will output 'N' when verifying the returned results. If $PK(flag) \neq PK(flag')$ and the rest are the same, the number of returned results is not equal to N, and the Verify Algorithm 4 will output 'N'. If the number of $flag = randA$ is the same as the number of $flag' = randA$ in the returned VI, it is also necessary to ensure that the v_i corresponding to the two are the same, which indicates that the attacker needs to obtain the verification information from the data owner, but VL is private to the data owner, and the probability of information leakage can be almost ignored. If $H(F) \neq H(F')$ and the rest are the same, in this case $F \neq F'$, the Verify Algorithm 4 will output 'N'.

(3) VI $\neq$ VI', C(w) $\neq$ C'(w)

Assume that the cloud server does not update the security index and ciphertext after receiving the update token from the data owner. If the data user performs a Search operation (Algorithm 3), the cloud server returns the un-updated results to the user. In the system model architecture (Figure 1), before performing the Search operation, the data user needs to send the latest VI request for the searched keyword to the data owner. The data owner searches VL and returns the latest VI of the keyword to the data user. After receiving the VI, the data user uses the Verify Algorithm 4 to compare the un-updated VI with the latest. If any inconsistency is found, the Verify Algorithm 4 directly outputs 'N'.

The above shows that if the cloud server does not update the security index and ciphertext to save computing or storage resources, our scheme can verify the verification information and return results through the verification algorithm to find the un-updated situation in time. Therefore, the v-PADSSE scheme proposed by us meets the updated reliability.

5.2. Verifiability Analysis

In this section, we assume that the attacker can forge $(C'(w), VI')$ so that the returned results pass the Verify Algorithm 4. Assuming that the correct results and verification information are $(C(w), VI)$, we will compare the forged information with the real information to prove that the probability of the attacker passing the Verify Algorithm 4 through forging verification information is negligible.

We will consider the following three scenarios to demonstrate the verifiability of the v-PADSSE.

(1) VI = VI', C(w) $\neq$ C'(w)

Attackers forge $VI' = PK(flag) + PK(VI) + H(F')$, while proper verification information $VI = PK(flag) + PK(VI) + H(F)$. This makes:

$PK(flag') + PK(v_i') + H(F') = PK(flag) + PK(v_i) + H(F)$;

In this case, because N, V, $flag$, and v_i are encrypted using the user's public key, the cost of forgery is relatively small. At this point, we can consider:

$H(F') = H(F)$;

According to the properties of the hash function, $F' = F$ is certain. In this case, $C'(w) = C(w)$, which is not consistent with the assumption. Therefore, the probability of an attacker passing the Verify Algorithm 4 in this way is almost negligible.

(2) VI $\neq$ VI', C(w) = C'(w)

The attacker forges the ciphertext $C'(w)$ to be consistent with the correct ciphertext. According to the design of the v-PADSSE, the verification information contains $H(F)$. At this point, we can consider:

$PK(v_i') + PK(flag') \neq PK(v_i) + PK(flag)$;

According to the above situation, $PK(V) = PK(\sum v_i) = PK(\sum v_i')$; when $PK(flag') \neq PK(flag)$, if the number of $flag = randA$ is not equal to the number of $flag' = randA$, the known probability of information leakage of VL can be ignored. In this case, the probability of the number of returned results being N is negligible, and the Verify Algorithm 4 will output 'N'. Therefore, the probability of the above situation passing the Verify Algorithm 4 can also be ignored.

(3) VI $\neq$ VI', C(w) $\neq$ C'(w)

In this case, the data user will spend a communication after sending the trapdoor to the data owner to request the latest verification information N, V of the keyword. Therefore, under this assumption, as long as any of the verification information is different, or the encrypted files returned are different, $H(F)$ is inconsistent, which will make the Verify Algorithm 4 output 'N'. Therefore, the probability of the attacker passing the verification can be ignored under this condition.

The above three scenarios show that if a malicious attacker forges ciphertext or verification information, our scheme can also determine which information is forged and give feedback. Therefore, our scheme satisfies verifiability.

6. Performance and Experiments

In this section, we will analyze the performance of the proposed v-PADSSE scheme. The basic logic of the experiment was written in C++, and the running environment was Windows 10 equipped with a 2.40 GHz 12th Gen Intel(R) Core(TM) i7 CPU and 4.0 GB RAM.

Index construction efficiency. We evaluated the bitmap index proposed in the scheme and the verification list construction efficiency. Figure 4 shows the time spent to build the security index and verification list when the number of keywords is set to 10,000 and the number of privacy files changes from 1000 to 10,000. In the scheme, the security index adopts the form of a bitmap index, the number of rows is the number of keywords, and the number of columns is the number of document identifiers of privacy files. When the number of rows in the bitmap index is fixed and the number of private files increases, the number of columns in the bitmap also needs to increase, and the time cost of building a secure index also increases. Figure 5 shows the time spent to construct the security index and verification list when the number of privacy files is 10,000 and the number of keywords contained in the privacy files changes from 1000 to 10,000. When the number of secure index columns is fixed, the increase in the number of keywords leads to an increase in the number of rows in the bitmap index, and the time cost of building the secure index Algorithm 1 also increases. During secure index construction, the number of nodes is related to the number of keywords and privacy files. Therefore, when the number of privacy files or keywords increases, the number of columns or rows of the bitmap index will also increase, and the time cost of building a security index will also increase. Since the number of nodes in VL is only related to the number of keywords contained in the privacy file, when the number of keywords increases, the number of nodes in VL increases, and the time cost of building VL (Algorithm 2) increases at the same time.

Update token generation efficiency. Figure 6 shows the time cost of generating update tokens (Algorithm 5) (modify token, delete token, and add token) in the scheme. Since the generation of the update token involves the document identification and the number of keywords contained in the privacy file after the document identification of the modified file is determined, the latest update times of the file need to be obtained from VL. Therefore, the generation efficiency of update tokens is linearly related to the number of nodes in VL, and the higher the number, the longer the token generation time. However, since the added token may involve increasing the number of VL nodes, the generation time will be slightly longer.

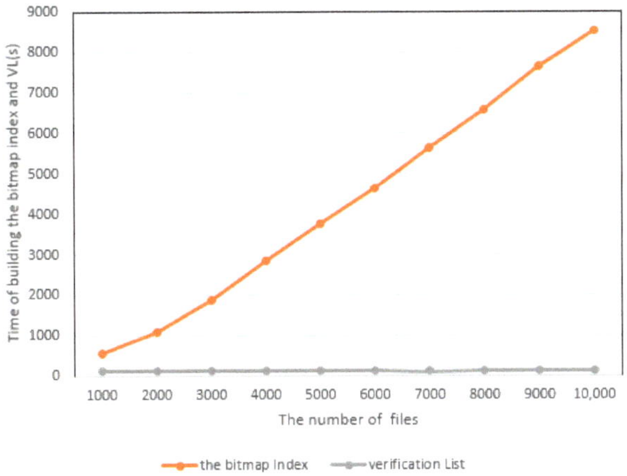

Figure 4. Security index and VL construction time cost.

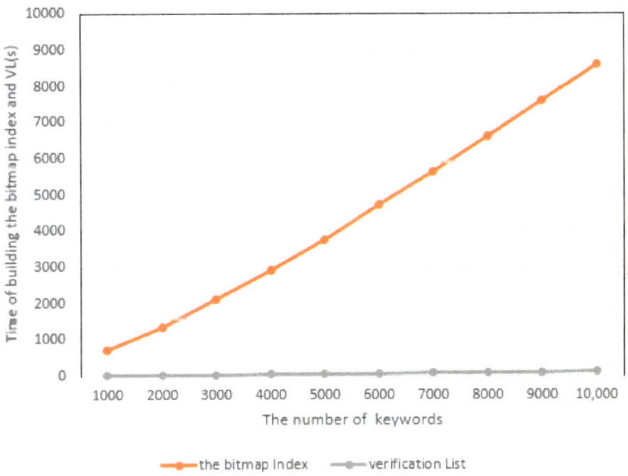

Figure 5. Security index and VL construction time cost.

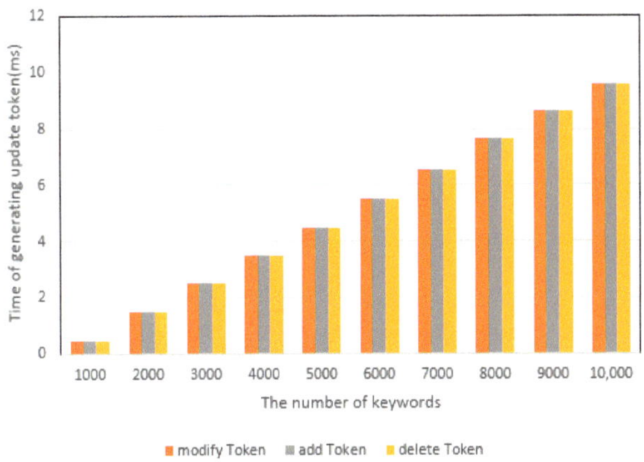

Figure 6. The update token generation time cost.

Search efficiency analysis. The VL obtains the latest verification information and generates an update token. After receiving the update token, the cloud server searches for it in the security index. Figure 7 shows the time cost of performing a search operation in the security index when the number of keywords is 10,000 and the number of private files changes from 1000 to 10,000. It can be seen that when the number of rows in the security index is fixed, that is, the number of keywords is fixed, the time cost of searching the index increases linearly with the increase in the number of columns, that is, the number of privacy files. Figure 8 shows the time cost of searching (Algorithm 3) the VL and the secure index when the number of privacy files is 10,000 and the number of keywords changes from 1000 to 10,000. Since the number of nodes in VL is equal to the number of keywords, the search time also increases linearly when the number of keywords increases. When the number of columns in the security index is fixed and the number of rows in the bitmap index increases as the number of keywords increases, the search time cost increases.

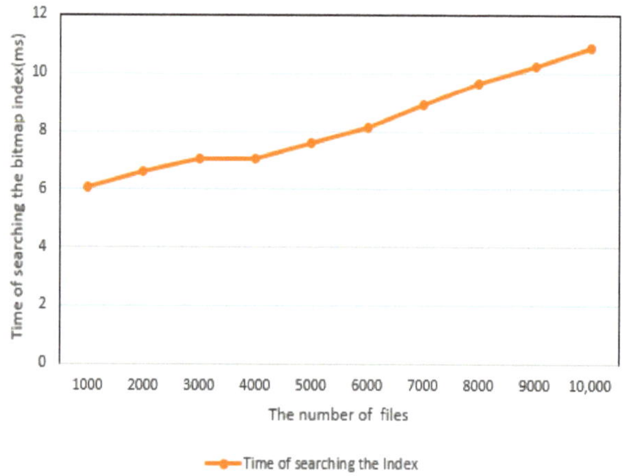

Figure 7. Search secure index time cost.

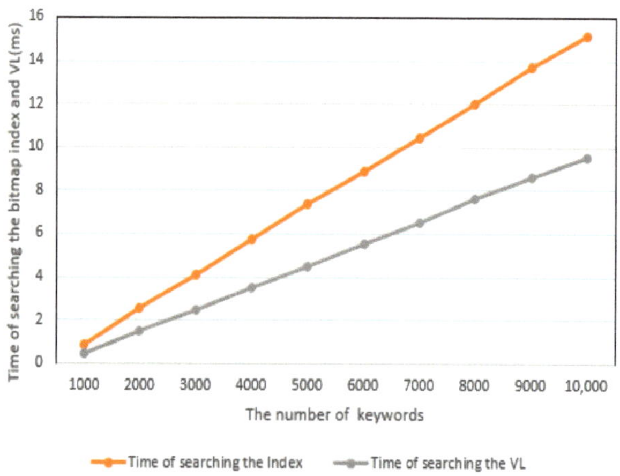

Figure 8. Search secure index and VL time cost.

In this section, we compare this scheme with what is generally regarded as the most typical verifiable SSE scheme [54] in terms of verification efficiency and update efficiency.

Verify efficiency analysis. We made a comparative analysis of the verification (Algorithm 4) time cost of our scheme and scheme [54]. As can be seen from Figure 9, the verification time cost of our scheme is lower than scheme [54]. Scheme [54] used a bilinear mapping accumulator to verify search results, which is based on asymmetric key encryption. Our scheme is based on a VL; the number of file updates is stored in the VL, which is more efficient than the accumulator. As shown in Figure 9, when the number of privacy files containing search keywords is 200, the verification time cost of scheme [54] is roughly 5 ms, and the verification time cost of our scheme is 0.3725 ms. When the number of search keywords is 2000, the verification time cost of scheme [54] is about 48 ms, and the verification time cost of our scheme is about 9.2437 ms. As can be seen from Figure 10, the number of CPU clock cycles of our scheme is lower than that of scheme [54]. Therefore, the verification efficiency of our scheme is higher than that of scheme [54].

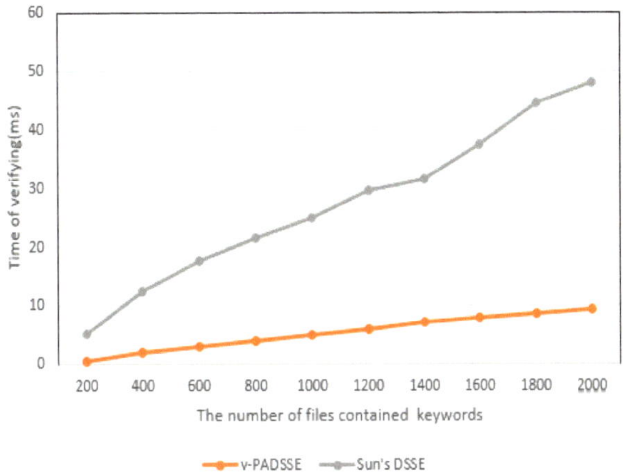

Figure 9. Verification efficiency comparison.

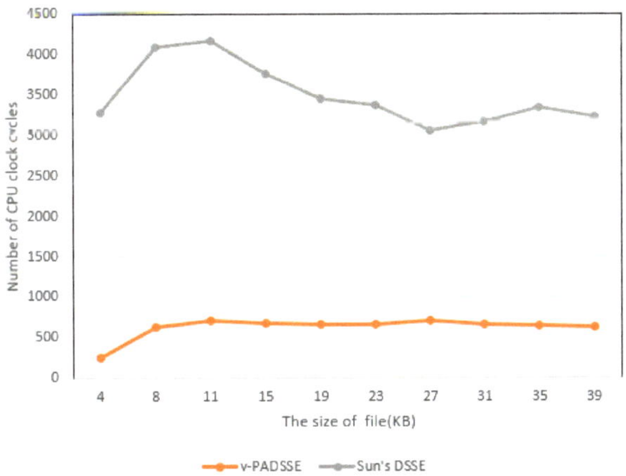

Figure 10. CPU clock cycles of per data comparison.

Update efficiency analysis. After receiving the update token, the cloud server needs to perform the corresponding Update operation (Algorithm 6) on the security index. As can be seen from Figures 11–13, the number of columns or rows in the security index needs to be increased due to the add and modify operation, and the time cost is slightly larger than the delete operation. The cloud server deletes the corresponding column in the security index when it performs the delete operation, and the time cost is lower. As can be seen from Figures 11–13, the update efficiency of our scheme is better than scheme [54].

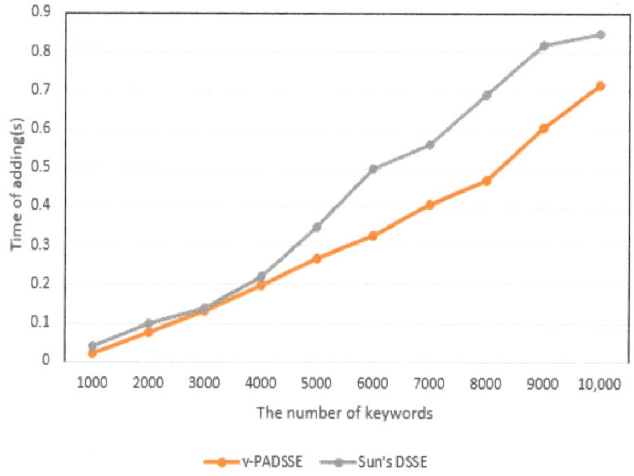

Figure 11. The comparison of add operation time cost.

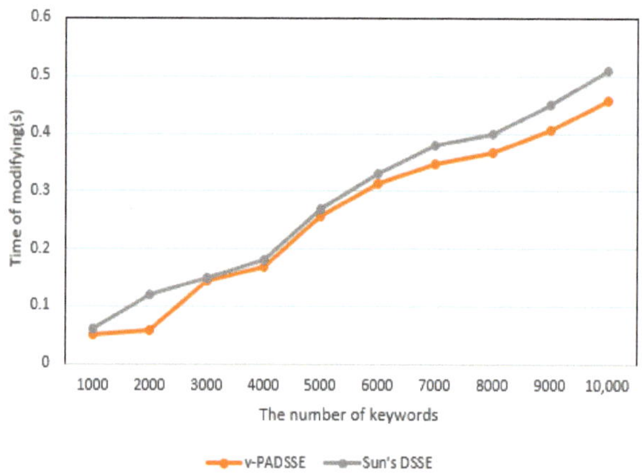

Figure 12. The comparison of modify operation time cost.

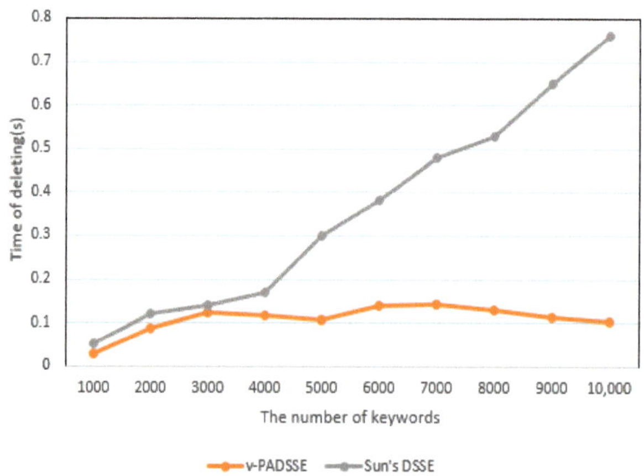

Figure 13. The comparison of delete operation time cost.

7. Discussion

In this section, we analyze the advantages and disadvantages of schemes [18,19,43,51], as shown in Table 3. $\Sigma o\phi o\varsigma$ [51], Zhang's scheme [43], and Gao's scheme [19] realize the dynamic update and searchability of data through constructing an inverted index. If the update file contains many keywords, the update efficiency is relatively low. None of the above four schemes involve key management securely. $\Sigma o\phi o\varsigma$ [51] uses a one-way trap gate to realize forward security, but the calculation cost is high. Zhang's scheme [43] is improved on the basis of $\Sigma o\phi o\varsigma$ [51], using random states to achieve forward safety and improve efficiency. However, the correctness of the returned results is not verified; that is, the update reliability proposed in this scheme is not satisfied. Gao's scheme [19] requires third-party TPA to verify the integrity of search results, which requires TPA to honestly implement the verification algorithm, which requires a trap gate, data block number, RAL, and authenticator to perform related calculations, which is relatively complex. Both Ge's scheme [18] and our scheme used a bitmap to construct the security index, which has high updating efficiency. However, the accumulated authentication tags (AATs) in Ge's scheme [18] contain ciphertext data blocks, which consume additional storage resources. In our scheme, the verification process does not involve complex operations, and the verification information is simple, which makes the verification efficiency high, but the scheme also needs to consume communication resources once more. In conclusion, compared with the above schemes, our scheme is relatively efficient in the process of searching, updating, and verifying.

Table 3. Advantages and disadvantages.

Schemes	Advantages	Disadvantages
$\Sigma o\phi o\varsigma$ [51]	Effectively implement forward security.	The calculation of trapdoor replacement is costly.
Zhang's scheme [43]	The multi-level hash function is used to replace the one-way permutation function, and the update efficiency is improved significantly.	The correctness of the returned result is not verified.
Gao's scheme [19]	The verification process effectively hides the relation between the keywords and the encrypted files to avoid statistical attacks.	The verification process is complex, and TPA must perform the verification process honestly.
Ge's scheme [18]	The verification of the returned results consumes only one AAT resource, which has high efficiency.	AAT contains ciphertext data blocks, which consume additional storage resources.
our scheme	The verification procedure is simple and does not involve complex operations, which has high efficiency.	The verification process consumes an additional communication resource.

8. Conclusions

In this paper, we first studied the research status of the DSSE scheme and analyzed the advantages and disadvantages of different schemes. Since most schemes do not involve key management, we proposed a verifiable DSSE scheme based on the public key cryptosystem which can realize secure key management. In Section 3, we defined the security model, design goals, core algorithm, and security analysis of the V-PDSSE scheme. In Section 4, we described the bitmap index and verification list construction of the scheme in detail and explained the core algorithm steps of the scheme. Finally, we compared the time complexity with schemes [18,19,43,51] to prove that the implementation efficiency of our scheme is high. In Section 5, a security analysis was carried out on the reliability and verifiability of our scheme to prove that our scheme meets the security requirements. In Section 6, we tested the efficiency of the core algorithms and compared the efficiency of scheme [54] in security index construction, verification list construction, searching, search result verification, and updating. The results show that our scheme has high efficiency and strong feasibility. In Section 7, we analyzed the advantages and disadvantages of schemes [18,19,43,51].

Compared with previous schemes, the functional design of this scheme is more comprehensive. The verification process does not involve complex operations, the verification information structure is simple, and the execution efficiency is high. Our scheme can solve the problems of dynamic searchability, forward security, integrity, and correct verification of search results and key management well. In future work, given the rapid development of quantum computers and verifiable DSSE schemes, how to deal with quantum attacks effectively will become a key direction of our research.

Author Contributions: Writing—original draft preparation, G.D.; writing—review and editing, S.L. All authors have read and agreed to the published version of the manuscript.

Funding: This work is supported by the Natural Science Foundation of Ningxia (No. 2021AAC03068) and the Key R&D Program of Ningxia (No. 2021BEG03071).

Data Availability Statement: Not applicable.

Acknowledgments: The authors would like to thank the editor and the anonymous reviewers for their valuable comments and suggestions that improved the quality of this paper.

Conflicts of Interest: The authors declare no conflict of interest. The funders had no role in the design of the study; in the collection, analyses, or interpretation of data; in the writing of the manuscript; or in the decision to publish the results.

References

1. Xu, L.; Xu, C.G.; Liu, Z.Y.; Wang, Y.L.; Wang, J.F. Enabling comparable search over encrypted data for IoT with privacy-preserving. *Comput. Mater. Contin.* **2019**, *60*, 675–690. [CrossRef]
2. Song, D.X.; Wagner, D.; Perrig, A. Practical techniques for searches on encrypted data. In Proceedings of the 2000 IEEE Symposium on Security and Privacy, Berkeley, CA, USA, 14–17 May 2000; pp. 44–55.
3. Islam, M.S.; Kuzu, M.; Kantarcioglu, M. *Access Pattern Disclosure on Searchable Encryption: Ramification, Attack and Mitigation*; Proc.NDSS: New York, NY, USA, 2012; pp. 1–15.
4. Zhang, Y.P.; Katz, J.; Papamanthou, C. All your queries are belong to us: The power of file-injection attacks on searchable encryption. *IACR Cryptol. Eprint Arch.* **2016**, *172*, 707–720.
5. Cash, D.; Grubbs, P.; Perry, J.; Ristenpart, T. Leakage-abuse attacks against searchable encryption. In Proceedings of the ACM SIGSAC Conference on Computer and Communications Security (CCS'15), Denver, CO, USA, 12–16 October 2015; pp. 668–679.
6. Kamara, S.; Papamanthou, C.; Roeder, T. Dynamic searchable symmetric encryption. In Proceedings of the ACM Conference on Computer and Communications Security (CCS 2012), Raleigh, NC, USA, 16–18 October 2012; pp. 965–976.
7. Kamara, S.; Papamanthou, C. Parallel and dynamic searchable symmetric encryption. In Proceedings of the 17th International Conference on Financial Cryptography and Data Security (FC 2013), Okinawa, Japan, 1–5 April 2013; Sadeghi, A.-R., Ed.; Springer: Berlin/Heidelberg, Germany, 2013; pp. 258–274.
8. Guo, C.; Chen, X.; Jie, Y.M.; Fu, Z.J.; Li, M.C.; Feng, B. Dynamic multi-phrase ranked search over encrypted data with symmetric searchable encryption. *IEEE Trans. Serv. Comput.* **2017**, *13*, 1034–1044. [CrossRef]
9. Xia, Z.H.; Wang, X.H.; Sun, X.M.; Wang, Q. A secure and dynamic multi-keyword ranked search scheme over encrypted cloud data. *IEEE Trans. Parallel Distrib. Syst.* **2016**, *27*, 340–352. [CrossRef]
10. Liu, Q.; Nie, X.H.; Liu, X.H.; Peng, T.; Wu, J. Verifiable ranked search over dynamic encrypted data in cloud computing. In Proceedings of the 2017 IEEE/ACM 25th International Symposium on Quality of Service (IWQoS), Vilanova i la Geltrú, Spain, 14–16 June 2017; pp. 1–6.
11. Nie, X.H.; Liu, Q.; Liu, X.H.; Peng, T.; Lin, Y.P. Dynamic verifiable search over encrypted data in untrusted clouds. In *Algorithms and Architectures for Parallel Processing*; Springer: Cham, Switzerland, 2016; pp. 557–571.
12. Zhu, X.Y.; Liu, Q.; Wang, G.J. A novel verifiable and dynamic fuzzy keyword search scheme over encrypted data in cloud computing. In Proceedings of the 2016 IEEE Trustcom/BigDataSE/ISPA, Tianjin, China, 23–26 August 2016; pp. 845–851.
13. Liu, Q.; Tian, Y.; Wu, J.; Peng, T.; Wang, G. Enabling verifiable and dynamic ranked search over outsourced data. *IEEE Trans. Serv. Comput.* **2022**, *15*, 69–82. [CrossRef]
14. Jiang, X.X.; Yu, J.; Yan, J.B.; Hao, R. Enabling efficient and verifiable multi-keyword ranked search over encrypted cloud data. *Inf. Sci.* **2017**, *403–404*, 22–41. [CrossRef]
15. Chen, F.; Xiang, T.; Fu, X.W.; Yu, W. User differentiated verifiable file search on the cloud. *IEEE Trans. Serv. Comput.* **2018**, *11*, 948–961. [CrossRef]
16. Wan, Z.G.; Deng, R.H. VPSearch: Achieving verifiability for privacy preserving multi-keyword search over encrypted cloud data. *IEEE Trans. Depend. Sec. Comput.* **2018**, *15*, 1083–1095. [CrossRef]
17. Kurosawa, K.; Ohtaki, Y. How to update documents verifiably in searchable symmetric encryption. In *Cryptology and Network Security*; Springer: Cham, Switzerland, 2013; pp. 309–328.

18. Ge, X.; Yu, J.; Zhang, H.; Hu, C.; Li, Z.; Qin, Z.; Hao, R. Towards achieving keyword search over dynamic encrypted cloud data with symmetric-key based verification. *IEEE Trans. Dependable Secur. Comput.* **2021**, *18*, 490–504. [CrossRef]
19. Gao, X.; Yu, J.; Chang, Y.; Wang, H.; Fan, J. Checking only when it is necessary: Enabling integrity auditing based on the keyword with sensitive information privacy for encrypted cloud data. *IEEE Trans. Dependable Secur. Comput.* **2021**, *19*, 3774–3789. [CrossRef]
20. Yu, J.; Ren, K.; Wang, C. Enabling cloud storage auditing with key-exposure resistance. *IEEE Trans. Inf. Forensics Secur.* **2015**, *10*, 1167–1179.
21. Zhang, Y.; Yu, J.; Hao, R.; Wang, C.; Ren, K. Enabling efficient user revocation in identity-based cloud storage auditing for shared big data. *IEEE Trans. Dependable Secur. Comput.* **2018**, *17*, 608–619. [CrossRef]
22. Shacham, H.; Waters, B. Compact Proofs of Retrievability. In Proceedings of the 14th Annual International Conference on the Theory and Application of Cryptology & Information Security, Melbourne, Australia, 7–11 December 2008; pp. 90–107.
23. Miao, Y.B.; Ma, J.F.; Liu, X.M.; Li, X.H.; Jiang, Q.; Zhang, J.W. Attribute-based keyword search over hierarchical data in cloud computing. *IEEE Trans. Serv. Comput.* **2017**, *13, 985–998*. [CrossRef]
24. Miao, Y.B.; Ma, J.F.; Liu, X.M.; Weng, J.; Li, H.W.; Li, H. Lightweight fine-grained search over encrypted data in fog computing. *IEEE Trans. Serv. Comput.* **2018**, *12*, 772–785. [CrossRef]
25. Liu, X.; Yang, G.; Mu, Y.; Deng, R.H. Multi-user verifable searchable symmetric encryption for cloud storage. *IEEE Trans. Dependable Secur. Comput.* **2020**, *17*, 1322–1332. [CrossRef]
26. Xu, P.; Wu, Q.; Wang, W.; Susilo, W.; Domingo-Ferrer, J.; Jin, H. Generating searchable public-key ciphertexts with hidden structures for fast keyword search. *IEEE Trans. Inf. Forensics Secur.* **2015**, *10*, 1993–2006.
27. Fu, Z.J.; Xia, L.L.; Sun, X.M.; Liu, A.X.; Xie, G.W. Semantic aware searching over encrypted data for cloud computing. *IEEE Trans. Inf. Forensics Secur.* **2018**, *13*, 2359–2371. [CrossRef]
28. Zhang, W.; Xiao, S.; Lin, Y.P.; Zhou, T.; Zhou, S.W. Secure ranked multi-keyword search for multiple data owners in cloud computing. In Proceedings of the 2014 44th Annual IEEE/IFIP International Conference on Dependable Systems and Networks, Atlanta, GA, USA, 23–26 June 2014; pp. 276–286.
29. Fu, Z.J.; Sun, X.M.; Linge, N.; Zhou, L. Achieving effective cloud search services: Multi-keyword ranked search over encrypted cloud data supporting synonym query. *IEEE Trans. Consum. Electron.* **2014**, *60*, 164–172. [CrossRef]
30. Naveed, M.; Prabhakaran, M.; Gunter, C.A. Dynamic searchable encryption via blind storage. In Proceedings of the 2014 IEEE Symposium on Security and Privacy, Berkeley, CA, USA, 18–21 May 2014, pp. 639–654.
31. Zhang, R.; Xue, R.; Liu, L. Searchable encryption for healthcare clouds: A survey. *IEEE Trans. Serv. Comput.* **2018**, *11*, 978–996. [CrossRef]
32. Xu, C.; Wang, N.; Zhu, L.; Sharif, K.; Zhang, C. Achieving searchable and privacy-preserving data sharing for cloud-assisted E-healthcare system. *IEEE Internet Oftings J.* **2019**, *6*, 8345–8356. [CrossRef]
33. Emura, K.; Miyaji, A.; Omote, K. A timed-release proxy re-encryption scheme. *IEICE-Trans. Fundam. Electron. Commun. Comput. Sci.* **2011**, *E94-A*, 1682–1695. [CrossRef]
34. Yang, Y.; Ma, M. Conjunctive keyword search with designated tester and timing enabled proxy Re-encryption function for E-health clouds. *IEEE Trans. Inf. Forensics Secur.* **2016**, *11*, 746–759. [CrossRef]
35. Watanabe, Y.; Shikata, J. Timed-release computational secret sharing and threshold encryption. *Des. Codes Cryptogr.* **2018**, *86*, 17–54. [CrossRef]
36. Emura, K.; Hayashi, T.; Ishida, A. Group signatures with timebound keys revisited: A new model, an efcient construction, and its implementation. *IEEE Trans. Dependable Secur. Comput.* **2020**, *17*, 292–305. [CrossRef]
37. Xu, P.; He, S.; Wang, W.; Susilo, W.; Jin, H. Lightweight searchable public-key encryption for cloud-assisted wireless sensor networks. *IEEE Trans. Ind. Inform.* **2018**, *14*, 3712–3723. [CrossRef]
38. Xiong, H.; Wang, Y.; Li, W.; Chen, C.M. Flexible, efficient, and secure access delegation in cloud computing. *ACM Trans. Manag. Inf. Syst. (TMIS)* **2019**, *10*, 2. [CrossRef]
39. Miao, Y.; Tong, Q.; Deng, R.H.; Choo, K.K.R.; Liu, X.; Li, H. Verifiable searchable encryption framework against insider keyword-guessing attack in cloud storage. *IEEE Trans. Cloud Comput.* **2020**, *10*, 835–848. [CrossRef]
40. Wu, D.N.; Gan, Q.Q.; Wang, X.M. Verifiable public key encryption with keyword search based on homomorphic encryption in multi-user setting. *IEEE Access* **2018**, *6*, 42445–42453. [CrossRef]
41. Chai, Q.; Gong, G. Verifiable symmetric searchable encryption for semi-honest-but-curious cloud servers. In Proceedings of the 2012 IEEE International Conference on Communications (ICC), Ottawa, ON, Canada, 10–15 June 2012; pp. 917–922.
42. Yang, L.; Zheng, Q.; Fan, X. Rspp: A reliable, searchable and privacy-preserving e-healthcare system for cloud-assisted body area networks. In Proceedings of the IEEE INFOCOM 2017-IEEE Conference on Computer Communications, Atlanta, GA, USA, 1–4 May 2017; pp. 1–9.
43. Zhang, Z.; Wang, J.; Wang, Y.; Su, Y.; Chen, X. Towards efficient verifiable forward secure searchable symmetric encryption. In *Computer Security-ESORICS 2019*; Springer International Publishing: Cham, Switzerland, 2019; Volume 11736, pp. 304–321.
44. Deepa, N.; Perumal, P. Hybrid context aware recommendation system for e-health care by merkle hash tree from cloud using evolutionary algorithm. *Soft. Comput.* **2020**, *24*, 7149–7161. [CrossRef]
45. Zhu, J.; Li, Q.; Wang, C.; Yuan, X.; Wang, Q.; Ren, K. Enabling generic, verifiable, and secure data search in cloud services. *IEEE Trans. Parallel Distrib. Syst.* **2018**, *29*, 1721–1735. [CrossRef]

46. Chen, C.; Zhu, X.; Shen, P.; Hu, J.; Guo, S.; Tari, Z.; Zomaya, A.Y. An efficient privacy-preserving ranked keyword search method. *IEEE Trans. Parallel Distrib. Syst.* **2015**, *27*, 951–963. [CrossRef]
47. Cheng, H.; Wang, H.; Liu, X.; Fang, Y.; Wang, M.; Zhang, X. Person re-identification over encrypted outsourced surveillance videos. *IEEE Trans. Dependable Secur. Comput.* **2019**, *18*, 1456–1473. [CrossRef]
48. Guo, Y.; Zhang, C.; Jia, X. Verifiable and forward-secure encrypted search using blockchain techniques. In Proceedings of the 2020 IEEE International Conference on Communications (ICC), Dublin, Ireland, 7–11 June 2020; pp. 1–7.
49. Wang, Q.; He, M.; Du, M.; Chow, S.; Lai, R.; Zou, Q. Searchable encryption over feature-rich data. *IEEE Trans. Depend. Sec. Comput.* **2018**, *15*, 496–510. [CrossRef]
50. Du, M.; Wang, Q.; He, M.; Weng, J. Privacy-preserving index-ing and query processing for secure dynamic cloud storage. *IEEE Trans. Inf. Forensics Secur.* **2018**, *13*, 2320–2332. [CrossRef]
51. Bost, R. Σοφος: forward secure searchable encryption. In Proceedings of the 2016 ACM SIGSAC Conference on Computer and Communications Security (CCS 2016), Vienna, Austria, 24–28 October 2016; Weippl, E.R., Katzenbeisser, S., Kruegel, C., Myers, A.C., Halevi, S., Eds.; ACM: New York, NY, USA, 2016; pp. 1143–1154.
52. Cao, N.; Wang, C.; Li, M.; Ren, K.; Lou, W. Privacy-preserving multi-keyword ranked search over encrypted cloud data. *IEEE Trans. Parallel Distrib. Syst.* **2014**, *25*, 222–233. [CrossRef]
53. Li, J.; Huang, Y.; Wei, Y.; Lv, S.; Liu, Z.; Dong, C.; Lou, W. Searchable Symmetric Encryption with Forward Search Privacy. *IEEE Trans. Dependable Secur. Comput.* **2021**, *18*, 464–465. [CrossRef]
54. Sun, W.H.; Liu, X.F.; Hou, W.J.L.Y.T.; Li, H. Catch you if you lie to me: Efficient verifiable conjunctive keyword search over large dynamic encrypted cloud data. In Proceedings of the 2015 IEEE Conference on Computer Communications (INFOCOM), Hong Kong, China, 26 April–1 May 2015; pp. 2110–2118.

electronics

Article

CANARY: An Adversarial Robustness Evaluation Platform for Deep Learning Models on Image Classification

Jiazheng Sun [1,2], Li Chen [3], Chenxiao Xia [3], Da Zhang [1], Rong Huang [1], Zhi Qiu [1], Wenqi Xiong [1], Jun Zheng [1,2,*] and Yu-An Tan [1,2]

[1] School of Cyberspace Science & Technology, Beijing Institute of Technology, Beijing 100081, China; jiazheng.sun@bit.edu.cn (J.S.); tan2008@bit.edu.cn (Y.-A.T.)
[2] Beijing Key Laboratory of Software Security Engineering Technology, Beijing 100081, China
[3] School of Computer Science & Technology, Beijing Institute of Technology, Beijing 100081, China
* Correspondence: zhengjun@bit.edu.cn

Abstract: The vulnerability of deep-learning-based image classification models to erroneous conclusions in the presence of small perturbations crafted by attackers has prompted attention to the question of the models' robustness level. However, the question of how to comprehensively and fairly measure the adversarial robustness of models with different structures and defenses as well as the performance of different attack methods has never been accurately answered. In this work, we present the design, implementation, and evaluation of Canary, a platform that aims to answer this question. Canary uses a common scoring framework that includes 4 dimensions with 26 (sub)metrics for evaluation. First, Canary generates and selects valid adversarial examples and collects metrics data through a series of tests. Then it uses a two-way evaluation strategy to guide the data organization and finally integrates all the data to give the scores for model robustness and attack effectiveness. In this process, we use Item Response Theory (IRT) for the first time to ensure that all the metrics can be fairly calculated into a score that can visually measure the capability. In order to fully demonstrate the effectiveness of Canary, we conducted large-scale testing of 15 representative models trained on the ImageNet dataset using 12 white-box attacks and 12 black-box attacks and came up with a series of in-depth and interesting findings. This further illustrates the capabilities and strengths of Canary as a benchmarking platform. Our paper provides an open-source framework for model robustness evaluation, allowing researchers to perform comprehensive and rapid evaluations of models or attack/defense algorithms, thus inspiring further improvements and greatly benefiting future work.

Keywords: AI security; adversarial robustness evaluation; adversarial attack; deep model

Citation: Sun, J.; Chen, L.; Xia, C.; Zhang, D.; Huang, R.; Qiu, Z.; Xiong, W.; Zheng, J.; Tan, Y.-A. CANARY: An Adversarial Robustness Evaluation Platform for Deep Learning Models on Image Classification. *Electronics* **2023**, *12*, 3665. https://doi.org/10.3390/electronics12173665

Academic Editors: Cheng-Chi Lee and George A. Tsihrintzis

Received: 25 July 2023
Revised: 28 August 2023
Accepted: 28 August 2023
Published: 30 August 2023

1. Introduction

Nowadays, deep learning is widely used in image classification tasks and plays an irreplaceable role in security-sensitive areas such as autonomous driving [1], medical diagnosis [2–4], software security [5], and military reconnaissance [6]. However, small perturbations crafted by attackers can disturb image classification models to produce erroneous inference results [7]. It has been pointed out that there is an "arms race" between attack [8–10] and defense [11–13]. With a large number of means of attacks and defenses being proposed, how to fully and fairly measure the adversarial robustness of models with different structures and defense methods as well as the performance, strengths, and weaknesses of different attack methods has always been a challenge for researchers.

In order to comprehensively evaluate the security of deep learning models, some research [14–22] has proposed evaluation metrics, method libraries, and evaluation platforms. Works such as CleverHans [14] and FoolBox [15] integrated the most common attack and defense methods, but the neglect of code quality made some of them incorrectly developed or even unworkable. DeepSec [18] first proposed a series of evaluation metrics for both attack and defense methods but needed to exhaustively validate the effectiveness of these metrics and set a baseline and rank these methods based on the metrics. RealSafe [20] abandoned these metrics and instead used two complementary robustness curves as the primary evaluation metrics, focusing on the misclassification rate of attacks under different perturbation budgets. In fact, the evaluation strategy of RealSafe did not always work for attacks that limit the reduction of the misclassification rate while optimizing perturbations (e.g., Boundary Attack) or for attacks that are difficult to precisely limit the scale of perturbations (e.g., CW [23]). AISafety [22] attempted to extend the work of both. However, it neglected the universality of the evaluation metrics, and its interpretability and neuron traversal evaluation were difficult to widely adapt to models with different structures. Furthermore, almost all work evaluated only a few models (e.g., RealSafe only evaluated ResNet [24] and Inception, while DeepSec only evaluated ResNet, and AISafety only evaluated VGG [25] and WRN [26]), which left us with a lack of knowledge on the performance of attack and defense methods on models with different structures. The evaluation frameworks proposed by these works also lacked sufficient flexibility and universality in the face of new methods, thus limiting their further role.

We note that evaluation metrics are still dominated by the misclassification rate and norm metrics, even in the latest work on adversarial methods. Researchers drew different conclusions based on different models and different parameters and claimed that their findings were in a sense the best (we have already revealed that attack methods can perform very differently on different models, see Section 5.5 for further discussion). Clearly, the results of such evaluations may be biased, and incomplete evaluations could not provide them with convincing conclusions.

In this work, hoping to facilitate future research, we develop a comprehensive, generic scoring framework of 26 (sub)metrics to evaluate the adversarial robustness of models. First, we define a valid example selection strategy that avoids iterative testing of different perturbations, allows for faster conclusions than RealSafe, and can be adapted to a wider range of attack methods. Second, we propose a two-way evaluation strategy of "Attack Effectiveness–Model Robustness", which allows us to fully understand the performance of existing attacks on different models and the robustness of existing models in the face of different attacks. We finally propose a novel integrated capability measure based on Item Response Theory (IRT [27]) for the first time, which can adequately measure the difficulty and differentiation of metrics based on Markov Chain Monte Carlo (MCMC [28]), and can give an "Attack Effectiveness–Model Robustness" capability score for attacks and models.

We integrate a large number of classical and SOTA attacks for bi-directional evaluation, including 12 white-box attacks and 12 black-box attacks. These attacks cover the widest range of attack paths, attack means, and distance measures, including (1) gradient-based attacks, transfer-based attacks, score-based attacks, and decision-based attacks; (2) frequency-domain- and time-domain-based attacks; and (3) attacks based on L_0, L_2, L_∞. To fully demonstrate the differences in robustness between models with different structures, we selected the 15 most representative models ranging from AlexNet [29] to ConvNeXt [30] in the evaluation. We conducted large-scale experiments with these models and methods on the ImageNet [31] dataset. Using quantitative results, we show the differences in misclassification and imperceptibility capabilities between different attack methods and further analyze the competition between them; we also show the differences in the robustness of the different structural models and, furthermore, which attack methods work better or worse against which models. We also provide a more intuitive capability score to help researchers understand the robustness of different models and the differences in the effectiveness of different attack methods more clearly.

We developed a new adversarial robustness evaluation platform, Canary, on which we have based all our evaluation experiments. The structure is shown in Figure 1. We hope to open-source the platform, share all our evaluation data, and continue to integrate more attack and defense methods. We hope that more researchers will evaluate their work in the platform in order to provide a reliable benchmark, which we believe can help fellow researchers to better understand adversarial attacks and further improve the robustness of their models.

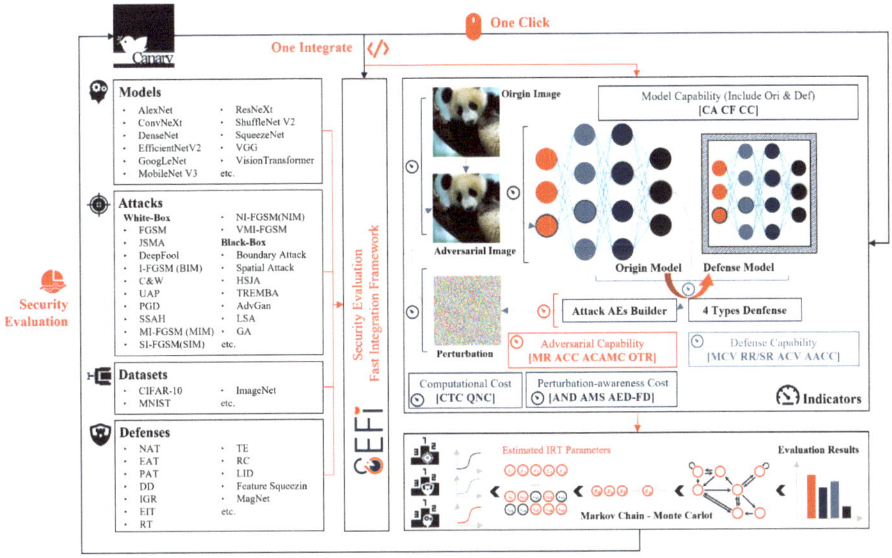

Figure 1. With 26 evaluation metrics, our comprehensive evaluation framework, Canary, is tested on 15 models against 12 white-box attacks and 12 black-box attacks. We measure the performance of the adversarial examples generated by the attack methods in terms of bias of label, confidence, activation mapping, and imperceptibility of perturbation and evaluate the robustness of the models in an adversarial setting.

Our contributions can be summarized as follows:

- We propose novel evaluation methods for model robustness, attack/defense effectiveness, and attack transferability and develop a scoring framework including 26 (sub)metrics. We first use IRT to calculate these metrics into scores that reflect their real capabilities, making it possible for us to compare and rank model robustness and the effectiveness of the attack method.
- We design and open-source an advanced evaluation platform called Canary, including 17K lines of code. The platform contains at least 30 attacks, including 15 white-box attacks and 15 black-box attacks. To our knowledge, this is one of the best platforms that can allow users to freely integrate any CNN model or any attack or defense method.
- Based on Canary and the scoring framework, we conducted the largest-scale cross-evaluation experiment of "model-attack" to date and obtained a series of interesting and insightful findings. In particular, we revealed the significantly different performances of different models under the same attack and the substantial differences of different attack methods in attacking the same model. These findings may promote the development of the adversarial learning field.
- We have collated the test results into a database and open-sourced it with a view to providing a valid baseline for other researchers, which will be the second baseline for model robustness since RobustBench.

Notations

For ease of understanding, we summarize the basic notations used in this paper in Table 1, and any notation mentioned in the table will not be subject to additional explanation.

Table 1. Base notations used in this paper.

Notations	Description
$x = \{x_1, \cdots, x_n\}$	x is the set of n original images, where x_i denotes the ith image in the set.
$y = \{y_1, \cdots, y_n\}$	y is the set of n original images corresponding to ground-truth labels, where y_i denotes the label of the ith image in the set x, and $y_i \in \{1, \cdots, k\}$.
$F : x_i \to y_i^*, y_i^* \in \{1, \cdots, k\}$	F is a deep-learning-based image k-class classifier that has $F(x_i) = y_i$ when classified correctly.
$P : x_i \to \{P(1), \cdots, P(k)\}$	P is the Softmax layer of F, $F(x_i) = \arg\max_j P(x_i)_j$.
$P(x_i)_j$	$P(x_i)_j$ denotes the probability that x_i is inferred to be j by F, also known as the confidence level, where $j \in \{1, \cdots, k\}$.
x^a	x^a is the adversarial example, where x is generated by the attack method.
y^{adv}	For targeted attacks only, y^{adv} is the label of the specified target.

2. Related Works

In this section, we will provide a brief overview of existing works on adversarial attacks and defenses and those on adversarial robustness evaluation.

2.1. Methods of Adversarial Attack and Defense

Formally, an adversarial example can be defined as follows: Given an original image x (where $x \in \mathbb{R}^{w \times h \times c}$, w and h are the dimensions of the image and c is the number of its channels) and F is a classification model trained from a set of clean images, then $F(x)$ is the inference of the original image x. If the perturbation $\delta(x)$ required to make x cross the decision boundary of F can be found such that $x^a = x + \delta(x)$ and $F(x) \neq F(x^a)$, then the image x^a can be an adversarial example of F. Carlini and Wagner argue that the optimal adversarial example generation algorithm needs to ensure the following two conditions: (1) $\delta(x)$ is as small as possible (usually $\delta(x)$ uses l_P-norm, $p \in \{1, 2, \infty\}$ to measure), while being as imperceptible to the human eye as possible; and (2) x^a should be as effective as possible to make the F classification produce errors [23]. For target attacks, the confidence level in the errors should also be sufficiently high.

Considering the attacker's knowledge of the target model, it can be classified as either (1) a white-box attack or (2) a black-box attack. For white-box attacks, the attacker has full access to the model, can obtain the model structure, and can often obtain a high misclassification rate at a small perturbation cost, which is often used to evaluate the effectiveness of defense methods or the robustness of the model under adverse conditions. The most common white-box attacks are generally based on gradients to optimize perturbations and generate adversarial examples. For black-box attacks, the attacker only has access to the input and output information of the model but not its structure, and the main implementation methods are transfer-based and query-based attacks.

Query-based attacks rely on the model inference scores, increasing the misclassification rate at the cost of high accesses. Depending on the amount of information obtained, they can be further divided into decision-based attacks, which can only obtain hard-label, and score-based attacks, which can obtain a continuous inference score (i.e., the confidence level for each classification, soft-label). We have summarized many important adversarial attack algorithms based on the above definitions and descriptions. For more details see Appendix A: Details of the main adversarial attack algorithms in our evaluations.

The defense methods can be broadly classified into three categories: adversarial training, image processing, and adversarial example detection. For adversarial training, we consider the defended model F_D to have a similar structure to the original model F_O but with differences in the weight hyperparameters; for image processing, we consider $F_D(x) = F_O(\varphi(x))$, where φ is the image processing method; and for adversarial example detection, there is generally no modification to the model itself.

In this paper, we evaluate the following attack methods, shown in Table 2.

Table 2. Main adversarial attack algorithms in computer vision in our experiment.

Algorithm	Perturbation Measurement	Attacker's Knowledge	Attack Approach
FGSM [32]	L_∞	white-box	gradient
JSMA [33]	L_0	white-box	gradient
DeepFool [34]	L_0, L_2, L_∞	white-box	gradient
I-FGSM (BIM) [35]	L_∞	white-box	gradient
C&W Attack [23]	L_0, L_2, L_∞	white-box	gradient
Projected Gradient Descent (PGD) [36]	L_1, L_∞	white-box	gradient
MI-FGSM (MIM) [37]	L_∞	transferable black-box	transfer, gradient
SI-FGSM (SIM) [38]	L_∞	transferable black-box	transfer, gradient
NI-FGSM (NIM) [38]	L_∞	transferable black-box	transfer, gradient
VMI-FGSM (VMIM) [39]	L_∞	transferable black-box	transfer, gradient
Elastic-Net Attack (EAD) [40]	L_1	white-box	gradient
SSAH [41]	-	white-box	gradient
One pixel Attack (OPA) [42]	L_0	black-box query, score	Soft Label
Local Search Attack (LSA) [43]	L_0	black-box query, score	Soft-Label
Boundary Attack (BA) [44]	L_2	black-box query, decision	Hard-Label
Spatial Attack (SA) [45]	-	black-box query	Hard-Label
Hop Skip Jump Attack (HSJA) [46]	L_2, L_∞	black-box query, decision	Hard-Label
Gen Attack (GA) [47]	L_2, L_∞	black-box query, score	Soft-Label
SPSA [48]	L_∞	black-box query, score	Soft-Label
Zeroth-Order Optimization (ZOO) [49]	L_2	black-box query, score	Soft-Label
AdvGan [50]	L_2	black-box query, score	Soft-Label
TREMBA [51]	-	black-box query, score	Soft-Label

2.2. *The Robustness Evaluation of DL Model*

Many different evaluation frameworks have been proposed to evaluate DL-model security comprehensively. These efforts can be broadly classified into three categories, namely the attack/defense toolsets represented by CleverHans [14], FoolBox [15], and ART [16]; the benchmarking methods/platforms represented by RealSafe [20] (upgraded version is Ares) and DEEPSEC [18]; and the evaluation database represented by RobustBench [21].

CleverHans is the first proposed library of DL-model attack and defense methods. Similarly, FoolBox and ART provide additional attack and defense methods and support running on various DL learning frameworks. Unfortunately, CleverHans has suspended updating maintenance and support since 2021 and has significantly fewer methods than the other method libraries. Attack method libraries such as FoolBox rely on community contributions and lack the necessary checks in late version iterations, leaving the correctness of the code open to question and controversy. These studies mainly focused on building open-source libraries for adversarial attacks and defenses and did not provide a comprehensive strategy for evaluating the security of DL models.

DEEPSEC provides a unified platform for adversarial robustness analysis of DL models, containing 16 attack methods and 10 attack-effectiveness metrics, 13 defense methods, and 5 defense-effectiveness metrics. Similarly, RealSafe and AISafety [22] add additional evaluation metrics to those described in DEEPSEC and update the attack and defense methods. However, while AISafety provides a variety of interpretable, neuronal coverage-related evaluation metrics, it relies heavily on specific attack methods and models and is difficult to apply to other models. Similarly, DEEPSEC provides a variety of attack and defense methods, but adding new attack/defense methods and models is relatively difficult, which makes it difficult to adapt to the latest attack/defense methods. To our knowledge, all such platforms do not analyze the evaluation metrics for level of difficulty and differentiation, nor do they provide a widely recognized ranking of the final evaluation results. While these studies provide evaluation methods and implementations, they still need to improve in terms of universality, ease of use, and interpretation of results.

RobustBench provides a widely recognized benchmark for evaluating the robustness of DL models. RobustBench uses the AutoAttack [52] attack method to evaluate and rank the security of multiple DL models trained on CIFAR-10. However, whether RobustBench can be used as a robustness evaluation metric that can be generalized to practical applications is still questioned by researchers. The RobustBench evaluation of model robustness is only tested by a single attack method, AutoAttack, which severely weakens the credibility and applicability of the evaluation results. Lorenz et al. proposed that detecting adversarial perturbations generated by the AutoAttack method itself is relatively easy, and other attack methods are better at concealment under the same misclassification rate. Also, the resolution of the CIFAR-10 dataset is too low, making it unable to be well generalized to higher-resolution images [53].

In terms of universality, the test metrics proposed by many test platforms impose harsh requirements on the structure of the models to be tested, making it difficult to be widely used; moreover, many attack libraries contain attack or defense algorithms that are limited by various conditions, making them difficult to adapt to all deep learning models; furthermore, due to the possible inability to find pre-defined execution logic, existing test platforms and some method libraries also have serious difficulties in integrating new models or attack and defense methods.

In terms of validity, many test platforms chose adversarial evaluation metrics that later proved ineffective or outdated. For example, the Neuron Coverage series of metrics were first used in DeepGauge [54] and integrated into frameworks such as AISafety. However, experiments by Yan et al. on these frameworks demonstrated the very limited correlation between these metrics and the security and robustness of neural networks [55].

In terms of completeness, there is a lack of correlation between different test platforms and method libraries, which makes them cover only a small number of attack and defense methods as well as a lack of different cross-tests and comparative tests. To our knowledge, apart from a few database platforms, such as RobustBench, other platforms do not yet provide benchmark evaluation databases and lack the necessary baselines for measurement. Furthermore, due to the lack of corresponding strategies, the evaluation results are also mostly a simple list of metrics and do not lead to conclusions worthy of attention.

In this paper, we replicate and evaluate the following models: AlexNet [29], VGG [25], GoogLeNet [56], InceptionV3 [57], ResNet [24], DenseNet [58], SqueezeNet [59], MobileNetV3 [60], ShuffleNetV2 [61], MNASNet [62], EfficientNetV2 [63], VisionTransformer (ViT) [64], RegNet [65], SwinTransformer (SwinT) [66], and ConvNeXt [30]. All of the above 15 models have a wide range of applications.

3. Measurement Metrics and Evaluation Methods

In order to effectively measure model security and the effectiveness of the attack and defense algorithms known to date, we have developed a universal, valid, and interpretable framework for evaluating the robustness of models and the effectiveness of attack and defense algorithms, which contains a total of 26 evaluation metrics (with sub-metrics) that can be widely used. A Python framework that has implemented all the evaluation metrics is also provided for researchers to use in their studies (see Section 4). In this section, we introduce our evaluation metrics framework and evaluation methodology while describing how these metrics can be used in combination to measure model robustness and attack/defense capabilities.

3.1. Measurement Metrics

The metrics framework we have designed for evaluation can be broadly divided into four parts: Model Capability Oriented, Adversarial Effect Oriented, Adversarial Cost Oriented, and Defense Effect Oriented. In this section, we will provide a detailed explanation of the rationale for selecting the metrics and their definitions and expressions.

3.1.1. Model Capability Measurement Metrics

We know that adversarial reinforcement learning generally improves the generalization of models to make them more robust against adversarial examples, but the inferential capability of the models may be negatively affected by this. It is, therefore, necessary to consider the models' performance when ranking their overall ability and to give higher scores to models that perform better and are safer. In addition to this, the models themselves need to be taken into account when trying to compare attack or defense methods tested on different models. We consider the following measurement metrics:

Clean Example Accuracy (Clear Accuracy, CA): The accuracy of the model for the classification of the clean dataset. CA can be expressed as:

$$\mathrm{CA} = \frac{1}{n}\Sigma_{i=1}^{n} count(F(x_i) = y_i) \tag{1}$$

Clean Example F1 score (Clear F1, CF): The F1 score of the model for classification of the clean dataset. Let $TP_i = \Sigma_{k=1}^{n} count(F(x_i) = y_k, y_i = y_k)$; $FP_i = \Sigma_{k=1}^{n} count(F(x_i) = y_k, y_i \neq y_k)$; $FN_i = \Sigma_{k-1}^{n} count(F(x_i) \neq y_k, y_i = y_k)$, and the recall can be expressed as $Recall_i = \frac{TP_i}{TP_i+FN_i}$, the precision can be expressed as $Precision_i = \frac{TP_i}{TP_i+FP_i}$, and CF can be expressed as:

$$\mathrm{CF} = \frac{1}{n}\sum_{i=1}^{n} \frac{2 \times Precision_i \times Recall_i}{Precision_i + Recall_i} \tag{2}$$

Clear Confidence (CC): The average confidence that the model classifies the clean dataset. CC can be expressed as:

$$\mathrm{CC} = \frac{1}{n}\Sigma_{i=1}^{n} P(x_i)_{y_i} \tag{3}$$

3.1.2. Attack Effectiveness Measurement Metrics

The attack effectiveness measurement metrics directly reflect the threat capability of the attack method. By comparing the confidence bias before and after the attack, it indicates the effective interference caused by the adversarial attack, while a higher misleading ability and transferability rate mean that this attack method brings more security pressure to the model.

We define $P(x)$ as the Softmax output of $f(x)$, the confidence matrix, and $F(x)$ as the Hardmax output of $f(x)$, the label. To be fair, all metrics in this subsection are considered only for examples x_i that satisfy $F(x_i) = y_i$, and others will be discarded.

We define the following metrics in detail to evaluate the effectiveness of the attack:

Misclassification Ratio (MR) for adversarial examples: The proportion of images that are misclassified as any other class after the attack than before the attack. For targeted attacks, we additionally consider **Targeted Attack Success (TAS)** to help measure the effectiveness of targeted attacks. To avoid interference, the image label of a targeted attack must not be the same as the attack target. MR can be expressed as:

$$\mathrm{MR} = \frac{1}{n}\Sigma_{i=1}^{n} count(F(x_i^a) \neq y_i) \quad (4)$$

TAS can be expressed as:

$$\mathrm{TAS} = \frac{1}{n}\Sigma_{\mathrm{i}=1}^{n} count\left(F(x_i^a) \neq y_i^{adv} \middle| y_i^{adv} \neq y_i\right) \quad (5)$$

Adversarial Example Confidence Change (ACC): The confidence change in the model inference before and after the attack, which measures the degree of misclassification of the attack on the model identification results. Compared to MR, ACC is able to reveal further and measure the efforts made by the attack method to achieve the purpose of the attack. ACC consists of two sub-metrics, Average Increase in Adversarial-class Confidence (AIAC) and Average Reduction in True-class Confidence (ARTC), which reveals the extent to which the attack tricks the classifier into classifying the attacked image as an adversarial category or makes a misclassification from the true category. AIAC and ARTC can be expressed as:

$$\mathrm{AIAC} = \frac{1}{n}\Sigma_{\mathrm{i}=1}^{n}\left[P(x_i)_{F(x_i^a)} - P(x_i^a)_{F(x_i^a)}\right] \quad (6)$$

$$\mathrm{ARTC} = \frac{1}{n}\Sigma_{\mathrm{i}=1}^{n}\left[P(x_i)_{y_i} - P(x_i^a)_{y_i}\right] \quad (7)$$

Clearly, for any adversarial example, if both IAC and RTC are negative, the attack must fail; however, for examples where the attack fails, IAC or RTC is not necessarily negative.

Average Class Activation Mapping Change (ACAMC): The cosine similarity of the model's activation mapping before and after the attack. The Grad-CAM proposed by Selvaraju et al. is able to analyze the area of interest of the model for a category [67], and based on this theory, we can analyze whether the attack makes the model focus on the wrong features or information. Specifically, the category c area of interest of the model, for example, x can be expressed as $L_x^c = ReLU\left(\sum_k a_k^c A^k\right)$, where: A^k is the data of channel k in A. A is generally the feature layer of the last convolutional layer output; a_k^c is the weight, which can be expressed as $\frac{1}{Z}\sum_i \sum_j \frac{\partial P_c}{\partial A_{ij}^k}$, where P_c is the inference score of category c; A_{ij}^k is the data at ij in channel k in A; and Z is the area of A. In this paper, we focus on the following two offsets: the offset $\mathrm{ACAMC_A}$ of the area corresponding to the model inference class before and after the attack, which can be expressed as:

$$\mathrm{ACAMC_A} = \frac{1}{n}\Sigma_{\mathrm{i}=1}^{n} S\left(L_{x_i}^{F(x_i)}, L_{x_i^a}^{F(x_i^a)}\right) \quad (8)$$

and the offset $\mathrm{ACAMC_T}$ of the area corresponding to the original label class before and after the attack, which can be expressed as:

$$\mathrm{ACAMC_T} = \frac{1}{n}\Sigma_{\mathrm{i}=1}^{n} S\left(L_{x_i}^{y_i}, L_{x_i^a}^{y_i}\right) \quad (9)$$

$\mathrm{S}(a,\mathrm{b})$ is the cosine similarity of a to b.

Observable Transfer Rate (OTR): The proportion of adversarial examples generated by an attack against a particular target model that is misclassified by other models. Since it is impossible to exhaust all models, the scale is derived only from the observable standard model under test. The OTR can be expressed as:

$$\text{OTR} = \frac{1}{n(m-1)} \Sigma_{\delta=1,\delta\neq\hat{\delta}}^{m-1} \Sigma_{i=1}^{n} count\left(F_{\delta}(x_i^a) \neq y_i \middle| A\left(F_{\hat{\delta}}, x_i\right) \rightarrow x_i^a, F_{\hat{\delta}}(x_i^a) \neq y_i\right) \tag{10}$$

where m is the number of models under test, $F_{\hat{\delta}}, F_{\delta} \in \{F_1, \ldots, F_m\}$, and $A(F, x) \rightarrow x^a$ is the adversarial example x^a generated from the original image x via attack algorithm A based on model F. OTR counts the global proportion of adversarial examples generated by attack algorithm A based on a specific model $F_{\hat{\delta}}$ that remains adversarial after transfer to other models F_{δ}.

To simplify the computation, here, OTR uses the adversarial examples generated by the attack on one model and observes the transfer misclassification rate of these examples on other models. We also provide a full version of the OTR calculation, and other comprehensive test methods for adversarial example transferability testing, see Section 3.2.4.

3.1.3. Cost of Attack Measurement Metrics

The cost of an adversarial attack can be divided into two aspects: computational cost and perturbation-awareness cost, which can effectively reflect the strengths and weaknesses of different attack algorithms in achieving the same attack target.

(1) Computational cost

The computational cost metrics of an adversarial example directly reflect the time and computational equipment cost to perform the attack. Faster attacks with fewer model queries mean a greater threat. We consider the following measurement metrics:

Calculation Time Cost (CTC): The time an attack method takes to compute the output of an adversarial example. Since this metric is affected by the model, data processing batch, computing device, etc., we only count the time spent on attacks running a single time on the same device, the same model, or the same group of models, and assign them five levels of ranking after sorting to ensure that the conclusions are universal.

Query Number Cost (QNC): The average model query cost of an attack method calculating and generating an adversarial example. In this part, we record all queries of the model during the attack, including the Forward and Backward operations of the model, and use QNC_F and QNC_B to distinguish. The black-box attack QNC_B must be 0, otherwise, the attack will be considered a white-box attack.

(2) Perturbation-awareness cost

The perturbation-awareness cost metrics of an adversarial example directly reflect the quality of the adversarial example. Subject to the attack's success, a smaller awareness cost means better attack concealment, which means that these examples are less likely to be detected and defended against in the test. The robustness of a model is evaluated based on the adversarial examples generated by the attack method from a clean dataset. Therefore, the measurement of the perceived perturbation of the adversarial examples can help us understand both the imperceptibility of the adversarial method and the security of the model. We introduce the following state-of-the-art metrics to measure the level of perturbation awareness of the adversarial example dataset by evaluating the magnitude of the difference before and after the image attack:

Average Norm Distortion (AND): The norm distance of the images before and after the attack. With full consideration of the graphical implications of the norm paradigm, AND consists of three sub-metrics: Average Maximum Distortion (AMD), Average Euclidean Distortion (AED), and Average Pixel Change Ratio (APCR). AMD is the maximum deviation of the pixel modified by the adversarial example compared with the original image, which is often used as a perturbation constraint for the attack method and can be expressed as:

$$\text{AMD} = \frac{1}{n} \sum_{i=1}^{n} \|x_i^a - x_i\|_{\infty} \tag{11}$$

AED is the Euclidean distance between the original image and the adversarial example, which can be expressed as:

$$\mathrm{AED} = \frac{1}{n}\sum_{i=1}^{n} \|x_i^a - x_i\|_2 / \sqrt{\|x_i\|_0} \tag{12}$$

APCR is the number of pixels modified by the adversarial example compared with the original image, which can be expressed as:

$$\mathrm{APCR} = \frac{1}{n}\sum_{i=1}^{n} \|x_i^a - x_i\|_0 / \|x_i\|_0 \tag{13}$$

The lower values of AMD, AED, and APCR indicate that the adversarial attack produces fewer changes to the image.

Average Euclidean Distortion in Frequency Domain (AED-FD): The average Euclidean distance between the high and low-frequency components of the image before and after the attack after differentiating in the frequency domain. From a frequency domain perspective, Luo et al. showed that the high-frequency components representing noise and texture are more imperceptible than the low-frequency components containing the basic object structure, so the additional consideration of AED-FD is not only an effective measure of how attacks from the frequency domain alter the image but also reveals the location of traditional attacks in the frequency domain, thus providing a better explanation and estimate of the imperceptibility of these attacks. Based on the discrete wavelet transform (DWT [68]), AED-$\mathrm{FD_L}$ is defined as the AED of the reconstructed image for the low-frequency component, which can be expressed as:

$$\mathrm{FD_L} = \frac{1}{n}\sum_{i=1}^{n} \|\phi_{ll}(x_i^a) - \phi_{ll}(x_i)\|_2 \tag{14}$$

AED-FD_H is defined as the AED of the reconstructed image for the high-frequency component, which can be expressed as:

$$\mathrm{FD_H} = \frac{1}{n}\sum_{i=1}^{n} \|\phi_{lh+hl+hh}(x_i^a) - \phi_{lh+hl+hh}(x_i)\|_2 \tag{15}$$

where $\phi_{lh+hl+hh}(x) = L^T(LxH^T)H + H^T(HxL^T)L + H^T(HxH^T)L$ and $\phi_{ll}(x) = L^T(LxL^T)L$, with L and H being the low-pass and high-pass filters of the orthogonal wavelet, respectively. Smaller AED-$\mathrm{FD_L}$ means that the perturbation is less likely to be perceived by humans.

Average Metrics Similarity (AMS): The extent to which features such as color, structure, texture, etc., are shifted before and after the attack. Attacks on different structures of the image have different effects on image distortion, e.g., key disturbed pixels will be particularly visible in flat areas, which cannot be adequately measured by AND. An Image Quality Assessment (IQA) of the image before and after the attack can measure the degradation of the original image from a perspective more in line with human visual awareness. In IQA-related studies, metrics such as Structural Similarity (SSIM [69]) and Peak Signal to Noise Ratio (PSNR [70]) can measure image similarity based on low-dimensional features such as image structure information and pixel statistics; while Zhang et al. pointed out that human judgments of image similarity rely on higher-order image structure and context. To comprehensively measure the feature similarity of the adversarial examples, AMS consists of two sub-metrics, Average Deep Metrics Similarity (ADMS) and Average Low-level Metrics Similarity (ALMS).

We define ALMS as the Multiple Scales Gradient Magnitude Similarity Deviation (MS-GMSD [71]) of all successfully attacked adversarial examples. Xue et al. considered image gradient information as an important low-level feature, and their proposed GMSD [72] used only image gradient as a feature and used the standard deviation instead of the mean value of SSIM. Based on this, Zhang et al. introduced a masking degree term in the similarity index and introduced multi-scale to better evaluate luminance distortion, showing optimal performance in similarity measurement based on low-level features. ALMS can be expressed as:

$$\text{ALMS} = \frac{1}{n}\sum_{i=1}^{n} G(x_i^a, x_i) \tag{16}$$

where $G(x,y) = \sqrt{\sum_{i=1}^{n} \omega_j \sigma_j(x,y)^2}$, $\sigma_j(x,y)$ is the GMSD score on the jth scale, and ω_j is the weight of different scales. The lower value of ALMS indicates that the adversarial attack is less likely to be perceived by humans, and on the contrary, the higher the value is, the less imperceptible the attack is.

We define ADMS as the Deep Image Structure and Texture Similarity (DISTS [73]) of all successfully attacked adversarial examples. Ding et al. found that the full-reference IQA models represented by SSIM, GMSD, and LPIPS [74] are too sensitive to the point-to-point deviation between identical texture images [75]. However, for a human observer, two examples of the same texture are almost identical even if there are significant differences in the pixel arrangement of the features, and their proposed DISTS can measure image similarity more accurately than the above methods. Like LPIPS, DISTS also extracts image features based on the VGG model, calculates the similarity between texture and structure of the feature mapping, and balances it with a set of learnable weights, thus effectively combining sensitivity to structural distortion and tolerance to texture resampling. ADMS can be expressed as:

$$\text{ADMS} = \frac{1}{n}\sum_{i=1}^{n} D(x_i^a, x_i) \tag{17}$$

where $D(x,y) = 1 - \sum_{i=0}^{m}\sum_{j=1}^{n_i}\left(a_{ij} l\left(\tilde{x}_j^{(i)}, \tilde{y}_j^{(i)}\right) + \beta_{ij} s\left(\tilde{x}_j^{(i)}, \tilde{y}_j^{(i)}\right)\right)$, $l\left(\tilde{x}_j^{(i)}, \tilde{y}_j^{(i)}\right)$ is the texture similarity measurement, which can be expressed as $\frac{2\mu_{\tilde{x}_j}^{(i)}\mu_{\tilde{y}_j}^{(i)} + c_1}{\left(\mu_{\tilde{x}_j}^{(i)}\right)^2 + \left(\mu_{\tilde{y}_j}^{(i)}\right)^2 + c_1}$. $s\left(\tilde{x}_j^{(i)}, \tilde{y}_j^{(i)}\right)$ is the structural similarity measurement, which can be expressed as $\frac{2\sigma_{\tilde{x}_j\tilde{y}_j}^{(i)} + c_2}{\left(\sigma_{\tilde{x}_j}^{(i)}\right)^2 + \left(\sigma_{\tilde{y}_j}^{(i)}\right)^2 + c_2}$. $\{a_{ij}, \beta_{ij}\}$ are learnable weights and satisfy $\sum_{i=0}^{m}\sum_{j=1}^{n_i}(a_{ij} + \beta_{ij}) = 1$. A lower value of ADMS means that the adversarial attack is less likely to be perceived by humans, and on the contrary, the higher the value is, the less imperceptible the attack is.

3.1.4. Effectiveness of Defense Measurement Metrics

Defense effectiveness measurement metrics directly reflect the resistance of the defense method and its negative impact on the model. A good defense solution ensures security without unduly sacrificing model capabilities. We measure the effectiveness of defense by comparing the model capability measurement metrics and the adversarial attack effectiveness metrics before and after defense to reflect the security enhancement and performance loss of the model before and after the implementation of the defense. We use X_F to denote the value of a given metric X on model F.

In general, for the measurement of adversarial training, we regenerate adversarial examples based on F_D, which is denoted as x_i^{aD} to distinguish it from the adversarial example x_i^a generated based on F_O; for the measurement of adversarial example detection for image processing defenses, we do not regenerate adversarial examples.

We define the following metrics in detail to evaluate the effectiveness of both types of defenses for adversarial training and image processing:

Model Capability Variance (MCV): The loss of inference capability of a model before and after the defense. Considering model capability measurement metrics, MCV consists of three sub-metrics, Accuracy Variance (AV), F1-Score Variance (FV), and Mean Confidence Variance (CV), which can be generically expressed as $X_{Def} - X_{Ori}(X \in \{CA,CF,CC\})$.

Rectify/Sacrifice Ratio (RR/SR): The change of the model's inference capability before and after defense. To further evaluate how defense affects the model's inference result, we define RR as the proportion of test data classified incorrectly before defense but correctly after defense, and SR as the proportion of test data classified correctly before defense but incorrectly after defense [18]. RR can be expressed as:

$$\mathrm{RR} = \frac{1}{n}\Sigma_{i=1}^{n} count(F_O(x_i) \neq y_i, F_D(x_i) = y_i) \tag{18}$$

and SR can be expressed as:

$$\mathrm{SR} = \frac{1}{n}\Sigma_{i=1}^{n} count(F_O(x_i) = y_i, F_D(x_i) \neq y_i) \tag{19}$$

Attack Capability Variance (ACV): The difference in misclassification rate and perturbation perception of an attack on the model before and after defense. Considering the attack effectiveness measurement metrics, ACV consists of three sub-metrics, MR Variance (MRV), AND Variance (ANDV), and AMS Variance (AMSV), which can be generically expressed as $X_{Def} - X_{Ori}(X \in \{\mathrm{MR, AMD, AED, APCR, ADMS, ALMS}\})$.

Average Adversarial Confidence Change (AACC): The amount of change in the confidence of the adversarial example generated by the model before and after defense, which is used to measure the degree of impact of the defense on the attack. The AACC consists of two sub-metrics, Average Reduction in Adversarial-class Confidence (ARAC) and Average Increase in True-class Confidence (AITC), revealing the extent to which the defense mitigates the attack's deception of the classifier, which means the attacked picture is classified as an adversarial class or deviates from the true class. ARAC and AITC can be expressed as:

$$\mathrm{ARAC} = \frac{1}{n}\Sigma_{\mathrm{i}=1}^{n}\left[P_O(x_i^a)_{F_O(x_i^a)} - P_D\left(x_i^{aD}\right)_{F_D(x_i^{aD})}\right] \tag{20}$$

$$\mathrm{AITC} = \frac{1}{n}\Sigma_{\mathrm{i}=1}^{n}\left[P_O(x_i^a)_{y_i} - P_D\left(x_i^{aD}\right)_{y_i}\right] \tag{21}$$

3.2. *Evaluation Methods*

3.2.1. Evaluation Example Selection

In order to calculate the multi-class evaluation metrics mentioned in Section 3.1 to evaluate the security of the model and the effectiveness of the attack and defense methods, we will generate multiple adversarial examples on the target model using the selected attack methods and use the model to infer the mentioned adversarial examples. Apart from early single-step attacks, methods for generating adversarial examples can be broadly classified into two categories:

Perturbation restriction: restricting the perturbation and iterating to obtain the best misclassification rate under the current perturbation, as in method A in Figure 2a;

Misclassification rate restriction: restricting the attack misclassification rate and iterating to obtain the optimal perturbation under the current misclassification rate, as in method B in Figure 2a.

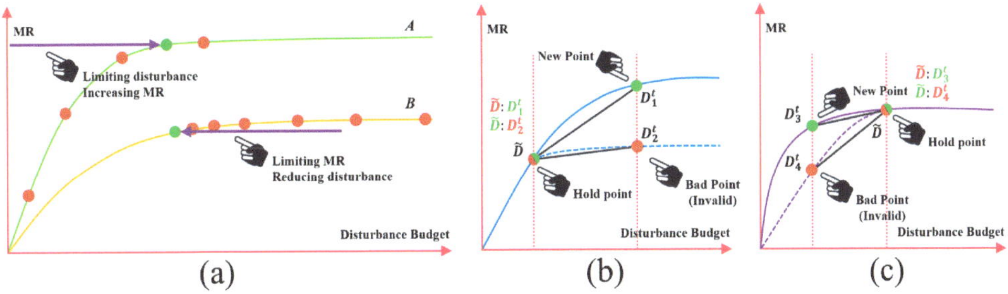

Figure 2. (**a**) The attack represented by A is to limit the perturbation to rise by iterations to reach the maximum MR under a certain perturbation limit; the attack represented by B is to limit the MR to fall by iterations to reach the minimum perturbation under a certain MR limit. For A: (**b**) finds appropriate example points by gradually raising the perturbation limit. If the MR changes significantly after the perturbation limit is raised, the current point is dropped, and the point that is increased after the perturbation is taken as the new point; otherwise, the current point is not changed; (**c**) finds the appropriate example point by gradually decreasing the perturbation. If the MR changes significantly after the perturbation is decreased, the current point is not changed; otherwise, the current point is dropped, and the point decreased after the perturbation is taken as the current point. For B: the appropriate example points can be found automatically.

The evaluation example selection scheme for these two types of algorithms is as follows:

1. When restricting the perturbations of the evaluation examples, inappropriate perturbation restrictions may prevent the attack method from achieving its full performance. As in Figure 2b,c, the data point $\widetilde{D}$ to be determined is measured under a randomly selected perturbation, and we cannot determine whether it is an appropriate evaluation example based on this point alone. As in Figure 2b, when we add perturbations, there are two possibilities at this point:
   (1) The new data point is D_1^t. Since D_1^t has a significantly higher misclassification rate compared to $\widetilde{D}$, it can be argued that the perturbation restriction prevents the misclassification rate from increasing, and using $\widetilde{D}$ for the evaluation would compromise the fairness of the evaluation. Therefore, the pending point is updated to D_1^t and the perturbation test needs to continue to be added.
   (2) The new data point is D_2^t. As there is no significant change in the misclassification rate of D_2^t compared to $\widetilde{D}$, it can be argued that $\widetilde{D}$ has reached its limit, and the significant increase in the perturbation budget has degraded the example quality, and using D_2^t would compromise the fairness of the evaluation. Therefore, the point to be determined remains $\widetilde{D}$ unchanged.

   Similarly, as in Figure 2c, when we reduce the perturbation, the pending point is updated from $\widetilde{D}$ to D_3^t if the new data point is D_3^t; if the new data point is D_4^t, then the pending point remains $\widetilde{D}$ unchanged. After adding a perturbation, if the pending point has not changed, then we reduce the perturbation until it does not change anymore, and the reached point is the appropriate evaluation example point; if the pending point changes, then we continue to increase until it does not change anymore, and the reached point is the appropriate evaluation example point.
2. In limiting the misclassification rate of the evaluation examples, we note that some of the attack methods limit the failure of examples, i.e., reduce the adversarial perturbation budget while always ensuring that the examples can attack successfully, thus we default to no upper limit on the misclassification rate of the attacks, and the final iteration completed is the appropriate evaluation example point.

3.2.2. Evaluation Data Collection

We will use multiple attack methods to generate multiple adversarial examples on multiple target models and will use the target model to infer these adversarial examples. The red blocks of data shown in Figure 3 are the evaluation data obtained through this process. To measure the transferability of the attack algorithm, we can also use other models that do not match the target model to infer the above adversarial examples, and the resulting evaluation data is marked with grey blocks. After applying the above method to the K attack methods on M models, we can form a data matrix of $K \times M \times M$, denoted as Δ_{KM^2}.

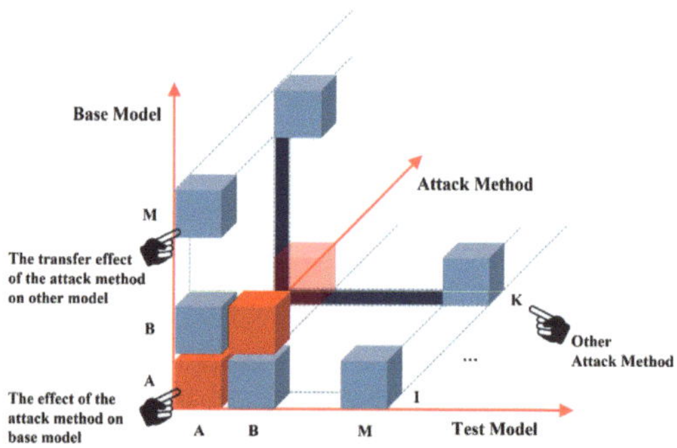

Figure 3. Schematic diagram of the evaluation data matrix, where the model includes A, B, ..., M and the attack-method include I, II, ..., K. Gray blocks indicate transfer tests (the generated base model is different from the test model), and red blocks indicate non-transfer tests (the generated base model is the same as the test model).

3.2.3. Two-Way "Attack Effectiveness–Model Robustness" Evaluation Strategy

Clearly, the multiple types of evaluation metrics mentioned in Section 3.1 measure both the attack method's capability and the model's robustness. For models, the more robust the model, the lower the attack effectiveness metrics such as MR, AIAC, and ARTC, and the higher the attack perturbation perception cost metrics such as AND and AMS should be when attacked by the same method; for attack methods, the better the performance of the attack method, the higher the attack effectiveness metrics and the lower the attack perturbation perception cost metrics should be when attacking the same model.

For Δ_{KM^2}, if the transferability evaluation is not considered, only all the red data blocks marked in Figure 3 can be taken for evaluation, and the data matrix is then denoted as Δ_{KM}. As shown in Figure 4a, when considering model robustness evaluation, we squeeze the data of Δ_{KM} along the recursive direction of K, thus combining the evaluation results of multiple attack methods against the same model to obtain the data sequence $\Delta_{\tilde{M}}$, i.e., the data blocks labeled green. This process allows us to measure model robustness at the same threat strength by avoiding the potential bias caused by a single attack method to the maximum extent. Similarly, when considering the effectiveness of the attack method, we squeeze along the progression of M to obtain the data sequence $\Delta_{\overline{K}}$, i.e., the data blocks labeled yellow. By performing a ranking analysis on $\Delta_{\tilde{M}}$, we achieve the measurement of the robustness of the M models. By performing a ranking analysis on $\Delta_{\overline{K}}$, we achieve the measurement of the effectiveness of the K attack methods.

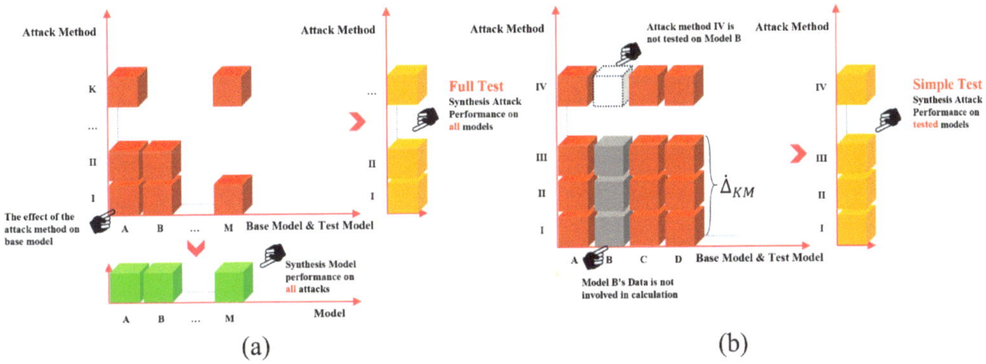

Figure 4. (**a**) Two-way evaluation strategy. The model includes A, B, . . ., M and the attack-method include I, II, . . ., K. After collecting the data, taking the mean value of the data along the attack-method axis, we will get the difference in model robustness independent of the attack method; taking the mean value of the data along the model axis, we will get the difference of attack-method effectiveness independent of the model. (**b**) Fast test mode. After establishing the baseline, if the new attack method IV is added, IV can quickly draw conclusions without completing the full model evaluation, although this may introduce errors, and the more experiments IV completes, the smaller the errors will be.

Based on this, we only need to establish a benchmark Δ_{KM^2} that makes it as inclusive as possible of models and attack methods that are currently widely used in academia and can effectively give their relative ranking when measuring the effectiveness of new attacks or the robustness of models, thus revealing whether these attacks or models have achieved SOTA, and through which provide a widely accepted standard for adversarial robustness evaluation and the effectiveness of adversarial methods. As shown in Figure 4b, due to the independence of the data blocks from each other, researchers do not need to complete all the testing tasks initially but only need to exclude incomplete items to obtain a quick ranking, which saves researchers' time and allows them to devote their efforts to other areas rather than repeatedly testing known data.

3.2.4. Transferability Evaluation

Adversarial examples can generate attacks on models with different structures and parameters, i.e., an attacker can use an adversarial example generated on an alternative model to attack an unknown target model. For Δ_{KM^2}, considering transferability evaluation, all the grey data blocks marked in Figure 3 are taken for evaluation, at which point the data matrix is noted as $\Delta_{\underset{KM^2}{\leftrightarrow}} = \Delta_{KM^2} - \Delta_{KM}$.

As shown in Figure 5a, for one of the K attack methods, we squeeze $\Delta_{\underset{M^2}{\leftrightarrow}}$ to obtain the matrix of observable transferrable metrics $\Delta^{B}_{\underset{M}{\leftrightarrow}}$ for different alternative models if squeezed along the transfer test model direction and $\Delta^{T}_{\underset{M}{\leftrightarrow}}$ for different transfer test models if squeezed along the generation model direction. $\Delta^{B}_{\underset{M}{\leftrightarrow}}$ can reveal on which model the method generates a better adversarial example with and $\Delta^{T}_{\underset{M}{\leftrightarrow}}$ can reveal which models are more vulnerable to the transfer attack of the method. Squeezing $\Delta^{B}_{\underset{M}{\leftrightarrow}}$ or $\Delta^{T}_{\underset{M}{\leftrightarrow}}$ again yields an observable metric of transferability for the attack method.

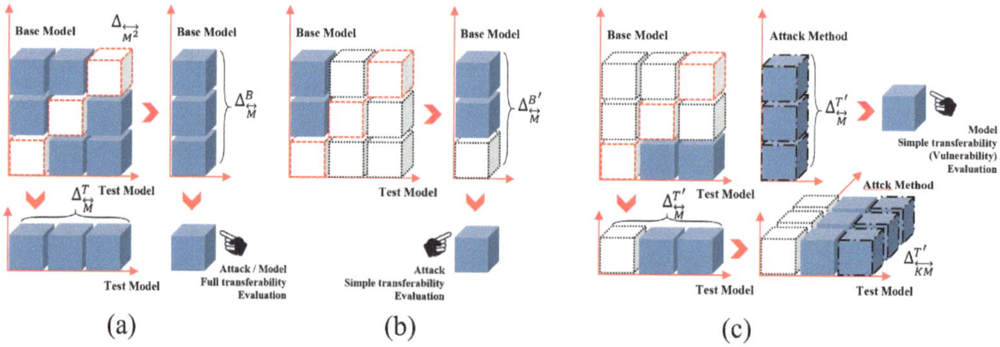

Figure 5. Complete transferability evaluation: e.g., (**a**) the results are averaged over all the transferability results, which are the transferability evaluation results. Simple transferability evaluation: e.g., (**b**) using the adversarial examples generated by a certain attack on all models to test on a certain model, and taking the mean value of the results as the transferability simple test evaluation result of the attack; e.g., (**c**) using the adversarial examples generated by a certain attack on a certain model to test on all models, counting all attacks, and taking the mean value of all transferability attack results on a certain test model as the transfer vulnerability evaluation result of the model.

In $\Delta_{\underset{M^2}{\leftrightarrow}}$, the transferability is based on the observations of all models except itself, which means that the data size will increase rapidly as the number of models evaluated increases. In order to quickly measure the transferability of an attack method, we design a simple evaluation model of attack transferability, as shown in Figure 5b. In this model, the transferability of an attack method will be observed by a specified test model, denoted as $\Delta^{B'}_{\underset{M}{\leftrightarrow}}$. Using $\Delta^{B'}_{\underset{M}{\leftrightarrow}}$ instead of $\Delta^{B}_{\underset{M}{\leftrightarrow}}$, the simple metric of transferability for the method is obtained. The simple mode will reduce the comprehensiveness and credibility of the evaluation due to the choice of model, but it still gives a general indication of the difference in transferability of different attack methods.

Considering M models subject to K attack methods, calculate $\Delta^{T}_{\underset{M}{\leftrightarrow}}$ for each attack method separately and combine them into $\Delta^{T}_{\underset{KM}{\leftrightarrow}}$, where for a given model, $\Delta^{T}_{\underset{K}{\leftrightarrow}}$ reveals which transfer attack it is more susceptible to. By squeezing $\Delta^{T}_{\underset{K}{\leftrightarrow}}$, we obtain a threat metric for the model's transfer attack. To quickly measure this metric, we devise a simple model transfer attack threat evaluation mode as shown in Figure 5c. All models except itself will observe the transfer misclassification rate of an attack method in this model, but only the adversarial examples generated based on a particular model, denoted as $\Delta^{T'}_{\underset{M}{\leftrightarrow}}$. Using $\Delta^{T'}_{\underset{M}{\leftrightarrow}}$ instead of $\Delta^{T}_{\underset{M}{\leftrightarrow}}$ gives the model's simple transfer attack threat metric. Unlike the use of $\Delta^{T}_{\underset{M}{\leftrightarrow}}$, the calculation of $\Delta^{T'}_{\underset{M}{\leftrightarrow}}$ results in the selected transfer example generating model $\Delta^{T}_{\underset{K}{\leftrightarrow}}$ being zero, and, therefore, the simple mode results in the transferability of a given model not being tested. In addition, empirically, there is significant variation in the transferability of adversarial attacks, and if the majority of attacks in K have poor transferability, this will also have an impact on the differentiation of the metric, so it is recommended that only attacks with good transferability are used for this evaluation.

3.3. Evaluation Results Ranking

We consider the model, the attack, and the defense methods all as subjects. A good measure should, as far as possible, serve to differentiate between subjects when it is meaningful in its own right. This is an issue that has not been rigorously considered in other studies. At the same time, the question of how to rank test takers who have completed the test has yet to be addressed. The simplest and most easily understood approach would be to simply add up the participants' scores on each item to obtain a total score and then rank them according to the total score. However, this approach ignores the differences in difficulty and differentiation between test items, making the results less rigorous.

We might consider the testing of models, attacks, and defenses as an examination of the students. The statistical model of Item Response Theory (IRT) is often used by researchers to analyze test scores or questionnaire data, assuming that the subject has a measurable "latent trait" (generally referred to as a latent ability in tests). If we use θ to represent this, then as a subject's level of ability changes, the expected score on an item, $Score(\theta_i)$, changes accordingly. This mathematical model of the relationship between potential ability levels and item response outcomes is known as the Item Characteristic Function (ICF) and is represented graphically as the Item Characteristic Curve (ICC) [27].

IRT is based on several assumptions:

a. Unidimensionality Assumption: This assumption posits that various test items in the evaluation collectively measure a single latent trait encompassed within all test items. The subject's performance on the assessment can be explained solely by one underlying trait.
b. Local Independence Assumption: This assumption posits that the subjects' responses to the test items are influenced solely by their individual ability levels and specific properties, without affecting other subjects or their reactions to other test items. In other words, the ability factor in the item response model is the sole factor influencing the subject's responses to the test items.
c. Monotonicity Assumption: This assumption posits that the expected scores of the subjects on the test items are expected to increase monotonically with their ability levels.

It is generally believed that the unidimensionality assumption and the local independence assumption are equivalent, with local independence being a necessary outcome of the unidimensionality assumption [27].

Based on IRT theory, we can learn that there are two main factors that influence their test scores on items: the first aspect is the level of ability of the subjects themselves; the second aspect is the measurement properties of the test items, such as item difficulty, item discrimination, and guessability. We may let the θ_i parameter denote the ability of the ith subject, the a_j parameter denote the discrimination of the jth test item, the β_j parameter denote the difficulty of the jth test item, the c_j parameter denote the guessing parameter of the jth test item, and the event X_{ij} denote that subject i got test item j correctly (means a full score on test item j). On the jth test, item parameters are a_j, β_j, c_j, and the ability of the ith subject is θ_i, the probability of subject i doing test item j correctly (score expectation on j) is:

$$P(\theta_i; a_j, \beta_j, c_j) = c_j + (1 - c_j)\frac{e^{Da_j(\theta_i - \beta_j)}}{1 + e^{Da_j(\theta_i - \beta_j)}} \tag{22}$$

where D is a constant. When D takes a value of 1.702, the difference in the probability density of this function between the normal shoulder type curve is less than 0.01, so D generally takes a value of 1.702.

We wish to estimate the parameters in the formula, i.e., the discrimination, difficulty, and guessability of each test metric in a measurement sense, based on a set of actual data from the subjects (i.e., data from the model or method's evaluation), while measuring each subject's latent ability. Based on Bayes' theorem, there is $p(\Theta|X) \propto p(X|\Theta)p(\Theta)$, where Θ is the parameter to be estimated, X is the actual data, and the expectation of the posterior distribution, $p(\Theta|X)$, is exactly the value of the parameter we wish to estimate. In the Logistic model, the prior distribution of the parameters $p(\Theta)$ is generally: $\theta \sim N(0,1)$, $Log(a) \sim N(0,1)$, $b \sim N(0,1)$, $c \sim B(5,17)$. We may consider the final score as the probability expectation of getting a full or zero score on this test item in order for it to satisfy the binomial distribution. Since each example is independent, by Bernoulli's theorem, we easily know that $P(X|\Theta) = \prod_{1}^{n} P(\Theta)^{Score}(1 - P(\Theta))^{1-Score}$. At this point, $p(\Theta|X)$ can be determined by the prior distribution of all parameters and the likelihood function of the subjects' responses. We can take the M-H (Metropolis-Hastings) algorithm under Gibbs sampling based on the Markov Chain Monte Carlo (MCMC) method to generate a Markov chain with a smooth distribution of exactly $P(X|\Theta)$, and then draw example points on the chain and use their means as estimates of the parameter Θ. Since the parameter Θ consists of four covariates together, the subject parameter θ_i and the item parameters $a_j, \beta_j, c_j, \theta_i$ is only related to the subject and a_j, β_j, c_j are only related to the test item, we may assume that θ_i is known to estimate a_j, β_j, c_j, and then assume that a_j, β_j, c_j are known to estimate θ_i, and keep repeating this process until the final result converges. The specific algorithm is formulated as Algorithm 1.

Algorithm 1. MCMC-based parameter estimation algorithm for the IRT model

Input: Number of subjects N, Number of test items m, Subject score matrix $X_{i=1\to N, j=1\to m}$, Markov Chain length L and stability period M

for k $\in Ldo$

At the kth moment, sampling $\theta_i^k \sim N\left(\theta_i^{k-1}, C_\theta^2\right)$ for each subject (i = 1,2,. . .,N)

Sampling from uniform distribution $u \sim Uniform[0,1]$

if $u \leq \alpha\left(\theta_i^{k-1}, \theta_i^k\right)$ [1] **then**

Accept to transfer, $\theta_i^k = \theta_i^k$

else

Reject to transfer, $\theta_i^k = \theta_i^{k-1}$

Sampling of each item parameter (j=1,2,. . .,m):

$$a_j \sim N\left(a_j^{k-1}, C_a^2\right), \beta_j \sim N\left(\beta_j^{k-1}, C_\beta^2\right), c_j \sim N\left(c_j^{k-1}, C_c^2\right)$$

Sampling from uniform distribution $u \sim Uniform[0,1]$

if $u \leq \alpha\left(\left(a_j^{k-1}, \beta_j^{k-1}, c_j^{k-1}\right), \left(a_j^k, \beta_j^k, c_j^k\right)\right)$ [1] **then**

Accept to transfer, $\left(a_j^k, \beta_j^k, c_j^k\right) = \left(a_j^k, \beta_j^k, c_j^k\right)$

else

Reject to transfer, $\left(a_j^k, \beta_j^k, c_j^k\right) = \left(a_j^{k-1}, \beta_j^{k-1}, c_j^{k-1}\right)$

Discarding the burn-in period data, we obtain:

$$\theta_i = \frac{1}{M} \sum_{L-M \leq k < L}^{k} \theta_i^k$$

$$\left(a_j, \beta_j, c_j\right) = \frac{1}{M} \sum_{L-M \leq k < L}^{k} \left(a_j^k, \beta_j^k, c_j^k\right)$$

Output: $\theta_{i=1\to N}; a_{j=1\to m}, \beta_{j=1\to m}, c_{j=1\to m}$

[1] This is the transfer condition for the Markov Chain in the algorithm for estimating IRT parameter values using the MCMC method.

In the MCMC algorithm, $\alpha(i,j)$ is generally referred to as the acceptance rate, with a value between [0,1]. Specifically, the equation for $\alpha(i,j)$ in Algorithm 1 is:

$$\alpha\left(\theta_i^{k-1}, \theta_i^k\right) = \min\left\{\frac{p\left(X_{i,j=1\to m}\middle|\theta_i^k, a_j^{k-1}, \beta_j^{k-1}\right)p\left(\theta_i^k\right)}{p\left(X_{i,j=1\to m}\middle|\theta_i^{k-1}, a_j^{k-1}, \beta_j^{k-1}\right)p\left(\theta_i^{k-1}\right)}, 1\right\} \tag{23}$$

$$\alpha\left(\left(a_j^{k-1}, \beta_j^{k-1}, c_j^{k-1}\right), \left(a_j^k, \beta_j^k, c_j^k\right)\right) = \min\left\{\frac{p\left(X_{i=1\to N,j}\middle|\theta_i^k, a_j^k, \beta_j^k\right)p\left(a_j^k\right)p\left(\beta_j^k\right)p\left(c_j^k\right)}{p\left(X_{i=1\to N,j}\middle|\theta_i^k, a_j^{k-1}, \beta_j^{k-1}\right)p\left(a_j^{k-1}\right)p\left(\beta_j^{k-1}\right)p\left(c_j^{k-1}\right)}, 1\right\} \tag{24}$$

With the above algorithm, we obtain the subjects' ability Θ, which we use as a score that allows us to rank model robustness as well as attack- and defense-method effectiveness, thus giving a ranking and relative position for each model, attack, or defense method, which can significantly reveal differences in ability between models or methods and can provide future research with a view to enable better improvements. In the actual calculation process, we will first use IRT to calculate Θ for a large category (Sections 3.1.1–3.1.4) based on all the metrics under that category and then use IRT to calculate the final result based on Θ for the relevant large category. The first layer of computation will avoid the problem of bias due to inconsistency in the number of metrics in the broad categories.

Since some of the metrics listed in Section 3.1 take values that cannot simply be used as IRT scores, we normalize them to [0,1] for evaluation by using the "max-min" normalization method. This ensures that the values are not concentrated in a small interval, which would otherwise bias the IRT calculation.

4. Open-Source Platform

We are committed to providing an open, fair, and comprehensive set of metrics and want to build a platform that fully implements these metrics. The platform should make it extremely easy to introduce new attack/defense algorithms and DL models while ensuring that these algorithms can be tightly integrated with the models to produce model robustness scores and attack/defense algorithm effectiveness scores. At the same time, we want to build a large dataset that is closely related to the platform, including the results of all SOTA attack/defense algorithms on the most widely used models. This platform is named Canary, and an overview of the platform is detailed in Figure 1. The Canary platform is now available on GitHub (https://github.com/NeoSunJZ/Canary_Master, accessed on 1 August 2023).

The Canary platform consists of a web visualization interface, a data server, and the Security Evaluation Fast Integration (SEFI) framework. Researchers can construct attacks or defenses in the web interface or from the command line and visualize the query results with analysis reports at the end of execution, while SEFI executes the relevant commands defined by the web interface or by the researcher. For more about the platform, see Appendix B: Open-source platform structure and metrics calculation process. Basically, SEFI consists of four core components:

1. Component Modifiers. Component modifiers can modify four types of components: attack methods, defense methods, models, and datasets. The component modifiers allow researchers to easily test and evaluate their implementations of attacks, defenses, or models using SEFI. A large library of pre-built components, Canary Lib, is also available for researchers.
2. Security Testing Module. The security testing module consists of five sub-modules: Attack Unit, Model Inference Unit, Adv Disturbance-Aware Tester, Image Processing Unit, and Model Training Unit. The combination of these test modules will provide the necessary data to support the security evaluation.
3. Security Evaluation Module. The security evaluation module consists of three sub-modules: attack evaluation, model-baseline evaluation, and defense evaluation:
    (1) Attack Evaluation: This module contains the Attack Cost Evaluator (Adv Example Disturbance-aware and Cost Evaluator) and the Attack Deflection Capability Evaluator. In this module, we implement the calculation of 17 numerical metrics for adversarial attacks (see Sections 3.1.2 and 3.1.3 for details). The attack evaluation allows the user to evaluate how well the generated adversarial examples transfer the inference results of the target model, the quality of the examples themselves, and how well these adversarial examples transfer against non-target models.
    (2) Model-baseline Evaluation: This module contains the Model Inference Capability Analyzer. In this module, we implement three common baseline metrics of model inference capability (see Section 3.1.1 for details). The model-baseline

evaluation allows the user to evaluate the model's performance to be tested and to make better trade-offs between model quality and robustness.

(3) Defense Evaluation: This module contains the Defense Capability Analyzer. In this module, we have implemented four (classes of) common baseline metrics of model inferential capabilities (see Section 3.1.4 for more details; due to the nature of defense evaluation, most of the relevant sub-metrics are presented in the form of pre- and post-defense differences, so we will not repeat them here). The defense evaluation allows the user to evaluate the effectiveness of the defense method to be tested.

4. System Module. The system modules include the SQLite access module, the disk file access module, the web service module, the exception detection module, the interruption recovery module, and so on. These modules are mainly used to access test data, interact with experimental data and progress to the visualization interface, provide error information when an error occurs, and resume the experimental task from the point of interruption.

The private VUE-based GUI of Canary and SpringBoot-based Basic Information Data Server is now available on GitHub (GUI: https://github.com/NeoSunJZ/Canary_View, accessed on 1 August 2023; Data Sever: https://github.com/NeoSunJZ/Canary_Server, accessed on 1 August 2023).

In order to provide a benchmark for testing and evaluation, we have additionally provided a library of presets and a benchmark database:

1. A library of pre-built components. The in-built library is integrated using component modifiers. The presets library contains three types of components that have been pre-implemented:
    (1) Attack methods. We have integrated 30 adversarial attack methods in the presets library, including 15 white-box attacks and 15 black-box attacks. These attack methods have been selected, considering attack specificity, attack paths, and perturbation characteristics to make the coverage as comprehensive as possible.
    (2) Defense methods. We have integrated 10 adversarial defenses in the pre-built library, including 4 image processing defenses, 4 adversarial training, and 2 adversarial example identification defenses. The selection of these methods takes into account the path of defense, the target of the defense, and the cost of the defense so that the coverage is as comprehensive as possible.
    (3) Models. We integrated 18 artificial intelligence models in the pre-built library and provided them with pre-training parameters based on ImageNet, CIFAR-10/100 datasets.

    In selecting these pre-built components, we focused on the importance of discussion and relevant contributions in the open-source community and finally selected those algorithms, models, and datasets that are being widely discussed and used.
2. In-built benchmarking database. We have conducted a comprehensive cross-test of 15 models and 20 attack methods and constructed the results into an open benchmark database. For details, please refer to Section 5 of this paper.

Currently, some similar frameworks or toolkits are already in use. A detailed comparison of our framework with mainstream adversarial attack and defense tools is described in Table 3.

Table 3. A detailed comparison of our framework with adversarial attack and defense tools. Legend '×' indicates that the item is not applicable to this tool.

Tool	Type	Publication Time	Researcher	Support Framework [3]	Test Dataset [3]	Defense Algorithm [3]	Defense Algorithm [3]	Number of Evaluation Metrics [3]	In-built Model [3]	Filed
CleverHans [14]	Method Toolkit	2016	Pennsylvania State University	3	×	16	1	×	×	Image Classification
Foolbox [15]	Method Toolkit	2017	University of Tübingen	3	×	>30	1	3	×	Image Classification
ART [16]	Method Toolkit	2018	IBM Research Ireland	10	×	28 [1]	**>20** [1]	6	×	Image Classification Target Detection Target Tracking Speech Recognition
AdverTorch [17]	Evolution Framework	2019	Borealis AI	1	×	21	7	×	×	Image Classification
DEEPSEC [18]	Evolution Framework	2019	Zhejiang University	1	2	16	13	14	4	Image Classification
AdvBox [19]	Method Toolkit	2020	Baidu Inc.	7	×	10	6	×	×	Image Classification Target Detection
Ares [20]	Evolution Framework	2020	Tsinghua University	1	2	19	10	2	15	Image Classification
RobustBench [21]	Evolution Framework	2021	University of Tübingen	×	3	1	×	×	**120+** [2]	Image Classification
AISafety [22]	Evolution Framework	2023	Beijing University of Aeronautics and Astronautics	1	2	20	5	23	3	Image Classification
Canary (Ourselves)	Evolution Framework	2023	Beijing Institute of Technology	1	**4**	**>30**	10	**26**	18	Image Classification

[1] We only counted algorithms belonging to image classification. [2] This is a baseline platform that allows researchers to self-share their evaluation data. [3] This information is counted in August 2023, most of the tools (including ourselves) are still adding new or removing old attack and defense algorithms, the actual supported frameworks, number of embedded algorithms, etc. are based on the latest situation.

5. Evaluations

In this section, we first test the performance of a range of attack methods, then evaluate the models' security and explore the best defense options. Specifically, we have conducted a comprehensive cross-test of 15 models and 20 attack methods, generating about 250,000 adversarial examples and the white-box attack data matrix $\Delta^{w}_{(8)(15)}$, the black-box attack data matrix $\Delta^{b}_{(8)(15)}$, and the transfer attack data matrix $\Delta^{wt}_{(4\times2)(15)}$.

Note that all experimental code has been integrated into Canary's in-built libraries, and specific experimental parameters are given in the Canary documentation, which you can find on GitHub. All experiments were performed on an Nvidia RTX 3090 GPU, and the results database has been open-sourced, which you can find in Canary's in-built pre-test dataset.

5.1. Experimental Setup

We used the most popular 1000 classification dataset, ImageNet, which more closely resembles a real-life image classification task compared to MNIST and CIFAR-10. To fully evaluate the effectiveness of all methods, we used 15 of the most widely used models to date, encompassing a wide range of model structures from simple to complex. We used the best pre-trained weight data provided by PyTorch [76] Torchvision, and the models all achieved near SOTA accuracy on the ImageNet dataset.

The experimental images were segmented using standard training/test segmentation and rescaled in ImageNet to $224 \times 224 \times 3$. We converted the range of image pixels from [0,255] to the input domain required by the model (in this experiment, the model input domain was [0,1]) and entered the attack method, then cropped the resulting perturbed image to the input domain and restored it to [0,255]. We note that although such a conversion is almost equivalent, this process will inevitably lead to subtle effects due to the floating point arithmetic used for the pixels. In this experiment, the magnitude of the effect on a single pixel is about 1×10^{-5}. For very few special attack methods, this can cause a reduction in the misclassification rate of the attack. Similarly, if we truncate all fractional parts to store these images as image files, the impact is more severe. In our experiments, we store all generated perturbed images separately as image and floating-point array files and evaluate them based on the array files only.

Our evaluation method is as follows. First, we take 1000 images from the test set of the ImageNet dataset for the white-box attack and 600 images for the black-box attack. When counting, we only count the images that can be correctly classified on the corresponding model. Then, for each attack method, we generate 1000 (white-box attack) or 600 (black-box attack) adversarial examples on the 15 models using the extracted images. Next, using the security evaluation and security testing modules of the Canary platform, we monitor the adversarial example generation process, cross-test these adversarial examples on the 15 models, and obtain all the information needed to calculate the metrics. Finally, we calculate all the test metrics and estimate the capability of the attack algorithm using the MCMC method and further get the IRT-score.

Our parameter configuration principles are as follows: For all integrated attack methods, we prioritized the relevant code open-sourced by the authors or available on CleverHans and Foolbox, and for attack methods for which the original code was completely unavailable, we reproduced it as described in the authors' paper. In our evaluation, we gave priority to the hyperparameters suggested by the method authors in their paper or the open-source code.

We followed the requirements of Section 3.2.1 regarding the selection of evaluation examples, adjusting some of the parameters so that the resulting adversarial examples are suitable for evaluation. Subject to these requirements, we set the limit to 1/255 (smaller perturbation) or 16/255 (larger perturbation) for all methods that use L_∞ to limit the size of the perturbation; for black-box methods, we limit the maximum query budget to 10,000 per image. For targeted attacks, the target class for each target is chosen among the labels other than the original labels chosen randomly and evenly.

5.2. Evaluation of Adversarial Attack Effectiveness

We use the correlation method in Section 3.2 to squeeze the data matrix $\Delta^{w}_{(8)(15)}$, $\Delta^{b}_{(8)(15)}$, and $\Delta^{wt}_{(4\times2)(15)}$ along the model direction, making it possible to ignore the model factors and transform to the data series $\Delta^{w}_{\overline{(8)}}$, $\Delta^{b}_{\overline{(8)}}$, and $\Delta^{wt}_{\overline{(4\times2)}}$.

Our evaluation results for the attack are displayed in two tables, where the Effects Part is shown in Table 4, and the Cost Part is shown in Table 5.

Table 4. Effectiveness evaluation results of all adversarial attacks on 15 models.

Attack			Attack Effects						
Attack Type	Attacks		MR	ACC		ACAMC		OTR [1]	
				AIAC	ARTC	$ACAMC_A$	$ACAMC_T$	Simple	Full
White Box	FGSM		79.1%	21.4%	64.3%	0.895	0.900	32.47%	-
	JSMA		75.3%	23.1%	45.1%	0.811	0.955	6.86%	-
	DeepFool		99.9%	38.3%	49.7%	0.893	0.985	0.61%	-
	I-FGSM		96.9%	80.6%	74.6%	0.841	0.871	3.22%	-
	C&W Attack		98.4%	33.6%	43.7%	0.884	0.987	0.61%	-
	PGD		96.4%	78.8%	74.4%	0.843	0.880	3.23%	-
	EAD		99.4%	45.5%	59.4%	0.904	0.956	5.98%	-
	SSAH		78.4%	20.1%	62.2%	0.930	0.841	1.74%	-
Black Box (Transferable Attack)	MI-FGSM	$\epsilon = 1$	95.6%	70.5%	74.2%	0.886	0.841	3.84%	-
		$\epsilon = 16$	100.0%	96.0%	75.8%	0.829	0.612	-	39.1%
	VMI-FGSM	$\epsilon = 1$	93.8%	62.4%	73.4%	0.890	0.850	4.53%	-
		$\epsilon = 16$	99.9%	95.3%	75.8%	0.838	0.605	-	62.1%
	NI-FGSM	$\epsilon = 1$	97.2%	82.3%	74.6%	0.872	0.839	3.39%	-
		$\epsilon = 16$	100.0%	96.4%	75.8%	0.828	0.597	-	33.2%
	SI-FGSM	$\epsilon = 1$	95.2%	71.0%	73.8%	0.886	0.835	4.36%	-
		$\epsilon = 16$	100.0%	96.4%	75.8%	0.826	0.596	-	38.3%
Black Box	AdvGan		94.8%	50.6%	69.5%	0.808	0.896	26.92%	-
	LSA		55.1%	6.8%	35.2%	0.931	0.963	22.63%	-
	BA		73.1%	12.1%	44.3%	0.907	0.978	1.15%	-
	SA		42.6%	12.3%	21.5%	0.958	0.975	12.05%	-
	SPSA		58.5%	20.2%	44.9%	0.937	0.959	10.05%	-
	HSJA		51.2%	−18.3%	55.4%	0.916	0.946	32.05%	-
	GA		22.0%	−20.1%	35.8%	0.956	0.975	4.50%	-
	TREMBA		61.8%	32.5%	32.7%	0.932	0.976	3.63%	-

[1] Legend '-' indicates that mutually exclusive metrics have been calculated.

Table 5. Cost evaluation results of all adversarial attacks on 15 models.

Attack			Calculate Cost				Disturbance-Aware Cost					
Attack Type	Attacks		CTC [1]	QNC [1]		APCR	AND		AED-FD		AMS	
				QNC_F	QNC_B		AED (10^{-2})	AMD (10^{-1})	FD_L (10^{-2})	FD_H (10^{-2})	ADMS (10^{-1})	ALMS (10^{-1})
White Box	FGSM		Very Fast	1	1	98.3%	3.528	0.627	6.840	0.831	2.611	0.994
	JSMA		Slow	~1300	~1300	0.7%	1.434	7.890	3.174	1.387	0.872	0.499
	DeepFool		Very Fast	~100	~100	32.3%	0.091	0.089	0.241	0.055	0.041	0.007
	I-FGSM		Very Fast	~100	~100	76.2%	0.186	0.039	0.443	0.097	0.139	0.015
	C&W Attack		Very Slow	-	-	11.0%	0.033	0.116	0.137	0.035	0.020	0.003
	PGD		Very Fast	~100	~100	77.0%	0.188	0.039	0.441	0.098	0.134	0.015
	EAD		Slow	~10,000	~5000	9.3%	0.930	1.972	2.667	1.345	0.448	0.150
	SSAH		Fast	-	-	68.9%	0.351	0.289	0.869	0.027	0.268	0.016
Black Box (Transferable Attack)	MI-FGSM	$\epsilon = 1$	Fast	~100	~100	85.1%	0.203	0.039	0.477	0.103	0.166	0.017
		$\epsilon = 16$				99.0%	2.996	0.627	5.953	0.873	2.213	0.877
	VMI-FGSM	$\epsilon = 1$	Slow	~2000	~2000	84.3%	0.202	0.039	0.477	0.103	0.185	0.017
		$\epsilon = 16$				97.4%	2.992	0.628	5.990	0.903	2.369	0.980
	NI-FGSM	$\epsilon = 1$	Very Fast	~100	~100	77.0%	0.188	0.039	0.448	0.099	0.146	0.016
		$\epsilon = 16$				99.4%	2.165	0.627	4.638	0.660	1.861	0.617
	SI-FGSM	$\epsilon = 1$	Fast	~300	~300	80.2%	0.194	0.039	0.465	0.103	0.176	0.016
		$\epsilon = 16$				99.4%	2.262	0.627	4.736	0.709	1.946	0.681
Black Box	AdvGan		-	-	-	93.0%	2.462	2.868	5.814	0.938	2.778	0.589
	LSA		Normal	~200	0	5.3%	5.310	9.125	9.384	3.527	1.963	1.404
	BA		Normal	~10,000	0	81.3%	1.117	0.815	1.756	0.188	0.597	0.129
	SA		Very Fast	~120	0	96.0%	17.058	9.591	16.919	25.327	2.458	3.058
	SPSA		Slow	~200	0	97.3%	2.617	0.688	4.475	0.746	1.756	0.419
	HSJA		Very Fast	~200	0	93.0%	8.865	1.891	13.031	1.420	3.526	1.387
	GA		Normal	~10,000	0	95.6%	2.244	0.629	3.840	0.452	1.589	0.311
	TREMBA		-	-	-	97.2%	0.846	0.157	2.009	0.287	0.894	0.151

[1] Legend '-' indicates that the metric is not applicable to this algorithm.

5.2.1. Evaluation of Attack Effectiveness

We quantified and analyzed the effectiveness of the attacks on the adversarial examples in terms of ACC, MR, OTR, and ACAMC.

For the ACC metric, AIAC and ARTC reflect the reduction in the confidence of the attack method on the true label and the increase in the confidence of the adversarial label, respectively. We argue that the confidence bias metric can reveal how the attack works: examples with higher ARTC are less likely to be inferred by the model to the true category, i.e., "hide themselves"; examples with higher AIAC are more effective in inducing the model to converge to a particular label, i.e., "misleading enhancement". Considering the ACC metric, for most of the attack methods, the ARTC is significantly higher than or stays the same as AIAC, which means that when the misclassification rate or perturbation budget reaches a critical state, the perturbation optimization goal is to "hide themselves"; after reaching a critical value (e.g., setting the perturbation budget of methods such as MI-FGSM to $\epsilon = 16$), the goal of perturbation optimization changes to "misleading enhancement" as the ARTC is already approaching its peak with the perturbation budget continues to increase. In addition, we found that most of the attacks derived from FGSM exhibit an excellent ability to "hide themselves", which may be one of the reasons why FGSM-like methods are more transferable at higher perturbation budgets.

Considering the MR metric, the misclassification rate of black-box attacks is about 51.6%, while the misclassification rate of white-box attacks is about 93.5%, significantly higher than that of black-box attacks, and iterative attacks always outperform non-iterative attacks. We found that for the 15 models of the ImageNet dataset, the MR of most of the white-box attacks can achieve approximately 100%, while the MR of black-box attacks achieves close to 60%. Combined with the confidence bias metric, the ARTC is only slightly lower for most black-box attacks than for white-box attacks, but the AIAC is significantly lower than for white-box attacks, suggesting that the lack of access to model gradient data hinders black-box attacks in terms of "misleading enhancement" and is one of the bottlenecks that limit their misclassification rate.

For the ACAMC metric, $ACAMC_A$ and $ACAMC_T$ reflect the deviation of the model's attention to the inferred and true labels before and after the attack from the perspective of model interpretability. Considering the ACAMC metric, none of the attack methods tested have an $ACAMC_A$ below 0.8, indicating that although the attack effectively deviated from the label results, it did not produce a substantial deviation of their attention regions, i.e., the attack would have caused the model to misperceive within similar attention regions. The black-box ACAMC metric is significantly higher than the white-box attack, i.e., the black-box attack is more difficult to alter the model's attention area, further demonstrating the dilemma of the black-box attack in terms of "misleading enhancement". Similar to the findings revealed by the ACC metric, the $ACAMC_T$ also shows that further increases in the perturbation budget can lead to a larger transfer in the attention area of the true class, thus enhancing misleadingness.

For the OTR metric, we performed a full test for the methods used primarily for transferrable attacks, giving their full results for cross-testing on all models. Simple results are given for all methods other than these based on the DenseNet model test. Considered in conjunction with the OTR and AND metrics, an increase in the perturbation magnitude AMD leads to higher transferability, and examples such as VMI-FGSM and black-box attacks using partially simulated gradients to implement the attack also suggest that enriching the diversity of gradients to avoid the attack "over-fitting" to a particular attacked model can generate adversarial examples with higher transferability.

5.2.2. Evaluation of Computational Cost

To evaluate the computational cost of the attacks, we tested the running time CTC and the number of model queries QNC that the attack methods used to generate an adversarial example on average over the 15 models. It would be unfair to compare their running times directly due to various complex factors (e.g., code implementation, support for batch computing or not, and different computing devices). We, therefore, only give empirically based five-level grading results in our evaluation, and we note that CW, JSMA, EAD, VMI-FGSM, and SPSA are significantly slower than other attacks. In particular, we have dropped the evaluation of the black-box methods ZOO and One-pixel in this paper because they are too slow to compute.

For the model query quantity QNC, we restrict the upper limit of QNC for the black-box model to 10,000, but no lower limit; meanwhile, the QNC_B for the black-box model must be 0. In fact, for white-box iterative attacks, QNC is closely related to the configuration of the number of iterations of the attack method. For fairness, QNC will be taken as the minimum value after the misclassification rate of the attack method reaches its limit, and the lower limit of iterations of the attack method is 100, but no upper limit. For the black-box methods, we note that the BA and GA queries are significantly higher than other attacks. For the white-box methods, we note that both JSMA and EAD require more rounds to reach the limit; when the number of iterations is 100, in order to enhance their transferability, VMI-FGSM, and SI-FGSM have higher query numbers compared to MI-FGSM, etc.

In addition, we cannot give average runtime data and model query number data for all attacks that require prior training, regardless of whether they are adversarial patches or generative models. In the case of AdvGan, once the generator has been trained, it can generate adversarial examples in a very short time, and the number of adversarial examples generated will determine the dilution of the training time, so we cannot use CTC as a simple measurement for such methods. Also, AdvGan does not call the original model during the attack, so neither the CTC nor the QNC part is available.

5.2.3. Evaluation of Perturbation-Awareness Cost

We quantified and analyzed the perturbation-awareness cost of the adversarial examples in terms of AND, AED-FD, and AMS. Collectively, the perturbation-awareness cost of the black-box model is significantly higher than that of the white-box attack. For the same attack method, a higher perturbation-awareness cost will lead to a higher MR before the MR reaches its limit, which does not necessarily hold for different attack methods.

The work of Carlini et al. states that a successful attack needs to satisfy: a. the gap between the adversarial example and the corresponding clean example should be as small as possible; b. the adversarial example should make the model misclassify with as high a confidence level as possible [23]. The experimental results show a competitive relationship between the effectiveness of the attack and the perturbation imperceptibility of the same attack method. In perturbation-limited attacks, such as I-FGSM and its derivative methods, the misclassification loss is often included in the loss function used to optimize the perturbation, while the perturbation magnitude is limited using gradient projection, gradient truncation, etc. The perturbation always limits the misclassification rate from increasing further until the misclassification rate reaches the limit of the method. In misclassification rate first attacks, such as BA, HJSA, etc., they further optimize the perturbation by discarding failed examples to limit the misclassification rate. After the perturbation has been reduced to the method limit, the misclassification rate always limits further reductions of the perturbation. This limitation is precisely caused by competition, i.e., there is a limit bound consisting of both misclassification rate and perturbation perception, which is the best that the method can achieve. In addition to the above attacks, some of the attacks represented by CW and EAD incorporate both the misclassification rate and the perturbation limit into the optimization objective. CW, for example, makes use of a dichotomous lookup weight parameter c to measure the ratio of the two effects at the cost of a significant sacrifice in computational speed, but when we gradually increase the trade-off constant k from 0, the perturbation-awareness cost metrics of CW both increase significantly, suggesting that a competitive relationship between the two still exists. Furthermore, we found that in perturbation-limited attacks, the perturbation imperceptibility was not further optimized after the misclassification rate reached its limit but always fully reached the perturbation-limited value and that poor perturbation limits would seriously affect the conclusions of this class of methods in terms of perturbation-awareness cost evaluation.

The AMS class metrics are based on norm definitions since existing attacks often use norms to measure and constrain perturbation magnitude. We note that their choice of metric norm has better metric performance than other norms. For example, infinite norm-based attacks perform better in the AMD metric but perform more mediocrely in the AED and APCR.

AMS-like metrics are more sensitive to human perception than AND-like metrics. In general, AMS-like metrics have a similar trend to AED and AMD, which means that attacks based on L2 norm or infinite norm restrictions produce more visually imperceptible adversarial examples than those produced by other attacks. In addition, the AMS also depends on the characteristics of the attack method itself, e.g., the SSAH method based on frequency domain attacks does not achieve a worse AMS, although its AMD, AED, and APCR are all significantly larger than those of algorithms such as FGSM. We find that relatively balanced AMD metrics, i.e., attack methods with low and balanced AMD, AED, and APCR, have a lower AMS. Similar to the AND metrics, the AMS includes metrics with inconsistent performance between ADMS and ALMS: ADMS is more concerned with changes in the textural nature of the picture, as in the case of HSJA, AdvGan, and FGSM in Figure 6, where perturbations produce more severe texture problems, and their ADMS ranking is worse than other methods, while ALMS is more concerned with changes in the gradient of the picture, such as significant unsmooth noise, as shown below for LSA, HSJA, and FGSM, which produce significantly higher noise pixel variability than other methods.

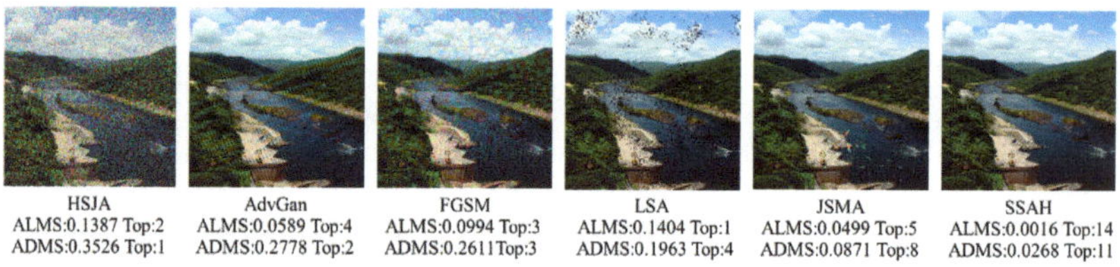

Figure 6. ALMS and ADMS values and rankings of the adversarial example generated by 6 methods based on the AlexNet model.

In particular, attack methods that involve fundamental transformation of the image, such as SA, which relies on rotating and translating the picture rather than adding perturbations to achieve the attack, although they do not differ significantly from the original image in terms of content, are easily perceived and identified because they significantly twist the picture, and the perturbation-awareness cost, in this case, cannot be simply measured by the AND or AMS metrics.

5.3. Evaluation of Transferability

To reveal which models are more vulnerable to transfer attack threats and which models based on which generated adversarial examples have more transferability, we generate adversarial examples based on 15 models using the 4 methods MI-FGSM, VMI-FGSM, NI-FGSM, and SI-FGSM under $\epsilon = 16$ and perform a full transfer test in the above models to generate the transfer matrix $\Delta_{(4)(15)^2}^{\leftrightarrow}$.

The performances of the selected models on the four methods mentioned above are shown in Table 6.

Table 6. Transferability evaluation results of 4 attacks on 15 models. We excluded all data generated on a certain model and tested on this model, i.e., the blank squares in the heat map of the transferability matrix.

Attacks		Observable Transfer		
		MR	ACC	
			AIAC	ARTC
MI-FGSM	Hot Map	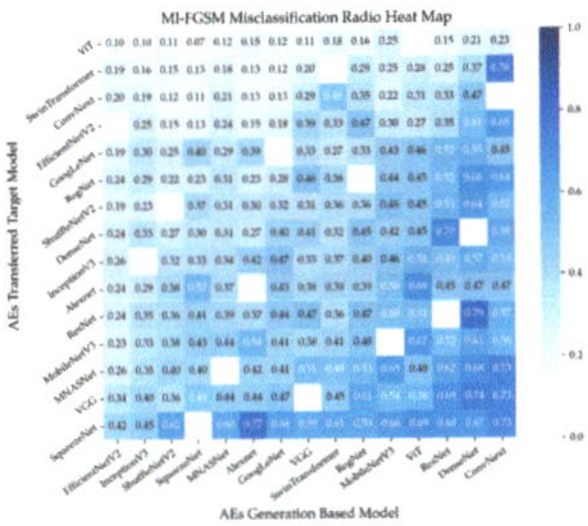	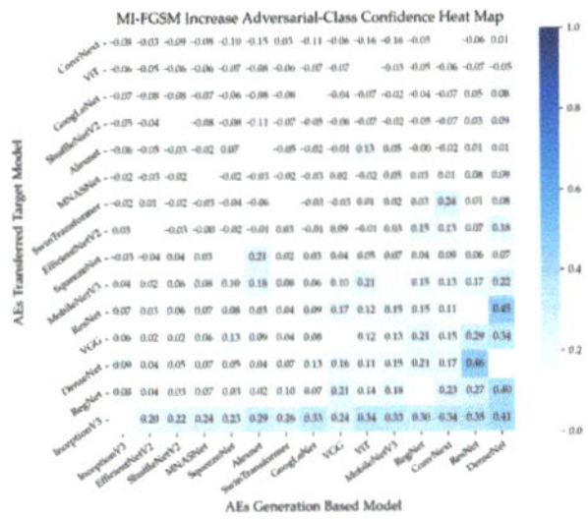	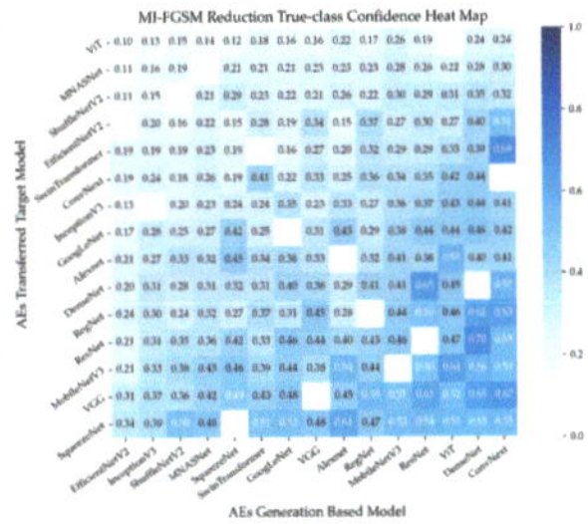
	Average	39.113%	5.310%	34.187%
NI-FGSM	Hot Map	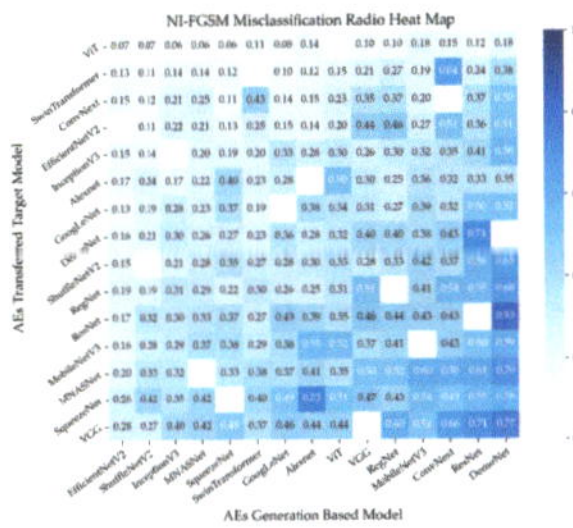	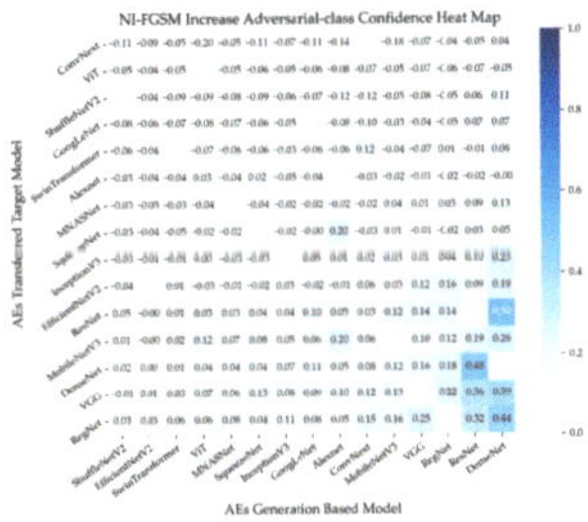	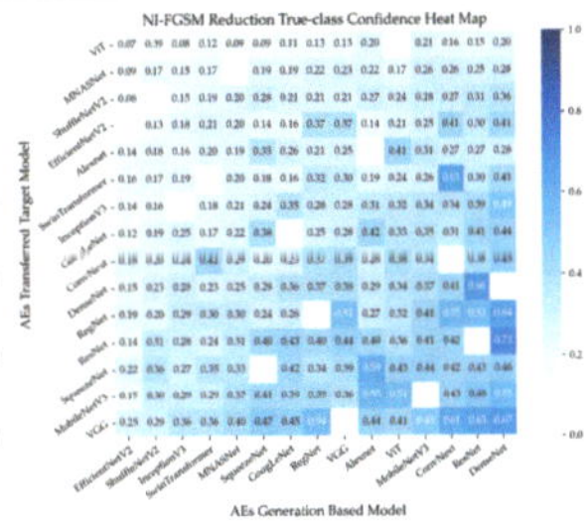
	Average	33.175%	2.190%	30.077%
SI-FGSM	Hot Map	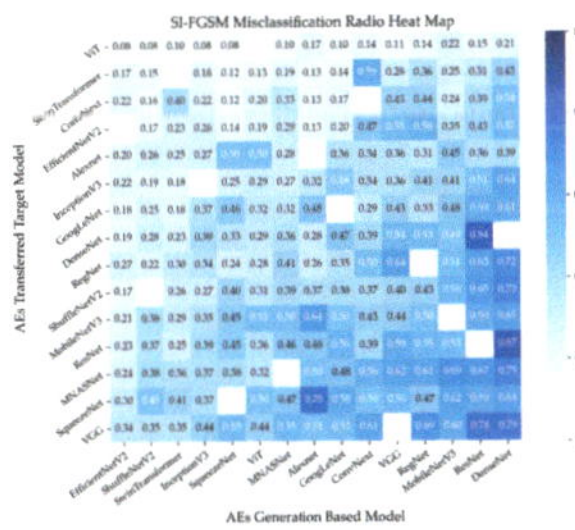	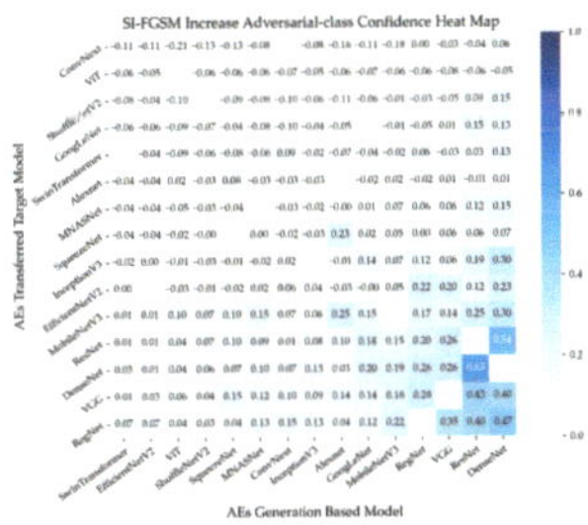	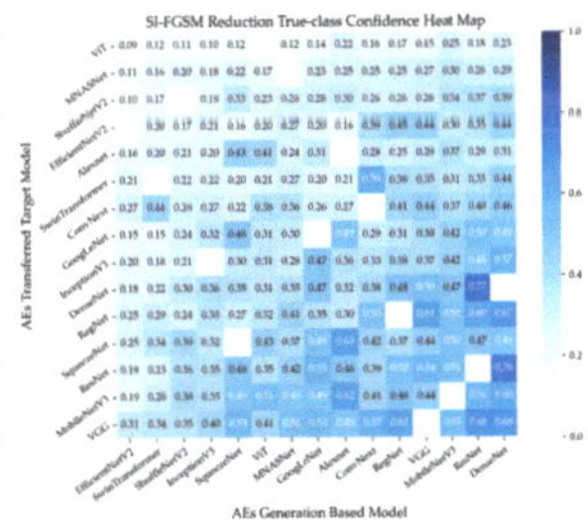
	Average	38.256%	4.320%	34.247%
VMI-FGSM	Hot Map	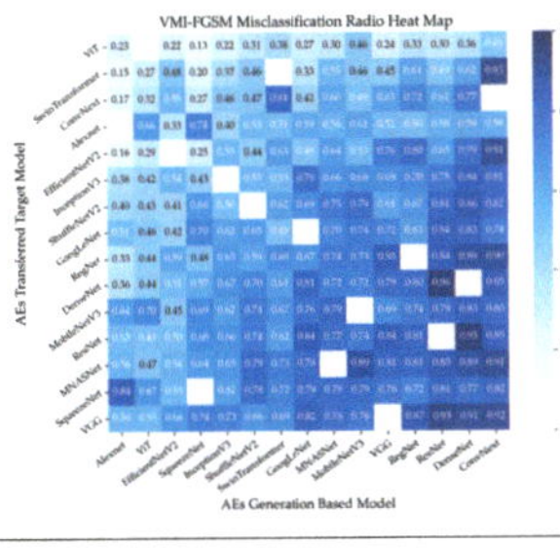	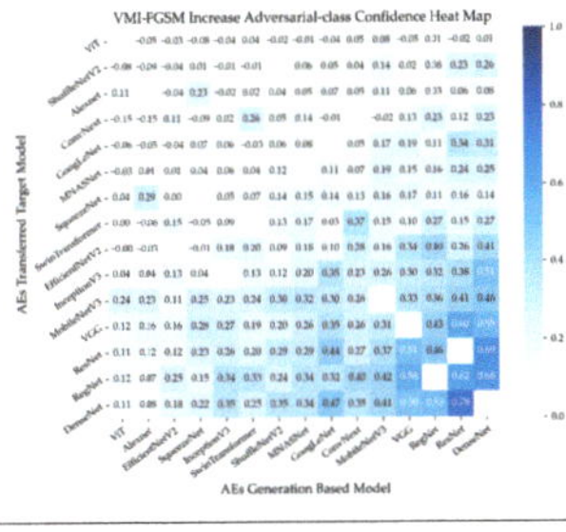	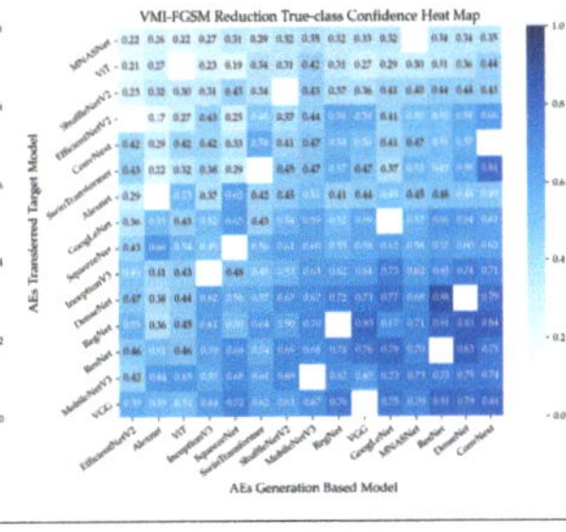
	Average	62.132%	17.287%	51.870%

In terms of attack methods, VMI-FGSM (VMIM) achieves significantly better transfer rates, while SI-FGSM (SIM) and NI-FGSM (NIM) do not achieve better results than MI-FGSM (MIM). This is because the improvement of SIM and NIM over MIM is that a higher misclassification rate can be achieved with fewer iterations, whereas the number of rounds and perturbations we have chosen makes the number of iterations of these methods the same, and all have reached the upper limit, in which case there is no significant advantage for SIM and NIM. In terms of the confidence bias metric, the ARTC for all attacks is significantly higher than the AIAC, i.e., the transfer attack relies heavily on "hiding themselves" rather than "misleading enhancement". Also, the stronger the transfer attack, the better the "hide themselves" effect.

In terms of models, the adversarial examples based on ResNet, DenseNet, and ConvNeXt have stronger transferability, while those based on EfficientNetV2 and ShuffleNetV2 generally have poor transferability. Meanwhile, ViT and SwinTransformer show stronger resistance to transfer-based attacks, but it seems that the adversarial examples generated by MIM or VMIM based on the ConvNeXt alternative model can effectively erode SwinTransformer. VGG, SqueezeNet, and MNASNet are more vulnerable to transfer-based attacks than other models. As we can find in Section 5.4, this does not correlate with the misclassification rate of non-transfer attacks for these models.

5.4. Evaluation of Model Robustness

We use the method related in Section 3.2 to squeeze the data matrix $\Delta^{w}_{(8+4)(15)}, \Delta^{b}_{(8)(15)}$ along the direction of the attack. So that it ignores the attack method itself and transforms into a data sequence $\Delta^{w}_{\underset{(15)}{\sim}}, \Delta^{b}_{\underset{(15)}{\sim}}$.

Our evaluation results for the model are displayed in two tables, where the Capabilities Part is shown in Table 7 and the Under Attack Effectiveness Part is shown in Table 8.

Table 7. Model capabilities results of all models.

Model	Model Capability		
	CA	CF	CC
AlexNet	53.6%	0.413	44.3%
VGG	72.4%	0.612	65.1%
GoogLeNet	68.5%	0.567	54.3%
InceptionV3	79.1%	0.694	68.4%
ResNet	74.4%	0.643	67.2%
DenseNet	78.8%	0.692	73.4%
SqueezeNet	54.8%	0.441	43.3%
MobileNetV3	71.7%	0.611	66.6%
ShuffleNetV2	74.2%	0.636	38.2%
MNASNet	77.0%	0.672	29.9%
EfficientNetV2	87.0%	0.813	63.2%
VisionTransformer	73.9%	0.627	60.0%
RegNet	81.2%	0.723	76.6%
SwinTransformer	84.0%	0.766	72.2%
ConvNeXt	85.0%	0.781	57.6%

Table 8. Model under attack effectiveness results of all models.

	Model	Attack Effects						Disturbance-Aware Cost					
			ACC		ACAMC			AND		AED-FD		AMS	
		MR	AIAC	ARTC	$ACAMC_A$	$ACAMC_T$	APCR	AED (10^{-2})	AMD (10^{-1})	FD_L (10^{-2})	FD_H (10^{-2})	ADMS (10^{-1})	ALMS (10^{-1})
White	AlexNet	96.5%	50.3%	65.9%	0.925	0.950	65.1%	0.815	1.221	1.805	0.432	0.620	0.204
	VGG	98.2%	70.4%	76.1%	0.886	0.938	59.5%	0.700	1.016	1.574	0.302	0.725	0.147
	GoogLeNet	96.1%	45.3%	65.2%	0.933	0.942	60.8%	0.749	1.148	1.675	0.328	0.614	0.218
	InceptionV3	90.3%	53.8%	73.5%	0.923	0.920	59.7%	1.063	1.300	2.370	0.530	0.678	0.270
	ResNet	96.5%	66.7%	74.4%	0.924	0.963	60.3%	0.767	1.160	1.684	0.360	0.687	0.198
	DenseNet	96.1%	71.4%	77.2%	0.933	0.970	61.3%	0.777	1.178	1.708	0.392	0.725	0.219
	SqueezeNet	98.4%	57.3%	64.7%	0.931	0.969	60.3%	0.743	1.253	1.611	0.330	0.609	0.176
	MobileNetV3	97.0%	69.1%	77.7%	0.880	0.852	62.3%	0.752	1.022	1.757	0.306	0.716	0.200
	ShuffleNetV2	94.5%	34.1%	42.7%	0.807	0.862	56.2%	0.681	1.035	1.557	0.264	0.486	0.137
	MNASNet	91.2%	31.3%	31.7%	0.801	0.882	57.4%	0.700	0.971	1.574	0.346	0.643	0.150
	EfficientNetV2	82.1%	48.4%	57.3%	0.766	0.884	58.9%	0.921	1.114	2.287	0.784	0.527	0.211
	ViT	86.8%	40.5%	61.7%	0.754	0.837	66.6%	0.978	1.296	2.326	0.822	0.703	0.278
	RegNet	95.4%	70.5%	78.5%	0.889	0.953	59.8%	0.745	1.080	1.568	0.314	0.682	0.160
	SwinT	91.9%	63.8%	68.7%	0.877	0.880	55.8%	0.847	1.297	1.743	0.399	0.654	0.188
	ConvNeXt	91.6%	49.6%	55.7%	0.575	0.898	61.7%	0.812	1.156	1.792	0.582	0.579	0.168
Black	AlexNet	67.8%	13.6%	49.8%	0.938	0.961	81.1%	4.922	3.130	6.636	4.715	1.760	0.899
	VGG	63.6%	15.2%	52.6%	0.910	0.962	79.0%	4.900	3.130	6.573	4.385	1.729	0.888
	GoogLeNet	55.7%	−0.5%	42.8%	0.971	0.989	82.1%	5.561	3.271	7.456	4.868	1.893	0.996
	InceptionV3	39.1%	−6.3%	43.0%	0.968	0.984	78.9%	6.770	3.995	8.996	5.294	1.910	1.186
	ResNet	49.9%	5.0%	40.0%	0.967	0.986	80.8%	5.251	3.205	7.037	4.635	1.812	0.959
	DenseNet	53.2%	12.4%	43.9%	0.975	0.989	81.2%	5.632	3.289	7.534	4.802	1.920	1.018
	SqueezeNet	74.9%	14.4%	50.4%	0.954	0.977	79.2%	4.471	3.010	5.973	4.497	1.575	0.810
	MobileNetV3	53.5%	8.6%	46.8%	0.912	0.952	81.5%	5.199	3.209	7.236	4.337	1.816	0.975
	ShuffleNetV2	50.5%	−1.4%	26.6%	0.937	0.977	80.4%	5.240	3.223	7.150	4.307	1.004	0.955
	MNASNet	49.0%	−1.4%	19.7%	0.949	0.978	80.4%	5.196	3.191	7.033	4.646	1.787	0.961
	EfficientNetV2	32.9%	−0.6%	25.2%	0.943	0.976	78.6%	6.597	4.069	8.604	4.702	1.761	1.138
	ViT	50.7%	6.3%	35.5%	0.817	0.872	80.8%	5.974	3.365	8.091	4.737	1.966	1.087
	RegNet	50.9%	12.4%	44.0%	0.934	0.978	80.7%	5.392	3.230	7.214	4.710	1.900	0.977
	SwinT	44.1%	8.1%	33.0%	0.972	0.987	81.1%	5.995	3.426	8.243	4.453	2.022	1.064
	ConvNeXt	37.8%	1.6%	25.0%	0.868	0.950	81.0%	6.116	3.422	8.327	4.637	2.006	1.075

5.4.1. Evaluation of Model Capabilities

The capabilities of the tested models are demonstrated in Table 7.

5.4.2. Evaluation of Under-Attack Effectiveness

We quantified and analyzed the model's effectiveness under attack in terms of both the under-attack effect and the perturbation budget. The results are as Table 8.

Considering the MR, the average misclassification rate of the white-box attacks is 93.5%, while that of the black-box attacks is 51.6%. For white-box attacks, models such as SwinTransformer, ConvNeXt, MNASNet, InceptionV3, ViT, and EfficientNetV2 performed relatively well, with an average MR of 89%; other models performed poorly, with an average MR of 97%. In terms of black-box attacks, SqueezeNet, AlexNet, and VGG models performed the worst with an average MR of 69%; SwinTransformer, InceptionV3, ConvNeXt, and EfficientNetV2 models performed the best with an average MR of 39%; other models performed more similarly with an average MR of 52%.

Considering the structure and performance of the models themselves, we found that the robustness of the models generally improves further as the depth, width, and resolution of the model network increase. AlexNet, which consists of a simple overlay of five large kernel convolutional layers, is less robust. To achieve lightweight, SqueezeNet significantly reduces the size of its convolutional layers, and although it uses Fire to maintain a similar misclassification rate with AlexNet, there is a significant dip in robustness, with the highest MR obtained in both white-box and black-box attacks; VGG also uses several smaller convolutional kernels instead of the large convolutional kernels in AlexNet, but VGG increases the network depth to ensure the learning of more complex patterns, so the robustness is hardly significantly different from AlexNet. ResNet greatly increases the number of network layers by stacking residual networks, and DenseNet further reduces the number of parameters and enhances feature reuse, allowing for more complex feature pattern extraction and thus better robustness than models such as AlexNet, EfficientNet; on the other hand, scales depth, width, and resolution uniformly through a fixed set of scaling factors, significantly improving its robustness and obtaining the lowest MR in both white-box and black-box attacks. Similarly, GoogLeNet further balances network depth and width as it evolves to InceptionV3, which also results in better robustness.

Further, we note that the model's ability to perceive image information from a more global and diverse perspective will help improve its robustness. For example, Vit divides the input image into multiple 16 $\times$ 16 patches and then projects them as fixed-length vectors, thus modeling the long-range dependency in the image using the self-attentive mechanism in Transformer. Similar to ViT, SwimTransformer uses a self-attentive mechanism based on moving windows, while ConvNeXt changes the parameters of the Stem layer convolution kernel of ResNet to rasterize the image in the manner of Transformer, dividing the image into patches before processing. All three models adopt a similar approach to segmenting images, obtaining different information about the input image, and building a comprehensive perception. This approach, while improving model performance, also increases the difficulty of correctly classifying against adversarial perturbation, and such models consequently exhibit lower MR than other models. For example, ConvNeXt shows better robustness than ResNet, and the Inception family of models uses convolutional kernels of different sizes to extract image features and obtain diverse information, showing better robustness than their contemporaries.

The higher consistency of the misclassification rate ranking under black- and white-box attacks suggests that the more robust models can resist both attacks. We also found that the misclassification rate ranking showed an inverse relationship with the model accuracy. This may be due to the researchers' enhanced feature learning capability and global sensing capability to improve the model inference capability, resulting in improved model robustness as well.

5.4.3. IRT-Based Comprehensive Evaluation

We used IRT to synthesize the tested models' robustness evaluation results to obtain the scores, which are shown in Table 9. When evaluating model robustness using IRT, we first calculate the Model Capability Θ_1, Attack Effects Θ_2, and Disturbance-aware Cost Θ_3, respectively, and then use Θ_1, Θ_2, and Θ_3 to calculate the comprehensive results.

Table 9. CA, MR, and IRT results of all models on 20-attacks.

Model	CA ↑ Rank [1]	MR ↓		IRT ↑			
		White Rank [1]	Black Rank [1]	White		Black	
				Score (Θ)	Rank [1]	Score (Θ)	Rank [1]
SqueezeNet	2	1	1	0.07	2	0	1
MobileNet V3	4	3	5	0	1	0.35	4
VGG	5	2	3	0.08	3	0.2	3
AlexNet	1	4	2	0.18	5	0.1	2
ShuffleNet V2	7	9	9	0.16	4	0.47	6
MNASNet	9	12	11	0.38	7	0.52	7
ResNet	8	5	10	0.38	7	0.55	8
ConvNeXt	14	11	14	0.31	6	0.76	12
GoogLeNet	3	6	4	0.4	9	0.57	9
ViT	6	14	8	0.76	13	0.36	5
RegNet	12	8	7	0.47	10	0.6	10
DenseNet	10	7	6	0.67	12	0.66	11
SwinT	13	10	12	0.59	11	0.91	13
Inception V3	11	13	13	0.99	14	1	15
EfficientNet V2	15	15	15	1	15	0.93	14

[1] "↑" indicate that the smaller the item's value, the smaller the rank, and "↓" indicate that the larger the item's value, the smaller the rank. The smaller the rank, the worse the adversarial robustness.

5.4.4. Black- and White-Box Attack Differences

Considering the ACC, the ARTC is always higher than the AIAC, regardless of whether the attack is carried out using a black-box or white-box approach, i.e., the contribution of a significant reduction in the confidence in the true classification of the model to the success of the attack is higher than the contribution of a significant increase in the confidence in the adversarial classification, which is particularly evident in the black-box attack. Furthermore, for the same model, the white-box attack achieves significantly better results than the black-box attack, both in terms of confidence and attention bias, due to the direct access to the gradient. In terms of perturbability, the white-box attack can achieve smaller perturbations, and the perturbations are primarily concentrated in the low-frequency domain, making the white-box attack's perturbations more difficult to perceive by the human eye. In comparison, the perturbations of the black-box attack are about seven times larger than those of the white-box, and there is no significant difference in the ratio of high-frequency to low-frequency perturbations, which reflects the lack of effective planning of the perturbations of the black-box attack and makes them more easily detected by the human eye.

5.5. Attack vs. Model

To reveal which attacks the models are more vulnerable to and which models the attacks are more sensitive and effective against, we counted 3 attacks with the best MR and 3 attacks with the worst MR in each of the 15 models, respectively, and the results are shown in Figure 7.

Rank / Attack Method / Model	FGSM	JSMA	DeepFool	I-FGSM	C&W Attack	PGD	EAD	SSAH	MI-FGSM	MI-FGSM (T)	VMI-FGSM	VMI-FGSM (T)	NI-FGSM	NI-FGSM (T)	SI-FGSM	SI-FGSM (T)	AdvGan	LSA	BA	SA	SPSA	HSJA	GA	TREMBA
Alexnet	☆1	☆2										★1						☆2		☆1	☆2	★3		
VGG	☆3			☆1		☆1		☆3	☆2		☆2		☆1		☆1			☆3		☆3			☆2	☆1
GoogLeNet			☆2					★1									★3							-
InceptionV3		★3	☆1	★3	★1	★3	☆2	-	★3	★2	★3		★3	★3	★3		☆2	★3	★1			★1		
ResNet								☆1		☆3		☆3		☆2		☆2					★1	★2		
DenseNet	★2							★3		☆2		☆2		☆1		☆1				★3	☆3			
SqueezeNet	☆2	☆3		☆2	★3	☆2			☆1		☆1		☆2		☆2			☆1		☆2	☆1	☆3	☆1	☆2
MobileNetV3			☆3	☆3	★2	☆3			☆3		☆3		☆3		☆3	☆3			★2				☆3	☆3
ShuffleNetV2							☆1			★3				★2		★2	☆3							
MNASNet																	★1		★3			☆1		★3
EfficientNetV2	★1	★1		★2		★2	★1	★2	★2	★1	★2	★3	★2	★1	★2	★1	★2	★1		★1	★3		★1	-
ViT		☆1		★1	☆3	★1	★1	-	★1		★1	★2	★1		★1				☆2					
RegNet							☆3	☆2									☆1				★2			
SwinT		★2			☆2		★1	-								★3			☆1			☆2	★3	★2
ConvNext	★3				☆1		★1			☆1		☆1		☆3				★2	☆3	★2			★2	★1

Figure 7. Performance of different attacks on different models. Legend ☆ indicates poor performance. Legend ★ indicates good performance, and numbers indicate ranking. Legend '-' indicates that due to the features of the algorithm, the test was not run on the model. Superscript (T) means that the evaluation using this method is based on Transfer.

We note an interesting phenomenon that the researchers proposing these methods seem to prefer to use those models in their articles with the best performance of their attacks for testing. For example, it can be seen through our experiments that SSAH has the best misclassification rate for ResNet, RegNet, and VGG, and coincidentally, the authors also developed experiments based on ResNet and observed its transferability based on ResNet and VGG; TREMBA has the best misclassification rate for VGG, SqueezeNet, and MobileNet, and the authors of the paper also happened to include VGG and MobileNet. In addition, another thing worth exploring is that the misclassification rates reported by the authors are often higher than our measurements (even significantly higher, but never lower). We believe that this could be caused by differences in test models and dataset selection or could be related to parameter configuration. However, it is undeniable that researchers prefer to choose models or datasets that have a lower attack difficulty and a higher attack misclassification rate to prove that their attacks are effective and better.

6. Discussion

After conducting extensive experiments with these models and attack methods using our comprehensive evaluation framework, we will explore the differences from other works and the value, limitations, and future of our work.

Additional Related Work. Attack methods for image classification are constantly being innovated, and various evaluation metrics and methods exist. Although the adversarial attack and defense library [14,15,17,19] covers a variety of attack and defense algorithms, the consistency of the experimental conditions and metrics in conducting adversarial robustness evaluation cannot be guaranteed, which makes it difficult to compare the adversarial robustness from model to model and before and after the model defense. We built Canary, a model robustness evaluation framework, to comprehensively integrate various attack and defense algorithms, datasets, and evaluation metrics, and to analyze the model's ability to defend against adversarial attacks and the effectiveness of the attacks at multiple levels and fine-grains, following a consistent evaluation strategy in a standardized environment.

Firstly, in terms of metric selection, we considered universality as the first priority of metrics and effectiveness as the second priority. Thus, we propose a set of generic, quantifiable, and comprehensive adversarial robustness evaluation metrics, including 26 (sub)metrics. This means that when considering a set of valid metrics, we will first select the ones with more remarkable universality. To ensure the metrics' universality, we primarily rely on the Softmax Output of the model to measure the effectiveness of the attack to make it broadly applicable; for interpretability evaluation, we use the most widely applicable Grad-CAM as part of the construction of the evaluation metrics; and for image quality evaluation, we cover the three main paradigms that are widely used by attacking methods. Unlike previous work [18,20,22], this allows our evaluation metrics to be measured without relying on any particular attack method or model and will enable researchers to use the Canary evaluation framework to integrate customized new models and attack methods with just a few Python decorators, without having to make any extensive modifications to them.

When designing the metrics, we also focused on the validity of the metrics. Previous research [18,22] used methods such as SSIM [69] to measure the visual difference between the adversarial examples and the original images. However, their performance was not good, so we chose the newest and best-performing IQA methods, MS-GMSD [71] and DISTS [73], as a replacement; the confidence level of the adversarial examples is regarded as an essential metric to measure the effectiveness of the adversarial examples. However, we found that the confidence level of the adversarial examples generated by the same attack method on different models and the confidence level of the original images are inconsistent and cannot be compared, so we chose the confidence change to evaluate it better. In addition, we also considered the performance of the adversarial perturbation in the frequency domain with different norm distances to further enhance the comprehensiveness of the evaluation. Given that the experiments of Yan et al. [55] on the DeepGauge framework [54] demonstrated a minimal correlation between Neuron Coverage metrics [54] and neural network safety and robustness and that some of the Neuron Coverage metrics impose constraints on the model structure, we dropped all the metrics in question.

Secondly, we noted that many evaluation methods/frameworks, as represented by the work [18], simply provide a table consisting of multiple metrics upon completion of the evaluation, which often leaves researchers with only rough and vague judgments of strengths and weaknesses. Therefore, after proper processing, we used the IRT algorithm to compute these metrics into scores that reflect the score of the effectiveness of the attack and defense methods or model robustness, making it possible for us to compare and rank model robustness and the effectiveness of the attack method. To our knowledge, this is the first application of IRT in the field of AI robustness evaluation.

Finally, in terms of the evaluation subject and evaluation scale, considering that related work [18,20,22] focused on the evaluation of the effectiveness of attack methods (using the same structural model to evaluate several different attack/defense methods), and related work [21] focused on the evaluation of the robustness of the model (using one attack method to test multiple structural models), we believe that these works do not fully reveal the model robustness and the effectiveness of attack methods and may introduce biases. Therefore, we conducted the largest experimental study to date on the effectiveness and transferability of 10 white-box attacks, 8 query black-box attacks, 4 transferable black-box attacks, and the robustness of 15 models (a total of $15 \times (14 \times 1000 + 8 \times 600)$ adversarial examples were generated and tested, within approximately 1960 man-hours), which, in contrast to the above work, allows us to focus the large differences in the performance of each of the 22 attacks on 15 different models (rather than just on different training datasets of the same model). At the same time, our open access to this part of the data (the baseline) allows researchers to perform comprehensive evaluations by simply integrating and testing their own models or attack methods to understand the performance ranking of the model or method, thus providing strong support for their work.

Limitations and Future Work. Firstly, although we tried to cover as many attacks and models as possible, we were still unable to exhaust and replicate everything, which may lead to some new conclusions and observations. Therefore, we have open-sourced Canary Lib, containing all our chosen testing methods and models. We encourage researchers to test their attacks, defenses, and models based on Canary and to upload their results to the platform to provide benchmarks and help more people.

Secondly, we defined an optimal parameter setting for each attack in the evaluation. Specifically, we prioritized the validity of the evaluation example, and to ensure validity, we kept the exclusivity parameters in the attack the same or similar to the original paper and standardized generic parameters (such as perturbation budget) to ensure fairness of comparison. If the computing power is sufficient, researchers can also use Canary to try more combinations of parameters to find the best parameters for a given attack. We have yet to focus on comparing model defense methods in the current development. Researchers can also integrate and try multiple defense scenarios based on Canary to compare the performance of the models before and after the defense.

Thirdly, adding or removing any metrics from the list of metrics will eventually lead to a change in the computation of IRT. In the actual experiments, we adopted a two-layer computation method to maintain its robustness, i.e., removing or adding a small number of metrics in the broad categories will not disrupt the evaluation results. However, further investigation into the robustness of the IRT algorithm may still be necessary, and researchers can conduct other studies from a quantitative perspective or mathematical principles.

Finally, in the experimental part, we tried to analyze the reasons for the differences in model robustness. However, we still have not entirely determined the internal mechanism, especially since specific attack methods seem to have very different effectiveness and transferability on various models, which leaves plenty of room for future theoretical research work on the existence mechanism of adversarial examples, and the vulnerability and interpretability of deep learning models, etc.

Application of Work. We believe that this work has the potential to play a significant role in the design and training of artificial intelligence models. It assists researchers in accurately evaluating the strengths and weaknesses of model robustness, thus promoting fundamental improvements in model design and training methods. This work can also help people understand the actual robustness of models to avoid using low-robustness models in security-sensitive domains. In addition, the designers of attack or defense methods can use this platform to measure whether their proposed methods are truly effective and to what extent they are effective, thereby advancing the development of this field.

7. Conclusions

In this work, we establish a framework for evaluating model robustness and effectiveness of attack/defense methods that includes 26 metrics that consider model capabilities, attack effects, attack costs, and defense costs. We also give a complete evaluation scheme as well as a specific method IRT to calculate the ability scores of models or attack/defense methods based on the metrics results for ranking. In addition, we provide an open-source model robustness evaluation platform, Canary, which can support users to freely integrate any CNN model and attack/defense method and evaluate them comprehensively. To fully demonstrate the effectiveness of our framework, we conducted large-scale experiments using 8 white-box attacks, 8 query black-box attacks, and 4 transfer black-box attacks on 15 models trained by the ImageNet dataset using an open-source platform. The experimental results reveal the very different behaviors of different models when subjected to the same attack, the huge difference between different attack methods when attacking the same model as well as other very interesting conclusions. Finally, we present a discussion that comprehensively contrasts our work with other related work and explores limitations, future work, and applications. The work aims to provide a comprehensive evaluation framework and method that can rigorously evaluate the robustness of the model. We hope that our paper and the Canary platform will help other researchers better understand adversarial attacks and model robustness as well as further improve them.

Author Contributions: Conceptualization, J.S., J.Z. and Y.-A.T.; Methodology, J.S., L.C., C.X. and R.H.; Software, J.S., L.C., C.X., D.Z., Z.Q. and W.X.; Validation, J.S., C.X., D.Z., Z.Q. and W.X.; Formal analysis, J.S.; Resources, J.S.; Data curation, J.S. and L.C.; Writing—original draft, J.S., C.X. and D.Z.; Writing—review & editing, J.S., D.Z., R.H., Z.Q., W.X. and J.Z.; Visualization, J.S., C.X. and R.H.; Supervision, J.Z. and Y.-A.T.; Project administration, J.Z. and Y.-A.T. All authors have read and agreed to the published version of the manuscript.

Funding: This work was supported by the National Natural Science Foundation of China under Grant U1936218 and 62072037.

Data Availability Statement: The analysis result data used to support the findings of this study have been deposited in the Canary GitHub repository (https://github.com/NeoSunJZ/Canary_Master). The raw data (Approximately 1TB in Total) used to support the findings of this study are available from the corresponding author upon request.

Acknowledgments: The authors would like to thank the editors and anonymous reviewers for their useful contributions to improving the quality of the paper. The authors sincerely thank Heng Ye, Dongli Tan, Guanting Wu, Shujie Hu, Jing Liu, and Jiayao Yang for their contributions to the open-source system, Ruinan Ma for his suggestions on the revision of this paper, and Zijun Zhang for his suggestions on the language improvement of the paper.

Conflicts of Interest: The authors declare no conflict of interest.

Appendix A. Details of the Main Adversarial Attack Algorithms in Our Evaluations

Appendix A.1. White-Box Attacks

The white-box approach of generating adversarial examples is based on the gradient of the neural network, adding perturbations to the pixels to generate adversarial examples. Szegedy et al. first identified adversarial examples that could be misclassified by deep learning models using the L-BFGS [7] method. Goodfellow et al. proposed a gradient-based attack method, the fast gradient (FGSM [32]) algorithm. Based on this, Kurakin et al. proposed an iterative fast gradient (I-FGSM [35], also known as BIM) algorithm based on improved FGSM. BIM can generate more effective adversarial examples than FGSM by gradually increasing the loss function in small iterative steps. Since FGSM is a single-step attack, i.e., adding gradients only once against an image, this method has a low misclassification rate for a complex non-linear model. Therefore, Madry et al. considered multiple small steps instead of one large step in FGSM and proposed the Project Gradient Descent (PGD [36]) attack. Compared to I-FGSM, PGD increases the number of iteration rounds and adds a layer of randomization. Furthermore, Dong et al. proposed a momentum-based iterative method (MI-FGSM [37], also known as MIM) attack based on FGSM and I-FGSM. MIM can accelerate gradient descent by accumulating velocity vectors on the gradient of the loss function. Derivatives of FGSM also include TI-FGSM [77], SI-FGSM [38], NI-FGSM [38], VMI-FGSM [39], etc.

In contrast to the idea of FGSM, Moosavi-Dezfooli et al. proposed an iterative algorithm, DeepFool [34], which generates perturbations by an iterative method that iteratively moves pixels within the classification boundary to outside the boundary until the whole picture is misclassified. Based on DeepFool, Moosavi-Dezfooli et al. also found that the method could be extended to find a universal adversarial perturbation on a batch of images such that all images are misclassified, a method known as universal adversarial perturbations (UAP [78]). Papernot et al. proposed a saliency map-based method, JSMA [33], which assigns a salient value to each dimension of the input and generates a Jacobi saliency map, thereby capturing the most sensitive features that affect the neural network's inference result and selectively modifying image pixels. Notably, Carlini et al. proposed an optimization-based attack method (C&W [23]) algorithm that comprehensively measured accuracy versus perturbation budget in the hope that the presence of an attack can be imperceptible when the adversarial example can make the model misclassified. This concept has also been widely adopted in many subsequent works, such as the EAD [40] proposed by Chen et al., which followed the objective function of the C&W attack while adding elastic L_1 and L_2 norm regularisation terms to enhance attack transfer capability and promoting perturbation sparsity by measuring L_1 loss.

While the attackers in the above approaches generally base their analysis on the spatial information of image pixels, Luo et al. showed that the attack could also be performed in the frequency domain. They proposed the SSAH [41] attack based on semantic similarity, using a low-frequency constraint to limit the noise to the high-frequency space and to effectively reduce the human visual perception of the perturbation.

In Section 5, the FGSM, BIM, PGD, DeepFool, JSMA, C&W, EAD, and SSAH algorithms and their improved derivatives are experimented with and evaluated.

Appendix A.2. Query-Based Black-Box Attacks

In this section, we consider the query-based black-box attacks.

In decision-based attacks, the attacker only has access to the hard-label by inference, and optimization-based attacks, boundary attacks, and other methods are proposed to perform the attack. The core idea of decision-based was first proposed by Brendel et al. in the Boundary Attack (BA [44]) algorithm. BA first generates an initial adversarial example x'_0 that makes the target model misclassify. The randomly generated x'_0 differs significantly from the original example x and is not an ideal adversarial example, so BA takes x'_0 as the initial point and conducts a random walk along the boundary between the adversarial and non-adversarial regions, moving in two steps at a time towards the orthogonal and target directions. After k iterations, it will result in a sufficient reduction in the distance between x'_k and image x while maintaining adversarial. However, as determining the optimal boundary location requires multiple walk iterations, BA requires a massive query of the target model. Similarly, the Hop Skip Jump Attack (HSJA [46]) algorithm proposed by Chen et al. uses a dichotomous search to reach the boundary, followed by a Monte Carlo method to estimate the approximate gradient direction at the boundary and then a step search through geometric progression. HSJA demonstrates that a suitable step length optimizes the final result to a fixed point. Furthermore, the work of Engstrom et al. showed that simple image transformations such as translation or rotation are sufficient to deceive neural network-based visual models on a large proportion of the input, and their proposed Spatial Attack (SA [45]) can also rely solely on inferential labeling queries of the target model to achieve the attack.

In the score-based class, the attacker can obtain probabilities for one or all classes and use spatial search, gradient estimation, and other means to carry out the attack. For spatial search, the Local Search Attack (LSA [43]) proposed by Narodytska et al. iteratively modifies a single pixel or a small number of pixels to generate sub-images, uses a greedy algorithm to search, and retains the best example to achieve the attack. Further on, the One Pixel Attack (OPA [42]) proposed by Su et al. uses a differential evolutionary algorithm to search and retain the best sub-image for attack based on the fitness function. However, all such algorithms suffer from a large search volume, and image size can severely affect the effectiveness of these algorithms.

In terms of gradient estimation, Chen et al. proposed a zero-order optimization attack (ZOO [49]) to estimate the gradient of the target model to generate an adversarial example. ZOO uses a differential numerical approximation to estimate the gradient of the target function with respect to the input and then uses a gradient-based approach to perform the attack. Similarly, Uesato et al. proposed a method to perform an attack using the Simultaneous Perturbed Stochastic Approximation (SPSA [48]) algorithm for gradient estimation, which achieves higher efficiency than ZOO through feature reduction and random sampling; Alzantot et al. proposed a gradient-free optimization attack (Gen Attack, GA [47]), which uses a genetic algorithm to generate adversarial examples with several orders of magnitude fewer queries than ZOO; Huang et al. proposed the TREMBA [51] attack, which uses a pre-trained codec to generate low-dimensional embeddings, and then uses NSE to search for valid examples in the embedding space to attack the black-box model, which can effectively improve the misclassification rate of the black-box attack and significantly reduce the number of queries.

In addition, Xiao et al. proposed an AdvGan [50] attack based on generative adversarial networks by mapping clean examples to adversarial perturbations through a perturbation generator G, superimposing perturbations to clean examples and inputting them into a discriminator D to determine whether they are adversarial examples, and at the same time querying the model to measure the loss of the adversarial target, and finally optimizing the above objective function using the mini-max game and obtaining G. The adversarial examples are directly generated using G in the following process. Derivative methods of AdvGan also include AdvGan++ [79], etc.

In Section 5, the BA, HSJA, LSA, SPSA, GA, AdvGan, TREMBA, and SA algorithms are experimented with and evaluated. Attack algorithms such as ZOO and OPA are also replicated in this paper but are not fully experimented with and evaluated due to the prohibitive time cost.

Appendix A.3. Transferable Black-Box Attacks

In this section, we consider the transfer-based class of black-box attacks. There are three main types of transfer-based black-box attacks, namely Gradient-based Attack, which improves transferability by designing new gradient updates; Input Transformations Attack, which improves transferability by increasing the diversity of data using input transformations; and Feature-Level Attack, which improves transferability by attacking intermediate layer features.

Regarding optimal gradient updating, the gradient calculation methods of FGSM and I-FGSM effectively improved the transferability of the adversarial examples. On this basis, Dong et al. proposed MI-FGSM [37], which integrates the momentum term into the iterative process of the attack to stabilize the update direction and get rid of undesirable local maxima during the iterative process to further improve the transferability. Lin et al. proposed NI-FGSM [38] to modify the MI-FGSM gradient information and adopted Nesterov accelerated gradients to enhance the attack transferability. Further, Wang et al. proposed VMI-FGSM [39], where instead of directly using the current gradient for momentum accumulation in each iteration of the gradient calculation, the current gradient is further adjusted by considering the variance of the gradient from the previous iteration, and the variance-based adjustment method can improve the transferability of the gradient-based attack.

In terms of input transformations, Xie et al. proposed DIM [80] to increase data diversity by randomly resizing and padding the input data, and Dong et al. proposed the TIM [77] attack based on translation invariance to improve transferability by using a predefined kernel to convolve the gradients of untranslated images to moderate the different discriminative regions between different models. Similarly, Lin et al. proposed a SIM [38] attack based on image scaling invariance, which computes the gradient of a single image scaled multiple times and approximates the final gradient, which is also effective in improving the transferability of the attack. For intermediate layer feature modification, Wang et al. proposed the FIA [81] attack, which significantly enhances the transferability of the adversarial examples by corrupting the key object-perceptual features that dominate the decisions of different models.

In Section 5, the MI-FGSM (MIM), NI-FGSM (NIM), SI-FGSM (SIM), and VMI-FGSM (VMIM) algorithms are experimented with and evaluated.

Appendix B. Open-Source Platform Structure and Metrics Calculation Process

We envisage that the Canary platform should follow the following design guidelines:

- Fairness—the platform's evaluation of model security and attack and defense effectiveness should be conducted on an equal footing or with the introduction of necessary parameters to eliminate discrepancies, resulting in a fair score and ranking.
- Universality—the platform should include comprehensive and rigorous metrics that can be universally applied to all types of models and the most representative baseline models, attack, and defense methods to draw comprehensive conclusions.
- Extensibility—the platform should be fully decoupled from the attack/defense methods library, making it easy to integrate new attack/defense methods while reducing intrusion into the target code.
- Clearness—the platform should give intuitive, clear, and easy-to-understand final evaluation results and be able to accurately measure the distance of the model or method under test against a baseline and against other models or methods.
- Quick Deployability—the platform should be quickly deployable to any device without the need for cumbersome configuration and coding and without creating baselines, repeatedly allowing for rapid evaluation results.

Accordingly, we designed and developed the Canary platform. The platform consists of a component modifier, a security testing module, a security evaluation module, and a system module. The security evaluation module includes attack evaluation, model-baseline evaluation, and defense evaluation. The evaluation process and structure can be expressed as follows:

Canary SEFI calculates the metrics presented in Section 3.1 based on the component modifier, security test module, and security evaluation module. Specifically, SEFI divides the metrics collection into four phases.

As shown in Figure A1, in the model capability testing phase, SEFI will test and collect Grad-CAM data and confidence matrix data for the model based on a randomly selected set of picture examples $\chi = \{x_1, x_2, \cdots, x_n\}$ and calculate all the metrics in Section 3.1.1.

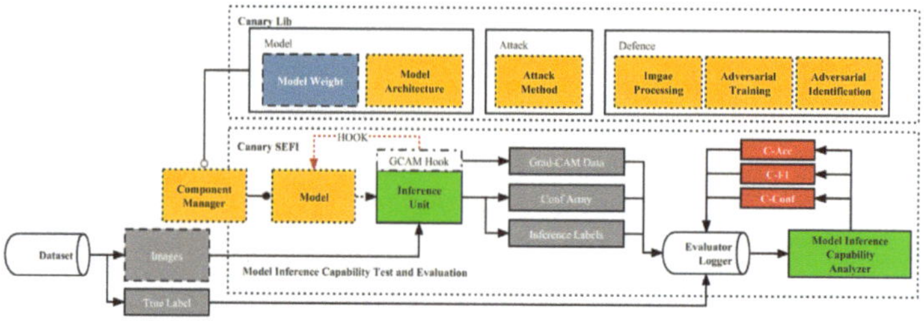

Figure A1. Schematic diagram of the process of testing and evaluating model inference capability. The component manager collects and builds model objects sent to the inference unit after the Hook. The inference results, confidence, and Grad-CAM data are obtained after inferring the test dataset, stored in the database, and finally, the metrics are calculated by the analyzer.

As shown in Figure A2, in the adversarial example generation phase, an adversarial example χ^a is generated from χ based on the target model using the specified attack method, and data on the number of model queries and the time of adversarial example generation are collected and stored.

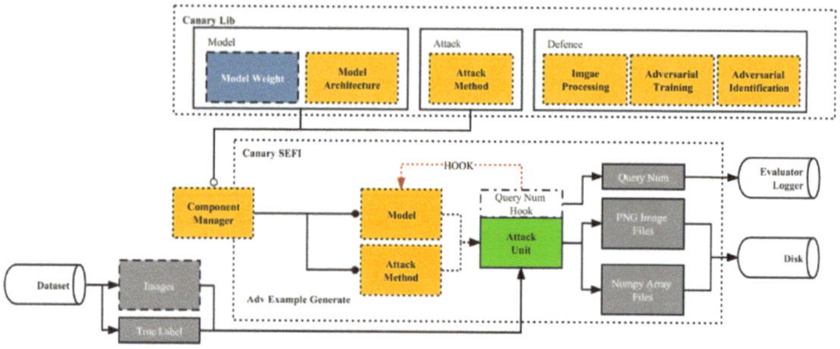

Figure A2. Schematic diagram of the process of adversarial example generation. The component manager collects and constructs the model object and attack method object, the model object is sent to the attack unit with the attack method object after the Hook, and the model query number, time, and adversarial example images are obtained after generating the adversarial examples based on the test dataset. Finally, they are stored in the database and disk respectively.

As shown in Figure A3, in the evaluation phase, SEFI first tested and collected Grad-CAM data and confidence matrix data for the model based on χ^a and compared them with the data collected during the model capability testing phase to calculate the metrics in Section 3.1.2; then evaluated the difference between χ^a and χ, and further calculated the metrics in Section 3.1.3.

As shown in Figure A4, in the defense phase, for the adversarial classification defense, the adversarial example classification model capability can be evaluated based on χ^a; for the image processing defense, the image processing result $\varphi(\chi^a)$ can be generated and stored, and the evaluation phase can be completed using $\varphi(\chi^a)$, comparing χ^a to measure the image processing defense capability and calculating the applicable metrics in Section 3.1.4. For adversarial training, the weights can be stored and used for post-defense model capability testing, adversarial example generation and evaluation, comparing the pre-defense model to measure the adversarial training defense capability, and calculating the applicable metrics in Section 3.1.4.

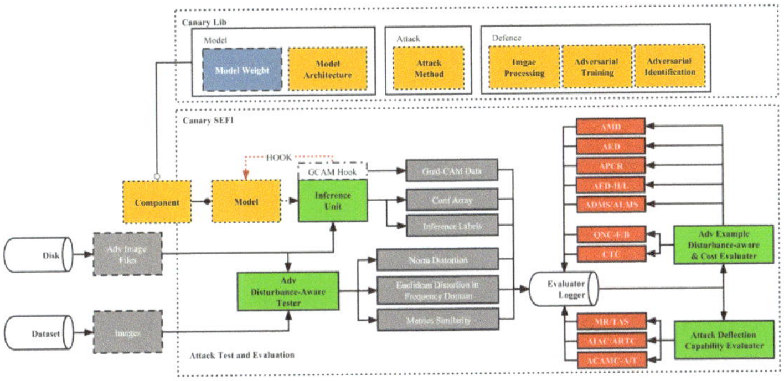

Figure A3. Schematic diagram of the process of attack testing and evaluation. The component manager collects and constructs model objects, which are sent to the inference unit after the Hook. The inference results, confidence, and CAM Data are obtained after inference of the generated adversarial examples and stored in the database. Finally, the analyzer calculates the metrics by comparing the change in quality and inference results of the images before and after the attack (original images and adversarial examples).

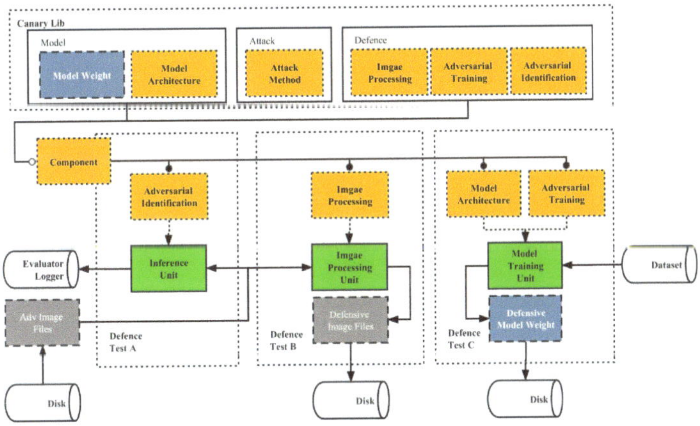

Figure A4. Schematic diagram of the defense testing process. The component manager collects and builds defense method objects and model objects. The defense methods can be divided into three categories according to different defense routes: Adversarial Identification (Test A), Image Processing (Test B), and Adversarial Training (Test C). The objects of the adversarial identification are sent to the inference unit to evaluate the identification capability; the objects of the image processing are sent to the image processing unit to process the generated adversarial examples and store the defense results to disk, and finally apply the process shown in Figure A3 for comparative analysis; the objects of the adversarial training are sent to the model training unit together with the structure of the model to be defended, to train the model based on the dataset and store the weight to disk, and finally apply the process shown in Figures A1–A3 for comparative analysis.

References

1. Hu, Y.; Yang, J.; Chen, L.; Li, K.; Sima, C.; Zhu, X.; Chai, S.; Du, S.; Lin, T.; Wang, W. Planning-oriented autonomous driving. In Proceedings of the IEEE/CVF Conference on Computer Vision and Pattern Recognition, Vancouver, BC, Canada, 18–22 June 2023; pp. 17853–17862.
2. Liu, Y.; Yang, J.; Gu, X.; Guo, Y.; Yang, G.-Z. EgoHMR: Egocentric Human Mesh Recovery via Hierarchical Latent Diffusion Model. In Proceedings of the 2023 IEEE International Conference on Robotics and Automation (ICRA), ExCel, London, UK , 29 May–2 June 2023; pp. 9807–9813.
3. Shin, H.; Kim, H.; Kim, S.; Jun, Y.; Eo, T.; Hwang, D. SDC-UDA: Volumetric Unsupervised Domain Adaptation Framework for Slice-Direction Continuous Cross-Modality Medical Image Segmentation. In Proceedings of the IEEE/CVF Conference on Computer Vision and Pattern Recognition, Vancouver, BC, Canada, 18–22 June 2023; pp. 7412–7421.
4. Liu, F.; Wu, X.; Ge, S.; Fan, W.; Zou, Y. Exploring and distilling posterior and prior knowledge for radiology report generation. In Proceedings of the IEEE/CVF Conference on Computer Vision and Pattern Recognition, Nashville, TN, USA, 19–25 June 2021; pp. 13753–13762.
5. Jaszcz, A.; Połap, D. AIMM: Artificial intelligence merged methods for flood DDoS attacks detection. *J. King Saud Univ.-Comput. Inf. Sci.* **2022**, *34*, 8090–8101. [CrossRef]
6. Du, B.; Huang, Y.; Chen, J.; Huang, D. Adaptive Sparse Convolutional Networks with Global Context Enhancement for Faster Object Detection on Drone Images. In Proceedings of the IEEE/CVF Conference on Computer Vision and Pattern Recognition, Vancouver, BC, Canada, 18–22 June 2023; pp. 13435–13444.
7. Szegedy, C.; Zaremba, W.; Sutskever, I.; Bruna, J.; Erhan, D.; Goodfellow, I.J.; Fergus, R. Intriguing properties of neural networks. In Proceedings of the 2nd International Conference on Learning Representations, ICLR 2014, Banff, AB, Canada, 14–16 April 2014.
8. Huang, H.; Chen, Z.; Chen, H.; Wang, Y.; Zhang, K. T-sea: Transfer-based self-ensemble attack on object detection. In Proceedings of the IEEE/CVF Conference on Computer Vision and Pattern Recognition, Vancouver, BC, Canada, 18–22 June 2023; pp. 20514–20523.
9. Wei, Z.; Chen, J.; Wu, Z.; Jiang, Y.-G. Enhancing the Self-Universality for Transferable Targeted Attacks. In Proceedings of the IEEE/CVF Conference on Computer Vision and Pattern Recognition, Vancouver, BC, Canada, 18–22 June 2023; pp. 12281–12290.
10. Wang, X.; Zhang, Z.; Tong, K.; Gong, D.; He, K.; Li, Z.; Liu, W. Triangle attack: A query-efficient decision-based adversarial attack. In Proceedings of the European Conference on Computer Vision, Tel Aviv, Israel, 23–28 October 2022; pp. 156–174.
11. Frosio, I.; Kautz, J. The Best Defense is a Good Offense: Adversarial Augmentation against Adversarial Attacks. In Proceedings of the IEEE/CVF Conference on Computer Vision and Pattern Recognition, Vancouver, BC, Canada, 18–22 June 2023; pp. 4067–4076.
12. Addepalli, S.; Jain, S.; Sriramanan, G.; Venkatesh Babu, R. Scaling adversarial training to large perturbation bounds. In Proceedings of the European Conference on Computer Vision, Tel Aviv, Israel, 23–28 October 2022; pp. 301–316.
13. Połap, D.; Jaszcz, A.; Wawrzyniak, N.; Zaniewicz, G. Bilinear pooling with poisoning detection module for automatic side scan sonar data analysis. *IEEE Access* **2023**, *11*, 72477–72484. [CrossRef]
14. Papernot, N.; Faghri, F.; Carlini, N.; Goodfellow, I.; Feinman, R.; Kurakin, A.; Xie, C.; Sharma, Y.; Brown, T.; Roy, A. Technical report on the cleverhans v2. 1.0 adversarial examples library. *arXiv* **2016**, arXiv:1610.00768.
15. Rauber, J.; Brendel, W.; Bethge, M. Foolbox: A python toolbox to benchmark the robustness of machine learning models. *arXiv* **2017**, arXiv:1707.04131.
16. Nicolae, M.-I.; Sinn, M.; Tran, M.N.; Buesser, B.; Rawat, A.; Wistuba, M.; Zantedeschi, V.; Baracaldo, N.; Chen, B.; Ludwig, H. Adversarial Robustness Toolbox v1. 0.0. *arXiv* **2018**, arXiv:1807.01069.
17. Ding, G.W.; Wang, L.; Jin, X. AdverTorch v0. 1: An adversarial robustness toolbox based on pytorch. *arXiv* **2019**, arXiv:1902.07623.
18. Ling, X.; Ji, S.; Zou, J.; Wang, J.; Wu, C.; Li, B.; Wang, T. Deepsec: A uniform platform for security analysis of deep learning model. In Proceedings of the 2019 IEEE Symposium on Security and Privacy (SP), San Francisco, CA, USA, 20–22 May 2019; pp. 673–690.
19. Goodman, D.; Xin, H.; Yang, W.; Yuesheng, W.; Junfeng, X.; Huan, Z. Advbox: A toolbox to generate adversarial examples that fool neural networks. *arXiv* **2020**, arXiv:2001.05574.
20. Dong, Y.; Fu, Q.-A.; Yang, X.; Pang, T.; Su, H.; Xiao, Z.; Zhu, J. Benchmarking adversarial robustness on image classification. In Proceedings of the IEEE/CVF Conference on Computer Vision and Pattern Recognition, Seattle, WA, USA, 13–19 June 2020; pp. 321–331.
21. Croce, F.; Andriushchenko, M.; Sehwag, V.; Debenedetti, E.; Flammarion, N.; Chiang, M.; Mittal, P.; Hein, M. Robustbench: A standardized adversarial robustness benchmark. *arXiv* **2020**, arXiv:2010.09670.
22. Guo, J.; Bao, W.; Wang, J.; Ma, Y.; Gao, X.; Xiao, G.; Liu, A.; Dong, J.; Liu, X.; Wu, W. A comprehensive evaluation framework for deep model robustness. *Pattern Recognit.* **2023**, *137*, 109308. [CrossRef]
23. Carlini, N.; Wagner, D. Towards evaluating the robustness of neural networks. In Proceedings of the 2017 IEEE Symposium on Security and Privacy (SP), San Jose, CA, USA, 22–24 May 2017; pp. 39–57.
24. He, K.; Zhang, X.; Ren, S.; Sun, J. Deep residual learning for image recognition. In Proceedings of the IEEE Conference on Computer Vision and Pattern Recognition, Las Vegas, USA, NV, 27–30 June 2016; pp. 770–778.
25. Simonyan, K.; Zisserman, A. Very deep convolutional networks for large-scale image recognition. *arXiv* **2014**, arXiv:1409.1556.
26. Zagoruyko, S.; Komodakis, N. Wide Residual Networks. In Proceedings of the British Machine Vision Conference 2016, BMVC 2016, York, UK, 19–22 September 2016.
27. Embretson, S.E.; Reise, S.P. *Item Response Theory*; Psychology Press: Vermont, UK, 2013.

28. Geyer, C.J. Practical markov chain monte carlo. *Stat. Sci.* **1992**, *7*, 473–483. [CrossRef]
29. Krizhevsky, A.; Sutskever, I.; Hinton, G.E. Imagenet classification with deep convolutional neural networks. *Commun. ACM* **2017**, *60*, 84–90. [CrossRef]
30. Liu, Z.; Mao, H.; Wu, C.-Y.; Feichtenhofer, C.; Darrell, T.; Xie, S. A convnet for the 2020s. In Proceedings of the IEEE/CVF Conference on Computer Vision and Pattern Recognition, New Orleans, LA, USA, 18–24 June 2022; pp. 11976–11986.
31. Deng, J.; Dong, W.; Socher, R.; Li, L.-J.; Li, K.; Fei-Fei, L. Imagenet: A large-scale hierarchical image database. In Proceedings of the 2009 IEEE Conference on Computer Vision and Pattern Recognition, Miami, FL, USA, 20–25 June 2009; pp. 248–255.
32. Goodfellow, I.J.; Shlens, J.; Szegedy, C. Explaining and Harnessing Adversarial Examples. In Proceedings of the 3rd International Conference on Learning Representations, ICLR 2015, San Diego, CA, USA, 7–9 May 2015.
33. Papernot, N.; McDaniel, P.; Jha, S.; Fredrikson, M.; Celik, Z.B.; Swami, A. The limitations of deep learning in adversarial settings. In Proceedings of the 2016 IEEE European Symposium on Security and Privacy (EuroS&P), Congress Center Saar, Saarbrücken, Germany, 21–24 March 2016; pp. 372–387.
34. Moosavi-Dezfooli, S.-M.; Fawzi, A.; Frossard, P. Deepfool: A simple and accurate method to fool deep neural networks. In Proceedings of the IEEE Conference on Computer Vision and Pattern Recognition, CVPR 2016, Las Vegas, NV, USA, 27–30 June 2016; pp. 2574–2582.
35. Kurakin, A.; Goodfellow, I.J.; Bengio, S. Adversarial examples in the physical world. In *Artificial Intelligence Safety and Security*; Chapman and Hall/CRC: Boca Raton, FL, USA, 2018; pp. 99–112.
36. Madry, A.; Makelov, A.; Schmidt, L.; Tsipras, D.; Vladu, A. Towards Deep Learning Models Resistant to Adversarial Attacks. In Proceedings of the 6th International Conference on Learning Representations, ICLR 2018, Vancouver, BC, Canada, 30 April–3 May 2018.
37. Dong, Y.; Liao, F.; Pang, T.; Su, H.; Zhu, J.; Hu, X.; Li, J. Boosting adversarial attacks with momentum. In Proceedings of the IEEE Conference on Computer Vision and Pattern Recognition, CVPR 2018, Salt Lake City, UT, USA, 18–23 June 2018; pp. 9185–9193.
38. Lin, J.; Song, C.; He, K.; Wang, L.; Hopcroft, J.E. Nesterov Accelerated Gradient and Scale Invariance for Adversarial Attacks. In Proceedings of the 8th International Conference on Learning Representations, ICLR 2020, Addis Ababa, Ethiopia, 26–30 April 2020.
39. Wang, X.; He, K. Enhancing the transferability of adversarial attacks through variance tuning. In Proceedings of the IEEE/CVF Conference on Computer Vision and Pattern Recognition, CVPR 2021, Nashville, TN, USA, 20–25 June 2021; pp. 1924–1933.
40. Chen, P.-Y.; Sharma, Y.; Zhang, H.; Yi, J.; Hsieh, C.-J. Ead: Elastic-net attacks to deep neural networks via adversarial examples. In Proceedings of the AAAI Conference on Artificial Intelligence, AAAI 2018, New Orleans, LA, USA, 2–7 February 2018.
41. Luo, C.; Lin, Q.; Xie, W.; Wu, B.; Xie, J.; Shen, L. Frequency-driven imperceptible adversarial attack on semantic similarity. In Proceedings of the IEEE/CVF Conference on Computer Vision and Pattern Recognition, CVPR 2022, New Orleans, LA, USA, 18–24 June 2022; pp. 15315–15324.
42. Su, J.; Vargas, D.V.; Sakurai, K. One pixel attack for fooling deep neural networks. *IEEE Trans. Evol. Comput.* **2019**, *23*, 828–841. [CrossRef]
43. Narodytska, N.; Kasiviswanathan, S.P. Simple black-box adversarial perturbations for deep networks. *arXiv* **2016**, arXiv:1612.06299.
44. Brendel, W.; Rauber, J.; Bethge, M. Decision-Based Adversarial Attacks: Reliable Attacks Against Black-Box Machine Learning Models. In Proceedings of the 6th International Conference on Learning Representations, ICLR 2018, Vancouver, BC, Canada, 30 April–3 May 2018.
45. Bhagoji, A.N.; He, W.; Li, B.; Song, D. Exploring the space of black-box attacks on deep neural networks. *arXiv* **2017**, arXiv:1712.09491.
46. Chen, J.; Jordan, M.I.; Wainwright, M.J. Hopskipjumpattack: A query-efficient decision-based attack. In Proceedings of the 2020 IEEE Symposium on Security and Privacy (SP), San Francisco, CA, USA, 18–21 May 2020; pp. 1277–1294.
47. Alzantot, M.; Sharma, Y.; Chakraborty, S.; Zhang, H.; Hsieh, C.-J.; Srivastava, M.B. Genattack: Practical black-box attacks with gradient-free optimization. In Proceedings of the Genetic and Evolutionary Computation Conference, CECCO 2019, Prague, Czech Republic, 13–17 July 2019; pp. 1111–1119.
48. Uesato, J.; O'donoghue, B.; Kohli, P.; Oord, A. Adversarial risk and the dangers of evaluating against weak attacks. In Proceedings of the International Conference on Machine Learning, ICML 2018, Jinan, China, 26–28 May 2018; pp. 5025–5034.
49. Chen, P.-Y.; Zhang, H.; Sharma, Y.; Yi, J.; Hsieh, C.-J. Zoo: Zeroth order optimization based black-box attacks to deep neural networks without training substitute models. In Proceedings of the 10th ACM Workshop on Artificial Intelligence and Security, AISec 2017, Dallas, TX, USA, 3 November 2017; pp. 15–26.
50. Xiao, C.; Li, B.; Zhu, J.-Y.; He, W.; Liu, M.; Song, D. Generating Adversarial Examples with Adversarial Networks. In Proceedings of the Twenty-Seventh International Joint Conference on Artificial Intelligence, IJCAI 2018, Stockholm, Sweden, 13–19 July 2018; pp. 3905–3911.
51. Huang, Z.; Zhang, T. Black-Box Adversarial Attack with Transferable Model-based Embedding. In Proceedings of the 8th International Conference on Learning Representations, ICLR 2020, Addis Ababa, Ethiopia, 26–30 April 2020.
52. Croce, F.; Hein, M. Reliable evaluation of adversarial robustness with an ensemble of diverse parameter-free attacks. In Proceedings of the International Conference on Machine Learning, ICML 2020, Virtual Event, 13–18 July 2020; pp. 2206–2216.

53. Lorenz, P.; Strassel, D.; Keuper, M.; Keuper, J. Is robustbench/autoattack a suitable benchmark for adversarial robustness? *arXiv* **2021**, arXiv:2112.01601.
54. Ma, L.; Juefei-Xu, F.; Zhang, F.; Sun, J.; Xue, M.; Li, B.; Chen, C.; Su, T.; Li, L.; Liu, Y. Deepgauge: Multi-granularity testing criteria for deep learning systems. In Proceedings of the 33rd ACM/IEEE International Conference on Automated Software Engineering, ASE 2018, Montpellier, France, 3–7 September 2018; pp. 120–131.
55. Yan, S.; Tao, G.; Liu, X.; Zhai, J.; Ma, S.; Xu, L.; Zhang, X. Correlations between deep neural network model coverage criteria and model quality. In Proceedings of the 28th ACM Joint Meeting on European Software Engineering Conference and Symposium on the Foundations of Software Engineering, ESEC/FSE 2020, Virtual Event, 8–13 November 2020; pp. 775–787.
56. Szegedy, C.; Liu, W.; Jia, Y.; Sermanet, P.; Reed, S.; Anguelov, D.; Erhan, D.; Vanhoucke, V.; Rabinovich, A. Going deeper with convolutions. In Proceedings of the IEEE Conference on Computer Vision and Pattern Recognition, CVPR 2015, Boston, MA, USA, 7–12 June 2015; pp. 1–9.
57. Szegedy, C.; Vanhoucke, V.; Ioffe, S.; Shlens, J.; Wojna, Z. Rethinking the inception architecture for computer vision. In Proceedings of the IEEE Conference on Computer Vision and Pattern Recognition, CVPR 2016, Las Vegas, NV, USA, 27–30 June 2016; pp. 2818–2826.
58. Huang, G.; Liu, Z.; Van Der Maaten, L.; Weinberger, K.Q. Densely connected convolutional networks. In Proceedings of the IEEE Conference on Computer Vision and Pattern Recognition, CVPR 2017, Honolulu, HI, USA, 21–26 July 2017; pp. 4700–4708.
59. Iandola, F.N.; Han, S.; Moskewicz, M.W.; Ashraf, K.; Dally, W.J.; Keutzer, K. SqueezeNet: AlexNet-level accuracy with 50x fewer parameters and< 0.5 MB model size. *arXiv* **2016**, arXiv:1602.07360.
60. Howard, A.; Sandler, M.; Chu, G.; Chen, L.-C.; Chen, B.; Tan, M.; Wang, W.; Zhu, Y.; Pang, R.; Vasudevan, V. Searching for mobilenetv3. In Proceedings of the IEEE/CVF International Conference on Computer Vision, ICCV 2019, Seoul, Republic of Korea, 27 October–2 November 2019; pp. 1314–1324.
61. Ma, N.; Zhang, X.; Zheng, H.-T.; Sun, J. Shufflenet v2: Practical guidelines for efficient cnn architecture design. In Proceedings of the European Conference on Computer Vision (ECCV), Munich, Germany, 8–14 September 2018; pp. 116–131.
62. Tan, M.; Chen, B.; Pang, R.; Vasudevan, V.; Sandler, M.; Howard, A.; Le, Q.V. Mnasnet: Platform-aware neural architecture search for mobile. In Proceedings of the IEEE/CVF Conference on Computer Vision and Pattern Recognition, CVPR 2019, Long Beach, CA, USA, 15–20 June 2019; pp. 2820–2828.
63. Tan, M.; Le, Q. Efficientnetv2: Smaller models and faster training. In Proceedings of the International Conference on Machine Learning, ICML, Virtual Event, 18–24 July 2021; pp. 10096–10106.
64. Dosovitskiy, A.; Beyer, L.; Kolesnikov, A.; Weissenborn, D.; Zhai, X.; Unterthiner, T.; Dehghani, M.; Minderer, M.; Heigold, G.; Gelly, S. An image is worth 16x16 words: Transformers for image recognition at scale. *arXiv* **2020**, arXiv:2010.11929.
65. Radosavovic, I.; Kosaraju, R.P.; Girshick, R.; He, K.; Dollár, P. Designing network design spaces. In Proceedings of the IEEE/CVF Conference on Computer Vision and Pattern Recognition, CVPR 2020, Seattle, WA, USA, 13–19 June 2020; pp. 10428–10436.
66. Liu, Z.; Lin, Y.; Cao, Y.; Hu, H.; Wei, Y.; Zhang, Z.; Lin, S.; Guo, B. Swin transformer: Hierarchical vision transformer using shifted windows. In Proceedings of the IEEE/CVF International Conference on Computer Vision, ICCV, Montreal, QC, Canada, 11–17 October 2021; pp. 10012–10022.
67. Selvaraju, R.R.; Cogswell, M.; Das, A.; Vedantam, R.; Parikh, D.; Batra, D. Grad-cam: Visual explanations from deep networks via gradient-based localization. In Proceedings of the IEEE international Conference on Computer Vision, ICCV 2017, Venice, Italy, 22–29 October 2017; pp. 618–626.
68. Shensa, M.J. The discrete wavelet transform: Wedding the a trous and Mallat algorithms. *IEEE Trans. Signal Process.* **1992**, *40*, 2464–2482. [CrossRef]
69. Wang, Z.; Bovik, A.C.; Sheikh, H.R.; Simoncelli, E.P. Image quality assessment: From error visibility to structural similarity. *IEEE Trans. Image Process.* **2004**, *13*, 600–612. [CrossRef]
70. Huynh-Thu, Q.; Ghanbari, M. Scope of validity of PSNR in image/video quality assessment. *Electron. Lett.* **2008**, *44*, 800–801. [CrossRef]
71. Zhang, B.; Sander, P.V.; Bermak, A. Gradient magnitude similarity deviation on multiple scales for color image quality assessment. In Proceedings of the 2017 IEEE International Conference on Acoustics, Speech and Signal Processing (ICASSP), ICASSP 2017, New Orleans, LA, USA, 5–9 March 2017; pp. 1253–1257.
72. Xue, W.; Zhang, L.; Mou, X.; Bovik, A.C. Gradient magnitude similarity deviation: A highly efficient perceptual image quality index. *IEEE Trans. Image Process.* **2013**, *23*, 684–695. [CrossRef]
73. Ding, K.; Ma, K.; Wang, S.; Simoncelli, E.P. Image quality assessment: Unifying structure and texture similarity. *IEEE Trans. Pattern Anal. Mach. Intell.* **2020**, *44*, 2567–2581. [CrossRef] [PubMed]
74. Zhang, R.; Isola, P.; Efros, A.A.; Shechtman, E.; Wang, O. The unreasonable effectiveness of deep features as a perceptual metric. In Proceedings of the IEEE Conference on Computer Vision and Pattern Recognition, CVPR 2018, Salt Lake City, UT, USA, 18–22 June 2018; pp. 586–595.
75. Ding, K.; Ma, K.; Wang, S.; Simoncelli, E.P. Comparison of full-reference image quality models for optimization of image processing systems. *Int. J. Comput. Vis.* **2021**, *129*, 1258–1281. [CrossRef] [PubMed]
76. Paszke, A.; Gross, S.; Chintala, S.; Chanan, G.; Yang, E.; DeVito, Z.; Lin, Z.; Desmaison, A.; Antiga, L.; Lerer, A. Automatic differentiation in pytorch. In Proceedings of the Thirty-First Conference on Neural Information Processing Systems, NeurIPS 2017, Long Beach, CA, USA, 4–9 December 2017.

77. Dong, Y.; Pang, T.; Su, H.; Zhu, J. Evading defenses to transferable adversarial examples by translation-invariant attacks. In Proceedings of the IEEE/CVF Conference on Computer Vision and Pattern Recognition, CVPR 2019, Long Beach, CA, USA, 16–20 June 2019; pp. 4312–4321.
78. Moosavi-Dezfooli, S.-M.; Fawzi, A.; Fawzi, O.; Frossard, P. Universal adversarial perturbations. In Proceedings of the IEEE Conference on Computer Vision and Pattern Recognition, CVPR 2017, Honolulu, HI, USA, 21–26 July 2017; pp. 1765–1773.
79. Jandial, S.; Mangla, P.; Varshney, S.; Balasubramanian, V. Advgan++: Harnessing latent layers for adversary generation. In Proceedings of the IEEE/CVF International Conference on Computer Vision Workshops, ICCVW 2019, Seoul, Republic of Korea, 27 October–2 November 2019.
80. Xie, C.; Zhang, Z.; Zhou, Y.; Bai, S.; Wang, J.; Ren, Z.; Yuille, A.L. Improving transferability of adversarial examples with input diversity. In Proceedings of the IEEE/CVF Conference on Computer Vision and Pattern Recognition, CVPR 2019, Long Beach, CA, USA, 16–20 June 2019; pp. 2730–2739.
81. Wang, Z.; Guo, H.; Zhang, Z.; Liu, W.; Qin, Z.; Ren, K. Feature importance-aware transferable adversarial attacks. In Proceedings of the IEEE/CVF International Conference on Computer Vision, ICCV 2021, Montreal, QC, Canada, 10–17 October 2021; pp. 7639–7648.

electronics

Article

A Novel Traffic Obfuscation Technology for Smart Home

Shuo Zhang, Fangyu Shen, Yaping Liu *, Zhikai Yang and Xinyu Lv

Cyberspace Institute of Advanced Technology, Guangzhou University, Guangzhou 510006, China; szhang18@gzhu.edu.cn (S.Z.); 2112006189@e.gzhu.edu.cn (F.S.); 2112006047@e.gzhu.edu.cn (Z.Y.); 2112006171@e.gzhu.edu.cn (X.L.)

* Correspondence: ypliu@gzhu.edu.cn

Abstract: With the widespread popularity of smart home devices and the emergence of smart home integration platforms such as Google, Amazon, and Xiaomi, the smart home industry is in a stage of vigorous development. While smart homes provide users with convenient and intelligent living, the problem of smart home devices leaking user privacy has become increasingly prominent. Smart home devices give users the ability to remotely control home devices, but they also reflect user home activities in traffic data, which brings the risk of privacy leaks. Potential attackers can use traffic classification technology to analyze traffic characteristics during traffic transmission (e.g., at the traffic exit of a smart home gateway) and infer users' private information, such as their home activities, causing serious consequences of privacy leaks. To address the above problems, this paper focuses on research on privacy protection technology based on traffic obfuscation. By using traffic obfuscation technology to obscure the true traffic of smart home devices, it can prevent malicious traffic listeners from analyzing user privacy information based on traffic characteristics. We propose an enhanced smart home traffic obfuscation method called SHTObfuscator (Smart Home Traffic Obfuscator) based on the virtual user technology concept and a virtual user behavior construction method based on logical integrity. By injecting traffic fingerprints of different device activities into the real traffic environment of smart homes as obfuscating traffic, attackers cannot distinguish between the real device working status and user behavior privacy in the current home, effectively reducing the effect of traffic classification attack models. The protection level can be manually or automatically adjusted, achieving a balance between privacy protection and bandwidth overhead. The experimental results show that under the highest obfuscation level, the obfuscation method proposed in this paper can effectively reduce the classification effect of the attack model from 95% to 25%.

Keywords: smart home privacy; traffic obfuscation; traffic fingerprint

Citation: Zhang, S.; Shen, F.; Liu, Y.; Yang, Z.; Lv, X. A Novel Traffic Obfuscation Technology for Smart Home. *Electronics* **2023**, *12*, 3477. https://doi.org/10.3390/electronics12163477

Academic Editors: Daniele Riboni, Athanasios D. Panagopoulos and Myung-Sup Kim

Received: 21 June 2023
Revised: 31 July 2023
Accepted: 7 August 2023
Published: 17 August 2023

1. Introduction

In recent years, the smart home industry is in a rapid development stage. According to research conducted by relevant institutions, it is predicted that by 2025, 21.3% of households worldwide will use smart home devices, and the total number of smart home devices will reach 5.44 billion units [1]. While smart home devices provide users with convenient and intelligent living experiences, they also pose privacy risks by reflecting users' home activities in traffic data. Smart home devices are typically limited in functionality and designed for specific purposes. The changes in traffic patterns are highly correlated with user behavioral activities. Potential attackers can exploit this by performing traffic classification attacks to identify the activity states of users' devices, as illustrated in Figure 1, particularly in the traffic exit of smart home gateways. Therefore, it is relatively easy to identify user activities and infer privacy information from smart home traffic data, leading to significant privacy risks in this regard.

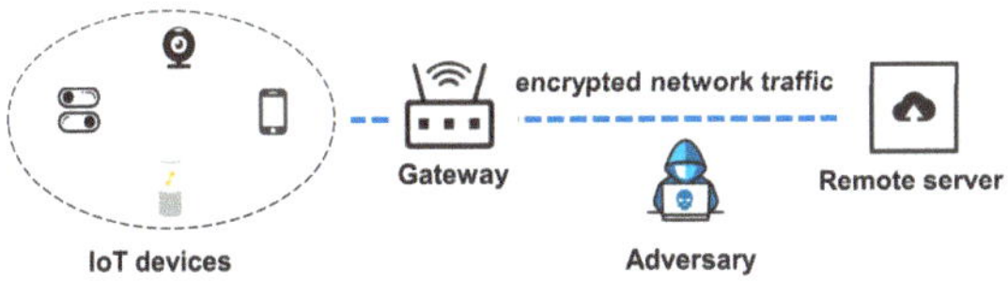

Figure 1. Overview of the privacy threat model.

Relevant studies [2] have shown that even with data encryption, attackers can infer users' privacy-sensitive information from traffic data, as each device has unique traffic characteristics and corresponding activity events. Information such as device types, actions, statuses, and user behaviors can be deduced from the traffic, making it possible to identify user activity even during interactions with smart home devices, such as conversing with voice assistants, opening/closing smart door locks, or watching smart TVs. Detecting changes in traffic rates, averages, and other features can reveal user behavioral patterns and activity states. In specific cases, even the traffic variations in a smart light can provide insights into a household's daily routines, including when users come home, when children go to bed, or whether a user stays up late. Such privacy-sensitive information can potentially facilitate further attacks, such as break-ins when no one is home, crimes targeting individuals living alone, or the sale of personal information to criminals for profit.

Previous traffic classification techniques for smart home traffic have primarily relied on the concept of traffic fingerprints according to [3–6]. Based on relevant information about smart home devices and their operational traffic data, traffic data are transformed into representative feature vectors. These feature vectors are used to construct traffic fingerprints for each device and even for specific device behaviors within the target household. By matching and detecting traffic fingerprints, the behavior of devices can be identified, and user privacy can be inferred.

In this paper, we focus on the side channel attacks where adversaries monitor the incoming/outgoing network traffic to/from smart homes, infer activities of smart home devices with traffic classification algorithms, and gain advantages in conducting subsequent severe attacks. We propose the use of traffic obfuscation techniques at the traffic exit of smart home gateways to obfuscate the actual traffic generated by devices, thereby preventing attackers from inferring users' privacy information based on traffic characteristics. To identify the appropriate timing for traffic injection, we adopted the concept of virtual users. The concept of virtual users in this research is inclined towards constructing a logically coherent and realistic user behavior pattern that is projected onto the household traffic, rather than a combination of individual or a few device behaviors. This approach aims to ensure that the injected false traffic is more deceptive, thereby preventing attackers from extracting genuine user privacy information. The key challenge lies in developing an adaptive strategy for generating virtual user behaviors.

Furthermore, considering the cost and bandwidth constraints in real smart home environments, another significant research focus in recent years has been on achieving a defense mechanism that can be adjusted based on the current network conditions. For example, one approach proposes adjusting the intensity of noise addition by altering the privacy budget [7], allowing users to select an appropriate defense level according to their specific circumstances. This addresses the practicality of implementing effective defense measures while considering the limitations of smart home environments.

Overall, we propose an enhanced smart home traffic obfuscation method called SHTObfuscator (Smart Home Traffic Obfuscator). The method utilizes the concept of virtual users and injects obfuscated traffic to construct a "realistic" user behavior trajectory within the smart home traffic data. Additionally, a smart home traffic privacy protection system, SHTProtector (Smart Home Traffic Protector), is designed and implemented. The functionality of each module in the system is tested through experiments, validating the feasibility and effectiveness of the SHTObfuscator approach. The specific research work is as follows:

The contribution of this paper is as follows:

(1) The proposal of an enhanced smart home traffic obfuscation method called SHTObfuscator based on the virtual user technology concept. By injecting traffic fingerprints of different device activities into the real traffic environment, we effectively reduce the effect of traffic classification attack models.
(2) A smart home traffic privacy protection system SHTProtector is designed and implemented. Experiments of device identification monitoring, device fingerprint extraction, traffic obfuscation effect and traffic obfuscation overhead are carried out in the real environment of smart home, and the effectiveness of the proposed method is verified.
(3) Achieved the balance between privacy preserving and communication overhead in accordance with the network condition.

The organizational structure of this paper is as follows. We introduce the related work of traffic obfuscation for smart homes in Section 2, and the motivation in Section 3. We propose the design and simulation of our mechanism in Section 4 and the experimental evaluation in Section 5. We conclude this paper in Section 6.

2. Related Work

Attackers can infer the privacy of smart homes through traffic classification. However, traffic obfuscation techniques can confuse real traffic, thereby preventing attackers from inferring users' private information based on traffic characteristics. Current research on smart home traffic obfuscation techniques, both domestically and internationally, mainly includes packet padding, traffic shaping, fake traffic injection, and virtual user.

Yao ZJ [8] proposed an evaluation framework for assessing the effectiveness of traffic obfuscation methods. The evaluation metrics for traffic obfuscation methods include stealthies, computational overhead, and deployment difficulty.

Stealthies refers to the ability of network traffic to be obfuscated in order to evade detection by observers. Computational overhead refers to the number of resources consumed during the obfuscation process, including computational time, number of computations, and required physical resources. Additionally, the deployment difficulty of obfuscation techniques is also an important factor that affects user experience. Therefore, when selecting suitable traffic obfuscation techniques, it is necessary to consider a comprehensive range of factors, including stealthies, computational overhead, and deployment difficulty.

In order to minimize privacy breaches in smart homes, in 2019, Nicolazzo S et al. [9] proposed a privacy-preserving solution for mitigating feature disclosure in a multiple IoT environment, which draws inspiration from concepts in database theory, specifically k-anonymity and t-closeness. Additionally, in 2022, Corradini E et al. [10] proposed a two-tier Blockchain framework to increase the security and autonomy of smart objects in the IoT by implementing a trust-based protection mechanism. They have implemented robust privacy measures to safeguard the personal information of IoT devices.

Packet padding primarily targets attack methods that rely on packet size features, while traffic shaping focuses on overall statistical features of data flows, including temporal patterns, periodicity, and rates of traffic.

In 2018, Pinheiro A J et al. [11] summarized and compared the obfuscation strategies for packet length, and proposed a lightweight packet filling mechanism, which adopted the combination of maximum filling and random filling, and reduced the accuracy of traffic classification algorithm from 92% to 30.38% at the cost of delay increase of approximately 19.8%. The limitation lies in less experimental settings and the need to use VPN.

In 2019, Apthorpe et al. [12] improved and proposed a new traffic shaping algorithm Stochastic Traffic Padding (STP), which allowed users to make a trade-off between cost and privacy. STP performed traffic shaping during user activities and selectively injected confused traffic in other time periods, which improved the disadvantage of constant rate traffic classifier that the cost of no user activities was too high.

Xiong et al. [13] introduced the concept of differential privacy for data packet padding. The authors employed a differential privacy model to obfuscate the traffic of each smart home device. They adjusted the level of obfuscation flexibly by defining different privacy levels, allowing for different obfuscation strengths for low-bandwidth and high-bandwidth devices. This approach aimed to meet the usage requirements of different smart home users.

In 2020, Pinheiro et al. [14] improved upon the static data packet padding mechanism proposed in 2018. To address the high overhead issue, they proposed an adaptive data packet padding method based on Software-Defined Networking (SDN). This method adjusts the number of inserted data packets based on changes in the utilization of the home network. The padding mechanism is set by an SDN application that monitors network traffic variations, with the goal of dynamically balancing privacy protection and communication overhead.

Wang et al. [15] introduced the concept of differential privacy for traffic obfuscation. The authors modeled the distribution of packet inter-arrival times and packet sizes and used privacy parameters to determine the level of privacy protection provided by differential privacy. The advantage of this method is its controllable overhead. However, the drawback is that the obfuscation noise increases the latency of the data packets, which may impact the normal operation of devices.

In 2021, Prates N et al. [16] proposed a defense mechanism that combines active monitoring and passive defense. It includes two modules: a vulnerability monitoring module that collects traffic from smart home devices and extracts requests exchanged between the devices and the gateway along with their timestamps. Possible privacy leaks are inferred using time-based statistical algorithms. The traffic shaping module introduces delays to the traffic of devices experiencing privacy leaks, making it difficult for attackers to perform inference attacks. The limitation of this method is also the lack of in-depth exploration of the impact of delays on the normal operation of devices.

In traffic shaping methods, there are also smart home traffic obfuscation schemes based on adversarial learning, which typically utilize Generative Adversarial Networks (GANs), Deep Convolutional GANs (DCGANs), and similar techniques to generate obfuscation noise for traffic. Relevant research in this area includes:

In 2020, Ibitoye et al. [17] proposed a privacy protection scheme for smart homes based on GANs, specifically addressing the privacy issues of audio devices such as smart speakers. In the face of audio-based inference attacks, this method effectively defends against inference attacks while preserving the semantics of audio samples.

In the same year, Ranieri et al. [18] focused on defense methods against traffic attacks on smart devices, particularly targeting smart speakers. The authors built a testbed for the smart home environment to evaluate the effectiveness of deep adversarial learning techniques. The experiments validated the effectiveness of using Additive White Gaussian Noise (AWGN) for traffic shaping, but the limitation is the lack of further optimization regarding the method's overhead.

Packet padding and traffic shaping aim to blur the characteristics of real traffic by adjusting its features, thus preventing attackers from extracting users' private information from the traffic. On the other hand, the purpose of fake traffic injection is to mimic the traffic generated by real devices by injecting fake traffic, thereby concealing the users' actual activities, and preventing attackers from analyzing their network behavior. These methods have a relatively low deployment difficulty since they do not require modifications at the protocol or device level.

Fake traffic injection can be divided into two types: random injection and adaptive injection. Random injection involves injecting randomly generated fake traffic into the real traffic, making it difficult for attackers to distinguish between genuine and fake traffic. This method can effectively increase the cost of attacks and reduce the success rate but may also increase the false positive rate and potentially impact the normal operation of some smart home devices.

In 2017, Apthorpe et al. [19] explored the feasibility and implementation methods of privacy protection through injecting dummy traffic. The authors suggested that injecting virtual traffic could be done on the device itself or on the smart home gateway. The challenge lies in determining the timing of injection, ensuring that the distribution of the generated fake events is similar to that of real events without creating logical conflicts.

In 2019, Hafeez et al. [20] proposed a method of constructing virtual traffic. To conceal background traffic, they suggested sending a constant stream of traffic on the upstream link regardless of the actual activity of smart home devices. When the devices are inactive, virtual traffic representing device activity is sent on the upstream link, preventing adversaries from identifying the real activities of the smart home devices. The limitation of this method also lies in the increased network overhead.

In 2021, Zhu et al. [21] proposed different traffic injection strategies for devices with different bandwidths. The authors divided smart home devices into two categories: high-bandwidth devices and low-bandwidth devices, allowing for better cost planning. Additionally, the proposed method does not modify the original traffic, which has the advantage of not introducing latency to device traffic and not affecting normal device communication.

In 2022, Xu et al. [22] addressed the attack of traffic classification based on device behavior fingerprints, as proposed by Trimananda et al. [5]. They proposed a low-cost defense method by adding noise to these device behavior fingerprints using mechanisms such as random noise. For example, for a smart outlet, the sequence pattern of its on/off events may have only slight differences, so incorporating them into the same pattern would not incur significant overhead. If the on/off events have the same device behavior fingerprint, attackers would not be able to distinguish between the events occurring on the device.

Virtual users are an optimization method proposed in recent years, based on the concept of fake traffic injection, and utilizing adaptive injection techniques. The limitation of traditional fake traffic injection methods is that attackers can use causal relationship analysis or context integrity detection to infer the occurrence of fake events. This is especially true for random injection methods, which can lead to logical conflicts between the behavior of virtual devices and real devices. Therefore, virtual users are more inclined to construct a logically coherent and realistic user behavior pattern that is projected into the household traffic, rather than a combination of individual or a few device behaviors. This ensures that the injected fake traffic is more deceptive and prevents attackers from prying into the real users' privacy information.

In 2021, Liu et al. [23] proposed a defense mechanism against privacy leakage in smart home wireless networks by constructing virtual users. They improved the deception of virtual users based on real users' behavioral patterns, achieving a good obfuscation effect. However, the limitation of their study is that they only obfuscated the unidirectional traffic from the gateway to the devices, which somewhat weakened the defense effectiveness.

In the same year, Yu et al. [24] presented a low-cost and open-source user defense system targeting user activity attack models based on machine learning and deep learning. The authors employed device behavior fingerprint learning using random forests, user behavior modeling based on LSTM, and device behavior fingerprint injection to obfuscate users' home privacy. The defense system showed promising results but lacked a balance between defense effectiveness and bandwidth consumption.

Based on the above analysis, this study believes that the smart home traffic obfuscation method based on the concept of virtual users has great potential for development. However, further optimization is needed in terms of method design and bandwidth consumption.

3. Motivation

In this section, we first present the threat model, which includes the smart home environment and attackers that we consider. Next, we describe the goals and design challenges.

3.1. Threat Model

Our threat model assumes that the attacker knows which IoT devices are in a home, the identity (e.g., MAC addresses) of the IoT device, and the size and time of the packets each device is sending. We assume all packet payloads are encrypted. The goal of the adversaries is to extract the fingerprint of device events and infer privacy from user events. This goal is intentionally broad to encompass different types of devices. For example, a user event for a sleep monitor might be someone falling asleep or waking up.

Although most packets of smart home devices are encrypted, traffic metadata (e.g., timestamps, lengths, and directions) is still available to attackers. Attackers also have access to unencrypted packet headers, which are used to extract valuable information such as Network and MAC addresses. Via side-channel analysis, attackers can use these data to infer privacy-sensitive information about the target home, such as IoT device types, device states, and user behaviors. For the small number of IoT devices that send unencrypted packets, attackers can see the meaningful information about an IoT device from the payload directly and thus need not use any side-channel analysis method [25]. Countermeasures against information leakage from unencrypted packets are out of the scope of this work.

IoT generates traffic different from traffic generated by other individual devices, such as smartphones, routers, or tablets. Besides, traffic of the IoT network follows a stable pattern and the generated network traffic being very predictable which is different from the traffic in ISPs. Among the many threats to privacy introduced by IoT devices, network traffic classification based on side-channel information, such as packet length, interval between packets, flow direction, and transmission rate, represents a major concern as it can lead to leaks of user data and behavior.

Attackers may sniff the export traffic and extracted the device event fingerprints based on the length packet length with machine learning algorithms. The fingerprints will be used for matching device events and furthermore, inferring user privacy information. For example, the use of the packet size alone in machine learning techniques enables inferring if an individual has sleep disorders or health conditions and/or engages in sexual or extra-marital activities. Along these lines, blackmail and extortion become clear threats that stand to violate and detrimentally affect an individual's autonomy, which is one of the most important aspects of privacy [26]. Therefore, it is essential to provide mechanisms that prevent personal information from IoT devices from being compromised or leaked and potentially used to maliciously make inferences about the private life of individuals.

Based on the analysis mentioned above, the main steps and objectives of the smart home traffic privacy attacker in this study are depicted in Figure 2:

(1) The attacker captures the outgoing traffic from the gateway of the target smart home by sniffing, and uses relevant classification features and algorithms to identify the types of devices present in the household, such as smartphones, computers, and smart home devices such as smart lights, smart cameras, and smart speakers.

(2) After identifying the various devices in the target home, the attacker extracts packet-level features for each behavior of the devices based on relevant classification algorithms. They construct corresponding device behavior fingerprints and infer the behaviors of smart home devices, such as turning on/off smart lights and taking photos or videos with cameras. This allows them to obtain the behaviors of different types of devices and their corresponding timestamps within a certain period.

(3) The attacker performs logical analysis of device behaviors and, using machine learning or deep learning algorithms, establishes mapping relationships between device behaviors and user behaviors. This enables them to infer the underlying user behaviors behind the device behaviors. By continuously observing the target household over a period (e.g., a week or a month), the attacker can also deduce more in-depth privacy information about the user, such as the time when the user leaves the house or the periods when the camera is turned off.

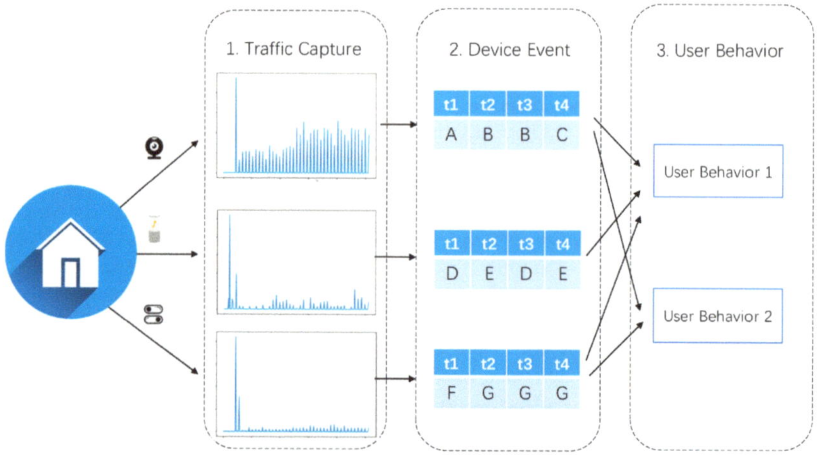

Figure 2. Attackers' goals of smart home traffic analysis.

3.2. Feature Selection

For traffic fingerprint training, there are various features can be extracted at the packet level, flow level, and behavior level. Packet-level features are those features which are extracted from each packet. These packet-level features including source and destination port, packet length, and packet payload length. A network flow is defined by its 5-tuples, which are source IP address, destination IP addresses, source port number, destination port number, and transport layer protocol [27]. A network flow usually represents one complete message exchange between a client and a server. Flow level features including flow length, flow ratio, flow payload length, flow duration. There are few features in each IoT device, which is independent of packet-level or flow-level features but depends on the application behavior of devices and are called behavioral level features. The behavior level features including NTP interval, DNS interval, transmission rate, DNS queries, cipher suites and sleep time.

For the features above, packet length, flow length, flow ratio, and transmission rate are often used for extracting device event fingerprint and infer privacy. Therefore, padding mechanism based on packet length should be an effective solution.

3.3. Goals and Challenges

Due to the relatively small scale of smart home device traffic data compared to network traffic and the high accuracy and real-time nature of packet-level features [28], most of the related research utilizes classification algorithms based on packet-level features for traffic classification by attackers. Therefore, this study designs attack models that infer user privacy information based on packet-level traffic fingerprints of smart home devices to demonstrate the feasibility and potential harm of smart home traffic classification attacks. These attack models are used to evaluate the effectiveness of the proposed SHTObfuscator defense method. It should be noted that SHTObfuscator also alters features such as transmission speed and data flow size, thereby providing a certain level of defense against attack models that rely on data flow-level features as well.

Our goals are as follows:

(1) Injecting traffic fingerprints of different device behaviors into the smart home traffic environment as obfuscation traffic, constructing a flow behavior trajectory for a virtual user, which can effectively reduce the effectiveness of user privacy inference models.

(2) The behavior logic of the virtual user is self-consistent and does not conflict with real user behavior, making it difficult for attackers to uncover the virtual user through

logical inference. Additionally, the injection of obfuscation traffic does not interfere with the normal operation of smart home devices and the daily lives of real users.

(3) The privacy protection level can be adjusted to control the number of obfuscated packets injected, achieving a balance between privacy protection and bandwidth overhead.

4. Design

4.1. Overall Design

The main idea of the proposed smart home traffic obfuscation method, SHTObfuscator is as follows:

As mentioned earlier, attackers can use traffic fingerprinting techniques to launch traffic classification attacks on smart home. Similarly, injecting obfuscation traffic based on device traffic fingerprints into real smart home traffic can reduce the classification effectiveness of traffic classification models. This makes it difficult for attackers to distinguish which traffic is generated by the devices, thus hindering their ability to infer the real user's behavior privacy, and ensuring user privacy to a large extent.

Meantime, previous research has shown that if the injected obfuscation traffic only involves a single device, or if the virtual device behavior lacks logical consistency or conflicts with the real user's behavior, attackers can use causal analysis or logic integrity checks to discern the virtual device behavior corresponding to the obfuscation traffic. Once attackers identify the obfuscation traffic, the defense mechanism of traffic obfuscation becomes ineffective. Therefore, to achieve better defense, simply simulating device behavior and injecting fake traffic from the device level is insufficient. Since a smart home user's behavior may involve interactions among multiple devices, simulating behavior at the user level is more effective in defense and deception.

Based on the above analysis, before generating obfuscation traffic, SHTObfuscator follows a series of steps to construct a logically consistent sequence of virtual user behaviors. It generates corresponding virtual device behavior sequences based on the mapping relationship between the target user's behavior and device behavior. Finally, using the fingerprint data saved in the smart home device traffic fingerprint library, obfuscation traffic is generated using a traffic generation tool and injected into the gateway traffic of the target smart home. This creates a seemingly realistic user behavior trajectory within the smart home traffic data, making it difficult for attackers to distinguish between inferred behaviors of real users and virtual users, thus ensuring user privacy.

As the number of virtual devices and behaviors increases, attention must be given to the increase in bandwidth overhead. To address this concern, this paper proposes a "tunable" privacy protection level for the traffic obfuscation scheme, allowing users to dynamically balance privacy protection and cost overhead based on their home's bandwidth conditions and requirements.

The traffic obfuscation process of SHTObfuscator consists of three functional stages: traffic fingerprint extraction, virtual user generation, and obfuscation traffic injection. The processes and detailed steps of each functional stage are depicted in Figure 3.

4.2. Event Fingerprint Extraction

Obviously, an adversary could easily use traffic rate changes to infer user activities. There are many works trying to classify different smart home devices based on their traffic characteristics. Features in different resolutions, including packet level, flow level and behavior level are extracted as fingerprints and then fed into machine learning models to identify the type of the device which generates the traffic [29].

For example, Trimananda et al. [5] proposed a smart home device activity classification method. By extracting the size and direction characteristics of smart home traffic data packets, a unique fingerprint was established for each activity of each device, and the activities (such as light bulb on/off) were classified by detecting the fingerprint. They identified the traffic flows that occurred immediately after each event and observed that certain pairs of packets with specific lengths and directions followed each ON/OFF event:

the same pairs consistently showed up for all events of the same type (e.g., ON), but were slightly different across event types (ON vs. OFF). The pairs were comprised of a request packet in one direction, and a reply packet in the opposite direction. Intuitively, this makes sense: if the smart home device changes state, this information needs to be sent to (request), and acknowledged by (reply), the cloud server to enable devices that are not connected to the home network to query the smart home device's current state.

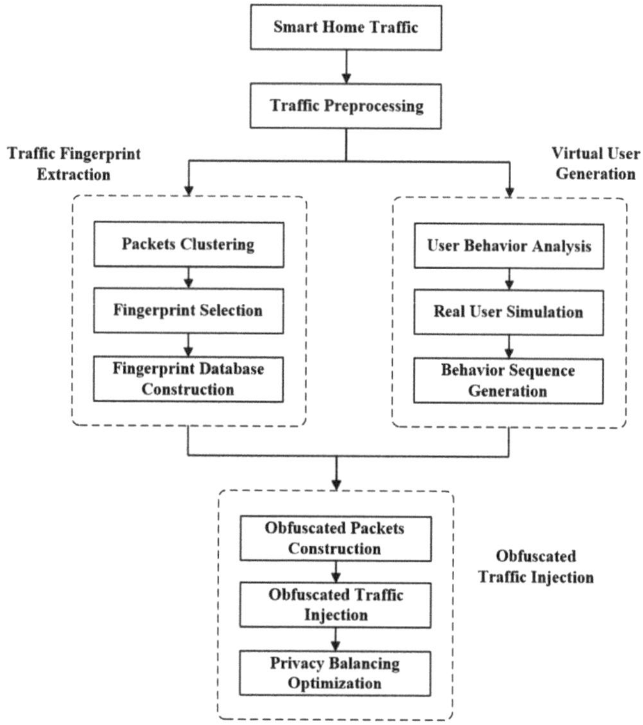

Figure 3. Processes of our proposal.

With the approach of [5], we extracted the stream on/off fingerprints of Xiaomi smart camera, as shown in Figure 4, we observed an exchange of 2 TLS Application Data packets between the plug and an Internet host where the packet lengths were 115, 299, 364 and 1061 when the stream was toggled ON, but 445 and 442 for OFF. This preliminary analysis indicates that each type of event is uniquely identified by the exchange of pairs (or longer sequences) of packets of specific lengths.

Once the candidate fingerprints are selected, their usability as device behavior fingerprints is verified using a detection algorithm. If the maximum number of device behaviors detected using the device behavior fingerprint is the same (or similar) as the actual number of device behaviors, and the timestamps of the detected device behaviors match the timestamps of the events recorded during the training period, the device behavior fingerprint is finally determined to be a valid device behavior fingerprint and stored in the device behavior fingerprint file.

Device behavior fingerprints can be generated for multiple devices and their different behaviors, forming a dynamically maintained device behavior fingerprint library. The device behavior fingerprint library includes the device types and traffic fingerprints of various behaviors. Since device behavior fingerprints may change with changes in manufacturer software or protocol versions, regular updates and maintenance are required.

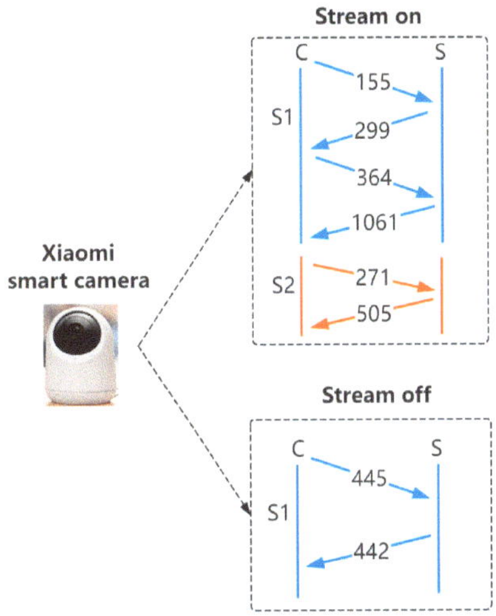

Figure 4. Stream on/off event fingerprints of Xiaomi smart camera.

4.3. *Virtual User Generation*

4.3.1. User Behavior Analysis

The design objective of the virtual user is to make the attacker perceive them as a real person living in the home based on the traffic characteristics. Therefore, the behavior associations or habits of the virtual user should closely resemble those of the target home's real user. At the same time, the behavior of the virtual user should be sufficiently different from that of the real user to prevent the attacker from distinguishing between the two. The behavior of the virtual user should be logically consistent and not conflict with the behavior of the real user.

The effectiveness of the virtual user concept lies in how to construct a reasonable sequence of home behaviors for the virtual user. Before doing so, it is important to clarify which smart home devices and their corresponding behavior activities are associated with each user behavior pattern. This may vary significantly for different users due to their individual behavioral habits. Therefore, it is necessary to establish a mapping relationship between user behaviors and device behaviors in the target home, ensuring that each user behavior includes a sequence of behaviors from one or more devices. This device behavior sequence not only includes different types of devices but also captures the sequential relationships between behaviors of different devices. Therefore, the behavior B_a of a real user a in a smart home can be represented by the Formula (1).

$$B_a = \{< D_1,\ Event_1,\ Time_1 >, \ldots,\ < D_i,\ Event_i,\ Time_i >\} \quad (1)$$

The D_i represents the smart home devices present in the household, $Event_i$ represents the associated device behavior, and $Time_i$ represents the occurrence time of the device behavior. These three parameters can be used to describe the behavior of a smart home user. In order to model the behavior of smart home users and virtual users in future research, it is important to have a clear understanding of their actions and patterns.

Since the captured traffic data are continuous, it is necessary to segment the device behavior streams in the traffic files to ensure that each segmented device behavior stream accurately represents a user behavior and establish the mapping relationship. Then, based on these segments, the device-level features of user behavior are extracted, allowing for the selection of activities to be built for the virtual user and the generation of obfuscated traffic based on identifiers. Therefore, the first step is to reasonably segment the device behavior streams in the traffic data.

(1) Device Behavior Segmentation

Due to the variety and granularity of current smart home devices, directly identifying and classifying device behaviors from raw device traffic data can be complex. Therefore, it is possible to first divide the scenarios of smart home users' daily life patterns. For example, the user's daily pattern can be divided into scenarios such as waking up, cooking, leaving home, coming back home, and sleeping based on time relationships. The main types of devices involved in each pattern can be predefined. For instance, the "coming back home" pattern often involves changes in the status of devices such as smart locks, smart lights, and smart cameras. Then, based on the captured traffic transmission time, the current user scenario X_i can be preliminarily determined, and the approximate range of devices can be defined. The corresponding device traffic fingerprints can be extracted from the fingerprint database, and device behaviors can be identified and classified by matching the traffic fingerprints. This approach can greatly improve the efficiency of segmentation.

Specifically, device traffic can be divided into $B_a = \{b_1, \ldots, b_i\}$, where b_i represents a user behavior, denoted as $b_i = \{e_1, \ldots, e_j\}$, and e_j is one device behavior within it. The segmentation is based on three factors: time intervals between traffic fingerprints, proximity between traffic fingerprints, and the frequency of occurrence of traffic fingerprints [30], as described below:

(i) Time intervals between traffic fingerprints: By observing the time intervals between traffic fingerprints, device behaviors can be divided into different time periods or stages. For example, device behaviors with short time intervals can be grouped together, indicating that the user performed multiple consecutive device operations within a short period. Device behaviors with long time intervals can be grouped separately, indicating that the user performed the next device operation after a longer time.

(ii) Proximity between traffic fingerprints: This factor measures the correlation and continuity between device behaviors. If there is a strong proximity between the user's device behaviors, they can be grouped together. For example, if the user sequentially turns on the TV, sound system, and lights, indicating a high proximity between these devices, they can be grouped together.

(iii) Frequency of occurrence of traffic fingerprints: By observing the frequency of occurrence of traffic fingerprints, device behaviors can be categorized. For example, if a user frequently turns on a particular device, those frequently occurring device behaviors can be grouped together, while infrequently occurring device behaviors can be grouped separately.

By considering these three factors, device behavior streams can be effectively segmented and classified.

(2) User Behavior Feature Extraction

Based on segmenting and classifying device behavior streams, we can deduce which device behaviors belong to the same user behavior and establish an initial mapping relationship. However, to make the mapping relationship more comprehensive and complete, further exploration of user behavior features is needed.

Firstly, through observation and analysis, it is evident that smart home user behavior data exhibit symmetry. This symmetry refers to the regularity and consistency in user device operations. Specifically, the symmetry behavior features of smart home users can be manifested in the following aspects:

(i) Symmetry in turning on and off: The symmetry behavior feature of smart home users can be reflected in the activation and deactivation of devices. For example, if a user turns on the lights in the living room at a certain time, according to the symmetry feature, the user is likely to turn off the lights at some future time to maintain the symmetry of device behavior.

(ii) Symmetry in temporal patterns: The symmetry behavior feature of smart home users can also be observed in the temporal patterns of device operations. User behaviors may exhibit symmetry within specific time periods during the day. For instance, if a user turns on the bedroom air conditioner at a specific time in the evening, according to the symmetry feature, the user may also turn off the air conditioner during the subsequent same time period.

(iii) Symmetry in device combinations: The symmetry behavior feature of smart home users can be reflected in device combinations. User behaviors may exhibit symmetry when simultaneously using multiple devices. For example, if a user turns on the television, they may also turn on the stereo system simultaneously, and then turn them off after a certain period to maintain the symmetry of device behavior.

Therefore, the behavior symmetry parameter M can be introduced to describe this user behavior feature.

Furthermore, based on relevant research [31], due to the significant randomness in smart home user behavior, the device behaviors within the same user behavior class can be divided into deterministic behaviors and non-deterministic behaviors. For example, consider a smart motion-sensing light installed at the entrance of a kitchen in a household. The user's cooking behavior would involve both deterministic and non-deterministic behaviors. When the motion sensor detects the user passing by, the light turns on. This device behavior is deterministic, occurring every time the user engages in cooking. Apart from deterministic behaviors, there are other behaviors as well. For instance, during the cooking process, the use of a microwave, refrigerator, or kettle is not always certain. These uncertain behaviors represent variation and randomness, while deterministic behaviors constitute inherent characteristics of user behavior. In such cases, the device behaviors associated with a specific user behavior can be represented as $db \cup nb$, where db represents deterministic behaviors and nb represents non-deterministic behaviors.

In summary, the mapping relationship BD between user behavior and device behavior can be described using the formula:

$$BD = ((db + M_{db}) \cup (nb + M_{nb})) \tag{2}$$

(3) User Behavior Connections Exploration

In real smart home environments, user behaviors often follow certain patterns known as behavioral habits. To effectively protect the privacy of target households' user behaviors, this study creates deceptive virtual users whose behaviors differ from real users. To achieve this, it is necessary to uncover the regularities and patterns of real users' behavioral habits. This study considers two main types of associations in the target household's behaviors: the association between user behaviors and time, and the association between user behaviors themselves.

The association between behavior and time represents the relationship between a behavior and the time it occurs, such as the user's habit of performing a specific action at a certain time of the day. Based on relevant studies [32], the probability of a behavior occurring at a specific time can be calculated by analyzing the behavioral records from the previous three days or a week, using a time unit of two hours. This probability, denoted as P_1, serves as a parameter for capturing the temporal relationships when constructing virtual user behaviors.

The association between user behaviors represents the occurrence of other behaviors when a particular behavior takes place, capturing the temporal order of behaviors based on real users' habits. The probability of two behaviors occurring together can be obtained through statistical analysis of the associations between user behaviors. This probability, denoted as P_2, serves as a parameter for capturing the behavioral relationships when constructing virtual user behaviors.

Based on the above probability parameters, a preliminary model can be developed to represent the behavioral habits of real users in smart home environments. This enables the generation of virtual user behaviors that are more aligned with real users, thus enhancing the deceptive nature of the generated behaviors. However, it should be noted that this model is still based on probabilistic parameters derived from statistical analysis and cannot accurately predict the specific behaviors of each user. Therefore, it is important to consider other practical factors to improve the accuracy and realism of the generated virtual user behaviors.

4.3.2. Behavior Sequence Generation

(1) Construction of Virtual User Behaviors

Based on the previous three steps and after obtaining the required information from the target smart home, the construction of virtual user behaviors begins. This study adopts a top-down approach to build virtual users. Firstly, the behavior sequences of virtual users are constructed. Then, for each user behavior, the corresponding sequences of device behaviors are generated. Finally, traffic fingerprints are extracted from the fingerprint library corresponding to each device behavior, and obfuscated traffic is injected into the target home.

According to Equation (1), based on the behavior patterns B_a of real user a, the daily behavior of virtual user a, denoted as V_a, can be described as:

$$V_a = \{< V_{e0},\ Time_0 >, \ldots, < V_{ei},\ Time_i >\} \quad (3)$$

V_{ei} represents a virtual user behavior, and $Time_i = < T_{begin},\ T_{end} >$ represents its time information, including the start time T_{begin} and end time T_{end}. For example, the behavior pattern "having breakfast from 7 a.m. to 8 a.m. and cooking from 11 a.m. to 12 p.m." is part of the user behavior pattern. To avoid suspicion from attackers, it is necessary to generate dynamic behaviors for virtual users each day. Based on the real users' behavioral habits learned in the target household, a function F is used to determine the virtual user's behavior V_{ei} and its occurrence time $Time_i$:

$$< V_{ei},\ Time_i >= F(X_i,\ P_1,\ P_2, Past_i,\ M_i) \quad (4)$$

X_i is the user's current context at time t_i, P_1 and P_2 are the probabilities of a certain user behavior occurring, obtained from the analysis of real user behavior habits in terms of time and behavioral associations, respectively. These probabilities can be derived from statistical analysis of the learned real user behavior patterns in the target home. $Past_i$ represents the behaviors that the virtual user has already performed at a specific time, and M_i is the result of the symmetry analysis of the real user's already occurred behaviors. By considering multiple factors, it is possible to simulate the real user's behavior and ensure the logical integrity of the virtual user's own behavior.

If there is a high similarity between real and virtual users, attackers may still be able to infer the real user's behavior [33]. Therefore, the behavior patterns of virtual users should be different from those of real users. Planning the occurrence time of virtual user behaviors ensures that real and virtual users are engaged in different activities. Based on the behavioral associations and temporal relationships described earlier, the next behavior of the virtual user is determined based on the previous behavior and its duration. Thus, the assigned behaviors to virtual users are logically reasonable.

Furthermore, to strike a balance between smart home privacy protection and bandwidth consumption, a privacy protection level f can be introduced. Different privacy protection levels correspond to different quantities of generated virtual user behaviors. As the privacy protection level f decreases, the number of generated virtual user behaviors decreases accordingly. This is because under high privacy protection levels, the generated virtual user behaviors should closely resemble those of real users to ensure effective obfuscation of real user traffic. However, in situations where network resources are scarce, an excessive number of virtual user behaviors can have a negative impact on network performance. Therefore, it is necessary to control the quantity of virtual user behaviors. Based on the analysis above, the daily behavior V_a of a virtual user can be generated using the following Equation (5):

$$V_a = D\ (F,\ f,\ < V_{e0},\ Time_0 >) \quad (5)$$

In the above statement, F is the function used to generate virtual user behaviors and their corresponding time. f is the adjustable privacy protection level, and V_{e0} represents the first behavior of the day, typically waking up. For a virtual user, the time of their waking up behavior, $Time_0$ can be randomly generated within a certain range. The algorithm for function D is shown in Algorithm 1. Throughout the day, based on the generated initial behaviors of the virtual user and referring to the probabilities of real user behavior habits and the already occurred user behaviors, the virtual user's behaviors are constructed step by step in chronological order.

Algorithm 1. Virtual User Behavior Generation

INPUT: Initial behavior of virtual user $<Ve_0, Time_0>$
Real user behavior probabilities P_1, P_2
Current context mode X_i, symmetry test parameter M_i
Confusion level parameter f
OUTPUT: Virtual user's daily behavior pattern
$Va = <Ve_0, Time_0>, \ldots, <Ve_n, Time_n>$
DATA: SQLite Fingerprint Database *DB*

Initialize $C(f)$ as the threshold for the number of virtual user behaviors under the predetermined f level
$count = 1$
$Va = <Ve_0, Time_0>$
for $Hour_i \in [0,23]$ **do**
if $C(f)/24 >= count$ **then**
$Past_i = <Ve_0, Time_0>, \ldots, <Ve_i, Time_{i-1}>$
$<Ve_i, Time_i> = F(X_i, P_1, P_2, Past_i, M_i)$
add $<Ve_i, Time_i>$ to V_a
$count = count + 1$
end
end

(2) Device Event Sequence Generation

After constructing the virtual user's behavior sequence for a day, the next step is to generate the corresponding device behavior sequence based on the established mapping relationship. One key challenge is to ensure the contextual consistency and logical integrity of the device behavior sequence. Device behaviors are not only influenced by the current behavior but also by previous behaviors. For example, if the virtual user has previously turned on the lights in the living room, they should turn off the lights when leaving the room to maintain the coherence and consistency of device behaviors. Therefore, a symmetry test is also required for device behaviors.

The symmetry test for device behaviors can effectively reduce the occurrence of two unfavorable situations for privacy protection:

(i) Continuous virtual device behaviors that may unintentionally leak user privacy. For example, the sequence of three device behaviors: (real user) turn on the lights → (virtual user) turn off the lights → (virtual user) turn on the lights. In this case, an attacker can still determine the real state of the lights. To address this, when generating virtual user device behaviors, we can check if the previous behavior was a real "turn on" behavior and ensure that subsequent behaviors logically match it.

(ii) Logical conflicts between consecutive virtual device behaviors that render the confusion ineffective. For example, the sequence of three device behaviors: (virtual user) turn off the lights → (virtual user) turn off the lights → (virtual user) turn off the lights. When the same behavior occurs consecutively, an attacker may realize the presence of a virtual user, which could compromise the privacy protection. To mitigate this, when the virtual user attempts to turn off a device that is already off, a symmetry test can be performed to validate and correct the logical behavior.

Additionally, continuous monitoring of the target smart home is necessary. This includes monitoring the real home environment to ensure the virtual user's behavior aligns with the real user's behavior and promptly detecting any anomalous behaviors. In the same smart home environment, device behaviors should not create logical conflicts between home users (real and virtual), so the virtual user's behavior model needs to be updated accordingly.

The algorithm for generating the virtual user's device behavior sequence is presented in Algorithm 2. It involves symmetry behavior testing and deterministic behavior analysis based on the obtained user behavior sequence. The occurrence times of device behaviors are then sorted according to Equation (4), resulting in the final corresponding virtual device behavior sequence.

Algorithm 2. Device Behavior Sequence Generation

INPUT: Virtual user behavior sequence V_a
Symmetry test parameter M_i
Association between user behavior and device behavior *BD*
Confusion level parameter *f*
OUTPUT: Device behavior sequence $E_a = \{de_1, de_2, \ldots, de_n\}$

Decompose V_a into user behavior and time sequence
<Ve_0, $Time_0$>, . . ., <Ve_m, $Time_m$>.
count = 1
while $count \leq m$ **do**
i = *count*
$de_i = F\ (d_0, t_0, BD)$
if M_i
add de_i to *Ea*
else
continue
count = *count* + 1
end

4.4. Obfuscated Traffic Injection

After generating the behavior of virtual users and the corresponding device behavior sequences, the corresponding device behavior traffic fingerprints will be extracted from the fingerprint library and injected into the smart home outbound traffic through the gateway.

The construction process of obfuscating data packets is as follows: based on the captured original network traffic, the packet size and direction are determined according to the traffic fingerprint. By using MAC addresses that are similar or identical to real devices, attackers can be misled in the first step of identifying all device types within a home, thus affecting the subsequent stages of behavior identification. Additionally, virtual devices can be constructed using MAC addresses that are identical to real devices, effectively obfuscating the device behavior of a specific device and making it difficult for attackers to distinguish whether the identified device behavior comes from a real device. The obfuscated data packets use the same destination/source IP, port numbers, etc., as the real device traffic. The payload can be filled using relevant packet construction tools and dynamically adjusted.

Many smart home devices have bidirectional traffic interactions, such as smart voice assistants, which frequently exchange data with device cloud services during operation. The behavior traffic fingerprints of such devices are mostly bidirectional. To simulate this bidirectional interaction at the gateway exit, traffic obfuscation units can be deployed on both the local gateway and remote servers. When the gateway transmits traffic outward, the remote server masquerades as a role in the smart home device cloud service, responding to the "traffic demands" of the local virtual devices by sending obfuscated traffic to the gateway server. Within the limits of cost, the number of remote servers can be increased, establishing a many-to-one mapping relationship with the smart home gateway. This way, if one remote server is unable to work due to an attack or other reasons, other servers can still provide obfuscation support, ensuring the reliability and stability of privacy protection methods. By injecting bidirectional traffic between the gateway and cloud services, the obfuscated traffic becomes more covert, making it difficult for attackers to differentiate between real and virtual device traffic and thus making it challenging for attackers to target smart homes.

Based on the above, traffic obfuscation methods often incur certain network bandwidth overhead, which may increase the latency of smart home devices and affect user experience. For sensitive devices such as smart speakers that require high network performance, excessive network latency can also impact the normal functionality of the device. Therefore, to strike a better balance between privacy protection in smart homes and bandwidth overhead, SHTObfuscator provides three different levels of obfuscation intensity: Level I, Level II, and Level III. Under different obfuscation levels, the density of virtual user behaviors will correspondingly increase or decrease, resulting in flexible changes in the bandwidth overhead caused by obfuscated traffic. Smart home users can dynamically adjust the obfuscation intensity based on the current network conditions at home to achieve the best outcome.

According to related research [34], real smart home users generate an average of 30 behaviors per day. Therefore, for Level I obfuscation, approximately 15 user behaviors can be generated for each virtual user per day. For Level II obfuscation, approximately 30 user behaviors can be generated per virtual user per day. For Level III obfuscation, approximately 45 user behaviors can be generated per virtual user per day. By changing the obfuscation intensity to modify the number of user behaviors, the required size of obfuscated traffic can be adjusted, achieving a balance between privacy protection and bandwidth consumption optimization.

Based on observations of laboratory smart home devices, it has been found that the effectiveness of the attack model varies between day and night, with less privacy information exposed during the night. This is because fewer smart home devices are active during the night when users are asleep. Therefore, it is possible to reduce the obfuscation intensity during nighttime to save costs. Since there is a significant difference in the number of user behaviors between daytime and nighttime for real users, and the purpose of designing virtual users is to make attackers perceive them as real individuals, it is unnecessary to obfuscate the traffic patterns of daytime and nighttime into the same pattern. This functionality can be implemented in the subsequent system implementation to be automatically handled by the system itself without requiring manual switching by users. Of course, this should be done under the premise of confirming that the user is not staying up late or has already fallen asleep.

Meanwhile, in the subsequent system implementation, an adaptive obfuscation method can be designed to allow the system to determine the current time and automatically adjust the obfuscation intensity based on different time periods, thereby ensuring the balance between the security of privacy information and cost-effectiveness. For example, during nighttime periods, the system can choose to appropriately reduce the obfuscation intensity to reduce resource consumption, while during daytime periods, the system can use stronger obfuscation intensity to ensure the security of privacy information.

This adaptive obfuscation method can be implemented in the system through programming languages. The current time can be obtained using modules such as "datetime" in Python, and then the obfuscation intensity can be adjusted based on conditional statements according to the time period. At the same time, the actual usage patterns of users, such as their sleep time and habits, should be considered during the implementation process to avoid excessive or insufficient obfuscation when users need to use smart home devices.

In conclusion, the adaptive obfuscation method can balance the security of privacy information while saving network bandwidth resources and improving the cost-effectiveness of the system. During implementation, the user's usage habits and time factors should be considered to make the system more intelligent and flexible.

5. Experimental Evaluation

5.1. Experimental Setup

The padding process is application independent and can be performed at the transport, network, and link layers. The padding mechanism can be implemented in software, acting as a middlebox on devices, such as a home router and gateway.

The experimental environment topology, as shown in Figure 5, consists of seven types of smart home devices such as smart cameras and smart speakers, as well as non-smart home devices such as smartphones and computers. These devices are connected to the smart home gateway via WiFi and interact with a cloud server, forming a smart home living scenario. The smart home gateway is deployed with the SHTProtector traffic privacy protection system, and the remote server supports bidirectional injection of obfuscated traffic.

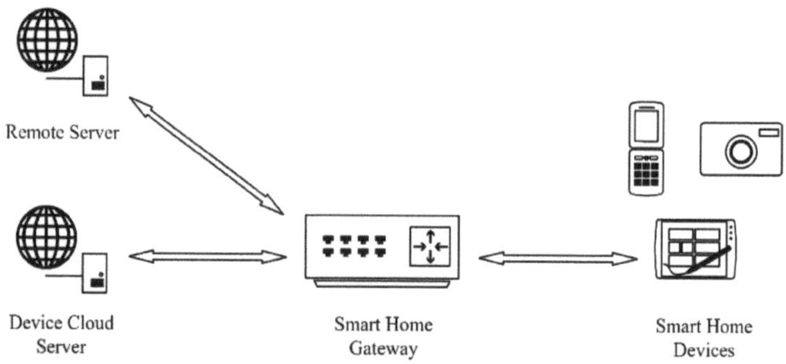

Figure 5. Experimental environment.

The hardware and software information of the smart home gateway based on OpenWrt is provided in Table 1.

Table 1. Hardware and Software Information.

Component	Specifications
CPU	i5-8400
RAM	8 GB
OpenWrt	19.07
DNSmasq	2.8.5
Hostapd	v2.10-devel

The real environment of the experiments is shown in Figure 6, including the smart home gateway and smart home devices (including cameras, smart speakers, and smart sensors).

The dataset used to generate traffic fingerprints consists of device traffic captured in the real laboratory environment. The laboratory environment dataset includes behavioral traffic and idle traffic from 10 devices. The device types include 7 smart home devices and 3 non-smart home devices, as shown in Table 2. The collection time for idle traffic is 10 min, while the collection of behavioral traffic is manually triggered based on the functional behaviors of each device. During the collection process, only the target smart home devices and non-smart home devices are in an active state. Each device behavior is triggered 30 times, with each trigger lasting 10 s, and the time of each behavior trigger is recorded.

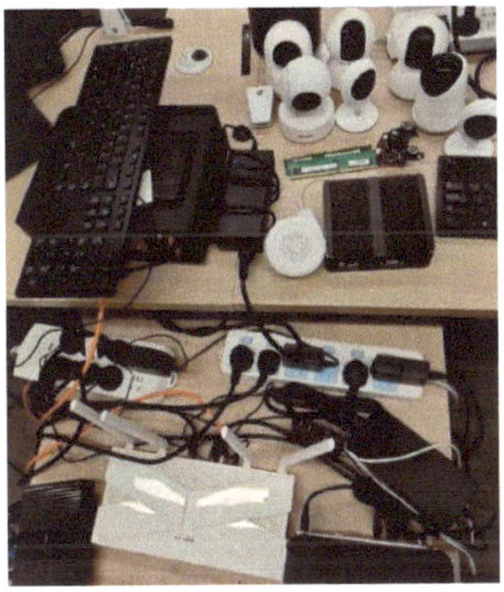

Figure 6. Real environment of experiments.

Table 2. Laboratory Device Information.

Manufacturer	Name	Function	Device Behavior
Lenovo	Camera	Fingerprinting	View monitoring
Xiaomi	Smart Pan-Tilt Camera	Fingerprinting	Recording
Hikvision	Ezviz Camera	Fingerprinting	Recording
Baidu	Xiaodu Speaker	Fingerprinting	Conversation
Aqara	Smart Light	Fingerprinting	On/Off
Aqara	Motion Sensor	Fingerprinting	Motion detection
Aqara	Smart Switch	Fingerprinting	On/Off
Huawei	Mate20 Smartphone	Background	Video browsing
Lenovo	IdeaPad 16 Laptop	Background	File downloading
Lenovo	ThinkPad Laptop	Background	Standby

To evaluate the functionalities of the SHTProtector smart home privacy protection system, the following experiments were designed to validate the effectiveness of various modules, including the deceptive nature of virtual traffic, the effectiveness of traffic obfuscation methods, and the efficacy of privacy balancing optimization.

5.1.1. Traffic Obfuscation Effectiveness Experiment

This experiment consists of two parts: device behavior recognition experiment and user behavior inference experiment.

(i) Device Behavior Recognition Experiment: The objective is to verify the deceptive nature of virtual traffic. Assume that an attacker extracts device behavior fingerprints from the dataset and trains a random forest classification model, this model is used to detect whether injected packets can be identified by the attacker as the expected device behavior and whether fake packets can be distinguished from real packets.

(ii) User Behavior Inference Experiment: The purpose is to validate the effectiveness of the obfuscation methods. Using a commonly used Hidden Markov Model (HMM) in the smart home domain, user behavior inference is performed to evaluate the obfuscation effect of the proposed traffic obfuscation method on the user behavior inference model.

5.1.2. Traffic Obfuscation Overhead Experiment

The goal of this experiment is to test the obfuscation effect and bandwidth overhead under different defense levels, in order to verify the balance between privacy protection strength and bandwidth overhead. The experiment evaluates the obfuscation effect and household traffic size under different defense levels and includes a control group for comparison, aiming to validate the effectiveness of privacy balancing optimization.

5.2. Efficiency of Obfuscation

Assume that attackers extract device behavior fingerprints from a dataset, they trained a random forest classification model. This model is used to detect whether injected packets can be recognized by the attacker as the intended device behavior and whether fake packets can be distinguished from real ones.

The results of the device behavior inference experiment are presented in Table 3. The recall rate of device behavior inference represents the ratio of successfully inferred behaviors to the total number of behaviors. The precision of device behavior inference represents the ratio of correctly inferred events to the total number of inferred events. The F1 score is the harmonic mean of both metrics. From the experimental results, it can be observed that the recall rate and F1 score of virtual packets used for confusion are very similar to those of real packets. This indicates that attackers tend to identify the behavior of virtual users as real device behavior, thus validating the high deceptive nature of the generated confusing traffic based on the proposed method in this paper. It effectively confuses attackers in real-world scenarios.

Table 3. Device Behavior Recognition Results.

Device Behavior		Real	Virtual
Device	**Behavior**	**F1 Score (%)**	**F1 Score (%)**
Xiaomi Camera	Record	91.7	91.1
Aqara Switch	Turn On	98.0	98.3
Xiaodu Speaker	Talk	91.5	93.0
Smart Light	Turn On	97.4	96.3
Motion Sensor	Sensor	96.6	96.5

After inferring device behavior, attackers need to construct a new classification model to infer user behavior. Previous research [35] has shown that Hidden Markov Models (HMMs) perform well in inferring user behavior in smart home environments. Based on observations and usage of smart home devices in a laboratory environment, the following analysis is presented:

In a smart home environment, user behavior typically involves multiple smart home devices. For example, the user's behavior of returning home may involve actions such as unlocking the door, turning on lights, adjusting the thermostat, and activating smart plugs. In such cases, attackers can use HMMs to infer user behavior from the states of smart home devices. The fundamental assumption of HMMs is that the hidden state forms a Markov chain, meaning that the current hidden state only depends on the previous hidden state and is independent of previous states. Therefore, when attackers observe a sequence of states from smart home devices, they can use HMMs to predict the sequence of hidden states (i.e., user behavior) and infer the user's privacy information.

Since the effectiveness of classifying device behavior attacks has been experimentally validated in the previous step, it is possible to identify the device behavior sequence within a specific time period in the home using a classification model. Therefore, a training dataset can be created, which includes sequences of device behavior and their corresponding user behaviors. Attackers can use this dataset to train an HMM and utilize the HMM to infer user behavior.

Table 4 shows the user behaviors and the underlying device behaviors involved. As shown in Table 5, the experimental results of user behavior inference before and after traffic obfuscation demonstrate that the proposed traffic obfuscation method has a good effect on confusing the classification model for user behavior inference. It effectively reduces the inference accuracy of the classification model for user behaviors such as leaving home, returning home, sleeping, waking up, and walking. The detailed experimental results can be found in the Appendix A.

Table 4. User and Device Behavior.

User Behavior	Relevant Device Behavior
Control Smart Light	Turn on, turn off, change color, adjust brightness
Control Smart Plug	Turn on, turn off
Talk to Smart Speaker	Turn on and engage in conversation with smart speaker
Sleep	Activate camera, turn on motion sensor, turn off smart light
Wake Up	Turn off motion sensor, turn off camera, turn on speaker
Leave Home	Turn off motion sensor, turn on camera, turn off light, unlock/lock door
Back Home	Unlock/lock door, turn on light, turn on motion sensor, turn off camera

Table 5. User Behavior Recognition Results under Different Defense Levels.

	Original	Level I	Level II	Level III
Behavior	**F1 Score (%)**			
Leave Home	92.2	31.4	27.3	22.6
Return Home	91.4	29.1	23.1	21.4
Sleep	90.6	28.0	24.6	19.3
Wake Up	91.3	26.3	22.7	18.0
Walk	94.5	25.6	22.8	19.5

Based on the key steps of the proposed SHTObfuscator method, the traffic obfuscation process was simulated on the dataset. The obfuscated traffic was then tested using the HMM user behavior inference model mentioned earlier. In addition, packet padding and traffic shaping methods were included as a comparison. The detailed experimental results, shown in Figure A1, demonstrate that the three obfuscation levels of the SHTObfuscator method significantly reduce the F1 scores of the attack model for all seven user behaviors, indicating effective privacy protection.

Among the compared traffic obfuscation methods, the effectiveness of packet padding surpasses that of obfuscation levels I and II. This is likely due to the ability of packet padding to directly alter the fundamental feature of packet size, providing more direct obfuscation for simple user behaviors such as controlling a single device. However, packet padding requires high granularity and results in significant bandwidth consumption.

Under the highest obfuscation level III, SHTObfuscator outperforms packet padding in obfuscating complex user behaviors, and the obfuscation levels I and II also yield better results compared to traffic shaping. Through these experimental comparisons, it is confirmed that the SHTObfuscator method exhibits excellent privacy protection performance.

5.3. Overhead Evaluation

The traffic obfuscation overhead experiment primarily focuses on comparing the network bandwidth consumption of SHTProtector at different obfuscation levels and testing the functionality of the privacy balancing module. The experiment involves collecting and comparing the sizes of traffic generated by smart home devices and their corresponding obfuscation effects (measured by the F1 score of the obfuscated attack model) over the course of one week after deploying the gateway. The average values are calculated for each obfuscation level.

Table 6 presents the results of the privacy balancing optimization experiment. For the three different levels of traffic obfuscation, the SHTProtector privacy protection system incurs approximately 6.7–17.8% additional bandwidth consumption, resulting in a decrease in the F1 score of the attack model from around 95% to 29.4–20.6%, with an average of approximately 25%. Compared to the control group methods such as packet padding, traffic shaping, and fake traffic injection, SHTProtector achieves a good balance between obfuscation effectiveness and lower bandwidth consumption.

Table 6. Overhead Evaluation of Padding Strategy.

Method	Effectiveness (%)	Traffic	Overhead (%)
Original Traffic	-	310 MB	-
Obfuscation Level I	29.4	331 MB	6.7
Obfuscation Level II	25.5	346 MB	11.6
Obfuscation Level III	20.6	365 MB	17.8
Packet Padding	21.3	-	87.5
Traffic Shaping	33.2	-	29.0
Fake Traffic Injection	28.3	-	31.1

Compared to existing related research, our study has made significant improvements to the smart home traffic obfuscation method based on the concept of virtual users. We have adopted a bidirectional traffic injection approach, enabling the obfuscated traffic to more realistically simulate the interactions among smart home devices. By injecting obfuscated traffic into the network, we increase the difficulty for attackers to analyze and identify traffic patterns, thereby enhancing the effectiveness of privacy protection.

It is worth noting that we have carefully considered the issue of logical integrity during the process of injecting obfuscated traffic. The obfuscated traffic not only effectively hides the users' real behaviors but also ensures that it does not cause system anomalies or data loss. Through a well-designed bidirectional traffic injection strategy, we maintain the coherence and interpretability of the traffic, making the obfuscated traffic more realistic and less detectable by potential attackers.

In addition to improving the quality of obfuscated traffic, this study also addresses the problem of bandwidth consumption during the traffic obfuscation process. We have achieved adaptive control of traffic obfuscation, allowing users to choose appropriate levels of protection based on their specific needs and privacy requirements. This balanced approach between privacy protection and cost control provides smart home users with more personalized privacy protection solutions.

Overall, the proposed smart home traffic obfuscation method based on virtual users not only enhances privacy protection but also considers the feasibility and practicality of traffic obfuscation. It offers an effective and feasible solution for data security and privacy protection in smart home environments, providing strong support for the security and privacy of future smart home systems.

6. Conclusions and Prospect

In recent years, the smart home industry has experienced rapid growth. While smart home devices provide users with convenient and intelligent living experiences, they also reflect users' household behaviors in traffic data, which poses privacy risks. To address the issue of smart home traffic privacy protection, this paper proposes an enhanced smart home traffic obfuscation method called SHTObfuscator, and designs and implements a smart home traffic privacy protection system called SHTProtector. The main contributions of this paper are as follows:

(1) Based on the concept of virtual users, an improved traffic obfuscation method, SHTObfuscator, is proposed. This method injects traffic fingerprints of different device behaviors into the real traffic environment of smart homes as obfuscated traffic. It effectively prevents attackers from distinguishing the real device operation status and user behavior privacy in the home, thereby reducing the effectiveness of traffic classification attack models. It also provides different levels of protection to achieve a balance between privacy protection and bandwidth overhead.

(2) A virtual user behavior construction method based on logical integrity is proposed. This paper classifies the different behaviors of virtual users and their corresponding device behaviors and considers the logical relationship between virtual user behaviors and real user behaviors. The method ensures that the constructed virtual user behaviors have a high level of deception while performing traffic obfuscation.

(3) The design and testing of an adaptive smart home traffic privacy protection system. Based on the SHTObfuscator traffic obfuscation method, a smart home traffic privacy protection system, SHTProtector, is designed and implemented. It includes functions such as device identification, traffic fingerprint extraction, obfuscated traffic injection, and privacy balance optimization. Experiments are conducted in an experimental environment composed of smart home gateways and smart home devices to evaluate device identification monitoring, traffic fingerprint extraction, traffic obfuscation effectiveness, and traffic obfuscation overhead, thereby validating the effectiveness of the proposed methods.

Based on the research on smart home traffic obfuscation methods, further exploration is needed in the following areas:

(1) It is necessary to continue investigating the bandwidth consumption introduced by the virtual user based smart home traffic obfuscation method in real environments and find a better balance between privacy protection strength and bandwidth consumption.

(2) This paper primarily focuses on the case of a single virtual user. Further research is needed to explore obfuscation methods for constructing multiple virtual users.

(3) For smart home privacy protection systems, further research is needed on how to make the system more intelligent in adjusting traffic obfuscation modes to achieve more efficient utilization of computational resources.

Author Contributions: Conceptualization, S.Z., F.S. and Y.L.; Methodology, S.Z. and F.S.; Software, F.S.; Validation, F.S.; Formal analysis, F.S. and Z.Y.; Investigation, Y.L.; Resources, S.Z.; Data curation, F.S.; Writing—original draft, F.S.; Writing—review & editing, S.Z., Y.L., Z.Y. and X.L.; Visualization, F.S., Z.Y. and X.L.; Supervision, Y.L.; Project administration, S.Z., Y.L., Z.Y. and X.L.; Funding acquisition, S.Z. and Y.L. All authors have read and agreed to the published version of the manuscript.

Funding: This work is supported by The Major Key Project of PCL (Grant No. PCL2022A03), Key-Area Research and Development Program of Guangdong Province (No. 2019B010137005).

Data Availability Statement: Owing to the policies and confidentiality agreements adhered to in our laboratory, the data presented in this study are available on request from the corresponding author.

Conflicts of Interest: The authors declare no conflict of interest.

Appendix A

The detailed experimental results are shown in Figure A1.

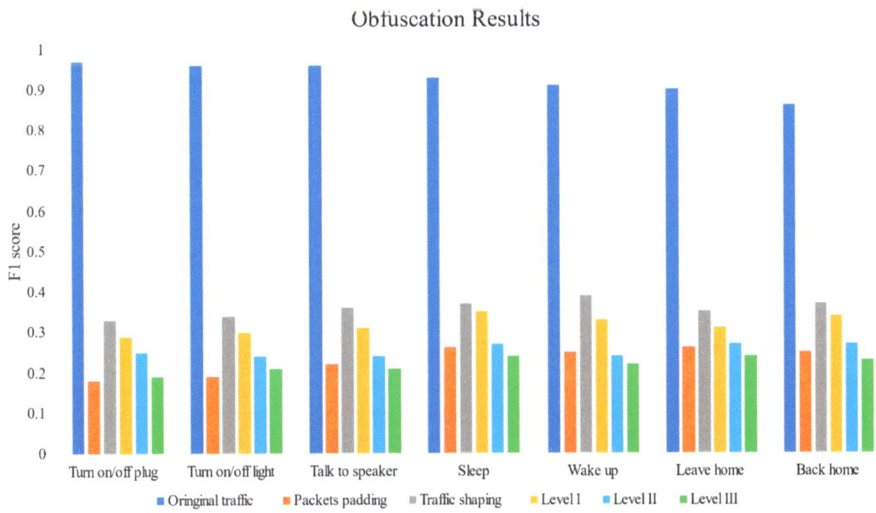

Figure A1. Detailed obfuscation results.

References

1. Cisco, U. *Cisco Annual Internet Report (2018–2023) White Paper*; Cisco: San Jose, CA, USA, 2020.
2. Acar, A.; Fereidooni, H.; Abera, T.; Sikder, A.K.; Miettinen, M.; Aksu, H.; Conti, M.; Sadeghi, A.R.; Uluagac, S. Peek-a-Boo: I See Your Smart Home Activities, Even Encrypted! In Proceedings of the 13th ACM Conference on Security and Privacy in Wireless and Mobile Networks, Linz, Austria, 8 July 2020; ACM: New York, NY, USA, 2020; pp. 207–218.
3. Salman, O.; Elhajj, I.H.; Kayssi, A.; Chehab, A. A Review on Machine Learning Based Approaches for Internet Traffic Classification. *Ann. Telecommun.* **2020**, *75*, 673–710.
4. Alshehri, A.; Granley, J.; Yue, C. Attacking and Protecting Tunneled Traffic of Smart Home Devices. In Proceedings of the Tenth ACM Conference on Data and Application Security and Privacy, New Orleans, LA, USA, 16–18 March 2020; pp. 259–270.
5. Trimananda, R.; Varmarken, J.; Markopoulou, A. Packet-Level Fingerprints for Smart Home Devices. In Proceedings of the 2020 Network and Distributed System Security Symposium, San Diego, CA, USA, 23–26 February 2020; pp. 1084–8045. [CrossRef]
6. Copos, B.; Levitt, K.; Bishop, M.; Rowe, J. Is Anybody Home? Inferring Activity from Smart Home Network Traffic. In Proceedings of the 2016 IEEE Security and Privacy Workshops, San Jose, CA, USA, 22–26 May 2016.
7. Dong, S.; Li, Z.; Tang, D.; Chen, J.; Sun, M.; Zhang, K. Your Smart Home Can't Keep a Secret: Towards Automated Fingerprinting of IoT Traffic with Neural Networks. In Proceedings of the 15th ACM Asia Conference on Computer and Communications Security, Taipei, Taiwan, 5–9 October 2020.
8. Yao, Z.J.; Ge, J.G.; Zhang, X.D.; Zheng, H.B.; Zou, Z.; Sun, K.K.; Xu, Z.H. Research review on traffic obfuscation and its corresponding identification and tracking technologies. *J. Softw.* **2018**, *29*, 3205–3222. (In Chinese)
9. Nicolazzo, S.; Nocera, A.; Ursino, D.; Virgili, L. A privacy-preserving approach to prevent feature disclosure in an IoT scenario. *Future Gener. Comput. Syst.* **2020**, *105*, 502–519. [CrossRef]
10. Corradini, E.; Nicolazzo, S.; Nocera, A.; Ursino, D.; Virgili, L. A two-tier Blockchain framework to increase protection and autonomy of smart objects in the IoT. *Comput. Commun.* **2022**, *181*, 338–356. [CrossRef]
11. Pinheiro, A.J.; Bezerra, J.M.; Campelo, D.R. Packet Padding for Improving Privacy in Consumer IoT. In Proceedings of the 2018 IEEE Symposium on Computers and Communications (ISCC), Natal, Brazil, 25–28 July 2018.
12. Apthorpe, N.; Reisman, D.; Sundaresan, S.; Narayanan, A.; Feamster, N. Spying on the smart home: Privacy attacks and defenses on encrypted iot traffic. *arXiv* **2017**, arXiv:1708.05044.
13. Xiong, S.; Sarwate, A.D.; Mandayam, N.B. Defending against packet-size side-channel attacks in IoT networks. In Proceedings of the 2018 IEEE International Conference on Acoustics, Speech and Signal Processing (ICASSP), Calgary, AB, Canada, 15–20 April 2018; pp. 2027–2031.
14. Pinheiro, A.J.; de Araujo-Filho, P.F.; Bezerra, J.D.M.; Campelo, D.R. Adaptive packet padding approach for smart home networks: A tradeoff between privacy and performance. *IEEE Internet Things J.* **2020**, *8*, 3930–3938.
15. Wang, C.; Kennedy, S.; Li, H.; Hudson, K.; Atluri, G.; Wei, X.; Sun, W.; Wang, B. Fingerprinting encrypted voice traffic on smart speakers with deep learning. In Proceedings of the 13th ACM Conference on Security and Privacy in Wireless and Mobile Networks, Linz, Austria, 8–10 July 2020; pp. 254–265.
16. Prates, N.; Vergütz, A.; Macedo, R.T.; Santos, A.; Nogueira, M. A defense mechanism for timing-based side-channel attacks on IoT traffic. In Proceedings of the GLOBECOM 2020—2020 IEEE Global Communications Conference, Taipei, Taiwan, 7–11 December 2020; pp. 1–6.
17. Ibitoye, O.; Matrawy, A.; Shafiq, M.O. A GAN-based Approach for Mitigating Inference Attacks in Smart Home Environment. *arXiv* **2020**, arXiv:2011.06725.
18. Ranieri, A.; Caputo, D.; Verderame, L.; Merlo, A.; Caviglione, L. Deep adversarial learning on google home devices. *arXiv* **2021**, arXiv:2102.13023.
19. Apthorpe, N.; Reisman, D.; Feamster, N. Closing the blinds: Four strategies for protecting smart home privacy from network observers. *arXiv* **2017**, arXiv:1705.06809.
20. Hafeez, I.; Antikainen, M.; Tarkoma, S. Protecting IoT-environments against traffic analysis attacks with traffic morphing. In Proceedings of the 2019 IEEE International Conference on Pervasive Computing and Communications Workshops (PerCom Workshops), Kyoto, Japan, 11–15 March 2019; pp. 196–201.
21. Zhu, Q.; Yang, C.; Zheng, Y.; Ma, J.; Li, H.; Zhang, J.; Shao, J. Smart home: Keeping privacy based on Air-Padding. *IET Inf. Secur.* **2021**, *15*, 156–168.
22. Xu, Z.; Khan, H.; Muresan, R. TMorph: A Traffic Morphing Framework to Test Network Defenses Against Adversarial Attacks. In Proceedings of the 2022 International Conference on Information Networking (ICOIN), Jeju-si, Republic of Korea, 12–15 January 2022; pp. 18–23.
23. Liu, X.; Zeng, Q.; Du, X.; Valluru, S.L.; Fu, C.; Fu, X.; Luo, B. Sniffmislead: Non-intrusive privacy protection against wireless packet sniffers in smart homes. In Proceedings of the 24th International Symposium on Research in Attacks, Intrusions and Defenses, San Sebastian, Spain, 6–8 October 2021; pp. 33–47.
24. Liu, X.; Zeng, Q.; Du, X.; Valluru, S.L.; Fu, C.; Fu, X.; Luo, B. Privacyguard: Enhancing smart home user privacy. In Proceedings of the 20th International Conference on Information Processing in Sensor Networks (Co-Located with CPS-IoT Week 2021), Nashville, TN, USA, 18–21 May 2021; pp. 62–76.
25. Apthorpe, N.; Reisman, D.; Feamster, N. A smart home is no castle: Privacy vulnerabilities of encrypted iot traffic. *arXiv* **2017**, arXiv:1705.06805.

26. Datta, T.; Apthorpe, N.; Feamster, N. A developer-friendly library for smart home IoT privacy-preserving traffic obfuscation. In Proceedings of the 2018 Workshop on IoT Security and Privacy, Budapest, Hungary, 20 August 2018; pp. 43–48.
27. Dyer, K.P.; Coull, S.E.; Ristenpart, T.; Shrimpton, T. Peek-a-boo, i still see you: Why efficient traffic analysis countermeasures fail. In Proceedings of the 2012 IEEE Symposium on Security and Privacy, San Francisco, CA, USA, 20–23 May 2012; pp. 332–346.
28. Asif, M.; Khan, T.A.; Taleb, N.; Said, R.A.; Siddiqui, S.Y.; Batool, G. A Proposed Architecture for Traffic Monitoring & Control System via LiFi Technology in Smart Homes. In Proceedings of the 2022 International Conference on Business Analytics for Technology and Security (ICBATS), Dubai, United Arab Emirates, 16–17 February 2022; pp. 1–3.
29. Apthorpe, N.; Huang, D.Y.; Reisman, D.; Narayanan, A.; Feamster, N. Keeping the smart home private with smart (er) iot traffic shaping. *Proc. Priv. Enhancing Technol.* **2019**, *2019*, 128–148.
30. Liu, J.; Zhang, C.; Fang, Y. Epic: A differential privacy framework to defend smart homes against internet traffic analysis. *IEEE Internet Things J.* **2018**, *5*, 1206–1217.
31. Jmila, H.; Blanc, G.; Shahid, M.R.; Lazrag, M. A survey of smart home iot device classification using machine learning-based network traffic analysis. *IEEE Access* **2022**, *10*, 97117–97141. [CrossRef]
32. Yoshigoe, K.; Dai, W.; Abramson, M.; Jacobs, A. Overcoming invasion of privacy in smart home environment with synthetic packet injection. In Proceedings of the 2015 TRON Symposium (TROnShOW), Tokyo, Japan, 9–11 December 2015; pp. 1–7.
33. Yoshigoe, K.; Dai, W.; Abramson, M.; Jacobs, A. Anomaly traffic detection and correlation in smart home automation IoT systems. *Trans. Emerg. Telecommun. Technol.* **2022**, *33*, e4053.
34. Uddin, M.; Nadeem, T.; Nukavarapu, S. Extreme SDN Framework for IoT and Mobile Applications Flexible Privacy at the Edge. In Proceedings of the 2019 IEEE International Conference on Pervasive Computing and Communications, Kyoto, Japan, 11–15 March 2019.
35. Hussain, A.M.; Oligeri, G.; Voigt, T. *The Dark (and Bright) Side of IoT: Attacks and Countermeasures for Identifying Smart Home Devices and Services*; Springer: Berlin/Heidelberg, Germany, 2021.

electronics

Article

An APT Event Extraction Method Based on BERT-BiGRU-CRF for APT Attack Detection

Ga Xiang *, Chen Shi and Yangsen Zhang

School of Information Management, Beijing Information Science and Technology University, Beijing 100192, China
* Correspondence: xiangga@bistu.edu.cn

Abstract: Advanced Persistent Threat (APT) seriously threatens a nation's cyberspace security. Current defense technologies are typically unable to detect it effectively since APT attack is complex and the signatures for detection are not clear. To enhance the understanding of APT attacks, in this paper, a novel approach for extracting APT attack events from web texts is proposed. First, the APT event types and event schema are defined. Secondly, an APT attack event extraction dataset in Chinese is constructed. Finally, an APT attack event extraction model based on the BERT-BiGRU-CRF architecture is proposed. Comparative experiments are conducted with ERNIE, BERT, and BERT-BiGRU-CRF models, and the results show that the APT attack event extraction model based on BERT-BiGRU-CRF achieves the highest F1 value, indicating the best extraction performance. Currently, there is seldom APT event extraction research, the work in this paper contributes a new method to Cyber Threat Intelligence (CTI) analysis. By considering the multi-stages, complexity of APT attacks, and the data source from huge credible web texts, the APT event extraction method enhances the understanding of APT attacks and is helpful to improve APT attack detection capabilities.

Keywords: network security; event extraction; deep learning; APT event; BERT-BiGRU-CRF

check for updates

Citation: Xiang, G.; Shi, C.; Zhang, Y. An APT Event Extraction Method Based on BERT-BiGRU-CRF for APT Attack Detection. *Electronics* **2023**, *12*, 3349. https://doi.org/10.3390/electronics12153349

Academic Editor: Myung-Sup Kim

Received: 30 June 2023
Revised: 30 July 2023
Accepted: 2 August 2023
Published: 4 August 2023

1. Introduction

APT refers to the sustained and effective attack activities of an organization against specific objects. It is defined as attackers with complex technologies to create opportunities with rich resources to achieve their own purposes [1]. APT aims to attack infrastructure and steal sensitive intelligence and has a strong national strategic intention so that the network security threat has evolved from a random attack to a purposeful, organized, and premeditated group attack [2]. APT seriously threatens the nation's cyberspace security. In recent years, organized APT attacks continue to occur at a high rate [3]. APT attacks are rampant and frequent, so it is urgent to carry out more research to improve detection and defense technology.

Current APT defense solutions include detection based on APT attack life cycle, big data analysis, and dynamic behavior analysis [4–12]. Unfortunately, current defense technologies are unable to detect an APT attack accurately in time, since APT attacks are highly targeted, have strong concealment, and have a long duration. More work is needed to understand APT attack features for effective detection. Currently, the APT sample data are not sufficient and the features for detection are not clear.

Except for traditional attack detection methods, there is a new direction as CTI has appeared. Threat intelligence information is analyzed and shared to improve detection accuracy, shorten response time, and reduce defense costs. CTI research includes the following: (1) CTI sharing; there are some works on CTI sharing [13–15] whereby researchers have studied the CTI sharing framework and format. (2) CTI analysis; to analyze CTI automatically from huge sources, Information Extraction (IE) attracts researchers' interest naturally.

Knowledge Graphs (KG) and Indicators of Compromise (IOC) are extracted from unstructured CTI texts [16,17]. It should be noted that most CTI research is in English. More CTI research in Chinese is needed.

Regarding CTI analysis research, currently, there is seldom specific CTI research for APT attacks. CTI analysis for APT attacks will bring benefit to understanding APT attack features. This is definitely helpful for APT detection. From the previous investigation, it was observed that many reports and articles on APT-related vulnerabilities, security reports, event analysis, corresponding organizations, and attack alarms are published from authoritative network security technology centers, major manufacturers, research institutions, honker organizations, forums, etc. They are good data sources for APT CTI analysis. At the same time, sometimes organizations are alarmed that they will launch an APT to a specific field or affiliation at a specific time, even with some details described. In addition, the same APT attack sometimes can be launched at different times in different fields. Such important information is worth analyzing carefully to strengthen the APT detection ability. To collect big data and accelerate data analysis, it is imperative to study automatic information exaction methods.

This paper explores a new APT event extraction method based on deep learning with orienting APT Web texts in Chinese. We address the following objectives:

(1) An APT event schema is proposed based on analyzing APT attack stages. Event schemas are different in different fields. For APT events, it needs to define a proper schema to extract effective information.
(2) An APT event dataset in Chinese is constructed to train models. There is no APT event dataset although there are many event datasets. It is necessary to construct a corresponding dataset to train extraction models.
(3) An APT event extraction method based on the BERT-BiGRU CRF model is proposed. This offers numerous advantages, which are helpful for solving the issues of insufficient attack sample data and low detection accuracy.

This research provides a novel CTI analysis method to extract APT events from credible web texts. The current CTI analysis is mainly about KG construction and IOC extraction. There is little CTI analysis of APT event extraction. Event extraction is proper to extract APT attack features, since event types are proper to express different APT attack stages, and rich event arguments are applicable to extract APT attack signatures. At the same time, this paper studies the APT event extraction from Chinese web texts. Most of the existing CIT analysis is in English. In the Chinese language, there is no blank space between words in a sentence. It needs to first cut words. The accuracy of cut words impacts downstream extraction tasks. In addition, Chinese word semantics are richer, and sentence structures are more complex than English ones.

The remainder of this paper is organized as follows: Section 2 describes related works. Section 3 details our proposal for APT event extraction. Section 4 reports the results of our experiments. Finally, the conclusion and discussion are presented in Section 5.

2. Related Works

2.1. APT Attack Detection Method

From the perspective of the APT attack detection method, the traditional solutions mainly focus on three aspects: (1) Detection based on the APT attack lifecycle. Yang [4] proposed a classification frame of APT attack behavior based on phased characteristics to fully understand APT attack behavior. In article [5], it is proposed that a classification and evaluation method of APT attack behavior is based on stage characteristics. (2) Detection based on big data analysis. Fu [6] analyzed four APT attack detection technologies based on big data analysis. Chen [7] analyzed large data processing technologies to solve the real-time restoration and analysis of high-performance network traffic. Wang [8] analyzed data on user access control, data isolation, data integrity, privacy protection, security audit, advanced persistent attack prevention, etc. (3) Detection based on dynamic behavior analysis. Sun [9] applied the method that runs virus samples in the sandbox or virtual machine to analyze the dynamic behavior of the APT virus. Sun [10] proposed a new APT detection model by combining MapReduce and the support vector machine (SVM) algorithm to reduce calculation costs. Eslam [11] studied the dynamic Windows malicious code detection method based on context understanding analysis of API calls. Hamid [12] proposed a method of deep learning for static and dynamic malware detection. Zhang [18] proposed a mathematical backdoor model to summarize all kinds of backdoor attacks.

2.2. CTI Analysis

In addition to the above methods, in recent years CTI research appears which provides a new direction for carrying out the cyber-attack defense. CTI research mainly includes CTI sharing and analysis. CTI sharing studies the sharing format, standard, and framework [13–15,19,20]. As for CTI analysis, there are many types of research based on IE from Nature Language Processing (NLP). IE and textual data mining of open-source intelligence on the Web have become increasingly important topics in cyber security [16]. Liao [21] proposed iACE, a new solution for fully automated IOC extraction to obtain IP, MD5, and other IOC-like strings in the articles. Husari [22] developed automated and context-aware analytics of CTI to accurately learn attack patterns from commonly available CTI sources. Zhu [23] designed a network security knowledge ontology to construct KG from CTI sources. While inconsistencies exist in the constructed KG, Jo [16] studied semantic inconsistencies in finding methods. There is research on IOC extraction, malware KG construction, inconsistency checks, etc. While there is no specific APT-related CTI information extraction.

2.3. Event Extraction

For IE, it includes entity, entity relations, event, and event relation extractions. Event and relation extraction methods include the following: (1) Pattern matching, such as [24–27]. (2) Pattern matching and machine learning combination, such as [28–31]. (3) Deep learning, such as [32–36]. In [37], a tree-based neural network model is proposed to learn syntactic features automatically. The bidirectional recurrent neural networks described in [38] with a joint framework show good extraction performance. At the same time, event extraction data source and application fields are extended. Ritter presented a novel approach for discovering important event categories and classifying extracted events based on latent variable models from Twitter [39]. Lu studied event extraction in question-and-answer tasks and proposed a question–generation model to generate questions [40]. There are some IE works to unify the extraction model. The various IE predictions are unified into a linearized hierarchical expression under a GLM model [41]. There are many event extraction works but few for APT event extraction. Since APT is complex with multiple stages, it is meaningful to apply event extraction technology to describe the stages and features of APT attacks accurately.

To train extraction models, event extraction corpora and datasets are needed. There are many event corpora [42–45] but no APT-related event dataset.

In conclusion, it is interesting to extract APT events from CTI web texts based on deep learning technology. Considering APT defense's existing issues, namely, weak penetration protection, low detection accuracy, difficulty in obtaining evidence of attack range, and unknown new attack response, it is worth studying to extract information from unstructured APT-related texts, which can help understand APT attacks more completely. In this paper, based on current CTI analysis and event extraction technology, an APT event schema is proposed, an APT event dataset is constructed, and an APT event extraction method is proposed based on BERT-BiGRU-CRF.

3. Materials and Methods

The overview of the APT event extraction method is shown in Figure 1.

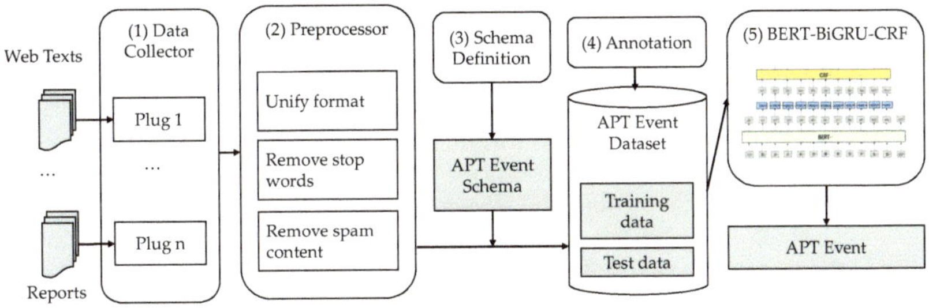

Figure 1. Overview of the APT event extraction.

It consists of a data collector, preprocessor, schema definition, annotation, and extraction model. (1) The data collector collects data from different sources, including web texts and reports. Different plugs are designed to handle multiple data sources. (2) Data are preprocessed to unify format and remove stop words, etc. (3) APT event types and schema are defined. (4) According to the schema, the APT event dataset is constructed for further model training. (5) The BERT-BiGRU-CRF model is trained to extract APT events.

3.1. Data Source and Preprocess

At first, corresponding data are collected and preprocessed. The key point is to find credible data sources for APT texts. As shown in Table 1, they are some credible websites that can provide potential APT information sources.

Table 1. APT information sources.

Types of Web Sites	Detail Information
Authoritative network security technology center	https://www.cert.org.cn/ * https://www.cnvd.org.cn/ * https://cve.mitre.org/ https://nvd.nist.gov/ https://www.cvedetails.com/
Major manufacturers	https://www.oracle.com/security-alerts/ https://msrc.microsoft.com/update-guide/ *
Research institutions	https://www.kaspersky.com.cn/ * https://www.nsfocus.com.cn/ * https://www.qianxin.com/ *
Forum	honker or hacker organizations and forums
APT dataset	https://github.com/cyber-research/APTMalware

Note: The links with * mean that the web texts are in Chinese.

The APT data collector is designed to acquire APT-related vulnerabilities, security reports, event analysis, corresponding organizations, alarms, etc. A distributed webpage crawler system based on the Scrapy framework is designed and implemented. The following rules are considered: (1) A distributed structure is used to improve crawling speed by easily adding hosts. (2) Modularization architecture is used for improved scalability. When adding a new target website, it can focus on creating a specific code for the website's crawling, parsing, and loading rules, while no big change is required for the common module. (3) It shall be easy to deploy. (4) There is real-time monitoring. (5) It has high performance.

Data preprocessing is necessary. It includes the following steps: (1) Remove the html label such as <a, <font, etc. Such labels are filtered and real content is obtained. (2) Download a file if a downloadable file is found. (3) Cut words and remove stop words. A word dictionary and stop word table are built for APT texts. The APT dictionary includes huge

network security words of APT attacks, new APT technologies, related affiliations, addresses, and period reference pronouns. At the same time, a customized stop word table is created for APT attacks. These are intended to improve word cutting accuracy. (4) Remove the spam content, such as advertisements.

The acquisition of APT attack texts mainly adopts crawler technology, using the requests library in Python to request page data from web pages. For example, for the Qi'anxin Threat Intelligence Center, the BeautifulSoup library is used to complete the parsing of page data. After downloading, each article is named with the title of each event, and the content includes the title, time, and description of the APT attack. Afterward, further processing is carried out on the crawled information, such as removing duplicate content. For some websites, an anti-crawler mechanism exists, so a manual copy is used.

3.2. APT Attack Stages and Event Schema

The APT attack has a complex long duration and is hard to detect. There are some existing works that studied the APT stages. In [46], it described an APT attack tree model, including reconnaissance, establishing a foothold, lateral movement, exfiltration or impediment, and post-exfiltration or post-impediment stages. In [47–49], the APT lifecycle is divided into three stages: attack prelude, intrusion implementation, and subsequent attacks.

According to the APT lifecycle, when defining the event schema for APT, it is necessary to consider APT stages. We define the APT event categories, which match the stages. The lifecycle of an APT attack includes three stages, as shown in Figure 2. In different stages, it has different key features or signatures, which can be defined as APT event arguments.

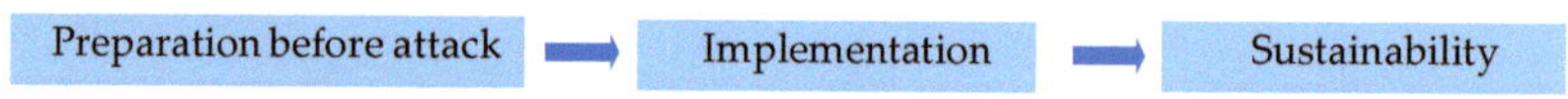

Figure 2. The lifecycle of APT attacks.

In our research, to simplify the problem, we focus on the stages of preparation before attack and implementation. By analyzing the stages, we define the schema: (1) Define two event categories: preparation and implementation. (2) In each category, according to typical APT attack types, we define nine APT event types. (3) For each APT event type, we define the corresponding arguments. The schema of the APT event is defined below in Table 2.

Table 2. APT categories, event types, and arguments.

NO.	Event Category	Event Type	Argument Role1	Argument Role2	Argument Role3	Argument Role4	Argument Role5
1	Preparation	Spear phishing attack	Fake file	True file	Attacker	Target	Attack tactics
2		Water hole attack	Fake file	True file	Attack weapon		
3		Scan	Target				
4		Steal information	Attacker	Target	Stolen target	Attack weapon	
5	Implementation	Trojan	Attacker	Target	Attack weapon	Attack tactics	
6		Worm	Attacker	Target	Attack weapon		
7		Back door	Attacker	Target	Attack weapon		
8		Virus	Attacker	Target	Attack weapon	Attack tactics	
9		Vulnerability exploitation	Attacker	Target	Attack weapon	Attack tactics	

3.3. APT Dataset Construction

At present, there are many event datasets, but unfortunately, there is no existing event dataset for APT events. To train the model, it needs to construct an APT event dataset. Referring to the annotation method of DuEE1.0 (Chinese event extraction dataset) from Baidu released in 2020, we annotated APT event samples of an APT dataset. This annotation method is beneficial to define different event types and the flexibility of the corresponding arguments.

An example template of annotation for a single APT attack event is shown in Figure 3. The annotated events are saved in the data exchange format JSON, which is not only convenient for conversion but also easy to read.

```
{
  "text": " ",
  "event_list": [{
          "event_type":" ",
          "trigger":" ",
          "trigger_start_index": ,
          "arguments":[{
                      "argument_start_index": ,
                      "role":" ",
                      "argument":" ",
                      "alias":[]
           },{
                      "argument_start_index": ,
                      "role":" ",
                      "argument":" ",
                      "alias":[]
        }],
        "class":" "
  },{
          "event_type":" ",
          "trigger":" ",
          "trigger_start_index":,
          "arguments":[ ],
          "class":" "
         }]
}
```

Figure 3. Example template of one APT attack event annotation.

The annotated events are saved in a JSON tree structure. There are many indentations, line breaks, and spaces that take up a lot of space. To save space, we save each annotated event as a single line. Therefore, when annotating events and writing them into a JSON file, the JSON is compressed by setting the attributes (setting the dump() function's indent = 4, separators = (',', ':')). Each line of the generated JSON file is the extraction result of one event, and the new line is another event. As in Figure 4.

```
{"text": "近日，红雨滴团队研究人员对国外厂商披露为海莲花的样本进行了深入
{"text": "近日，红雨滴团队研究人员在日常威胁狩猎中再次捕获到一例针对Linu
{"text": "MuddyWater组织的攻击通常始于向组织发送有针对性的电子邮件，然
{"text": "近日，奇安信威胁情报中心红雨滴在日常的威胁狩猎捕获一起 Donot
{"text": "双尾蝎组织具有Windows和Android双平台攻击武器，且仅Windows平
{"text": "近日，奇安信威胁情报中心在日常样本分析研判中捕获到多个以印度国
{"text": "近日，奇安信红雨滴团队在日常样本狩猎过程中捕获到一批使用了与海
{"text": "近日，奇安信威胁情报中心红雨滴团队在日常的威胁狩猎中捕获了该组
{"text": "奇安信威胁情报中心在日常威胁发现过程中发现一个专门针对贸易行业
{"text": "近日，奇安信威胁情报中心红雨滴团队在日常的威胁狩猎中捕获了该组
{"text": "近日，奇安信威胁情报中心红雨滴在日常的威胁狩猎捕获一起Donot A
{"text": "2021年11月11日，奇安信威胁情报中心红雨滴团队披露了SideCopy组
```

Figure 4. APT attack event dataset.

Finally, the APT event dataset is constructed, resulting in a total of 130 event information types. Although the size is not big, it covers the main APT attack stages, attack types, etc. It is divided into training sets, validation sets, and testing sets in a ratio of 8:1:1.

3.4. APT Attack Event Extraction Based on BERT-BiGRU-CRF

The event extraction tasks for an APT attack include the identification of event types according to the defined APT event type and arguments schema, and the extraction of all related arguments. After our investigation and large experiments, the BERT-BiGRU-CRF model is constructed to extract APT events and shows good performance. The overview of the APT event extraction model based on BERT-BiGRU-CRF is shown in Figure 5 as follows:

(1) BERT layer. At first, the BERT model is applied to pre-train word vectors. The BERT encoding layer is located at the bottom of the model. In the encoding layer, tokens are

segmented from the input of APT texts, and the segmented tokens are transformed into corresponding word vectors by extracting the semantic feature.

(2) BiGRU layer. Secondly, it connects with BiGRU to carry out the APT trigger word and event argument extraction. The pre-trained word vector is fed into the BiGRU layer, which will continue to extract its features and obtain the emission matrix of its sequence. The final output is the predicted label (APT-related trigger word or arguments defined in the schema) corresponding to each word.

(3) CRF layer. The obtained result is then constrained by the CRF layer and its transfer matrix is obtained. Ultimately, the optimal label sequence is output.

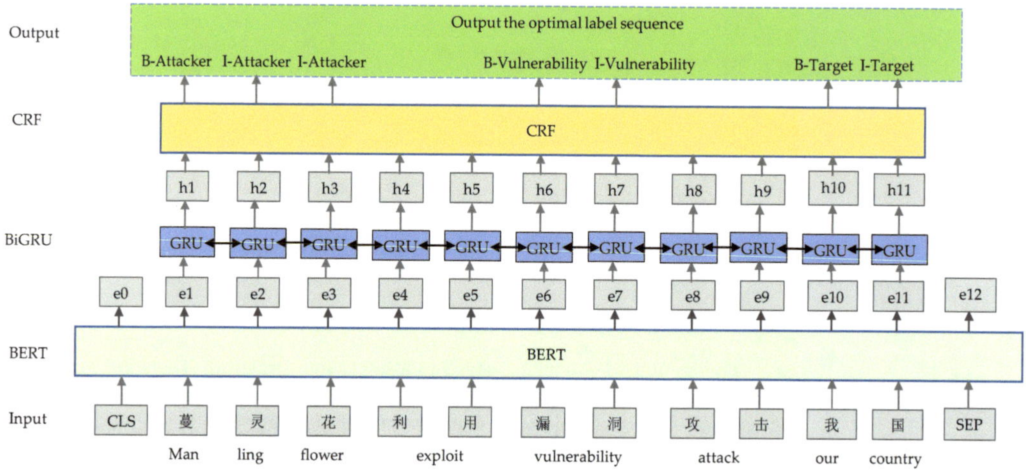

Figure 5. Overview of the APT event extraction model based on BERT-BiGRU-CRF.

3.4.1. BERT Pre-Training Layer

To improve extraction performance, BERT is applied as a pre-training model.

As shown in Figure 6, using the text "蔓灵花利用漏洞 (Manling flower exploits vulnerability)" as an example, the input text is first cut into single Chinese words, and the CLS mark is added at the beginning of the sentence, and the SEP mark is added at the end. Then, through multi-layer transformers, the vectors of word, clause, and position are obtained, and they are integrated together. Finally, it serves as the input vector for the BiGRU layer.

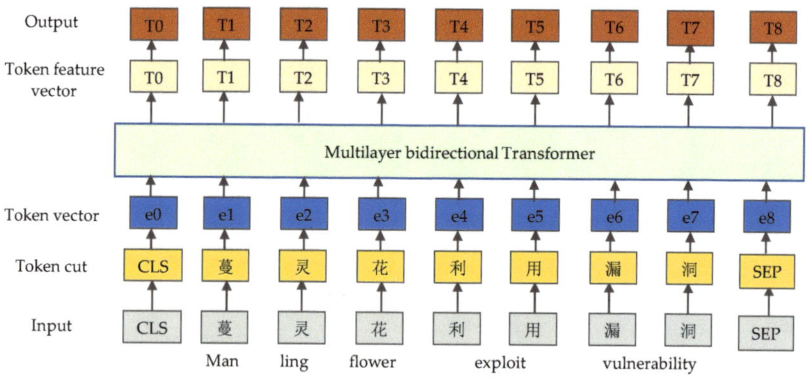

Figure 6. BERT layer structure.

3.4.2. BiGRU Layer

The input of the BiGRU layer is a word vector pre-trained by the BERT layer, and the output is the score of the predicted label corresponding to each word (as shown in Figure 7).

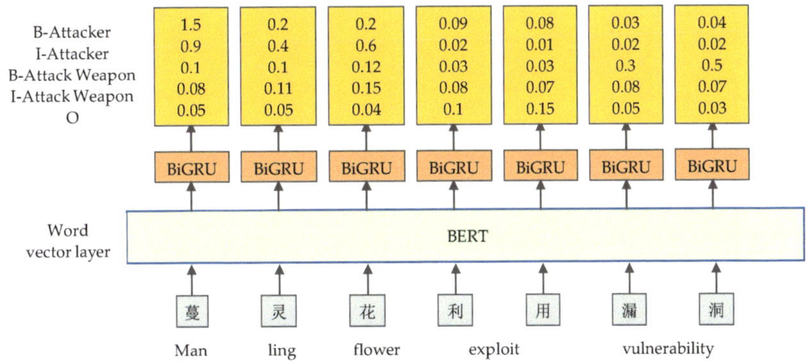

Figure 7. Output of BiGRU layer-1.

The output of the BiGRU layer is also known as the emission matrix. It consists of emission scores. Each score represents the value of each label corresponding to the character. Using the word "蔓 (Man)" as an example, the outputs through the BiGRU level are 1.5 (B-Attacker), 0.9 (I-Attacker), 0.1 (B-Attack Weapon), 0.08 (I-Attack Weapon), and 0.05 (O). These numbers are the scores given to the word "蔓" based on each label. That is, for the word "蔓", its score of the label "B-Attacker" is 1.5 which is the highest one, and the score of the label "I-attacker" is 0.9, and so on. The higher the score, the greater the likelihood of representing this category. The character "蔓" has the highest score in the "B-Attacker" category, so the word "蔓" is temporarily labeled as "B-Attacker". The matrix that combines the emission scores of each word together is called the emission matrix, which will also serve as the input to the CRF layer.

3.4.3. CRF Layer

Even without the CRF layer, we can still train an event extraction model based on BERT-BiGRU, because the BiGRU model provides scores for each label corresponding to each word. We can choose the label with the highest score (marked in red) as the prediction result. For example, if the character "灵 (Ling)" has the highest score of "I-attacker" (0.4), then we can choose "I-attacker" as the prediction result. However, the actual situation may result in the following predicted results (as shown in Figure 8).

The CRF layer can add some constraints to ensure the effectiveness of the final prediction result. The constraints can be automatically learned by the CRF layer during data training. Possible constraints include the following:

(1) The beginning of the sentence should be "B-" or "O", not "I-"; as shown in Figure 8, the sentence cannot start with "I-Attack Weapon".
(2) B-lablel1 I-label2 I-label3… "In this case, categories 1, 2, and 3 should be the same entity category." For example, "B-attacker I-attacker" is correct, while "B-attacker I-attack weapon" is incorrect.
(3) "O I-Attack Weapon" is incorrect, the beginning of the named entity should be "B-" instead of "I-".

With the above useful constraints, erroneous prediction sequences will be greatly reduced. The CRF layer mainly utilizes a transition matrix to ensure these constraints. The transition score is the score transferred from one label to another label, as shown in Table 3.

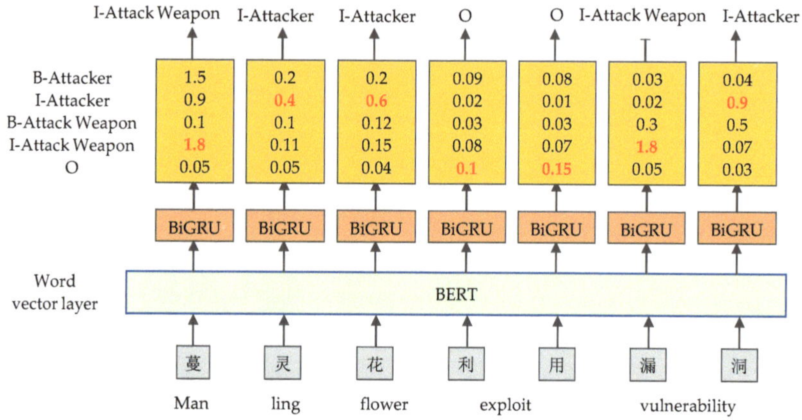

Figure 8. Output of BiGRU Layer-2.

Table 3. Transition matrix.

Transition Matrix	0	B-Attacker	I-Attacker	B-Attack Weapon	I-Attack Weapon
0	0.8	0.07	0	0.12	0
B-Attacker	0	0	1	0	0
I-Attacker	0.18	0	0.85	0	0
B-Attack Weapon	0	0	0	0	1
I-Attack Weapon	1	0	0	0	0

Using the third row and third column in Table 3 as an example, 0.85 represents the score for transitioning from the label "I-Attacker" to the label "I-Attacker".

Finally, combining the emission matrix obtained from the BiGRU layer and the transition matrix obtained from the CRF layer, we can calculate the tag path with the highest score, as shown in Figure 9.

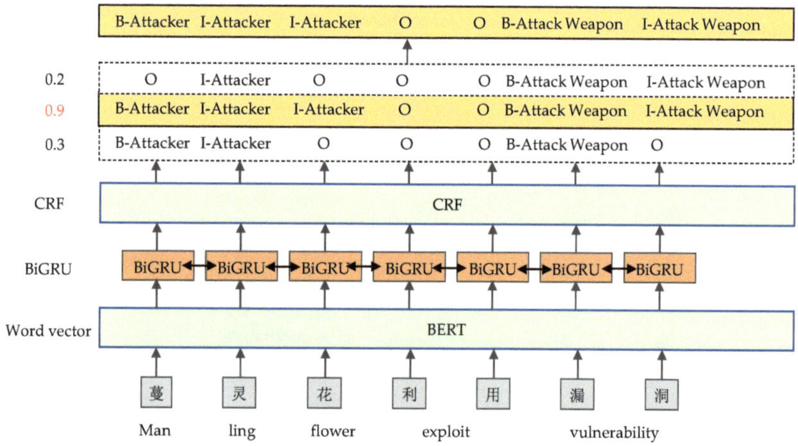

Figure 9. The final output of the BERT-BiGRU-CRF model.

The tag path of "B-Attacker I-Attacker I-Attacker O O B-AttackWeapon I-Attack Weapon" has a score of 0.9 (marked in red), which is the highest score. Therefore, this path is the final output.

4. Experimental Results

4.1. Model Construction and Training

When implementing the models of the APT event extraction described in Section 3, the deep learning framework of Baidu PaddlePaddle is applied. It integrates the functions of model training, inference framework, and basic model library. BERT-BiGRU-CRF models are constructed based on the PaddlePaddle. The specific training parameters are shown in Table 4.

Table 4. Specific training parameters.

Parameter Name	Values
num_epoch(training rounds)	60
learnin_rate(learning_rate)	5×10^{-5}
weight_decay(weight decay)	0.01
warmup_proportion(warmup proportion)	0.1
gru_hidden_size(gru hidden size)	300

4.2. Experimental Results

4.2.1. Comparison with Other Models

The evaluation indicators will use the following three indicators as references:

1. Precision = number of correct predictions with "Positive"/number of predictions with "Positive", mainly focusing on the accuracy of the results predicted by the model. The formula is as shown below:

$$\text{Precision} = \frac{\text{TP}}{\text{TP} + \text{FP}} \tag{1}$$

For TP, FP, etc., the meanings are as shown in Table 5.

2. Recall = number of correctly predicted items with "Positive"/number of manually annotated items with "Positive", mainly focusing on what the model missed. The formula is as shown below:

$$\text{Recall} = \frac{\text{TP}}{\text{TP} + \text{FN}} \tag{2}$$

3. F1 = 2 × Precision × Recall/(Precision + Recall), the formula is calculated as follows:

$$\text{F1} = \frac{2 \times \text{Precision} \times \text{Recall}}{\text{Precision} + \text{Recall}} \tag{3}$$

Table 5. Confusion matrix.

True/False Examples	Prediction	
	Positive	Negative
True	TP	FN
False	FP	TN

We compared several models with BERT-BiGRU-CRF to extract APT events. The results are as shown in Table 6.

From Table 6, for APT trigger word detection, it can be seen that the F1 values are 1.00 for ERNIE and BERT, and 0.9951 for BiGRU-CRF. The F1 values for trigger word extraction are all very high. This is because the trigger words of APT attacks are not huge, or relatively concentrated, so models show high precision and recall performance to identify APT trigger words.

Table 6. Comparison of experimental results.

Model	Trigger Word Detection			APT Event Argument Recognition		
	Precision	Recall	F1	Precision	Recall	F1
ERNIE	**1.00**	**1.00**	**1.00**	0.5859	0.8189	0.6831
BERT	**1.00**	**1.00**	**1.00**	0.5812	0.8813	0.7004
BiGRU-CRF	0.9903	1.00	0.9951	0.5211	**0.8462**	0.6451
BERT-BiGRU-CRF	**1.00**	**1.00**	**1.00**	**0.7013**	0.8011	**0.7479**

The APT event argument recognition is harder than the APT trigger word detection. It can be seen that the F1 value of BERT-BiGRU-CRF is 0.7479, which is better than the F1 values of BERT (0.7004) and BiGRU-CRF (0.6451). From Table 6, without BERT as a pre-training model, the final extraction F1 value can be seen as lower by about 10% than our proposed model.

From our experiment, it is found that pre-training improves the final extraction performance for APT events. ERNIE and BERT can both be used as the pre-training model. For our APT event extraction, BERT pre-training shows better performance. Therefore, we ultimately used the BERT model for the pre-training of word vectors, and then connected it to the BiGRU-CRF model.

Firstly, we applied BERT as a pre-training model. The BERT model can effectively learn the underlying information of the sequence, and if the data volume is small, it is also recommended to pre-train word vectors.

Secondly, it connected with the BiGRU model, which learned the sequence information well, resulting in better learning of the APT semantics. The BiGRU model can effectively solve the problem of long sentences, enabling better learning of deep semantics, and ultimately using the CRF model for constraints.

At last, we applied CRF to carry out constraints to improve accuracy.

In summary, for APT attack events, according to the experimental results, the BERT-BiGRU-CRF model has the best extraction effect and the highest event extraction efficiency.

4.2.2. Performance Analysis of BERT-BiGRU-CRF Model for APT Attack Event Extraction

For the BERT-BiGRU-CRF model, during training for APT attack event extraction, the corresponding F1 values are shown in Figure 10, showing the F1 change trend during the training process.

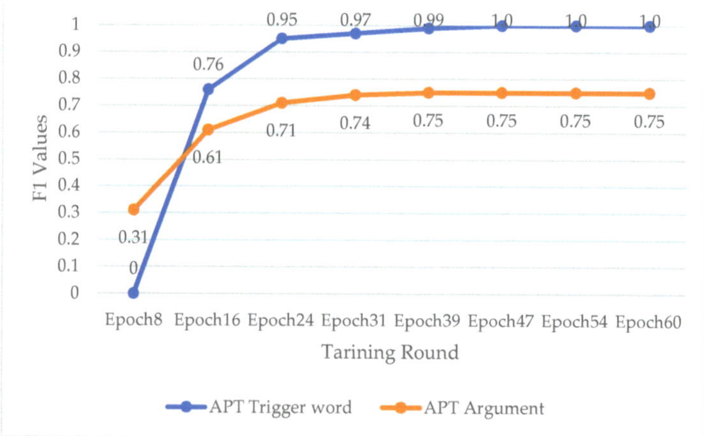

Figure 10. F1 values of BERT-BiGRU-CRF training.

As shown in Figure 10, the F1 value of the trigger words significantly increased at Epoch16, reaching a peak of 1.0 at Epoch16. The argument character also showed a significant increase in F1 value at Epoch16, ultimately reaching a peak of 0.75 at Epoch39.

4.2.3. Case Study

After the model training is finished, it can be used to carry out event extraction. The process of APT extraction is shown in Figure 11.

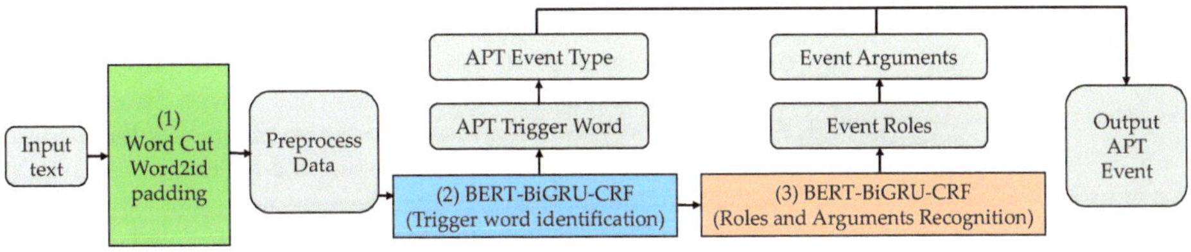

Figure 11. APT event extraction based on BERT-BiGRU-CRF model.

Using a case for example, the input text is as follows:
"南亚次大陆地区的响尾蛇组织被发现利用CVE-2019-2215漏洞针对安卓终端目标用户实施移动端的APT攻击。" (Translation: it is found that the Rattlesnake organization in the subcontinent of South Asia implemented mobile APT attacks against target users of Android terminal exploiting the CVE-2019 2215 vulnerability.)

(1) The input data were preprocessed including word cut, word2id, long text cut, and short text padding.
(2) The preprocessed data were input to the first BERT-BiGRU-CRF model to extract the trigger word. In this case, the trigger word is "漏洞利用" ("exploit vulnerability"), and the corresponding event type is "攻击实施-漏洞利用" ("Attack implementation-Vulnerability exploitation").
(3) According to the APT event type, the event roles are decided. Data are input to the second BERT-BiGRU-CRF model to extract the corresponding arguments.

All the outputs are merged to generate the final APT event for this text, as shown below:

event0–event_type: 攻击实施-漏洞利用 (attack implementation–vulnerability exploitation), trigger: 漏洞利用 (exploit vulnerability)

role_type: 攻击者 (Attacker), argument: 响尾蛇组织 (Rattlesnake organization)

role_type: 攻击武器 (Attack weapon), argument: CVE-2019 2215漏洞 (vulnerability)

role_type: 受害目标 (Target), argument: 安卓终端目标用户 (target users of Android terminal).

5. Conclusions and Discussion

This paper defines APT event types and templates, constructs an APT attack event extraction dataset, and builds an APT attack event extraction model based on BERT-BiGRU-CRF. Through comparative experiments with ERNIE, BERT, and BiGRU-CRF models, it was found that the APT attack event extraction model based on BERT-BiGRU-CRF had the highest F1 value, with an F1 value of 1.00 for trigger word extraction and 0.75 for argument role extraction, indicating the best extraction effect. This model first uses the BERT model to pre-train word vectors, then connects the BiGRU model for feature extraction, and then connects the CRF model for constraints, ultimately completing event extraction.

Considering there is little APT event extraction research, the work in this paper is a valuable contribution to CTI analysis and APT detection. It proposes a novel CTI analysis method by extracting APT events from Chinese web texts. During the APT event schema design, it considers the APT multi-stages and complexity, which is good for deeply understanding APT attacks. This is beneficial to improve APT attack detection ability.

There is a limitation to this research. For dataset construction, although there are some event datasets, unfortunately, there is no APT event dataset. During the research, we constructed the APT attack event dataset. The annotation cost is not low. Limited by the annotation resources, the annotation dataset is not big. This causes the following: (1) Event type numbers are not balanced. For example, much threat intelligence started with the spear-phishing attack as the starting point, the constructed dataset has a high proportion of "Attack preparation" and "Spear-phishing attack" events. (2) The trigger words related to APT are not completely included, indirectly resulting in some complex APT attack event information not being able to be extracted well.

Although the extraction method is effective, the potential weak point is that the model is a pipeline model, which separates trigger word extraction from argument role extraction. For APT attack events, there is some correlation between trigger words and argument roles, so using a joint extraction model may be worth studying further.

To remove the limitation and weak point, the next steps include the following: (1) Expand the data sources, obtain more unstructured information related to APT attack events on multiple websites, and make the constructed dataset contain complete event types and APT-related trigger words. (2) Consider applying the few-shot learning method to mitigate the data sparse issue. (3) Improve the use of a joint model for extraction.

Author Contributions: Conceptualization, G.X.; funding acquisition, G.X. and Y.Z.; methodology, G.X. and C.S.; software, C.S.; validation, G.X. and C.S.; writing—original draft, G.X. and C.S.; writing—review and editing, Y.Z. All authors have read and agreed to the published version of the manuscript.

Funding: This research was funded by the R&D Program of Beijing Municipal Education Commission, grant number KM202311232014, and the National Natural Science Foundation of China, grant number 62176023.

Conflicts of Interest: The authors declare that there is no conflict of interest regarding the publication of this paper.

References

1. National Institute of Standards and Technology. *SP800—53 Managing Information Security Risks*; National Institute of Standards and Technology: Gaithersburg, MD, USA, 2013.
2. Zhang, Y.; Pan, X.; Liu, Q.; Cao, J.; Luo, Z. APT attacks and defenses. *J. Tsinghua Univ. (Sci. Technol.)* **2017**, *57*, 1127–1133.
3. Chinese CNCERT. 2020 China Cybersecurity Analysis, [EB/OL]. (2021-5-26) [2021-6-4]. Available online: https://www.cert.org.cn/publish/main/upload/File/2020%20CNCERT%20Cybersecurity%20Analysis.pdf (accessed on 1 May 2023).
4. Yang, H. Research on APT Attack of Behavior Analyzing and Defense Decision. Master's Thesis, Information Engineering University, Zhengzhou, China, 2017.
5. Yang, H.; Wang, K. Phase-based classification and evaluation of APT attack behaviors. *Comput. Eng. Appl.* **2017**, *53*, 97–104, 234.
6. Fu, Y.; Li, H.; Wu, X.; Wang, J. Detecting APT attacks: A survey from the perspective of big data analysis. *J. Commun.* **2015**, *36*, 1–14.
7. Chen, X.; Zeng, X.; Wang, W.; Shao, G. Big Data Analytics for Network Security and Intelligence. *Adv. Eng. Sci.* **2017**, *39*, 112–129.
8. Wang, D.; Zhao, W.; Ding, Z. Review of Big Data Security Critical Technologies. *J. Beijing Univ. Technol.* **2017**, *43*, 335–349.
9. Sun, L. Research on Key Technology of APT Detection Based on Malicious Domain Name. Master's Thesis, Harbin Engineering University, Harbin, China, 2017.
10. Sun, J.; Wang, C. Research on APT attack detection based on behavior analysis. *Electron. Des. Eng.* **2019**, *27*, 142–146.
11. Eslam, A.; Ivan, Z. A dynamic Windows malware detection and prediction method based on contextual understanding of API call sequence. *Comput. Secur.* **2020**, *92*, 101760. [CrossRef]
12. Hamid, D.; Sajad, H.; Ali, D.; Sattar, H.; Hadis, K.; Reza, P.; Raymond, C. Detecting Cryptomining Malware: A Deep Learning Approach for Static and Dynamic Analysis. *J. Grid Comput.* **2020**, *18*, 293–303. [CrossRef]
13. Yang, P.; Wu, Y.; Su, L.; Liu, B. Overview of Threat Intelligence Sharing Technologies in Cyberspace. *Comput. Sci.* **2018**, *45*, 9–18, 26.
14. Ramsdale, A.; Shiaeles, S.; Kolokotronis, N. A Comparative Analysis of Cyber-Threat Intelligence Sources, Formats and Languages. *Electronics* **2020**, *9*, 824. [CrossRef]
15. Lin, Y.; Liu, P.; Wang, H.; Wang, W.; Zhang, Y. Overview of Threat Intelligence Sharing and Exchange in Cybersecurity. *J. Comput. Res. Dev.* **2020**, *57*, 2052–2065.

16. Jo, H.; Kim, J.; Porras, P.; Yegneswaran, V.; Shin, S. GapFinder: Finding Inconsistency of Security Information from Unstructured Text. *IEEE Trans. Inf. Forensics Secur.* **2021**, *16*, 86–99. [CrossRef]
17. Christian, R.; Dutta, S.; Park, Y.; Rastogi, N. An Ontology-driven Knowledge Graph for Android Malware. In Proceedings of the 2021 ACM SIGSAC Conference on Computer and Communications Security, Virtual, 15–19 November 2021; pp. 2435–2437.
18. Zhang, Q.; Ma, W.; Wang, Y.; Zhang, Y.; Shi, Z.; Li, Y. Backdoor Attacks on Image Classification Models in Deep Neural Networks. *Chin. J. Electron.* **2022**, *31*, 199–212. [CrossRef]
19. Li, Y.; He, J.; Li, J.; Yu, Y.; Tan, F. US Cyber Threat Intelligence Sharing Technology Analysis of Framework and Standards. *Secrecy Sci. Technol.* **2016**, *6*, 16–21.
20. Wagner, T.; Mahbub, K.; Palomar, E.; Abdallah, A. Cyber threat intelligence sharing: Survey and research directions. *Comput. Secur.* **2019**, *87*, 10158. [CrossRef]
21. Liao, X.; Yuan, K.; Wang, X.; Li, Z.; Xing, L.; Beyah, R. Acing the IOC game: Toward automatic discovery and analysis of open-source cyber threat intelligence. In Proceedings of the 2016 ACM SIGSAC Conference on Computer and Communications Security, Vienna, Austria, 24–28 October 2016; pp. 755–766.
22. Husari, G.; Al-Shaer, E.; Ahmed, M.; Chu, B.; Niu, X. TTPDrill: Automatic and accurate extraction of threat actions from unstructured text of CTI sources. In Proceedings of the 33rd Annual Computer Security Applications Conference, Orlando, FL, USA, 4–8 December 2017; pp. 103–115.
23. Shang, W.; Zhu, P.; Wang, B.; Cao, Z.; Zhang, M. Key Technologies for Building Knowledge Graphs for Threat Intelligence. *Autom. Panor.* **2023**, *40*, 15–19.
24. Khoo, C.S.; Kornfilt, J.; Oddy, R.N.; Myaeng, S.H. Automatic extraction of cause-effect information from newspaper text without knowledge-based inferencing. *Lit. Linguist. Comput.* **1998**, *13*, 177–186. [CrossRef]
25. Khoo, C.S.; Chan, S.; Niu, Y. Extracting causal knowledge from a medical database using graphical patterns. In Proceedings of the 38th Annual Meeting of the Association for Computational Linguistics, Hong Kong, China, 1–8 October 2000; pp. 336–343.
26. Hashimoto, C.; Torisawa, K.; De Saeger, S.; Oh, J.H. Excitatory or inhibitory: A new semantic orientation extracts contradiction and causality from the web. In Proceedings of the 2012 Joint Conference on Empirical Methods in Natural Language Processing and Computational Natural Language Learning, Jeju, Korea, 12–14 July 2012; pp. 619–630.
27. Sadek, J.; Meziane, F. Extracting Arabic Causal Relations Using Linguistic Patterns. *ACM Trans. Asian Lang. Inf. Process.* **2016**, *15*, 14. [CrossRef]
28. Girju, R. Automatic detection of causal relations for question answering. In Proceedings of the ACL 2003 workshop on Multilingual Summarization and Question Answering, Sapporo, Japan, 11–12 July 2003; pp. 76–83.
29. Blanco, E.; Castell, N.; Moldovan, D. Causal relation extraction. In Proceedings of the Sixth International Conference on Language Resources and Evaluation, Marrakech, Morocco, 26 May–1 June 2008.
30. Wang, H.; Shi, Y.; Zhou, X.; Zhou, Q.; Shao, S.; Bouguettaya, A. Web service classification using support vector machine. In Proceedings of the 2010 22nd IEEE International Conference on Tools with Artificial Intelligence, Arras, France, 27–29 October 2010; Volume 1, pp. 3–6.
31. Zhao, S.; Liu, T.; Zhao, S.; Chen, Y.; Nie, J.Y. Event causality extraction based on connectives analysis. *Neurocomputing* **2016**, *173*, 1943–1950. [CrossRef]
32. De Silva, T.N.; Zhibo, X.; Rui, Z.; Kezhi, M. Causal relation identification using convolutional neural networks and knowledge based features. *Int. J. Comput. Syst. Eng.* **2017**, *11*, 696–701.
33. Jin, G.; Zhou, J.; Qu, W.; Long, Y.; Gu, Y. Exploiting Rich Event Representation to Improve Event Causality Recognition. *Intell. Autom. Soft Comput.* **2021**, *30*, 161–173. [CrossRef]
34. Gao, J.; Luo, X.; Wang, H. Chinese causal event extraction using causality-associated graph neural network. *Concurr. Comput. Pract. Exp.* **2022**, *34*, e6572. [CrossRef]
35. Xu, J.; Zuo, W.; Liang, S.; Wang, Y. Causal Relation Extraction Based on Graph Attention Networks. *J. Comput. Res. Dev.* **2020**, *57*, 16.
36. Tan, Y.; Peng, H.; Qin, J.; Xue, Y. Chinese causality analysis based on weight calculation. *J. Huazhong Univ. Sci. Technol. (Nat. Sci. Ed.)* **2022**, *50*, 112–117. [CrossRef]
37. Fei, H.; Ren, Y.; Ji, D. A tree-based neural network model for biomedical event trigger detection. *Inf. Sci.* **2020**, *512*, 175–185. [CrossRef]
38. Nguyen, T.; Cho, K.; Grishman, R. Joint event extraction via recurrent neural networks. In Proceedings of the 2016 Conference of the North American Chapter of the Association for Computational Linguistics: Human Language Technologies, San Diego, CA, USA, 12–17 June 2016; pp. 300–309.
39. Ritter, A.; Mausam; Etzioni, O.W.; Clark, S. Open domain event extraction from twitter. In Proceedings of the 18th ACM SIGKDD International Conference on Knowledge Discovery and Data Mining, Beijing, China, 12–16 August 2012; pp. 1104–1112.
40. Lu, D.; Ran, S.; Tetreault, J.; Jaimes, A. Event Extraction as Question Generation and Answering. *arXiv* **2023**, arXiv:2307.05567.
41. Fei, H.; Wu, S.; Li, J.; Li, B.; Li, F.; Qin, L.; Zhang, M.; Zhang, M.; Chua, T. Lasuie: Unifying information extraction with latent adaptive structure-aware generative language model. *Adv. Neural Inf. Process. Syst.* **2022**, *35*, 15460–15475.
42. Pustejovsky, J.; Hanks, P.; Sauri, R.; See, A.; Gaizauskas, R.; Setzer, A.; Radev, D.; Sundheim, B.; Day, D.; Ferro, L. The timebank corpus. *Corpus Linguist.* **2003**, *2003*, 40.

43. Doddington, G.R.; Mitchell, A.; Przybocki, M.A.; Ramshaw, L.A.; Strassel, S.; Weischedel, R.M. The Automatic Content Extraction (ACE) Program-Tasks, Data, and Evaluation. *LREC* **2004**, *2*, 837–840.
44. Wang, X. Event-Oriented Text Knowledge Discovery and Representation. Ph.D. Thesis, Shanghai University, Shanghai, China, 2017. Available online: https://kns.cnki.net/KCMS/detail/detail.aspx?dbname=CDFD0911&filename=2010252946.nh (accessed on 15 May 2023).
45. Mariko, D.; Akl, H.A.; Labidurie, E.; Mazancourt, H.; El-Haj, M. Financial document causality detection shared task. *arXiv* **2020**, arXiv:2012.02505.
46. Drury, B.; Gonçalo Oliveira, H.; De Andrade Lopes, A. A survey of the extraction and applications of causal relations. *Nat. Lang. Eng.* **2020**, *28*, 361–400. [CrossRef]
47. Alshamrani, A.; Myneni, S.; Chowdhary, A.; Huang, D. A survey on advanced persistent threats: Techniques, solutions, challenges, and research opportunities. *IEEE Commun. Surv. Tutor.* **2019**, *21*, 1851–1877. [CrossRef]
48. Auty, M. Anatomy of an advanced persistent threat. *Netw. Secur.* **2015**, *2015*, 13–16. [CrossRef]
49. Chen, P.; Desmet, L.; Huygens, C. A study on advanced persistent threats. In *Lecture Notes in Computer Science*; Springer: Berlin/Heidelberg, Germany, 2014; Volume 8735, pp. 63–72. [CrossRef]

electronics

MDPI

Article

DB-YOLOv5: A UAV Object Detection Model Based on Dual Backbone Network for Security Surveillance

Yuzhao Liu [1], Wan Li [1,*], Li Tan [1,2], Xiaokai Huang [1], Hongtao Zhang [1] and Xujie Jiang [1]

[1] School of Computer Science and Engineering, Beijing Technology and Business University, Beijing 100048, China; jsjlyz21@st.btbu.edu.cn (Y.L.); tanli@th.btbu.edu.cn (L.T.); huangxk@st.btbu.edu.cn (X.H.); zhanghongtao@st.btbu.edu.cn (H.Z.); myishailong@gmail.com (X.J.)

[2] Chongqing Institute of Microelectronics Industry Technology, University of Electronic Science and Technology of China, Chongqing 400031, China

* Correspondence: wanli@btbu.edu.cn

Abstract: Unmanned aerial vehicle (UAV) object detection technology is widely used in security surveillance applications, allowing for real-time collection and analysis of image data from camera equipment carried by a UAV to determine the category and location of all targets in the collected images. However, small-scale targets can be difficult to detect and can compromise the effectiveness of security surveillance. In this work, we propose a novel dual-backbone network detection method (DB-YOLOv5) that uses multiple composite backbone networks to enhance the extraction capability of small-scale targets' features and improve the accuracy of the object detection model. We introduce a bi-directional feature pyramid network for multi-scale feature learning and a spatial pyramidal attention mechanism to enhance the network's ability to detect small-scale targets during the object detection process. Experimental results on the challenging UAV aerial photography dataset VisDrone-DET demonstrate the effectiveness of our proposed method, with a 3% improvement over the benchmark model. Our approach can enhance security surveillance in UAV object detection, providing a valuable tool for monitoring and protecting critical infrastructure.

Keywords: object detection; UAV; security surveillance; feature pyramid network; attention mechanism

check for updates

Citation: Liu, Y.; Li, W.; Tan, L.; Huang, X.; Zhang, H.; Jiang, X. DB-YOLOv5: A UAV Object Detection Model Based on Dual Backbone Network for Security Surveillance. *Electronics* **2023**, *12*, 3296. https://doi.org/10.3390/electronics12153296

Academic Editors: Yu-an Tan, Qikun Zhang, Yuanzhang Li and Xiao Yu

Received: 28 June 2023
Revised: 28 July 2023
Accepted: 29 July 2023
Published: 31 July 2023

1. Introduction

The use of drones for remotely detecting and tracking persons or vehicles has become increasingly prevalent in the field of security surveillance, particularly in urban areas. However, the widespread use of drones also raises concerns about network security and privacy. Due to their small size and limited power supply performance, UAVs have low computing power, which poses significant challenges for accurate object detection tasks [1]. In 2012, the introduction of the deep convolutional neural network (CNN) by Krizhevsky et al. [2] revolutionized the field of computer vision, leading to the development of more efficient and accurate object detection models, such as the RCNN model proposed by Girshick et al. [3] in 2015. Since then, deep learning-based object detection technology has undergone rapid development, providing significant potential for enhancing security surveillance capabilities while also requiring careful consideration of network security and privacy concerns. Recent studies such as [4] have focused on developing AI-driven solutions to address network security and privacy challenges in the context of UAV object detection.

Currently, object detection methods based on deep learning can be mainly divided into two-stage and one-stage categories. Among them, the two-stage method is based on target candidate regions for detection. This method extracts candidate regions and performs deep learning on the corresponding regions, which has high classification accuracy of detection results. This type of algorithm mainly includes a series of methods such as RCNN [3], Fast R-CNN [5], Faster R-CNN [6], R-FCN [7], CoupleNet [8], Mask RCNN [9], Cascade

RCNN [10], Libra R-CNN [11], Reasoning-RCNN [12], EfficientDet [13], D2Det [14], De-Feat [15], MViTv2 [16], and AdaMixer [17]. Otherwise, the one-stage method can directly calculate the category probability and position coordinate value of the object through regression, including SSD [18], DSSD [19], FSSD [20], ScratchDet [21], ExtremeNet [22], MimicDet [23], I3Net [24], SaFT [25], CapDet [26], YOLO [27], YOLOv2 [28], YOLOv3 [29], YOLOv4 [30], YOLOv5, YOLOx [31], YOLOF [32], YOLOv6 [33], YOLOv7 [34], YOLOv8, and other methods. The detection result is directly obtained after single detection, which greatly improves the speed of the model. For example, the YOLOv5 model improves the accuracy and speed of YOLOv4. The training phase of the model includes improvements such as mosaic data enhancement, adaptive image scaling, and adaptive anchor box calculation.

With the successive birth of various object detection models with superior performance and improved experimental results on the MS COCO dataset, object detection for UAV has also attracted increasing attention as an important computer vision task. UAV object detection plays an important role in understanding long-range images. Unlike general object detection, the aerial photography angles of UAVs all look down, which leads to a small scale and many targets in the image. Therefore, object detection models that are suitable for general data sets cannot achieve high robustness in UAV aerial photography. As shown in Figure 1, when the YOLOv5 model for object detection is employed in the VisDrone UAV dataset, pedestrian targets with small scales are more likely to be missed compared to vehicle targets with larger scales, which leads to weak generalization ability of the UAV object detection model.

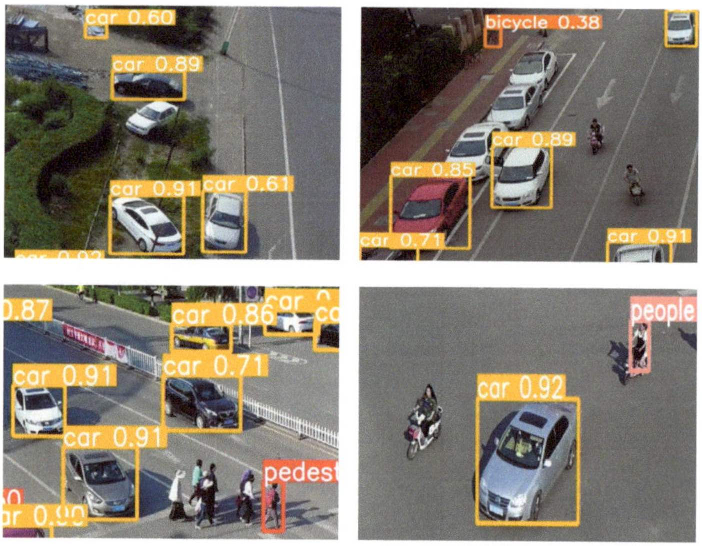

Figure 1. After the YOLOv5 model performs object detection on the VisDrone dataset, there is a phenomenon of both missed detection and false positives. The figure shows the detected targets marked with positioning boxes of different colors, but many vehicles and pedestrians are still not detected or are incorrectly identified.

In general, small-scale targets can be defined as the size range of objects in an image that are smaller than the minimum detectable size threshold of the object detection model. One way to define this threshold is to use the concept of object coverage ratio, which refers to the proportion of the image area covered by an object. For example, a commonly used threshold for object detection is 0.005, which means that an object must occupy at least 0.5% of the image area to be detected by the model. In this case, too-small scales would refer to objects that are smaller than the minimum size required to achieve an object coverage ratio of 0.005.

Based on the above discussion, our paper proposes a DB-YOLOv5 object detection model that is suitable for UAV, aiming at the problem of too-small targets in UAV. The model adopts a composite backbone network, which connects multiple identical backbone networks in a composite manner and fuses high-level and low-level features of multiple backbone, which expands the receptive field of the network. The bi-directional feature pyramid network structure is also introduced in the feature extraction stage, which can fuse multi-scale features conveniently, quickly, and effectively to improve the detection accuracy of small-scale targets. The spatial pyramid attention mechanism is used in the output stage, which can maintain the feature representation and spatial location information of the target and further strengthen the ability to identify and locate small targets. Finally, EIoU_loss is used to further optimize the bounding box of the small-scale target to improve the bounding box problem in small target detection.

The main contributions of this paper are as follows:

1. The dual-backbone network model DB-YOLOv5 is proposed. Aiming at the problem of missed and false detection of small targets in UAV images, the model integrates the high-level and low-level features of multiple identical backbone networks to expand the receptive field of the network for small target features.
2. The model uses a bi-directional feature pyramid network, which fuses multi-scale features through the bottom-up and top-down approaches to strengthen the network's multi-scale feature fusion for small targets.
3. The spatial pyramid attention mechanism enables the model to maintain both the feature information and the location information of small targets, which strengthens their identification and positioning.

The remainder of this paper is organized as follows. Section 2 presents the related work. Section 3 details the proposed method. The experiments and results analyses are provided in Section 4 while introducing the selected dataset and evaluation indicators. Finally, conclusions are drawn in Section 5.

2. Related Work

With the increasing demand for security surveillance, object detection models are being used more frequently in aerial remote sensing to detect potential security threats. However, one of the major challenges in this field is detecting small targets in aerial images. To address this problem, researchers have proposed various multi-angle improvements to different general object detection models with the aim of enhancing the robustness and generalization ability of the detection models for aerial photography datasets in the context of network security and privacy. For example, Cheng et al. [35] proposed a concept of coarse-grained density maps for the problem of dense small objects and uneven distribution in aerial remote sensing images and designed a density map-based clustering region generation algorithm. They improved the Mosaic data augmentation method to divide the image into multiple sub-regions so that dense small objects could be adjusted to a reasonable scale. This method improved the detection performance of rare objects and difficult samples and alleviated the foreground–background and class imbalances. Huang et al. [36] designed a unified foreground assembly and multi-agent detection network for the problem of dense small targets and target shape similarity in aerial images. The method combines the subregions provided by the coarse detector to suppress the background by clustering, and this method then assembles the resulting subregions into mosaics for a single inference. The method models the object distribution in a fine-grained manner by using multi-agent learning, thereby significantly reducing the overall time cost and improving the efficiency and accuracy of detection. Wang et al. [37] proposed a model based on multiple center points to solve the problem of small target detection in images. The method first located multiple center points and then estimated the offset and scale of multiple corresponding targets, which can improve the detection performance of small targets. Xu et al. [38] aimed at the detection of small targets in aerial images and believed that IoU, as the most commonly used indicator in object detection tasks, was not suitable for small targets. They proposed a simple and effective dot distance method, which was defined as the normalized Euclidean distance between the center points of the two bounding boxes. This method was suitable for small target detection and achieved better detection performance. Tan et al. [39] proposed the YOLOv4_Drone method based on YOLOv4, aiming at the problems of small targets, complex background, and mutual occlusions of targets in UAV images. This method employed the concept of hole convolution. It introduced an ultra-lightweight subspace attention mechanism and soft-nms to resample the same feature map, which implemented multi-scale feature representation, to solve the problem of missed detection caused by adjacent or even occluded targets captured by drones. In order to improve the precision of UAV object detection while satisfying the lightweight feature, Yang et al. [40] modified the YOLOv5s model. To address the small object detection problem, a prediction head is added to better retain small object feature information. The CBAM attention module is also integrated to better find attention regions in dense scenes. The original IOU-NMS is replaced by NWD-NMS in post-processing to alleviate the sensitivity of IOU to small objects.

Although the above algorithms have carried out various studies and explorations on the problem of small targets in UAV images, the proposed models still cannot obtain real-time and efficient detection results of small targets in practical UAV applications. Therefore, based on the YOLOv5 algorithm, this paper introduces a composite backbone network, a bidirectional feature pyramid network structure, and a spatial pyramid attention mechanism and proposes the UAV image object detection model DB-YOLOv5.

The YOLOv5 model has excellent speed and accuracy in the detection algorithm due to using the CSPDarknet53 backbone network to extract features. The CSPDarknet53 is based on the Darknet53 in YOLOv3, which combines the CSPNet [41] to develop the backbone structure. This network contains five CSP modules, which are composed of convolution kernels with a size of 3×3 and a stride of 2, so it can play a role in downsampling. Thus, the model adopts the CSPDarknet53 backbone network, which can enhance the feature learning ability of network, maintain the model accuracy while remaining lightweight, and reduce the computational cost of the model. In addition, the input of the model adopts the mosaic method for data enhancement, which splices four pictures through random scaling, cropping, and arrangement. This method is highly effective for small target detection. In the Neck stage of YOLOv5, the PANet [42] structure of FPN + PAN [43] is adopted, with which the model can strengthen the multi-scale feature fusion ability, accurately save the location information of small targets, and contribute to locating the target correctly. Although the DB-YOLOv5 model focuses on improving object detection in low-altitude aerial images, there are also several studies addressing other challenges in video surveillance. Sun et al. [44] proposed a dynamic partial-parallel data layout (DPPDL) for green video surveillance storage, which aims to reduce energy consumption and improve storage efficiency. Similarly, Yu et al. [45] introduced an extra-parity energy-saving data layout for video surveillance, which reduces energy consumption and optimizes storage utilization. These studies demonstrate the importance of developing efficient and sustainable solutions for video surveillance, which can have significant implications for various applications, such as security and public safety. Zhang et al. [46] conducted research on backdoor attacks on deep neural network models used in image classification. They analyzed the impact of these attacks on classification accuracy and proposed a defense mechanism to mitigate them. This study emphasizes the importance of developing secure and robust deep neural network models for reliable image classification.

In low-altitude aerial images, the visual information contained in tiny targets is limited by the condition of looking down, which results in significant difficulties in aerial target detection. Therefore, improving the detection performance of small and ambiguous targets and reducing the occurrence of missed and false detections is an urgent problem for UAV image object detection. This paper is dedicated to providing an effective solution to this purpose, namely, the UAV image object detection model DB-YOLOv5.

3. Methods

3.1. Overall Structure

The DB-YOLOv5, which the UAV object detection model proposed, improves the capabilities of feature extraction and fusion by introducing a composite backbone network, a bidirectional feature pyramid network, and a spatial pyramid attention mechanism. The problem of false and missed detection because the scale of targets in the UAV environment is too small can be solved by this model. Thus, the model can improve the accuracy of small targets. The structure of DB-YOLOv5 is shown in Figure 2.

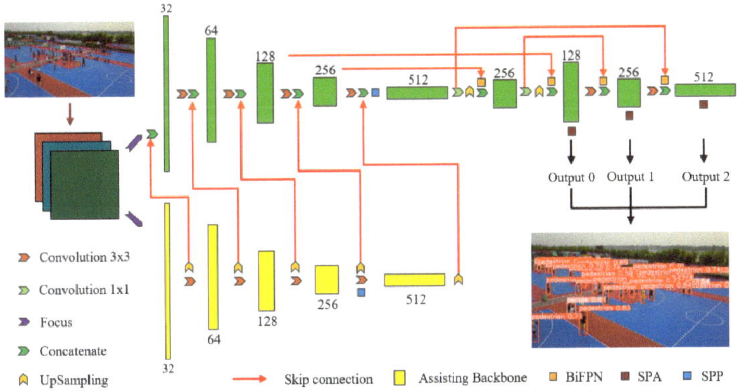

Figure 2. The overall architecture of the DB-YOLOv5 object detection model. The green module represents the image feature obtained through the model network; the number above the module represents the channel number of the feature.

The model performs data enhancement using the Mosaic operation in the image preprocessing stage, scales the input UAV image to the prescribed input size of 640 × 640 for this network model, and performs data preprocessing operations such as normalization. After that, Focus slicing and convolution are performed on the input image to obtain 320 × 320 × 32 feature maps. In the N-layer assisting backbone network (yellow part in Figure 1), the H × W × C feature map of layer $N-1$ can be obtained after 3 × 3 convolution and normalization operations to obtain the H/2 × W/2 × 2C N-layer feature map. To clarify, in the N-layer main backbone network (green part in Figure 1), the process to obtain the Nth-layer H × W × C feature map involves superimposing and fusing the 2H × 2W × C/2 feature maps of the N − 1st-layer and the Nth-layer feature maps in the assisting backbone network. This process is shown in Equation (1), where x^N_{main} and x^{N-1}_{main} denote the feature maps of the main backbone network at layer N and layer $N-1$, respectively; x^N_{assist} denotes the feature map of the assisting backbone network at layer N; and $UP(\cdot)$ denotes the UpSampling operation. The value of N used in this paper is 5.

$$x^N_{main} = x^{N-1}_{main} \oplus UP\left(x^N_{assist}\right) \tag{1}$$

where n is the feature fusion stage with N' output scales, and the dimension H × W × C of the N'th output feature map is obtained by fusing the N' − 1st output feature map with a scale of 2H × 2W × C/2 and the feature maps of the same H × W × C dimensions in the shallow network processed by the bidirectional feature pyramid network, as shown in Equation (2), where $x^{N\prime}_{fpn}$ and $x^{N\prime-1}_{fpn}$ denote the N'th and N' − 1st feature fusion output, respectively; $x^{N\prime}_{backward}$ denotes the feature map of the same size as the N′th output in the shallow network; and $Bi(\cdot)$ denotes the bidirectional feature pyramid network. In this paper, the value of N' is taken as 3.

$$x^{N\prime}_{fpn} = x^{N\prime-1}_{fpn} \oplus Bi\left(x^{N\prime}_{backward}\right) \tag{2}$$

The feature maps after feature extraction and multiscale fusion are adaptively averaged pooled at three scales of 80 × 80, 40 × 40, and 20 × 20 through a spatial pyramid structure to generate an attention map. The generated attention maps are weighted by a combination of a fully connected layer and a sigmoid activation layer to generate attention weights in the corresponding feature maps, which label the small targets in the original images more accurately.

3.2. Composite Backbone Network Based on CSPDarknet53

The backbone of the YOLOv5 model adopts the CSPDarknet53 network combined with the CSP structure. However, the feature extraction ability of this network for small-scale targets cannot achieve satisfactory results. Most of the current research on the backbone network focuses on deepening or widening the backbone. To deepen the network of the model without introducing additional pre-training overhead, we introduce the structure of the composite backbone network (CBNet) in the backbone stage of DB-YOLOv5. The structure aims to superimpose multiple layers of the same type of backbone to expand the feature receptive field of the network, thereby enhancing capability of the backbone's feature extraction for the small target in UAV.

CBNet is divided into two types: the main backbone and the assisting backbone. The purpose of using the assisting backbone is to complement the features extracted by the main backbone. Each backbone has L stages, which contain a series of layers of convolution and have the same size of feature maps. The nonlinear transformation implemented in the lth stage is defined as F^l. The output of the lth stage of the assisting backbone (denoted as x^l_{assist}) is fused with the output of the $l-1$st stage of the main backbone (x^{l-1}_{main}), which is the input in the parallel stage (l) of the main backbone, as shown in Equation (3):

$$x^l_{main} = F^l_{main}\left(x^{l-1}_{main} + g\left(x^l_{assist}\right)\right), l \geq 2 \tag{3}$$

where $g(\cdot)$ represents a layer of 1 × 1 convolution and a layer of batch normalization, whose purpose is to concatenate the features of the main and assisting backbones.

As shown in Figure 3, after the 80 × 80 feature image obtained by convolution in the assisting CSPDarknet53 backbone is input to the main backbone, it is superimposed and fused with the feature image obtained after the 640 × 640 original image is processed by Focus slicing, and the obtained result is input as the input content to the starting position of the main backbone. The 40 × 40 feature image obtained by convolution processing in the assisting backbone model and the 80 × 80 feature image in the main backbone model are then superimposed and fused, and the result is used as the input to continue the next convolution process. Finally, the 20 × 20 feature image output by the assisting backbone is superimposed and fused with the 40 × 40 feature image in the main backbone model, and the result is input to the main backbone model to continue the convolution operation. Thus, the obtained feature image is passed to the next module. After that, the feature information extracted from the backbone network is used as the input in Section 3.3 to perform multi-scale stacking and processing of features through the bidirectional feature pyramid network. Using the features learned by the network, combined with the spatial pyramid attention mechanism in Section 3.4, the objects in the input images of the model are classified and localized.

Meanwhile, to further enhance the operating efficiency and cut down on time cost, we no longer connect the low-level features of the first two layers in the composite backbone network module and only connect and stack the features of the last two layers of backbone networks. The high-level semantic feature information is further saved and learned while retaining lower-level location information, thereby easing the contradiction between time and accuracy to a certain extent. We named this module CBNet-tiny, as shown in Figure 4.

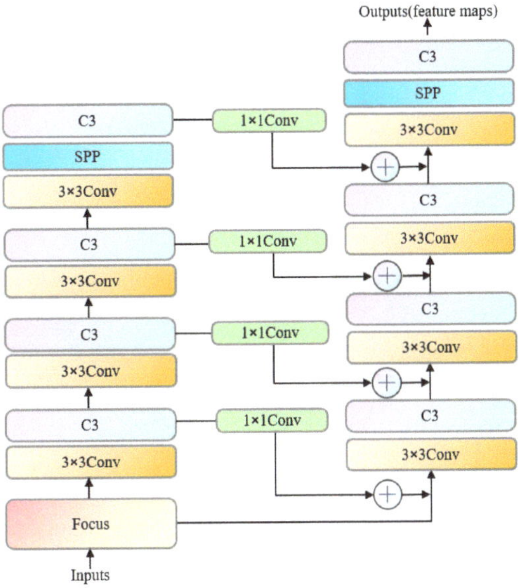

Figure 3. Diagram of the CBNet module's structure.

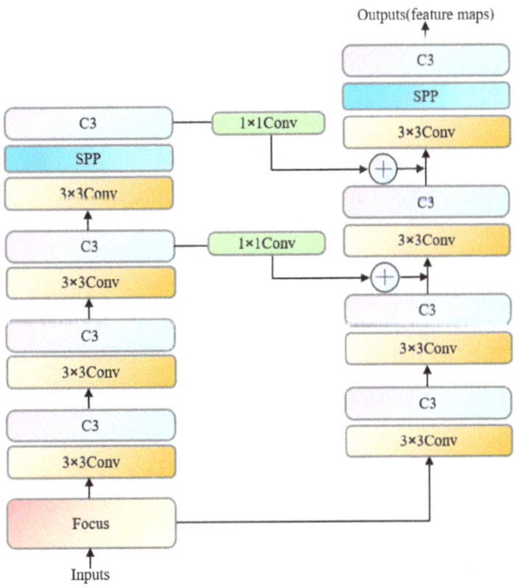

Figure 4. Diagram of the CBNet-tiny module's structure.

3.3. Bidirectional Feature Pyramid Network

The feature information extracted by the composite backbone network in Section 3.2 is also deviated in sensitivity to small targets according to the different feature extraction scales. In order to coordinate the feature information extracted from different scales, the model needs to combine the extracted features for multi-scale fusion and learning—that is, to take methods to further represent and process multi-scale features effectively, which is also one of the difficulties in target detection. Early detection models usually make predictions through a pyramid structure directly, which is based on features extracted from the backbone. In this process, the feature pyramid network plays an important role, proposing the idea of combining multi-scale features in a top-down manner. Inspired by this idea, PANet, based on FPN, adds a bottom-to-top path to further aggregate the feature information. However, it also consumes a lot of time, especially in the training phase, but achieves good performance. Since the contribution of nodes—only one input edge—to the fusion feature network is small, the Bi-FPN removes the intermediate nodes of P3 and P7 in PANet to form a simplified bidirectional network to reduce model overhead. Additionally, this module adds a skip connection between input nodes to output nodes at the same scale, incorporating more features without increasing excessive computational overhead. At the same time, the model regards the Bi-FPN module, which achieves feature fusion through a bidirectional path, as a network layer and reuses it many times to achieve better feature fusion, as shown in Figure 5.

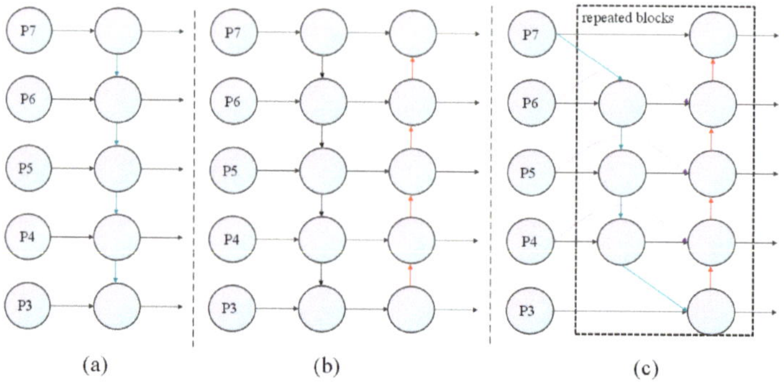

Figure 5. Comparison among different feature extraction modules. (**a**) Top-down FPN structure; (**b**) top-down and bottom-up PANET structure; (**c**) BiFPN structure with bidirectional path.

In the bidirectional feature pyramid network, the output results of each node are shown in Equations (4)–(6):

$$x^l_{fpn} = F_{conv}\left(x^l + F_{conv}\left(x^{l+1}\right)\right). \quad (4)$$

$$x^l_{fpn} = F_{conv}\left(x^l + F_{conv}\left(x^l + F_{conv}\left(x^{l+1}\right)\right) + x^{l-1}_{fpn}\right). \quad (5)$$

$$x^l_{fpn} = F_{conv}\left(x^l + x^{l-1}_{fpn}\right). \quad (6)$$

where $F_{conv}(\cdot)$ represents the convolutional layer, x^l represents the input features of the bidirectional pyramid network, and x^l_{fpn} represents the output features. Equation (4) represents the output result of node P3 in Figure 5, Equation (5) represents the output result of node P7 in Figure 5, and Equation (6) represents the output result of the intermediate node in Figure 5. Although the PANet structure of YOLOv5 can fuse multi-scale target feature information, it can easily cause missing features in the process of feature fusion between small and large targets, thus affecting the ability of the model to detect small-scale targets. To address this, we use the Bi-FPN module four times in DB-YOLOv5 to bi-directionally fuse multi-scale feature information multiple times on the three output branches to further strengthen the model's feature fusion and extraction capabilities for small targets and ensure the accuracy of positioning and classification of small targets in the model.

3.4. Spatial Pyramid Attention Mechanism

Although the model can strengthen the feature fusion and extraction capabilities of small objects through the bidirectional feature pyramid network described in Section 3.3, it may still be challenging to fully grasp the mechanism involved. However, in practical applications, the model also needs to be able to ignore the complex background and other interfering information features in the image and identify the desired feature information of the small target. To achieve accurate classification and positioning to avoid the problem of missed detection and false detection in the detection of small targets in the drone environment, we use the spatial pyramid attention network (SPANet) in DB-YOLOv5. The introduction of an attention mechanism makes our model focus on the small target part in the image and selectively extract key information from images while ignoring the interference of irrelevant information, such as the background. This improves the localization and classification performance of the entire model for small-scale targets and the accuracy of the detection model.

The feature processing process of the spatial pyramid attention mechanism is shown in Equation (7):

$$x_{weight} = sigmoid\Big(F_{fc}(P_{1\times1}(x) + P_{2\times2}(x) + P_{4\times4}(x))\Big) \quad (7)$$

Among them, $F_{fc}(\cdot)$ represents the fully connected layer; sigmoid($\cdot$) represents the activation function layer; $P_{1\times1}(\cdot)$, $P_{2\times2}(\cdot)$, and $P_{4\times4}(\cdot)$ represent the 1×1, 2×2, and 4×4 adaptive average pooling layers, respectively; and x_{weight} represents the output weight. The spatial pyramid attention mechanism locates the information of interest by using the structure of the spatial pyramid instead of global average pooling, which consists of two parts. As shown in Figure 6, the input feature maps are passed through a spatial pyramid structure, which is adaptively average pooled at three scales, to generate attention maps. Among them, the purpose of the 1×1 adaptive average pooling layer is to obtain the key information of the category in the feature map, the 2×2 pooling layer is used to save the less important key feature information in the image, and the 4×4 average pooling can effectively obtain the key position information in the feature map. Afterwards, the generated attention map is passed through a weight module, which is composed of a fully connected layer and a sigmoid activation layer, to generate the attention weights in the corresponding feature map. Thus, through the attention weight output by the attention module, the small objects in the original image are more accurately marked.

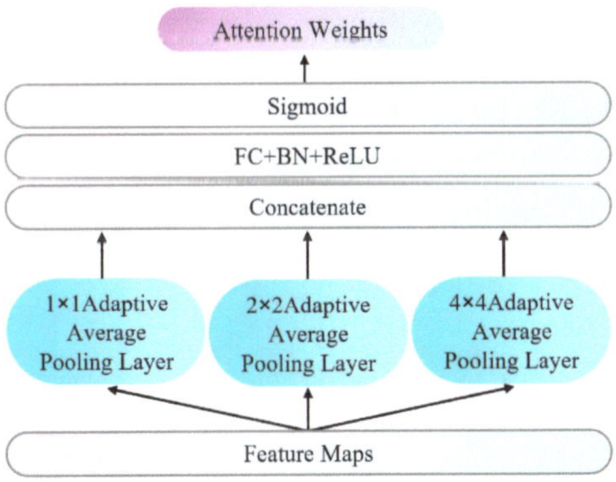

Figure 6. The structure of the spatial pyramid attention mechanism.

4. Experiments

4.1. Datasets

The data selected for the experiments were from the VisDrone-DET dataset. This dataset was collected by the AISKYEYE team at the Machine Learning and Data Mining Laboratory of Tianjin University, China. The dataset consisted of 10,209 still images captured by various drone-mounted cameras, including different locations (taken from 14 different cities that were thousands of kilometers apart in China), different environments (urban and rural), different objects (pedestrians, vehicles, bicycles, etc.), and different densities (sparse and crowded scenes). There were mainly 10 categories of objects. The number of samples for each category is shown in Figure 7.

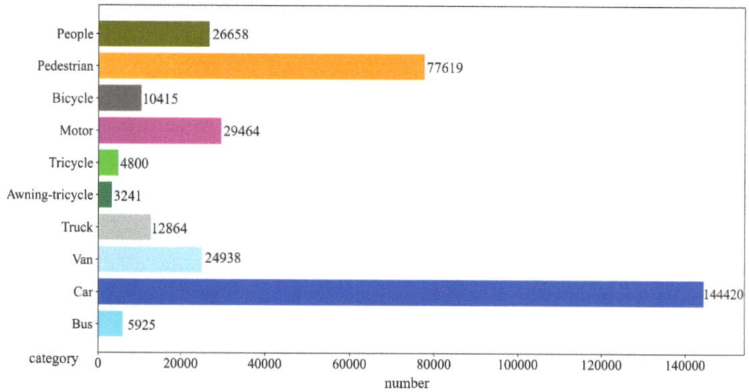

Figure 7. The number of samples in the categories in the VisDrone-DET dataset.

4.2. Experimental Details

We conducted our experiment using 6471 images from VisDrone2019-DET-train as the training set, 548 images from VisDrone2019-DET-val as the validation set, and 1610 images from VisDrone2019-DET-test-dev as the test set.

For DB-YOLOv5, we set the model input image size to 640 × 640, the batch size was 16, the confidence threshold was 0.25, and the Intersection over Union threshold was 0.45. The learning rate was initialized to 10–4 and halved after every 50% training batch. We implemented our model on the Torch 1.8.0 platform and conducted 300 epochs of training experiments on the training and validation sets on a single NVIDIA GeForce RTX 3070.

4.3. Quantitative Experiments

To verify the detection effect of the model proposed in the paper, we compared our model with other models in the field of object detection. The detection results are shown in Table 1.

Table 1. Experimental results of different object detection models on the VisDrone-DET dataset.

Method	mAP	Ped	People	Bicycle	Car	Van	Trunk	Tricycle	Awn. *	Bus	Motor
Corner Net [47]	17.41	20.43	6.55	4.56	40.94	20.23	20.54	14.03	9.25	24.39	12.1
Light-R CNN [48]	16.53	17.02	4.83	5.73	32.39	22.12	18.39	16.63	11.91	29.02	11.93
FPN [42]	16.51	15.69	5.02	4.93	38.47	20.82	18.82	15.03	10.84	26.72	12.83
Cascade RCNN [10]	16.09	16.28	6.16	14.85	4.18	37.29	17.11	14.48	12.37	20.38	24.31
Sparse R-CNN [48]	36.70	26.50	18.40	11.80	56.00	35.80	25.40	19.50	12.20	43.30	26.10
YOLOv4 [30]	40.99	15.20	11.50	22.40	65.40	60.70	59.40	33.60	52.60	71.40	22.10
YOLOv4_Drone [39]	45.67	18.00	13.00	23.00	69.00	62.00	68.00	42.00	60.00	76.00	26.00
YOLOv5	48.44	49.20	24.80	25.90	74.30	62.20	69.60	31.40	30.50	73.40	43.10
DB-YOLOv5	51.53	52.70	28.10	28.40	77.10	72.30	65.40	33.80	33.90	76.60	47.00

* The meaning of awn. is awning-tricycle.

It can be seen from the mean average precision (mAP) results in Table 1 that, compared with the anchor-based method adopted by DB-YOLOv5, the anchor-free detection model CornerNet [47] was not suitable for UAV detection. At the same time, the comparison of our model with FPN [42] also verifies that the BiFPN structure of the bidirectional path combined with the composite backbone network method could achieve more excellent results than basic FPN in UAV object detection. The comparison of Cascade RCNN [10] and Sparse R-CNN [48] shows that the one-stage method outperformed the two-stage method for the detection of small targets of UAVs. Obviously, compared with YOLO series models such as YOLOv4 [30] and YOLOv4_Drone [39], our model improved the overall detection performance and the performance of various categories. For example, in the three categories of "pedestrian", "people", and "motor", our model obtained an improvement of

346% and 292%, 244% and 216%, and 213% and 180%, respectively, which verifies the high accuracy of our model for the detection of small objects like pedestrians and motorcycles. However, it can also be observed that our model had lower accuracy on the three target categories of "trunk", "tricycle", and "awning-tricycle". After analysis, it is believed that the detection ability of small targets with similar semantics will be enhanced after the detection ability of our model for small targets is further improved. Due to the semantic similarity between tricycles and bicycles, trunks and vans, and awning-tricycles and cars, it is a significant challenge to distinguish them through the model during the learning process. Through the above experiments, the effectiveness of the improvement idea of our proposed target detection method applicable to small targets of UAVs can be seen, so we also hope that the improvement method proposed in this thesis can be applied to the same kind of YOLO algorithm and make performance breakthroughs on these versions as well, which is the work we will continue to study in depth in the future.

4.4. Qualitative Experiments

The detection results of the DB-YOLOv5 model are visualized in Figure 8. The figure includes the detection results under various conditions of insufficient light, sufficient light, dark, blurred image, and top-down angle. We can see that our method could better detect small and dense objects, especially in the central region. The target in the image is marked by a bounding box, whose color was randomly generated, and the same category in an image is marked with the same color, whereas different categories are marked with different colors.

Figure 8. The detection effect of the DB-YOLOv5 model in different scenarios. The images on the left are the original images in the dataset, and the images on the right are the output images of the model. (**a**) The detection effect under insufficient light; (**b**,**c**) the detection results when it is dark; (**d**,**g**) the detection results when the light is sufficient; (**e**) the detection effect when the light is sufficient but the image is blurred; (**f**,**h**) the detection effect diagram from the top-down angle when the light is sufficient; (**i**,**j**) the detection results from the top-down angle when it is dark.

4.5. Ablation Experiment

4.5.1. Influence of the Number of Backbone Networks

In the composite backbone network module of DB-YOLOv5, the visualization of the experimental results shows that the effect of using two backbone networks was better than three backbone networks in this model, as shown in Figure 9. Therefore, in this paper, we connected the two CSPDarknet53 backbone networks through the connection module to strengthen the main backbone with the assisting backbone, thereby improving the capability of feature extraction in the backbone.

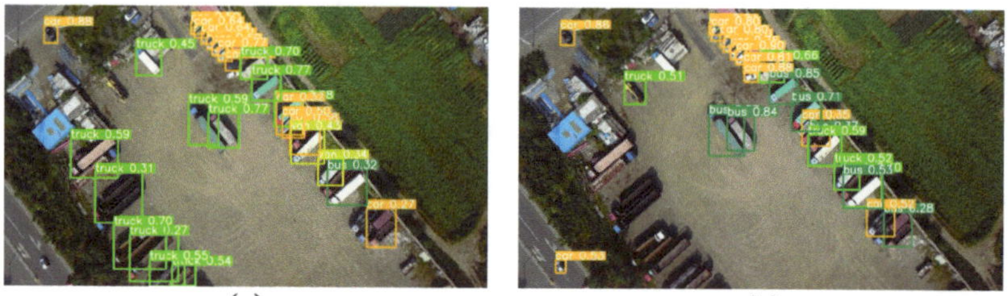

(a) (b)

Figure 9. Schematic diagram of the detection results of two backbone networks (**a**) and three backbone networks (**b**) in the composite backbone network. From the comparison of the two figures, the number of targets detected in (**b**) is significantly less than in (**a**), which proves that the effect of the two backbone networks in the composite backbone network is better than that of the three backbone networks.

4.5.2. Influence of Composite Backbone Network on Model Parameters

In the module of CBNet, we improved the ability of the backbone network to extract image features by adding two identical CSPDarknet53 backbone networks. However, the introduction of two backbone networks into the model caused an exponential increase in the parameters of the entire network model. Our experiment demonstrated that our proposed improvements can meet the requirements of high precision and short time consumption for UAV object detection. The parameter comparison after the improved model is shown in Table 2. Based on the above results, although the introduction of a composite backbone network structure in the model led to a significant improvement in parameters, it did not increase by multiples. At the same time, we can see that the floating point operations (FLOPs) computing power of the model was doubled. Therefore, after experimental verification, it can be concluded that the method of adding a composite backbone network structure in the model has feasibility and practical application prospects.

Table 2. Comparison of parameters of different detection models.

Model	Size (Pixels)	Params (M)	FLOPs@640 (B)
YOLOv5s	640	7.2	12.6
DB-YOLOv5s	640	12.9	41.6
YOLOv5m	640	21.2	49.0
DB-YOLOv5m	640	32.8	102.6
YOLOv5l	640	46.5	109.1
DB-YOLOv5l	640	88.4	220.3
YOLOv5x	640	86.7	205.7
DB-YOLOv5x	640	176.5	440.6

4.5.3. The Influence of Each Module on the Model

To verify the performance of the improved detection model, we compared the proposed model with the original YOLOv5 model and calculated the mean average precision (mAP) index for evaluation. As discussed in Section 3, we refer to the model with the CBNet module as YOLOv5_cb, the model with the CBNet-tiny module is YOLOv5_cbty, the YOLOv5_cb model with the BiFPN module is YOLOv5_bi, and the model proposed in this paper is DB-YOLOv5. The experimental results are shown in Table 3.

Table 3. Ablation experiment results of the model on the VisDrone-DET dataset.

Model	CBNet-tiny	CBNet	Bi-FPN	SPANet	mAP
YOLOv5					48.44%
YOLOv5_cbty	✓				49.26%
YOLOv5_cb		✓			49.65%
YOLOv5_bi		✓	✓		50.74%
DB-YOLOv5		✓	✓	✓	51.53%

It can be seen from the results in Table 3 that the three improved methods proposed in this paper significantly increased the detection accuracy of the categories in the UAV dataset VisDrone-DET. Compared with the baseline model, after adding the faster CBNet-tiny module, the YOLOv5_cbty model achieved an 0.82% improvement on the mAP indicator. At the same time, the mAP index of the model with a complete CBNet module had a 1.21% improvement compared to the benchmark model and a 0.4% performance improvement compared to the YOLOv5_cbty model. On this basis, the model obtained by adding the BiFPN module also had a 2.3% improvement in performance indicators compared to the benchmark model and a 1.1% performance improvement based on the YOLOv5_cb model. Moreover, our proposed model DB-YOLOv5 had a performance improvement of nearly 3.1% compared to the benchmark model and a 0.8% improvement compared to YOLOv5_bi. The contribution of the three modules to our model from high to low were CBNet, BiFPN, and SPA.

5. Conclusions

In this paper, we proposed a DB-YOLOv5 UAV object detection algorithm to address the issue of detecting small targets in UAV images. We built the model on top of YOLOv5 by incorporating a composite backbone network, bidirectional feature pyramid, and pyramid attention mechanism, which improved the network's capability for multi-scale feature fusion and small target detection. Our experiments on the VisDrone-DET dataset demonstrated that the proposed model achieved better performance in terms of objective detection metrics, making it suitable for small target detection tasks in UAV images. The proposed method has significant implications for security surveillance, particularly in the field of network security and privacy. By identifying small targets in UAV images, our approach can aid in detecting potential security threats, such as identifying security vulnerabilities in critical infrastructure and monitoring public events for potential security risks. Overall, this research provides a valuable contribution to the field of security surveillance by enhancing the capabilities of object detection algorithms for small target detection in UAV images, ultimately improving network security and privacy. Our next step is to develop a practical platform based on the simulation experiments. However, since we need to collect image data before learning, this process may be relatively slow. Our ultimate goal is to create a real-time platform and conduct experiments in a real environment. These are the directions for our future work.

Author Contributions: Conceptualization: L.T. and Y.L.; methodology: Y.L. and X.H.; formal analysis and investigation: Y.L.; writing—original draft preparation: Y.L.; writing—review and editing: Y.L., W.L., L.T., H.Z., X.H. and X.J.; supervision: L.T. and Y.L. All authors have read and agreed to the published version of the manuscript.

Funding: This research was funded by the Natural Science Foundation of Chongqing (CSTB2022NSCQ-MSX1415).

Data Availability Statement: The dataset used during the current study is available at: http://aiskyeye.com/download/object-detection-2/ (accessed on 27 June 2023).

Conflicts of Interest: All authors have read the final manuscript, have approved the submission to the journal, and have accepted full responsibilities pertaining to the manuscript's delivery and contents. The authors declare that they have no known competing financial interests or personal relationships that could have appeared to influence the work reported in this paper.

References

1. Erdelj, M.; Natalizio, E.; Chowdhury, K.R. Help from the sky: Leveraging UAVs for disaster management. *IEEE Pervasive Comput.* **2017**, *16*, 24–32. [CrossRef]
2. Krizhevsky, A.; Sutskever, I.; Hinton, G.E. Imagenet classification with deep convolutional neural networks. *Commun. ACM* **2017**, *60*, 84–90. [CrossRef]
3. Girshick, R.; Donahue, J.; Darrell, T. Region-based convolutional networks for accurate object detection and segmentation. *IEEE Trans. Pattern Anal. Mach. Intell.* **2015**, *38*, 142–158. [CrossRef]
4. Zou, Z.; Shi, Z.; Guo, Y. Object detection in 20 years: A survey. *Proc. IEEE* **2023**, *111*, 257–276. [CrossRef]
5. Girshick, R. Fast r-cnn. In Proceedings of the IEEE International Conference on Computer Vision (ICCV), Santiago, Chile, 7–13 December 2015; IEEE Press: Piscataway, NJ, USA, 2015; pp. 1440–1448.
6. Ren, S.; He, K.; Girshick, R. Faster r-cnn: Towards real-time object detection with region proposal networks. *IEEE Trans. Pattern Anal. Mach. Intell.* **2017**, *39*, 1137–1149. [CrossRef] [PubMed]
7. Dai, J.; Li, Y.; He, K. R-fcn: Object detection via region-based fully convolutional networks. *Adv. Neural Inf. Process. Syst. (NIPS)* **2016**, *29*, 379–387.
8. Zhu, Y.; Zhao, C.; Wang, J. Couplenet: Coupling global structure with local parts for object detection. In Proceedings of the IEEE International Conference on Computer Vision (ICCV), Venice, Italy, 22–29 October 2017; pp. 4126–4134.
9. He, K.; Gkioxari, G.; Dollár, P. Mask r-cnn. *IEEE Trans. Pattern Anal. Mach. Intell.* **2018**, *42*, 386–397. [CrossRef] [PubMed]
10. Cai, Z.; Vasconcelos, N. Cascade r-cnn: Delving into high quality object detection. In Proceedings of the IEEE Conference on Computer Vision and Pattern Recognition (CVPR), Salt Lake City, UT, USA, 18–22 June 2018; pp. 6154–6162.
11. Pang, J.; Chen, K.; Shi, J. Libra r-cnn: Towards balanced learning for object detection. In Proceedings of the IEEE/CVF Conference on Computer Vision and Pattern Recognition (CVPR), Long Beach, CA, USA, 15–20 June 2019; pp. 821–830.
12. Xu, H.; Jiang, C.; Liang, X. Reasoning-rcnn: Unifying adaptive global reasoning into large-scale object detection. In Proceedings of the IEEE/CVF Conference on Computer Vision and Pattern Recognition (CVPR), Long Beach, CA, USA, 15–20 June 2019; pp. 6412–6421.
13. Tan, M.; Pang, R.; Le, Q.V. EfficientDet: Scalable and efficient object detection. In Proceedings of the IEEE/CVF Conference on Computer Vision and Pattern Recognition (CVPR), Seattle, WA, USA, 13–19 June 2020; pp. 10778–10787.
14. Cao, J.; Cholakkal, H.; Rao, M.A. D2Det: Towards high quality object detection and instance segmentation. In Proceedings of the IEEE/CVF Conference on Computer Vision and Pattern Recognition (CVPR), Seattle, WA, USA, 13–19 June 2020; pp. 11482–11491.
15. Guo, J.; Han, K.; Wang, Y. Distilling object detectors via decoupled features. In Proceedings of the IEEE/CVF Conference on Computer Vision and Pattern Recognition (CVPR), Nashville, TN, USA, 19–25 June 2021; pp. 2154–2164.
16. Li, Y.; Wu, C.Y.; Fan, H. Improved multiscale vision transformers for classification and detection. In Proceedings of the IEEE/CVF Conference on Computer Vision and Pattern Recognition (CVPR), New Orleans, LA, USA, 18–24 June 2022; pp. 4794–4804.
17. Gao, Z.; Wang, L.; Han, B. AdaMixer: A fast-converging query-based object detector. In Proceedings of the IEEE/CVF Conference on Computer Vision and Pattern Recognition (CVPR), New Orleans, LA, USA, 18–24 June 2022; pp. 5354–5363.
18. Liu, W.; Anguelov, D.; Erhan, D. Ssd: Single Shot Multibox Detector. In Proceedings of the Computer Vision–ECCV 2016: 14th European Conference (ECCV), Amsterdam, The Netherlands, 11–14 October 2016; Springer International Publishing: Amsterdam, The Netherlands, 2016; pp. 21–37.
19. Fu, C.Y.; Liu, W.; Ranga, A. Dssd: Deconvolutional single shot detector. *arXiv* **2017**, arXiv:1701.06659.
20. Li, Z.; Zhou, F. FSSD: Feature fusion single shot multibox detector. *arXiv* **2017**, arXiv:1712.00960.
21. Zhu, R.; Zhang, S.; Wang, X. ScratchDet: Training single-shot object detectors from scratch. In Proceedings of the IEEE/CVF Conference on Computer Vision and Pattern Recognition (CVPR), Long Beach, CA, USA, 15–20 June 2019; pp. 2263–2272.
22. Zhou, X.; Zhuo, J.; Krahenbuhl, P. Bottom-up object detection by grouping extreme and center points. In Proceedings of the IEEE/CVF Conference on Computer Vision and Pattern Recognition (CVPR), Long Beach, CA, USA, 15–20 June 2019; pp. 850–859.
23. Lu, X.; Li, Q.; Li, B. MimicDet: Bridging the gap between one-stage and two-stage object detection. In Proceedings of the Computer Vision–ECCV 2020: 16th European Conference (ECCV), Glasgow, UK, 23–28 August 2020; Springer International Publishing: Glasgow, UK, 2020; pp. 541–557.
24. Chen, C.; Zheng, Z.; Huang, Y. I3Net: Implicit instance-invariant network for adapting one-stage object detectors. In Proceedings of the IEEE/CVF Conference on Computer Vision and Pattern Recognition (CVPR), Nashville, TN, USA, 19–25 June 2021; pp. 12571–12580.
25. Zhao, Y.; Guo, X.; Lu, Y. Semantic-aligned fusion transformer for one-shot object detection. In Proceedings of the IEEE/CVF Conference on Computer Vision and Pattern Recognition (CVPR), New Orleans, LA, USA, 18–24 June 2022; pp. 7591–7601.
26. Long, Y.; Wen, Y.; Han, J. CapDet: Unifying dense captioning and open-world detection pretraining. *arXiv* **2023**, arXiv:2303.02489.
27. Redmon, J.; Divvala, S.; Girshick, R. You only look once: Unified, real-time object detection. In Proceedings of the IEEE Conference on Computer Vision and Pattern Recognition (CVPR), Las Vegas, NV, USA, 27–30 June 2016; pp. 779–788.

28. Redmon, J.; Farhadi, A. YOLO9000: Better, Faster, Stronger. In Proceedings of the IEEE Conference on Computer Vision and Pattern Recognition (CVPR), Honolulu, HI, USA, 21–26 July 2017; pp. 7263–7271.
29. Redmon, J.; Farhadi, A. Yolov3: An incremental improvement. *arXiv* **2018**, arXiv:1804.02767.
30. Bochkovskiy, A.; Wang, C.Y.; Liao, H.Y.M. Yolov4: Optimal speed and accuracy of object detection. *arXiv* **2020**, arXiv:2004.10934.
31. Ge, Z.; Liu, S.; Wang, F. Yolox: Exceeding yolo series in 2021. *arXiv* **2021**, arXiv:2107.08430.
32. Chen, Q.; Wang, Y.; Yang, T. You only look one-level feature. In Proceedings of the IEEE/CVF Conference on Computer Vision and Pattern Recognition (CVPR), Nashville, TN, USA, 19–25 June 2021; pp. 13034–13043.
33. Li, C.; Li, L.; Jiang, H. YOLOv6: A single-stage object detection framework for industrial applications. *arXiv* **2022**, arXiv:2209.02976.
34. Wang, C.Y.; Bochkovskiy, A.; Liao, H.Y.M. YOLOv7: Trainable bag-of-freebies sets new state-of-the-art for real-time object detectors. *arXiv* **2023**, arXiv:2207.02696.
35. Cheng, D.; Zhi, W.; Chi, Z. CMDNet: Coarse-grained density map guided object detection in aerial images. In Proceedings of the IEEE/CVF Conference on Computer Vision and Pattern Recognition (CVPR), Nashville, TN, USA, 19–25 June 2021; pp. 2789–2798.
36. Huang, Y.; Chen, J.; Huang, D. UFPMP-Det: Toward accurate and efficient object detection on drone imagery. *Proc. AAAI Conf. Artif. Intell.* **2022**, *36*, 1026–1033.
37. Wang, J.; Yang, W.; Guo, H. Tiny object detection in aerial images. In Proceedings of the 2020 25th International Conference on Pattern Recognition (ICPR), Milan, Italy, 10–15 January 2021; pp. 3791–3798.
38. Xu, C.; Wang, J.; Yang, W. Dot distance for tiny object detection in aerial images. In Proceedings of the IEEE/CVF Conference on Computer Vision and Pattern Recognition (CVPR), Nashville, TN, USA, 19–25 June 2021; pp. 1192–1201.
39. Tan, L.; Lv, X.; Lian, X. YOLOv4_Drone: Uav image target detection based on an improved yolov4 algorithm. *Comput. Electr. Eng.* **2021**, *93*, 107261. [CrossRef]
40. Yang, J.; Yang, H.; Wang, F. A modified yolov5 for object detection in uav-captured scenarios. In Proceedings of the 2022 IEEE International Conference on Networking, Sensing and Control (ICNSC), Shanghai, China, 15–18 December 2022; pp. 1–6.
41. Wang, C.; Mark, L.; Wu, Y. CSPNet: A new backbone that can enhance learning capability of cnn. In Proceedings of the IEEE/CVF conference on computer vision and pattern recognition workshops (CVPR), Seattle, WA, USA, 13–19 June 2020; pp. 1571–1580.
42. Liu, S.; Qi, L.; Qin, H. Path aggregation network for instance segmentation. In Proceedings of the IEEE Conference on Computer Vision and Pattern Recognition (CVPR), Salt Lake City, UT, USA, 18–22 June 2018; pp. 8759–8768.
43. Lin, T.; Dollár, P.; Girshick, R. Feature pyramid networks for object detection. In Proceedings of the IEEE Conference on Computer Vision and Pattern Recognition (CVPR), Honolulu, HI, USA, 21–26 July 2017; pp. 2117–21257.
44. Sun, Z.; Zhang, Q.; Li, Y.; Tan, Y.A. DPPDL: A Dynamic Partial-Parallel Data Layout for Green Video Surveillance Storage. *IEEE Trans. Circuits Syst. Video Technol.* **2018**, *28*, 193–205. [CrossRef]
45. Yu, X.; Zhang, C.; Xue, Y.; Zhu, H.; Li, Y.; Tan, Y.A. An Extra-Parity Energy Saving Data Layout for Video Surveillance. *Multimed. Tools Appl.* **2018**, *77*, 4563–4583.
46. Zhang, Q.; Ma, W.; Wang, Y. Backdoor Attacks on Image Classification Models in Deep Neural Networks. *Chin. J. Electron.* **2022**, *31*, 199–212. [CrossRef]
47. Law, H.; Deng, J. Cornernet: Detecting objects as paired keypoints. In Proceedings of the European Conference on Computer Vision (ECCV), Munich, Germany, 8–14 September 2018; pp. 734–750.
48. Sun, P.; Zhang, R.; Jiang, Y. Sparse r-cnn: End-to-end object detection with learnable proposals. In Proceedings of the IEEE/CVF Conference on Computer Vision and Pattern Recognition (CVPR), Nashville, TN, USA, 19–25 June 2021; pp. 14454–14463.

electronics

Article

Industrial Internet Intrusion Detection Based on Res-CNN-SRU

Zengyu Cai [1], Yajie Si [1], Jianwei Zhang [2,*], Liang Zhu [1], Pengrong Li [1] and Yuan Feng [1]

[1] School of Computer and Communication Engineering, Zhengzhou University of Light Industry, Zhengzhou 450001, China; czy@zzuli.edu.cn (Z.C.); 332107020571@email.zzuli.edu.cn (Y.S.); lzhu@zzuli.edu.cn (L.Z.); 332207030629@email.zzuli.edu.cn (P.L.); fy@zzuli.edu.cn (Y.F.)

[2] School of Software Engineering, Zhengzhou University of Light Industry, Zhengzhou 450001, China

* Correspondence: ing@zzuli.edu.cn

Abstract: Nowadays, the industrial Internet is developing rapidly, but at the same time it faces serious information security risks. At present, industrial Internet data generally have the problems of complex attack sample types, large numbers, and high feature dimensions. When training a model, the complexity and quantity of attack samples will result in a long detection time for the intrusion detection algorithm, which will fall short of the system's real-time performance. Due to the high feature dimension of the data, shallow feature extraction will be unable to extract the data's more significant features, which will render the model's overall detection capacity insufficient. Aiming at the above problems, an industrial Internet intrusion detection method based on Res-CNN-SRU is proposed. This method not only considers the temporality of network traffic data but can also effectively capture the local features in the data. The dataset used in the experiment is the gas pipeline industry dataset proposed by Mississippi State University in 2014. Experiments show that the algorithm can effectively improve the recognition rate of the system and reduce the false-alarm rate. At the same time, the training time required for this method is also greatly shortened, and it can perform efficient intrusion detection on the industrial Internet.

Keywords: intrusion detection; deep learning; industry Internet; residual connection

check for updates

Citation: Cai, Z.; Si, Y.; Zhang, J.; Zhu, L.; Li, P.; Feng, Y. Industrial Internet Intrusion Detection Based on Res-CNN-SRU. *Electronics* **2023**, *12*, 3267. https://doi.org/10.3390/electronics12153267

Academic Editor: Juan-Carlos Cano

Received: 19 June 2023
Revised: 13 July 2023
Accepted: 25 July 2023
Published: 29 July 2023

1. Introduction

Today's digital and Internet technology is profoundly changing our way of production and life. The traditional industrial control system mostly runs on the isolated Intranet, and almost does not need to consider the threat of the external network to hardware, protocols, deployment, etc. However, with the rapid development of communication, Internet of Things and other technologies, it has brought great changes to the application of industrial automation control systems and the business and technical architecture in the industrial environment and formed a new industrial platform, that is, the industrial Internet platform [1–3]. Driven by industrial Internet technology, in order to improve production efficiency, more enterprises have begun to realize the digitization, networking, and intelligence of production processes. However, with the continuous improvement in industrial equipment interconnection and intelligent technology, industrial Internet systems are also facing various attacks from the network, including computer viruses, malware, distributed denial-of-service attacks, and so on. These attacks can cause systems to crash, data to be compromised, or industrial equipment to be remotely controlled. At the same time, the industrial Internet involves a large amount of data transmission and storage, including production data, sensitive information and trade secrets. Hackers may attempt to steal these data for malicious purposes, such as industrial espionage, extortion, or theft of intellectual property. In February 2021, a water treatment plant system was attacked in Florida, the United States. The attacker remotely logged into the system by stealing credentials, obtained SCADA access, and then started an HMI program to send attack signals, destroy the liquid level control and dosage setting process, and increase the concentration of sodium hydroxide to 111 times the normal value, directly threatening the safety of citizens [4]. Therefore, industrial Internet intrusion detection has become more and more important.

Industrial Internet intrusion attacks may not only cause losses to the production and economy of enterprises but also have an irreversible impact on society. Therefore, intrusion detection for the industrial Internet is a major challenge to be solved urgently. Industrial Internet intrusion detection refers to discovering intrusion attacks by monitoring network traffic, identifying abnormal behaviors and threats, and taking corresponding measures to prevent and respond to attacks.

Nowadays, the combination of deep learning methods and network intrusion detection has become more and more popular. The convolutional neural network is a deep learning model that has been widely used in the field of image and speech processing. It can realize intrusion detection by analyzing and modeling network traffic data. In addition, due to the successful application of recurrent neural networks in the field of sequence data processing, more and more researchers have begun to apply it to network intrusion detection in recent years. Based on RNN, SRU (simplified recurrent unit) is a new recurrent neural network structure with fast operation and better representation ability.

The main contributions of this paper are as follows.

- A depth feature extraction method for high dimensional network traffic is proposed, which can extract local features without losing time features, and add residual connections, which not only alleviates the problem of gradient disappearance but also improves the convergence speed of the network.
- Combination with a parallel algorithm of SRU abnormal traffic detection. Compared with the traditional LSTM model, the SRU model has the advantages of high computational efficiency, fast training, strong sequence modeling ability, low memory utilization rate, and is able to train the accuracy of the model faster.
- Experiments show that the proposed method has high detection accuracy and low time consumption, and can effectively detect complex malicious response injection attacks, denial-of-service attacks, reconnaissance attacks and other attack types in the industrial Internet environment.

2. Related Work

In recent years, China and other nations have attached great importance to industrial Internet security and carried out a great deal of intrusion detection theory and technology research, among which the most representative is the intrusion detection method based on machine learning, especially the deep learning method, which can reduce false-positive rates and improve detection rates and adaptability.

2.1. Industrial Internet Intrusion Detection Based on Machine Learning

Machine learning has been widely used in computer vision, natural language processing, biometric identification, search engines, data mining and other fields. In the field of intrusion detection, machine learning also plays an important role, including support vector machine [5,6], K-means clustering algorithm [7] and Bayesian network model [8]. R. Zhang et al. [9] proposed a network intrusion detection scheme based on an improved SVM algorithm. This method simplifies the intrusion detection system through sample classification and selects the optimal parameters as the basis of intrusion detection through iterative processing. Simon D. Duque Anton et al. [10] used an anomaly detection algorithm based on machine learning and time series to analyze network data containing industrial operations to detect attacks that introduce the data. To detect attacks, two machine learning-based algorithms, SVM and random forest, are used. Both perform well and solve the problem of feature extraction and selection and processing of missing data.

Through sample categorization and iterative processing, this technique chooses the best parameters to serve as the intrusion detection system's foundation. However, as a nonparametric model, SVM is mainly used for the classification and verification of small datasets. With the increasing interconnection of modern heavy industry and manufacturing, the scale of integration is gradually expanding, and the traffic in the industrial Internet is also developing to a larger order of magnitude. In the face of the industrial Internet with huge data, support vector machines face problems such as high time overhead, reduced detection efficiency, and difficulty in obtaining hyperplanes. Ahsan Al Zaki Khan et al. [11] employed machine learning algorithms using WEKA to develop a misuse intrusion detection system designed to identify attacks on a SCADA system network of a gas pipeline infrastructure. They used naïve Bayes, rule-based and tree-based classifiers in supervised learning mode for classifying the attacks. Majed Al-Asiri et al. [12] presented a case study simulating a natural gas pipeline dataset to compare the effectiveness of decision tree classifiers for various types of features in SCADA systems. Oliver Eigner et al. [13] improved the K nearest neighbors algorithm and applied it to the industrial Internet, successfully detecting an attack. S. Jaiswal et al. [14] improved the KNN model by using the ant colony optimization algorithm, and conducted experiments on the KDD99 dataset. The above experiments of applying KNN to intrusion detection have indeed achieved certain results, but the KNN model is applied to industrial control systems, especially when the industry is large, because KNN has to calculate the distance from all data for each test sample and has the problem of high time overhead and poor performance.

In summary, the machine learning algorithm has good detection when dealing with fewer feature dimensions. However, due to the massive and high-dimensional characteristics of industrial Internet network data, traditional machine learning has been unable to meet this demand. Therefore, it is imperative to carry out deep learning research.

2.2. Industrial Internet Intrusion Detection Based on Deep Learning

Since traditional machine learning methods can no longer meet the needs of increasingly complex networks, many researchers use deep learning to replace traditional machine learning methods. Deep learning has been well applied in many fields, such as image, video recognition, natural language processing and robot technology. Nowadays, deep learning application scenarios are more and more extensive, and it has been proved that deep learning has certain advantages over traditional machine learning methods in industrial Internet intrusion detection. The development of deep learning has brought new possibilities to intrusion detection. Xia W et al. [15] optimized the BP neural network and used the Adaboost algorithm to obtain the optimal weight and threshold by continuously adjusting the weight of training samples, which effectively solves the problem of intrusion detection. Aiming at the security problem of the Internet of Things, Yang Aimin et al. [16] proposed an LM-BP neural network model by improving the BP network, and applied it to the intrusion detection system. However, the BP neural network model has a single structure, and a large number of parameters will be generated when fitting complex functions, which will easily lead to overfitting and performance degradation, so the detection results are not ideal. Y Li, Y Xu et al. [17] proposed a multi-CNN fusion-based intrusion detection system. The processed data showed a better training result for deep learning.

Chuanlong Yin et al. [18] proposed a deep learning approach for intrusion detection using recurrent neural networks. The RNN-IDS model improves the accuracy of intrusion detection and provides a new research method for intrusion detection. Bipraneel Roy et al. [19] presented a novel deep learning technique for detecting attacks within the IoT network using a bidirectional long short-term memory recurrent neural network. The experimental outcome showed that BLSTM RNN was highly efficient for building a high-accuracy intrusion detection model and offered a novel research methodology. Song Zhiwen [20] used a genetic algorithm to obtain the optimal selection for the training set and test set, and combined convolutional neural network and gated loop unit to propose a CNN-GRU intrusion detection method based on a genetic algorithm.

Zhou et al. [21] proposed a variational long short-term memory (VLSTM) learning model for intelligent anomaly detection based on reconstructed feature representation to solve the industrial Internet's imbalance in data distribution in high-dimensional anomaly detection for industrial applications. RH Hwang, MC Peng et al. [22] proposed an intrusion detection model based on word embedding and long short-term memory network, which can classify malicious traffic. The experimental results show that the method has a significant classification effect in normal and malicious binary classification detection. Jie Ling, Zhishen Zhu et al. [23] proposed an intrusion detection method based on a bidirectional simple recurrent unit. With skip connections employed, the optimized bidirectional structure in the SRU neural network is able to alleviate the vanishing gradient problem and improve training effectiveness. As mentioned above, these detection algorithms have achieved some success, but the RNN model they use has many parameters and the performance is not good enough. It is easy to cause gradient disappearance or gradient explosion, and compared with the convolution model, it has no advantage in the final recognition rate.

Therefore, compared with traditional machine learning methods, deep learning performs well in processing large-scale and high-dimensional data, and deep learning can automatically learn and extract features, but there are still problems such as limited feature learning ability and gradient disappearance, so further optimization is needed.

In summary, traditional machine learning methods cannot extract features very accurately in the field of industrial Internet intrusion detection. Therefore, for the industrial Internet with large network traffic, its detection accuracy is usually low. This paper proposes an industrial Internet intrusion detection model based on 1D CNN with residual structure and a simple recurrent unit algorithm to solve this problem using 1D CNN to extract features and improve the accuracy of data classification. The residual structure can make the model deeper and more powerful, which helps to improve the accuracy of intrusion detection. It also can improve the generalization ability of the model, avoid the problem of gradient disappearance through skip connection, and reduce overfitting. Compared with the traditional LSTM model, the SRU model has faster training and lower memory consumption, and can train a model with high accuracy faster.

Combined with the Mississippi natural gas pipeline dataset for experiments, it can be found that the proposed convolutional neural network and simple recurrent unit model combined with residual structure are more efficient than other algorithms in intrusion detection. While improving the detection accuracy, it also takes into account the stability of the model. After many experiments, it is proved that the improved model has better detection.

3. Proposed Method

This paper proposes an industrial Internet intrusion detection model based on Res-CNN-SRU. A deep neural network hybrid model is constructed by fusing 1D CNN and a simple recurrent unit network. One-dimensional CNN combines the direct connection structure of the residual network. The direct connection of the residual structure can avoid the disappearance of the depth gradient. The SRU will further screen the data after convolution extraction and mine the timing information. Specifically, the intrusion detection process is regarded as a classification problem, and the traffic characteristics in the network are classified to determine whether there is an attack in the network.

3.1. Intrusion Detection Model Based on Res-CNN-SRU

The method consists of three parts: one-dimensional convolutional neural network, residual connection, and simple recurrent unit.

3.1.1. One-Dimensional Convolutional Neural Network

A convolutional neural network (CNN) is a kind of feedforward neural network with convolution calculation and deep structure [24]. Among them, 1D CNN is often used in the field of natural language processing [25], while 2D CNN and 3D CNN are often used in image recognition [26], Mandarin speech recognition [27], face recognition [28] and other fields. The traditional neural network uses matrix multiplication to establish the connection by using the input data and the neural network parameter matrix. Each input unit interacts with the output unit through the parameters in the parameter matrix. However, CNN reduces the number of network model parameters by local connection and weight sharing, which not only reduces the computational complexity of the model but also makes the network easy to optimize [29].

The 1D CNN is a convolutional neural network that uses one-dimensional convolution to extract features from one-dimensional time series, which can ensure that local features are extracted without losing time series features [30].

Convolutional neural networks usually comprise three layers:

1. Convolution layer. In order to achieve the effect of feature extraction, the input features are scanned by the convolution kernel, subjected to matrix operations in the "receptive field," and superimposed with deviations [31].
2. Pooling layer. The pooling layer has a variety of different forms of nonlinear pooling functions. It divides the input image into several rectangular regions and outputs the maximum value for each subregion. The pooling layer will continuously reduce the space size of the data, so the number of parameters and the amount of calculation will also decrease, which also controls the overfitting to a certain extent.
3. Fully connected layer. The extracted features are nonlinearly combined and output to other fully connected layers. The convolution layer and pooling layer can achieve the purpose of automatically extracting local features of data, while the fully connected layer can achieve feature learning.

The one-dimensional convolution formula is shown in Equation (1).

$$Z^{m+1} = [Z^{m} * w^{m+1}] + d = \sum_{z=1}^{m} [Z_{k}^{m}(s_0 + x) w_{k}^{m+1}(x)] + d \quad (1)$$

The maximum pooling formula is shown in Equation (2).

$$A_{i}^{m+1}(j) = \max_{(j-1)W+1 \le t \le jW} \{F_{i}^{m}(t)\} \quad (2)$$

In the formula, Z^m is the value of the convolution input of the m layer, Z^{m+1} is the value of the convolution output of the $m + 1$ layer, d is the value of the deviation, w_k^{m+1} is the value of the weight of the corresponding node of the $m + 1$ layer, f is the value of the convolution kernel size of the convolution layer, s_0 is the value of convolution step size of the convolution layer, $F_i^l(t)$ is the value of the t neuron in the i feature of the m layer, W is the value of the pooled area, A_i^{m+1} is the value of the output of the $m + 1$ layer neuron.

3.1.2. Residual Connection

It is found that with the deepening of the number of the network layer, not only will the gradient disappearance problem occur but also the network degradation will lead to the occurrence of overfitting. Residual connection can effectively solve the above problems. The idea of residual connection is derived from the gating idea of LSTM, which expresses the output as a linear superposition of a nonlinear transformation of input and input [32,33], as shown in Figure 1.

The traditional neural network layer can be expressed as $y = F(x)$, where $F()$ is the mapping function of the network layer. Suppose there is a residual block whose input is x and output is $H(x)$. In the residual network, we hope to learn the residual $F(x)$ through the residual connection so that the output can be expressed as $y = H(x) + F(x)$. Through the residual connection, we can optimize the network by learning the residual $F(x)$. If the network can successfully learn the identity mapping, that is, $f(x) = H(x)$, then the residual $F(x)$ is close to zero and the output of the network is close to the input. In this way, the network can gradually optimize the performance of the model by adjusting the residual part.

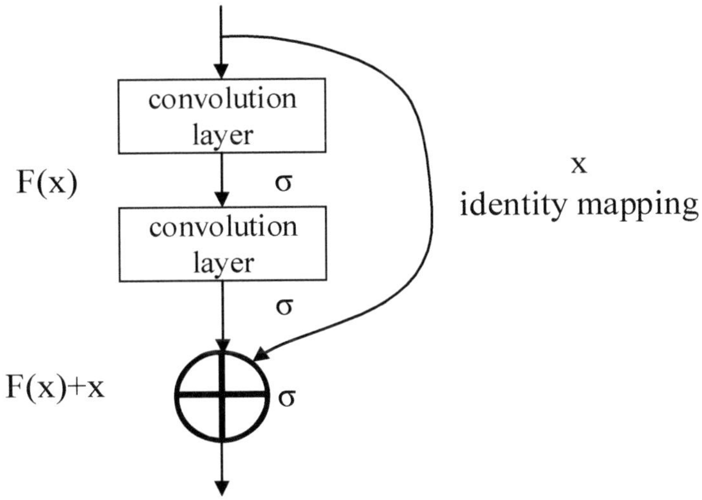

Figure 1. Residual block.

The output formula of the residual block is shown in Equation (3).

$$x_{m+1} = x_m + F(x_{ml}, w_m) \tag{3}$$

In the formula, x_{m+1} is the output of the $m + 1$ layer, x_m is the input of the layer m, $f(x_m, w_m)$ is the residual of layer m.

In summary, residual connection is a design that introduces skip connections. It allows the input of the previous layer to be added directly to the output of the subsequent layer, making it easier for the network to learn the residual part, thereby improving the performance and training effect of the network. Through residual connections, information can flow more freely in the network, and gradient signals can also spread more easily. The introduction of this structure makes it possible to train deeper networks, improve the performance of the model, and solve the problem of gradient disappearance and gradient explosion in deep neural networks.

3.1.3. Simple Recurrent Unit

Many advances in the field of deep learning come from enhanced modeling capabilities and related computing capabilities, which usually involve deeper neural networks. While the deep neural network brings significant improvements, it also has certain drawbacks, that is, it requires a lot of training time. Simplified recurrent unit is a sequence modeling method for processing time series data, such as text and voice data. It is a model similar to recurrent neural network, but it has a simpler structure and more efficient calculation. Traditional RNN has some problems, such as difficulty in capturing long-term dependencies, low computational efficiency, and difficulty in parallel computing. The SRU structure is simple and contains only two key operations: reset gate and update gate. Most importantly, SRU has parallel computing capabilities. When calculating each time step, the traditional RNN needs to rely on the results of the previous time step, which makes it difficult to perform parallel computing. SRU does not have this limitation, and can process the entire input sequence in parallel, thus speeding up the training. The structure of SRU is shown in Figure 2.

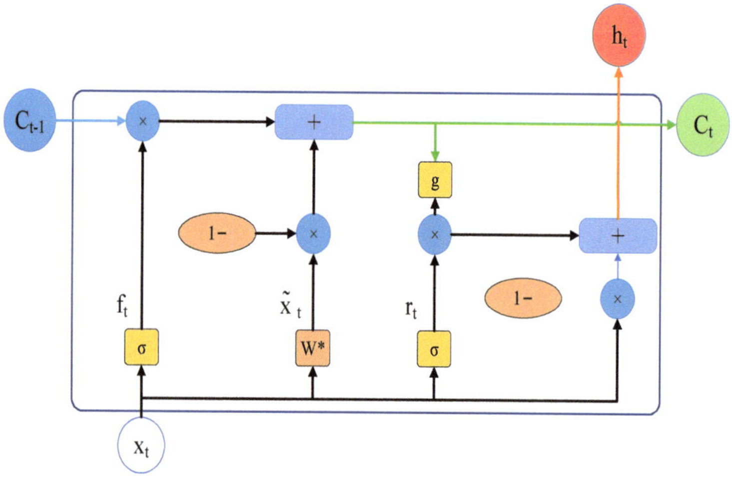

Figure 2. Structure diagram of SRU.

The SRU model is roughly divided into two parts: the light recurrence component and the highway network component. The light recurrence section computes the sequence of states ct while reading the input vectors x_t one at a time in order to collect sequential data. The input x_t and the state c_t generated by the light recurrence are adaptively combined using the reset gate r_t. The skip connection technique is used to calculate the hidden state ht of the highway network unit.

The light recurrence component is mainly manifested in the following two ways. First, in order to reduce the degree of recursion, its two gating units, the forgetting gate and the reset gate, no longer depend on the hidden state h_{t-1} at the previous moment, but depend on the intermediate state c_{t-1} at the previous moment; second, in order to reduce the amount of calculation, the Hadamard product is used instead of the matrix product. The specific implementation process is as follows.

First, the input $\mathrm{x_t}$ is linearly transformed, as shown in Equation (4).

$$\widetilde{\mathrm{x_t}} = \mathrm{Wx_t} \tag{4}$$

The forget gate of SRU is a vector that controls forgetting based on current information and past information. It obtains sequence information by reading the input vector x_t in order and calculates the state vector C_t. The calculation as shown in Equation (5).

$$\mathrm{f_t} = \sigma(\mathrm{W_f x_t} + \mathrm{v_f} \odot \mathrm{C_{t-1}} + \mathrm{b_f}) \tag{5}$$

In the formula, $\odot$ represents the element-by-element multiplication, σ represents the sigmoid function, b_f represents the offset term, and the intermediate state C_t synthesizes the information of the past state and the information of the current input. How much past information is retained depends on the calculated forgetting gate f_t, as shown in Equation (6).

$$\mathrm{C_t} = \mathrm{f_t} \odot \mathrm{C_{t-1}} + (1 - \mathrm{f_t}) \odot \widetilde{\mathrm{x_t}} \tag{6}$$

The highway network unit directly incorporates the input x_t into the calculation, which is equivalent to a crossover of the input in the residual network, as shown in Equations (7) and (8).

$$\mathrm{r_t} = \sigma(\mathrm{W_r x_t} + \mathrm{v_r} \odot \mathrm{C_{t-1}} + \mathrm{b_r}) \tag{7}$$

$$h_t = r_t \odot g(C_t) + (1 - r_t) \odot x_t \tag{8}$$

Here, b_r represents the offset term, and $(1 - r_t)\odot x_t$ is a skip connection, which can optimize the gradient propagation. When the network depth increases, the gradient will not disappear because the propagation distance is too far.

In the above formula, although the dependence of the previous moment is removed, there is still a certain bottleneck, that is, the operation of three matrix multiplications, which provides a deeper optimization strategy matrix multiplication. Batch processing can be performed at all time steps, which can significantly improve the intensity of calculation and improve the utilization of GPU. In the above formula, matrix multiplication can be combined into one, and subsequent processing can be found according to the index, as shown in Equation (9).

$$U^T = \begin{pmatrix} W \\ W_f \\ W_r \end{pmatrix} [x_1, x_2, .x_n] \tag{9}$$

Among them, $U \in R^{n\times 3D}$ is the calculated matrix, d is the hidden state size, and n is the sequence length of the input data.

3.2. Detection Model

LSTM and GRU can suppress gradient disappearance and gradient explosion to a certain extent when capturing long-distance related information, and their effects are better than traditional SimpleRNN. However, as variants of SimpleRNN, they have the disadvantage of the RNN structure itself, that is, parallel computing cannot be performed. SRU can realize parallel computing of hidden layer dimension, with less calculation, fewer parameters and fast training. In industrial Internet intrusion detection, CNN can locally perceive network traffic data through convolution operation and capture local features and signs of attack in the data so as to realize sensitive detection of intrusion behavior. In addition, CNN can adaptively learn and optimize network weights through the backpropagation algorithm in the training process, thereby improving the generalization ability of the model and the ability to detect unknown attacks. However, as the number of layers of the model network becomes deeper and deeper, the problem of gradient disappearance will inevitably become more obvious, which will consume a lot of computing resources. Thus, we introduce the residual connection. The residual connection allows information to be transmitted across layers in the network, avoiding the problem of gradient disappearance and gradient explosion. This direct connection method can maintain the information integrity of the input data and enable the network to learn and model complex intrusion behaviors more deeply.

The detection model based on Res-CNN-SRU intrusion constructed in this paper is shown in Figure 3. The process is as follows.

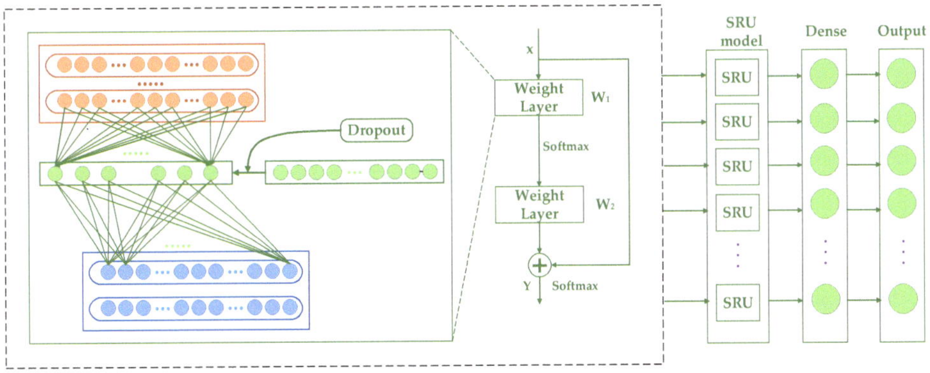

Figure 3. Intrusion detection model based on Res-CNN-SRU.

1. Firstly, the original gas pipeline traffic is preprocessed, and the preprocessed data are input into the convolution layer.
2. Feature extraction. In the 1D residual block, the input has two paths. In the first path, the data are first extracted by the convolutional layer, and then the features are convoluted to summarize the output. Within the residual structure, feature reuse is completed through weight sharing. The second path is where the data are directly output after shortcut processing, and the final output is the sum of two parts. The obtained results are then passed through 1 BN layer, Conv1D layer and maximum pooling layer, and finally the extracted features are obtained. Finally, we use the output vector as the input of the SRU to predict the subsequent features.
3. First, a time series is generated for the input data so that the input data become sequence data with a time step. After the time series traffic is generated, we set the learning rate attenuation to control the learning rate in segments, in order to achieve more efficient learning at different stages and train the neural network. We use small batches of random gradient descent for training. The output obtained by the SRU is passed through the fully connected layer. In order to prevent overfitting, a dropout layer is added. Finally, the classification is performed through the softmax layer.

Dropout function is set after the pooling layer, and some neuron nodes are randomly discarded during the training process, with a probability of 0.2. The mechanism of randomly discarding some neurons is equivalent to training different neural networks in each iteration, which can effectively suppress the occurrence of overfitting. The vector operation of the dropout function is expressed in Equation (10).

$$dropout\left(x_j^{l'}\right) = x_j^{l'} \circ m \tag{10}$$

where $x^i{}_j$ is the value of the input vector, m is the value of the random mask vector, and $\circ$ represents the product of elements, that is, the multiplication of the same elements. When the corresponding position element of the mask matrix or vector is 1, the input element is retained. When the corresponding position element is 0, the input element is discarded.

The classification stage uses the features learned by the model based on Res-CNN-SRU to mark the input instance. At this stage, a fully connected output layer maps the learned features to the output class. The output of this stage is controlled by the softmax function, as shown in Equation (11).

$$\mathrm{y(x)} = \mathrm{softmax}(\varphi) \tag{11}$$

where φ is the output of the dropout layer.

4. Experiment

In this section, we first introduce the dataset used in the experiment, then describe the implementation and evaluation indicators of data preprocessing and carry out multiple comparative tests by constantly adjusting parameters.

4.1. Experimental Dataset

In 2014, Mississippi State University published a set of industrial control system intrusion detection standard datasets from the network layer data of a natural gas pipeline control system [34]. Compared with the KDD CUP99 dataset, the data collected in Mississippi are the data collected in the industrial network, which have higher dimensions and more types of attacks. The attack types of the dataset are shown in Table 1.

4.2. Data Preprocessing

Data preprocessing plays an important role in the experiment and testing of the industrial Internet intrusion detection model, which affects the performance and detection accuracy of the intrusion detection model. The data preprocessing in this paper is mainly divided into three steps: low-variance filter, normalization, and one-hot encoding.

Table 1. Description of datasets.

Attack Type	Description	Label	Number
Normal	Normal data	0	61,156
NMRI	Naive malicious response injection attack	1	2763
CMRI	Complex malicious response injection attack	2	15,466
MSCI	Malicious state command injection attack	3	782
MPCI	Malicious parameter command injection attack	4	7637
MFCI	Malicious function command injection attack	5	573
DOS	Denial-of-service attack	6	1837
Recon	Reconnaissance attack	7	6805

4.2.1. Low-Variance Filter

Our dataset is complex and variable, with many eigenvalues, but not every eigenvalue is well distinguished, that is, it has a very low variance. Such eigenvalues have no analytical value, so we choose to remove them directly. For example, if a feature of a column accounts for 95% of the instance value of all input samples, it can be considered not very useful. If 100% is 1, then this feature is meaningless. This paper chooses to remove the nine feature columns with the smallest variance, and finally obtains a dataset with 17-dimensional effective eigenvalues.

4.2.2. Normalization

The gas pipeline dataset has high-dimensional features, and the maximum and minimum intervals of these features are large. We set the data eigenvalues in a small specific interval. We use min max normalization to map the features to the range [0, 1]. The normalization formula is as shown in Equation (12).

$$x'_p = \frac{x_q - min(x_p)}{\max(x_p) - min(x_p)} \tag{12}$$

4.2.3. One-Hot Encoding

The classifier cannot directly process the disordered discrete features of the natural gas pipeline dataset. We use one-hot coding to establish a mapping table for discrete feature data to make them ordered and continuous. The dataset has eight classification results. They can be encoded as (1,0,0,0,0,0,0,0), (0,1,0,0,0,0,0,0), (0,0,1,0,0,0,0,0), (0,0,0,1,0,0,0,0), (0,0,0,0,1,0,0,0), (0,0,0,0,0,0,0,1,0,0), (0,0,0,0,0,0,0,0,1,0), (0,0,0,0,0,0,0,0,0,0,0,1), as shown in Equation (13).

$$One-hot\ encoding = \begin{cases} (1,\ 0,\ 0,\ 0,\ 0,\ 0,\ 0,\ 0),\ if\ the\ result\ is\ Normal(0). \\ (0,\ 1,\ 0,\ 0,\ 0,\ 0,\ 0,\ 0),\ if\ the\ result\ is\ NMRI(1). \\ (0,\ 0,\ 1,\ 0,\ 0,\ 0,\ 0,\ 0),\ if\ the\ result\ is\ CMRI(2). \\ (0,\ 0,\ 0,\ 1,\ 0,\ 0,\ 0,\ 0),\ if\ the\ result\ is\ MSCI(3). \\ (0,\ 0,\ 0,\ 0,\ 1,\ 0,\ 0,\ 0),\ if\ the\ result\ is\ MPCI(4). \\ (0,\ 0,\ 0,\ 0,\ 0,\ 1,\ 0,\ 0),\ if\ the\ result\ is\ MFCI(5). \\ (0,\ 0,\ 0,\ 0,\ 0,\ 0,\ 1,\ 0),\ if\ the\ result\ is\ DOS(6). \\ (0,\ 0,\ 0,\ 0,\ 0,\ 0,\ 0,\ 1),\ if\ the\ result\ is\ Recon(7). \end{cases} \tag{13}$$

4.3. *Benchmarking Metrics*

Accuracy, precision, recall and F1 are used as key performance indicators to evaluate the proposed method. The calculation methods of these four indicators are as shown in Equations (14)–(17).

$$\text{Accuracy} = \frac{TN + TP}{TP + FP + TN + TP} \tag{14}$$

$$\text{Precision} = \frac{TP}{TP + FP} \tag{15}$$

$$\text{Recall} = \frac{TP}{FN + TP} \tag{16}$$

$$\text{F1} = \frac{2TP}{2TP + FP + FN} \tag{17}$$

Among them, *TP* represents the abnormal flow instance of correct classification, *TN* represents the normal flow instance of correct classification, *FP* is the normal flow instance of wrong classification, and *FN* represents the abnormal flow instance of wrong classification.

4.4. Performance Comparison

The performance of the proposed algorithm is evaluated and analyzed, mainly involving detection time, detection accuracy and loss.

4.4.1. Experimental Parameter Settings

This method is compared with three traditional machine learning methods (SVM, naïve Bayes and REPtree) and three deep learning methods based on RNN. The experiment is carried out on a workstation with Intel Core i7-9700H CPU, NVIDIA GeForce GTX745 GPU, 32GB RAM and Windows 10 64-bit operating system. We use the 2.3.1 version of the Keras package to implement our model. Experiments are carried out under the same hardware, software environment and algorithm parameters. The ratio of the training set to the test set is 8:2. We conducted four experiments under different dataset partitions with an average accuracy of 98.7%, similar to the results described in the paper. The specific parameters of the simulation platform are shown in Table 2.

Table 2. Experimental parameters.

Parameter Name	Description	Value
depth	Hidden layer size	4
optimizer	Gradient descent algorithm	RMSprop
activation	Activation function	softmax
epochs	Iteration size	100
batch_size	Samples per epoch	100
unit	Hidden unit size	128
dropout	Random deactivation rate	0.2

4.4.2. Hyperparameter Optimization

In this paper, we use the hyperparameter optimization of grid search to obtain the best performance. This method can evaluate each possible permutation of the selected hyperparameters. This paper focuses on the selection of activation function, optimizer and batch size.

Activation function is an important part of neural network design that directly affects the performance of neural network. Each activation function has different effects on the overall performance and convergence of the neural network, so the choice of activation function is very important. In this paper, we choose three most commonly used activation functions for experiments, namely, rectified linear unit (ReLU), softmax, and hyperbolic tangent (Tanh).

One cycle of learning and adjusting the network weights is called an epoch, and the number of samples used in another iteration becomes the batch size. Different batch sizes affect the convergence speed and convergence effect of this model. In this paper, we choose 10 and 100 as the batch size for hyperparameter search.

In the training process, the choice of the optimizer also affects the best solution to the model parameters. A suitable optimizer can make the model fall into overfitting and achieve global optimization. In this paper, we choose three optimizers, such as Adam, SGD, and RMSprop, to conduct experiments.

Table 3 shows the performance of each hyperparameter combination. By adjusting the hyperparameters, the model with the highest accuracy of 98.79% is obtained. The activation function to achieve the optimal result is softmax, the optimization method is RMSprop, and the batch size is 100.

Table 3. The effect of different hyperparameters on model accuracy.

Activation	Optimizer	Batch_Size	Accuracy (%)	Precision (%)	Recall (%)	F1 (%)
ReLU	Adam	10	98.5	94.06	94.01	94.05
ReLU	Adam	100	96.51	79.67	77.41	78.44
ReLU	SGD	10	90.71	62.26	62.2	62.26
ReLU	SGD	100	78.43	31.58	63.15	42.1
ReLU	RMSprop	10	97.78	88.04	86.91	87.42
ReLU	RMSprop	100	96.26	95.38	95.49	95.42
softmax	Adam	10	98.54	94.35	94.07	94.21
softmax	Adam	100	98.55	94.25	94.23	94.24
softmax	SGD	10	94.54	78.48	78.09	78.26
softmax	SGD	100	90.71	62.27	62.31	62.26
softmax	RMSprop	10	98.55	94.26	94.27	94.26
softmax	RMSprop	100	98.79	95.34	95.04	95.19
Tanh	Adam	10	98.66	94.72	94.70	94.73
Tanh	Adam	100	98.35	93.77	93.08	93.41
Tanh	SGD	10	87.51	60.15	60.22	60.19
Tanh	SGD	100	90.71	62.26	62.31	62.27
Tanh	RMSprop	10	98.42	93.09	92.63	92.83
Tanh	RMSprop	100	98.63	95.15	93.84	94.46

4.4.3. Comparison of Methods

Table 4 shows the performance comparison of our method with the other six methods, including three classical machine learning methods and three deep learning methods based on RNN. The results show that compared with the other methods, the intrusion detection method based on Res-CNN-SRU has the highest accuracy, precision, recall rate and F1 on the gas pipeline dataset, and the training time is the shortest. This means that our proposed method achieves the best intrusion detection results on the gas pipeline dataset.

Table 4. Comparison with other methods.

Paper	Method	Accuracy (%)	Precision (%)	Recall (%)	F1 (%)	Training Time (s)
[10]	SVM	92.5	78.2	93.6	85.2	-
[11]	Naïve Bayes	71.94	70.6	71.9	71.24	-
[12]	Decision Tree	84.9	86.1	84.9	87	-
[18]	RNN	94.95	78.89	78.17	77.98	-
[19]	BLSTM	97.36	89.59	89.36	90.1	102
[20]	CNN-GRU	94.69	78.94	78.92	75.45	107
	Ours	98.79	95.34	95.04	95.38	89

Figure 4 shows the comparison of training accuracy and loss between our method and three RNN-based deep learning methods. All models train 100 epochs. In contrast, our method converges faster in the training process and can obtain higher accuracy.

Experiments are performed on normal data and various types of attack data, as shown in Figure 5. The results show that the RNN algorithm has low accuracy for CMRI and DOS data, the BLSTM algorithm has low accuracy for DOS data, and the CNN-GRU algorithm has low accuracy for NMRI, CMRI, DOS and Recon data. Compared with other algorithms, our method has better performance on all kinds of data in the gas pipeline dataset, and the accuracy of DOS data is significantly higher than other algorithms.

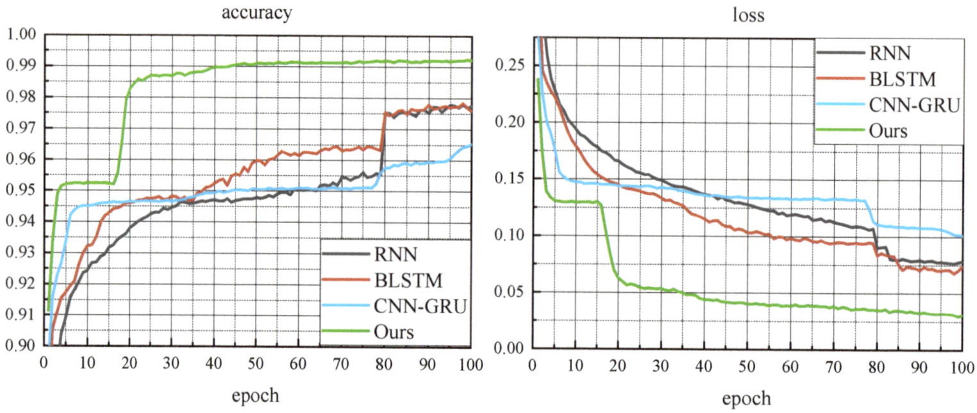

Figure 4. Training accuracy and loss.

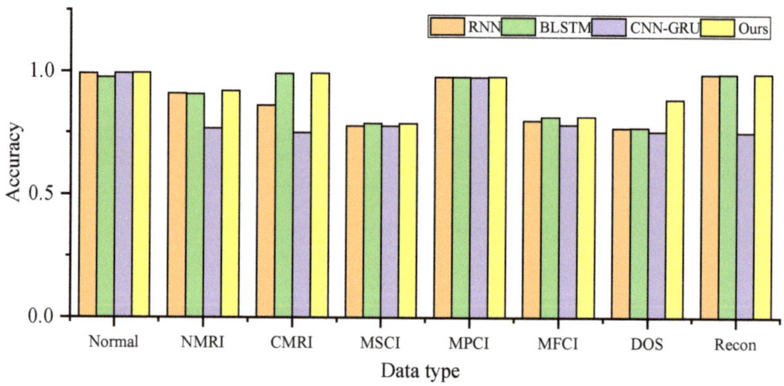

Figure 5. Accuracy of normal data and various types of attack data.

The output vector based on 1D CNN with residual connection is put into a time-varying model based on RNNs. These four models are SimpleRNN, LSTM, GRU and SRU. We use the softmax activation function and RMSprop optimizer.

In Figure 6, SRU has the highest accuracy of the methods. In Figure 7, the training time of SRU is significantly shorter than that of LSTM and GRU. SimpleRNN has the least training time because of its simplest internal structure. However, SimpleRNN is prone to gradient disappearance and gradient explosion. It can be seen from the above results that the accuracy of SRU is the highest among the models, and the training time is shorter than LSTM and GRU.

We conducted a model ablation study to verify the effect of our model. Specifically, verification improvements come from each component. Each component is removed from the Res-CNN-SRU-based model in turn and compared with the complete model based on Res-CNN-SRU.

The results of the ablation study are shown in Figure 8. This proves that whatever components are removed from the model, the final accuracy, precision recall and F1 will decline. Among them, the accuracy of the model based on Res-CNN-SRU is 0.9879, the precision is 0.9534, the recall is 0.9504, and the F1 is 0.9519. If there is no CNN, the accuracy rate is obviously lagging behind and becomes the worst result. After deleting the SRU or residual connection part, all performance indicators also decreased. This shows that the use of CNN can effectively and automatically extract the features of industrial Internet network traffic and improve the accuracy of intrusion detection.

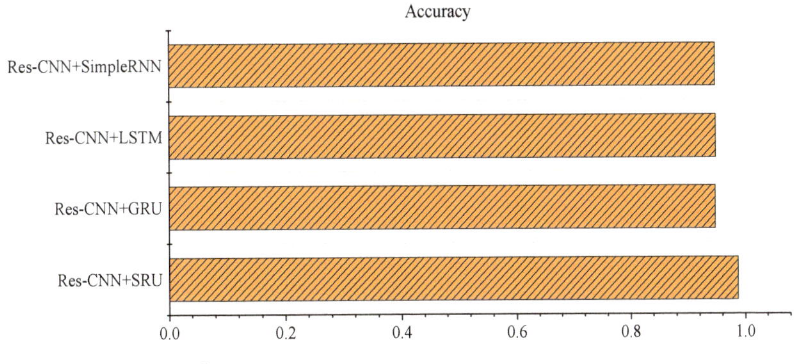

Figure 6. Comparison of accuracy.

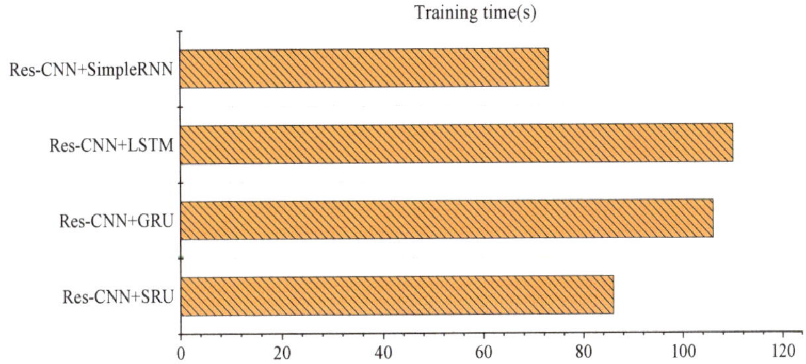

Figure 7. Comparison of training time.

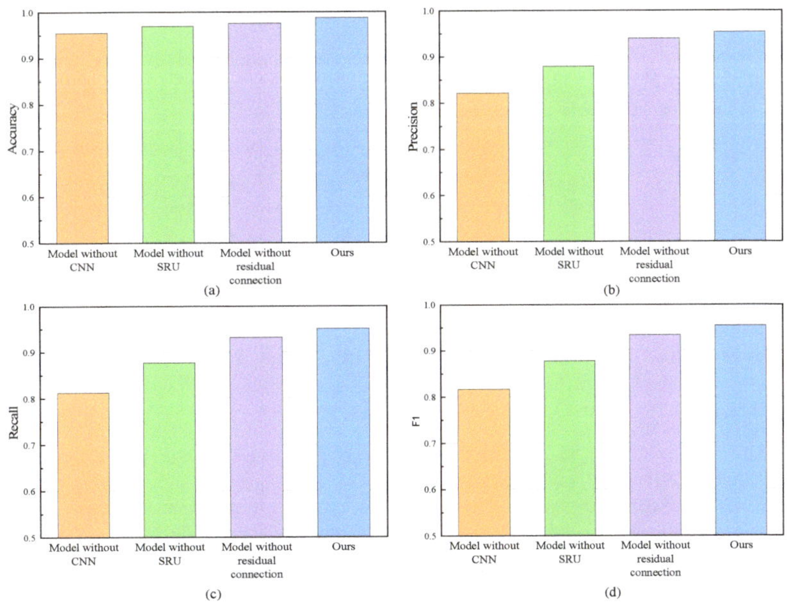

Figure 8. Ablation experimental results. (**a**) Accuracy; (**b**) precision; (**c**) recall; (**d**) F1.

5. Conclusions

Aiming at the problems of large industrial network traffic and difficult processing of features, this paper proposes an industrial Internet intrusion detection method based on Res-CNN-SRU. Our main contribution is to introduce a deep feature extraction method that combines spatial and temporal dimensions. Firstly, we propose a 1D CNN for spatial feature extraction of high-dimensional network traffic, which can extract local features without losing temporal features. At the same time, residual connection can not only alleviate the problem of gradient disappearance but also improve the convergence speed of the network. Then, a parallel computing SRU anomaly traffic detection algorithm is proposed. Compared with the traditional LSTM model, the SRU model has the advantages of efficient calculation, fast training, strong sequence modeling ability and low memory usage, and can train a model with high accuracy faster. Finally, using the gas pipeline dataset, the performance test and ablation experiment of the proposed intrusion detection model are carried out. The experimental results show that the accuracy of this method on the Mississippi natural gas pipeline dataset can reach 0.9879, the precision is 0.9534, the recall is 0.9504, and the F1 is 0.9519, giving higher accuracy and calculation efficiency than the existing method. This proves the performance advantages and effectiveness of our method on the gas pipeline dataset. In real life, the application of industrial Internet intrusion detection can detect and respond to intrusion events in time to reduce potential risks and losses. Early detection and response can prevent attackers from causing more damage to industrial systems and reduce downtime and production disruptions.

However, with the rapid development of the Internet, network intrusion behaviors are ever-changing, and many new attacks have emerged. Due to the lack of sufficient sample data to train machine learning models or detect the characteristics of new attacks, the encryption of network traffic and privacy protection measures may limit the visibility of intrusion detection systems to attack activities. The detection effect of this system against unknown attacks is not ideal. The detection of unknown type attacks is a complex and challenging problem. In the future, we will adopt a combination of supervised learning and unsupervised learning. For the attacks that cannot be identified by the classification model, unsupervised learning will be adopted to perform cluster analysis so as to enhance the detection ability of the intrusion detection system to unknown-type attacks.

Author Contributions: Conceptualization, Z.C. and Y.S.; methodology, Z.C. and Y.S.; validation, J.Z., L.Z. and P.L.; data curation, Y.F. All authors have read and agreed to the published version of the manuscript.

Funding: This research was funded by the National Natural Science Foundation of China (62072416), Key Research and Development Special Project of Henan Province (221111210500), and Key Technologies R&D Program of Henan Province (232102211053, 222102210170).

Data Availability Statement: Not applicable.

Conflicts of Interest: The authors declare no conflict of interest.

References

1. Dai, M.; Deng, H.; Chen, B.; Su, G.; Lin, X.; Wang, H. Design of binary erasure code with triple simultaneous objectives for distributed edge caching in industrial Internet of Things networks. *IEEE Trans. Ind. Inform.* **2019**, *16*, 5497–5504. [CrossRef]
2. Huang, X.; Hong, S.H.; Li, Y. Hour-ahead price based energy management scheme for industrial facilities. *IEEE Trans. Ind. Inform.* **2017**, *13*, 2886–2898. [CrossRef]
3. Zhang, Y.; Guo, Z.; Lv, J.; Liu, Y. A framework for smart production-logistics systems based on CPS and industrial IoT. *IEEE Trans. Ind. Inform.* **2018**, *14*, 4019–4032. [CrossRef]
4. Awotunde, J.B.; Chakraborty, C.; Adeniyi, A.E. Intrusion detection in industrial internet of things network-based on deep learning model with rule-based feature selection. *Wirel. Commun. Mob. Comput.* **2021**, *2021*, 7154587. [CrossRef]
5. Bhavsar, Y.B.; Waghmare, K.C. Intrusion detection system using data mining technique: Support vector machine. *Int. Emerg. Technol. Adv. Eng.* **2013**, *3*, 581–586.
6. Kuang, F.; Xu, W.; Zhang, S. A novel hybrid KPCA and SVM with GA model for intrusion detection. *Appl. Soft Comput.* **2014**, *18*, 178–184. [CrossRef]

7. Kumar, V.; Chauhan, H.; Panwar, D. K-means clustering approachto analyze NSL- KDD intrusion detection dataset. *Int. J. Soft Comput. Eng.* **2013**, *3*, 1–4.
8. Zhao, H.; Liu, I. Research on test data generation method of complex event big data processing system based on Bayesian network. *Comput. Appl. Res.* **2018**, *35*, 155–158,162.
9. Zhang, R.; Song, Y.; Wang, X. Network Intrusion Detection Scheme Based on IPSO-SVM Algorithm. In *Proceedings of the 2022 IEEE Asia-Pacific Conference on Image Processing, Electronics and Computers (IPEC), Dalian, China, 14–16 April 2022*; IEEE: Piscataway, NJ, USA, 2022; pp. 1011–1014.
10. Anton, S.D.D.; Sinha, S.; Schotten, H.D. Anomaly-Based Intrusion Detection in Industrial Data with SVM and Random Forests. In *Proceedings of the 2019 International Conference on Software, Telecommunications and Computer Networks (SoftCOM), Split, Croatia, 19–21 September 2019*; IEEE: Piscataway, NJ, USA, 2019; pp. 1–6.
11. Khan, A.A.Z. Misuse Intrusion Detection Using Machine Learning for Gas Pipeline SCADA Networks. In Proceedings of the International Conference on Security and Management (SAM), The Steering Committee of The World Congress in Computer Science, Computer Engineering and Applied Computing (WorldComp), Las Vegas, NV, USA, 29 July–1 August 2019; pp. 84–90.
12. Al-Asiri, M.; El-Alfy, E.S.M. On using physical based intrusion detection in SCADA systems. *Procedia Comput. Sci.* **2020**, *170*, 34–42. [CrossRef]
13. Eigner, O.; Kreimel, P.; Tavolato, P. Detection of Man-in-the-Middle Attacks on Industrial Control Networks. In *Proceedings of the 2016 International Conference on Software Security and Assurance (ICSSA), Saint Pölten, Austria, 24–25 August 2016*; IEEE: Piscataway, NJ, USA, 2016; pp. 64–69.
14. Aiswal, S.; Saxena, K.; Mishra, A.; Sahu, S.K. A KNN-ACO approach for intrusion detection using KDDCUP'99 dataset. In *Proceedings of the 2016 3rd International Conference on Computing for Sustainable Global Development (INDIACom), New Delhi, India, 16–18 March 2016*; IEEE: Piscataway, NJ, USA, 2016; pp. 628–633.
15. Xia, W.; Neware, R.; Kumar, S.D.; Karras, D.A.; Rizwan, A. An optimization technique for intrusion detection of industrial control network vulnerabilities based on BP neural network. *Int. J. Syst. Assur. Eng. Manag.* **2022**, *13* (Suppl. S1), 576–582. [CrossRef]
16. Yang, A.; Zhuansun, Y.; Liu, C.; Li, J.; Zhang, C. Design of intrusion detection system for Internet of Things based on improved BP neural network. *IEEE Access* **2019**, *7*, 106043–106052. [CrossRef]
17. Li, Y.; Xu, Y.; Liu, Z.; Hou, H.; Zheng, Y.; Xin, Y.; Zhao, Y.; Cui, L. Robust detection for network intrusion of industrial IoT based on multi-CNN fusion. *Measurement* **2020**, *154*, 107450. [CrossRef]
18. Yin, C.; Zhu, Y.; Fei, J.; He, X. A deep learning approach for intrusion detection using recurrent neural networks. *IEEE Access* **2017**, *5*, 21954–21961. [CrossRef]
19. Roy, B.; Cheung, H. A Deep Learning Approach for Intrusion Detection in Internet of Things Using Bi-Directional Long Short-term Memory Recurrent Neural Network. In Proceedings of the 2018 28th International Telecommunication Networks and Applications Conference (ITNAC), Sydney, NSW, Australia, 21–23 November 2018; IEEE: Piscataway, NJ, USA, 2018; pp. 1–6.
20. Cao, B.; Li, C.; Song, Y.; Qin, Y.; Chen, C. Network intrusion detection model based on CNN and GRU model. *Appl. Sci.* **2022**, *12*, 4184. [CrossRef]
21. Zhou, X.; Hu, Y.; Liang, W.; Ma, J.; Jin, Q. Variational LSTM enhanced anomaly detection for industrial big data. *IEEE Trans. Ind. Inform.* **2020**, *17*, 3469–3477. [CrossRef]
22. Hwang, R.H.; Peng, M.C.; Nguyen, V.L.; Chang, Y.L. An LSTM-based deep learning approach for classifying malicious traffic at the packet level. *Appl. Sci.* **2019**, *9*, 3414. [CrossRef]
23. Ling, J.; Zhu, Z.; Luo, Y.; Wang, H. An intrusion detection method for industrial control systems based on bidirectional simple recurrent unit. *Comput. Electr. Eng.* **2021**, *91*, 107049. [CrossRef]
24. Xu, Y.; Jin, T.; Xu, Y.; Shi, X.; Chen, S.; Sun, W.; Xue, Y.; Wu, H. Transformer image recognition system based on deep learning. *J. Shanghai Electr. Power Univ.* **2021**, *37*, 51–56.
25. Mahmoud, A.; Zrigui, M. Sentence embedding and convolutional neural network for semantic textual similarity detection in Arabic language. *Arab. J. Sci. Eng.* **2019**, *44*, 9263–9274. [CrossRef]
26. Zhang, K.; Guo, Y.; Wang, X.; Yuan, J.; Ding, Q. Multiple feature reweight densenet for image classification. *IEEE Access* **2019**, *7*, 9872–9880. [CrossRef]
27. Huang, J.T.; Li, J.; Gong, Y. An Analysis of Convolutional Neural Networks for Speech Recognition. In *Proceedings of the IEEE International Conference on Acoustics, Speech and Signal Processing, South Brisbane, QLD, Australia, 19–24 April 2015*; IEEE: Piscataway, NJ, USA, 2015; pp. 4989–4993.
28. Krizhevsky, A.; Sutskever, I.; Hinton, G.E. Imagenet Classification with Deep Convolutional Neural Networks. In Proceedings of the 2012 Advances in Neural Information Processing Systems (NIPS2012), Lake Tahoe, NV, USA, 3–6 December 2012; pp. 1097–1105.
29. Wang, H.; Shi, H.; Chen, X.; Zhao, L.; Huang, Y.; Liu, C. An improved convolutional neural network based approach for automated heartbeat classification. *J. Med. Syst.* **2020**, *44*, 35. [CrossRef] [PubMed]
30. Zhao, L.; Ma, Y. Fault diagnosis of gear box based on one dimensional convolutional neural networks. *J. Test Meas. Technol.* **2019**, *33*, 302–306.
31. Qu, J.; Yu, L.; Yuan, T.; Tian, Y.; Gao, F. Adaptive fault diagnosis algorithm for rolling bearings based on one-dimensional convolutional neural network. *Chin. J. Sci. Instrum.* **2018**, *39*, 134–143. [CrossRef]

32. Shaikh, A.; Gupta, P. Real-time intrusion detection based on residual learning through ResNet algorithm. *Int. J. Syst. Assur. Eng. Manag.* **2022**, 1–15. [CrossRef]
33. He, K.M.; Zhang, X.Y.; Ren, S.Q.; Sun, J. Deep Residual Learning for Image Recognition. In *Proceedings of the 2016 IEEE Conference on Computer Vision and Pattern Recognition (CVPR), Las Vegas, NV, USA, 27–30 June 2016*; IEEE: Piscataway, NJ, USA, 2016.
34. Morris, T.; Gao, W. Industrial Control System Traffic Data Sets for Intrusion Detection Research. In *Critical Infrastructure Protection VIII. ICCIP 2014. IFIP Advances in Information and Communication Technology*; Springer: Berlin/Heidelberg, Germany, 2014; pp. 65–78.

electronics

MDPI

Article

HoaKV: High-Performance KV Store Based on the Hot-Awareness in Mixed Workloads

Jingyu Liu [1], Xiaoqin Fan [1], Youxi Wu [1], Yong Zheng [2] and Lu Liu [3,*]

1 School of Artificial Intelligence, Hebei University of Technology, Tianjin 300400, China; liujy@hebut.edu.cn (J.L.); 202122802058@stu.hebut.edu.cn (X.F.); wuc@scse.hebut.edu.cn (Y.W.)
2 State Grid Energy Saving Service Co., Ltd., Beijing 100052, China; zhengyong@sgecs.sgcc.com.cn
3 School of Computer Science, Beijing Institute of Technology, Beijing 100081, China
* Correspondence: liulu@bit.edu.cn

Abstract: Key–value (KV) stores based on the LSM-tree have become the mainstream of contemporary store engines, but there are problems with high write and read amplification. Moreover, the real-world workload has a high data skew, and the existing KV store lacks hot-awareness, leading to its unreliable and poor performance on the highly skewed real-world workload. In this paper, we propose HoaKV, which unifies the key design ideas of hot issues, KV separation, and hybrid indexing technology in a system. Specifically, HoaKV uses the heat differentiation in KV pairs to manage the hot data and the cold data and conducts real-time dynamic adjustment data classification management. It also uses partial KV separation technology to manage differential KV pairs for large and small KV pairs in the cold data. In addition, HoaKV uses hybrid indexing technology to index the hot data and the cold data, respectively, to improve the performance of reading, writing, and scanning at the same time. In the mixed read and write workloads experments show that HoaKV performs significantly better than several state-of-the-art KV store technologies such as LevelDB, RocksDB, PebblesDB, and WiscKey.

Keywords: key–value store; LSM-tree; hash indexing; hot-awareness; KV separation

check for updates

Citation: Liu, J.; Fan, X.; Wu, Y.; Zheng, Y.; Liu, L. HoaKV: High-Performance KV Store Based on the Hot-Awareness in Mixed Workloads. *Electronics* **2023**, *12*, 3227. https://doi.org/10.3390/electronics12153227

Academic Editor: Andrei Kelarev

Received: 19 June 2023
Revised: 21 July 2023
Accepted: 24 July 2023
Published: 26 July 2023

1. Introduction

Persistent KV stores are an essential part of modern store infrastructure [1,2]. KV stores are used in a wide variety of applications due to its excellent horizontal scalability and access speed and support for unstructured data stores, such as web search [3–6], e-commerce, social networking, data deduplication [7], and graph stores [8]. KV stores, organizes, and manages data in the form of KV pairs, usually providing a set of simple interfaces for data operation: write, read, and scan. With the development of Internet applications, the scale of user access and data are growing rapidly. Compared with relational databases, KV stores can better support mass user access.

The Log-Structured Merge-tree (LSM-tree) [9] is the main structure of persistent KV stores, such as the classic Google LevelDB [10]; Facebook RocksDB [11], which is a multi-threaded improvement based on LevelDB; Amazon DynamoDB [12]; the Apache-distributed database Cassandra [13]; the large-scale KV store HBase [3]; and BigTable [4]. The LSM-tree is a persistent index structure optimized for write-intensive workloads. The core idea is to improve write efficiency by sacrificing partial read performance and converting random write requests into sequential writes. The LSM-tree has the advantages of efficient write performance, efficient range query performance, and scalability. Compression operation is the key technology to ensure the read speed of the LSM-tree, but a large number of compression operations will reduce the system performance and lead to write amplification, which has always been the main limitation of the LSM-tree. Therefore, the previous research directions of KV store optimization based on the LSM-tree mainly include write amplification, compression operation optimization [14], adaptation to new hardware problems [15], special workload [16], secondary index or memory optimization [17,18], etc. Reducing the write amplification [19] is often accompanied by a decline in query performance or the use of large memory. Thus, the full performance potential of KV stores are still constrained by the inherent multi-level-based LSM-tree design.

Among KV store workloads in the real world, delete-intensive and update-intensive workloads dominate many store scenarios, including server log cleaning [20] and online transaction processing [21]. Therefore, hot issues in mixed workloads (that is, a small number of projects frequently visited in highly skewed workloads) [22] are a common problem in real scenarios and have been extensively studied in the literature [23,24]. Many store systems, such as LevelDB [10] and RocksDB [11], use KV stores in memory to manage hot projects. UniKV [25] takes the latest incoming data as the hot data and uses the hash index in memory to index the hot data, to achieve efficient access performance. HotRing [26] is optimized for massively concurrent access to a small portion of items and dynamically adapts to the shift of hotspots by pointing bucket heads to frequently accessed items. However, how to accurately judge the hot and cold of the currently accessed file block has always been a research difficulty. In recent years, with the development of machine learning technology, various classification algorithms have been increasingly applied to the field of system structure design. Therefore, the use of machine learning algorithms, to predict the hot and cold of the file block and is applied to the cache optimization mechanism, is a problem worth studying. In addition, the access frequency of data changes dynamically, so it is meaningful to take timely response measures to the access of data.

To this end, we design a novel KV store. Based on the differentiated key-value management scheme, mixed index method, and a variety of well-designed technologies, HoaKV achieves high read, write, and scan performance for large KV stores with mixed workloads. Our main contributions are summarized as follows:

- We propose HoaKV, which coordinates the differential management of the hot data and the cold data to effectively adapt to mixed workloads. Specifically, HoaKV divides KV pairs according to the frequency of read and write access (i.e., heat), preferentially allocates system resources for the hot data to achieve fast access, and further carries out special management for the cold data according to its size.
- We propose a dynamic adjustment technology for the hot and cold data to achieve high scalability in large KV stores. Specifically, we timely adjust the classification of data and change its store management method according to the heat of real-time data changes.
- We propose a hybrid index method, namely the three-level hash index method in memory designed for the hot data and the three-level direct index technology on disk designed for the cold data, to improve I/O performance and reduce memory overhead.
- We propose a fine-grained partial KV separation and distinguish between small and large KV pairs in the cold data management to reduce the I/O overhead caused by frequent value movement caused by the compression operation of large KV pairs in the LSM-tree. In order to improve the performance of reading, writing, and scanning, we also propose a dynamic value grouping method to effectively manage the large KV pairs.
- We implemented a HoaKV prototype on LevelDB [10] and evaluated its performance using micro-benchmark and YCSB [24]. For micro-benchmark testing, HoaKV achieved efficient loading throughput, compared to LevelDB [10], RocksDB [11], WiscKey [19], and PebblesDB [27]. It also achieved significant throughput improvements in updates and reads.

2. Related Work

HoaKV is based on the previous work of building and optimizing KV stores. This section briefly introduces the previous work and the work close to HoaKV.

LSM-tree. Many persistent KV stores are built on the LSM-tree to solve scanning and scalability problems. In addition to building KV stores on new hardware such as nonvolatile memory or describing the real-world KV store workload, some research focuses on optimizing the write performance of the LSM-tree KV store, including optimizing the structure of the LSM-tree [27,28], KV separation [19,29,30], and reducing the compression overhead [31,32]. The main problem of write performance is the write amplification caused by the merge operation. For this reason, many researchers focus on how to optimize the merge operation. This can be roughly divided into two directions. One is the separation of key and value. WiscKey [19] uses the KV separation strategy to directly write the value into the value log and write the key and its corresponding value address into the LSM-tree. Helen H.W. Chan et al. put forward HashKV [29] based on WiscKey. Its core idea is to use the hash to group KV pairs, store the KV pairs in the corresponding segment group, and use the segment group as the unit when performing GC, thus reducing the GC overhead. However, its write performance is not ideal. Another research direction is reducing the write amplification by relaxing the requirement of data ordering in the same layer. DiffKV [28] utilizes a new structure, vTree, for value management with partial ordering. PebblesDB [31] proposes a fragmented LSM-tree, which relaxed the complete sorting of KV pairs by dividing each level into multiple non-overlapping segments and allowing KV pairs in each segment to not be sorted. UniKV [25] unifies hash indexing and the LSM-tree in a single system and leverages data locality with a layered design and dynamic range partitioning.

Hot-awareness. HashKV [29] proposes a distinction strategy between hot keys and cold keys. HashKV stores the hot keys in the segment of vLog, and separates the cold key, stores in the disk then. HotRing [26] proposes a novel hotspot-aware KVS, named HotRing, which is optimized for massively concurrent access to a small portion of items. Based on the cost–benefit model, uCleaner [33] proposes a method to separate the hot and cold data to reduce the I/O traffic caused by the phenomenon of valid data movement during GC.

Hybrid indexing. UniKV [25] aims to simultaneously achieve high performance in read, write, and scan, while supporting scalability, and it is also deployable in commodity store devices (e.g., SSDs). Data Calculator [34] and Continuums [35] focus on unifying the major different data structureto achieve self-designed KV stores. HiKV [36] and NoveLSM [37] designed a new index structure for nonvolatile memory. KVS_Top [38] uses a combination of hash and b-tree technologies to support the high-speed search of a large number of keys (40 million). DPPDL [39] adopts a dynamic partial-parallel strategy, which dynamically allocates the storage space with an appropriate degree of partial-parallelism according to performance requirements.

HoaKV also adopts the mixed index method. Different from the above hybrid index technology, HoaKV aims to achieve high-performance read, write, and scan, and supports scalability at the same time. HoaKV combines log structure and KV stores based on hash and sorting and uses a compact hash table to reduce the memory usage of each key. That is to say, HoaKV divides the data into the hot data and the cold data. Different methods are used for indexing the hot data and the cold data. In order to achieve fast read/write performance of the hot data, we use the hash index in memory. At the same time, for the index of the cold data, we use a common index that does not consume memory resources.

3. HoaKV Design

We propose HoaKV, which divides KV pairs into the hot data and the cold data, and further divides them into the large KV pairs and the small KV pairs according to the size of the cold data to achieve differential management of KV pairs. It supports efficient read and write through the hash index and the normal index. The data classification is adjusted through the dynamic change of the key value to the heat, to realize the dynamic scalable and high-performance KV store.

3.1. Architectural Overview

HoaKV consists of two parts as shown in Figure 1. The first part is called the HotStore, which stores the hottest part of KV pairs, and that is the data with the highest recent read/write access frequency. The second part is called the ColdStore, which stores KV pairs differentiated by value size. Our insight is to calculate the heat of data using the read and write frequencies of KV pairs. The hot data are the largest part of the read–write ratio and accounts for only a small fraction of all KV pairs, so we keep them in the HotStore (fully sorting by heat) and index them directly with in-memory hash indexing for fast reads and writes. Meanwhile, we keep the remaining large amount of cold KV pairs in the ColdStore for efficient scans and scalability. HoaKV realizes the idea via the following techniques:

- Hot-awareness splitting. HoaKV stores the hot data in the HotStore. When KV pairs in a data block are written from in-memory, we calculate the heat of each KV pair and compare it with the minimum heat of the HotStore, then, if it is large, we store it in the HotStore.
- Hot KV indexing. To improve read performance, HoaKV stores the keys and values of the hot data separately. Also, HoaKV designs lightweight three-level hash hot indexing to balance memory usage and hash collisions. The hash indexing tables indexes keyTag, heat, and vTableID.
- Partial KV separation. To efficiently manage KV pairs in the ColdStore, HoaKV presents a partial KV separation scheme. The cold data are divided into small KV pairs and large KV pairs. Furthermore, a differentiated and fine-grained key-value management mechanism is implemented in the ColdStore to avoid frequent value movement in the merge process.
- Dynamic value grouping. To achieve high read and write performance in large KV stores, HoaKV proposes a value grouping scheme that dynamically splits KV pairs into multiple groups that are independently managed according to the key ranges, to expand a KV store in a scale-out manner.
- Cold KV indexing. In order to quickly find the location of the values of KV pairs and update the heat of the cold data in real-time, HoaKV uses the cold indexing table to record keys, heat, and group ID, where the value is located.

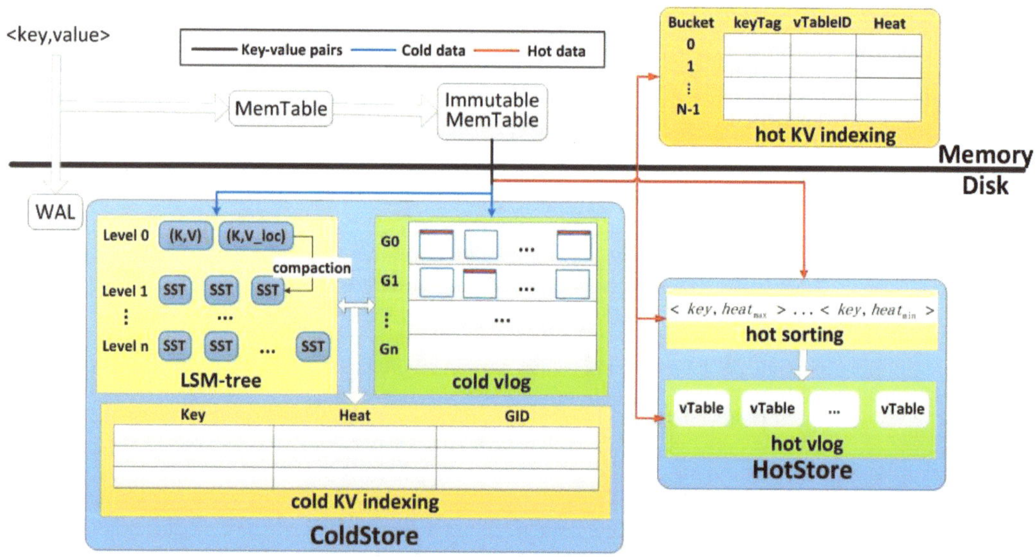

Figure 1. System overview.

3.2. Hot-Awareness Splitting

HoaKV divides all KV pairs into the hot data and the cold data. The hot data, which are the most frequently read–write accessed part of the data, accounts for a small portion of all key value pairs. The remaining data are the cold data, which accounts for the majority of the total data, and the cold data has less read and write access in a short time. HoaKV stores the hot data in the HotStore, and KV pairs are sorted by heat, that is, the data with the highest heat achieves the fastest read–write access efficiency. To reduce sorting overhead for the hot data, HoaKV stores the keys and values of the hot data separately.

We define the frequency of read–write access to KV pairs per unit time as heat, whose probability density function is as follows:

$$heat = (PW_i + PR_i)/T \quad (1)$$

where PW_i and PR_i represent the write frequency and read frequency of the ith KV pair, respectively, in the time T, and T is time. Data blocks are passed in from memory and the heat of each KV pair in the data block is calculated. HoaKV limits the size of the heat. When a KV pair has a heat greater than or equal to the predetermined threshold *HeatLimit*, the KV pair is the hot data, and HoaKV stores the KV pair in the HotStore. The KV pairs in the HotStore are sorted by heat, and the heat of KV pairs changes dynamically. The HotStore needs to sort the KV pairs frequently. To reduce sorting overhead, the HotStore stores the key and value of the hot data separately. The HotStore stores the key and the corresponding heat in the heat sorting and stores the value separately in the hot vlog.

Figure 2 depicts the hot-awareness splitting design. The data block are passed in from in-memory, and HoaKV updates and calculates the heat of each KV pair. If the heat of a KV pair is greater than or equal to *HeatLimit*, the KV pair is the hot data and are stored in the HotStore. For frequent read–write access to the hot data, the HotStore stores the keys and heat of the hot data in the hot sorting and sorts by heat. To reduce sorting overhead, the HotStore stores the values of the hot data in the hot vlog. The hot vlog is composed of multiple vTables, and the value of the hot data is stored in the vTable. The value of *HeatLimit* in the HotStore is dynamic. *HeatLimit* represents the minimum heat of the hot data. Due to the size of the HotStore being fixed, when the heat of the newly inserted KV pair is greater than *HeatLimit*, the KV pair corresponding to *HeatLimit* is redefined as the cold data, which is extracted from the HotStore and transferred into the ColdStore as the cold data. Then, the minimum heat in the latest sorting result is taken as *HeatLimit*, so the value of *HeatLimit* is dynamic.

The cold and hot data adjustment. The read and write access of KV pairs will increase the heat. The hot and cold data are not fixed, so they need to be adjusted dynamically. As shown in Algorithm 1, when a KV pair is inserted into the disk, we use a hash function to calculate the keyTag based on the key. Then, we search for the keyTag in the hot indexing table first. If it exists, it indicates that the KV pair is the hot data. We update its corresponding heat and perform a new hot sorting. The motivation proposed in this article is suitable for highly tilted workloads, so it is necessary for the efficient processing of the hot data. According to real-time reading and writing accesses of the data, we will timely update the location of the hot data in the disk through the heat sorting, so that the hot data that we need is accessed at the fastest speed and improves the performance of the storage engine. Furthermore, we require a higher time complexity for the sorting of the hot data, and the space complexity is not high. According to Algorithm 1, if the keyTag is in the hot indexing table, the system will update the heat of the hot data. As it is only updated and then sorted, the heat order sequence is basically orderly and decreasing, and the heat update of the hot data has been increasing. Therefore, based on the above characteristics, we have chosen the best sorting algorithm suitable for this situation for the hot sorting. Specifically, after updating the heat of the hot data, we start to compare and move forward from the position of the key to the previous node until the heat is less than the previous node. Therefore, in the worst case, the time complexity of this sorting algorithm is O

(N), and the space complexity is O (N). If corresponding to a read operation, the value corresponding to the key is returned from the hot vlog based on the vTableID in the hot indexing table. If it is a write operation, due to the real-time requirement for processing the hot data, we find the corresponding value from the hot vlog based on the vTableID and recycle the invalid value directly, where we then store the written value in the location of the old value. If the keyTag is in the cold indexing table and represents the KV pair as the cold data, we update its heat in the cold indexing table and compare it with *HeatLimit*. If it is greater than *HeatLimit*, we update it to the hot data. Specifically, we find the key with the lowest heat from the hot sorting, calculate the keyTag, find the vTableID from the hot indexing table, and then return the value from the hot vlog based on the vTableID. (this is the process of taking the heat minimum KV pair). Then, we update it to the cold data, compare its value to the threshold *Value_Size* (if greater than the threshold, take the key value separation technique, otherwise store the KV pair directly in LSM-tree). Then, we insert the new hot data into the hot sorting to further redo the hot sorting. Specifically, we calculate the keyTag of the new hot data, store the heat in the hot indexing table, store the value of the hot data in the vTable of the hot vlog, and then return the vTableID which is stored in the indexing entry of the hot indexing table. For the read operation, the value of the hot data is returned directly when the new hot data are inserted into the HotStore. For the write operation, we insert the latest value directly into the vTable of the hot vlog. If the keyTag is not in the cold indexing table, we insert it directly into the ColdStore. For read operation, we return the null values directly. For write operation, we write directly when the KV pair is inserted into the ColdStore. This enables dynamic adjustment of the cold and hot data.

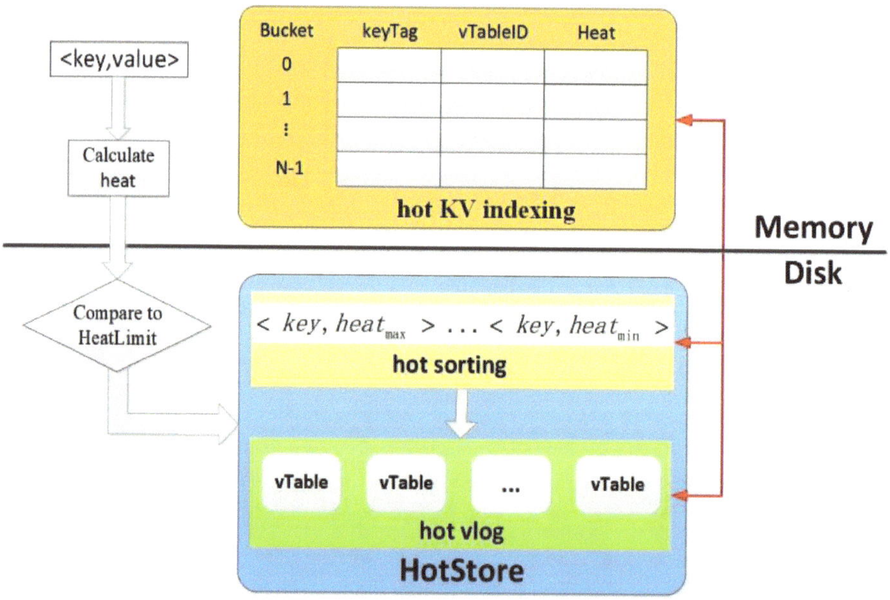

Figure 2. Hot-awareness splitting.

Algorithm 1: Flow chart of dynamic adjustment of the cold and hot data

```
Input: KV pairs <key, value>
Calculate the keyTag
if the keyTag in the hot indexing table then
    update heat in the hot sorting and the hot indexing table
    adjust heat sorting
    read the vTableID according to the keyTag
    if operation == read then
        read value according to the vTableID in the hot vlog
        return value
    else if operation == write then
        find the value from the hot vlog based on the vTableID
        recycle the invalid value
        store the written value in the location of the old value
    end if
else if the keyTag in the cold indexing table then
    update heat
    if heat > HeatLimit then
        take the heat minimum KV pair
        calculate the keyTag
        update it to the cold data
        if value > Value_Size then
            take the key value separation technique
        else
            store the KV pair directly in the LSM-tree
        end if
        insert the new hot data into the HotStore
        redo the hot sorting
        if operation == read then
            return the value of the new hot data
        else if operation == write then
            insert the latest value directly into the vTable
        end if
    end if
else
    insert it directly into the ColdStore
    if operation == read then
        return null
    else if operation == write then
        write value
    end if
end if
```

3.3. Hot KV Indexing

For data management in memory, HoaKV adopts a similar method to the traditional KV store based on the LSM-tree and ensures data durability using write-ahead logging (WAL). That is, the KV pairs are first appended to the log on the disk for crash recovery and then inserted into the MemTable, which is organized into a skiplist in memory. When the MemTable is full, it is converted into an Immutable MemTable. Then, according to the heat, a part of KV pairs, that is, the hot data, are refreshed to the HotStore on the disk via a background process.

Keys and values of KV pairs in the HotStore are stored separately; keys and the latest heat are stored in hot sorting via a heat-sorted manner; values are stored separately in the vTable of the hot vlog; and keys and values are indexed using a hash index in memory. To update and read the latest value in time, HoaKV also stores the heat in the hash index table. Its constituent level: <keyTag, vTableID, heat>. The keyTag stores the upper two bytes of the hash result calculated with the different hash functions. The vTableID is the location of the hot data stored in the vTable of the hot vlog. The heat is the frequency of read–write access to KV pairs per unit time.

At the same time, in order to reduce the use of memory, HoaKV establishes a lightweight hash index, which uses a three-level hash. In addition, HoaKV uses the hash chain and cuckoo hashing method to solve the hash conflicts problem. As shown in Figure 3, the hash index contains N buckets. Each bucket stores the index entries of KV pairs with cuckoo hashing, so it may append one or several overflowed index entries due to hash conflicts. When we create an index item for a KV pair, we search the bucket according to the hash results calculated using N hash functions (from the general hash function library), i.e., (h_1, h_2, . . ., h_e, . . ., h_E) (*key*)% N, until we find an empty bucket. Note that we can use up to N hash functions in this cuckoo hash scheme. If we cannot find an empty bucket among N buckets, we will generate an overflow index entry and append it to the bucket located using h_E (*key*)% N.

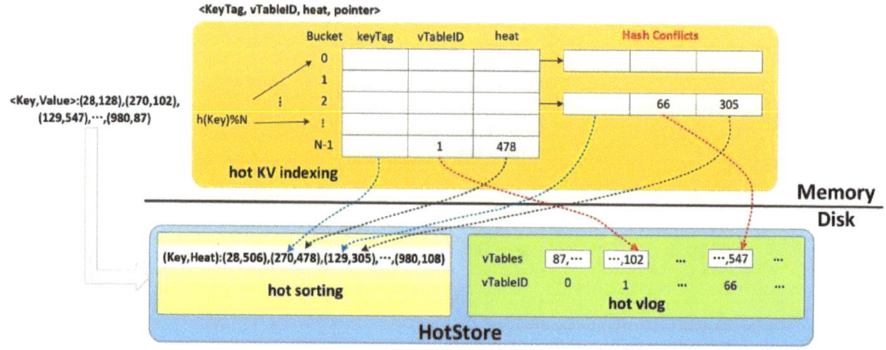

Figure 3. Hot indexing.

After finding a bucket, we record the keyTag and vTableID of the hot data in the selected index entry. Each index entry contains four attributes:<keyTag, vTableID, heat, pointer>. The keyTag stores the upper two bytes of the hash result calculated using the different hash functions, that is, h_{n+1} (*key*). It is used to quickly filter out index entries during key searching. The vTableID uses two bytes to store a vTableID. We can index 128 GB of vTables in the HotStore, each of which is 2 MB in size. The heat uses two bytes to store the latest value. The pointer uses two bytes to point to the next index entry in the same bucket.

The finding key and updating heat process works as follows: First, we use h_{n+1} (*key*) to calculate the keyTag. Then, we search for candidate buckets from h_n (*key*)% N to h_1 (*key*)% N until we find the hot data and update the heat. For each candidate bucket, the latest overflow entry is appended to the tail. Therefore, we compare the keyTag with the index entry belonging to the bucket from the tail of the overflow entry. Once we find a matching keyTag, we will use the vTableID to retrieve the metadata of the vTable andchange the heat value of the hot data. Note that due to the hash conflicts of h_{n+1} (*key*), the queried KV pair may not exist in this vTable, i.e., different keys have the same keyTag. Finally, if the KV pair is not found in the HotStore, it indicates that it is the cold data andwe need to further search in the ColdStore.

We now analyze the memory cost of the hash index. Each KV pair in the HotStore will consume an index entry, and each index entry will consume 8 bytes of memory. Therefore, for every 1 GB of hot data in the HotStore and the size of 1 KB KV pairs, it has about 1 million index entries. Considering that in our experiment, the bucket utilization is about 80%, it requires about 10 MB of memory. This memory usage is less than 1% of the data size in the HotStore. Note that for very small KV pairs, hash indexing may incur a large memory overhead. However, since all the data stored in the HotStore are the hot data, that is, frequent read and write operations will occur in a short period, the large memory overhead caused by very small KV pairs is acceptable.

Our hash index scheme is a tradeoff in design. On the one hand, when we allocate buckets for KV pairs, there may be hash conflicts, i.e., different keys have the same hash value *h*(*key*) and are allocated to the same bucket. Therefore, we need to store the key information in the index entry so that the key can be distinguished during the lookup. On the other hand, storing a complete key wastes memory. In order to balance memory usage and read performance, HoaKV uses three hash values and reserves only a 2-Byte hash as a keyTag. This greatly reduces the probability of hash conflicts, which is also demonstrated in our experiment. Even if hash conflicts occur, we can still resolve them by comparing the keys stored on the disk.

3.4. Partial KV Separation

Recall that HoaKV stores a small number of hot data KV pairs in the HotStore and indexes with an in-memory hash index, which incurs additional memory overhead. The data that are not frequently read or written recently are defined as the cold data, which accounts for the majority of KV pair sequences. HoaKV stores the cold data in the ColdStore, that is, the data whose key value to heat is less than *HeatLimit*. As the size of KV pairs in the cold data is not uniform, if the large KV pairs data are directly stored in the LSM-tree, as in the traditional LSM-tree based KV store, it may cause great I/O overhead. As a result, the existing KV pairs in the LSM-tree need to be read and written back after merging. Therefore, how to reduce the merging cost of the cold data is a challenging, key problem for HoaKV. To improve the range query performance, HoaKV proposes a partial KV separation strategy, that is, the cold data are further divided according to its KV pair size; the key and value address of the large KV pair is stored in the LSM-tree; the value is stored separately in the cold vlog; and the key and value of the small KV pair are retained in the LSM-tree.

After the KV pairs sequence is split by the heat, the remaining KV pairs are the cold data, and we further classify the cold data. Depending on the size of the value, HoaKV categorizes the cold data as the small KV pairs and the large KV pairs. Differentiated fine-grained key-value management mechanisms are implemented for the different types of KV pairs. As shown in Algorithm 2, according to the threshold value which we set as *Value_Size*, HoaKV classifies the cold data KV pairs. Specifically, all KV pairs whose values are smaller than *Value_Size* are classified as the small KV pairs. KV pairs whose value is larger than *Value_Size* are classified as the large KV pairs. HoaKV uses different store and garbage collection mechanisms for different KV pairs. At the same time, HoaKV uses the heat index table on the disk to index the heat and the key and value for each KV pair.

Algorithm 2: Partial KV separation

```
Input: Cold KV pairs <key, value>
if value > Value_Size then
    store value in the cold vlog
    return value location
    store key and value location in the LSM-tree
else
    store key and value in the LSM-tree
end if
```

For the small KV pairs, HoaKV always stores the keys and values together in the SST file of the LSM-tree without KV separation. For the small KV pairs, KV separation will not bring obvious benefits, but will exacerbate issues such as read–write amplification and GC costs. The core of the key value separation technology is to store the key and the address of the value in the LSM-tree and store the value alone in the value log. For the garbage collection of the key value, which uses the key value separation technology, we need to find the corresponding address from the LSM-tree, find the value from the value log according to the address, and then perform the garbage collection. This process increases the garbage collection cost of the storage system. Therefore, we need to reduce the cost of garbage collection as much as possible, and the garbage collection of the small key value is in the compaction process of LSM-tree. At the same time, due to the value of the small key value being relatively small, it has a small impact on the scale of the LSM-tree. This strategy reduces the system's garbage collection cost to a certain extent and retains the advantages of LSM-tree technology, including excellent insertion and search performance, and at the same time, alleviates the problem of I/O amplification. Therefore, the key value separation technology for small key values can lead to reading and writing amplification and GC costs. For the large KV pairs, HoaKV always performs a KV separation mechanism. HoaKV stores the value of the large KV pairs in the cold vlog, and the value in the LSM-tree is the location information of the value in the cold vlog. Therefore, for the large KV pairs, merging operations between levels on the LSM-tree only need to rewrite keys and metadata and do not need to move values, greatly reducing the write magnification of the large KV pairs.

3.5. *Dynamic Value Grouping*

With the data size growth of HoaKV, if we simply add more levels to large-scale stores as most existing LSM-tree based KV stores, moving data from a lower level to a higher level will lead to frequent compaction operations during write process, and trigger multi-level access during read process. Therefore, HoaKV proposes a dynamic value grouping scheme to expand the store horizontally. The scheme stores the values of the large KV pairs in different groups and manages them independently according to different key ranges.

The dynamic value grouping scheme works as follows (shown in Figure 4): Initially, HoaKV writes the value in a group (i.e., G0). Once the size of the group exceeds the predetermined threshold GroupSize, HoaKV will divide the group into two groups according to the key range and manage them independently (for example, G0 is divided into G0 and G1). For the value grouping strategy, the main feature is that the keys corresponding to the values stored in two groups are not overlapping. Therefore, how to split a group is crucial.

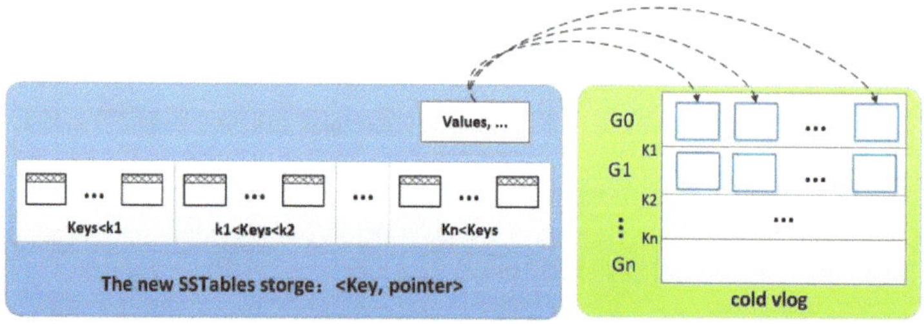

Figure 4. Dynamic value grouping.

To split the values in the cold vlog, HoaKV first locks them and stops the write request. Note that the unit of locking is a group, that is, HoaKV locks the entire group and stops all writes to the group during splitting. Then, it sorts all the keys corresponding to the values to avoid overlapping between groups. It first reads all the SSTable files related to the large KV pairs from the LSM-tree, sorts the keys, divides the sorted keys into two parts, and records the boundary key as *K* between the two parts. Note that the boundary *K* acts as a dividing point, that is, if the key of a large KV pair is less than *K*, its value is put into G0, and the remaining values are stored in G1. By dividing the points, HoaKV divides the values in the cold vlog into two groups whose keys do not overlap. Finally, HoaKV stores the value position with the corresponding key in the pointer, writes the key and pointer back to the corresponding SSTable file, and updates the value grouping information in the index table. HoaKV releases the lock and resumes processing the write request after splitting the value.

3.6. Cold KV Indexing

KV pairs in the ColdStore are managed differently by size. For large KV pairs, the KV separation strategy is implemented by storing the key and the address of the value in the LSM-tree and the true value in the cold vlog. For small KV pairs, the KV separation strategy is not implemented, and the key and value are stored directly in the LSM-tree. The data stored in the ColdStore are the cold data, but the heat of the data is changing. We need to adjust the store location and key-value management according to the heat of the data. We use an index structure to index the heat, key, and grouping number of the values.

To reduce disk usage, we build a lightweight index with three levels. Its constituent level: < heat, key, GID >. The heat is the frequency of read–write access to KV pairs per unit time. The key is the unique identification of the KV pair. The GID is the ID of the large KV pair in the cold data which is stored in the group. The hash index of the hot data uses the hash results calculated by the hash function to store the bucket. Unlike this, although the index structure also contains N buckets, it uses the direct indexing method. Considering that for large-scale store engines, if the direct indexing method is used purely, the search efficiency of the system will be reduced. Therefore, in order to speed up the search efficiency, we have improved the direct indexing method. The value of the cold data is stored in a dynamic grouping mode, so multiple values are stored in a group and the keys corresponding to these values are in the same range. Therefore, as shown in Figure 5, we store relevant information in the index structure according to the grouping sequence number (GID) of the cold data value, and HoaKV stores the heat information in the same bucket as the GID. Different values have the same GID, which will cause conflicts in the index structure. We use the link method to resolve conflicts. Therefore, one or more overflow index entries may be appended to each bucket due to the conflict of the GID. When we create an index item for a KV pair, we search the bucket according to the GID corresponding to the value. Note that in this scheme, if the bucket we find according to the GID is not empty, we will generate an overflow index entry and attach it to the bucket located by the GID.

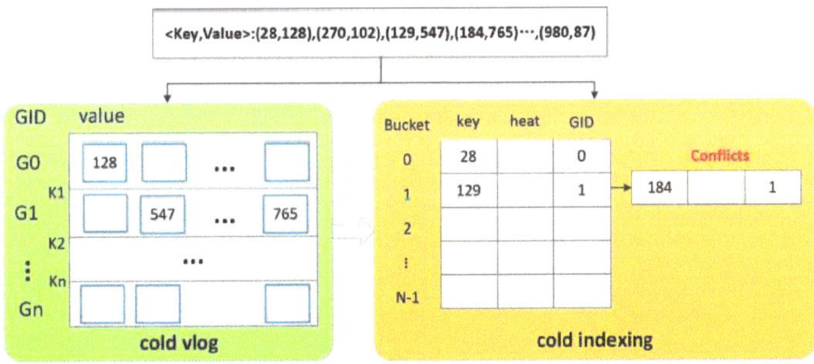

Figure 5. Cold indexing.

4. Evaluation

In this section, we evaluate the performance of HoaKV using real-workload-based benchmarks. In particular, we compare the throughput and scalability of HoaKV with several state-of-the-art KV stores: LevelDB, RocksDB, PebblesDB, and WiscKey. We also provide detailed evaluations to demonstrate the effectiveness of the major designs adopted by HoaKV.

4.1. Setup

We run all experiments on a machine with a 20 core Intel Xeon Silver 4210 2.20 GHz CPU which made by Intel Corporation from California, USA, 64 GB RAM, and a 4 TB SSD. The machine runs Ubuntu 20.04.6 LTS, with the 64-bit Linux 5.4 kernel and the ext4 file system.

For LevelDB, RocksDB, PebblesDB, and WiscKey, we use the same default parameters. Specifically, we set memtable_size as 64 MB (same as RocksDB by default), bloom_bits as 10 bits, and open_files as 1000. For block_cache_size, HoaKV sets it as 20 MB by default, while other KV stores set it as 170 MB to match the size of HoaKV's hash index for fair comparisons. The remaining memory is used as the page cache of the kernel. For the other parameters of different KV stores, we use their default values. For other parameters of HoaKV, by default, to balance write performance and memory costs, we set the group size to 40 GB. To limit the hash index in the HotStore, we set the size of the HotStore to 4 GB. For GC operations, HoaKV uses a single GC thread. In each test, if no other specification is made, we will use the default setting: 32 threads. We allow other KV stores to use all available capacity in our SSD RAID volume so that their major overheads come from read and write amplifications in the LSM-tree management. Finally, HoaKV uses YCSB [24] to generate various types of workloads. Generally, HoaKV sets the size of KV pairs to 1 KB and the key size to 24-Byte. HoaKV makes a request based on the Zipfian distribution, where the Zipfian constant defaults to 0.99 in YCSB.

4.2. Micro-Benchmarks

We evaluate the performance of the different KV stores, including the performance of load, read, update, and scan under the single-thread operations and the size of the KV stores. Specifically, we use YCSB to generate the workload and set the size of each KV pair to 1 KB, which consists of 8-Byte metadata (including key/value size fields and retention information), a 24-Byte key, and a 992-Byte value. We first randomly load 100 M KV pairs (approximately 100 GB). We then evaluate the performance of 10 M read operations, 100 M update operations, and 1 M scan operations that scan 50 GB of data. In addition, HoaKV sets some parameters, such as HotStore Size, Group Size, *HeatLimit*, and Value_size. During the evaluation of the micro-benchmarks, HoaKV takes the values of these parameters as: HotStore Size is 16 GB, Group Size is 20 GB, *HeatLimit* is 0.95:0.05, and Value_size is 32 KB.

Experiment 1 (the Performance of Load). We evaluate the load throughput for different KV stores and HoaKV. Figure 6a shows the load throughput of each KV store. Compared to other KV stores, it shows that HoaKV's load performance is 9.6 times that of LevelDB, 6.2 times that of RocksDB, 1.8 times that of PebblesDB, and 0.8 times that of WiscKey. It is important to note that HoaKV is implemented based on LevelDB, but its performance is higher than other specifically optimized KV stores except WiscKey. This is because WiscKey separates each KV pair, so the LSM-tree has the least amount of data and therefore has a higher load throughput than HoaKV. The load throughput of HoaKV is much greater than LevelDB because HoaKV uses partial KV separation. There are more KV pairs in the same layer, which also makes HoaKV have more I/O resources to service user requests, so HoaKV has a much higher load performance than LevelDB. Load performance is mainly affected by write amplification, so the comparison results of load performance are similar to those of write amplification.

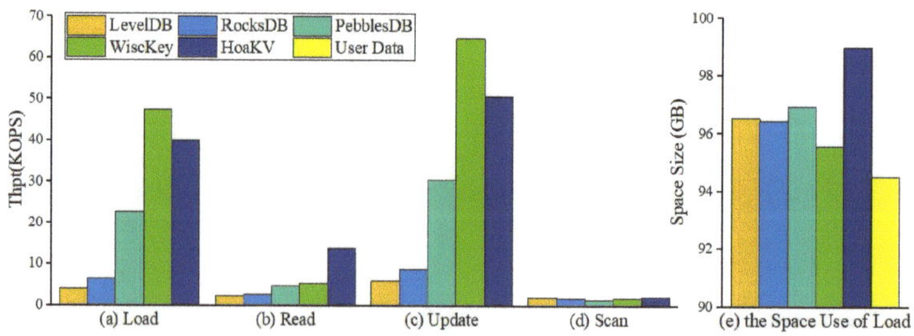

Figure 6. Micro-benchmark performance.

Experiment 2 (the Performance of Read). We then evaluate the performance of 10 M read operations on various KV stores. Figure 6b shows the throughput of each KV store performing read operations. As can be seen, HoaKV has the best-read performance. The read performance of HoaKV is better than WiscKey, mainly because for HoaKV, the small KV pairs in the cold data do not perform KV separation, and there is no need to issue another I/O request during reading. The read throughput of HoaKV increases by nearly five times compared to LevelDB, which is also because HoaKV's differentiated key-value management strategy allows the LSM-tree to store more KV pairs per layer than LevelDB, with an average of fewer layers to search for a KV pair.

Experiment 3 (the Performance of Update). We evaluate the performance of 100 M update operations for different KV stores and HoaKV. As shown in Figure 6c, WiscKey has the highest update performance because it directly writes KV pairs to the value log without the need to update them to WAL files and memory tables. It also has the lowest update I/O volume and performs the best. HoaKV has a lower update performance than WiscKey, but its update throughput is 7.5 times higher than LevelDB. This is mainly because LevelDB's severe write amplification affects its update performance, while the write amplification problem of HoaKV is much better because it stores the value of the hot data in the hot vlog and stores the value of the large KV pairs in the cold data into the cold vlog.

Experiment 4 (the Performance of Scan). We also test the scan performance of various store systems. Figure 6d shows the scanning throughput of each store system. According to the results, LevelDB performs the best for scan operations as it stores all KV pairs in an orderly manner in the LSM-tree without performing KV separation. Compared with WiscKey which fully implements KV separation, HoaKV has a 12.5% improvement in scan performance. This is because most of the data in the LSM-tree is stored in the bottom two layers, while in the LSM-tree of HoaKV, small KV pairs do not perform KV separation, greatly improving scan performance.

Experiment 5 (the Usage of Space). Figure 6e shows the total KV store size for different KV stores after all load and update requests are issued. In addition, they have very similar KV store sizes, meaning that all systems consume similar store space during the loading phase. HoaKV incurs a slight additional store overhead, mainly used to store and record pointers to the value positions of the hot data and the large KV pairs in the cold data.

4.3. YCSB Evaluation

Experiment 6 (YCSB performance). Next, we evaluate the performance of various KV stores using the default workload of YCSB, which is an industry standard for evaluating KV stores. As shown in Table 1, YCSB provides four different core workloads (Workloads A-D), each representing a read–write mode in a real-world application scenario. Specifically, Workloads A and B are read–write mixed with 50% and 95% reads, respectively. Workload C is a read-only workload with 100% reads. Workload D also includes 95% reads, but reads queries for the latest values.

Table 1. YCSB Read/Update ratio.

Workload	Workload A	Workload B	Workload C	Workload D
Read	0.5	0.95	1	0.95
Update	0.5	0.05	0	0.05

We present the performance results of LevelDB, RocksDB, PePePebblesDB, WiscKey, and HoaKV under the default YCSB core workload. Figure 7 shows the total throughput of each KV store area under each YCSB workload. In both read–write-dominated workloads, HoaKV always performs better than other KV stores. In Workload A, compared to other KV stores, HoaKV is 4.7 times that of LevelDB, 1.2 times that of RocksDB, 3.2 times that of PebblesDB, and 2.2 times that of WiscKey, respectively. The performance of HoaKV and RocksDB is similar, mainly because under workloads with fewer updates, RocksDB no longer delays write operations to refresh the MemTable. It can better provide reads and updates through multi-threading optimization. Next, we consider Workload B, Workload C, and Workload D, all of which are read-intensive. HoaKV is 4.4–11.4 times that of LevelDB, 1.2–3.0 times that of RocksDB, 2.3–7.4 times that of PebblesDB, and 1.0–2.5 times that of WiscKey, respectively.

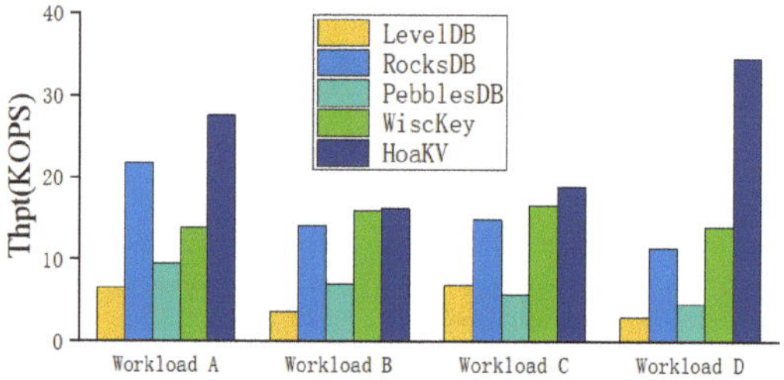

Figure 7. YCSB performance.

4.4. Performance Impact

Experiment 7 (Impact of the HotStore size). We investigate the effect of the HotStore size on HoaKV. We randomly load 100 M KV pairs and issue a 10 M read operation. Figure 8a shows the result of modifying the size of the HotStore from 1 GB to 16 GB when the fixed group size is 40 GB. As the size of the HotStore increases, the load throughput also increases, while the read performance remains almost unchanged. However, the memory cost of hash indexing for the HotStore will increase. Therefore, the size of the HotStore should be limited to balance performance and memory overhead.

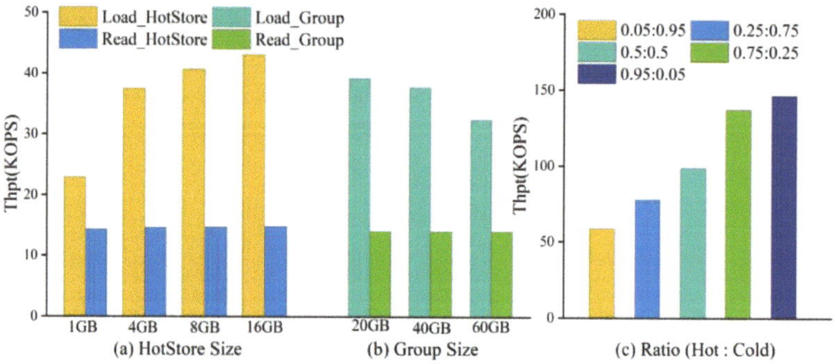

Figure 8. Performance Impact.

Experiment 8 (Impact of the Group size). We analyze the impact of the group size on HoaKV. We randomly load 100 M KV pairs again and issue a 10 M read. Figure 8b shows the result of changing the group size from 20 GB to 60 GB while fixing the store area size of the HotStore to 4 GB. The impact of group size on write performance is minimal, while it has almost no impact on read performance. The reason is that GC operates independently within each group. Therefore, the smaller the grouping, the more effective the GC operation. However, group size can affect memory costs, as HoaKV needs to allocate a MemTable for each group. Therefore, smaller groups may occupy more memory, so group size should be limited.

Experiment 9 (Impact of *HeatLimit*). We evaluate the impact of *HeatLimit* on HoaKV's update performance. The size of the heat threshold *HeatLimit* also represents the proportion of the hot data and the cold data in HoaKV, so we consider five different proportions of the hot data and the cold data, including 0.05:0.95, 0.25:0.75, 0.5:0.5, 0.75:0.25, and 0.95:0.05. Figure 8c shows the update throughput for the different ratios in the hot data and the cold data. Thus, as the proportion of the hot data becomes heavier, the update performance of HoaKV becomes higher. As the hot data indexes the keyTag, vTableID, and heat through a hash index table in memory, HoaKV can quickly find the corresponding KV pairs and update them.

Experiment 10 (Impact of Value_Size). We investigate the effect of KV size ranging from 256 B to 32 KB and maintained other parameter settings. Figure 9 shows the throughput of randomly loading 100 GB KV pairs, reading 10 GB, and updating 100 GB KV pairs. To better illustrate the performance trend of data access, the throughput shown in this graph is in MB/s. As the size of KV pairs increase, both HoaKV and PebblesDB have higher throughput due to their efficient sequential I/Os. HoaKV always outperforms PebblesDB in terms of load, read, and update performance. When the KV pair becomes larger, the improvement of HoaKV reduces the throughput of loading the KV store and increases the throughput of reads and updates. The reason is that as the size of KV pairs increase, PebblesDB maintains more SSTables in the first level. This reduces compression overhead but can cause read operations to check these SSTables one by one, resulting in a decrease in read performance.

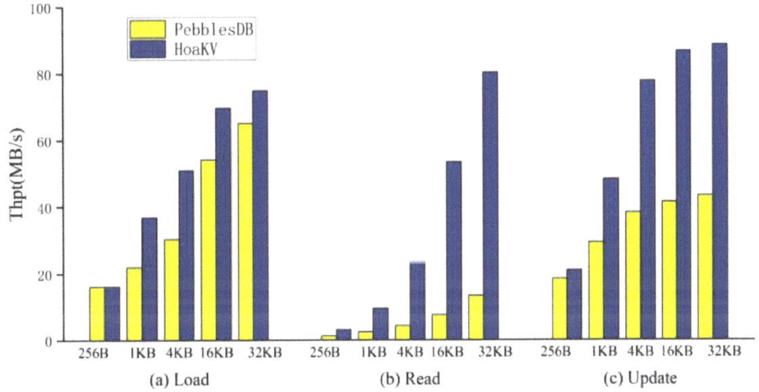

Figure 9. Impact of Value_Size.

5. Conclusions

In this paper, we propose HoaKV, which divides KV pairs into the hot data and the cold data, and further divides them into the large KV pairs and the small KV pairs according to the size of the cold data to achieve the differential management of KV pairs. It supports efficient read and write through the hash index and the normal index. The data classification is adjusted through the dynamic change of the key value to the heat, to realize the dynamic scalable and high-performance KV store. In HoaKV, the differentiated GC method is used for the two log files. Due to the unique characteristics of the hot data, the GC of the hot data requires timeliness. In order to reduce GC overhead, HoaKV proposes a delay method based on the number of invalid values in each packet of the cold vlog. The test experiment shows that HoaKV achieves efficient read, write, and scan performance and has low store cost. HoaKV achieves a balance of performance in all aspects.

Future research directions are as follows: the optimization of distributed KV storage systems. This article mainly focuses on optimizing KV storage systems on a single machine. For distributed KV storage systems, more issues need to be considered. In a distributed system, there may be load imbalance among nodes, which affects the overall performance of the distributed KV storage system. Therefore, we hope to conduct more in-depth research on data consistency and load balancing in distributed KV storage systems.

Author Contributions: Conceptualization, J.L., X.F. and Y.W.; methodology, J.L. and Y.Z.; software, J.L. and X.F.; validation, J.L., X.F. and L.L.; writing—original draft preparation, J.L.; writing—review and editing, J.L. and L.L.; supervision, Y.Z. and L.L. All authors have read and agreed to the published version of the manuscript.

Funding: This work was supported by the National Natural Science Foundation of China (no. U1936218 and 62072037). The funder is Chinese Government.

Data Availability Statement: The data presented in this study are available on request from the corresponding author. The data are not publicly available due to privacy.

Conflicts of Interest: The authors declare no conflict of interest.

References

1. Thakur, N.; Han, C.Y. An Intelligent Ubiquitous Activity Aware Framework for Smart Home. In Proceedings of the 3rd International Conference on Human Interaction and Emerging Technologies: Future Applications (IHIET 2020), Paris, France, 27–29 August 2020.
2. Thakur, N.; Han, C.Y. Country-Specific Interests Towards Fall Detection from 2004–2021: An Open Access Dataset and Research Questions. *Data* **2021**, *6*, 92. [CrossRef]
3. Apache. HBase. Available online: https://hbase.apache.org/ (accessed on 10 May 2023).
4. Chang, F.; Dean, J.; Ghemawat, S.; Hsieh, W.C.; Wallach, D.A.; Burrows, M.; Chandra, T. Bigtable: A Distributed Storage System for Structured Data. *Acm Trans. Comput. Syst.* **2008**, *26*, 1–26. [CrossRef]
5. Facebook. Memcached. Available online: http://memcached.org (accessed on 10 May 2023).
6. RedisLib. Redis. Available online: https://redis.io (accessed on 10 May 2023).
7. Lu, G.; Nam, Y.J.; Du, D.H. BloomStore: Bloom-Filter Based Memory-Efficient Key-Value Store for Indexing of Data Deduplication on Flash. In Proceedings of the 2012 IEEE 28th Symposium on Mass Storage Systems and Technologies (MSST), San Diego, CA, USA, 16–20 April 2012.
8. Elyasi, N.; Choi, C.; Sivasubramaniam, A. Large-Scale Graph Processing on Emerging Storage Devices. In Proceedings of the USENIX FAST 2019, Boston, MA, USA, 25–28 February 2019.
9. O'Neil, P.; Cheng, E.; Gawlick, D. The Log-Structured Merge-Tree (LSM-tree). *Acta Inform.* **1996**, *33*, 351–385. [CrossRef]
10. Sanjay, G.; Jeff, D. Leveldb. Available online: https://github.com/google/leveldb (accessed on 10 May 2023).
11. Facebook. Rocksdb, a Persistent Key-Value Store for Fast Storage Enviroments. Available online: http://RocksDB.org/ (accessed on 10 May 2023).
12. DeCandia, G.; Hastorun, D.; Jampani, M.; Kakulapati, G.; Lakshman, A.; Pilchin, A.; Sivasubramanian, S. Dynamo: Amazon's Highly Available Key-Value Store. *ACM SIGOPS Oper. Syst. Rev.* **2007**, *41*, 205–220. [CrossRef]
13. Lerner, R.M. Cassandra: A Decentralized Structured Storage System. *Linux J.* **2010**, *44*, 35–40.
14. Pan, F.F.; Yue, Y.L.; Xiong, J. Dcompaction: Speeding up Compaction of the LSM-Tree Via Delayed Compaction. *J. Comput. Sci. Technol.* **2017**, *32*, 41–54. [CrossRef]
15. Lim, H.; Andersen, D.G.; Kaminsky, M. Towards Accurate and Fast Evaluation of Multi-Stage Log-Structured Designs. In Proceedings of the 14th USENIX Conference on File and Storage Technologies (FAST 16), Santa Clara, CA, USA, 22–25 February 2016.
16. Qader, M.A.; Hristidis, V. High-Throughput Publish/Subscribe on Top of LSM-Based Storage. *Distrib. Parallel Databases* **2019**, *37*, 101–132. [CrossRef]
17. Yan, F.; Tan, Y.-A.; Zhang, Q.; Wu, F.; Cheng, Z.; Zheng, J. An Effective RAID Data Layout for Object-based De-duplication Backup System. *Chin. J. Electron.* **2016**, *25*, 832–840. [CrossRef]
18. Yu, X.; Zhang, C.; Xue, Y.; Zhu, H.; Li, Y.; Tan, Y.-A. An Extra-Parity Energy Saving Data Layout for Video Surveillance. *Multimed. Tools Appl.* **2018**, *77*, 4563–4583.
19. Lu, L.; Pillai, T.S.; Gopalakrishnan, H.; Arpaci-Dusseau, A.C. WiscKey: Separating Keys from Values in SSD-Conscious Storage. *ACM Trans. Storage* **2017**, *13*, 1–28. [CrossRef]
20. Aye, T.T. Web Log Cleaning for Mining of Web Usage Patterns. In Proceedings of the 2011 3rd International Conference on Computer Research and Development, Shanghai, China, 11–13 March 2011.
21. TPC. Tpc-C is an On-Line Transaction Processing Benchmark. Available online: http://www.tpc.org/tpcc/ (accessed on 10 May 2023).
22. Yu, X.; Tan, Y.-A.; Zhang, C.; Liang, C.; Khaled, A.; Zheng, J.; Zhang, Q. A High-performance Hierarchical Snapshot Scheme for Hybrid Storage Systems. *Chin. J. Electron.* **2018**, *27*, 76–85. [CrossRef]
23. Atikoglu, B.; Xu, Y.; Frachtenberg, E.; Jiang, S.; Paleczny, M. Workload Analysis of a Large-Scale Key-Value Store. In Proceedings of the 12th ACM SIGMETRICS/PERFORMANCE Joint International Conference on Measurement and Modeling of Computer Systems, London, UK, 11–15 June 2012.
24. Cooper, B.F.; Silberstein, A.; Tam, E.; Ramakrishnan, R.; Sears, R. Benchmarking Cloud Serving Systems with Ycsb. In Proceedings of the 1st ACM Symposium on Cloud Computing, Indianapolis, IN, USA, 10–11 June 2010.

25. Zhang, Q.; Li, Y.; Lee, P.P.; Xu, Y.; Cui, Q.; Tang, L. UniKV: Toward High-Performance and Scalable Kv Storage in Mixed Workloads Via Unified Indexing. In Proceedings of the 2020 IEEE 36th International Conference on Data Engineering (ICDE), Dallas, TX, USA, 20–24 April 2020.
26. Chen, J.; Chen, L.; Wang, S.; Zhu, G.; Sun, Y.; Liu, H.; Li, F. HotRing: A Hotspot-Aware in-Memory Key-Value Store. In Proceedings of the 18th USENIX Conference on File and Storage Technologies (FAST 20), Santa Clara, CA, USA, 24–27 February 2020.
27. Raju, P.; Kadekodi, R.; Chidambaram, V.; Abraham, I. PebblesDB: Building Key-Value Stores Using Fragmented Log-Structured Merge Trees. In Proceedings of the 26th Symposium on Operating Systems Principles, Shanghai, China, 29–31 October 2017.
28. Li, Y.; Liu, Z.; Lee, P.P.; Wu, J.; Xu, Y.; Wu, Y.; Tang, L.; Liu, Q.; Cui, Q. Differentiated Key-Value Storage Management for Balanced I/O Performance. In Proceedings of the 2021 USENIX Conference on USENIX Annual Technical Conference, Santa Clara, CA, USA, 14–16 July 2021.
29. Chan, H.H.; Li, Y.; Lee, P.P.; Xu, Y. HashKV: Enabling Efficient Updates in KV Storage Via Hashing. In Proceedings of the 2018 USENIX Conference on USENIX Annual Technical Conference, Boston, MA, USA, 11–13 July 2018.
30. Chen, H.; Zhang, H.; Dong, M.; Wang, Z.; Xia, Y.; Guan, H. Efficient and Available in-Memory KV-Store with Hybrid Erasure Coding and Replication. *USENIX Assoc.* **2017**, *13*, 1–30. [CrossRef]
31. Sears, R.; Ramakrishnan, R. bLSM: A General Purpose Log Structured Merge Tree. In Proceedings of the 2012 ACM SIGMOD International Conference on Management of Data, Scottsdale, AZ, USA, 20–24 May 2012.
32. Shetty, P.J.; Spillane, R.P.; Malpani, R.R.; Andrews, B.; Seyster, J.; Zadok, E. Building Workload-Independent Storage with VT-Trees. In Proceedings of the Presented as Part of the 11th USENIX Conference on File and Storage Technologies (FAST 13), San Jose, CA, USA, 12–15 February 2013.
33. Liu, M.; Gu, J. uCleaner: An Efficient Adaptive Garbage Collection Mechanism for KV-Separated LSM-Stores. In Proceedings of the 2022 5th International Conference on Data Science and Information Technology (DSIT), Shanghai, China, 22–24 July 2022.
34. Idreos, S.; Zoumpatianos, K.; Hentschel, B.; Kester, M.S.; Guo, D. The Data Calculator: Data Structure Design and Cost Synthesis from First Principles and Learned Cost Models. In Proceedings of the 2018 International Conference on Management of Data, Houston, TX, USA, 10–15 June 2018.
35. Idreos, S.; Dayan, N.; Qin, W.; Akmanalp, M.; Hilgard, S.; Ross, A.; Lennon, J.; Jain, V.; Gupta, H.; Li, D. Design Continuums and the Path toward Self-Designing Key-Value Stores That Know and Learn. In Proceedings of the Conference on Innovative Data Systems Research (CIDR 2019), Asilomar, CA, USA, 13–16 January 2019.
36. Xia, F.; Jiang, D.; Xiong, J.; Sun, N. HiKV: A Hybrid Index Key-Value Store for Dram-Nvm Memory Systems. In Proceedings of the 2017 USENIX Annual Technical Conference, Santa Clara, CA, USA, 12–14 July 2017.
37. Kannan, S.; Bhat, N.; Gavrilovska, A.; Arpaci-Dusseau, A.; Arpaci-Dusseau, R. Redesigning LSMs for Nonvolatile Memory with NoveLSM. In Proceedings of the 2018 USENIX Annual Technical Conference, Boston, MA, USA, 11–13 July 2018.
38. Puranik, S.; Barve, M.; Rodi, S.; Patrikar, R.J.E. FPGA-Based High-Throughput Key-Value Store Using Hashing and B-Tree for Securities Trading System. *Electronics* **2022**, *12*, 183. [CrossRef]
39. Sun, Z.; Zhang, Q.; Li, Y.; Tan, Y.-A. DPPDL: A Dynamic Partial-Parallel Data Layout for Green Video Surveillance Storage. *IEEE Trans. Circuits Syst. Video Technol.* **2018**, *28*, 193–205. [CrossRef]

electronics

MDPI

Article

Sentiment Analysis of Comment Data Based on BERT-ETextCNN-ELSTM

Lujuan Deng, Tiantian Yin *, Zuhe Li and Qingxia Ge

School of Computer and Communication Engineering, Zhengzhou University of Light Industry, Zhengzhou 450002, China; lujuandeng@163.com (L.D.); zuheli@zzuli.edu.cn (Z.L.); 332007040514@email.zzuli.edu.cn (Q.G.)

* Correspondence: 332007040532@email.zzuli.edu.cn

Abstract: With the rapid popularity and continuous development of social networks, users' communication and interaction through platforms such as microblogs and forums have become more and more frequent. The comment data on these platforms reflect users' opinions and sentiment tendencies, and sentiment analysis of comment data has become one of the hot spots and difficulties in current research. In this paper, we propose a BERT-ETextCNN-ELSTM (Bidirectional Encoder Representations from Transformers–Enhanced Convolution Neural Networks–Enhanced Long Short-Term Memory) model for sentiment analysis. The model takes text after word embedding and BERT encoder processing and feeds it to an optimized CNN layer for convolutional operations in order to extract local features of the text. The features from the CNN layer are then fed into the LSTM layer for time-series modeling to capture long-term dependencies in the text. The experimental results proved that compared with TextCNN (Convolution Neural Networks), LSTM (Long Short-Term Memory), TextCNN-LSTM (Convolution Neural Networks–Long Short-Term Memory), and BiLSTM-ATT (Bidirectional Long Short-Term Memory Network–Attention), the model proposed in this paper was more effective in sentiment analysis. In the experimental data, the model reached a maximum of 0.89, 0.88, and 0.86 in terms of accuracy, F1 value, and macro-average F1 value, respectively, on both datasets, proving that the model proposed in this paper was more effective in sentiment analysis of comment data. The proposed model achieved better performance in the review sentiment analysis task and significantly outperformed the other comparable models.

Keywords: sentiment analysis; BERT; long short-term memory; convolutional neural network

Citation: Deng, L.; Yin, T.; Li, Z.; Ge, Q. Sentiment Analysis of Comment Data Based on BERT-ETextCNN-ELSTM. *Electronics* **2023**, *12*, 2910. https://doi.org/10.3390/electronics12132910

Academic Editor: Yu-an Tan

Received: 22 March 2023
Revised: 16 June 2023
Accepted: 28 June 2023
Published: 3 July 2023

1. Introduction

With the rapid development and popularity of social media platforms such as Weibo, Zhihu, and Twitter [1–3], more and more users can post their views, attitudes, and emotions on certain topics on these social media platforms, resulting in a large amount of textual data consisting of comments with emotional overtones. Analyzing textual data with emotional overtones not only makes it possible to obtain information about the user's psychological state at the moment, his or her inclination to voice an opinion on various matters, and to understand the general views and attitudes of users, but the data also have potential economic value [4]. The analysis can even be used to monitor undesirable comments and thus ensure online safety. Therefore, sentiment analysis of text comment data has important research implications.

The three main methods for text sentiment analysis are based on sentiment dictionaries, machine learning, and deep learning [5]. The sentiment dictionary approach matches a dataset with words in a sentiment dictionary. It calculates the sentiment polarity of the text through weighting, but a complete dictionary is challenging to construct [6]. Machine learning [7] methods use algorithms such as Naive Bayes (NB) and Support Vector Machines (SVM) to achieve sentiment analysis. Still, traditional machine learning methods often fail to integrate contextual information, thoroughly affecting the accuracy of classification, so they are not well suited to a variety of scenarios. Both methods have apparent drawbacks, based on which deep learning-based approaches have been proposed [8]. Compared with traditional machine learning models, deep learning methods can actively extract text features [9–15], reduce the complexity of text construction features, and perform better on sentiment analysis tasks. This paper focuses on sentiment analysis using deep learning methods.

Typical neural network learning methods include Convolutional Neural Networks (CNN), Recurrent Neural Networks (RNN), Long Short-Term Memory (LSTM) networks, etc. Sentiment analysis methods based on deep learning can be subdivided into single neural network sentiment analysis methods, hybrid (combined, fused) neural network sentiment analysis methods, sentiment analysis with the introduction of attention mechanisms, and sentiment analysis using pre-trained models. This paper uses pre-trained models and optimized hybrid (combinatorial, fusion) neural networks for sentiment analysis to effectively address the problem of ignoring contextual semantics in traditional sentiment analysis methods and to better extract the semantic information of the corresponding words to achieve effective sentiment classification of text.

2. Related Studies

Sentiment analysis is an important research hotspot in the field of natural language processing and has a wide range of research areas in data mining, web mining, text mining, and opinion analysis. In recent years, sentiment analysis methods based on deep learning have been widely used, the most common of which are convolutional neural network [16] models and recurrent neural network models.

With the continuous development of deep learning technology, more and more researchers have started to apply deep learning research methods to sentiment analysis of text classes. For example, convolutional neural networks and recurrent neural networks have been widely used by Sun [17] and others have used recurrent neural networks to process text features in order to address the problem of sparse text features, achieving good results on Chinese datasets. However, because of the special structure of RNNs, gradient explosion and gradient dispersion problems are prone to occur. Therefore, variants of RNNs are generally used to deal with sentiment analysis problems at present.

Alhagr et al. [18] argued that sentiment analysis is essentially a sequence problem and so they used a Long Short-Term Memory network (LSTM) to deal with sequences and proposed six LSTM models with different parameters. These models have shown excellent performance on multiple datasets. However, it is difficult to accurately capture the local information of a sentence using only LSTM models, so some researchers have also explored combining deep learning methods such as CNN and LSTM to improve the accuracy of sentiment analysis.

The convolutional neural network model proposed by Kim [19] is one of the classic approaches in the field of sentiment analysis. The model used convolutional and max-pooling operations to extract features from the input text and fed the extracted features into a fully connected layer for classification. Kim applied the model to an IMDB movie review dataset and achieved the best performance at the time.

The recurrent neural network-based sentiment analysis method proposed by Zhuge et al. [20] in 2015 used a Long Short-Term Memory network model (LSTM) to encode text and then used a word vector and sentiment dictionary approach for text feature extraction. The method was applied to several datasets and achieved good performance.

Zhou et al. [21] proposed a deep learning-based sentiment analysis method, the Bidirectional Long Short-Term Memory Network (BiLSTM) model, for text encoding and an attention mechanism to adaptively select important text features. In sentiment analysis tasks, the model could accurately identify sentiment tendencies in text. In addition, the model had good generalization capabilities and could be applied to different datasets and tasks.

Later, Cheng et al. [22] proposed a method for simultaneous text reading comprehension and aspect-level-based sentiment analysis. The method used a Gated Recurrent Unit (GRU) to encode the text and a Multi-Head Attention mechanism to adaptively select the important features in the text. In addition, the method could simultaneously identify different aspects of the text and perform sentiment analysis separately, thus improving the accuracy and efficiency of sentiment analysis.

Munikar et al. [23] used a deep bidirectional language model based on the Transformer architecture, a pre-trained BERT model, and fine-tuned it. Their experiments showed that their model outperformed other popular models without the complex architecture.

Based on the above summary comparison, in the field of sentiment analysis [24], deep learning methods that have been developed in recent years [25–27] can automatically and quickly extract relevant features from large-scale text data and capture deep semantic information more easily, with better classification results. However, there are still limitations in word vector representation and the neural network feature extraction processes in deep learning methods [28–30], which may lead to incomplete feature extraction or failure to adequately capture semantic information, thus affecting the classification results. To address this problem, this paper constructed BERT and optimized an improved CNN-LSTM model as BERT-ETextCNN-ELSTM (BERT–Enhanced Convolution Neural Networks–Enhanced Long Short-Term Memory) to improve comment sentiment analysis with improved accuracy and efficiency. While retaining the advantages of CNN and LSTM models, the model was enhanced with the introduction of BERT and optimized CNN-LSTM for representation learning and generalization, aiming to further improve the accuracy and efficiency of sentiment analysis.

3. Model Construction

The flow of the model is shown in Figure 1. In this paper, a fused BERT and optimally improved TextCNN-LSTM model were constructed as BERT-ETextCNN-ELSTM. In the model architecture, a fusion mechanism was introduced to fuse BERT, text embedding, and CNN layer representations. This fusion allowed the model to take full advantage of the deep contextual understanding of BERT and the local feature extraction capabilities of CNN. The outputs of these different layers were integrated to capture a more comprehensive representation of the input text, effectively capturing both global and local semantic information. Exploiting the synergy of the strengths of the two approaches, BERT excelled in capturing long-term dependencies and global semantic information, while CNN enhanced the model's ability to capture local nuances and fine-grained features. This fusion enabled our model to effectively capture both macro and micro levels in sentiment analysis, resulting in better performance in sentiment analysis tasks.

3.1. Input Layer

(1) Data pre-processing: the original text data are cleaned, divided into words, and deactivated to obtain a data format that can be processed by the model.

(2) Text embedding layer: The text sequence after word separation is mapped into a high-dimensional vector representation, where each word corresponds to a vector $\{W_1, W_2,\ldots, W_{n-1}, W_n\}$, which is used to capture the semantic information of each word. In the model of this paper, a BERT [31] pre-training model was used for text embedding. The BERT model is shown in Figure 2.

3.2. Feature Extraction Layer

3.2.1. Enhanced Convolutional Neural Networks

A convolutional neural grid [19] contains convolutional layers, most commonly a two-dimensional convolutional layer. It has two spatial dimensions, height and width, which are often used to process image data, and it is currently widely used in sentiment analysis research [32–34], as shown in Figure 3. The processing of TextCNN in this paper used the Keras concatenate layer for the second part of the convolutional neural network to enhance processing and then put the second part of the six-layer convolutional neural network into the concatenate layer. Not only did this reduce the complexity of the model and loss of gradients due to model redundancy, but it also increased the number of output channels in the TextCNN network, allowing for better extraction of features from the data.

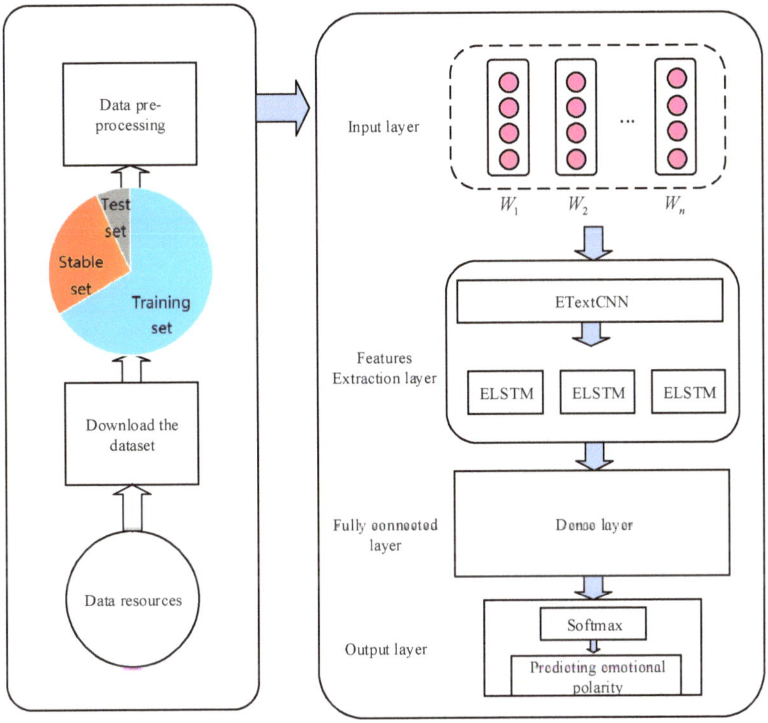

Figure 1. Flow chart of ETextCNN-ELSTM model.

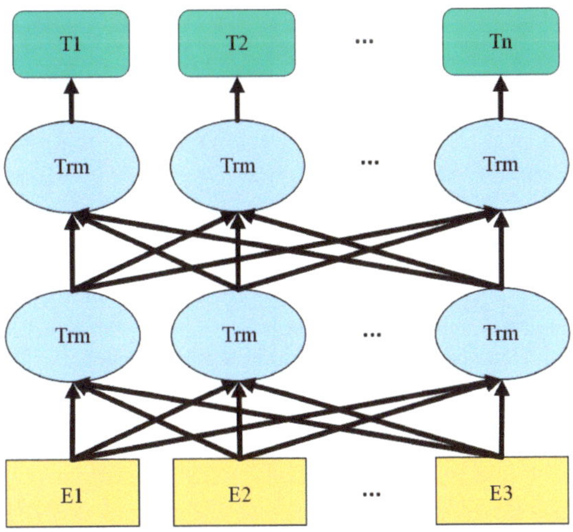

Figure 2. BERT architecture (Source: Adapted from [23]).

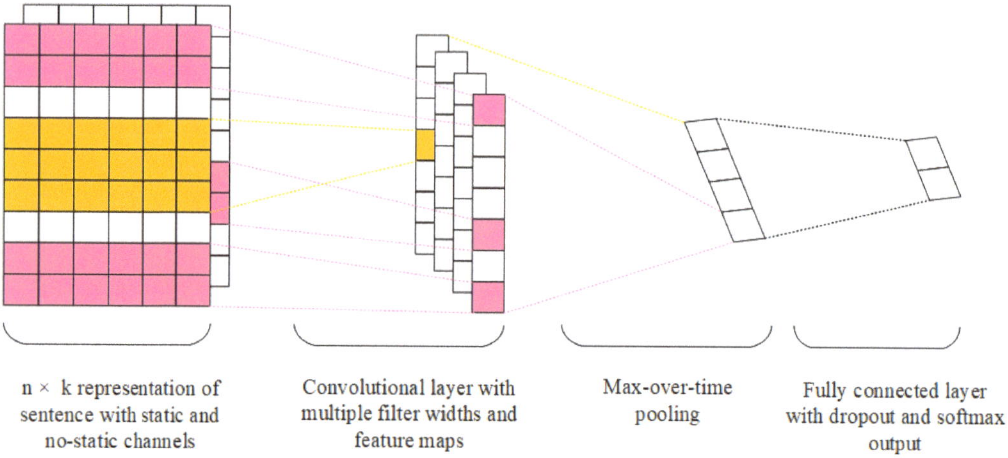

Figure 3. TextCNN neural network.

3.2.2. Enhanced Long and Short-Term Memory Neural Networks

In this paper, an LSTM model was considered and improved on top of the enhanced convolutional neural network. The LSTM [8] consists of oblivion, input, and output gates. The oblivion gate determines whether the information needs to be retained by the sigmoid function; the input gate filters the input information, ignores the information with the output feature dimension of 0, and updates the current cell state by combining the temporary and previous cell states; while the output gate selectively retains and ignores the information at the present moment and calculates the output result by the tanh function as the input information at the next moment. The structure of the LSTM network is shown in Figure 4, and the main calculation equations are as follows.

$$a_t = \tanh(W_a x_t + U_a h_{t-1} + b_a) \tag{1}$$

$$i_t = \sigma(W_i x_t + U_i h_{t-1} + b_i) \tag{2}$$

$$f_t = e_t \circ \sigma(W_f x_t + U_f h_{t-1} + b_f) \tag{3}$$

$$o_t = \sigma(W_o x_t + U_O h_{t-1} + b_o) \tag{4}$$

$$c_t = f_t \circ c_{t-1} + i_t \circ a_t \tag{5}$$

$$h_t = o_t \circ \tanh(c_t) \tag{6}$$

where the activation function σ is a sigmoid-like function such as $\sigma(x) = (1/1 + e^{-x})$; $\circ$ is a Hadamard product operator; U and W denote the weight matrix calculated from the output h_{t-1} of the previously hidden layer and the current input x_t, respectively; and b_* is the input bias of the three S-shaped functions. In the above equations, $i_t, f_t,$ and o_t denote the outputs of the input, oblivion, and output gates, respectively.

In this paper, the traditional LSTM was considered to rebuild the network model as Enhanced Long Short-Term Memory (ELSTM), as shown in Figure 5. Therefore, it can be seen that this paper considered adding a fully connected layer and a dropout layer on top of the LSTM to prevent the model from overfitting in the training process. Then, the two neural networks were put into the concatenate layer to form a strengthened

LSTM neural network. Then, the three strengthened neural networks were put into the concatenate layer to enhance the LSTM neural network and achieve better extraction of data features, as shown in Figure 4. The LSTM needed to be connected to a fully connected layer to transform the output of the LSTM into the desired result. The final product of this paper was a fully connected layer of four dimensions. Based on the extracted feature vectors, the output layer used a dropout mechanism combined with softmax for sentiment classification.

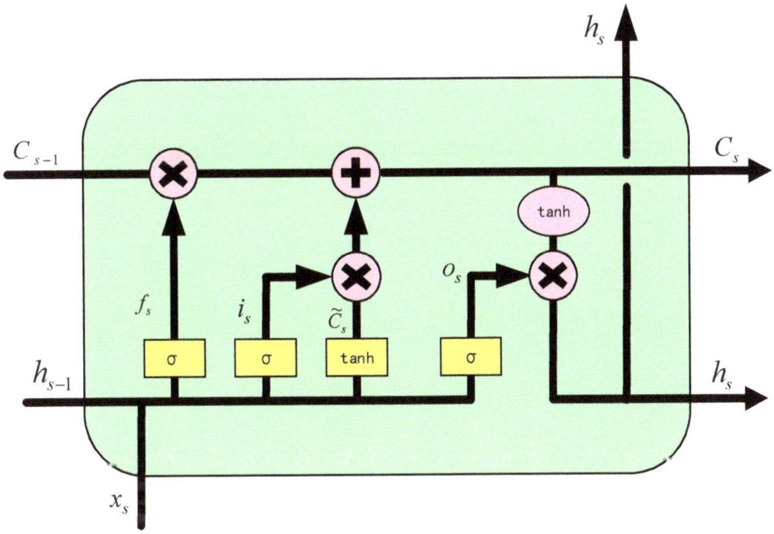

Figure 4. LSTM structure diagram (Source: Adapted from [20]).

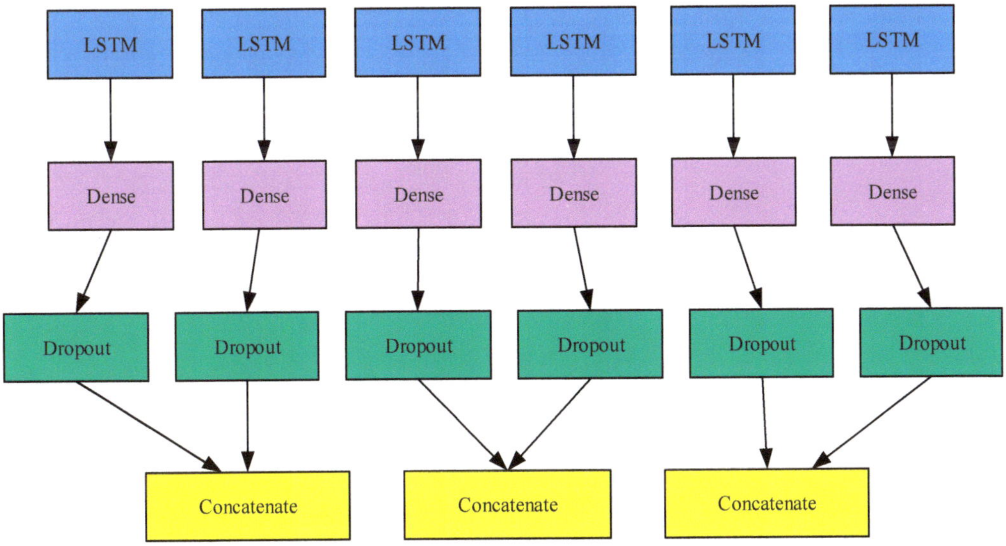

Figure 5. ELSTM structure diagram.

4. Experiment

4.1. Datasets and Pre-Processing

To more fully validate the applicability and stability of the model proposed in this paper, experiments were conducted on two Chinese datasets, namely the microblog review dataset simplifyweibo_4_moods and the hotel review dataset ChnSentiCorp_htl_all, which are described below.

The data were prepared from the official Weibo comment dataset simplifyweibo_4_moods downloaded from the web, containing four emotions: joy, anger, disgust, and depression. Each category had about 50,000 comments. The labeling methods and some of the data are shown in Tables 1 and 2. As each comment came from the web and used more symbolic language, regular expressions were applied to clean the comments. The words were split using Jieba in Python, and the length of each comment after breaking was calculated in preparation for creation of the splitter below. Figure 6 demonstrates that the number of reviews selected for each category in the chosen dataset was evenly distributed. The frequency histogram in Figure 7 shows the length of each sentence after the word splitting process, and it can be seen that the average size was 95 words and most comments were under 100 words, so the maximum number of words chosen for the next splitter was 100.

Table 1. Description of the simplifyweibo_4_moods dataset.

Field	Description
label	0 joy, 1 anger, 2 disgust, 3 depression
review	Microblog content

Table 2. Selected data from the simplifyweibo_4_moods dataset.

Serial Number	Label	Review
257031	2	It's a nasty feeling, I'm always too impulsive...
56901	0	Come and see my little pill stencil~ ~Wow, wow, wow, wow~
351395	3	The most complete one I've found. This is when you go to see your son in the north. Nostalgia. By the way, why am I wearing that torn shirt? So ugly...
249801	1	Poor, help this child to turn down, Hope will not be because of the alleged contact business what responsibility ah... is wanting fans to want crazy what situation ah? Want to...

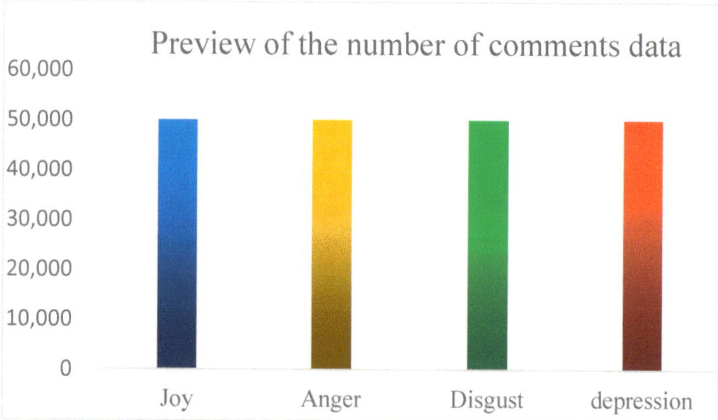

Figure 6. Preview of the number of comments in the dataset.

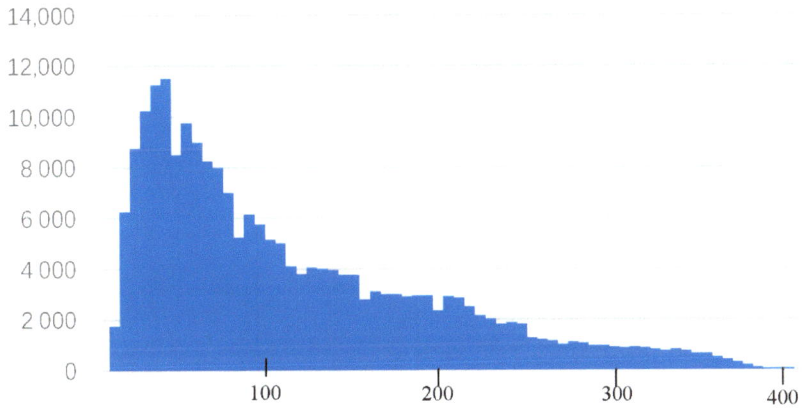

Figure 7. Preview of comment data length.

After the first part of the analysis, an understanding of the parameters of the word splitter was obtained. The Keras tokenizer was used to process the word-sorted data to obtain a matrix of training, stable, and test datasets, as well as a dictionary of the frequency and number of words corresponding to the occurrences. The dimensionality of the data processed by the sorter was 20,000 × 100 for the training set, 8000 × 100 for the stable set, and 2000 × 100 for the test set, which accounted for 66.7%, 26.7%, and 6.7% of the dataset, respectively.

The ChnSentiCorp_htl_all dataset was a dataset compiled by Mr. Songbo Tan with 7766 hotel reviews, including 5322 positive reviews and 2444 negative reviews. The allocation for the dataset was 4660 training samples, 1553 validation samples, and 1553 test samples for various sentiment analysis-related experiments. They accounted for 60%, 20%, and 20% of the dataset, respectively. The labeling methods and some of the comment data are shown in Tables 3 and 4.

Table 3. Description of the ChnSentiCorp_htl_all dataset.

Field	Description
label	1 indicates a positive comment, 0 indicates a negative comment
review	Content

Table 4. Selected data from the ChnSentiCorp_htl_all dataset.

Serial Number	Label	Review
5612	0	The room is unimaginably small, it is recommended that large people do not choose, the average sleeping feet can not be straight. The room is not more than 10 square feet, and the color TV is 14...
7321	0	Our family took the kids to the "May Day". The hotel is a great place to stay, but it seems to be wrong. 1. The hotel is in addition to...
3870	1	I went to the West Hill on Saturday to pick oranges and thought it would be a good hotel to stay at when I passed by...
4057	1	Convenient transportation is within walking distance to Fisherman's Wharf and Macau Ferry Terminal...
1452	1	It is a very nice hotel with a big bed and very comfortable. The hotel staff is very friendly.

4.2. Evaluation Indicators

This paper used accuracy, F1 score, Macro F1, and binary cross entropy loss function as evaluation metrics. Accuracy provided a clear judgment of the model's performance; F1 score was the summed average of accuracy and recall, which takes into account the accuracy and recall of the classification model; and Macro F1 was the average F1 score per category, providing an overview of the overall performance assessment. Below are the calculation formulas.

$$Accuracy = \frac{TP + TN}{TP + TN + FP + FN} \tag{7}$$

$$\text{Precision}(P) = \frac{TP}{TP + FP} \tag{8}$$

$$\text{Recall}(R) = \frac{TP}{TP + FN} \tag{9}$$

$$F_1 = 2 \times \frac{P \times R}{P + R} \tag{10}$$

$$\mathrm{H(p,q)} = -\sum \mathrm{p(x)log(q(x))} \tag{11}$$

where TP indicates the number of sentiment predictions that are positive and correct, and TN shows the number of sentiment predictions that are negative and correct. FP suggests the number of harmful category errors predicted as positive. FN indicates the number of positive category errors predicted as unfavorable. The loss function was calculated using Equation (11) where p and q represent the true distribution and the prediction, respectively.

4.3. Model Parameter Settings

The model parameters and their descriptions are shown in Table 5.

Table 5. Model parameter settings.

Name of Experimental Parameter	Parameter Values
Max Length of Sentences	100
Size of Word Vector	100
Batch Size	100
Window Size	3, 4, 5
Epochs	10
Dropout_rate	0.5
Optimizer	Adam
Learning_rate	0.001

4.4. Comparative Tests

To verify the validity of the hybrid neural network model, several classical models were selected for comparison experiments.

(1) TextCNN: Used for sentiment classification of text, it is a single basic convolutional neural network sentiment analysis method. In this paper, it was optimized by layer stacking.
(2) LSTM: Used for sentiment classification of text, it is a single basic long- and short-term memory neural network sentiment analysis method. In this paper, the LSTM was enhanced by increasing its number and complexity.
(3) TextCNN-LSTM: The text data are first transformed into word vectors through the embedding layer, and then features at different levels are extracted through multiple convolutional kernels in the TextCNN part. These extracted features are then

transformed into a time series and handed over to the LSTM part for subsequent processing.

(4) BiLSTM-ATT: First, the text sequence is transformed into a word vector through the embedding layer. Next, an attention mechanism is introduced for weighting the contribution of different words to the output of a given input text sequence to obtain more accurate and important information.

(5) Attention-Based Convolutional Neural Network (ABCNN): Combining the attention mechanism and CNN to sentence modeling, the goal is to construct a new sentence model containing sentence contextual relationships by taking into account the correlations between sentences through the attention mechanism.

(6) BERT-ETextCNN-ELSTM: First, the input text sentences are processed by the BERT pre-training model to obtain the corresponding word vector representation. Then, the TextCNN is optimally fused with an LSTM enhanced by increasing the number and complexity through layer stacking into an ETextCNN-ELSTM, after which the obtained word vectors are input into the ETextCNN-ELSTM to capture the features in the text sequence to different degrees through multiple convolutional kernels.

4.5. Analysis of Experimental Results

The error and accuracy obtained by the BERT-ETextCNN-ELSTM model trained on the simplifyweibo_4_moods and ChnSentiCorp_htl_all datasets at different numbers of iterations are shown in Figures 8 and 9. We can see that the accuracy of the model on the training set reached its highest at the 10th iteration, and therefore the number of iterations for this model was chosen to be 10.

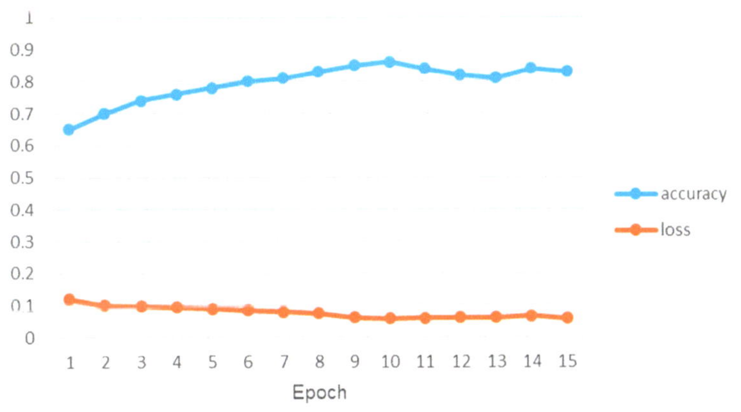

Figure 8. Loss and accuracy of the simplifyweibo_4_moods dataset.

From the above experiments, we can see that the number of iterations also affected the performance of the models, so we compared the results of each comparison model at different iterations to select the most appropriate number of iterations. Figures 10 and 11 show the experimental results for the six comparison models on the simplifyweibo_4_moods and ChnSentiCorp_htl_all datasets at different numbers of iterations.

From the above results, it can be seen that the BERT-ETextCNN-ELSTM model achieved the best sentiment analysis performance on both datasets compared to the other five comparison models, and it can also be seen that the best results were achieved when the number of iterations was 10, so the number of iterations for the model in this paper was set to 10.

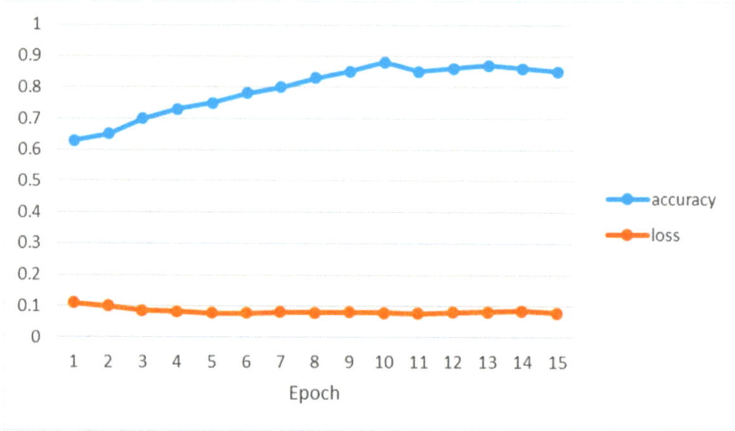

Figure 9. Loss and accuracy of the ChnSentiCorp_htl_all.

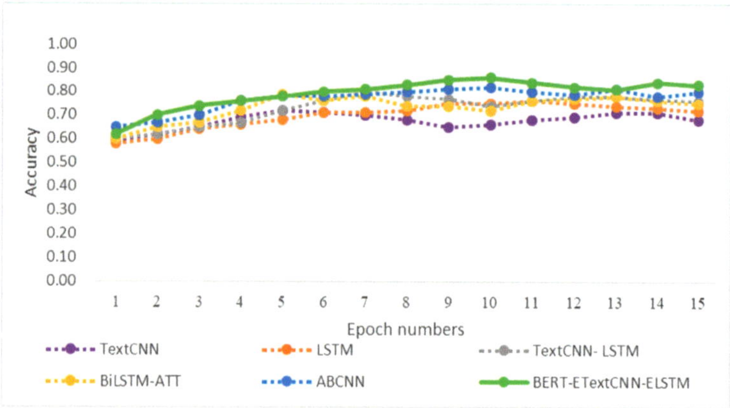

Figure 10. Accuracy of comparison models on the simplifyweibo_4_moods dataset.

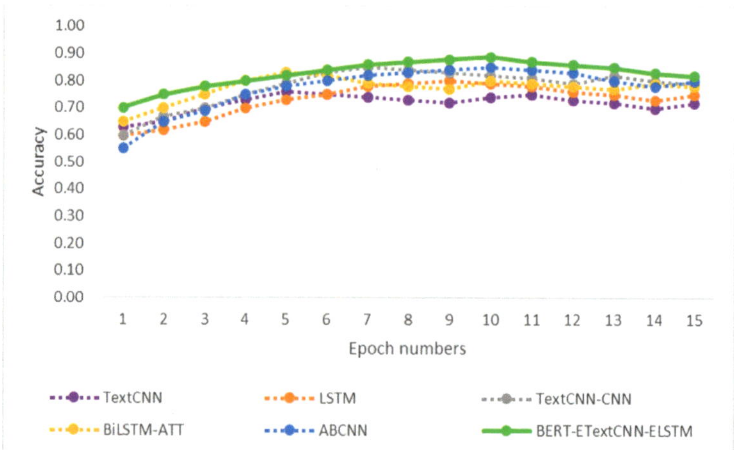

Figure 11. Accuracy of comparison models on the ChnSentiCorp_htl_all dataset.

In the training process of the model, this experiment introduced the dropout method. The dropout value is an important parameter, and a suitable value can make the model converge better, prevent the model from overfitting, and improve the performance of the model. Therefore, we chose different dropout values for training. The dropout values set in this experiment were [0.2, 0.3, 0.4, 0.5, 0.6, 0.7], and the best dropout value was selected from the training results of the model. The experiments were conducted on the simplifyweibo_4_moods dataset and the results of the experiments on the simplifyweibo_4_moods and ChnSentiCorp_htl_all dataset are shown in Figures 12 and 13. Through the results we can see that only the LSTM model worked best when the dropout value was 0.6, while the rest of the models achieved the best results when the dropout value was 0.5. The dropout value at this time could guarantee the accuracy of the results on the premise of the dropout value effectively preventing the model from overfitting, so the dropout value of the model in this paper was set to 0.5.

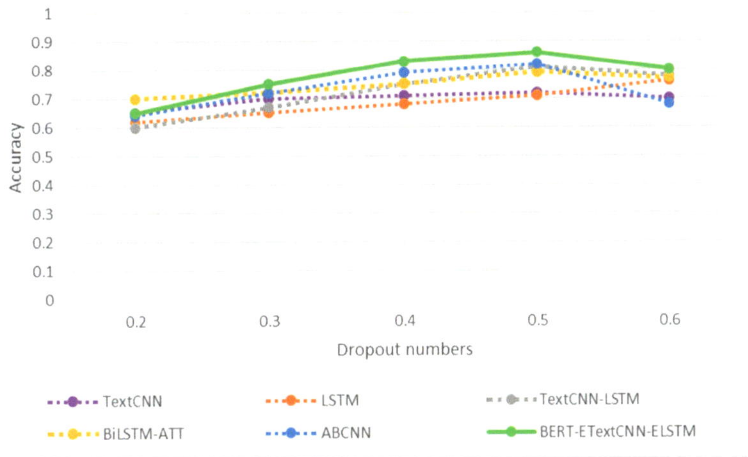

Figure 12. Accuracy of each model for the simplifyweibo_4_moods dataset for different dropout values.

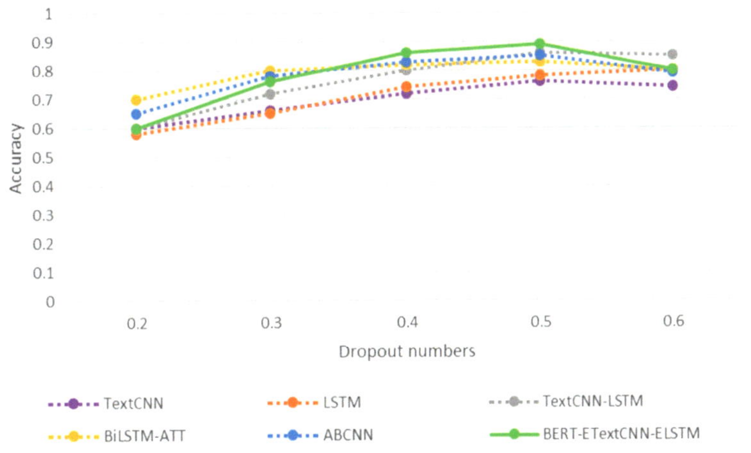

Figure 13. Accuracy of each model for the ChnSentiCorp_htl_all dataset for different dropout values.

In the process of gradient back propagation to update the parameters of the neural network, the optimizer used in this experiment was Adam. The Adam optimization algorithm is computationally efficient and converges quickly. To better exploit the efficiency of this algorithm, this paper chose different learning rate values to conduct experiments on the simplifyweibo_4_moods and ChnSentiCorp_htl_all datasets. The results on the simplifyweibo_4_moods and ChnSentiCorp_htl_all datasets are shown in Figures 14 and 15. From the experimental results, it can be seen that the model had the highest accuracy when the corresponding learning rate of Adam was 0.001. Therefore, the learning rate of the Adam optimizer in this paper was taken to be 0.001.

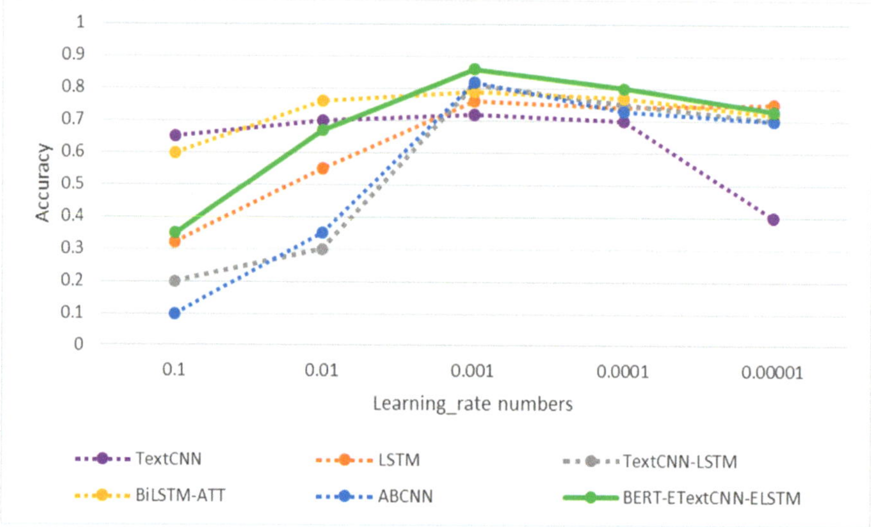

Figure 14. Accuracy of the simplifyweibo_4_moods dataset for each model at different learning rates.

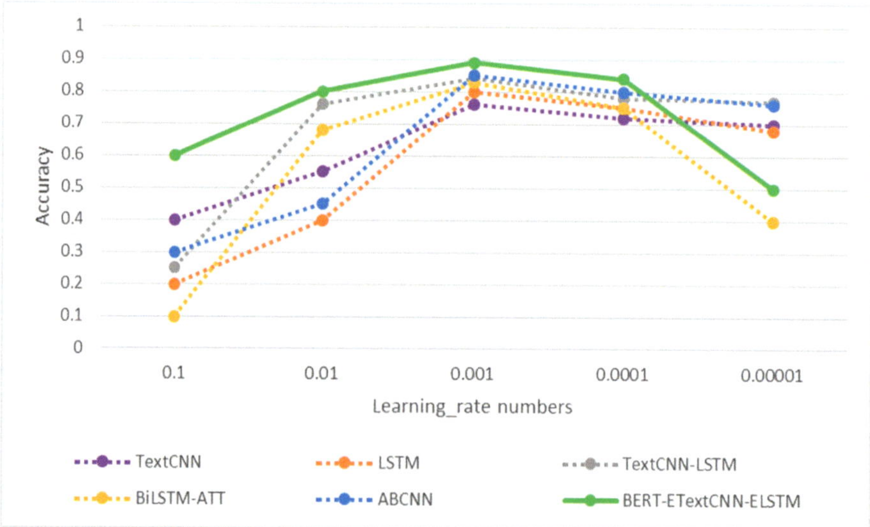

Figure 15. Accuracy of the ChnSentiCorp_htl_all dataset for each model at different learning rates.

The experimental results of the proposed model and other comparative models on the simplifyweibo_4_moods and ChnSentiCorp_htl_all datasets are shown in Tables 6 and 7 and Figure 16. To verify the effectiveness of the hybrid (combined, fused) neural network model proposed in this paper, using pre-trained models as well as optimized ones, several classical models were selected for comparison experiments. In the single neural network approach to sentiment analysis, the TextCNN and LSTM models were selected for comparison experiments. In the hybrid (combined, fused) neural network approach to sentiment analysis, among the sentiment analysis methods that introduce an attention mechanism, BiLSTM-ATT and Attention-Based Convolutional Neural Network (ABCNN) were chosen for comparison experiments. In both experiments, the best results of each model were selected for comparison.

Table 6. Table comparing experimental results on the simplifyweibo_4_moods dataset.

Model	Accuracy	F1 Score	Macro F1
TextCNN	0.72	0.71	0.69
LSTM	0.76	0.74	0.72
TextCNN-LSTM	0.81	0.79	0.78
BiLSTM-ATT	0.79	0.78	0.77
Attention-Based Convolutional Neural Network (ABCNN)	0.82	0.80	0.79
BERT-ETextCNN-ELSTM	0.86	0.85	0.84

Table 7. Table comparing experimental results on the ChnSentiCorp_htl_all dataset.

Model	Accuracy	F1 Score	Macro F1
TextCNN	0.76	0.75	0.74
LSTM	0.80	0.79	0.78
TextCNN-LSTM	0.86	0.85	0.83
BiLSTM-ATT	0.83	0.81	0.79
Attention-Based Convolutional Neural Network (ABCNN)	0.85	0.84	0.83
BERT-ETextCNN-ELSTM	0.89	0.88	0.86

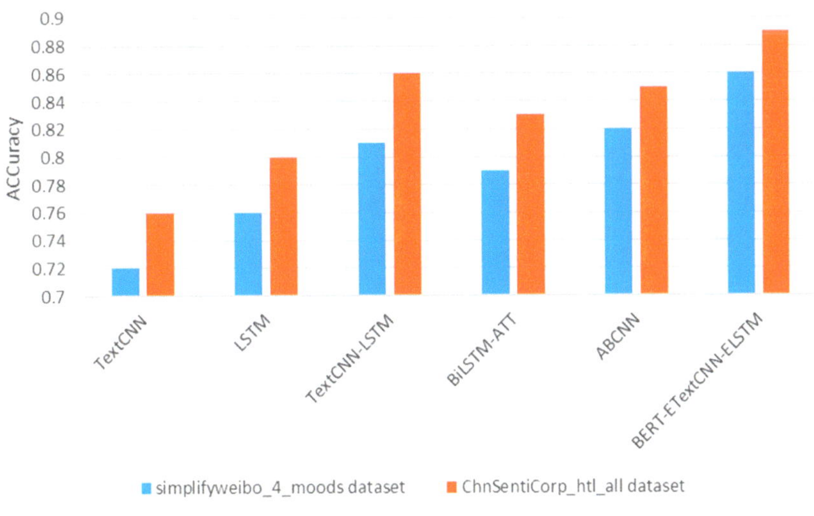

Figure 16. Accuracy of each model on different datasets.

From the experimental results, it can be seen that the BERT-ETextCNN-ELSTM model proposed in this paper achieved the best sentiment analysis performance on both the simplifyweibo_4_moods and ChnSentiCorp_htl_all datasets, with the highest accuracy, F1 value, and macro-average F1 value. From the results, it can be seen that the overall performances of TextCNN-LSTM, BiLSTM-ATT, Attention-Based Convolutional Neural Network (ABCNN), and the model in this paper, BERT-ETextCNN-ELSTM, were significantly higher than those of TextCNN and LSTM. Additionally, the hybrid (combined, fused) neural networks for sentiment analysis compared to single neural network approaches were studied, and the advantages of different approaches were considered before combining and improving these approaches. Their use for sentiment analysis achieved good results, indicating that this approach was significantly effective in alleviating the problem of reliance on the model's structure. Among the hybrid models, the performance of the model proposed in this paper, BERT-ETextCNN-ELSTM, was significantly higher than that of TextCNN-LSTM, BiLSTM-ATT, and ABCNN, indicating that the BERT model incorporated in this paper could better handle contextual information and deal with problems such as polysemy and ambiguity. In addition, the optimization of TextCNN-LSTM in this paper enabled the model to more fully exploit the deep semantic information of short textbooks, thus further improving sentiment analysis of comment data.

5. Conclusions

With the development of the Internet, comment data have become more diverse and the structure of comment data has become more complex. Traditional sentiment analysis methods are no longer able to produce results with great accuracy, and deep learning methods are constantly developing new models due to their ability to actively extract text features and their excellent performance in sentiment analysis tasks.

The research content of this paper aimed to address the shortcomings in deep learning and improve its sentiment analysis performance. The main contributions and findings of this thesis are as follows:

In response to the problem that traditional deep learning models cannot extract deep semantic information and that it becomes more difficult for traditional deep learning models to extract text features when the information from review data keeps changing, such as the emergence of new vocabulary, an optimized CNN-LSTM model was proposed to better complete the extraction of features. The model superimposed layers on the convolutional neural network, which not only reduced the complexity of the model and gradient disappearance due to redundancy of the model, but it also increased the output channels in the TextCNN network, enhanced the LSTM, increased the number and complexity of the LSTM, and achieved better extraction of data features.

By introducing the BERT model, our model could take full advantage of deep bidirectional contextual understanding to better capture the global semantic information of sentences. The pre-training capability of BERT and learning from a large corpus enabled our model to better understand Chinese text and perform an accurate analysis of sentiment. Experimental results on two publicly available datasets, simplifyweibo_4_moods and ChnSentiCorp_htl_all, validated the superiority of our model over current mainstream models and achieved better performance and results. This demonstrated the robustness and applicability of the model, as well as its effectiveness for Chinese sentiment analysis tasks. However, comment data from websites have complex issues such as imperfect expression and inaccuracy. This experiment will further refine the advancement of the algorithm since, for example, speech, images, and videos also intuitively express people's emotions, and the next work will also explore applications in the fields of speech, image, and video processing to improve the accuracy of the analysis.

Author Contributions: Conceptualization, L.D., T.Y. and Z.L.; Methodology, L.D. and T.Y.; Formal analysis, L.D., Z.L. and Q.G.; Software, L.D., T.Y., Q.G. and T.Y.; Validation, T.Y., Z.L. and Z.L.; Investigation, Z.L. and Q.G.; Resources, Q.G.; Writing-original draft, Q.G. All authors have read and agreed to the published version of the manuscript.

Funding: This paper was supported by the National Natural Science Foundation of China [Grant 61702462], the Henan Provincial Science and Technology Research Project [Grants 222102210010 and 222102210064], the Research and Practice Project of Higher Education Teaching Reform in Henan Province [Grants 2019SJGLX320 and 2019SJGLX020], the Undergraduate Universities Smart Teaching Special Research Project of Henan Province [Grant Jiao Gao (2021) No. 489-29], and the Academic Degrees & Graduate Education Reform Project of Henan Province [Grant 2021SJGLX115Y].

Data Availability Statement: The data presented in this study are openly available in https://datafountain.cn/datasets/54, (accessed on 30 August 2022).

Conflicts of Interest: The authors declare no conflict of interest.

References

1. Wang, X.; Wei, F.; Liu, X.; Zhou, M.; Zhang, M. Topic sentiment analysis in twitter: A graph-based hashtag sentiment classification approach. In Proceedings of the 20th ACM International Conference on Information and Knowledge Management, Glasgow, UK, 24–28 October 2011; pp. 1031–1040.
2. Brauwers, G.; Frasincar, F. A survey on aspect-based sentiment classification. *ACM Comput. Surv.* **2022**, *55*, 1–37. [CrossRef]
3. Jia, K. Sentiment classification of microblog: A framework based on BERT and CNN with attention mechanism. *Comput. Electr. Eng.* **2022**, *101*, 108032. [CrossRef]
4. Sun, B.; Tian, F.; Liang, L. Tibetan micro-blog sentiment analysis based on mixed deep learning. In Proceedings of the 2018 International Conference on Audio, Language and Image Processing (ICALIP), Shanghai, China, 16–17 July 2018; pp. 109–112.
5. Jia, K.; Li, Z. Chinese micro-blog sentiment classification based on emotion dictionary and semantic rules. In Proceedings of the 2020 International Conference on Computer Information and Big Data Applications (CIBDA), Guiyang, China, 17–19 April 2020; pp. 309–312.
6. Hong, X.; Shaohua, X. Analysis on Web Public Opinion Orientation Based on Syntactic Parsing and Emotional Dictionary. *J. Chin. Comput. Syst.* **2014**, *35*, 811–813.
7. García-Méndez, S.; de Arriba-Pérez, F.; Barros-Vila, A.; González-Castaño, F.J. Targeted aspect-based emotion analysis to detect opportunities and precaution in financial Twitter messages. *Expert Syst. Appl.* **2023**, *218*, 119611. [CrossRef]
8. Fang, L.; Shao, D. Application of long short-term memory (LSTM) on the prediction of rainfall-runoff in karst area. *Front. Phys.* **2022**, *9*, 790687. [CrossRef]
9. Sangeetha, K.; Prabha, D. Sentiment analysis of student feedback using multi-head attention fusion model of word and context embedding for LSTM. *J. Ambient. Intell. Humaniz. Comput.* **2021**, *12*, 4117–4126. [CrossRef]
10. Yadav, R.K.; Jiao, L.; Goodwin, M.; Granmo, O.C. Positionless aspect based sentiment analysis using attention mechanism. *Knowl. Based Syst.* **2021**, *226*, 107136. [CrossRef]
11. Li, Y.; Zhang, K.; Wang, J.; Gao, X. A cognitive brain model for multimodal sentiment analysis based on attention neural networks. *Neurocomputing* **2021**, *430*, 159–173. [CrossRef]
12. Banupriya, R.; Kannan, R. A convolutional neural network based feature extractor with discriminant feature score for effective medical image classification. *NeuroQuantology* **2020**, *18*, 1.
13. Febrian, R.; Halim, B.M.; Christina, M.; Ramdhan, D.; Chowanda, A. Facial expression recognition using bidirectional LSTM—CNN. *Procedia Comput. Sci.* **2023**, *216*, 39–47. [CrossRef]
14. Satrya, W.F.; Aprilliyani, R.; Yossy, E.H. Sentiment analysis of Indonesian police chief using multi-level ensemble model. *Procedia Comput. Sci.* **2023**, *216*, 620–629. [CrossRef]
15. Kale, A.S.; Pandya, V.; Di Troia, F.; Stamp, M. Malware classification with Word2Vec, HMM2Vec, BERT, and ELMo. *J. Comput. Virol. Hacking Tech.* **2022**, *19*, 1–16. [CrossRef]
16. Zheng, Y.; Zhang, R.; Wang, S.; Mensah, S.; Mao, Y. Anchored model transfer and soft instance transfer for cross-task cross-domain learning: A study through aspect-level sentiment classification. In Proceedings of the Web Conference 2020, Taipei, Taiwan, 20–24 April 2020; pp. 2754–2760.
17. Sun, L.; Lian, Z.; Tao, J.; Liu, B.; Niu, M. Multi-modal continuous dimensional emotion recognition using recurrent neural network and self-attention mechanism. In Proceedings of the 1st International on Multimodal Sentiment Analysis in Real-life Media Challenge and Workshop, Seattle, WA, USA, 16 October 2020; pp. 27–34.
18. Alhagry, S.; Fahmy, A.A.; El-Khoribi, R.A. Emotion recognition based on EEG using LSTM recurrent neural network. *Int. J. Adv. Comput. Sci. Appl.* **2017**, *8*, 355–358. [CrossRef]
19. Chen, Y. Convolutional Neural Network for Sentence Classification. Master's Thesis, University of Waterloo, Waterloo, ON, Canada, 2015.
20. Zhuge, Q.; Xu, L.; Zhang, G. LSTM Neural Network with Emotional Analysis for prediction of stock price. *Eng. Lett.* **2017**, *25*, 167–175.
21. Zhou, Q.; Wu, H. NLP at IEST 2018: BiLSTM-attention and LSTM-attention via soft voting in emotion classification. In Proceedings of the 9th Workshop on Computational Approaches to Subjectivity, Sentiment and Social Media Analysis, Brussels, Belgium, 31 October 2018; pp. 189–194.
22. Cheng, Y.; Sun, H.; Chen, H.; Meng, L.; Cai, Y.; Cai, Z.; Huang, J. Sentiment analysis using multi-head attention capsules with multi-channel CNN and bidirectional GRU. *IEEE Access* **2021**, *9*, 60383–60395. [CrossRef]

23. Munikar, M.; Shakya, S.; Shrestha, A. Fine-grained sentiment classification using BERT. In *2019 Artificial Intelligence for Transforming Business and Society (AITB)*; IEEE: Piscataway, NJ, USA, 2019; Volume 1, pp. 1–5.
24. Yu, L.; Chen, L.; Dong, J.; Li, M.; Liu, L.; Zhao, B.; Zhang, C. Detecting malicious web requests using an enhanced textcnn. In Proceedings of the 2020 IEEE 44th Annual Computers, Software, and Applications Conference (COMPSAC), Madrid, Spain, 13–17 July 2020; pp. 768–777.
25. Bengio, Y.; Ducharme, R.; Vincent, P. A neural probabilistic language model. *Adv. Neural Inf. Process. Syst.* **2000**, *13*, 1137–1155.
26. Mikolov, T.; Sutskever, I.; Chen, K.; Corrado, G.S.; Dean, J. Distributed representations of words and phrases and their compositionality. In Proceedings of the Advances in Neural Information Processing Systems 26 (NIPS 2013), Lake Tahoe, NV, USA, 5–10 December 2013; Volume 26.
27. Kumar, A.; nee Khemchandani, R.R. Self-attention enhanced recurrent neural networks for sentence classification. In Proceedings of the 2018 IEEE Symposium Series on Computational Intelligence (SSCI), Bengaluru, India, 18–21 November 2018; pp. 905–911.
28. Kota, V.R.; Munisamy, S.D. High accuracy offering attention mechanisms based deep learning approach using CNN/bi-LSTM for sentiment analysis. *Int. J. Intell. Comput. Cybern.* **2022**, *15*, 61–74. [CrossRef]
29. Sharma, A.K.; Chaurasia, S.; Srivastava, D.K. Sentimental short sentences classification by using CNN deep learning model with fine tuned Word2Vec. *Procedia Comput. Sci.* **2020**, *167*, 1139–1147. [CrossRef]
30. Ullah, F.; Chen, X.; Shah, S.B.H.; Mahfoudh, S.; Hassan, M.A.; Saeed, N. A Novel Approach for Emotion Detection and Sentiment Analysis for Low Resource Urdu Language Based on CNN-LSTM. *Electronics* **2022**, *11*, 4096. [CrossRef]
31. Liu, S.; Lee, I. Sequence encoding incorporated CNN model for Email document sentiment classification. *Appl. Soft Comput.* **2021**, *102*, 107104. [CrossRef]
32. Hui, L.; Yaqing, C. Fine-Grained Sentiment Analysis Based on Convolutional Neural Network. *Data Anal. Knowl. Discov.* **2019**, *3*, 95–103.
33. Sangeetha, J.; Kumaran, U. A hybrid optimization algorithm using BiLSTM structure for sentiment analysis. *Meas. Sens.* **2023**, *25*, 100619. [CrossRef]
34. Yin, W.; Schütze, H. Multichannel variable-size convolution for sentence classification. *arXiv* **2016**, arXiv:1603.04513.

electronics

MDPI

Article

Black-Box Evasion Attack Method Based on Confidence Score of Benign Samples

Shaohan Wu , Jingfeng Xue, Yong Wang * and Zixiao Kong

School of Computer Science and Technology, Beijing Institute of Technology, Beijing 100081, China; 3120201083@bit.edu.cn (S.W.); xuejf@bit.edu.cn (J.X.); 3120185534@bit.edu.cn (Z.K.)
* Correspondence: wangyong@bit.edu.cn

Abstract: Recently, malware detection models based on deep learning have gradually replaced manual analysis as the first line of defense for anti-malware systems. However, it has been shown that these models are vulnerable to a specific class of inputs called adversarial examples. It is possible to evade the detection model by adding some carefully crafted tiny perturbations to the malicious samples without changing the sample functions. Most of the adversarial example generation methods ignore the information contained in the detection results of benign samples from detection models. Our method extracts sequence fragments called benign payload from benign samples based on detection results and uses an RNN generative model to learn benign features embedded in these sequences. Then, we use the end of the original malicious sample as input to generate an adversarial perturbation that reduces the malicious probability of the sample and append it to the end of the sample to generate an adversarial sample. According to different adversarial scenarios, we propose two different generation strategies, which are the one-time generation method and the iterative generation method. Under different query times and append scale constraints, the maximum evasion success rate can reach 90.8%.

Keywords: adversarial examples; evasion attack; malware detection; artificial intelligence security

check for updates

Citation: Wu, S.; Xue, J.; Wang, Y.; Kong, Z. Black-Box Evasion Attack Method Based on Confidence Score of Benign Samples. *Electronics* **2023**, *12*, 2346. https://doi.org/10.3390/electronics12112346

Academic Editor: Aryya Gangopadhyay

Received: 7 April 2023
Revised: 12 May 2023
Accepted: 15 May 2023
Published: 23 May 2023

1. Introduction

Deep learning has shown great potential in several fields. In recent years, with the continuous deepening of its research, deep learning models have been introduced in many fields, and have achieved quite good results. However, it has been shown that deep learning models can be attacked by a specific class of inputs called adversarial examples [1]. Adversarial examples first appeared in the field of image classification. It is generated by adding some small perturbations to the original samples, which can deceive deep learning models and make them misclassified. With the development of research, the existence of adversarial examples has also been found in other fields. At present, the research on adversarial attack and defense has become a domain task, jointly promoting the development of deep learning models.

In the field of malware detection, traditional manual analysis methods require a lot of time and professional domain knowledge, which is difficult to cope with the ever-growing malware and a large number of variants. Additionally, deep learning—especially end-to-end deep learning models have excellent performance in the face of these problems. The most typical one is a convolutional neural network model called Malconv [2]. This model is a malware detection model for PE files jointly proposed by the Laboratory of Physical Sciences (LPS) and NVIDIA. It takes the first 2 M bytes of PE samples as input and has become one of the better detection models recognized in the field.

It is more difficult to generate adversarial examples in the malware detection adversarial field because it is necessary to ensure that the functions of the samples are not affected when adding adversarial perturbations and that the adversarial examples whose original functions are affected are meaningless. Therefore, the most commonly used method of adding perturbation is to append several bytes at the end of the sample, which can ensure the structural integrity of the PE file and minimize the probability that the function of the sample will be affected. Currently, many effective adversarial attack methods have been proposed based on this strategy, but most of them ignore the information contained in the feedback of the detection model to benign samples. Our method starts with the confidence score of a benign sample and extracts sequence fragments called benign payload from the benign sample. These sequence fragments will be used as training data for our RNN generation model after processing, helping the RNN generation model learn how to generate sequences that reduce the confidence score of the detection model. Finally, we use the end-byte sequence of the original malicious sample as an input to the RNN generation model to generate adversarial perturbations and append them to the end of the malicious sample, thereby generating adversarial examples.

Our study shows that it is possible to successfully craft adversarial examples that evade detection models with only some model feedback on benign examples. Furthermore, our method is not designed to help intruders evade detection models but to potentially help detection model researchers improve the robustness of models against adversarial attacks. At present, some methods have been proposed to improve the defense performance of detection models in the presence of adversarial examples, and all these methods require a large number of adversarial examples. We compare our method with several other methods, and the results show that our method has certain advantages in both evasion performance and perturbation scale.

2. Background and Related Work

2.1. Malware Detection Method Based on Machine Learning

Malware detection is gradually shifting from traditional rule-based methods to machine-learning-based and deep learning methods, which are heavily introduced to improve the detection capabilities of models. In this paper, we mainly focus on PE files [3] for the Windows platform. These methods can be divided into three categories, depending on how they process the input. The first category is image-based methods, which treat bytes as pixels, convert the entire software sample into a color or grayscale image, and apply image classification methods for detection. Nataraj et al. [4] first adopted this idea to convert software samples into grayscale images and used the K-nearest neighbor method to classify using the texture features of the image. Since then, more excellent image classification models have been introduced based on this idea, including VGGNet [5], ResNet [6], Inception-V3 [7], etc. The second category is disassembly-based methods. Such methods usually disassemble software samples first, then extract features such as control flow graph and function call graph from the assembly code, and finally use related methods of graph classification to detect and classify [8–11]. Some people also directly extract features from the disassembled assembly opcode sequence for detection [12,13]. The third category is to use raw binary byte sequences directly. Jain et al. [14] directly extract n-gram features from byte sequences and use traditional machine learning methods for detection. Raff et al. [15] proposed a detection model that only selects a few bytes of the header of the PE file as input, which can use less domain knowledge to achieve better results. Raff et al. [2] also proposed the first end-to-end shallow CNN model that allows almost the entire malware byte sequence (first 2 M bytes) as input, called Malconv. It can achieve 94.0% accuracy and 98.1% AUC after training on a dataset including 2 million PE files, so we choose this model as the target model for our adversarial attack.

2.2. Adversarial Attack

Adversarial attacks (also known as evasion attacks) are a popular research topic recently, and the goal of this task is to generate effective adversarial examples. For a certain sample x that the model can detect correctly, add an imperceptible small perturbation η to it to obtain the perturbed sample $\widetilde{x}$, if $\widetilde{x}$ can successfully evade the detection model, then $\widetilde{x}$

is an effective adversarial sample. According to the different information mastered by the attacker, the types of attacks can be simply divided into white-box attacks and black-box attacks. In a white-box attack, the attacker can obtain information, such as the model structure, parameters, training set, etc.; in a black-box attack, the attacker can only obtain the classification results of some samples by the model. Early research mainly focused on the field of image classification. Szegedy et al. [1] first proposed the concept of adversarial examples in 2014 and proved the existence of adversarial examples. They construct an adversarial perturbation based on the gradient information when the model classifies a certain sample, so that the classification result moves in the wrong direction as much as possible, thereby generating an adversarial sample. Subsequently, Goodfellow et al. [16] proposed the famous FGSM algorithm, which maximizes the prediction error of the model while ensuring that the input l_0 norm remains unchanged after the perturbation, and can find adversarial examples with low-performance overhead. In the field of black-box attacks, the intuitive idea is to transform unknown black-box attack problems into known white-box attacks. Papernot et al. [17] introduced this idea. They collect the prediction output of the target model for some samples and use these input and output to train a surrogate model, and then use the method of white-box attack on the surrogate model to generate adversarial examples. Xu et al. [18] introduced the idea of a genetic algorithm, they generate random perturbation samples and then make the samples evolve continuously based on the confidence scores of the model on these samples, and finally generate effective adversarial examples. Su et al. [19] adopted similar ideas to implement adversarial attacks that only change a few or even a single pixel.

In the field of malware detection, many methods have also been proposed to generate adversarial examples. Kreuk et al. [20] first migrated the FGSM method to the field of adversarial malware. They mapped discrete bytes into a continuous space to solve the problem that the gradient of the objective function cannot be obtained and introduced domain knowledge to ensure that the function of the adversarial sample remains unchanged. Kolosnjaji et al. [21] and Demetrio et al. [22] also proposed gradient-based white-box methods, where they added perturbations to the tail and head of PE files, respectively. Hu et al. [23] proposed a GAN-based black-box attack method where they trained a GAN with a surrogate model to indirectly generate adversarial examples that minimize the confidence score predicted by the detection model. Rosenberg et al. [24] focused on attacking malware classification models based on API calls. They still used alternative models plus white-box attacks to implement black-box attacks and proved the transferability of these attacks on different models. In order not to rely on the surrogate model and achieve a true black-box attack, genetic algorithms are introduced to solve this problem [25,26]. They use genetic algorithms to optimize random perturbations until the perturbed samples successfully evade the detector. Demetrio et al. [27] made further optimizations based on this idea. The perturbation they generated came from benign samples, and hyperparameters that control the scale of perturbation and the number of queries were introduced into the loss function. Another widely studied strategy is reinforcement learning [28–32]. This strategy is feasible when generating a small number of samples, but it is difficult to solve the problem of generating effective adversarial examples in large numbers. Park et al. [33] worked on attacking image-based malware classification models. They convert malware samples into images and employ FGSM or C&W methods to generate standard adversarial sample images, and then use dynamic programming algorithm to generate adversarial examples closest to standard samples. Ebrahimi et al. [34] proposed a black-box attack method based on the RNN model. They train the RNN model to learn the semantic features of benign samples, then generate adversarial perturbations with malicious samples as input and append them to the end to imitate benign samples, thereby evading the detection model. Chen et al. [35] proposed two methods for CNN-based detection models in white-box and black-box cases, respectively. In the white box case, the saliency vector is generated by the Grad-CAM method to divide the benign and malignant regions in the file, and the benign features are appended to the end of the malicious sample. In the case of a black box, the method of optimizing random perturbation is first used to attack, the successful attack trajectory is recorded, and the contribution of each data block to the success of the attack is calculated, which is used as a guide for subsequent attacks. After collating these studies, we find that most black-box attacks focus on the detection model's feedback on malicious samples, whether hard or soft labels, but ignore the confidence score feedback of the detection model on benign samples. Our method is able to collect this information and extract the features of benign samples contained in it, to train our RNN generation model, which will play a crucial role in subsequent adversarial attacks.

2.3. Generative RNN Model

Recurrent Neural Networks are a class of neural networks specialized for processing sequential data. Its basic structure is similar to that of a normal neural network, but at each moment t, a single node accepts a hidden state h_t affected by the previous moment in addition to the input x_t at the current moment and generates an output from it. These characteristics of RNN mean that it can record the historical information of the input, so it is especially suitable for data processing with sequential nature, including natural language processing [36], speech recognition, video analysis, etc. Considering the similarity between software data sequences and text sequences, the model can also be used in malware-related domains. There have been studies that have demonstrated the feasibility of using RNN models in the malware domain, whether for detection, classification, or adversarial attack [34,37–40]. The target model of our adversarial attack, Malconv, takes byte sequences as input, so we directly build the RNN model at the byte level. To control the scale of the input and output, we introduce the idea of a seq2seq model [41] with encoding and decoding layers between the input and output.

3. Proposed Method

The overall processing flow of our method is shown in Figure 1. Similar to other malware adversarial attack methods, we first introduce our threat model, followed by the benign payload we defined, and then the architecture design of the RNN model. Finally, based on the trained RNN model, according to the number of times the detection model is queried, we propose two different adversarial example generation methods, the one-time generation method, and the iterative generation method.

3.1. Threat Model

Our method focuses on the information obtained from the confidence scores of benign samples, and we focus on how to generate adversarial examples in batches with little impact on the original samples. The following is our threat model:

- **Adversary's Goal**: Generating batches of adversarial examples that can evade a deep learning-based malware detection model (the Malconv model in this paper), making the perturbation scale as small as possible under the premise of successful evasion.
- **Adversary's Knowledge**: The adversary cannot know the structure and parameters of the malware detection model, nor can it know the model's data set, training hyper-parameters, and other information, but it can obtain the confidence score feedback of some models for samples. Furthermore, in the one-time generation method, the adversary does not need to query the detection model, but in the iterative generation method, the adversary needs to conduct several confidence score queries to optimize adversarial perturbations.
- **Adversary's Capabilities**: Appending adversarial perturbations to the end of malware without changing sample functionality.

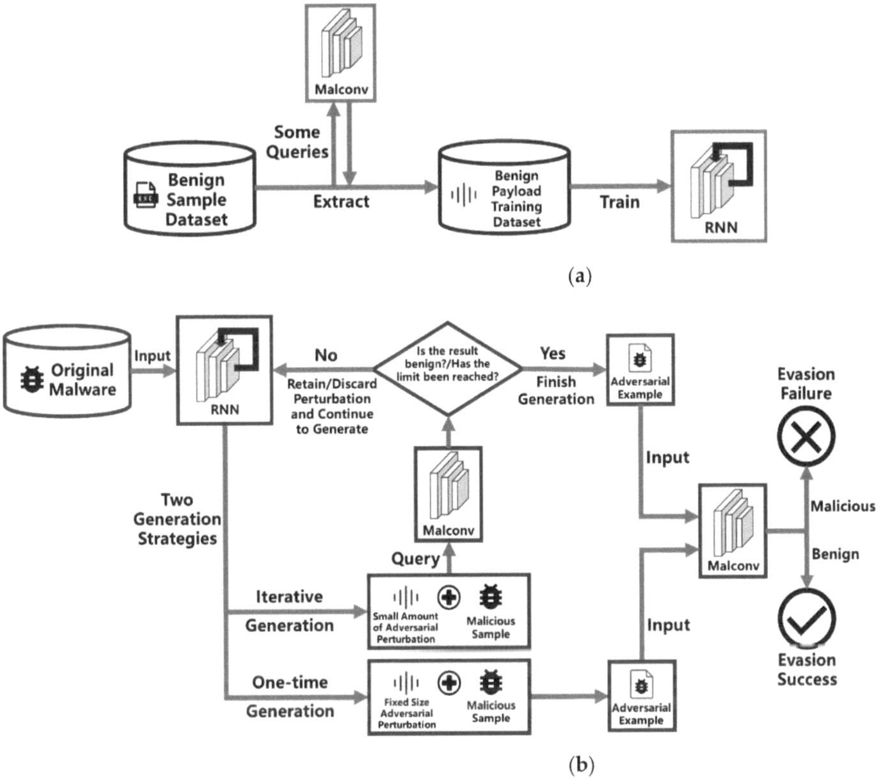

Figure 1. The overall processing flow chart of our method. (**a**) Flow of RNN generation model training; (**b**) flow of two adversarial example generation methods.

3.2. Benign Payload Extraction

Before introducing the definition of benign payload, we first illustrate our observations and thoughts on the deep learning-based end-to-end malware detection model and its adversarial examples. According to previous research on deep neural networks [1], the mapping from input space to output is discontinuous due to the use of a large number of nonlinear functions in neural networks. It is this discontinuity that leads to small perturbations that can change the results predicted by the model. We conducted experiments and observations on the Malconv model. The Malconv model can accept input of any length up to 2 M bytes. Therefore, we consider taking the first n bytes of the sample as input and observe the change trend of the confidence score of the Malconv model when n increases from small to large with a certain step size. Note that since the confidence score finally output by Malconv comes through the sigmoid layer, the sigmoid layer is sensitive to values near 0 but not to values at both ends, so we observe the original confidence score before the sigmoid layer. We found that there is indeed a sudden change in the confidence score with a small change in the value of n, as shown in Figure 2. These mutations may serve as an opening to attack the Malconv model. Our goal is to train an RNN model that generates perturbation sequences that reduce the confidence score of the Malconv model, and it is the sequence of bytes after the mutation point that makes the confidence score of the Malconv model significantly lower. From the effect point of view, this sequence is the key factor for the Malconv model to predict that the entire sample is benign, that is, the benign payload. Its detailed definition is as follows:

Let the target detection model be F, and we mainly focus on its original confidence score, which is the output of the model before passing through the sigmoid layer. If the output is less than 0, the model predicts it as a benign sample, and the smaller the output, the higher the probability that the model thinks it is a benign sample, and vice versa. As shown in Figure 3, select a split point c in the entire benign sample to obtain sequence a of arbitrary length and sequence b of fixed length. If the difference between $F(a)$ and $F(a+b)$ is greater than a certain threshold ε, the sequence b appended to sequence a is considered to be a benign payload that reduces its confidence score. We also record the difference by which the benign payload reduces the confidence score of the sample.

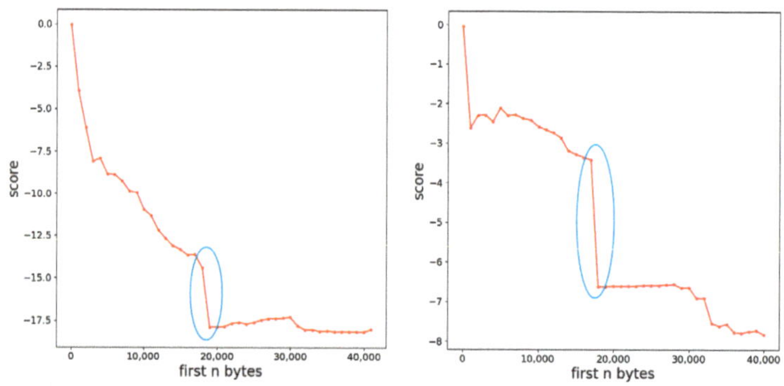

Figure 2. Two typical examples of sudden changes (in blue circle) in sample confidence scores for Malconv models.

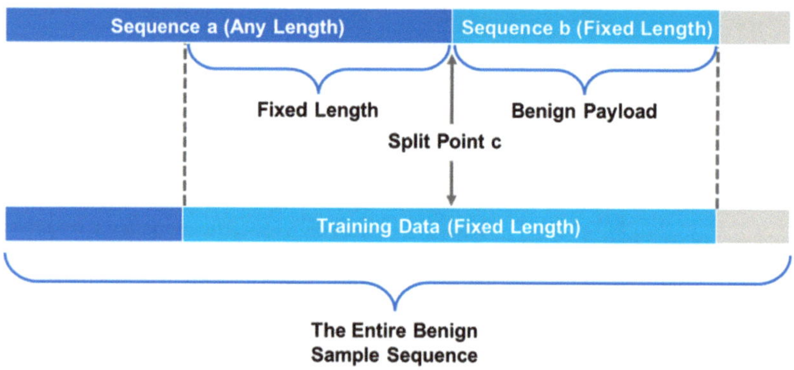

Figure 3. Extract training data from sequences of benign samples.

In order for the RNN model to learn how to generate perturbed sequences that degrade the model's confidence score, we take the benign payload and a fixed-length sequence before the benign payload as a training data sample of the RNN model and take several training data samples from several benign samples as the training set of the RNN model.

3.3. RNN Generation Model

The RNN model is especially suitable for dealing with sequence problems because the sequence is continuous, and the processing of the input of a certain node must not only use the information of the current node, but also combine the information of the previous sequence. In RNN, the information of the previous sequence is saved by the hidden state. Specifically, the hidden state h_t at each moment is given by the following formula:

$$h_t = f(Wh_{t-1} + Ux_t) \tag{1}$$

where h_{t-1} is the hidden state at the previous moment, W is the parameter matrix related to it, x_t is the input at the current moment, U is the parameter matrix related to the input, and f is the nonlinear activation function. That is, the hidden state is affected by the hidden state of the previous moment and the current input, and the output $\hat{y}_t$ at each moment is given by the following formula:

$$\hat{y}_t = f(Vh_t) \tag{2}$$

where h_t is the hidden state at the current moment, V is the parameter matrix associated with it, and f is the nonlinear activation function. In the above formula, W, U, and V are all parameters that the model needs to learn.

Similar to MalRNN [34], we also adopt the GRU model to learn the knowledge of benign payload. GRU is an improved RNN model proposed by Chung et al. [42], which can alleviate the problem of gradient disappearance when processing long sequences. Our model accomplishes the task of generating perturbed byte sequences from malware byte sequences, so we employ an encoder-decoder type of architecture. The encoder first embeds the original byte sequence into a low-dimensional feature vector, then the GRU also predicts the next possible output in the form of a feature vector, and finally, the decoder converts it into the corresponding byte sequence output. During model learning, the optimizer optimizes the following loss:

$$loss = \sum_t \mathcal{L}(\hat{y}_t, y_t) \tag{3}$$

where $\hat{y}_t$ is the predicted value of the model at position t, y_t is the real value of the sample sequence at position t, and $\mathcal{L}$ represents the function for calculating cross-entropy.

After the training is completed, the model accepts the input of a certain length of byte sequence at the end of the malicious sample and gives an adversarial perturbation sequence that may reduce the confidence score of the detection model. Our model adopts a random sampling strategy according to the probability distribution when giving prediction results, so the model may give different results for the same input.

During the experiment, we found that the perturbation sequence that can successfully reduce the confidence score of the model usually needs to have a certain complexity, that is, a large entropy value. Due to our random sampling strategy, the model occasionally outputs sequences with low entropy, such as sequences with a large number of repetitions of the same pattern or sequences with a large proportion of zero bytes. In order to further improve the evasion rate, we will calculate the entropy value of the perturbed sequence generated by the model, and the sequence with an entropy value lower than a certain threshold will be discarded and regenerated.

3.4. Adversarial Example Generation Method

After the RNN generation model training is completed, the generation model can be used to make adversarial examples. We have two different strategies for generating adversarial examples, the one-time generation method and the iterative generation method.

3.4.1. One-Time Generation Method

One-time generation methods do not need to query the detection model for feedback at generation time. Our generative RNN model employs an encoder-decoder architecture with variable-length inputs and outputs. Therefore, this method directly takes the byte sequence of a certain length at the end of the original malicious sample to be generated as an adversarial sample as the input of the RNN generation model, and directly adds the generated perturbation sequence of a certain length to the end of the original malicious sample.

This method is a straightforward use of a trained RNN generative model. It does not need to query the detection model when generating it, nor does it have any other complicated operations, which is especially suitable for occasions where there are not many restrictions on the perturbation scale and a large number of adversarial examples need to be produced.

We test the method's performance under different perturbation scales, respectively, and the results are detailed in Section 4.

3.4.2. Iterative Generation Method

In more practical scenarios, the perturbation scale of adversarial examples is usually limited. To reduce the perturbation scale, we propose the iterative generation method. The iterative generation method adopts the strategy of generating small perturbations multiple times. When generating adversarial examples, instead of generating large-scale adversarial perturbations at one time, a small-scale (such as 1 KB) perturbation is generated each time, and the guidance of the confidence score of the current perturbed sample is introduced during the generation process. If a single perturbation makes the model's confidence score of the perturbed sample drop beyond a certain threshold, the perturbation is retained; otherwise, the perturbation is discarded and regenerated. At the same time, due to the small scale of a single perturbation, there may be several consecutive failed perturbations. Our approach to this is to define an upper limit for the number of consecutive failures. If the number of consecutive failures reaches the upper limit, the last failure will be retained, and the generation will continue on this basis. The pseudocode of the iterative generation method is shown in Algorithm 1.

Algorithm 1: Iterative Generation Method

x: original malicious sample
$\widetilde{x}$: adversarial example
s: confidence score of the detection model for current sample
Q: maximum number of queries
P: maximum perturbation size
S: confidence score difference threshold for a single perturbation
F: maximum number of consecutive failures
$count_{ptb}$: current perturbation count
$count_{qry}$: current query count
$count_{fail}$: current consecutive failure count
l_{input}: input length for RNN model
l_{output}: output length for RNN model

Input: x, P, Q, S, F
Output: $\widetilde{x}$
$s \leftarrow Model.predict(x)$
$count_{ptb} \leftarrow 0,\ count_{qry} \leftarrow 0,\ count_{fail} \leftarrow 0$
$\widetilde{x} \leftarrow x$
while $count_{ptb} * l_{output} < P$ **and** $count_{qry} < Q$ **do**
  if $s < 0$
    return $\widetilde{x}$
  end if
  $ptb \leftarrow RNN.generate\left(\widetilde{x}\left[-l_{input}:\right]\right)$
  if $(s - Model.predict(x.append(ptb))) > S$ **or** $count_{fail} \geq F$ **then**
    $\widetilde{x} \leftarrow \widetilde{x}.append(ptb)$
    $s \leftarrow Model.predict(\widetilde{x})$
    $count_{fail} \leftarrow 0$
    $count_{ptb} \leftarrow count_{ptb} + 1$
  else
    $count_{fail} \leftarrow count_{fail} + 1$
  end if
  $count_{qry} \leftarrow count_{qry} + 1$
end while
return *False*

Generally speaking, when generating adversarial examples, the number of queries and the perturbation scale are mutually restrictive. On the premise of ensuring the successful generation of adversarial examples, limiting the number of queries will increase the scale of the perturbation, and limiting the scale of the perturbation requires more queries. Our approach allows users to flexibly define upper bounds on the perturbation scale and the number of queries and generate adversarial examples that successfully evade the detection model as much as possible while meeting these upper bounds. We have evaluated the performance of our method under a variety of different constraints, and the experimental results are detailed in Section 4.

4. Experiments Evaluation

4.1. Dataset

Our dataset contains both malware samples and benign software samples. The malware samples are a total of 6171 malicious PE files collected from VirusShare [43] websites in recent years. Benign samples are about 6000 benign PE files extracted from Windows 10 system files and commercial software from dozens of different software companies. Considering that the maximum input length of the Malconv model is 2 MB, we eliminated all files whose size exceeds 1.95 MB to avoid perturbed adversarial examples exceeding the maximum input length of Malconv. These excluded files accounted for a very small percentage of all files.

4.2. Detection Model Evaluation

We choose the Malconv model [2] as the target detection model we want to attack. The Malconv model is currently one of the most successful end-to-end malware detection models based on deep learning. Many adversarial attack methods use this model as the target detection model to attack. We reproduced the model using the Pytorch [44] library with a maximum input sequence length of 2,000,000, a 1D convolution filter size of 500, and a stride of 500. The data set is divided into training set, validation set, and test set according to 6:1:1. We conducted four experiments under different dataset partitions, with an average accuracy of 93.1% and an average AUC of 97.7%, similar to the results described in the paper.

4.3. Benign Payload Extraction and RNN Generation Model Training

Extracting the benign payload requires the help of the trained Malconv model. Our Malconv model can directly output its raw confidence score for a sample (that is, the score before passing through the sigmoid layer). A score less than 0 indicates benign, and greater than 0 indicates malicious, and the greater the absolute value, the higher the probability. We extract benign payloads on all benign samples with confidence scores less than −8.0. The size of the benign payload is fixed at 1 KB, and the entropy value of the sequence is first calculated before being sent to the detection model query. A sequence with too small entropy value will be considered to carry too little information to affect the prediction of the Malconv model and the query will be abandoned. If a benign payload is successfully found, it and its previous 1 KB sequence will be saved as the training data for our RNN generation model. We successfully extracted 2000 such sequences from the validation and training sets of the Malconv model.

The RNN generation model is trained on these training data sets, and its input and output sizes are fixed at 1 KB. After training, the RNN generation model will be used to generate perturbation sequences.

4.4. Evasion Performance Evaluation

Similar to other adversarial attack methods, we also use the evasion rate as the main indicator to evaluate the effect of our method. The evasion rate is the percentage of adversarial examples that successfully evade the detection model for all adversarial examples.

In order to ensure the invariance of the function of the adversarial examples, we will put the original malicious samples and the generated adversarial examples in the sandbox for behavioral analysis and comparison, and the samples that cannot run or whose behavior changes will be marked as failed to generate.

We randomly selected 500 malicious samples from the malicious samples that did not participate in Malconv training and were correctly classified by the Malconv model as the original malicious samples to evaluate the performance of our method. The average size of these samples is 282.3 KB.

4.4.1. One-Time Generation Method

The one-time generation method can generate the adversarial perturbation to be appended at one time. This method only uses the RNN generation model trained by the benign payload before and does not need to obtain any confidence scores during the generation process. This method takes several bytes at the end of the malicious sample as the input of the RNN generation model and appends the generated fixed-size perturbation bytes to the end of the original malicious sample, in order to try to make an adversarial example that evades the Malconv detection model.

We conduct experiments with perturbation sizes of 0.5 KB, 1 KB, 2 KB, 5 KB, 10 KB, and 20 KB, and record the evasion rate as well as the average confidence score of the generated adversarial examples on the detection model (these confidence scores are not disclosed to the generative model, they are only used for result analysis). The experimental results are shown in Table 1 and Figure 4.

Table 1. Results of the one-time generation method at different perturbation sizes.

Perturbation Size/KB	0	0.5	1	2	5	10	20
Evasion Rate	/	1.0%	3.8%	13.8%	35.4%	54.2%	66.8%
Mean Confidence Score	7.09	6.87	6.17	4.81	2.00	−0.29	−1.99

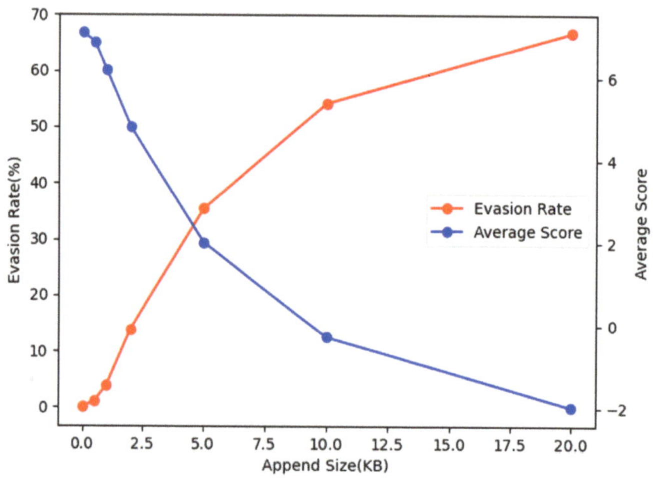

Figure 4. Evasion rate and average confidence score as a function of append size (KB) using the one-time generation method.

It can be seen from the figure that the evasion rate increases with the increase of the appended size, and the average confidence score decreases accordingly. The rising or falling trends of the two are basically the same, and they are gradually slowing down. This shows that as the appended size grows, the perturbation per KB is less effective. When the appended size reaches the maximum value of 20 KB set in our experiment, 66.8% of the adversarial examples successfully evade the target detection model, which can pose a certain threat to the target detection model as a black-box method.

4.4.2. Iterative Generation Method

The iterative generation method adopts the strategy of generating small perturbations multiple times. In our experiments, we use the RNN generative model to generate an adversarial perturbation with a fixed size of 1 KB each time and attach this perturbation to malicious samples. Then, we query the confidence score of the Malconv model for the current malicious sample and decide whether to keep this adversarial perturbation according to the difference between the confidence scores before and after adding this perturbation. Here, we set the threshold of the confidence score difference as 0.2, i.e., only adversarial perturbations that successfully reduce the confidence score by more than 0.2 will be retained. In addition, we made some restrictions in the experiment. The upper limit of the number of times to query the confidence score of the Malconv model is set to 50, and the upper limit of the total size of the adversarial perturbation is set to 20 KB. Our iterative generation method consumes the number of queries to optimize each adversarial perturbation until an adversarial example that can evade the detection model is successfully generated. If the number of queries or the size of the perturbation reaches the upper limit before then, the generation fails.

Under these conditions, 454 adversarial examples were successfully generated, and the evasion rate reached 90.8%. We counted the distribution of the number of queries and perturbation sizes required to successfully generate adversarial examples, as shown in Figure 5.

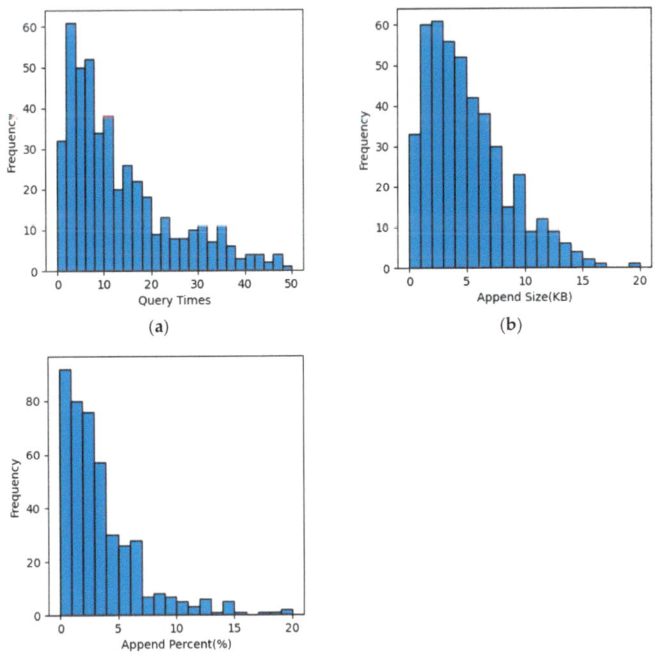

Figure 5. The distribution of conditions required to successfully generate adversarial examples. (**a**) The distribution of query times; (**b**) The distribution of perturbation sizes (KB); (**c**) The distribution of perturbation sizes (relative ratio).

It can be seen that the number of queries is mostly distributed within 1–20 times. The append size is mostly concentrated in 1–10 KB, and the peak value is around 3 KB. To reduce the influence of the size of the malicious sample itself on the perturbation scale, we also counted the relative ratio (%) of the perturbation scale and the malicious sample itself. It can be seen that the vast majority of perturbations only account for less than 10% of the original malicious samples, and those with an append size percentage of less than 5% account for more than 60% of all samples.

According to our statistics, among all the samples that successfully generate adversarial examples, the average number of queries is 13.87, the average size of the perturbation is 5541 bytes, and the average ratio of the perturbation size to the original sample size is 6.16%.

Since the evasion rate is affected by two factors, the number of queries and the appended size, we also counted and studied how the evasion rate is affected by these two factors, as shown in Figures 6 and 7.

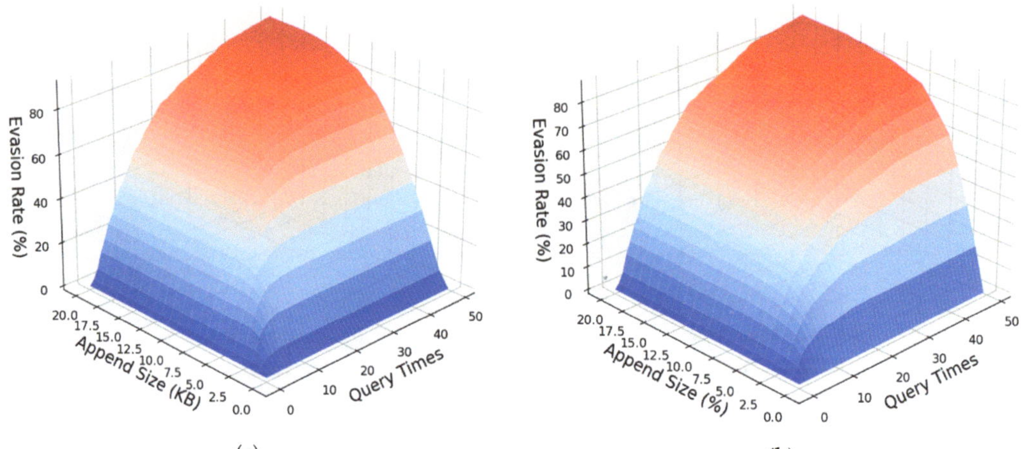

Figure 6. (**a**) Evasion rates under different append sizes (KB) and query times; (**b**) Evasion rates under different append percent (%) and query times.

From the comprehensive analysis and comparison of Figures 6 and 7, it can be seen that both the number of queries and the appended size have a significant marginal effect on the evasion rate. That is to say, with the improvement of these two abilities, the effect on the increase of evasion rate is getting weaker and weaker. Roughly speaking, when the number of queries reaches 30, increasing the number of queries has little effect on improving the evasion rate. Similarly, for the appended size, the improvement of the evasion rate is significantly weakened by adding the appended size after reaching 10 KB or 10% of the original sample size. In addition, the number of queries and the appended size will also interact with each other on the evasion rate results. Due to the settings of our method, each iteration of the query will generate at most 1 KB of adversarial perturbation. When the upper limit of the number of queries is much smaller than the upper limit of the perturbation size (KB), the generated adversarial perturbation will not reach the upper limit of the perturbation size, that is, the full ability of appending perturbation will not be exerted, and vice versa. Therefore, according to the experimental data and our experience, when the number of queries is about 3–4 times of the appended size (KB), better results can be obtained under the current conditions. Moreover, when the two increase simultaneously, the effect of increasing the evasion rate is more obvious, and the effect of improving a certain ability alone is limited.

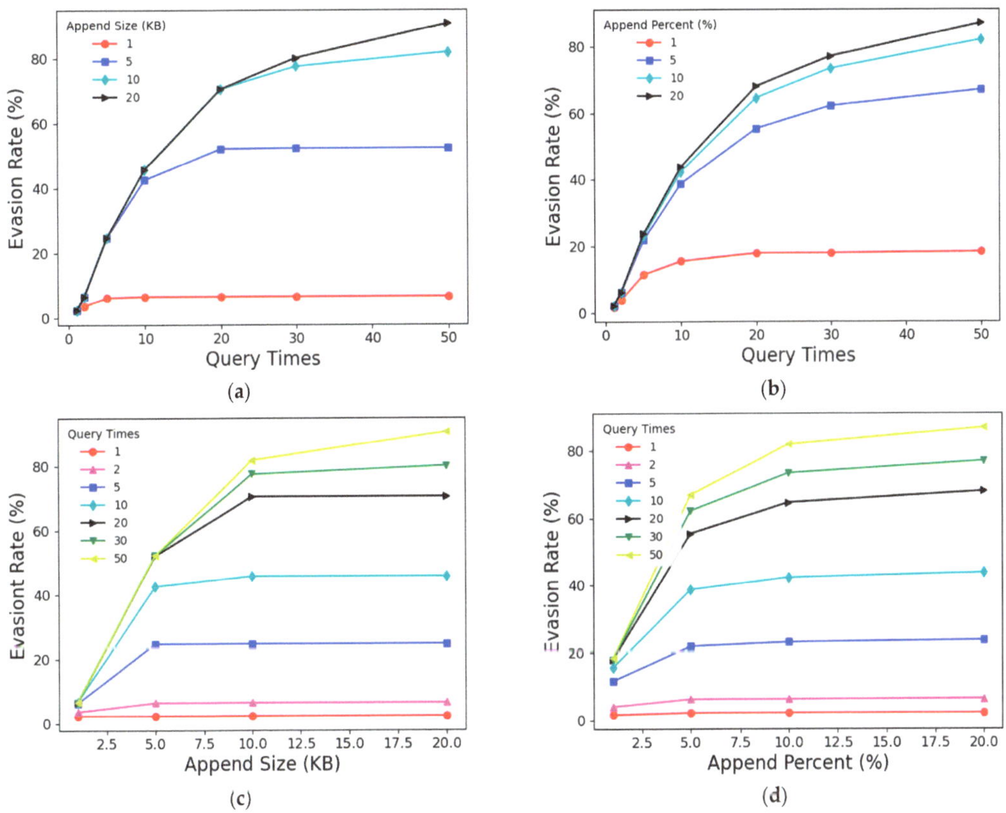

Figure 7. (**a**) Changes of evasion rate with query times under different append sizes (KB); (**b**) Changes of evasion rate with query times under different append percent (%); (**c**) Changes of evasion rate with append size (KB) under different query times; (**d**) Changes of evasion rate with append percent (%) under different query times.

In conclusion, our iterative generation method can achieve a 90.8% evasion rate under the maximum capacity condition we set (20 KB perturbation, 50 queries). Even if the ability is reduced by about half (10 KB perturbation, 20 queries), the evasion rate of 70.6% can still be achieved. Although each query needs to obtain the confidence score result given by the detection model, compared with the one-time generation method, the iterative method can more accurately find out the adversarial perturbation and can obtain a better evasion rate result at the lowest possible cost.

4.4.3. Comparison with Other Methods

We also compared it with other attack methods that employ the append strategies. We choose two white-box methods and two black-box methods to compare with our method.

- **Benign Features Append (BFA)**: It is a white box method proposed by Chen et al. [35], which introduces the Grad-CAM method proposed by Selvaraju et al. [45] to generate a saliency vector for the sample. A saliency vector, which contains features of a series of data blocks in an input binary file, can roughly show the benign and malicious regions of the file. Based on the saliency vector, they continuously select data blocks with benign features as perturbations to append to the end of the sample until the detection model is successfully evaded.

- **Enhanced BFA**: It is an improved version of the BFA method. This method [35] uses the important benign feature data blocks obtained from the BFA method as the initial perturbation of the FGSM method, which can more efficiently and quickly attract the attention of the model to obtain the backpropagation gradient. Compared with BFA method, it can significantly improve the success rate of evasion.
- **Random Append**: It is a relatively simple black-box adversarial method, which appends randomly generated perturbation bytes at the end of the sample to try to evade the detection model.
- **Experience Based Method**: It is a black box method proposed by Chen et al. [35]. This method first divides the benign sample into several data blocks and randomly appends the data blocks to the end of the malicious sample until the detection model is successfully evaded. Then, these attacks are repeated, and the contribution of each data block is calculated based on the trajectory of the successful attack. This contribution information replaces the saliency vector in the BFA method, and the subsequent attack process is the same as the BFA method.

Figure 8 shows the comparison results of evasion rates of several methods under different perturbation scales. First, our method achieves an evasion rate much higher than that of the random append method at any append size, indicating that the adversarial perturbation bytes generated by our method are targeted and the effect is relatively ideal. Furthermore, for the one-time generation method, it tends to vary with the perturbation size roughly the same as the experience-based method, but the evasion rate is slightly lower than that of the experience-based method. For the iterative generation method, when the perturbation size is less than 5 KB, its evasion rate is not as good as that of the experience-based method, but its evasion rate increases rapidly with the increase of the perturbation size. After it is greater than 5 KB, it has surpassed all other black-box methods, and gradually approaches the best white-box method in the figure, the enhanced BFA.

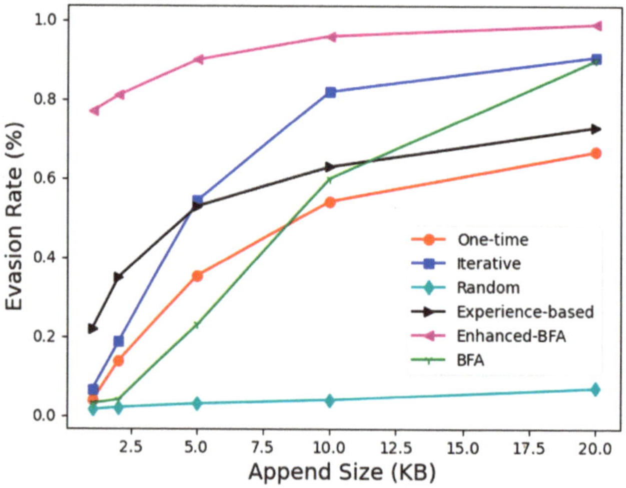

Figure 8. The evasion rate of each method under different append sizes.

In short, the one-time generation method is a basic method to directly use the RNN generation model to generate adversarial perturbation. The method is relatively simple and direct, and the information required is relatively small. Its evasion rate increases relatively steadily with the change in the perturbation scale. For the iterative generation method, since the perturbation size of our iteration is set to 1 KB, it is difficult to take advantage of iteration when the perturbation size is small (less than 5 KB), and the evasion rate at this time is not high. However, as the perturbation size grows, the evasion rate increases rapidly, surpassing the experience-based black-box method and gradually approaching the enhanced BFA white-box method.

5. Conclusions and Future Work

In this paper, we investigate the problem of insufficient robustness of current end-to-end malware detection models based on deep learning, especially the Malconv model. In recent years, these models, which do not require feature engineering and expert knowledge, are increasingly being used in automated anti-malware systems. Our research shows that under the condition of only obtaining the scores of some benign sample from the detection model, adversaries can train RNN generation models based on this information to generate adversarial perturbations, thereby making adversarial examples on a large scale. This is our one-time generation method, which achieves the highest evasion rate of 66.8%. If the score of the model on the intermediate samples can be obtained during the generation, the scale of additional perturbations can be further reduced and the success rate of evasion can be improved, that is, the iterative generation method, which achieves a maximum evasion rate of 90.8%. These results prove the vulnerability of the current deep learning-based malware detection model. Anti-malware systems usually do not pay enough attention to the detection and scoring information of benign samples, which may give adversaries an opportunity.

In the future, in terms of attack direction, due to the generality of our method, we will consider extending it to other models of the same type. While for other types of models, such as non-end-to-end, based on opcodes or other features, we still consider treating them as sequences and further transfer our method. In the direction of defense, we will consider the most basic adversarial training to improve the robustness of the model. Furthermore, in the introduction to the benign payload, we plot the model confidence score versus the first n bytes of the sample (Figure 2). Our research may imply that models with a smoother and less abrupt curve are more robust and harder to attack. In the future, we may start from this point to study how to improve the defense ability of detection models against adversarial attacks.

Author Contributions: Conceptualization, S.W.; Methodology, S.W.; Software, S.W.; Formal analysis, S.W.; Data curation, S.W. and Z.K.; Writing—original draft, S.W.; Writing—review & editing, S.W., Y.W. and Z.K.; Supervision, J.X. and Y.W.; Project administration, J.X. and Y.W.; Funding acquisition, J.X. All authors have read and agreed to the published version of the manuscript.

Funding: This research and the APC was funded by Major Scientific and Technological Innovation Projects of Shandong Province (2020CXGC010116), the National Natural Science Foundation of China (No. 62172042), and the National Key Research & Development Program of China (2020YFB1712104).

Data Availability Statement: Previously published articles were used to support this study and these prior studies and datasets are cited at relevant places within this article. The link to the datasets is https://virusshare.com/ (accessed on 26 March 2022).

Conflicts of Interest: The authors declare that there is no conflict of interest regarding the publication of this paper.

References

1. Szegedy, C.; Zaremba, W.; Sutskever, I.; Bruna, J.; Erhan, D.; Goodfellow, I.; Fergus, R. Intriguing properties of neural networks. In Proceedings of the International Conference on Learning Representations (ICLR), Banff, AB, Canada, 14–16 April 2014.
2. Raff, E.; Barker, J.; Sylvester, J.; Brandon, R.; Catanzaro, B.; Nicholas, C. Malware detection by eating a whole EXE. In Proceedings of the 32nd AAAI Workshops, New Orleans, LA, USA, 2–3 February 2018; pp. 268–276.
3. Pietrek, M. Peering Inside the PE: A Tour of the win32 (R) Portable Executable File Format. *Microsoft Syst. J.* **1994**, *9*, 15–38.
4. Nataraj, L.; Karthikeyan, S.; Jacob, G.; Manjunath, B. Malware images: Visualization and automatic classification. In Proceedings of the 8th International Symposium on Visualization for Cyber Security, Pittsburgh, PA, USA, 20 July 2011; pp. 1–7. [CrossRef]
5. Simonyan, K.; Zisserman, A. Very deep convolutional networks for large-scale image recognition. *arXiv* **2014**, arXiv:1409.1556.
6. Kaiming, H.; Xiangyu, Z.; Shaoqing, R.; Jian, S. Deep Residual Learning for Image Recognition. In Proceedings of the 2016 IEEE Conference on Computer Vision and Pattern Recognition (CVPR), Las Vegas, NV, USA, 27–30 June 2016; pp. 770–778. [CrossRef]

7. Szegedy, C.; Vanhoucke, V.; Ioffe, S.; Shlens, J.; Wojna, Z. Rethinking the inception architecture for computer vision. In Proceedings of the IEEE Conference on Computer Vision and Pattern Recognition, Las Vegas, NV, USA, 27–30 June 2016; pp. 2818–2826.
8. Hassen, M.; Chan, P. Scalable Function Call Graph-based Malware Classification. In Proceedings of the Seventh ACM Conference on Data and Application Security and Privacy(CODASPY), Scottsdale, AZ, USA, 22–24 March 2017; ACM: New York, NY, USA, 2017; pp. 239–248. [CrossRef]
9. Kinable, J.; Kostakis, O. Malware classification based on call graph clustering. *J. Comput. Virol.* **2011**, *7*, 233–245. [CrossRef]
10. Kong, D.; Yan, G. Discriminant malware distance learning on structural information for automated malware classification. In Proceedings of the 19th ACM SIGKDD International Conference on Knowledge Discovery and Data Mining, Chicago, IL, USA, 11–14 August 2013; pp. 1357–1365. [CrossRef]
11. Yan, J.; Yan, G.; Jin, D. Classifying malware represented as control flow graphs using deep graph convolutional neural network. In Proceedings of the 2019 49th Annual IEEE/IFIP International Conference on Dependable Systems and Networks (DSN), Portland, OR, USA, 24–27 June 2019; pp. 52–63. [CrossRef]
12. Santos, I.; Brezo, F.; Ugarte-Pedrero, X.; Bringas, P.G. Opcode sequences as representation of executables for data-mining-based unknown malware detection. *Inf. Sci.* **2013**, *231*, 64–82. [CrossRef]
13. Awad, Y.; Nassar, M.; Safa, H. Modeling malware as a language. In Proceedings of the 2018 IEEE International Conference on Communications (ICC), Kansas City, MO, USA, 20–24 May 2018; pp. 1–6. [CrossRef]
14. Jain, S.; Meena, Y.K. Byte level n–gram analysis for malware detection. In Proceedings of the International Conference on Information Processing, Shanghai, China, 13–17 November 2011; Springer: Berlin/Heidelberg, Germany, 2011; pp. 51–59. [CrossRef]
15. Raff, E.; Sylvester, J.; Nicholas, C. Learning the pe header, malware detection with minimal domain knowledge. In Proceedings of the 10th ACM Workshop on Artificial Intelligence and Security, Dallas, TX, USA, 3 November 2017; pp. 121–132. [CrossRef]
16. Goodfellow, I.; Shlens, J.; Szegedy, C. Explaining and harnessing adversarial examples. *arXiv* **2014**, arXiv:1412.6572.
17. Papernot, N.; McDaniel, P.; Goodfellow, I.; Jha, S.; Celik, Z.; Swami, A. Practical Black-Box Attacks against Machine Learning. In Proceedings of the 2017 ACM on Asia Conference on Computer and Communications Security (ASIACCS '17), Abu Dhabi, United Arab Emirates, 2–6 April 2017; Association for Computing Machinery: New York, NY, USA, 2017; pp. 506–519. [CrossRef]
18. Xu, W.; Qi, Y.; Evans, D. Automatically evading classifiers. In Proceedings of the 2016 Network and Distributed Systems Security Symposium, San Diego, CA, USA, 21–24 February 2016; p. 10.
19. Su, J.; Vargas, D.V.; Sakurai, K. One Pixel Attack for Fooling Deep Neural Networks. *IEEE Trans. Evol. Comput.* **2019**, *23*, 828–841. [CrossRef]
20. Kreuk, F.; Barak, A.; Aviv-Reuven, S.; Baruch, M.; Pinkas, B.; Keshet, J. Deceiving end-to-end deep learning malware detectors using adversarial examples. *arXiv* **2018**, arXiv:1802.04528.
21. Kolosnjaji, B.; Demontis, A.; Biggio, B.; Maiorca, D.; Giacinto, G.; Eckert, C.; Roli, F. Adversarial malware binaries: Evading deep learning for malware detection in executables. In Proceedings of the 26th European Signal Processing Conference (EUSIPCO), Rome, Italy, 3–7 September 2018; pp. 533–537. [CrossRef]
22. Demetrio, L.; Biggio, B.; Lagorio, G.; Roli, F.; Armando, A. Explaining vulnerabilities of deep learning to adversarial malware binaries. *arXiv* **2019**, arXiv:1901.03583.
23. Hu, W.; Tan, Y. Generating Adversarial Malware Examples for Black-Box Attacks Based on GAN. In *DMBD 2022: Data Mining and Big Data*; Communications in Computer and Information Science; Springer: Singapore, 2023; Volume 1745. [CrossRef]
24. Rosenberg, I.; Shabtai, A.; Rokach, L.; Elovici, Y. Generic black-box end-to-end attack against state of the art API call based malware classifiers. In *Research in Attacks, Intrusions, and Defenses, Proceedings of the 21st International Symposium, RAID 2018, Heraklion, Crete, Greece, 10–12 September 2018*; Proceedings 21; Springer International Publishing: Berlin/Heidelberg, Germany, 2018; pp. 490–510. [CrossRef]
25. Castro, R.L.; Schmitt, C.; Dreo, G. AIMED: Evolving Malware with Genetic Programming to Evade Detection. In Proceedings of the 18th IEEE International Conference on Trust, Security and Privacy in Computing and Communications/13th IEEE International Conference on Big Data Science and Engineering (TrustCom/BigDataSE), Rotorua, New Zealand, 5–8 August 2019; pp. 240–247. [CrossRef]
26. Castro, R.L.; Schmitt, C.; Rodosek, G.D. ARMED: How Automatic Malware Modifications Can Evade Static Detection. In Proceedings of the 5th International Conference on Information Management (ICIM), Cambridge, UK, 24–27 March 2019; pp. 20–27. [CrossRef]
27. Demetrio, L.; Biggio, B.; Lagorio, G.; Roli, F.; Armando, A. Functionality-Preserving Black-Box Optimization of Adversarial Windows Malware. *IEEE Trans. Inf. Forensics Secur.* **2021**, *16*, 3469–3478. [CrossRef]
28. Anderson, H.S.; Kharkar, A.; Filar, B.; Evans, D.; Roth, P. Learning to evade static PE machine learning malware models via reinforcement learning. *arXiv* **2018**, arXiv:1801.08917.
29. Chen, J.; Jiang, J.; Li, R.; Dou, Y. Generating Adversarial Examples for Static PE Malware Detector Based on Deep Reinforcement Learning. *J. Phys. Conf. Ser.* **2020**, *1575*, 012011. [CrossRef]
30. Song, W.; Li, X.; Afroz, S.; Garg, D.; Kuznetsov, D.; Yin, H. Mab-malware: A reinforcement learning framework for attacking static malware classifiers. *arXiv* **2020**, arXiv:2003.03100.
31. Li, X.; Li, Q. An IRL-based malware adversarial generation method to evade anti-malware engines. *Comput. Secur.* **2020**, *104*, 102118. [CrossRef]

32. Anderson, H.S.; Kharkar, A.; Filar, B.; Roth, P. Evading machine learning malware detection. In Proceedings of the Black Hat, Las Vegas, NV, USA, 22–27 July 2017.
33. Park, D.; Khan, H.; Yener, B. Generation and Evaluation of Adversarial Examples for Malware Obfuscation. In Proceedings of the 18th IEEE International Conference on Machine Learning and Applications (ICMLA), Boca Raton, FL, USA, 16–19 December 2019; pp. 1283–1290. [CrossRef]
34. Ebrahimi, M.; Zhang, N.; Hu, J.; Raza, M.T.; Chen, H. Binary black-box evasion attacks against deep learning-based static malware detectors with adversarial byte-level language model. *arXiv* **2020**, arXiv:2012.07994.
35. Chen, B.-C.; Ren, Z.-R.; Yu, C.; Hussain, I.; Liu, J.-T. Adversarial Examples for CNN-Based Malware Detectors. *IEEE Access* **2019**, *7*, 54360–54371. [CrossRef]
36. Takase, S.; Suzuki, J.; Nagata, M. Character n-Gram Embeddings to Improve RNN Language Models. *Proc. Conf. AAAI Artif. Intell.* **2019**, *33*, 5074–5082. [CrossRef]
37. Kolosnjaji, B.; Zarras, A.; Webster, G.; Eckert, C. Deep Learning for Classification of Malware System Call Sequences. In *AI 2016: Advances in Artificial Intelligence*; Kang, B., Bai, Q., Eds.; AI 2016. Lecture Notes in Computer Science; Springer: Cham, Switzerland, 2016; Volume 9992. [CrossRef]
38. Rosenberg, I.; Shabtai, A.; Elovici, Y.; Rokach, L. Defense methods against adversarial examples for recurrent neural networks. *arXiv* **2019**, arXiv:1901.09963.
39. Harun Babu, R.; Vinayakumar, R.; Soman, K.P. RNNSecureNet: Recurrent neural networks for Cyber security use-cases. *arXiv* **2019**, arXiv:1901.04281.
40. Zuo, F.; Li, X.; Young, P.; Luo, L. Neural machine translation inspired binary code similarity comparison beyond function pairs. *arXiv* **2018**, arXiv:1808.04706.
41. Cho, K.; Van Merriënboer, B.; Gulcehre, C.; Bahdanau, D.; Bougares, F.; Schwenk, H.; Bengio, Y. Learning phrase representations using RNN encoder-decoder for statistical machine translation. *arXiv* **2014**, arXiv:1406.1078.
42. Chung, J.; Gulcehre, C.; Cho, K.H.; Bengio, Y. Empirical evaluation of gated recurrent neural networks on sequence modeling. *arXiv* **2014**, arXiv:1412.3555.
43. Available online: https://virusshare.com/ (accessed on 26 March 2022).
44. Available online: https://pytorch.org/ (accessed on 20 March 2022).
45. Selvaraju, R.R.; Cogswell, M.; Das, A.; Vedantam, R.; Parikh, D.; Batra, D. Grad-cam: Visual explanations from deep networks via gradient-based localization. In Proceedings of the IEEE International Conference on Computer Vision (ICCV), Venice, Italy, 22–29 October 2017; pp. 618–626.

electronics

Article

The Same Name Is Not Always the Same: Correlating and Tracing Forgery Methods across Various Deepfake Datasets

Yi Sun [1,2], Jun Zheng [1], Lingjuan Lyn [3], Hanyu Zhao [1], Jiaxing Li [1], Yunteng Tan [1], Xinyu Liu [1] and Yuanzhang Li [1,*]

1 Beijing Institute of Technology, No. 5, South Street, Zhongguancun, Haidian District, Beijing 100811, China; 3120195532@bit.edu.cn (Y.S.); zhengjun@bit.edu.cn (J.Z.); 3220221483@bit.edu.cn (H.Z.); jiaxingxx@outlook.com (J.L.); 1120203017@bit.edu.cn (Y.T.); lxy1653300572@163.com (X.L.)
2 Department of Information Systems Technology and Design, Singapore University of Technology and Design, 8 Somapah Road, Singapore 487372, Singapore
3 Sony AI Inc., 1-7-1 Konan Minato-ku, Tokyo 108-0075, Japan; lingjuanlvsmile@gmail.com
* Correspondence: popular@bit.edu.cn

Abstract: Deepfakes are becoming increasingly ubiquitous, particularly in facial manipulation. Numerous researchers and companies have released multiple datasets of face deepfakes labeled to indicate different methods of forgery. However, naming these labels is often arbitrary and inconsistent, leading to the fact that most researchers now choose to use only one of the datasets for research work. However, researchers must use these datasets in practical applications and conduct traceability research. In this study, we employ some models to extract forgery features from various deepfake datasets and utilize the K-means clustering method to identify datasets with similar feature values. We analyze the feature values using the Calinski Harabasz Index method. Our findings reveal that datasets with the same or similar labels in different deepfake datasets exhibit different forgery features. We proposed the KCE system to solve this problem, which combines multiple deepfake datasets according to feature similarity. We analyzed four groups of test datasets and found that the model trained based on KCE combined data faced unknown data types, and Calinski Harabasz scored 42.3% higher than combined by forged names. Furthermore, it is 2.5% higher than the model using all data, although the latter has more training data. It shows that this method improves the generalization ability of the model. This paper introduces a fresh perspective for effectively evaluating and utilizing diverse deepfake datasets and conducting deepfake traceability research.

Keywords: deepfake; datasets; correlation; traceability; clustering; Calinski Harabasz

Citation: Sun, Y.; Zheng, J.; Lyn, L.; Zhao, H.; Li, J.; Tan, Y.; Liu, X.; Li, Y. The Same Name Is Not Always the Same: Correlating and Tracing Forgery Methods across Various Deepfake Datasets. *Electronics* **2023**, *12*, 2353. https://doi.org/10.3390/electronics12112353

Academic Editor: Miin-shen Yang

Received: 17 April 2023
Revised: 13 May 2023
Accepted: 17 May 2023
Published: 23 May 2023

1. Introduction

Facial recognition has become increasingly prevalent in recent years, with many applications utilizing it as the primary method for identity recognition. However, with the rapid development of deep learning-driven facial forgery technologies in recent years, such as deepfakes [1], there has been a rise in fraudulent practices within media and financial fields, which has sparked widespread social concern [2–4]. Consequently, there is a crucial need for the traceability of forged data.

Deepfake tracking methods can be broadly classified into traditional [5–7] and deep learning-based methods [8,9]. Traditional methods rely on techniques, such as image forensics and metadata analysis to detect signs of manipulation in a deepfake. These methods are based on analyzing the visual properties of an image or video, and they can include analyzing the distribution of colors, identifying inconsistencies in lighting and shadows, or detecting distortions in the image caused by manipulation. These traditional methods require extensive domain knowledge and specialized software to execute. On the other hand, deep learning-based methods rely on machine learning algorithms' power to detect deepfakes. These methods train deep neural networks on large datasets of real and fake images or videos, and they can detect deepfakes by analyzing the patterns in the data. Deep learning-based methods are highly effective at detecting deepfakes, but they require large amounts of training data and computing resources to execute. This paper mainly conducts related research based on the latter method.

Tracing the source of deep forgery relies on identifying the forgery algorithms used. However, the category labels in deepfake datasets fundamentally differ from those in the general computer vision field. In typical computer vision datasets, such as the CIFAR [10], ImageNet [11], and MNIST [12], the category labels are objective and have real-world meaning. For instance, the labels for salamander and setosa are assigned by biologists based on the biological characteristics of these species, or humans can accurately recognize facial expressions such as anger or happiness, as shown in Figure 1. These labels remain unchanged despite variations in camera equipment, lighting conditions, and post-processing of images. However, humans cannot classify deepfake pictures visually, and the images can only be named based on their forgery method. The names given to the forgery methods by different producers are highly subjective and arbitrary, as shown in Table 1. Many "wild datasets" do not provide forgery method labels. Furthermore, subsequent operations such as image compression and format conversion [13] may significantly alter the forgery characteristics of the images.

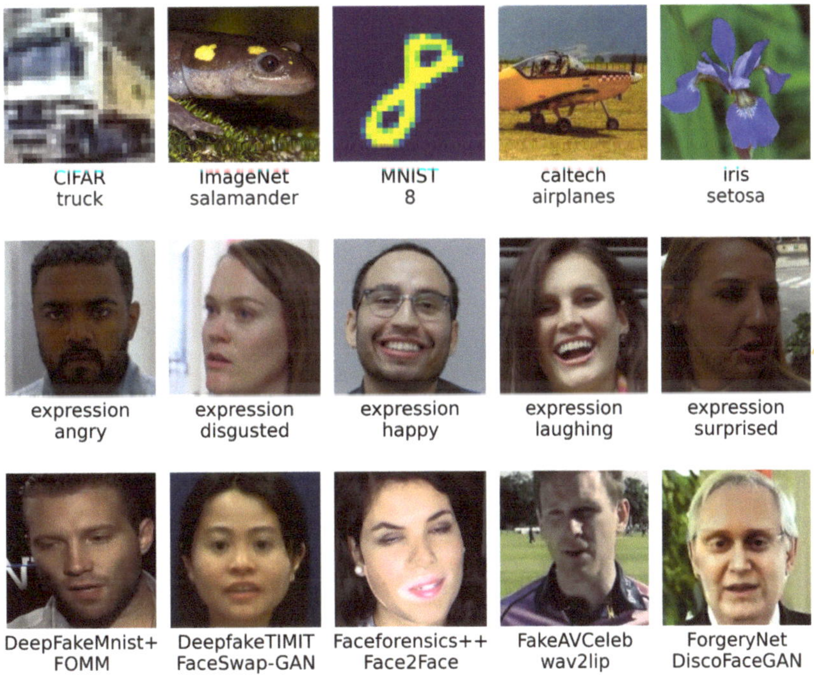

Figure 1. The first row shows the common CV dataset, the second row shows the human facial expression dataset, and the third row shows the deepfake dataset.

Improving facial forgery recognition and tracking technology relies on collecting and utilizing as many facial forgery datasets as possible. These datasets include ForgeryNet [14], DeepfakeTIMIT [15], FakeAVCeleb [16], DeeperForensics-1.0 [17], and others. Additionally, numerous "wild datasets" are gathered from the Internet. However, these datasets are published by different institutions, use varying forgery methods, and have different naming conventions. In some cases, the exact generation algorithm is not provided. This situation leads some researchers to use only one dataset in their experiments. Dealing with those with similar or identical names can create challenges for users when multiple datasets are employed.

Measuring the relevance of each deepfake dataset is crucial. To address this problem, we use the Xception model [18] as a forgery feature extractor, which is commonly used in the deepfake recognition field. We train both multi-classification and binary classification models that map various deepfake images into the feature space illustrated in Figure 2.

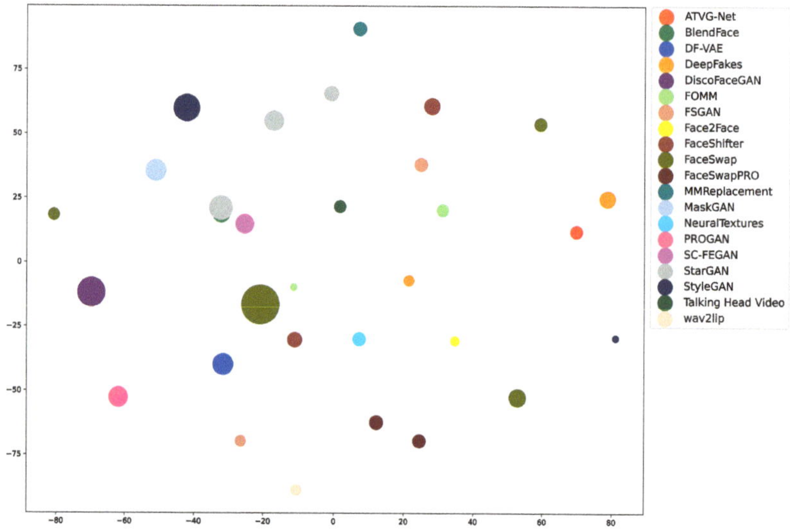

Figure 2. The circle's center represents the center position of this category of the dataset, and the area of the circle represents the rank of the Covariance Matrix of these datasets. Distances between the fake datasets represent the similarity of these fake features.

After mapping the deepfake datasets to feature space, we use PCA for dimensionality reduction and the K-means method for clustering. We use these cluster datasets to retrain the Xception model. We also combine these deepfake datasets based on forgery method labels and use them to train another Xception model as a control group. We perform a series of experiments on the test data using these models and use the Calinski Harabasz Index [19] as a measure to judge the performance of the models. To improve the credibility of the experimental results, we also repeat some experiments on The Frequency in Face Forgery Network (F3-Net) [9] and Residual Neural network (ResNet) [20].

Our main contributions are summarized as follows:

- We point out that the forgery category labels in the deepfake dataset lack objectivity. Our experiments prove that some forgery category labels of the same name differ significantly across different datasets.
- We establish the KCE-System. It is a deepfake dataset similarity evaluation index system that provides a measure of the similarity between different datasets and lays the foundation for subsequent researchers to use these datasets comprehensively.
- Our experiments confirm that when the forgery method of the deepfake dataset is unknown, the model can achieve better generalization performance by training on datasets that are merged based on closer feature distances.

2. Related Works

2.1. Deepfake Datasets

Numerous deepfake datasets have been created by researchers and institutions, including FaceForensics++ [21], Celeb-DF [22], DeepFakeMnist+ [15], DeepfakeTIMIT [1], FakeAVCeleb [16], DeeperForensics-1.0 [17], ForgeryNet [14], and Patch-wise Face Image

Forensics [23]. These datasets cover various forgery methods, have significant data scales, and are widely used. Please refer to Table 1 for more details.

Table 1. Common deepfake datasets, the symbol * represents the number of pictures.

Dataset	Real	Fake	Forgery Method
CelebDFv1 [22]	409	795	FaceswapPro
CelebDFv2 [22]	590	5639	FaceswapPro
DeeperForensics1.0 [17]	50,000	10,000	DeepFake Variational Auto-Encoder (DF-VAE) [24]
FakeAVCeleb [16]	178	11,833	Faceswap [25], Faceswap GAN (FSGAN) [26], Wav2Lip [27]
DeepFakeMnist+ [15]	10,000	10,000	First Order Motion Model for Image Animation (FOMM) [28]
DeepfakeTIMIT [1]	320	640	faceswap-GAN [29]
FaceForensics++ [21]	1000	5000	Faceswap [30], Deepfakes [31], Face2Face [32], FaceShifter [33], NeuralTextures [34]
DeepFakeDetection [35]	363	3068	Faceswap
ForgeryNet [14]	99,630	121,617	ATVG-Net [36], BlendFace, DeepFakes, DeepFakes-StarGAN-Stack, DiscoFaceGAN [37], FaceShifter [33], FOMM [28], FS-GAN [26], MaskGAN [38], MMReplacement, SC-FEGAN [39], StarGAN-BlendFace-Stack, StarGAN2 [40], StyleGAN2 [41], Talking Head Video [42]
Patch-wise Face Image Forensics [23]	* 25,000	* 25,000	PROGAN [43], StyleGAN2 [41]

2.2. *Deepfake Identification and Traceability*

2.2.1. Methods Based on Spectral Features

Many scholars consider upsampling to be a necessary step in generating most face forgeries. Cumulative upsampling can cause apparent changes in the frequency domain, and minor forgery defects and compression errors can be well described in this domain. Using this information can identify fake videos. Spectrum-based methods have certain advantages in generalization because they provide another perspective. Most existing image and video compression methods are also related to the frequency domain, making the method based on this domain particularly robust.

Chen et al. [44] proposed a forgery detection algorithm that combines spatial and frequency domain features using an attention mechanism. The method uses a convolutional neural network and an attention mechanism to extract spatial domain features. After the Fourier transform, the frequency domain features are extracted, and, finally, these features are fused for classification. Qian et al. [9] proposed a network structure called F3-Net (Frequency in Face Forgery Network) and designed a two-stream collaborative learning framework to learn the frequency domain adaptive image decomposition branch and image detail frequency statistics branch. The method has a significant lead over other methods on low-quality video. Liu et al. [45] proposed a method based on Spatial Phase Shallow Learning (SPSL). The method combines spatial images and phase spectra to capture upsampled features of facial forgery. For forgery detection tasks, local texture information is more critical than high-level semantic information. By making the network shallower, the network is more focused on local regions. Li et al. [46] proposed a learning framework based on frequency-aware discriminative features and designed a single-center loss function (SCL), which only compresses the intra-class variation of real faces while enhancing the inter-class variation in the embedding space. In this way, the network can learn more discriminative features with less optimization difficulty.

2.2.2. Methods Based on Generative Adversarial Network Inherent Traces

Scholars suggest that fake faces generated by generative adversarial networks have distinct traces and texture information compared to real-world photographs.

Guarnera et al. [47] proposed a detection method based on forgery traces, which uses an Expectation Maximization algorithm to extract local features that model the convolutional generation process. Liu et al. [48] developed GramNet, an architecture that uses global image texture representation for robust forgery detection, particularly against image disturbances such as downsampling, JPEG compression, blur, and noise. Yang et al. [49] argue that existing GAN-based forgery detection methods are limited in their ability to generalize to new training models with different random seeds, datasets, and loss functions. They propose DNA-Det, which observes that GAN architecture leaves globally consistent fingerprints, and model weights leave varying traces in different regions.

2.3. Troubles with Current Deepfake Traceability

Methods based on frequency domain and model fingerprints provide traceability for different forgery methods. Although researchers claim high accuracy rates in identifying and tracing related forgery methods, they typically only use a specific dataset for research. This approach reduces the comprehensiveness of traceability and the model's generalization ability. Therefore, researchers need to consider the similarity and correlation between samples in each dataset to make full use of these datasets.

However, this presents a significant challenge. Unlike typical computer vision datasets, deepfake datasets' labels are based on technical methods and forgery patterns rather than human concepts, making it impossible for humans to identify and evaluate them. The more severe problem is that the labels of forgery methods used in various deepfake datasets are entirely arbitrary. Some labels are based on implementation technology, while others are based on forgery modes. For example, many datasets have the label "DeepFakes". The irregularity and ambiguity of these labeling methods make it difficult to utilize the forged data of various deepfake datasets fully. Additionally, some deepfake datasets do not indicate specific forgery methods, such as "wild datasets".

3. Research Methods

3.1. K-Means and Calinski Harabasz Evaluation System

We trained an Xception model as a feature extractor using various deepfake datasets and real datasets as training sets. When examining different deepfake datasets in feature space, we observe that specific forgery methods are clustered together. In contrast, some forgery methods with similar names are separated, as shown in Figure 2. For example, one of the FOMM forgery methods is very close to the FaceSwap method but far from the other FOMM forgery methods. It shows that the forgery methods with the same name have a significant feature gap in different datasets, and different forgery methods will have relatively similar features. The same trend can be seen in the Cosine Similarity results in Figure 3. In order to evaluate the similarity between different forgery methods across various datasets. We assume that incorporating datasets that use the same forgery methods will beneficially enhance the model's performance. Conversely, merging different datasets or dividing the similar dataset into separate subsets may adversely affect the model's performance. We developed the K-means and Calinski Harabasz Evaluation System based on the above assumptions. For the sake of simplicity, we refer to it as the KCE-System for short.

The KCE-System incorporates unsupervised learning. The system divided the deepfake datasets into training sets and evaluation sets. Then it trains a deepfake recognition model using training sets, and extracting high-dimensional vectors from the middle layer of the model. After dimensionality reduction, the system used the K-means clustering method to merge various deepfake datasets. The system then trains the new Xception, F3-net, and ResNet models using these datasets. The trained models are then used to extract 2048-dimensional or 512-dimensional values from the evaluation set as feature values. Finally, the system uses the Calinski Harabasz Index method on the feature values after dimensionality reduction to evaluate The model's performance, as shown in Figure 4. Next, we will introduce several main parts of the system in detail.

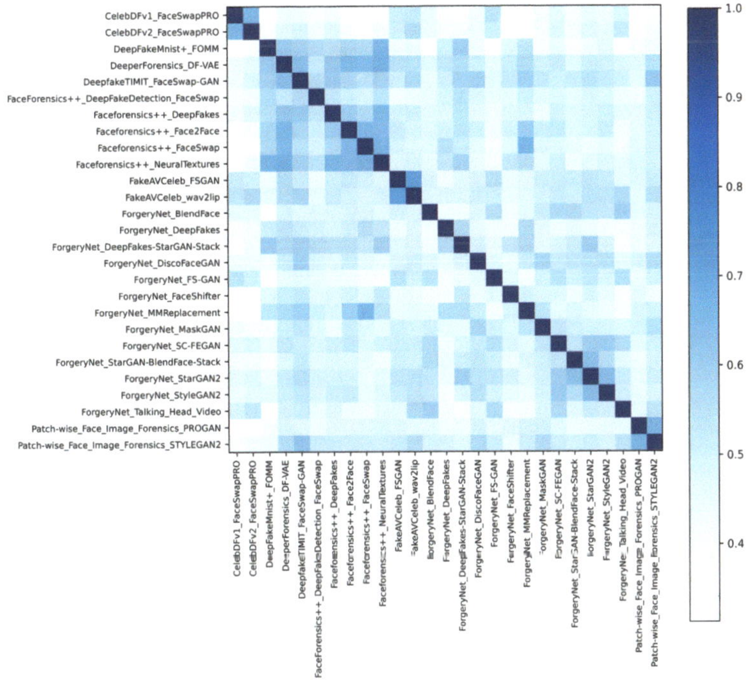

Figure 3. Similarity matrices for different forgery methods in each deepfake dataset.

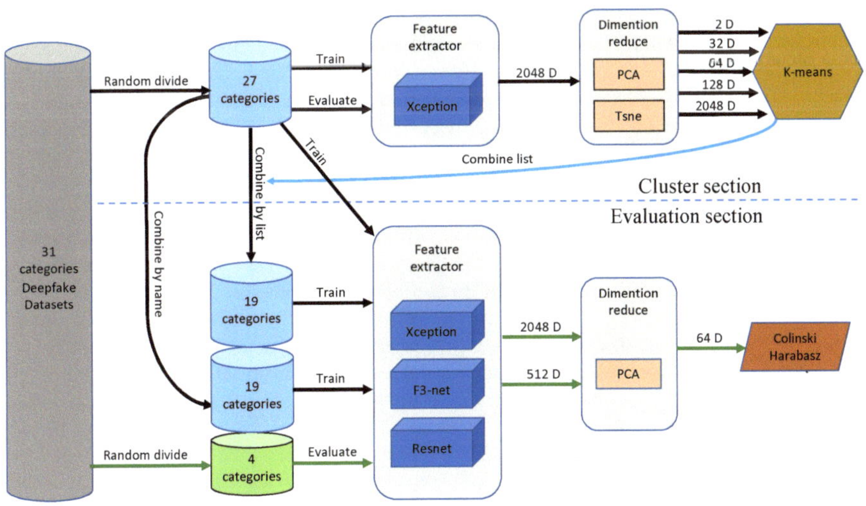

Figure 4. Overview of the KCE-System. The proposed architecture consists of two parts: the cluster section and the evaluation section.

3.2. Feature Extractor

Theoretically, when a model reaches a high classification accuracy for various categories of deep fake data, the model can extract the corresponding deepfake feature. We use the trained deepfake recognition model as a feature extractor, as the accuracy of these models in deepfake multi-classification tasks can reach more than 90%. For a comprehensive evaluation, we provide several representative models with different sizes.

The Xception [18] is a traditional CNN model based on separable convolutions with residual connections. The model has shown high accuracy when detecting deepfake videos. In terms of the training process of the feature extractor, the forgery method indicated in each dataset is used as a pseudo-labelling for multi-class training on the Xception. The training accuracy rate reaches 94%, and the model converges after three rounds of training. We use the trained model extract feature on the data of 27 categories of deepfake datasets. We take out its 2048-dimensional data as the sample's feature from the global pooling layer of Xception. Considering the trade-off between performance and efficiency, we select Xception as the baseline model.

The ResNet [20] is an improvement over the traditional deep neural network architecture that solves the problem of vanishing gradients and allows the training of much deeper networks. One of the main advantages of ResNet is its ability to handle deeper architectures, which leads to better accuracy in image classification tasks. Another notable model in facial forgery detection is the F3-Net, as proposed in [9]. This model leverages frequency domain analysis and comprises two branches, one focused on learning subtle forgery patterns via Frequency-aware Image Decomposition (FAD) and the other aimed at extracting high-level semantics from Local Frequency Statistics (LFS). Extensive experiments have demonstrated the effectiveness of the F3-Net in identifying low-quality forgery videos. Given the widespread applicability of the ResNet model in various computer vision fields and the unique position of the F3-Net in the domain of deepfake detection, we also select these two models as evaluation models and test them on half of the test group. To avoid the interference of the model itself on the experimental results to the greatest extent.

3.3. Dimensionality Reduction and Clustering

In this field, clustering algorithms, such as K-means [50], Gaussian Mixture, and DBSCAN [51] are commonly used. However, the DBSCAN algorithm is ineffective in controlling the number of clusters formed. In our system, we need to control the number of clusters formed for easy comparison with the data merged by name. The Gaussian Mixture algorithm is mainly designed for non-spherical clusters, while we focus more on the distance between categories in feature space, which emphasizes spherical clustering. Therefore, we chose to use the K-means clustering algorithm in our system.

The K-means algorithm uses Euclidean distance for clustering, but it can fail in high dimensions, so a dimension reduction method must be used. Two methods we utilized for comparison are PCA [52] and t-SNE [53]. PCA is stable but retains less information when reduced to two or three dimensions. When reducing dimensions to 64 using PCA, the interpretable variance contribution rate can be preserved at 95.2%. From Figure 5, we can see that it effectively preserves most of the information needed for clustering. The t-SNE supports low-dimensional reduction for visual analysis, but it has poor stability.

We utilize five different dimensionality reduction parameters to determine the most appropriate clustering dimension. We apply the t-SNE algorithm to reduce the high-dimensional feature data to 2 dimensions and use the PCA algorithm to reduce the dimensionality to 32, 64, and 128 dimensions. We also keep the 2048 dimensional original features without applying any dimensionality reduction algorithm. We then performed K-means clustering on each of these dimensions individually.

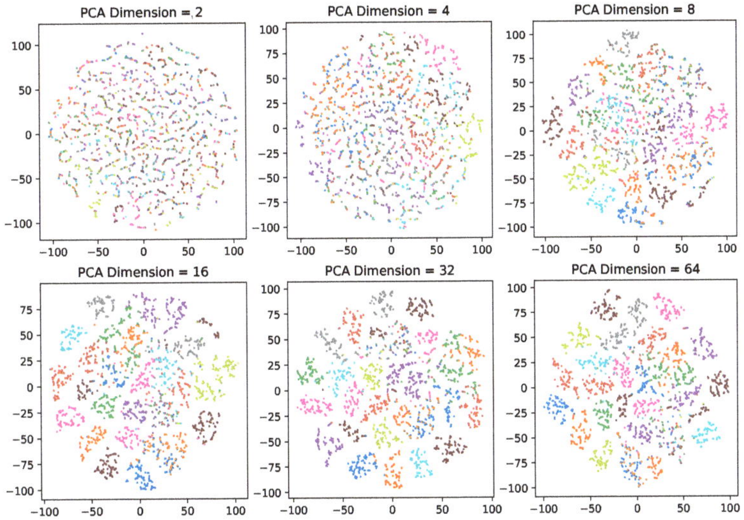

Figure 5. Illustration of dimensionality reduction using PCA. After using PCA to reduce the dimension, use the t-SNE method to reduce the dimension to two dimensions for display (Different colors indicate different forgery methods).

3.4. Selection of Evaluation Algorithms

We select four categories of deepfake datasets not involved in the training and clustering process as evaluation sets. We extract Xception, ResNet, and F3-net models' global pooling layer output and use the PCA algorithm reduces the data to 128 dimensions. An example of the results in Figure 6, demonstrating a clear distinction between the four unknown deepfake categories. This figure indicates that our model has indeed learned the relevant characteristics for identifying deepfakes.

Evaluating the performance of models trained with unreliably labeled or unlabeled data is difficult. We can not use precision and recall because we do not have a way to figure out whether each sample is classified correctly. To address this issue, we utilize the Calinski Harabasz Index [19], introduced by Calinski and Harabasz in 1974, as an effective evaluation method. This index is defined in Equation (1) as the ratio of the sum of between-cluster dispersion and inter-cluster dispersion for all clusters. Therefore, the Calinski Harabasz Index can be used to evaluate the models, with higher scores indicating that the model performs better on the test datasets.

For a set of data E of size n_E, which has been clustered into k clusters, the Calinski Harabasz score s is defined as the ratio of the between-cluster dispersion means and the within-cluster dispersion, as shown in Equation (1).

$$s = \frac{\mathrm{tr}(B_k)}{\mathrm{tr}(W_k)} \times \frac{n_E - k}{k - 1} \tag{1}$$

where $tr(B_k)$ is trace of the between group dispersion matrix and $tr(W_k)$ is the trace of the within-cluster dispersion matrix defined by:

$$B_k = \sum_{q=1}^{k} n_q (c_q - c_E)(c_q - c_E)^T \tag{2}$$

$$W_k = \sum_{q=1}^{k} \sum_{x \in C_q} (x - c_q)(x - c_q)^T \tag{3}$$

Here, C_q represents the set of points in cluster q, c_q represents the center of cluster q, c_E represents the center of E, and n_q represents the number of points in cluster q.

When using the Calinski Harabasz Index to evaluate clustering quality, it can be observed that the elbow points of the Calinski Harabasz Index tend to be around 3 or 4 of cluster number, as depicted in Figure 7. The results obtained from the Calinski Harabasz Index are consistent with the number of forged method categories in the actual evaluation set. This suggests that the Calinski Harabasz Index is a valuable method to assess the model's ability to identify new categories of deepfakes. When other training parameters remain the same, if a model's performance is outstanding, it indicates that the quality of the training set is excellent, with fewer incorrect labels. In other words, we effectively improve the reliability of these classification labels in the training set. Therefore, the Calinski Harabasz Index can effectively evaluate the correlation of these unreliable classification labels in our system.

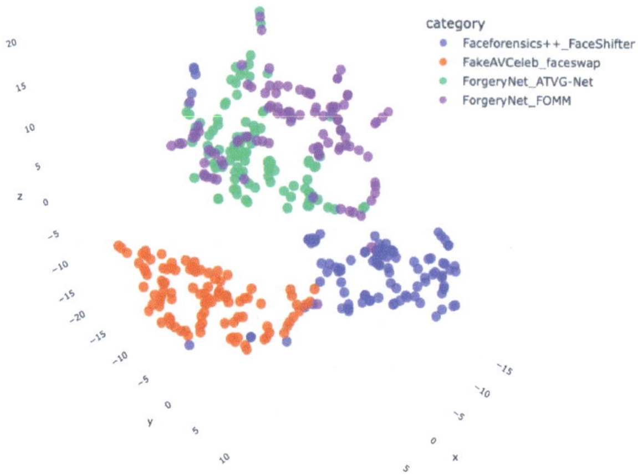

Figure 6. The model output of the evaluation sets, that be reduced to three dimensions using the t-SNE method for display.

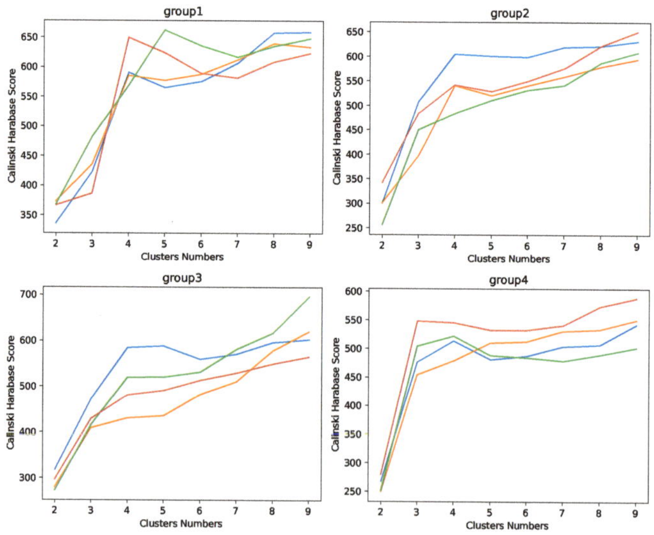

Figure 7. Using Calinski Harabasz Index to evaluate its clustering quality, it can be found that its elbow point is about 3 to 4.

4. Experiment

In this section, we first introduce the overall experimental setup. Our equipment includes four NVIDIA GeForce2080Ti GPUs. We use PyTorch to train and evaluate models, OpenCV to image data preprocessing, and Scikit-learn algorithm library for data analysis. We extract 620,000 fake face images from 10 deepfake datasets and train 40 models, including 32 Xception, 4 F3-net, and 4 ResNet models. The entire data preparation and experimental process spanned approximately 3 months.

4.1. Data Dividing and Preprocessing

We select 31 datasets labeled with forgery method names from CelebDF, DeeperForensics-1.0, DeepFakeMnist+, FaceForensics++, ForgeryNet, and FakeAVCeleb, see Table 1 for details. We use a random method to divide 31 deepfake categories into two sets, where the training set contains 27 categories, and the evaluation set contains four categories. We repeat the above division four times to obtain four sets of training sets and evaluation sets. See Table 2 for details.

Table 2. The table displays four sets of experimental data, each containing four evaluation datasets, with the remaining 27 datasets designated for training purposes.

Group	Evaluation Datasets
1	Faceforensics++_FaceShifter, FakeAVCeleb_FaceSwap, ForgeryNet_ATVG-Net, ForgeryNet_FOMM
2	DeeperForensics_DF-VAE, Faceforensics++_Face2Face, FakeAVCeleb_Wav2Lip, ForgeryNet_DiscoFaceGAN
3	DeepfakeTIMIT_FaceSwap-GAN, ForgeryNet_BlendFace, ForgeryNet_StarGAN2, Patch-wise-Face-Image-Forensics _PROGAN
4	CelebDFv2_FaceSwapPRO, Faceforensics++_ NeuralTextures, ForgeryNet_FS-GAN, ForgeryNet_Talking Head Video

We extract the frame data of each category according to the instructions of the relevant dataset and use the face detection model Retinaface [54] to intercept the face area. Then, we increase the side length of the image by a factor of 1.25. Finally, we randomly select 20,000 fake faces of each category and save these images as test data in png. format.

4.2. Merge Training Data Based on the Category Name

In order to verify our conjecture that there is large randomness in the naming of the forged methods in the deepfake dataset, we specially merged the training set data according to the principle of the same or close to the forged method names and used them as a control group. We use the following merging rules.

(a) Merge the FaceSwapPRO category in the CelebDFv1 dataset and the FaceSwapPRO category in the CelebDFv2 dataset.
(b) Merge the FOMM category in the DeepFakeMnist+ dataset and the FOMM category in the ForgeryNet dataset.
(c) Merge the FaceSwap-GAN category in the DeepfakeTIMIT dataset, the DeepFakeDetection FaceSwap category and the FaceSwap category in the FaceForensics++ dataset, and the faceswap category in the FakeAVCeleb dataset.
(d) Merge the DeepFakes category in the Faceforensics++ dataset and the DeepFakes category in the ForgeryNet dataset.
(e) Merge the FSGAN category in the FakeAVCeleb dataset and the FS-GAN category in the ForgeryNet dataset.
(f) Merge DeepFakes-StarGAN-Stack category, StarGAN-BlendFace-Stack category and StarGAN2 category in ForgeryNet dataset.
(g) Merge the StyleGAN2 category in the ForgeryNet dataset and the STYLEGAN2 category in the Patch-wise Face Image Forensics dataset.

We randomly sample corresponding proportions of data from the merged dataset and reassemble them into 20,000 images per category. The number of training set categories of the merged four groups is that Group 1 has a total of 19 categories, Group 2 has a total of 17 categories, Group 3 has a total of 19 categories, and Group 4 has a total of 19 categories.

4.3. Merge Training Data Based on the Results of K-Means Clustering

One of the purposes of our experiment is to determine the appropriate dimensionality for K-means clustering to address this type of problem. We need to ensure that we do not lose too many classification features due to excessive dimensionality reduction, nor do we cause the K-means algorithm to fail due to excessive dimensionality. Since we chose the Xception model as the baseline, we use the PCA algorithm to reduce the 2048-dimensional output to 128, 64, and 32 dimensions. We also reduce it to two dimensions using the t-SNE algorithm. For the F3-net and ResNet models, we only use the PCA algorithm to reduce the output feature value to 64 dimensions since we only need to verify that our method applies to these models.

In the previous section, we created training data for the control group based on name mergers. To facilitate comparison, we ensure that the number of categories of the experimental data for each group is identical. Therefore, we use the K-means clustering algorithm to cluster these training sets based on the specified number of clusters. Groups 1, 3, and 4 have 19 clusters, while Group 2 has 17 clusters. Finally, we use the results of the K-means clustering algorithm to combine the training set.

4.4. Experimental Results

We train Xception, F3-net, and ResNet models using training data merged by K-means clustering results and category names, respectively. For comparison, we also train the same models using the original training set without merging.

To obtain feature vectors for the validation set, we used these models as feature extractors and applied PCA to reduce them to 64 dimensions. We then calculated the Calinski Harabasz Index. Please refer to Table 3 for the result.

Table 3. The Calinski Harabasz Index results. The bold type indicates the best result for that group of tests.

Model	Train Data Merge by	Group 1 CH	Group 2 CH	Group 3 CH	Group 4 CH	Avg CH
Xception	Without merging	128.02825	**117.448499**	68.6994684	93.5723306	101.937137
Xception	Name	84.0837009	73.8172086	74.579957	61.2651927	73.4365148
Xception	K-means on 2048D	124.241305	105.070655	76.2218761	84.212058	97.4364735
Xception	K-means on t-SNE 2D	103.627829	87.1461055	66.6143003	76.5264273	83.4786656
Xception	K-means on PCA 64D	**137.241584**	101.192327	**85.2535376**	**94.2137508**	**104.4753**
Xception	K-means on PCA 128D	101.197038	101.502163	74.8441997	86.6358341	91.0448087
Xception	K-means on PCA 32D	114.247635	89.1934801	62.3932779	75.9596147	85.4485019
F3-net	Name			62.6592813	65.6510862	64.1551837
F3-net	K-means on PCA 64D			**85.361067**	**72.018708**	**78.6898875**
ResNet	Name			42.895651	47.9716533	45.4336522
ResNet	K-means on PCA 64D			**49.7529116**	**54.0786263**	**51.915769**

The Calinski Harabasz Index of the model trained on the data merged by K-means is 42.27% higher than that pooled by name. Furthermore, these scores are slightly higher than those directly using the original training set, even though the original set contains more data. At the same time, the Calinski Harabasz Index is also higher at 22.66% and 14.27% in F3-net and ResNet models. These prove an appropriate combination of deepfake datasets with similar features improves the model's generalization in the unknown forgery categories.

The Calinski Harabasz Index of merging by names is lower than by various cluster-based and original training sets, indicating significant differences in the characteristics of these same-name forgery methods. Merged by name harms the model.

Compared with the other three groups, the results of Group 2 are different. Furthermore, its Calinski Harabasz Index is lower than the training results on the original data. Because Group 2 has only 17 categories after the merger, with fewer training samples than other groups. More information loss can destroy the performance of the model.

5. Conclusions

This article starts with the traceability requirements of the deep forgery method. When using multiple deepfake datasets, we found many different deepfake datasets using the same or similar label names. Confusion arises in how to use these datasets comprehensively.

We leverage the Xception model to extract fake features from the deepfake dataset. Subsequently, PCA and t-SNE methods are employed to reduce dimensionality and perform K-means clustering. Then, combine the datasets based on the clustering results, and use the combined data to train Xception, F3-net, and ResNet models, respectively. Finally, we use these models to extract features from the evaluation set and evaluate the generalization of these models using the Calinski Harabasz index as an evaluation metric. Our contributions are mainly three-fold:

- We prove the labels of various deepfake datasets contain many randomnesses. If researchers use more than two deepfake datasets, combining these datasets only based on forgery labels will hurt the performance of the model.
- We propose K-means and Calinski Harabasz evaluation systems to evaluate the similarity of various deepfake datasets, laying the foundation for future researchers to use them comprehensively.
- We prove that the generalization ability of the deepfake recognition model in the face of new samples can be improved by merging datasets with high forgery feature similarity.

Our research is only a helpful exploration for entirely using various deep forgery datasets from the source of deep forgery methods. We mainly revealed the arbitrariness of label naming in deepfake datasets and the resulting troubles in the traceability of forgery methods. There is still a long way to go to solve this problem completely. In addition, different image compression algorithms and image resolutions significantly impact the fake features of deepfake datasets, which will seriously interfere with the model's extraction of fake features from deepfake datasets, and pose a significant challenge to the identifiability and traceability of deepfake datasets. We are committed to conducting further research to address these challenges effectively.

To ensure the healthy development of the field, research institutions and universities should standardize the label nomenclature of deepfake datasets. Additionally, legislation should require digital watermarking and blockchain technology to trace deepfake content to its source accurately. Our research is a helpful exploration of the use of various deep forgery datasets, and we hope it will inspire future work in this field.

Author Contributions: Conceptualization, Y.S.; Methodology, Y.S., J.Z. and J.L.; Software, Y.S., H.Z. and Y.T.; Validation, H.Z.; Formal analysis, Y.S.; Investigation, J.L. and X.L.; Resources, J.Z. and Y.L.; Data curation, L.L. and Y.T.; Writing—original draft, Y.S.; Writing—review & editing, J.Z. and L.L.; Visualization, Y.S. and H.Z.; Supervision, J.Z. and L.L.; Project administration, Y.L.; Funding acquisition, Y.L. All authors have read and agreed to the published version of the manuscript.

Funding: This work was funded by the National Key Research and Development Program of China under Grant 2018YFB1701402, National Natural Science Foundation of China (no. U1936218 and 62072037), Beijing Municipal Science & Technology Project (no. Z211100004121009), Sun Yi was supported by the China Scholarship Council for one year of study at Singapore University of Technology and Design (no. 202101750002).

Institutional Review Board Statement: Not applicable.

Informed Consent Statement: Not applicable.

Data Availability Statement: These data used in this paper were derived from the public domain. Data sharing is not applicable to this article as no new data were created or analyzed in this study.

Conflicts of Interest: The authors declare no conflict of interest.

References

1. Korshunov, P.; Marcel, S. Deepfakes: A new threat to face recognition? assessment and detection. *arXiv* **2018**, arXiv:1812.08685.
2. Chesney, B.; Citron, D. Deep fakes: A looming challenge for privacy, democracy, and national security. *Calif. L. Rev.* **2019**, *107*, 1753. [CrossRef]
3. Dixon, H.B., Jr. Deepfakes: More Frightening Than Photoshop on Steroids. *Judges' J.* **2019**, *58*, 35–37.
4. Feldstein, S. How Artificial Intelligence Systems Could Threaten Democracy. Available online: https://scholarworks.boisestate.edu/pubadmin_facpubs/102/ (accessed on 20 December 2022).
5. Verdoliva, L. Media forensics and deepfakes: An overview. *IEEE J. Sel. Top. Signal Process.* **2020**, *14*, 910–932. [CrossRef]
6. Xiang, Z.; Horváth, J.; Baireddy, S.; Bestagini, P.; Tubaro, S.; Delp, E.J. Forensic analysis of video files using metadata. In Proceedings of the IEEE/CVF Conference on Computer Vision and Pattern Recognition, Virtual, 19–25 June 2021; pp. 1042–1051.
7. Qureshi, A.; Megías, D.; Kuribayashi, M. Detecting deepfake videos using digital watermarking. In Proceedings of the 2021 Asia-Pacific Signal and Information Processing Association Annual Summit and Conference (APSIPA ASC), Tokyo, Japan, 14–17 December 2021; IEEE: Piscataway, NJ, USA, 2021; pp. 1786–1793.
8. Goodfellow, I.; Pouget-Abadie, J.; Mirza, M.; Xu, B.; Warde-Farley, D.; Ozair, S.; Courville, A.; Bengio, Y. Generative adversarial networks. *Commun. ACM* **2020**, *63*, 139–144. [CrossRef]
9. Qian, Y.; Yin, G.; Sheng, L.; Chen, Z.; Shao, J. Thinking in frequency: Face forgery detection by mining frequency-aware clues. In *Proceedings of the European Conference on Computer Vision*; Springer: Berlin/Heidelberg, Germany, 2020; pp. 86–103. [CrossRef]
10. Torralba, A.; Fergus, R.; Freeman, W.T. 80 million tiny images: A large data set for nonparametric object and scene recognition. *IEEE Trans. Pattern Anal. Mach. Intell.* **2008**, *30*, 1958–1970. [CrossRef] [PubMed]
11. Deng, J.; Dong, W.; Socher, R.; Li, L.J.; Li, K.; Fei-Fei, L. Imagenet: A large-scale hierarchical image database. In Proceedings of the 2009 IEEE Conference on Computer Vision and Pattern Recognition. Institute of Electrical and Electronics Engineers, Miami, FL, USA, 20–25 June 2009; pp. 248–255. [CrossRef]
12. Griffin, G.; Holub, A.; Perona, P. Caltech-256 Object Category Dataset. Available online: https://authors.library.caltech.edu/7694/ (accessed on 12 January 2023).
13. Schwarz, H.; Marpe, D.; Wiegand, T. Overview of the scalable video coding extension of the H. 264/AVC standard. *IEEE Trans. Circuits Syst. Video Technol.* **2007**, *17*, 1103–1120. [CrossRef]
14. He, Y.; Gan, B.; Chen, S.; Zhou, Y.; Yin, G.; Song, L.; Sheng, L.; Shao, J.; Liu, Z. Forgerynet: A versatile benchmark for comprehensive forgery analysis. In Proceedings of the IEEE/CVF Conference on Computer Vision and Pattern Recognition. Institute of Electrical and Electronics Engineers, Virtual, 19–25 June 2021; pp. 4360–4369. [CrossRef]
15. Huang, J.; Wang, X.; Du, B.; Du, P.; Xu, C. DeepFake MNIST+: A DeepFake Facial Animation Dataset. In Proceedings of the IEEE/CVF International Conference on Computer Vision, Nashville, TN, USA, 20–25 June 2021; IEEE: Piscataway, NJ, USA, 2021; pp. 1973–1982. [CrossRef]
16. Khalid, H.; Tariq, S.; Kim, M.; Woo, S.S. FakeAVCeleb: A novel audio-video multimodal deepfake dataset. *arXiv* **2021**, arXiv:2108.05080.
17. Jiang, L.; Li, R.; Wu, W.; Qian, C.; Loy, C.C. Deeperforensics-1.0: A large-scale dataset for real-world face forgery detection. In Proceedings of the IEEE/CVF Conference on Computer Vision and Pattern Recognition, Seattle, WA, USA, 13–19 June 2020; IEEE: Piscataway, NJ, USA, 2020; pp. 2889–2898. [CrossRef]
18. Chollet, F. Xception: Deep learning with depthwise separable convolutions. In Proceedings of the IEEE Conference on Computer Vision and Pattern Recognition (CVPR), Honolulu, HI, USA, 21–26 July 2017; IEEE: Piscataway, NJ, USA, 2017; pp. 1800–1807. [CrossRef]
19. Caliński, T.; Harabasz, J. A dendrite method for cluster analysis. *Commun. Stat.-Theory Methods* **1974**, *3*, 1–27. [CrossRef]
20. He, K.; Zhang, X.; Ren, S.; Sun, J. Deep residual learning for image recognition. In Proceedings of the IEEE Conference on Computer Vision and Pattern Recognition, Las Vegas, NV, USA, 27–30 June 2016; IEEE: Piscataway, NJ, USA, 2016; pp. 770–778. [CrossRef]
21. Rossler, A.; Cozzolino, D.; Verdoliva, L.; Riess, C.; Thies, J.; Nießner, M. Faceforensics++: Learning to detect manipulated facial images. In Proceedings of the IEEE/CVF International Conference on Computer Vision, Seoul, Republic of Korea, 27 October–2 November 2019; IEEE: Piscataway, NJ, USA, 2019; pp. 1–11. [CrossRef]
22. Li, Y.; Yang, X.; Sun, P.; Qi, H.; Lyu, S. Celeb-df: A large-scale challenging dataset for deepfake forensics. In Proceedings of the IEEE/CVF Conference on Computer Vision and Pattern Recognition, Seattle, WA, USA, 13–19 June 2020; IEEE: Piscataway, NJ, USA, 2020; pp. 3207–3216. [CrossRef]
23. Lee, J. This Dataset Is a Summary of the Datasets Used in the "A Study on Patch-Wise Deepfake Image Detection" Experiment Presented at the Winter Conference of the Korean Society of Telecommunications. Available online: https://github.com/Jeonghan57/A-Study-on-Patch-Wise-Deepfake-Image-Detection (accessed on 20 December 2022).

24. Kingma, D.P.; Welling, M. Auto-encoding variational bayes. *arXiv* **2013**, arXiv:1312.6114.
25. Korshunova, I.; Shi, W.; Dambre, J.; Theis, L. Fast face-swap using convolutional neural networks. In Proceedings of the IEEE International Conference on Computer Vision, Venice, Italy, 22–29 October 2017; IEEE: Piscataway, NJ, USA, 2017; pp. 3677–3685. [CrossRef]
26. Nirkin, Y.; Keller, Y.; Hassner, T. Fsgan: Subject agnostic face swapping and reenactment. In Proceedings of the IEEE/CVF International Conference on Computer Vision, Seoul, Republic of Korea, 27 October–2 November 2019; IEEE: Piscataway, NJ, USA, 2019; pp. 7184–7193. [CrossRef]
27. Prajwal, K.; Mukhopadhyay, R.; Namboodiri, V.P.; Jawahar, C. A lip sync expert is all you need for speech to lip generation in the wild. In Proceedings of the 28th ACM International Conference on Multimedia, New York, NY, USA, 12–16 October 2020; pp. 484–492. [CrossRef]
28. Siarohin, A.; Lathuilière, S.; Tulyakov, S.; Ricci, E.; Sebe, N. First order motion model for image animation. In *Proceedings of the Advances in Neural Information Processing Systems*; Curran Associates, Inc.: Red Hook, NY, USA, 2019; Volume 32.
29. Bshaoanlu. Faceswap-GAN. Available online: https://github.com/shaoanlu/faceswap-GAN (accessed on 12 January 2023).
30. Kowalski, M. FaceSwap. Available online: https://github.com/MarekKowalski/FaceSwap/ (accessed on 12 January 2023).
31. Deepfakes. Available online: https://github.com/deepfakes/faceswap (accessed on 9 January 2023).
32. Thies, J.; Zollhofer, M.; Stamminger, M.; Theobalt, C.; Nießner, M. Face2face: Real-time face capture and reenactment of rgb videos. In Proceedings of the IEEE Conference on Computer Vision and Pattern Recognition, Las Vegas, NV, USA, 27–30 June 2016; IEEE: Piscataway, NJ, USA, 2016; pp. 2387–2395. [CrossRef]
33. Li, L.; Bao, J.; Yang, H.; Chen, D.; Wen, F. Faceshifter: Towards high fidelity and occlusion aware face swapping. *arXiv* **2019**, arXiv:1912.13457.
34. Thies, J.; Zollhöfer, M.; Nießner, M. Deferred neural rendering: Image synthesis using neural textures. *ACM Trans. Graph. (TOG)* **2019**, *38*, 1–12. [CrossRef]
35. Dufour, N.; Andrew Gully, J. Contributing Data to Deepfake Detection Research. Available online: https://ai.googleblog.com/2019/09/contributing-data-to-deepfake-detection.html (accessed on 25 December).
36. Chen, L.; Maddox, R.K.; Duan, Z.; Xu, C. Hierarchical cross-modal talking face generation with dynamic pixel-wise loss. In Proceedings of the IEEE/CVF Conference on Computer Vision and Pattern Recognition, Long Beach, CA, USA, 15–20 June 2019; IEEE: Piscataway, NJ, USA, 2019; pp. 7832–7841. [CrossRef]
37. Deng, Y.; Yang, J.; Chen, D.; Wen, F.; Tong, X. Disentangled and controllable face image generation via 3d imitative-contrastive learning. In Proceedings of the IEEE/CVF Conference on Computer Vision and Pattern Recognition, Seattle, WA, USA, 13–19 June 2020; IEEE: Piscataway, NJ, USA, 2020; pp. 5154–5163. [CrossRef]
38. Lee, C.H.; Liu, Z.; Wu, L.; Luo, P. Maskgan: Towards diverse and interactive facial image manipulation. In Proceedings of the IEEE/CVF Conference on Computer Vision and Pattern Recognition, Seattle, WA, USA, 13–19 June 2020; IEEE: Piscataway, NJ, USA, 2020; pp. 5549–5558. [CrossRef]
39. Jo, Y.; Park, J. Sc-fegan: Face editing generative adversarial network with user's sketch and color. In Proceedings of the IEEE/CVF International Conference on Computer Vision, Seoul, Republic of Korea, 27 October–2 November 2019; IEEE: Piscataway, NJ, USA, 2019; pp. 1745–1753. [CrossRef]
40. Choi, Y.; Uh, Y.; Yoo, J.; Ha, J.W. Stargan v2: Diverse image synthesis for multiple domains. In Proceedings of the IEEE/CVF Conference on Computer Vision and Pattern Recognition, Seattle, WA, USA, 13–19 June 2020; IEEE: Piscataway, NJ, USA, 2020; pp. 8188–8197. [CrossRef]
41. Viazovetskyi, Y.; Ivashkin, V.; Kashin, E. Stylegan2 distillation for feed-forward image manipulation. In Proceedings of the European Conference on Computer Vision, Glasgow, UK, 23–28 August 2020; Springer: Berlin/Heidelberg, Germany, 2020; pp. 170–186. ._11. [CrossRef]
42. Fried, O.; Tewari, A.; Zollhöfer, M.; Finkelstein, A.; Shechtman, E.; Goldman, D.B.; Genova, K.; Jin, Z.; Theobalt, C.; Agrawala, M. Text-based editing of talking-head video. *ACM Trans. Graph. (TOG)* **2019**, *38*, 1–14. [CrossRef]
43. Gao, H.; Pei, J.; Huang, H. Progan: Network embedding via proximity generative adversarial network. In Proceedings of the 25th ACM SIGKDD International Conference on Knowledge Discovery & Data Mining, New York, NY, USA, 4–8 August 2019; pp. 1308–1316. [CrossRef]
44. Chen, Z.; Yang, H. Attentive semantic exploring for manipulated face detection. In Proceedings of the ICASSP 2021–2021 IEEE International Conference on Acoustics, Speech and Signal Processing (ICASSP), Toronto, ON, Canada, 6–11 June 2021; IEEE: Piscataway, NJ, USA, 2021; pp. 1985–1989. [CrossRef]
45. Liu, H.; Li, X.; Zhou, W.; Chen, Y.; He, Y.; Xue, H.; Zhang, W.; Yu, N. Spatial-phase shallow learning: Rethinking face forgery detection in frequency domain. In Proceedings of the IEEE/CVF Conference on Computer Vision and Pattern Recognition, Nashville, TN, USA, 20–25 June 2021; IEEE: Piscataway, NJ, USA, 2021; pp. 772–781. [CrossRef]
46. Li, J.; Xie, H.; Li, J.; Wang, Z.; Zhang, Y. Frequency-aware discriminative feature learning supervised by single-center loss for face forgery detection. In Proceedings of the IEEE/CVF Conference on Computer Vision and Pattern Recognition, Nashville, TN, USA, 20–25 June 2021; IEEE: Piscataway, NJ, USA, 2021; pp. 6454–6463. [CrossRef]
47. Guarnera, L.; Giudice, O.; Battiato, S. Deepfake detection by analyzing convolutional traces. In Proceedings of the IEEE/CVF Conference on Computer Vision and Pattern Recognition Workshops (CVPRW), Seattle, WA, USA, 14–19 June 2020; IEEE: Piscataway, NJ, USA, 2020; pp. 2841–2850. [CrossRef]

48. Liu, Z.; Qi, X.; Torr, P.H. Global texture enhancement for fake face detection in the wild. In Proceedings of the IEEE/CVF Conference on Computer Vision and Pattern Recognition, Seattle, WA, USA, 13–19 June 2020; IEEE: Piscataway, NJ, USA, 2020; pp. 8060–8069. [CrossRef]
49. Yang, T.; Huang, Z.; Cao, J.; Li, L.; Li, X. Deepfake Network Architecture Attribution. *Proc. AAAI Conf. Artif. Intell.* **2022**, *36*, 4662–4670. [CrossRef]
50. Hartigan, J.A.; Wong, M.A. Algorithm AS 136: A k-means clustering algorithm. *J. R. Stat. Soc. Ser. C (Appl. Stat.)* **1979**, *28*, 100–108. [CrossRef]
51. Ester, M.; Kriegel, H.P.; Sander, J.; Xu, X. Density-based spatial clustering of applications with noise. In Proceedings of the International Conference Knowledge Discovery and Data Mining, Portland, Oregon, 2–4 August 1996; Volume 240, pp. 11–30.
52. Hotelling, H. Analysis of a complex of statistical variables into principal components. *J. Educ. Psychol.* **1933**, *24*, 417. [CrossRef]
53. Van der Maaten, L.; Hinton, G. Visualizing data using t-SNE. *J. Mach. Learn. Res.* **2008**, *9*, 2579–2605.
54. Deng, J.; Guo, J.; Ververas, E.; Kotsia, I.; Zafeiriou, S. Retinaface: Single-shot multi-level face localisation in the wild. In Proceedings of the IEEE/CVF Conference on Computer Vision and Pattern Recognition, Seattle, WA, USA, 13–19 June 2020; IEEE: Piscataway, NJ, USA, 2020; pp. 5203–5212. [CrossRef]

electronics

MDPI

Article

Few-Shot Learning for Multi-POSE Face Recognition via Hypergraph De-Deflection and Multi-Task Collaborative Optimization

Xiaojin Fan [1], Mengmeng Liao [2,*], Lei Chen [3] and Jingjing Hu [1,*]

1 School of Computer Science and Technology, Beijing Institute of Technology, Beijing 100081, China
2 School of Mechatronic Engineering and Automation, Shanghai University, Shanghai 200444, China
3 School of Computer and Communication Engineering, University of Science and Technology Beijing, Beijing 100083, China
* Correspondence: mmliao16@fudan.edu.cn (M.L.); hujingjing@bit.edu.cn (J.H.)

Abstract: Few-shot, multi-pose face recognition has always been an interesting yet difficult subject in the field of pattern recognition. Researchers have come up with a variety of workarounds; however, these methods make it either difficult to extract effective features that are robust to poses or difficult to obtain globally optimal solutions. In this paper, we propose a few-shot, multi-pose face recognition method based on hypergraph de-deflection and multi-task collaborative optimization (HDMCO). In HDMCO, the hypergraph is embedded in a non-negative image decomposition to obtain images without pose deflection. Furthermore, a feature encoding method is proposed by considering the importance of samples and combining support vector data description, triangle coding, etc. This feature encoding method is used to extract features from pose-free images. Last but not the least, multi-tasks such as feature extraction and feature recognition are jointly optimized to obtain a solution closer to the global optimal solution. Comprehensive experimental results show that the proposed HDMCO achieves better recognition performance.

Keywords: few-shot learning; face recognition; pose variations; hypergraph

check for updates

Citation: Fan, X.; Liao, M.; Chen, L.; Hu, J. Few-Shot Learning for Multi-POSE Face Recognition via Hypergraph De-Deflection and Multi-Task Collaborative Optimization. *Electronics* **2023**, *12*, 2248. https://doi.org/10.3390/electronics12102248

Academic Editor: George A. Papakostas

Received: 28 March 2023
Revised: 6 May 2023
Accepted: 10 May 2023
Published: 15 May 2023

1. Introduction

Face recognition is a very important technology with a wide range of applications, such as video surveillance, forensics, and security [1–3]. Pose change is one of the difficulties in face recognition. Posture changes involved in images can cause images of one person to look like images of other people. That is to say, the change in pose will lead to an increase in intra-class difference and a decrease in inter-class difference, which will hinder the classifier from correctly recognizing the face images. One study shows that the performance of most algorithms decreases by more than 10% from frontal-frontal to frontal-profile face verification; however, there is only a small drop in the recognition performance of the human eye [4]. Therefore, it is of great significance to study face recognition involving pose change.

Many methods have been proposed to solve the multi-pose face recognition problem [5–11]. These methods can be divided into the following categories: face normalization, feature representation, spatial mapping, and pose estimation.

The method based on face normalization can better identify the image by normalizing the image with attitude deflection to the front image or the image close to the front image. For example, Ding et al. [12] transform images with pose deflection into frontal images by pose normalization. Luan et al. [13] take geometry preservation into account in GAN networks and exploit perceptual loss constraints along with norm loss to obtain the frontal images that preserve global and local information. Liu et al. [14] use pixel-level loss, feature space perception loss, and identity-preserving loss to generate real class-invariant frontal images. Yin et al. [15] embed the contextual dependency and the local consistency into GAN networks to extract the frontal images. Lin et al. [16] use the deep representation alignment network to extract the pose-invariant face feature. Yang et al. [17] use the multi-bit binary descriptor to extract the pose-invariant feature. Tu et al. [18] jointly optimize image inpainting and image frontalization to deal with the recognition of low-resolution face images involving pose variations.

Learning the effective feature representations of images can be beneficial for tackling the task of classification. For example, Zhou et al. [19] use the divide-and-strategy to deal with the representation and classification of samples, which can reduce the challenge of posture. Zhang et al. [20] use locality-constrained and label information to enhance the representational power of regression-based methods. Gao et al. [21] use the multi-modal hashing and discriminative correlation maximization analysis for feature representation learning to allow them to obtain the easily distinguishable feature representation of each pose image. Yang et al. [22] learn the more discriminative feature representations by imposing penalties on weighted vectors. Huang et al. [23] use the samples and feature centers to enhance the similarity of features between samples of the same class.

The method based on spatial mapping can reduce the intra-class differences and increase the inter-class differences by mapping samples into a new space, which is beneficial for classification. For example, He et al. [24] use the identity consistency loss and the pose-triplet loss to minimize the intra-class and maximize the inter-class. Wang et al. [25] use the divergence loss to increase the diversity among multiple attention maps. Furthermore, the attention sparsity loss is used to highlight the regions with strong discriminative power. He et al. [26] reduce the difference between images with different modes by applying adversarial learning to both image-level and feature level. Liu et al. [27] use the source domain data to improve the performance of target domain data so that the poses of two images with the same category from the source and target domains are markedly different. Sun et al. [28] use the equalized margin loss to reduce the impact of unevenly distributed data (uneven distribution of attitude deflection).

It is also a good way to estimate the attitude deflection angle of the image and use the information of the deflection angle to recognize the image. For example, Zhang et al. [29] use the pose-guided margin loss to estimate the head poses, then the recognition process can be completed in the same pose. Badave et al. [30] use multiple cameras for pose estimation and then use the estimated pose to recognize the face images. Wang et al. [31] combine the learned sub-classifiers into a classifier with a strong performance by learning the dictionaries and the sub-classifiers at the same time.

The above methods have good effects on face recognition involving small posture deflection or face recognition with a large number of samples. However, most face recognition is either few-shot face recognition or face recognition involving large pose deflection. It is difficult for these methods to learn the intrinsic relationship between multiple samples of the same category in the process of model learning, and the essential attributes of the samples of the same category summarized by the learned model are incomplete or inaccurate.

Hypergraphs can represent complex relationships between objects. Unlike ordinary graphs (where each edge of an ordinary graph can only connect two nodes), each edge of a hypergraph can connect multiple nodes. That is, a hypergraph can reveal complex relationships between multiple nodes. Furthermore, non-negative matrix factorization is widely used in the field of computer vision, such as feature extraction. A matrix can be decomposed into two matrices with different properties by non-negative matrix factorization. Inspired by non-negative matrix factorization, we can decompose each image involving attitude changes through non-negative matrix decomposition, and one matrix obtained by the decomposition is used as the image without attitude deflection, and the other matrix is used as the attitude change matrix. The image without pose deflection is finally obtained through multiple iterative decompositions. Inspired by the hypergraph, we treat each image as a node in the hypergraph and embed the hypergraph formed by multiple images into a non-negative matrix decomposition to extract images with better performance and no attitude deflection. A few-shot multi-pose face recognition method based on hypergraph de-deflection and multi-task collaborative optimization (HDMCO) is proposed in this paper. First, HDMCO uses the hypergraph and non-negative matrix factorization to obtain the images that are approximately frontal. Then, a novel feature encoding method based on the improved support vector data description is proposed, and it is jointly optimized with a dictionary learning-based classifier for feature extraction and feature classification. Figure 1 shows the flowchart of the proposed HDMCO.

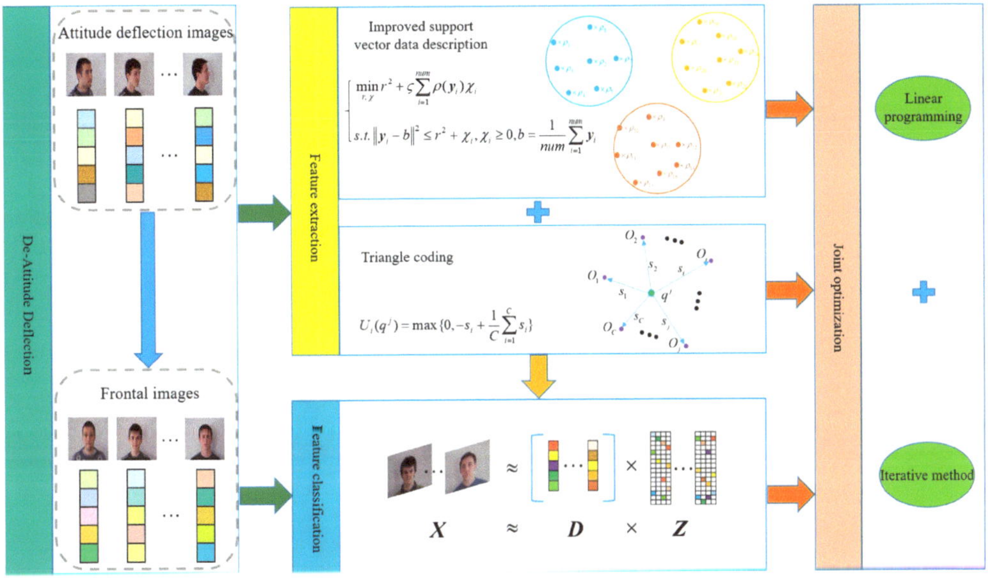

Figure 1. The flowchart of the proposed HDMCO. s_i represents the distance between the patch q^j and O_i, O_i is the center of the i -th SVDD sphere, $i = 1, 2, \cdots, C$. $\boldsymbol{X}$ is the training. Sample set, $\boldsymbol{D}$ is the dictionary, $\boldsymbol{Z}$ is the representation coefficient matrix.

In the de-attitude deflection phase of Figure 1, the image without attitude deflection is separated from the image with attitude deflection by non-negative matrix decomposition. In this process, the hypergraph is embedded in the non-negative decomposition to protect the structural information of the image. In the feature extraction phase, the improved support vector data description is used to obtain the clustering center and radius of each cluster, and triangle coding is used to encode features for each patch. Then, image coding can be obtained. In the feature classification phase, the dictionary learning-based classifier recognizes the features of the image and then determines the category of the image.

The main innovations of this paper are as follows.

(1) A novel multi-pose face recognition framework based on hypergraph de-deflection is proposed. The framework first isolates the pose-free deflection images, then utilizes the proposed feature coding method based on improved support vector data description to extract the features of the pose-free deflection images, and recognizes the extracted features.

(2) A new feature encoding method based on improved support vector data description is proposed. The feature encoding method utilizes the improved support vector data description and triangle encoding to make the extracted features more discriminative.

(3) An effective feature extraction and feature classification optimization model is constructed, which makes it easy to obtain a solution closer to the global optimum and helps to improve the recognition performance of the algorithm.

The subsequent sections of this article are arranged as follows: Section 2 introduces related studies. Section 3 describes the proposed method. Section 4 outlines the details of the experiments, and Section 5 presents the conclusion.

2. Relate Studies

This section will introduce some theories related to the proposed method. Specifically, few-shot face recognition, non-negative matrix factorization, and hypergraph theory will be introduced in turn.

2.1. Few-Shot Face Recognition

Few-shot face recognition has always been an interesting yet difficult research topic. Few-shot learning provides an effective solution to the very relevant and unavoidable problem of data scarcity in many applications. Prior knowledge is applied to small datasets so that few-shot learning can be generalized to new tasks and samples [32].

Researchers have proposed many methods to solve the problem of few-shot face recognition by using few-shot learning [33–35]. Masi et al. [36] propose the pose-aware model (PAM). PAM uses multiple networks to synthesize various pose images and uses the synthesized pose images to train the model to improve its recognition ability. However, this method needs a large amount of memory to store a large number of training images when using a variety of networks to generate a large number of images of various poses, so it is difficult to carry out during the actual process. Elharrouss et al. [37] propose the cascade networks (abbreviated as MCN) corresponding to multiple tasks to enhance the recognition ability of the recognition network for images involving pose variations. However, the diversity of attitude changes considered by this method is limited during model training, so the learned model is invalid when processing images involving other pose changes. Liu et al. [38] use multiple profile images to generate frontal images and use the Siamese network to learn the depth representation of the generated frontal images. The depth representation of the images is more easily recognized by the classifier, which helps to improve the recognition rate of the algorithm. Tao et al. [39] use the identity information of the images and the latent relationship between the frontal and profile images to model the distribution of the profile images and reduce the difference between the profile images and the frontal images. However, it is difficult to judge whether the underlying relationship between the frontal and profile images used is correct and comprehensive. Gao et al. [40] propose a multilayer locality-constrained structural orthogonal Procrustes regression (MLCSOPR) and use MLCSOPR to extract pose-robust features. This method only considers the horizontal change in the posture, but in practice, the image involves both the horizontal and vertical changes of the posture, so the application scope of this method is very narrow.

2.2. Non-Negative Matrix Factorization

Given any non-negative matrix X_0, it can be decomposed into two non-negative matrices $\overset{\leftrightarrow}{Y}$ and P^T.

$$\begin{cases} \min\limits_{\overset{\leftrightarrow}{Y},P^T} \|X_0 - \overset{\leftrightarrow}{Y}P^T\|_F^2 \\ s.t. \overset{\leftrightarrow}{Y} \geq 0, P \geq 0 \end{cases} \tag{1}$$

where $X_0 \in \Re^{m\times n}$ is the non-negative matrix, $\overset{\leftrightarrow}{Y} \in \Re^{m\times r}$ is the basis matrix, $P^T \in \Re^{r\times n}$ is the submatrix.

Then, $\overleftrightarrow{Y}$ and P^T can be updated by

$$\begin{cases} \overleftrightarrow{Y}_{ij} \leftarrow \overleftrightarrow{Y}_{ij} \frac{(XP)_{ij}}{(\overleftrightarrow{Y} P^T P)_{ij}} \\ (P^T)_{jk} \leftarrow (P^T)_{jk} \frac{(\overleftrightarrow{Y}^T X)_{jk}}{(\overleftrightarrow{Y}^T \overleftrightarrow{Y} P^T)_{jk}} \end{cases} \quad (2)$$

2.3. Hypergraph Theory

A hypergraph is very helpful for maintaining the internal structure of the data. Next, we will briefly introduce the hypergraph theory.

Hypergraph is defined as follows: Hypergraph G is an ordered binary group $G = (V, e)$, where V is a non-empty set with nodes or vertices as elements, which is called vertex set; e is a cluster of non-empty subsets whose elements are called hyperedges. Unlike ordinary graphs, each edge of the hypergraph can connect not only two vertices but also more vertices. Here, the hypergraph is undirected.

Given a hypergraph $G = (V, e)$, $V = \{v_1, v_2, \cdots, v_k\}$ is a set of finite data points, $v_i (i = 1, 2, \cdots, k)$ is a vertex. $e = \{e_1, e_2, \cdots, e_t\}$ is the set of hyperedges, e_j is a hyperedge.

The hyperedge set e satisfies the following two conditions:

(a) $e_j \notin \phi, j = 1, 2, \cdots, t$;

(b) $e_1 \cup e_2 \cup e_3 \cdots \cup e_t = V$;

Each hyperedge e_j has a corresponding weight w_j. Vertices hyperedges will form an association matrix $H \in \Re^{|V| \times |e|}$, any element in H can be calculated by Equation (3):

$$H_{ij} = \begin{cases} 1, v_i \in e_j \\ 0, v_i \notin e_j \end{cases} \quad (3)$$

To better understand the hypergraph theory, we take the hypergraph in Figure 2 as an example to illustrate the knowledge of the hypergraph. In Figure 2, the set of all vertices is denoted as $V = \{v_1, v_2, \cdots, v_8\}$, $e_1 = \{v_1, v_2, v_3\}$, $e_2 = \{v_4, v_5, v_6\}$ and $e_3 = \{v_7, v_8\}$ denote the three hyperedges of G. The set of all hyperedges is denoted as $e = \{e_1, e_2, e_3\}$. The value of each element in H can be obtained according to Equation (3) and shown in Figure 2. Each image serves as a data point and becomes a vertex in the hypergraph. Hyperedges are composed of several similar data points. Similar data points indicate images in which the contents of the images appear to be relatively close, such as two images of the same person with small differences in attitude.

The degree d_i of each vertex in the hypergraph is defined as the sum of the weights of the hyperedges to which it belongs, and the degree ρ_i of the hyperedges is defined as the number of nodes to which the hyperedge belongs. d_i and ρ_i are calculated as follows:

$$\begin{cases} d_i = \sum_{j=1}^{t} w_j H_{ij} \\ \rho_i = \sum_{i=1}^{k} H_{ij} \end{cases} \quad (4)$$

Let D_v denotes a diagonal matrix, whose main diagonal elements are $D_{v_{ii}} = d_i$, where $i = 1, 2, \cdots, k$. Similarly, let D_e and W be the diagonal matrices generated by ρ_j and w_j, respectively, where $j = 1, 2, \cdots, t$. Then, the non-regularized hypergraph Laplacian matrix can be calculated by Equation (5).

$$L^H = D_v - HWD_e^{-1}H \quad (5)$$

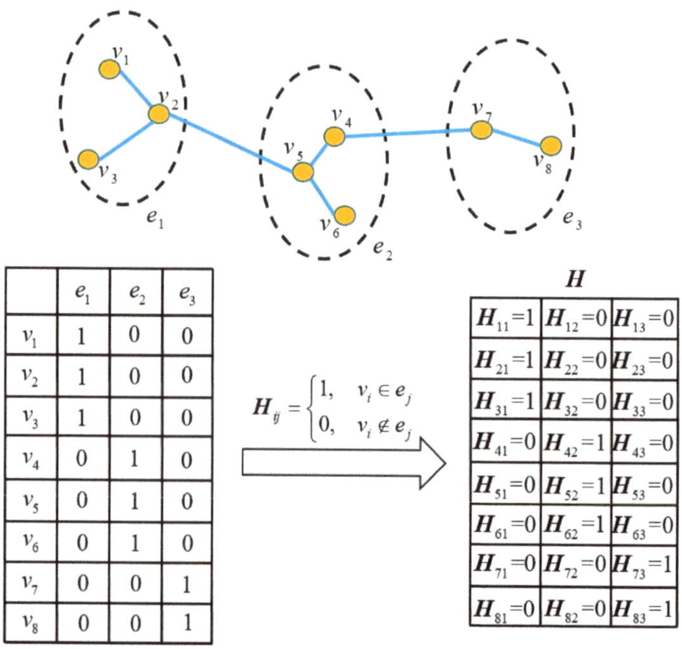

Figure 2. Examples of the hypergraph G. v_i is the vertex, $i = 1, 2, \cdots, 8$. e_j is the hyperedge, $j = 1, 2, 3$. $\boldsymbol{H}$ is the association matrix, $\boldsymbol{H}_{ij}$ is the element in row i and column j in $\boldsymbol{H}$.

3. Proposed Method

In this section, we introduce the proposed method (the few-shot, multi-pose face recognition method based on hypergraph de-deflection and multi-task collaborative optimization). The main idea of the proposed method is as follows. First, we propose a feature discrimination enhancement method based on non-negative matrix factorization and hypergraph embedding and use it to extract near-frontal images from pose-deflected images. After that, we propose a feature encoding method based on improved support vector data description and use it to extract the distinguishing features. Meanwhile, those distinguishing features are classified by the dictionary learning-based classifier. When performing feature extraction and feature classification, these two processes are jointly optimized. Hence, we mainly introduce the feature discrimination enhancement method based on non-negative matrix factorization and hypergraph embedding, feature encoding method, dictionary learning-based classifier, joint optimization of the feature extraction, and feature classification.

3.1. Feature Discrimination Enhancement Method Based on Non-Negative Matrix Factorization and Hypergraph Embedding

Suppose a given dataset is denoted as $\boldsymbol{Y} \in \Re^{m \times n}$, and each column in $\boldsymbol{Y}$ represents an image sample. First, we apply a Gaussian filter to each image in $\boldsymbol{Y}$ to remove the noise in the image. Next, we check whether the pixel value of each image is negative, change the negative value to 0 for the negative values, and keep the original value for the positive values, then obtain $\boldsymbol{Y}^W$. After that, we construct the deregularized hypergraph Laplacian matrix $\boldsymbol{L}^H$ of $\boldsymbol{Y}^W$. Assume that the number of hyperedges is t, the number of data in the hypergraph is N and t is equal to N. The number of vertices contained in each hyperedge is s. The vertices contained in each hyperedge are generated by $\boldsymbol{Y}_n^W$ itself and its nearest $s - 1$

neighbors, where Y_n^W is the nth column of Y^W. L^H is calculated according to Equation (5), where w_j can be calculated by Equation (6).

$$w_j = \sum_{Y_{n_1}^W, Y_{n_2}^W \in e_j} \exp\left(-\frac{\|Y_{n_1}^W - Y_{n_2}^W\|}{\delta^2}\right) \tag{6}$$

where $\delta = \frac{1}{s \times t} \sum_{j=1}^{t} \sum_{Y_{n_1}^W, Y_{n_2}^W \in e_j} \|Y_{n_1}^W - Y_{n_2}^W\|$.

After Y^W and L^H are obtained, the objective function is as follows.

$$\begin{cases} \min \|Y^W - \overleftrightarrow{Y} P^T\|_F^2 + \lambda Tr(P^T L^H P) \\ s.t. \overleftrightarrow{Y} \geq 0, P \geq 0 \end{cases} \tag{7}$$

where $Y^W \in \Re^{m \times n}$, $\overleftrightarrow{Y} \in \Re^{m \times n}$, $P \in \Re^{n \times n}$, $L^H \in \Re^{n \times n}$, $\|Y^W - \overleftrightarrow{Y} P^T\|_F^2$ represents the error resulting from the non-negative decomposition of Y^W. $Tr(P^T L^H P)$ is the hypergraph regular term, which can protect the local geometric structure of the data and improve the performance of the algorithm. The value of λ is set to 0.3.

It is difficult to solve Equation (7) directly, so an iterative solution method is adopted to solve this problem. The Lagrangian function corresponding to Equation (8) is:

$$\Delta = \|Y^W - \overleftrightarrow{Y} P^T\|_F^2 + \lambda Tr(P^T L^H P) + Tr(\Psi \overleftrightarrow{Y}^T) + Tr(\Phi P^T) \tag{8}$$

where Ψ is the matrix formed by the Lagrange multipliers of Ψ_{mk} for $\overleftrightarrow{Y}_{mk} \geq 0$, Φ is the matrix formed by the Lagrange multipliers of Φ_{nk} for $P_{mk} \geq 0$.

Δ in Equation (8) can be rewritten as

$$\begin{aligned} \Delta &= Tr(Y^{W^T} Y^W) - Tr(Y^{W^T} \overleftrightarrow{Y} P^T) - Tr(P \overleftrightarrow{Y}^T Y^W) \\ &+ Tr(P \overleftrightarrow{Y}^T \overleftrightarrow{Y} P^T) + \lambda Tr(P^T L^H P) + Tr(\Psi \overleftrightarrow{Y}^T) + Tr(\Phi P^T) \\ &= Tr(Y^{W^T} Y^W) - 2Tr(P \overleftrightarrow{Y}^T Y^W) + Tr(P \overleftrightarrow{Y}^T \overleftrightarrow{Y} P^T) \\ &+ \lambda Tr(P^T L^H P) + Tr(\Psi \overleftrightarrow{Y}^T) + Tr(\Phi P^T) \end{aligned} \tag{9}$$

By taking the partial derivatives of Δ with respect to $\overleftrightarrow{Y}$ and P, respectively, we obtain

$$\begin{cases} \frac{\partial \Delta}{\partial \overleftrightarrow{Y}} = -2Y^W P + 2\overleftrightarrow{Y} P^T P + \Psi \\ \frac{\partial \Delta}{\partial P} = -2Y^{W^T} \overleftrightarrow{Y} + 2P \overleftrightarrow{Y}^T \overleftrightarrow{Y} + 2\lambda L^H P + \Phi \end{cases} \tag{10}$$

According to the KKT conditions $\Psi_{mk} \overleftrightarrow{Y}_{mk} = 0$ and $\Phi_{nk} P_{nk} = 0$, we obtain

$$-(Y^W P)_{mk} \overleftrightarrow{Y}_{mk} + (\overleftrightarrow{Y} P^T P)_{mk} \overleftrightarrow{Y}_{mk} = 0 \tag{11}$$

$$-(Y^{W^T} \overleftrightarrow{Y})_{nk} P_{nk} + (P \overleftrightarrow{Y}^T \overleftrightarrow{Y})_{nk} P_{nk} + \lambda (L^H P)_{nk} P_{nk} = 0 \tag{12}$$

In Equations (11) and (12), the subscript of each variable indicates the number of iterations of the variable.

Then, $\overset{\leftrightarrow}{Y}_{mk}$ and P_{nk} can be updated by the following two equations.

$$\overset{\leftrightarrow}{Y}_{mk} \leftarrow \overset{\leftrightarrow}{Y}_{mk} \otimes \frac{(Y^W P)_{mk}}{(\overset{\leftrightarrow}{Y} P^T P)_{mk}} \tag{13}$$

$$P_{nk} \leftarrow P_{nk} \otimes \frac{(Y^{W^T} \overset{\leftrightarrow}{Y})_{nk} + (\lambda H W D_e^{-1} H P)_{nk}}{(P \overset{\leftrightarrow}{Y}^T \overset{\leftrightarrow}{Y})_{nk} + (\lambda D_v P)_{nk}} \tag{14}$$

The variables in Equations (13) and (14) have appeared before; please see the previous section for their definitions. The subscript of each variable indicates the number of iterations of the variable. $\otimes$ represents the element-wise multiplication of two matrices. The output $\overset{\leftrightarrow}{Y}$ is the image set with almost no attitude deflection. The features of each image with almost no attitude deflection can be obtained by using the proposed feature coding method, which has high-class discrimination.

Figure 3 shows the process of extracting near-frontal images from images involving pose variations. Y represents the original image set involving pose deflection, Y^W represents the image set after preprocessing Y, $\overset{\leftrightarrow}{Y}$ represents the image set of the approximate frontal image obtained by decomposition and iteration, P represents the pose change matrix. In Figure 3, we first preprocess each image in the original image set to obtain a non-negative image set without noise pollution. Then, the hypergraph is embedded into the non-negative matrix factorization to preserve the structure of the decomposed images. Finally, the image set with almost no deflection is obtained through matrix factorization and multiple iterative updates.

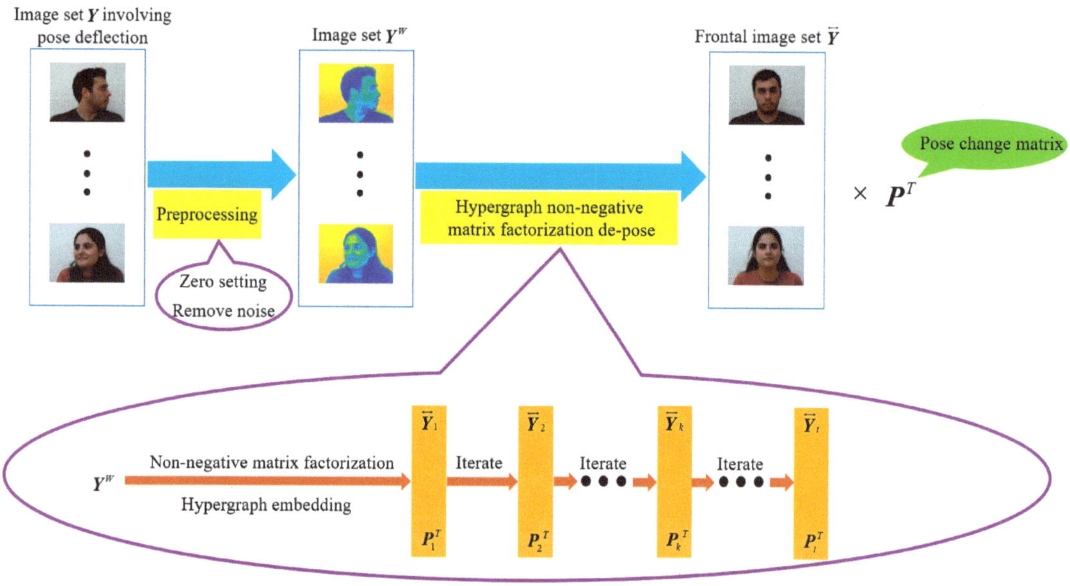

Figure 3. The process of extracting near-frontal images from images involving pose variations. Y is the original image set involving pose deflection, Y^W is the image set after preprocessing Y, $\overset{\leftrightarrow}{Y}$ is the image set of the approximate frontal image obtained by decomposition and iteration, P is pose change matrix, P^T is the transpose of P, $\overset{\leftrightarrow}{Y}_i$ is the value of $\overset{\leftrightarrow}{Y}$ at the i -th iteration, $P_i{}^T$ is the value of P^T at the i -th iteration.

3.2. Feature Coding Method Based on Improved Support Vector Data Description

The main idea of the proposed feature coding method based on improved support vector data description is as follows. First, we propose an improved support vector data description and use it to obtain the sphere center and radius of each cluster. After that, the radius and center of the ball corresponding to each cluster are used for feature encoding. The existing support vector data description considers that each data point plays the same role when calculating the radius of each cluster, which is not in line with reality. Hence, we assign a learned weight to each data in the model learning and propose an improved support vector data description; its model is as follows.

$$\begin{cases} \min\limits_{r,\chi} r^2 + \varsigma \sum\limits_{i=1}^{num} \rho(\boldsymbol{y}_i)\chi_i \\ s.t. \|\boldsymbol{y}_i - b\|^2 \le r^2 + \chi_i, \chi_i \ge 0, b = \frac{1}{num}\sum\limits_{i=1}^{num} \boldsymbol{y}_i \end{cases} \tag{15}$$

where r is the radius of the ball, $\boldsymbol{y}_i$ is the ith sample, $\rho(\boldsymbol{y}_i)$ is the weight of $\boldsymbol{y}_i$, b is the center of the ball, num is the number of the samples, χ_i is the slack variable. ς is a parameter whose value is set to 0.4.

The weight of any sample is calculated as follows.

First, we divide the whole data set into C clusters, and assume that the sample set of the kth cluster is denoted as $\left\{y_1^k, y_2^k, \cdots, y_{P_k}^k\right\}$, where y_i^k is the ith data point in $\left\{y_1^k, y_2^k, \cdots, y_{P_k}^k\right\}, i = 1, 2, \cdots, P_k$. P_k is the number of data points in $\left\{y_1^k, y_2^k, \cdots, y_{P_k}^k\right\}$, and $y_i^k = [v_1^{ki}, v_2^{ki}, \cdots, v_d^{ki}]^T \in \Re^{d\times 1}$.

Denote the average distance between two data points in $\left\{y_1^k, y_2^k, \cdots, y_{P_k}^k\right\}$ as m_k.

If the number of data points contained in $\left\{y_1^k, y_2^k, \cdots, y_{P_k}^k\right\}$ is greater than one, then

$$m_k = \frac{2}{p_k(p_k-1)} \sum_{i=1}^{p_k} \sum_{j=i+1}^{p_k} d(y_i^k, y_j^k) \tag{16}$$

$$d(y_i^k, y_j^k) = \sqrt{\left(v_1^{ki} - v_1^{kj}\right)^2 + \left(v_2^{ki} - v_2^{kj}\right)^2 + \cdots + \left(v_d^{ki} - v_d^{kj}\right)^2} \tag{17}$$

If the number of data points contained in $\left\{y_1^k, y_2^k, \cdots, y_{P_k}^k\right\}$ is equal to one, then

$$m_k = \frac{1}{\sum\limits_{i=1, i\neq k}^{C} p_k} \sum_{t=1, t\neq k}^{C} \sum_{i=1}^{P_t} d(y_1^k, y_i^t) \tag{18}$$

Generally speaking, the distances between data points in the same cluster are far less than the distances between data points in different clusters. Thus, we assume that data points in the same cluster have the same weight.

$$\rho_k = 1 - \frac{m_k}{\sum\limits_{i=1}^{C} m_i} \tag{19}$$

The Lagrange function of Equation (15) can be written as

$$\begin{aligned} \tilde{L}(r, \chi, \alpha, \beta) = r^2 + \varsigma \sum_{i=1}^{num} \rho(\boldsymbol{y}_i)\chi_i + \sum_{i=1}^{num} \alpha_i \\ \left\{ \left\|\boldsymbol{y}_i - \frac{1}{num}\sum_{j=1}^{num} \boldsymbol{y}_j\right\|^2 - r^2 - \chi_i \right\} - \sum_{i=1}^{num} \beta_i \chi_i \end{aligned} \tag{20}$$

Let $\frac{\partial \widetilde{L}}{\partial r} = 0$ and $\frac{\partial \widetilde{L}}{\partial \chi_i} = 0$, we can obtain

$$\begin{cases} \min\limits_{\boldsymbol{\alpha}} \frac{2}{num} \boldsymbol{\alpha} Q e - \boldsymbol{\alpha}^T \boldsymbol{\Omega} \\ s.t.\ \boldsymbol{\alpha}^T e = 1 \end{cases} \tag{21}$$

where $Q = (<\boldsymbol{y}_i, \boldsymbol{y}_j>)_{num \times num}$, $\boldsymbol{\Omega} = (<\boldsymbol{y}_i, \boldsymbol{y}_j>)_{num \times 1}$, $e = (1,1,1,\cdots,1)^T$, $\boldsymbol{y}_i$ and $\boldsymbol{y}_j$ are the ith sample and j^{th} sample in the dataset with attitude deflection removed, respectively, $\boldsymbol{\alpha} = [\alpha_1, \alpha_2, \cdots, \alpha_{num}]$. $\boldsymbol{\alpha}$ can be obtained by using the linear programming algorithm.

r can be obtained by using Equation (22).

$$r^2 = \boldsymbol{y}_i \cdot \boldsymbol{y}_j - 2 \sum_{i,j=1}^{\Upsilon} \alpha_i (\boldsymbol{y}_i \cdot \boldsymbol{y}_j) + \sum_{i,j=1}^{\Upsilon} \alpha_i \alpha_j (\boldsymbol{y}_i \cdot \boldsymbol{y}_j) \tag{22}$$

where Υ is the set of support vectors, the sample points used in Equation (22) are the support vectors. Whether the data point is a support vector, the following condition needs to be met: if the data point $\boldsymbol{y}_i$ is a support vector, its corresponding α_i is non-zero. $r = [r_1, r_2, \cdots, r_C]$, C is the number of clusters in the dataset.

Then, for each image with pose deflection removed, it is decomposed into $\widetilde{N}$ patches (each patch has the same size), and each patch is encoded. The schematic diagram of the image being divided into small pieces is shown in the Figure 4. For example, for an image q with attitude deflection removed, it is divided into $\widetilde{N}$ small patches. $\widetilde{N}$ is determined by our experience. For any small patch q^j, $j = 1,2,\cdots,\widetilde{N}$, it can be encoded as $U(q^j)$.

$$U(q^j) = \begin{bmatrix} U_1(q^j) & U_2(q^j) & \cdots & U_C(q^j) \end{bmatrix}^T \tag{23}$$

where $U_i(q^j) = \begin{bmatrix} U_{i,1}(q^j) & U_{i,2}(q^j) \end{bmatrix}$, $i = 1,2,\cdots,C$, $j = 1,2,\cdots,\widetilde{N}$, $U_{i,1}(q^j)$ and $U_{i,2}(q^j)$ are obtained by the triangle coding. $U_{i,1}(q^j) = \max\{0, d(s) - s_i(q^j)\}$, $s_i(q^j) = \|q^j - o_i\|_2$ represents the distance from q^j to o_i, $d(s)$ is the mean of all $s_i(q^j)$ values. $U_{i,2}(q^j) = \max\{0, A(m) - m_i(q^j)\}$, $m_i(q^j) = \frac{r_i}{\sum\limits_{k=1}^{C} r_k}$, $A(m)$ is the mean of all m_i values.

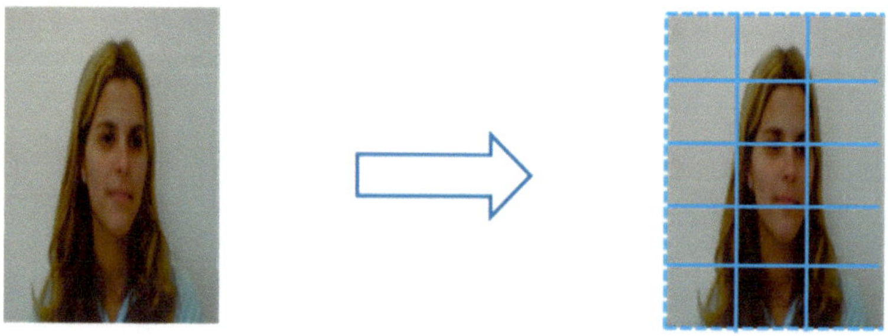

Figure 4. In the picture, each small grid represents a patch. The number of patches is chosen based on our experience.

Figure 5 shows the schematic diagram of the encoding. q^j represents the jth patch of the image q (The image q is divided into $\widetilde{N}$ patches). o_i denotes the center of the SVDD sphere formed by the jth cluster (multiple sample points are clustered into a cluster.), r_i.

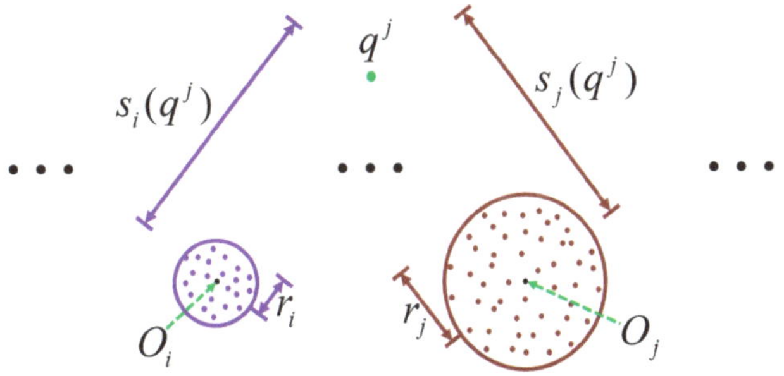

Figure 5. The schematic diagram of the encoding. o_i and o_j are the centers of the i -th and j -th SVDD balls, respectively. r_i and r_j are the radius of the i th and j th SVDD balls, respectively. $s_i(q^j)$ and $s_j(q^j)$ represent the distance from patch q^j to o_i and o_j, respectively. denotes the radius of the SVDD sphere formed by the ith cluster. $s_i(q^j)$ represents the distance between q^j and o_i. o_j denotes the center of the SVDD sphere formed by the jth cluster, r_j denotes the radius of the SVDD sphere formed by the jth cluster. $s_j(q^j)$ represents the distance between q^j and o_j. For the specific encoding of each patch, please refer to Equation (19).

Hence, the image q can be encoded as F_q, and the expression of F_q is as follows.

$$F_q = \begin{bmatrix} (U(q^1))^T & (U(q^2))^T & \cdots & (U(q^{\tilde{N}}))^T \end{bmatrix}^T \tag{24}$$

3.3. Dictionary Learning-Based Classifier

The de-deflection operations and feature encoding operations described above greatly reduce the influence of posture changes on face recognition. To further improve the recognition rate of the whole algorithm on this basis, we decided to learn the classifier, questioning which classifier can not only realize the learning function but also learn the characteristics related to the classified samples in the process of learning. Recent studies have shown that sparse representations have been successfully applied in many fields, such as image restoration and image classification. Dictionaries play an important role in sparse representation, and the quality of dictionaries greatly affects the performance of sparse representation. The latest research on dictionary learning shows that learning a desirable dictionary from the training data itself can usually yield good results for tasks on images or video [41]. Inspired by this, we are ready to learn the dictionary and use the learned dictionary to represent the test samples, and then determine the category of the test samples according to the representation residual.

The basic model of the dictionary learning-based classifier is as follows.

$$\begin{cases} \min\limits_{\boldsymbol{D},\boldsymbol{Z}} \|\boldsymbol{X} - \boldsymbol{D}\boldsymbol{Z}\|_F^2 + \eta\|\boldsymbol{Z}\|_1 \\ s.t. \|d_i\|_2^2 \le 1 \end{cases} \tag{25}$$

where $\boldsymbol{X}$ is the training samples, $\boldsymbol{D}$ represents the dictionary to be learned, $\boldsymbol{Z}$ is the representation coefficient, $\boldsymbol{d}_i$ represents the ith atom in $\boldsymbol{D}$. η is set to 0.3.

3.4. Joint Optimization of the Feature Extraction and Feature Classification

To obtain the globally optimal solution of HDMCO, we jointly optimized the feature extraction and feature classification.

The model for jointly optimizing the feature extraction and feature classification is as follows.

$$\begin{cases} \min\limits_{\boldsymbol{\alpha},\boldsymbol{D},\boldsymbol{Z}} \|\boldsymbol{X} - \boldsymbol{D}\boldsymbol{Z}\|_F^2 + \eta(\frac{2}{num}\boldsymbol{\alpha}^T\boldsymbol{Q}\boldsymbol{e} - \boldsymbol{\alpha}^T\boldsymbol{\Omega})\|\boldsymbol{Z}\|_1 \\ s.t. \boldsymbol{\alpha}^T\boldsymbol{e} = 1, \|\boldsymbol{d}_i\|_2^2 \le 1 \end{cases} \tag{26}$$

According to Equation (26), we can obtain $\boldsymbol{\alpha}$, $\boldsymbol{D}$ and $\boldsymbol{Z}$.

$\boldsymbol{\alpha}$ can be obtained by using Equation (27).

$$\begin{cases} \min\limits_{\boldsymbol{\alpha}} \eta(\frac{2}{num}\boldsymbol{\alpha}^T \boldsymbol{Q}\boldsymbol{e} - \boldsymbol{\alpha}^T \boldsymbol{\Omega})\|\boldsymbol{Z}\|_1 \\ s.t.\boldsymbol{\alpha}^T \boldsymbol{e} = 1 \end{cases} \tag{27}$$

Then, the value of $\boldsymbol{\alpha}$ can be obtained by using the linear programming algorithm.

$\boldsymbol{D}$ can be obtained by solving Equation (28).

$$\begin{cases} \min\limits_{\boldsymbol{D}} \|\boldsymbol{X} - \boldsymbol{D}\boldsymbol{Z}\|_F^2 \\ s.t.\|\boldsymbol{d}_i\|_2^2 \le 1 \end{cases} \tag{28}$$

Solving Equation (28) can be converted to solving Equation (29).

$$\begin{cases} \boldsymbol{D} = \underset{D}{\operatorname{argmin}} \|\boldsymbol{X} - \boldsymbol{D}\boldsymbol{Z}\|_F^2 + \vartheta\|\boldsymbol{D} - \boldsymbol{V} + \boldsymbol{J}\|_F^2 \\ \boldsymbol{V} = \underset{V}{\operatorname{argmin}} \vartheta\|\boldsymbol{D} - \boldsymbol{V} + \boldsymbol{J}\|_F^2, s.t.\|v^i\|_2^2 \le 1 \\ \boldsymbol{J} = \boldsymbol{J} + \boldsymbol{D} - \boldsymbol{V} \end{cases} \tag{29}$$

where ϑ is set to 0.2.

Then, $\boldsymbol{D}$ can be obtained by iteratively solving the variables in Equation (29).

$\boldsymbol{Z}$ can be obtained by solving Equation (30).

$$\min_{Z} \|\boldsymbol{X} - \boldsymbol{D}\boldsymbol{Z}\|_F^2 + \eta(\frac{2}{num}\boldsymbol{\alpha}^T \boldsymbol{Q}\boldsymbol{e} - \boldsymbol{\alpha}^T \boldsymbol{\Omega})\|\boldsymbol{Z}\|_1 \tag{30}$$

The solution to Equation (30) is as follows.

$$\boldsymbol{Z} = \operatorname{shrink}(\boldsymbol{D}^{-1}\boldsymbol{X}, \frac{\eta(\frac{2}{num}\boldsymbol{\alpha}^T \boldsymbol{Q}\boldsymbol{e} - \boldsymbol{\alpha}^T \boldsymbol{\Omega})}{2}) \tag{31}$$

where $\operatorname{shrink}(x, a) = \operatorname{signmax}(|x| - a, 0)$.

Figure 6 shows the schematic diagram of seeking a globally optimal solution.

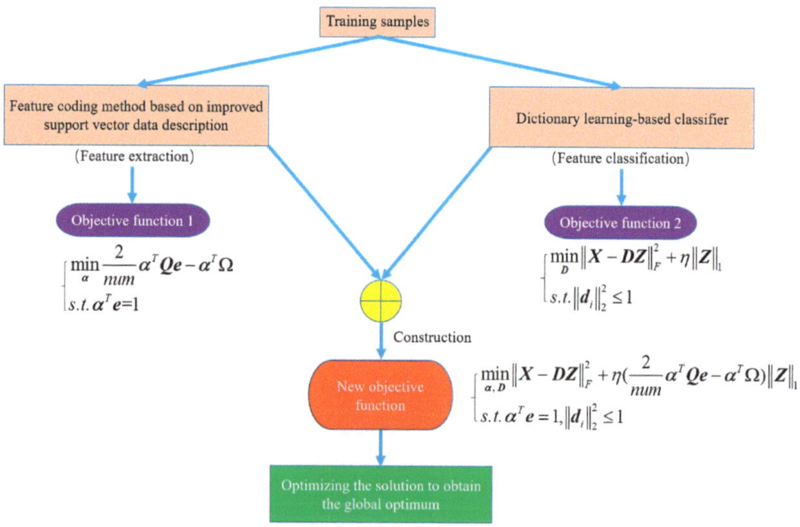

Figure 6. The schematic diagram of seeking a globally optimal solution.

4. Experiments

4.1. Dataset

Here, Multi-PIE [42], MegaFace [43], CAS-PEAL [44], YTF [45], CPLFW [46], and CVL [47] are used in experiments to verify the performance of HDMCO.

Multi-PIE mainly involves pose variations and illumination variations, and includes a total of more than 750,000 images of 337 different people. Figure 7a shows some samples of multi-PIE.

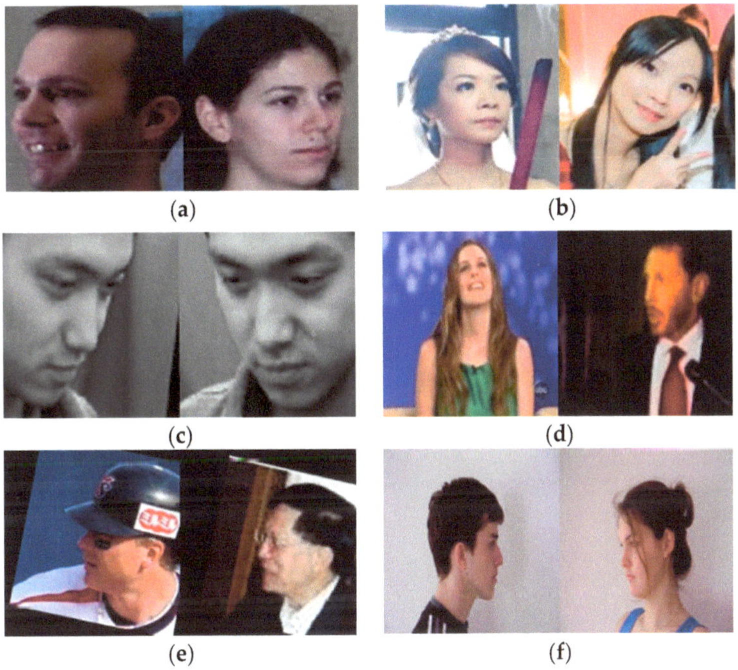

Figure 7. Example images from different datasets. (**a**) Multi-PIE (**b**) MegaFace (**c**) CAS-PEAL (**d**) YTF (**e**) CPLFW (**f**) CVL.

MegaFace is a challenging, large-scale face dataset. It contains the gallery set and the probe set. The gallery set contains more than 1 million face images, while the probe set contains 106,863 face images of 530 celebrities. Figure 7b shows some samples of MegaFace.

CAS-PEAL includes 99,450 images of 1040 different people, which mainly involve pose variations, expression variations, and lighting variations. Figure 7c shows some samples of CAS-PEAL.

YTF contains 3425 videos of 1595 subjects with diverse ethnicities. Figure 6d shows some samples of YTF.

CPLFW includes 11,652 images of 5749 different people, which mainly involves pose variations. Figure 7e shows some samples of CPLFW.

CVL contains 798 images of 114 different people, which mainly involves pose variations. Figure 7f shows some samples of CVL.

4.2. Experimental Results and Analysis

4.2.1. Comparison with State-of-the-Art Methods

Experimental Setup

Resnet [48], Duan's method [49], PGM-Face [29], PCCycleGAN [14], LDMR [20], MH-DNCCM [21], DRA-Net [16], TGLBP [35], MCN [37], 3D-PIM [50] WFH [17], mCNN [51],

HADL [31], RVFace [52], DTDD [53], ArcFace [54], VGG [55], and DeepID [56] are used as the comparison methods.

For multi-PIE, we choose images with pose deflection angles of -45°, -30°, -15°, 0°, 15°, 30°, 45° for experiments. In other words, a total of 2359 images of 337 subjects were used for the experiments. For images of each subject, we randomly selected three images for training and the remaining images for testing. It means that the number of training images accounted for 42.85% of the total number of images, and the number of testing images accounted for 57.15% of the total number of images.

For MegaFace, we selected the samples of categories with the number of images greater than or equal to two for experiments. For each class of samples used for experiments, we randomly selected one image for training and one image for testing. Namely, the number of training images accounted for 50% of the total number of images, and the number of testing images accounted for 50% of the total number of images.

For CAS-PEAL, we choose those images involving 800 subjects in three different poses (0°, -45° and 45°) for experiments. That is to say, each subject contains three images deflected at different angles. The image with a deflection angle of 0 degrees in each subject is used for training and the rest are used for testing. Specifically, the number of training images accounted for 33.33% of the total number of images and the number of testing images accounted for 66.67% of the total number of images.

For YTF, we selected 226 subjects with four or more videos available. Then, we selected 225 subjects from 226 subjects for experiments and divided the 225 subjects into five groups, each group involving 45 subjects. For each group, the first three videos of each subject as gallery sets and the remaining videos for testing. The results obtained from the five groups of experiments are averaged as the final experimental result. The number of training samples accounted for 43.29% of the total number of images, and the number of testing samples accounted for 56.71% of the total number of images.

For CPLFW, we selected the samples of 2000 classes to form a subset. For samples belonging to a certain class (each class) in this subset, we randomly selected one image as the training sample and one image as the test sample. Precisely, the number of training images accounted for 50% of the total number of images, and the number of testing images accounted for 50% of the total number of images.

For CVL, we choose three images in each class for training and the rest for testing. That is to say, the number of training images accounted for 42.85% of the total number of images, and the number of testing images accounted for 57.15% of the total number of images.

The images used in the experiments are cropped to 60×80.

Experimental Result

The Accuracies of different methods on different datasets are shown in Table 1. It can be seen from the experimental results on multi-PIE that ArcFace has the highest recognition rate, reaching 95.89%. This may be because the proportion of images involving large pose changes is relatively small, resulting in the difference between most training images and test images not being too large, and ArcFace can achieve good recognition results. Furthermore, almost all methods have achieved good results. The reason for this result is as follows. The Multi-PIE dataset involves relatively few images with large pose deflection. For example, the number of images with an attitude deflection of 45 degrees only accounts for two-sevenths of the total dataset, which means most of the images used for training have little difference from the test images. Then, the trained model can better identify the test samples.

Table 1. Accuracies (%) of Different Methods on Different Datasets.

Methods\Datasets	Multi-PIE [40]	MegaFace [41]	CAS-PEAL [42]	YTF [43]	CPLFW [44]	CVL [45]
Reset [48]	91.06	87.77	90.77	76.05	82.36	89.56
Duan [49]	87.68	82.55	89.37	73.88	81.06	85.17
PGM-Face [29]	90.23	85.33	90.01	73.20	78.58	88.06
PCCycleGAN [14]	88.99	85.01	88.85	75.16	80.66	87.38
LDMR [20]	91.33	86.23	92.29	77.22	85.06	90.23
MH-DNCCM [21]	91.78	85.89	90.46	76.11	82.50	87.98
DRA-Net [16]	93.06	83.99	93.16	76.47	82.97	90.01
TGLBP [35]	89.06	86.13	90.67	75.60	83.71	86.97
MCN [37]	92.01	86.24	91.37	77.05	85.20	88.31
3D-PIM [50]	93.02	86.31	91.79	78.05	85.07	89.22
WFH [17]	91.55	86.01	92.70	74.88	84.01	87.34
mCNN [51]	88.68	85.17	87.58	72.89	80.59	81.38
HADL [31]	90.82	85.35	90.47	75.95	84.35	86.40
RVFace [52]	92.10	88.03	93.17	78.05	85.97	90.03
DTDD [53]	90.39	88.37	93.55	77.35	86.23	88.80
ArcFace [54]	95.89	91.37	92.13	83.40	84.88	87.23
VGG [55]	95.14	89.29	90.92	81.05	83.06	85.71
DeepID [56]	93.88	87.58	88.15	78.45	83.46	85.12
HDMCO [ours]	95.19	90.67	95.88	80.34	88.41	92.19

For the experimental results on MegaFace, almost all methods based on deep learning achieved good results. The possible reasons are as follows: although the number of samples used for training in each category is not large, the difference between the large number of samples used for pre-training and the test samples is not too large. Thus, the final learned model has better classification ability for the test samples. Among all the methods, Duan's method has the worst performance, which may be because the performance of the method depends on finding the parts related to the pose. However, it cannot completely and correctly determine which parts of the image are related to the pose. Furthermore, this method mainly solves face recognition involving pose changes, while the MegaFace dataset involves not only pose changes but also other changes, so the recognition rate of this method on MegaFace is not very high.

The experimental results on YTF show that the recognition rate of all algorithms does not exceed 85%. This is because YTF datasets involve large changes (e.g., large pose changes, large expression changes), so their performance is not very good. Specifically, for methods based on deep learning, the pre-trained model is not suitable for the classification of test images. This is because a large number of samples used for pre-training are quite different from the images in the used dataset. For HADL, because the samples used for training may be quite different from the samples used for testing, the learned dictionary cannot accurately represent the test samples, which means that the algorithm cannot obtain a higher recognition rate. For Duan's method, because the samples used for training may be quite different from the samples used for testing, the learned characteristics of a certain category are quite different from those of the same category of images in the test set. Then, the recognition rate of the algorithm on the YTF dataset is not very high.

The experimental results on CPLFW show that the recognition rate of our method is higher than that of other algorithms. This may be because our proposed non-negative matrix factorization based on hypergraph embedding extracts the frontal images with better quality. In other words, we use hypergraph and non-negative matrix factorization to separate the frontal image from the profile image. The extracted pose-free features are then used to learn the dictionaries with strong performance, and the learned dictionaries are used to accurately represent the test samples, thereby greatly improving the recognition rate of the algorithm. The reasons why the recognition rate of the deep learning-based

Method is not as high as that of our method are as follows. A large number of samples used for pre-training are too different from the samples in the test set. For example, many samples used for pre-training are images with small attitude deflection, while many test samples are images with large attitude deflection. Then, the rules summarized for each category through training are not suitable for the rules of the same category of images in the test set.

The experimental results on CVL show that the recognition rate of our method is 92%, which is higher than that of other methods. The reasons for this result are as follows: the hypergraph is embedded in the non-negative matrix factorization so that the resulting images retain the intrinsic properties of the original images. Furthermore, triangular encoding is used to encode the obtained pose-free images, which makes the extracted features highly unique. Furthermore, we use the encoded features to train the dictionary, so that the learned dictionary has a stronger representation ability. Then, the test samples can be accurately represented by the dictionaries, thereby achieving the purpose of improving the recognition rate. The performance of deep learning-based methods is not the best among all methods, and the reasons for this result are as follows. The rules summarized for each category through pre-training are quite different from the rules of the same category of images in the test set. Therefore, the model obtained by training is not suitable for the classification of the test images, or the model obtained by training cannot correctly classify many test images. For HADL and LDMR, it is difficult for them to extract the pose-invariant features of the images when dealing with images with large pose changes, which makes it difficult for subsequent classifiers to correctly identify samples.

Tables 2 and 3 show the recall and precision of different methods on different datasets. The experimental results obtained are generally consistent with those in Table 1; HDMCO has the best effect.

Table 2. Recall (%) of Different Methods on Different Datasets.

Methods\Datasets	**Multi-PIE [40]**	**MegaFace [41]**	**CAS-PEAL [42]**	**YTF [43]**	**CPLFW [44]**	**CVL [45]**
Reset [48]	78.35	70.68	76.18	82.67	76.83	81.33
Duan [49]	76.02	65.43	72.67	77.61	73.25	78.69
PGM-Face [29]	79.66	73.14	75.68	75.60	77.25	80.39
PCCycleGAN [14]	81.64	72.95	77.62	73.08	76.89	76.28
LDMR [20]	83.58	76.89	72.99	75.03	75.88	79.01
MH-DNCCM [21]	82.05	73.91	70.03	73.26	74.19	80.06
DRA-Net [16]	85.11	80.34	77.68	79.32	80.64	81.39
TGLBP [35]	80.24	78.92	78.33	75.17	78.38	79.68
MCN [37]	83.67	80.20	81.08	77.68	80.34	78.18
3D-PIM [50]	85.02	81.35	81.69	79.67	77.58	76.64
WFH [17]	82.67	78.54	76.44	77.39	79.14	75.89
mCNN [51]	80.33	78.67	79.58	78.99	80.01	78.66
HADL [31]	78.89	80.59	79.44	79.88	78.46	80.62

Table 2. *Cont.*

Methods\Datasets	Multi-PIE [40]	MegaFace [41]	CAS-PEAL [42]	YTF [43]	CPLFW [44]	CVL [45]
RVFace [52]	82.24	80.30	77.89	79.01	81.33	80.23
DTDD [53]	80.95	80.68	79.25	79.31	80.64	82.07
ArcFace [54]	82.53	85.01	82.34	80.09	81.69	80.60
VGG [55]	79.28	81.02	78.08	75.89	79.88	79.47
DeepID [56]	81.08	82.16	79.66	81.06	81.06	78.30
HDMCO [ours]	88.37	85.67	86.17	85.60	88.32	88.97

Table 3. Precision (%) of Different Methods on Different Datasets.

Methods\Datasets	Multi-PIE [40]	MegaFace [41]	CAS-PEAL [42]	YTF [43]	CPLFW [44]	CVL [45]
Reset [48]	89.26	86.08	86.92	78.34	80.16	86.57
Duan [49]	85.06	80.38	88.15	75.06	79.68	86.23
PGM-Face [29]	89.32	86.42	88.95	75.01	77.19	86.27
PCCycleGAN [14]	86.27	85.39	86.19	77.12	79.18	85.61
LDMR [20]	88.97	85.09	90.87	75.80	83.97	87.18
MH-DNCCM [21]	88.39	82.17	88.69	78.02	80.05	85.10
DRA-Net [16]	90.86	82.34	92.05	75.24	80.34	87.19
TGLBP [35]	86.95	85.06	91.21	75.32	81.99	85.43
MCN [37]	90.67	83.97	89.68	76.38	83.97	87.32
3D-PIM [50]	90.98	85.11	90.08	75.86	83.46	87.68
WFH [17]	89.30	83.67	90.79	74.02	83.97	86.22
mCNN [51]	86.91	85.06	86.10	70.66	79.30	79.66
HADL [31]	88.69	84.39	88.67	76.08	83.97	85.88
RVFace [52]	90.68	86.92	91.86	78.68	85.02	88.60
DTDD [53]	88.67	87.08	92.43	76.18	85.15	87.67
ArcFace [54]	93.91	90.28	90.88	82.91	82.69	86.41
VGG [55]	95.86	88.06	88.67	79.38	81.67	85.02
DeepID [56]	93.05	86.14	85.97	77.68	81.97	84.67
HDMCO [ours]	96.08	91.35	94.86	81.57	88.05	92.30

4.2.2. Cross-Validation Experiment

In order to further verify the performance of HDMCO, cross-validation experiments are carried out in this section. For each data set, we selected the face image with an attitude deflection angle greater than 45°, and 5-fold cross-validation was performed. Specifically, the data set was divided into five parts, four of which were taken as training data and one as test data in turn, and the experiment was carried out. Each trial obtained the corresponding recognition rate. The average recognition rate of the results of five times was used as the estimation of the algorithm accuracy.

As can be seen from Table 4, the average recognition rate of many algorithms on the multi-PIE data set and CAS-PEAL data set is more than 80%. At the same time, it can also be seen that the recognition rate of the proposed HDMCO is higher than that of other algorithms.

Table 4. The Results (%) of Cross-validation.

Methods\Datasets	Multi-PIE [40]	MegaFace [41]	CAS-PEAL [42]	YTF [43]	CPLFW [44]	CVL [45]
Reset [48]	81.32	78.92	81.24	68.05	73.68	80.92
Duan [49]	80.68	75.60	80.38	63.58	71.99	78.96
PGM-Face [29]	77.68	79.31	77.59	72.38	68.56	77.90
PCCycleGAN [14]	76.82	75.66	74.97	68.33	69.98	78.62
LDMR [20]	80.38	83.29	80.64	73.20	76.82	80.93
MH-DNCCM [21]	81.60	81.32	83.67	64.51	71.93	79.71
DRA-Net [16]	83.64	83.16	81.46	66.49	74.69	80.97
TGLBP [35]	80.32	80.97	76.91	64.98	72.64	77.62
MCN [37]	80.06	79.86	80.46	71.61	71.62	78.59
3D-PIM [50]	81.30	80.61	78.67	70.38	73.92	78.61
WFH [17]	81.69	80.67	81.33	63.89	73.68	79.68
mCNN [51]	79.37	75.31	76.82	63.99	71.68	70.29
HADL [31]	80.34	73.97	80.34	73.61	73.61	77.85
RVFace [52]	77.31	76.89	83.89	75.06	75.38	79.33
DTDD [53]	78.39	80.67	82.58	73.68	78.99	78.99
ArcFace [54]	82.67	78.59	81.37	77.31	74.63	77.97
VGG [55]	80.69	77.98	80.59	73.68	73.91	76.89
DeepID [56]	83.99	77.86	78.61	71.68	77.35	77.95
HDMCO [ours]	89.30	85.07	85.99	78.95	83.93	83.97

4.2.3. The Effect of Feature Dimension on the Recognition Performance of the Algorithms

To illustrate the effect of feature dimension on the recognition rate of our method, we conducted experiments. DDTD, HADL, and PCCycleGAN are used as comparison methods. The experimental conditions are the same as the experimental conditions in Section 4.2.1. The only difference is that the dimension of the features ranges from 100 to 600. Figure 8 shows the effect of feature dimension on the recognition rate of different methods. It can be seen from Figure 8 that the recognition rates of all methods first gradually increase with the feature dimension and then remain unchanged. Furthermore, the recognition performance of our method is better than other methods.

4.2.4. The Display of the Extracted Frontal Images

To illustrate that our method can effectively separate pose-free images from pose-deflected images, we show the obtained separated images. In Figure 9, the left half of each subfigure shows the original image, and the right half shows the pose-free deflection image separated from the original image. As can be seen from Figure 9, the separated images are close to the frontal image. This shows that the proposed feature discrimination enhancement method based on non-negative matrix factorization and hypergraph embedding can indeed achieve the de-pose function.

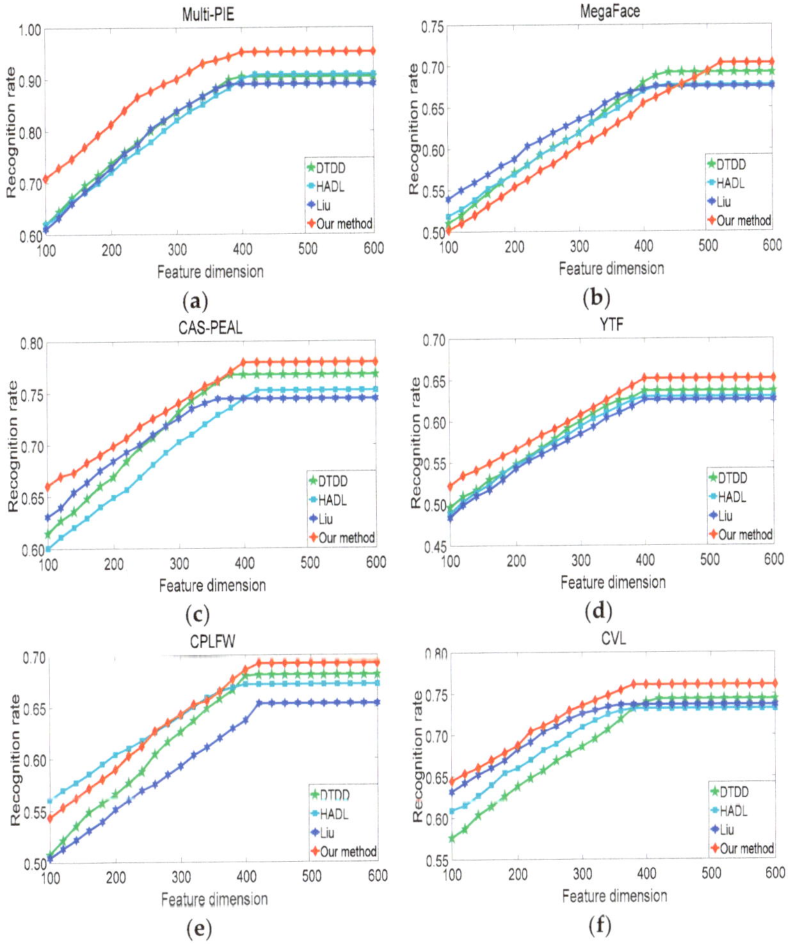

Figure 8. The effect of feature dimension on the recognition rate of different methods. (**a**) Multi-PIE (**b**) MegaFace (**c**) CAS-PEAL (**d**) YTF (**e**) CPLFW (**f**) CVL.

4.2.5. Ablation Experiment

To verify the role of each component in the proposed method, we performed ablation experiments. The main components of the method proposed in this paper are the "feature discrimination enhancement method based on non-negative matrix factorization and hypergraph embedding", the "feature coding method based on improved support vector data description", "dictionary learning-based classifier", and "joint optimization of the feature extraction and feature classification", which are abbreviated as de-deflection, feature coding, dictionary learning, and joint optimization.

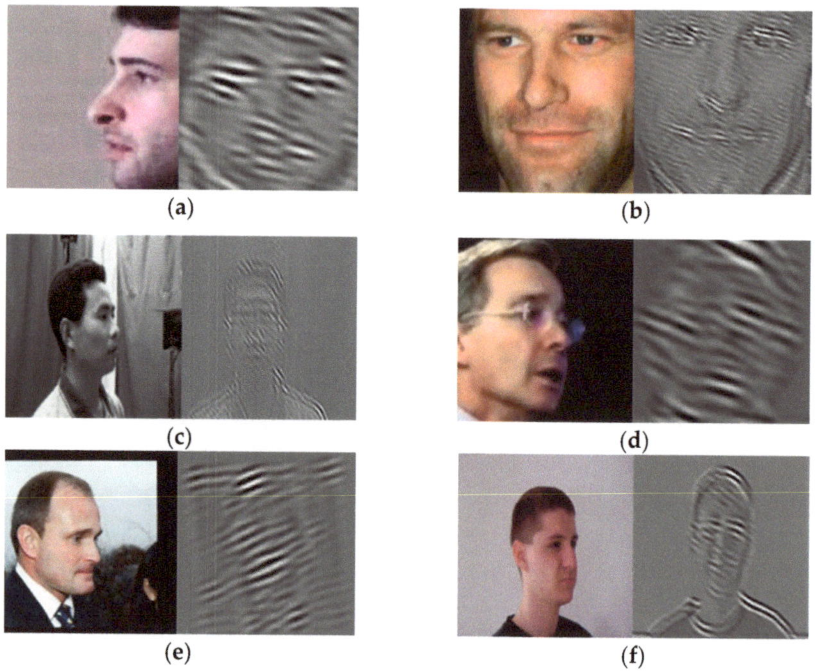

Figure 9. Images are separated by non-negative matrix factorization based on the hypergraph (a) Multi-PIE (b) MegaFace (c) CAS-PEAL (d) YTF (e) CPLFW (f) CVL.

Experimental Setup

The experimental conditions are the same as in Section 4.2.1.

Experimental Results

Figure 10 shows the results of ablation experiments. It can be seen from Figure 10a that using the de-deflection component can improve the recognition rate of the algorithm by about 2% on some datasets, and more on some datasets, such as 5% and 7%. As can be seen from Figure 10b, the use of feature encoding component improves the recognition rate of the algorithm by about 2% on almost all datasets. It can be seen from Figure 10c that the use of the dictionary learning component improves the recognition rate of the algorithm by about 1% on some datasets and by about 2% on others. It can be seen from Figure 10d that using the joint optimization component improves the recognition rate of the algorithm by about 3% on almost all datasets.

4.2.6. The Effect of Parameters on the Recognition Performance of HDMCO

In HDMCO, η and λ are the main parameters. To explore their impact on the recognition rate of HDMCO, we conducted experiments. The experimental conditions are the same as the experimental conditions in Section 4.2.1. The only difference is that η ranges from 0.1 to 0.6, and λ ranges from 0 to 1. Figure 11 shows the effect of the main parameters on the recognition rate of HDMCO. It can be seen from Figure 11 that the recognition rate of HDMCO is the highest when the value of η is about 0.3, and the recognition rate of HDMCO is the highest when the value of λ is about 0.5.

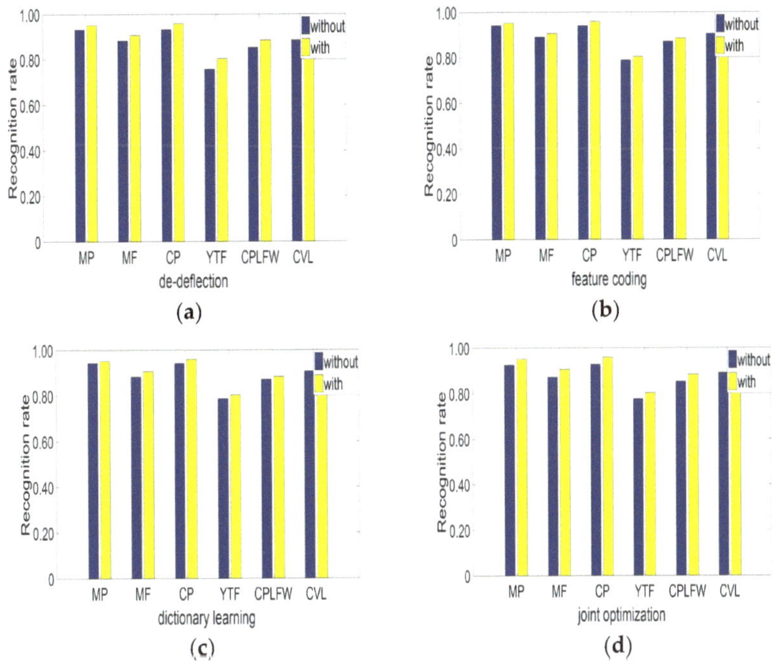

Figure 10. Results of ablation experiments. MP represents Multi-PIE, MF represents MegaFace, CP represents CAS-PEAL (**a**) de-deflection (**b**) feature learning (**c**) dictionary learning (**d**) joint optimization.

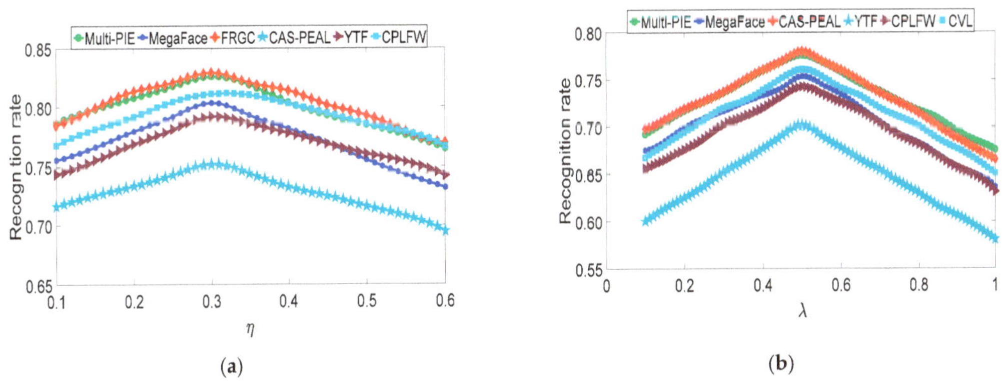

Figure 11. The effect of main parameters on the recognition rate of HDMCO. (**a**) η (**b**) λ.

4.2.7. Comparison of Computational Complexity

In this section, we analyze the computational complexity of the proposed algorithm and compare it with the computational complexity of several existing methods. The computational complexity of HDMCO is mainly dervived from solving $\boldsymbol{\alpha}$ using linear programming; meanwhile, the computational complexity of calculating $\boldsymbol{\alpha}$ is $o(n_0^2)$, and n_0 is the number of training samples. Thus, the computational complexity of HDMCO is $o(n_0^2)$. HADL [27] and LDMR [19] are used as comparative methods. The computational complexity of HADL is $O(M\tau(Kn_0^3 + K\max(L,K)))$, where τ is the iteration number, and L is the dimension of each sample, K is the number of atoms in the dictionary. M is the maximum number of the iteration number. The computational complexity of LDMR is $O(u_0v_0n_0^2 + n_0^3 + \tau(u_0v_0^2 + u_0v_0n_0))$, and u_0 and v_0 are the width and height of the image, respectively. It is easy to see from the computational complexity expressions of the three algorithms that the computational complexity of HDMCO is n_0^2, while the computational complexity of the other two algorithms is n_0^3. Hence, HDMCO has low computational complexity. Meanwhile, for example, the running time of HDMCO on the multi-PIE database is 713.45 s, while the running time of HADL and LDMR are 4397.45 s and 5813.24 s. The configuration of our computer is as follows: Intel Core i7-9700 K, 3.6 GHz, Nvidia GeForce RTX 2080 Ti.

5. Conclusions

In this paper, we propose a novel few-shot, multi-pose face recognition method based on hypergraph de-deflection and multi-task collaborative optimization (HDMCO). HDMCO uses the hypergraph theory and non-negative matrix decomposition to separate the frontal images from the attitude deflection images, and then uses the improved support vector data description and triangle coding to extract the features of the separated images without attitude deflection. Dictionary learning-based classifier is then also used to classify those features. The feature extraction process and feature classification process are jointly optimized. The large number of experimental results show that the proposed HDMCO does achieve good results. Although we have jointly optimized feature extraction and feature classification and achieved better results, since the separation of frontal images is separate from the subsequent feature extraction, the obtained recognition result is still not the ultimate optimal result of HDMCO. In future work, we will continue to explore the joint optimization of the separation of frontal images and feature extraction to obtain the ultimate optimal recognition effect of HDMCO.

Author Contributions: Conceptualization, X.F.; Methodology, X.F.; Validation, M.L.; Formal analysis, M.L.; Data curation, L.C.; Writing—review & editing, X.F.; Supervision, L.C.; Funding acquisition, J.H. All authors have read and agreed to the published version of the manuscript.

Funding: This work was funded in part by the Post-doctoral Innovative Talent Support Program (Grant no. BX20200048), and in part by the General Program of China Postdoctoral Science Foundation (Grant no. 2021M700405).

Data Availability Statement: Not applicable.

Conflicts of Interest: The authors declare no conflict of interest.

References

1. Jeevan, G.; Zacharias, G.C.; Nair, M.S.; Rajan, J. An empirical study of the impact of masks on face recognition. *Pattern Recognit.* **2022**, *122*, 108308. [CrossRef]
2. Solovyev, R.; Wang, W.; Gabruseva, T. Weighted boxes fusion: Ensembling boxes from different object detection models. *Image Vis. Comput.* **2021**, *107*, 104117. [CrossRef]
3. Wu, C.; Ju, B.; Wu, Y.; Xiong, N.N.; Zhang, S. WGAN-E: A generative adversarial networks for facial feature security. *Electronics* **2020**, *9*, 486. [CrossRef]
4. Sengupta, S.; Chen, J.C.; Castillo, C.; Patel, V.M.; Chellappa, R.; Jacobs, D.W. Frontal to profile face verification in the wild. In Proceedings of the 2016 IEEE Winter Conference on Applications of Computer Vision (WACV), Lake Placid, NY, USA, 7–10 March 2016; pp. 1–9.
5. Khrissi, L.; El Akkad, N.; Satori, H.; Satori, K. Clustering method and sine cosine algorithm for image segmentation. *Evol. Intell.* **2022**, *15*, 669–682. [CrossRef]
6. Zhao, J.; Xiong, L.; Cheng, Y.; Cheng, Y.; Li, J.; Zhou, L.; Xu, Y.; Karlekar, J.; Pranata, S.; Shen, S.; et al. 3D-aided deep pose-invariant face recognition. In Proceedings of the Twenty-Seventh International Joint Conference on Artificial Intelligence (IJCAI-18), Stockholm, Sweden, 13–19 July 2018; Volume 2, p. 11.
7. Zhao, J.; Xiong, L.; Li, J.; Xing, J.; Yan, S.; Feng, J. 3D-aided dual-agent gans for unconstrained face recognition. *IEEE Trans. Pattern Anal. Mach. Intell.* **2018**, *41*, 2380–2394. [CrossRef]
8. Zhao, J.; Cheng, Y.; Xu, Y.; Xiong, L.; Li, J.; Zhao, F.; Jayashree, K.; Pranata, S.; Shen, S.; Xing, J.; et al. Towards pose invariant face recognition in the wild. In Proceedings of the IEEE Conference on Computer Vision and Pattern Recognition, Salt Lake City, UT, USA, 18–22 June 2018; pp. 2207–2216.

9. Zhao, J.; Xiong, L.; Karlekar Jayashree, P.; Li, J.; Zhao, F.; Wang, Z.; Sugiri Pranata, P.; Shengmei Shen, P.; Yan, S.; Feng, J. Dual-agent gans for photorealistic and identity preserving profile face synthesis. In Proceedings of the 31st Conference on Neural Information Processing Systems (NIPS 2017), Long Beach, CA, USA, 4–9 December 2017.
10. Zhao, J. Deep Learning for Human-Centric Image Analysis. Ph.D. Thesis, National University of Singapore, Singapore, 2018.
11. Khrissi, L.; EL Akkad, N.; Satori, H.; Satori, K. An Efficient Image Clustering Technique based on Fuzzy C-means and Cuckoo Search Algorithm. *Int. J. Adv. Comput. Sci. Appl.* **2021**, *12*, 423–432. [CrossRef]
12. Ding, C.; Tao, D. Pose-invariant face recognition with homography-based normalization. *Pattern Recognit.* **2017**, *66*, 144–152. [CrossRef]
13. Luan, X.; Geng, H.; Liu, L.; Li, W.; Zhao, Y.; Ren, M. Geometry structure preserving based gan for multi-pose face frontalization and recognition. *IEEE Access* **2020**, *8*, 104676–104687. [CrossRef]
14. Liu, Y.; Chen, J. Unsupervised face frontalization for pose-invariant face recognition. *Image Vis. Comput.* **2021**, *106*, 104093. [CrossRef]
15. Yin, Y.; Jiang, S.; Robinson, J.P.; Fu, Y. Dual-attention gan for large-pose face frontalization. In Proceedings of the 2020 15th IEEE international conference on automatic face and gesture recognition (FG 2020), Buenos Aires, Argentina, 16–20 November 2020; pp. 249–256.
16. Lin, C.-H.; Huang, W.-J.; Wu, B.-F. Deep representation alignment network for pose-invariant face recognition. *Neurocomputing* **2021**, *464*, 485–496. [CrossRef]
17. Yang, H.; Gong, C.; Huang, K.; Song, K.; Yin, Z. Weighted feature histogram of multi-scale local patch using multi-bit binary descriptor for face recognition. *IEEE Trans. Image Process.* **2021**, *30*, 3858–3871. [CrossRef]
18. Tu, X.; Zhao, J.; Liu, Q.; Ai, W.; Guo, G.; Li, Z.; Liu, W.; Feng, J. Joint face image restoration and frontalization for recognition. *IEEE Trans. Circuits Syst. Video Technol.* **2021**, *32*, 1285–1298. [CrossRef]
19. Zhou, L.-F.; Du, Y.-W.; Li, W.-S.; Mi, J.-X.; Luan, X. Pose-robust face recognition with huffman-lbp enhanced by divide-and-rule strategy. *Pattern Recognit.* **2018**, *78*, 43–55. [CrossRef]
20. Zhang, C.; Li, H.; Qian, Y.; Chen, C.; Zhou, X. Locality-constrained discriminative matrix regression for robust face identification. *IEEE Trans. Neural Netw. Learn. Syst.* **2020**, *33*, 1254–1268. [CrossRef]
21. Gao, L.; Guan, L. A discriminative vectorial framework for multi-modal feature representation. *IEEE Trans. Multimed.* **2021**, *24*, 1503–1514.
22. Yang, S.; Deng, W.; Wang, M.; Du, J.; Hu, J. Orthogonality loss: Learning discriminative representations for face recognition. *IEEE Trans. Circuits Syst. Video Technol.* **2020**, *31*, 2301–2314. [CrossRef]
23. Huang, F.; Yang, M.; Lv, X.; Wu, F. Cosmos-loss: A face representation approach with independent supervision. *IEEE Access* **2021**, *9*, 36819–36826. [CrossRef]
24. He, M.; Zhang, J.; Shan, S.; Kan, M.; Chen, X. Deformable face net for pose invariant face recognition. *Pattern Recognit.* **2020**, *100*, 107113. [CrossRef]
25. Wang, Q.; Guo, G. Dsa-face: Diverse and sparse attentions for face recognition robust to pose variation and occlusion. *IEEE Trans. Inf. Forensics Secur.* **2021**, *16*, 4534–4543. [CrossRef]
26. He, R.; Li, Y.; Wu, X.; Song, L.; Chai, Z.; Wei, X. Coupled adversarial learning for semi-supervised heterogeneous face recognition. *Pattern Recognit.* **2021**, *110*, 107618. [CrossRef]
27. Liu, H.; Zhu, X.; Lei, Z.; Cao, D.; Li, S.Z. Fast adapting without forgetting for face recognition. *IEEE Trans. Circuits Syst. Video Technol.* **2020**, *31*, 3093–3104. [CrossRef]
28. Sun, J.; Yang, W.; Xue, J.H.; Liao, Q. An equalized margin loss for face recognition. *IEEE Trans. Multimed.* **2020**, *22*, 2833–2843. [CrossRef]
29. Zhang, Y.; Fu, K.; Han, C.; Cheng, P.; Yang, S.; Yang, X. PGM-face: Pose-guided margin loss for cross-pose face recognition. *Neurocomputing* **2021**, *460*, 154–165. [CrossRef]
30. Badave, H.; Kuber, M. Head pose estimation based robust multicamera face recognition. In Proceedings of the 2021 International Conference on Artificial Intelligence and Smart Systems (ICAIS), Coimbatore, India, 25–27 March 2021; pp. 492–495.
31. Wang, L.; Li, S.; Wang, S.; Kong, D.; Yin, B. Hardness-aware dictionary learning: Boosting dictionary for recognition. *IEEE Trans. Multimed.* **2020**, *23*, 2857–2867. [CrossRef]
32. Holkar, A.; Walambe, R.; Kotecha, K. Few-shot learning for face recognition in the presence of image discrepancies for limited multi-class datasets. *Image Vis. Comput.* **2022**, *120*, 104420. [CrossRef]
33. Guan, Y.; Fang, J.; Wu, X. Multi-pose face recognition using cascade alignment network and incremental clustering. *Signal, Image Video Process.* **2021**, *15*, 63–71. [CrossRef]
34. Zhang, Y.; Fu, K.; Han, C.; Cheng, P. Identity-and-pose-guided generative adversarial network for face rotation. *Neurocomputing* **2021**, *450*, 33–47. [CrossRef]
35. Qu, H.; Wang, Y. Application of optimized local binary pattern algorithm in small pose face recognition under machine vision. *Multimed. Tools Appl.* **2022**, *81*, 29367–29381. [CrossRef]
36. Masi, I.; Chang, F.J.; Choi, J.; Harel, S.; Kim, J.; Kim, K.; Leksut, J.; Rawls, S.; Wu, Y.; Hassner, T.; et al. Learning pose-aware models for pose-invariant face recognition in the wild. *IEEE Trans. Pattern Anal. Mach. Intell.* **2018**, *41*, 379–393. [CrossRef]
37. Elharrouss, O.; Almaadeed, N.; Al-Maadeed, S.; Khelifi, F. Pose-invariant face recognition with multitask cascade networks. *Neural Comput. Appl.* **2022**, *34*, 6039–6052. [CrossRef]

38. Liu, J.; Li, Q.; Liu, M.; Wei, T. CP-GAN: A cross-pose profile face frontalization boosting pose-invariant face recognition. *IEEE Access* **2020**, *8*, 198659–198667. [CrossRef]
39. Tao, Y.; Zheng, W.; Yang, W.; Wang, G.; Liao, Q. Frontal-centers guided face: Boosting face recognition by learning pose-invariant features. *IEEE Trans. Inf. Forensics Secur.* **2022**, *17*, 2272–2283. [CrossRef]
40. Gao, G.; Yu, Y.; Yang, M.; Chang, H.; Huang, P.; Yue, D. Cross-resolution face recognition with pose variations via multilayer locality-constrained structural orthogonal procrustes regression. *Inf. Sci.* **2020**, *506*, 19–36. [CrossRef]
41. Wang, H.; Kawahara, Y.; Weng, C.; Yuan, J. Representative selection with structured sparsity. *Pattern Recognit.* **2017**, *63*, 268–278. [CrossRef]
42. Gross, R.; Matthews, I.; Cohn, J.; Kanade, T.; Baker, S. Multi-pie. *Image Vis. Comput.* **2010**, *28*, 807–813. [CrossRef]
43. Kemelmacher-Shlizerman, I.; Seitz, S.M.; Miller, D.; Brossard, E. The megaface benchmark: 1 million faces for recognition at scale. In Proceedings of the IEEE Conference on Computer Vision and Pattern Recognition, Las Vegas, NV, USA, 27–30 June 2016; pp. 4873–4882.
44. Gao, W.; Cao, B.; Shan, S.; Chen, X.; Zhou, D.; Zhang, X.; Zhao, D. The CAS-PEAL large-scale chinese face database and baseline evaluations. *IEEE Trans. Syst. Man Cybern.-Part A Syst. Hum.* **2007**, *38*, 149–161.
45. Wolf, L.; Hassner, T.; Maoz, I. Face recognition in unconstrained videos with matched background similarity. In Proceedings of the CVPR 2011, Colorado Springs, CO, USA, 20–25 June 2011; pp. 529–534.
46. Zheng, T.; Deng, W. *Cross-Pose LFW: A Database for Studying Cross-Pose Face Recognition in Unconstrained Environments*; Technical Report; Beijing University of Posts and Telecommunications: Beijing, China, 2018; Volume 5.
47. Peer, P. CVL Face Database, Computer Vision Lab., Faculty of Computer and Information Science, University of Ljubljana, Slovenia. 2005. Available online: http://www.lrv.fri.uni-lj.si/facedb.html (accessed on 27 March 2023).
48. He, K.; Zhang, X.; Ren, S.; Sun, J. Deep residual learning for image recognition. In Proceedings of the IEEE Conference on Computer Vision and Pattern Recognition, Las Vegas, NV, USA, 27–30 June 2016; pp. 770–778.
49. Duan, X.; Tan, Z.-H. A spatial self-similarity based feature learning method for face recognition under varying poses. *Pattern Recognit. Lett.* **2018**, *111*, 109–116. [CrossRef]
50. Wu, H.; Gu, J.; Fan, X.; Li, H.; Xie, L.; Zhao, J. 3D-guided frontal face generation for pose-invariant recognition. *ACM Trans. Intell. Syst. Technol.* **2023**, *14*, 1–21. [CrossRef]
51. Zhao, J.; Li, J.; Zhao, F.; Nie, X.; Chen, Y.; Yan, S.; Feng, J. Marginalized CNN: Learning deep invariant representations. In Proceedings of the British Machine Vision Conference (BMVC), London, UK, 4–7 September 2017. [CrossRef]
52. Wang, X.; Wang, S.; Liang, Y.; Gu, L.; Lei, Z. RVFace: Reliable vector guided softmax loss for face recognition. *IEEE Trans. Image Process.* **2022**, *31*, 2337–2351. [CrossRef]
53. Zhong, Y.; Deng, W.; Fang, H.; Hu, J.; Zhao, D.; Li, X.; Wen, D. Dynamic training data dropout for robust deep face recognition. *IEEE Trans. Multimed.* **2021**, *24*, 1186–1197. [CrossRef]
54. Deng, J.; Guo, J.; Xue, N.; Zafeiriou, S. Arcface: Additive angular margin loss for deep face recognition. In Proceedings of the IEEE/CVF Conference on Computer Vision and Pattern Recognition, Long Beach, CA, USA, 16–20 June 2019; pp. 4690–4699.
55. Simonyan, K.; Zisserman, A. Very deep convolutional networks for large-scale image recognition. *arXiv* **2014**, arXiv:1409.1556.
56. Sun, Y.; Wang, X.; Tang, X. Deep learning face representation from predicting 10,000 classes. In Proceedings of the IEEE Conference on Computer Vision and Pattern Recognition, Columbus, OH, USA, 23–28 June 2014; pp. 1891–1898.

electronics MDPI

Article

Local Pixel Attack Based on Sensitive Pixel Location for Remote Sensing Images

Lu Liu [1,2], Zixuan Xu [1], Daqing He [2], Dequan Yang [3] and Hongchen Guo [2,*]

1 School of Computer Science, Beijing Institute of Technology, Beijing 100081, China
2 School of Cyberspace Science and Technology, Beijing Institute of Technology, Beijing 100081, China
3 Information Technology Center, Beijing Institute of Technology, Beijing 100081, China
* Correspondence: guohongchen@bit.edu.cn

Abstract: As deep neural networks (DNNs) are widely used in the field of remote sensing image recognition, there is a model security issue that cannot be ignored. DNNs have been shown to be vulnerable to small perturbations in a large number of studies in the past, and this security risk naturally exists in remote sensing object detection models based on DNNs. The complexity of remote sensing object detection models makes it difficult to implement adversarial attacks on them, resulting in the current lack of systematic research on adversarial examples in the field of remote sensing image recognition. In order to better deal with the adversarial threats that remote sensing image recognition models may confront and to provide an effective means for evaluating the robustness of the models, this paper takes the adversarial examples for remote sensing image recognition as the research goal and systematically studies vanishing attacks against a remote sensing image object detection model. To solve the problem of difficult attack implementation on remote sensing image object detection, adversarial attack adaptation methods based on interpolation scaling and patch perturbation stacking are proposed in this paper, which realizes the adaptation of classical attack algorithms. We propose a hot restart perturbation update strategy and the joint attack of the first and second stages of the two-stage remote sensing object detection model is realized through the design of the attack loss function. For the problem of the modification cost of global pixel attack being too large, a local pixel attack algorithm based on sensitive pixel location is proposed in this paper. By searching the location of the sensitive pixels and constructing the mask of attack area, good local pixel attack effect is achieved. Experimental results show that the average pixel modification rate of the proposed attack method decreases to less than 4% and the vanishing rate can still be maintained above 80%, which effectively achieves the balance between attack effect and attack cost.

Keywords: adversarial examples; remote sensing image object detection; vanishing attack

check for updates

Citation: Liu, L.; Xu, Z.; He, D.; Yang, D.; Guo, H. Local Pixel Attack Based on Sensitive Pixel Location for Remote Sensing Images. *Electronics* **2023**, *12*, 1987. https://doi.org/10.3390/electronics12091987

Academic Editor: Silvia Liberata Ullo

Received: 17 March 2023
Revised: 20 April 2023
Accepted: 20 April 2023
Published: 24 April 2023

1. Introduction

Remote sensing images have been an important data source for natural resource investigation, disaster monitoring, and public safety management. With the increasing computational power and the growing abundance of remote sensing data, deep convolutional neural networks have been more widely used in remote sensing image applications, such as image classification tasks [1–4] and target detection tasks related to image recognition [5–9] in the field of remote sensing. However, the vulnerability of deep neural networks has been exposed in recent years by the results of studies in which they are susceptible to well-designed adversarial samples [10] by attackers. An adversarial sample is a malicious input sample carefully generated by an attacker to deceive a deep learning model using an adversarial attack algorithm. The adversarial sample can cause the model to output wrong prediction results. Adversarial samples have subsequently gained the attention of many researchers in computer vision, and various adversarial attack algorithms have been developed rapidly in the following years. In the development process of adversarial attack techniques, Goodfellow et al. [11] proposed a fast method for generating adversarial samples, namely FGSM (Fast Gradient SignMethod), where the algorithm is optimized in the direction of the gradient sign generated by the target adversarial sample. The perturbation will always be in the direction of increasing the attack loss. Madry et al. [12] proposed the PGD algorithm, Kurakin et al. [13] proposed the iterative I-FGSM (Iterative-FGSM) method, and Dong et al. [14] proposed the MI-FGSM (Momentum-based I-FGSM) method that uses momentum to accelerate the convergence process. (Momentum-based Iterative FGSM) algorithm to accelerate the convergence process. Carlini and Wagner [15] proposed an optimization-based adversarial sample generation algorithm, C&W, whose innovation lies in defining an objective function that reduces the distance between the adversarial sample and the original sample while increasing the prediction error of the target model.

Remote sensing classification models have been proven unsafe by several researchers in the field of remote sensing image tasks [16–21]. Adversarial attacks against remote sensing image classification models were first proposed by Chen et al. [16]. Their study analyzed the adversarial sample problem in remote sensing image classification systems. The experimental results showed that remote sensing classification models are also vulnerable to adversarial sample attacks, proving the threat of adversarial samples to the security of remote sensing applications. Burnel et al. [18] generated adversarial samples with good transferability using generative adversarial networks. The experimental results in the paper have confirmed that the adversarial samples are still transferable on remote sensing classification models. The generated adversarial samples still have good attacks on black-box models. Czaja et al. [19] include in their research setup some practical factors that an attacker needs to consider when launching physical world attacks, providing the feasibility of physical world attacks. These studies make it possible to construct more realistic adversarial samples and further invisibility of adversarial samples when launching physical-world attacks. Xu et al. [20] conducted a systematic study of adversarial samples on remote sensing classification models, providing a baseline of the effectiveness of adversarial sample attacks on several common remote sensing image classification datasets. These studies only provided technical pavement for the study of adversarial samples on remote sensing image classification models but did not consider how to impose the attacks on remote sensing target detection models with more complex model structures. The studies that exist for adversarial attacks on remote sensing image target detection models include the study of adversarial patches proposed by Den et al. [21]. They disguised the adversarial patch on an aircraft object to help the aircraft escape from the YOLO V2 target detection model. The study has some limitations, firstly, the vanishing attack in the study only targets the aircraft category, and the study is weak in systematicity; in addition, the study only performed the attack on the more easily breached generic single-stage target detector and did not perform the attack study on the advanced remote sensing target detector.

In the field of adversarial samples for remote sensing image models, the research of adversarial attack algorithms for classification models is beginning to take shape. However, the implementation of adversarial attacks on remote sensing object detection models is complex due to the characteristics of remote sensing images that are different from close-up images and the complexity of remote sensing object detection models. It causes the research of adversarial attack algorithms for remote sensing object detectors to be still scarce, and large-scale systematic analysis and research are even more lacking, which is obviously not conducive to the model to deal with the security threats that may appear in the future. We propose well-performing adaptive improved adversarial attack algorithms based on the characteristics of remote sensing object detection models to construct transferable adversarial samples.

In view of the current situation of the lack of research on the countermeasure samples on the remote sensing object detector, this work first realizes the adaptation of the typical white-box attack algorithm, successfully implements the vanishing attack on the model, and builds a comparative baseline for the subsequent research, and then proposes the adaptive improved global pixel attack method and local pixel attack method according to the characteristics of the remote sensing target detector. Specifically, the contributions of this paper are as follows:

1. We design an attack adaptation method based on interpolation scaling and block-based perturbation superposition to successfully adapt a variety of typical white-box attacks to the remote sensing object detection, and we use a hot restart strategy to effectively solve the perturbation failure problem caused by image splitting preprocessing transformations. Moreover, through the design of the loss function, a joint attack on the two-stage remote sensing target detector RPN module and the classification refinement module is realized;
2. We propose an attack sensitivity mapping algorithm to realize the search for the location of sensitive pixel points and improve the attack effect;
3. We propose a local pixel attack algorithm (Sensitive Pixel Localization C&W, SPL-C&W) based on sensitive pixel point localization. By searching the location of attack-sensitive pixel points in the original image and constructing a technical scheme for mask extraction of the attack region, the local pixel attack is implemented while still adopting the hot restart perturbation update strategy, balancing the attack effect with the overhead of attacking the number of modified pixels.

2. Related Work

2.1. Remote Sensing Image Object Detection

Generic object detectors are divided into two-stage object detectors and single-stage object detectors. The two-stage object detector usually consists of two stages. Take Faster R-CNN [22] as an example, it consists of the following three modules: (1) Backbone network for extracting features. The feature information in the image is extracted by the convolution operation of this module to form a Feature Map and sent to the next stage. (2) Region Proposal Network (RPN). The function of this module is to distinguish the foreground from the background. (3) Classification refinement stage. In this stage, local features are extracted from the proposed regions sent in to achieve further classification refinement and position regression, obtain the specific categories and positions of objects, and obtain the final prediction results through postprocessing. The YOLO [23], as an example of a single-stage object detector, differs from the two-stage object detector in that it does not contain a module that distinguishes explicitly between the foreground and the background but directly regresses the class and location of the target to be detected in the output layer.

Remote sensing images differ in several ways from conventional images in real life. Firstly, they possess an enormous size; for example, the images in the DOTA dataset [24] range from 800 × 800 to 4000 × 4000. Secondly, the objects in remote sensing images are generally small and densely arranged, with some appearing in a formation and complex background. Thirdly, these images are primarily captured from an aerial view, leading to immense variability in the size, direction, and shape of the objects. Therefore, developing a remote sensing object detection model requires a unique approach. The rotational object detectors using deep neural networks are found to be suitable for remote sensing object detection due to its progress in deep learning technology and abundant data resources. In recent years, several excellent remote sensing object detectors based on deep neural networks have been developed [5,6,8] such as the two-stage Gliding Vertex [5] model and the ROI-Transformer [6] model, where ROI stands for Region of Interests. The Gliding Vertex model represents the location of the object using four points' offset on a horizontal frame. On the other hand, the ROI-Transformer model uses the two-stage object detector architecture for detection, and its final prediction stage's output is similar to that of a generic object detector—comprising the object's coordinate information and its category label. However, the coordinates for determining the rotation detection frame differ slightly from those of the Gliding Vertex model. Moreover, due to the massive size of remote sensing images, feeding the entire high-resolution image directly into the operation during training or testing is not possible using most GPUs. Therefore, most remote sensing object detection models perform preprocessing image transformations, cutting images into feasible sizes before training and testing. Overall, these unique characteristics of remote sensing images require the development of novel and robust remote sensing object detection models.

2.2. Adversarial Examples

The adversarial attack optimizes the loss function by adding small perturbations directly to the image pixels through an optimization algorithm, thus causing the modified sample detection results to deviate from the actual label. The attacks can be classified into global pixel attacks and local pixel attacks according to the number of image pixels involved. The global pixel attack involves the whole image, while the local pixel attack involves only some pixels. Almost all traditional attacks against image classification tasks are global pixel attacks, such as FGSM [11], I-FGSM [13], MI-FGSM [14], PGD [12], and C&W [15]. From the analysis of the above-mentioned related studies, it is clear that the specific implementation of category attacks that reduce the classification accuracy of object detectors should be the modules in the detectors involved in the classification process. In this paper, the subsequent research on the vanishing attack for remote sensing object detectors should also focus on these modules of the object detectors to achieve the attack effect. The effect of the attack on the target detector by the antagonistic sample can be briefly described as two: reduction of detector accuracy and vanishing attack. The DAG(Dense Adversary Generation) attack algorithm proposed by Xie et al. [25] and subsequently proposed by Chen et al. [7]. The ShapeShifter algorithm focuses the attack on the classification refinement phase of the two-stage object detector. The common goal of the vanishing attack is to make all objects in the image bypass the detection of the detector. The vanishing attack involves more orders of magnitude and is more difficult than an attack that misclassifies an object in the image. Vanishing attacks also reduce the detector's accuracy, target hiding is often more relevant, and the studies we have conducted have focused on vanishing attacks.

2.3. CAM

Among the interpretable approaches to neural networks, some studies on the visualization of image classification model predictions have commonly used the gradient information flowing back in the model [8,10]. In these studies, CNN predictions are visualized by highlighting pixels in the image that are "more important" for a particular class (i.e., changes in these pixels have the most significant impact on the prediction scores for that class). An example of the Class Activation Mapping (CAM) algorithm [8] on a GoogleNet classification model is shown in Figure 1. CAM uses the gradient information returned on the image classification model to obtain the response value of a layer of the feature map for a particular class, where a higher response value represents a higher contribution to the classification of that class. This way, a class activation map is obtained, and then the image regions most relevant to a particular class can be identified from the map by upsampling it.

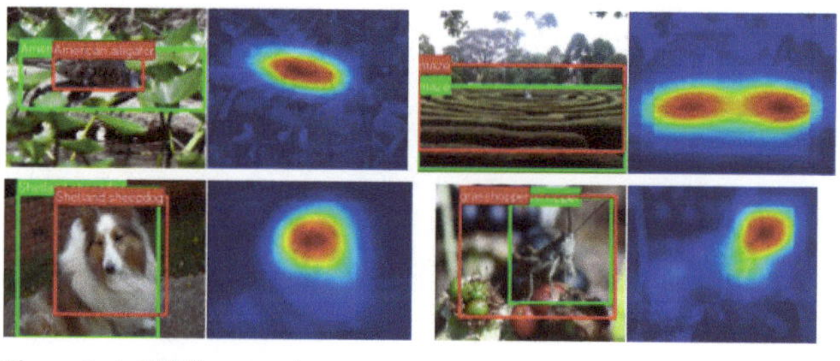

Figure 1. A CAM's example.

3. Attack Strategies

3.1. Problem Definition and Notation for Deep Neural Networks

First, the notation is defined by t to denote the number of the round of the multi-round attack, and the resulting adversarial sample is denoted as x_t^*; α denotes the step size of the multi-round attack, which represents the value of pixel modification at each round of the gradient-based attack algorithm; ε denotes the maximum value of pixel modification when using the L_∞ norm constraint; $J(\cdot)$ denotes the loss function of the adversarial attack, and $\nabla_x J(\cdot)$ denotes the gradient obtained by passing the attack loss back to the original image x. Y denotes the correct classification class of the image after the classification model Z, and Y' represents the target class set by the attack.

Our white-box attack is inspired by the formulation of the C&W attack. C&W [15] is an optimization-based adversarial attack algorithm. The algorithm proposes a new loss function that reduces the distance between the adversarial sample and the original sample while increasing the prediction error of the target model, i.e., subject to the L_2 norm. To facilitate optimization, the C&W algorithm first introduces the $tanh$ space variable w to represent the adversarial sample x^* , and the transformation range of x^* is transformed from $(0,1)$ to$(-\infty,+\infty)$. The variable w is calculated as follows:

$$x^* = \frac{1}{2}(tanh(w)+1). \tag{1}$$

The optimization expression for C&W against attacks consists of two parts, which are formulated as follows:

$$min||\delta||_2^2 + c \cdot f(x^*), \tag{2}$$

here, $||\delta||_2^2$ represents the Euclidean distance between the original image and the generated adversarial sample, and $f(\cdot)$ represents the probability distance between the category correctly predicted by the model and the category incorrectly predicted into the attack target. δ and $f(\cdot)$ represent the expressions respectively as follows:

$$\delta = x^* - x, \tag{3}$$

$$f(x^*) = max\big(max\{Z(x^*)_i : i \neq Y'\} - Z(x^*)_{Y'} \ , -k\big), \tag{4}$$

where c is a parameter measuring the loss function of the two components and k is the confidence that the model is misclassified, the larger the chance that the adversarial sample will be misclassified, but it will also be harder to find, and a better balance is usually achieved when it is greater than 40. The attack is usually implemented using the Adam optimizer to optimize the process.

3.2. Splitting Preprocessing

Due to the huge size of remote sensing images, most GPUs cannot support putting the whole high-resolution image directly on the GPU for calculation during training or prediction. If the image is scaled directly, some information will be lost. We take a single large image and split it into a collection of multiple subgraph splits that the GPU can process by some rules, i.e., we preprocess the image by splitting. The pseudo-code of the $Split$ algorithm is shown in Algorithm 1.

Given a remote sensing image x of size (w,h), the relevant parameters are as follows: (1) rate represents the rate of image scaling before cutting; (2) the Boolean type parameter padding for whether to perform a 0-pixel padding operation; (3) gap is represented by the distance between two adjacent slices; (4) the size of the single subgraph after cutting. The significance of the cutting parameters is as follows: rate represents the scaling ratio and the expected values are 1.0 and 0.5, where 1.0 means no image scaling and 0.5 means reducing the image size by half. When cutting the image, the split size is smaller than the set sub-size, and when the parameter padding is set to True, the pieces will be transformed by image padding, and the size will be expanded to the sub-size. The scaling transformation and the padding transformation are standard data enhancement tools used in image tasks, and these two parameters can be considered data enhancement operations in the cut preprocessing process.

Algorithm 1 The Framework of *Split*

Require: original remote sensing image x
Require: *rate, padding, gap, subsize*
Ensure: subgragh set $P = \{p_1, p_2, \ldots, p_n\}$
Let $(left, up) = (0, 0)$
resize x according to *rate* and update (w, h)
while $left \leq w$ **do**
  $up = 0$
  while $up \leq h$ **do**
    Split subgraph according to $(left, up)$
    Fill the subgragh based on the *padding* parameter
    Update P set
    if $up + subsize \geq h$ **then**
      Break
    end if
    Update up
  end while
  if $left + subsize \geq w$ **then**
    Break
  end if
  Update $left$
end while
return P

In addition, the target information at the edge of the slices may be missing during the cutting process. Therefore, the parameter gap is set to a certain overlap area between the adjacent subgraphs. This parameter is usually set to around 50% of the cut image size. The implementation process of the cutting preprocessing algorithm can be regarded as the process of sliding window cutting on the image. When updating the top-left coordinate $(left, up)$ of the subgraph corresponding to the original image during each slide, a judgment operation is needed. Taking the update of $left$ as an example, if $left + slide + subsize \leq w$, then the $left$ update is $left + slide$; otherwise, it is updated to $w - subsize$. The update of up is similar. The following is the process of the cutting preprocessing, as shown in the Figure 2. After the cutting preprocessing, we obtain a set of subgraphs $P = \{p_1, p_2, \ldots, p_n\}$.

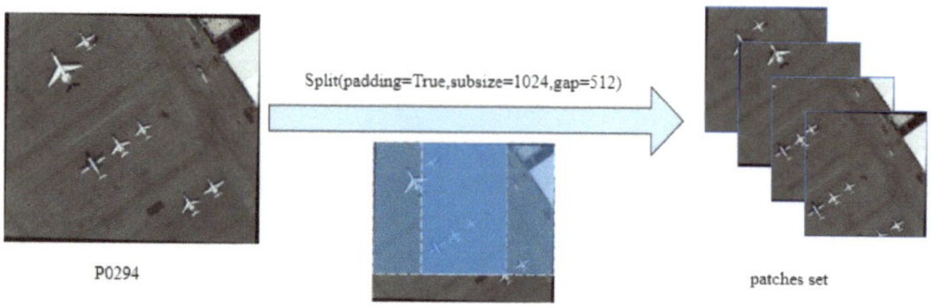

Figure 2. The process of the cutting preprocessing.

3.3. Hot Disturbance Update Strategy

The cutting preprocessing module, while ensuring smooth operation of the remote sensing algorithm, might reduce the effectiveness of the attack. Suppose all slices in the set of subgraph slices are attacked individually. In that case, all the perturbation blocks in the set are added to the original graph at once according to the corresponding positions of the subgraphs to generate the adversarial examples. However, as a result of the many overlaps between subgraphs, the overlap area of the perturbation blocks added in front will be covered by the perturbation blocks added later, resulting in partial loss of perturbation information. Finally, the generated adversarial examples are more biased towards the perturbation blocks added later, which is a kind of "local optimum" in the attack. If such an adversarial example is preprocessed by cutting and sent to the detector, the detection accuracy of the subgraph slices partially covered by the perturbation may not be reduced, and the accuracy of the final detection results obtained after merging the subgraph detection results will not be significantly reduced. The adversarial examples generated by this perturbation update strategy are less robust when using the cut preprocessing module. Therefore, when adding perturbations to the original image to generate the adversarial examples, instead of a one-time static addition, a dynamic approach should be taken to update the perturbations. To overcome this challenge, we propose a hot restart perturbation update strategy for dynamic updates of adversarial samples.

Hot restart is an approach where, after updating the perturbations for all subgraphs in the set P from the cutting preprocessing stage, the adversarial samples generated are reprocessed through cutting and preprocessing before the next attack round. It is important to note that the non-minimizable image transformation operation cuts off the backpropagation of the attack loss and makes the attack impossible to execute. Therefore, the cut preprocessing used in the attack is rewritten according to the cut preprocessing algorithm. This finer-grained perturbation update strategy can enhance the robustness of the generated perturbations. The drawback is that the update of the slice set is performed before each round of attack, and the perturbation update on the original image brought by a single attack on each slice in the slice set is calculated during each round of attack. Hence, the number of iterations of the attack increases, and the attack speed decreases.

The role of the RPN module in the two-stage target detector is to distinguish the foreground from the background and to fine-tune the object positions. Therefore, we can not only attack the classification refinement module to make it misclassified as a background class when performing a vanishing attack, but also attack the RPN module. The RPN module eventually sorts out the wrong proposed region (i.e., the background region) and sends it to the second stage, thus achieving the effect of the vanishing attack. The RPN module is understood as a binary classification model that distinguishes between foreground and background, and the confidence probability c is understood as the probability that the category is foreground. To accommodate the hot-restart strategy, the final attack process consists of two parts, the attack RPN module and the attack classification refinement module. Justifiably, the joint loss function J consists of two parts, J_{rpn} and J_{roi}. The loss function equation of the attack is expressed as follows:

$$J = \beta J_{rpn} + J_{roi}, \tag{5}$$

$$J_{roi} = -\sum_{i=1}^{m} logp(y_i'|b_i). \tag{6}$$

$$J_{rpn} = -\sum_{c\epsilon\{c_i|c_i>obj\}}^{n} log(1-c). \tag{7}$$

where β is the parameter to measure the proportion of J_{rpn} and J_{roi}. J_{roi} represents the loss of the attack classification refinement module, where the $b = \{b_1, b_2, \ldots, b_m\}$ denotes the number of detection frames sent to the second stage after filtering in the RPN stage, n. Y denotes the correct classification class of the image after the classification model. $Y' = \{y_1', y_2', \ldots, y_n'\}$ denotes the set attack target class label. Here is the background class with the label 0.

3.4. Sensitive Pixel Point Selection

The hot restart perturbation update strategy proposed above effectively solves the perturbation failure problem caused by the image cut preprocessing module in the remote sensing target detection model. It implements a global pixel attack with a high attack success rate on the remote sensing target detection model. However, the whole image is the range of modified pixels involved in the global pixel attack. The overhead of modified pixels in this attack can be accepted for conventional images with small sizes. If the size of a remote sensing image is 3000 × 3000, the number of modified pixels involved in a global pixel attack is 9,000,000, which is a large number. In order to balance the attack effect and the overhead, the number of pixels involved in the attack needs to be reduced as much as possible. Inspired by the Class Activation Mapping (CAM) algorithm [8] introduced above, an Attack Sensitivity Mapping (ASM) algorithm is proposed here, and the algorithm pseudo-code is shown in Algorithm 2. This algorithm can search for the pixel points in the original image that are more sensitive to the attack during the attack, and being more sensitive to the attack means that the modification of these pixels contributes more to the attack effect.

Algorithm 2 Attack Sensitivity Mapping (ASM)

```
Require: original image x, gradient graph on the original image ∇_x J
Require: K,kernel
Ensure: coordinates set of Top K sensitive pixels L = {l_1, l_2, ..., l_k}
for each x_(i,j) ∈ ∇_x J do
    Calculate the sensitivity s of each pixel
end for
Update sensitivity matrix S
S' = conv(S, kernel)
Pixels = Sort_desc(S')
Select Top K points from Pixels Set
for each k ∈ Top K do
    Map the index of k back to S
    Obtain sensitive pixels position coordinates
    Update Set L
end for
return L
```

The algorithm first performs the calculation of the attack sensitivity s. After back-propagating the attack loss J to the original image x, each pixel point $x_{(i,j)}$ is given its gradient, and the direction of the gradient represents the direction where the attack loss decreases fastest at this pixel point. The magnitude of the gradient represents the value of the decrease. The ASM algorithm determines the sensitivity of each pixel point in the image to the attack based on the magnitude of the gradient obtained by backpropagating the attack loss J to the original image x along the model network s. The expression for s is given as follows:

$$s = \sum_{n}^{c} \left| \left(\frac{\partial J}{\partial x} \bigg|_{x_{(i,j)}} \right) \right|, \tag{8}$$

where c represents the number of channels of the image, for a grayscale map with a single channel, $c = 1$, s is ultimately equal to the absolute value of the gradient size on the pixel point; for a color map with three channels of RGB, $c = 3$, s is ultimately equal to the sum of the absolute values of the gradient sizes of the three channels on the pixel point. So far, we can obtain the sensitivity matrix S with the same size as the original image, $S_{(i,j)}$ corresponds to the attack sensitivity information on the pixel $x_{(i,j)}$ in the original image.

The sensitivity matrix S can be regarded as a numerical sensitivity map. In order to make the selection result of sensitive pixel points more robust, the sensitivity matrix S is convolved here before the selection of sensitive pixel points. For the convolution operation, a 1×1 convolution kernel is used with a size of *kernel*, which is usually an odd number. The stride is set to 1.The matrix S' is obtained after the convolution process. All the points in the matrix S' are sorted in descending order according to their values, and the top K points are filtered out to obtain the *Top K* point set; for each point in the *Top K* point set, its position index is mapped back to S before the convolution process, thus obtaining the coordinate information of each point corresponding to *kernel* × *kernel* in the original image. The coordinate information of each point corresponds to *kernel* × *kernel* of sensitive pixels in the original image. After all the points in the *Top K* point set are processed, the coordinate information of the sensitive pixel points is retained and used for the construction of the attack region mask in next section. Finally, $L = \{l_1, l_2, \ldots, l_n\}$is used to denote the set of coordinates of the sensitive pixel points selected from the original image.

Using the ASM algorithm to search for sensitive pixel points in the original image, the sensitive pixel point localization maps for different values of K at $kernel = 1$ are shown in Figure 3. The K is taken as $K = 10, 50, 100, 500, 1000$, and the number of sensitive pixels accounts for 0.12%, 0.56%, 1.06%, 4.03%, and 5.35% of the original image, respectively. The distribution pattern of highly sensitive pixels in the image can be perceived from the changes of sensitive pixel location maps based on different K values. That is, most of the pixels that are highly sensitive to the attack are distributed in a particular area of the image containing the object to be detected, which should be focused on when performing local pixel attacks.

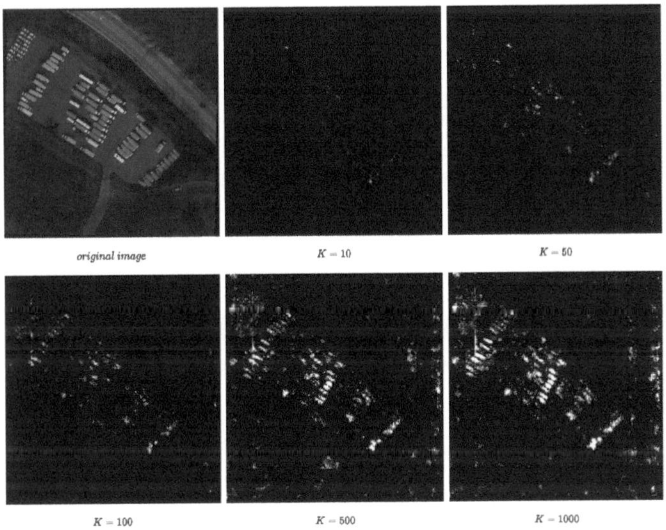

Figure 3. When $Kernel = 1$, the images of sensitive pixel location under different K values.

3.5. Construction of the Attack Area Mask

After searching the position information of *Top K* sensitive pixel points by the ASM algorithm, the position mask about these K pixel points can be constructed directly by setting the pixel value of the corresponding position to 1 and the remaining positions to 0, as shown in Figure 4. Suppose we use the obtained *Top K* sensitive pixel point position masks as attack region masks straightly. In that case, observation of the constructed position mask shows that there will be many isolated sensitive pixel points, especially at the edges of the image. It might be detrimental to future attack studies that might be conducted in the physical world. In addition, we can find that most pixel points susceptible to the attack are distributed within a specific area of the image containing the object to be detected. This phenomenon inspires us to construct the attack region mask by directly selecting the region containing the object to be detected. The detection frame information in the detection result of the original image by the target detection model can be used for construction. It is worth noting that the target detection model will use the contextual information to correct the classification results, so the attack range is only limited to the inside of the detection frame and may not be optimal; in addition, as the remote sensing target detection model adopts rotating frame detection, the detection frame is mostly a directed rectangular frame, so the edges of some objects with regular shapes will most likely overlap with the detection frame, and thus will not be included in the detection frame mask and finally, not in the attack area. Such a situation exists for the vehicle class in the DOTA dataset, and the contribution of the object's edge contour feature to the detection result cannot be ignored. Based on the above two points, a slight expansion of the detection frame area should be considered when constructing the mask. The graphical morphology method of expansion is used to slightly expand all the detection frame areas in the image so that part of the contextual information and the edge contours of the object can also be included in the mask range after processing. The parameter $kernel_0$ is the expanded convolution kernel used to perform the expansion operation. This scheme can eventually build a detection frame mask with a regular shape, but the number of pixels involved in the attack will be more significant.

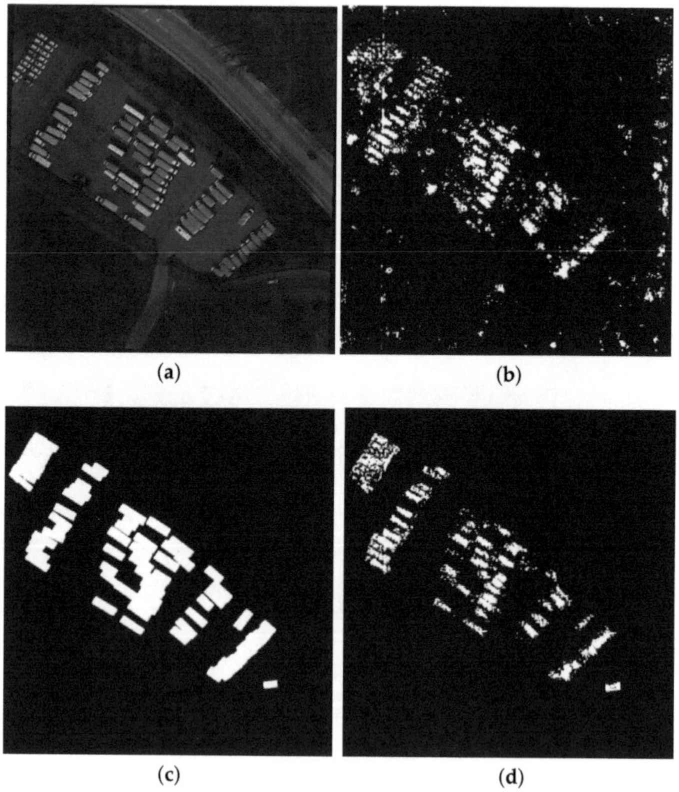

Figure 4. Attack area mask. (**a**) Original image; (**b**) $kernel = 3, K = 500$; (**c**) $M_b, kernel_0 = 7$; (**d**) M.

In summary, by fusing the ideas of the above two schemes, an attack region mask scheme that uses the detection frame mask to limit further the search range of *Top K* sensitive pixel points are designed here, and this attack region mask scheme will eventually filter out fewer sensitive pixel points. The detailed process of attack region mask construction is described below: firstly, the post-inflated detection frame mask M_b is constructed based on the detection frame information, and the gradient map $\nabla_x J$ is obtained by using M_b to mask the gradient map after passing back the attack loss to the original map, which is expressed as the following:

$$\nabla_x J' = \nabla_x J \odot M_b. \tag{9}$$

The ASM algorithm runs then, by which the search for *Top K* sensitive pixel points can be performed in the area already restricted by M_b so that the localized sensitive pixel points are more distributed in the object itself and around the object. The attack area masks

M can be constructed by constructing the localization map after obtaining the location information of *Top K* sensitive pixel points.

An example attack region mask constructed according to the above process is shown in Figure 4. Figure 4b represents an example map of sensitive pixel location obtained directly according to the ASM algorithm, where $kernel = 3$ and $K = 500$, and the number of sensitive pixels finally selected accounts for 6.09% of all pixels in the original image; Figure 4c represents an example map of detection frame mask constructed according to the detection frame information. Figure 4d represents the final attack region mask constructed according to the attack region mask scheme in this section, with the number of pixels in the attack region accounting for 4.73% of the original image. From Figure 4, it can be seen that the attack region mask constructed according to the scheme designed in this section can, on the one hand, make the attack focus more on the region where the object itself is located, and on the other hand, filter out the pixel points from these regions that are more sensitive to the attack, further reducing the overhead of modifying the number of pixels in the attack.

3.6. SPL-C&W

The process of implementing the vanishing attack by the Sensitive Pixel Localization C&W(SPL-C&W) algorithm proposed in conjunction with the above schemes is shown in Figure 5. The SPL-C&W algorithm performs the vanishing attack against the second-stage classification refinement module of the two-stage target detector.

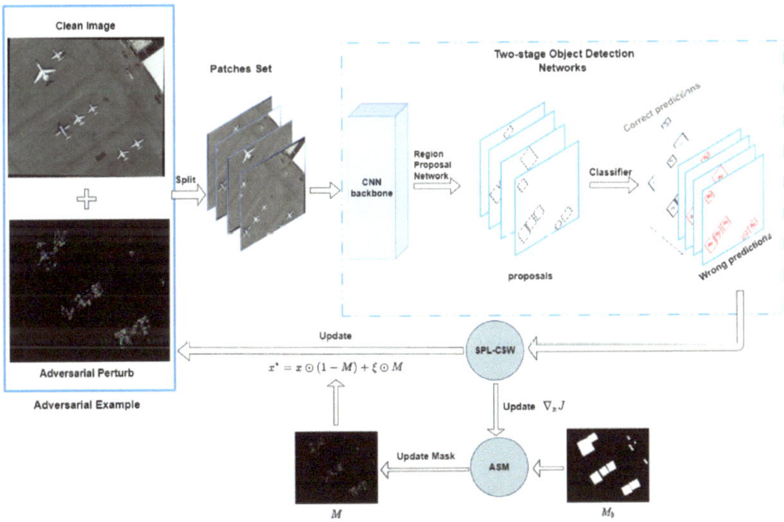

Figure 5. The overview of SPL C&W.

In order to generate an adversarial sample in the attack with splitting preprocessing, a hot restart perturbation update strategy is used in the algorithm. The ASM algorithm is utilized to search sensitive pixel points and construct the attack region mask during each round, explicitly targeting slicing in a single attack. The attack region mask makes it possible to update the perturbations only in the attack region and always keep the same initial value as the original image x for the pixel points outside the attack region. This adversarial sample optimization process can be expressed as follows:

$$x_t^* = x \odot (1 - M_t) + \xi_t \odot M_t, \tag{10}$$

where t represents the number of rounds of attacks, and ξ_t is used to denote the perturbation generated in the t th round of attacks, M_t represents the attack region mask updated from this round, and x_t^* represents the adversarial samples generated in the t th round of attacks.

In the multi-round iterative attack, the attack region mask is first updated at every single attack, and then the adversarial samples are optimized within the limits of the mask. In this way, the local pixel attack based on sensitive pixel point localization is finally achieved. The algorithmic framework of the SPL-C&W attack is shown in Algorithm 3.

Algorithm 3 The Framework of SPL-C&W

Require: real image x; the detector D; mask of the detection boxes M_b; patches set $P = \{p_1, p_2, \ldots, p_n\}$; proposal regions set $B = \{B_1, B_2, \ldots, B_n\}$ on P; detected label set $Y = \{Y_1, Y_2, \ldots, Y_n\}$; adversarial target label set $Y' = \{Y'_1, Y'_2, \ldots, Y'_n\}$

Require: iterations T; attack parameters c and k; ASM parameters K and $kernel$; construct mask parameters $kernel_0$

Ensure: adversarial example x^*

Let $x_0^* = x$; $P^* = Split(\ x_0^*)$
for $t = 0 \cdots T-1$ **do**
    $P_t^* = Split(x_t^*)$
    Input P_t^* to D
    Update Set B_t , Set Y_t and Set Y'_t
    if $Y_t == Y'_t$ **then**
        Break
    end if
    for each patch $p_{t_n}^* \in P_t^*$ **do**
        Input $p_{t_n}^*$ to D
        Attack $p_{t_n}^*$ by Attack method and backpropagation Loss J
        Optimize the ξ_t and obtain the gradient $\nabla_x J(p_{t_n}^*\ ,\ Y'_{t_n})$
        $\nabla_x J(p_{t_n}^*\ ,\ Y'_{t_n})' = \nabla_x J(p_{t_n}^*\ ,\ Y'_{t_n}) \odot M_b$
        // Search for the locations of sensitive pixels by ASM algorithm
        $L = \text{ASM}(x, \nabla_x J(p_{t_n}^*\ ,\ Y'_{t_n})')$
        Update Mask M according to L
        Update x_t^* according to $x_t^* = x \odot (1 - M) + \xi_t \odot M$
    end for
end for
return $x^* = x_T^*$

4. Evaluation

In this section, the SPL-C&W algorithm is used to perform the vanishing attack on two white-box remote sensing target detection models, and the rationality of the sensitive pixel point localization and attack region mask construction scheme proposed in this chapter is verified through comparative experiments; subsequently, it is verified that the SPL-C&W local pixel attack algorithm proposed in this chapter can balance between the attack success rate and the attack modification pixel overhead through comparison experiments with the attack effect of global pixel attack.

4.1. Setup

The experiments in this section are based on Pytorch and are conducted on a Linux server with a GeForce RTX2080 Ti graphics card and 64 GB of RAM. The adopted dataset uses validation set images from the DOTA V 1.0 remote sensing image dataset. The local pixel attack takes a long time to perform multiple searches for sensitive pixel points and the construction of attack region masks in each round of attack, and 100 images from the validation set are randomly selected for the experiments here.

In this chapter, the Gliding Vertex [5] with ROI-Transformer [6] detector is still used as the local white-box model on which the local pixel attack algorithm based on the feedback of sensitive pixel points is implemented. The R3Det [26] and BBAVectors [27] are used as the local black-box model, and Gliding Vertex and ROI-Transformer are mutually black-box models to verify the transferability of the generated adversarial samples. The four models of the experimental attack can operate normally locally before being attacked, and the detection performance on the 100 randomly selected images in this chapter is good, with the Gliding Vertex achieving 87.41% mAP (Mean Average Precision), the ROI-Transformer detector achieving 82.88% mAP, and the R3Det achieving 87.04% mAP, and BBAVectors can reach 88.79% mAP.

To compare with the global pixel attack method without ASM, the attack we use has the same parameters as follows: (1) normalize the original image from the pixel range of $[0, 255]$ to $[0, 1]$; (2) the attacks are constrained by the L_2 norm; (3) the maximum number of attack rounds $T = 50$ for multi-round attacks; (4) the model misclassification confidence $k = 50$ and the loss function parameter $c = 10$. It should be noted that in the experiment, a convolution operation was performed on the gradient map using the attack sensitivity algorithm with a convolution kernel of $kernel = 3$, and another parameter $K = 500$ was used for the ASM algorithm. The inflated convolution kernel $kernel_0 \in [1, 3, 5, 7, 9]$ detects the box mask when constructing the attack region mask.

4.2. Effectiveness Analysis of Sensitive Pixel Location

In order to verify the effectiveness of the sensitive pixel points positioned in the attack and the rationality of the attack region mask scheme, this section constructs different attack region masks for comparison experiments. It implements SPL-C&W local pixel attacks on the white-box Gliding Vertex model and ROI-Transformer model to analyze the differences in attack effects.

The descriptions of several groups of attack area masks used in the experiments are as follows: (1) Small squares of size 3×3 are randomly selected in the image several times to construct area masks. Then, local pixel attacks are performed, symbolically denoted as $randomK$, and K represents the number of randomly selected squares. The randomly selected 5000 and 10,000 small squares in the image correspond to the average modification rates of 4.27% and 8.26% in the images participating in the experiments, respectively, and the attacks have the same average image modification rates on the two white-box models; (2) using the ASM algorithm, the convolutional operation is performed using a convolutional kernel of $kernel = 3$ with parameters $k = 500$, constructing a position mask as the attack region mask for each round of SPL-C&W attack, symbolically denoted as conv3. The average image modification rate of the final attack is 7.63% on the Gliding Vertex model and 7.33% on the ROI-Transformer model; (3) Using the attack region mask scheme, the detection frame mask restriction ASM algorithm is added, searching the area range of $Top\ K$ sensitive pixel points. The detection box is not inflated here first to exclude the influence of other factors, and the parameter $kernel_0 = 1$ is symbolically represented as $box1conv3$. The final attack has an average image modification rate of 2.82% on the Gliding Vertex model and 2.29% on the ROI-Transformer model. Figure 6 shows the comparison of the local pixel attack effect under the above different attack region masks.

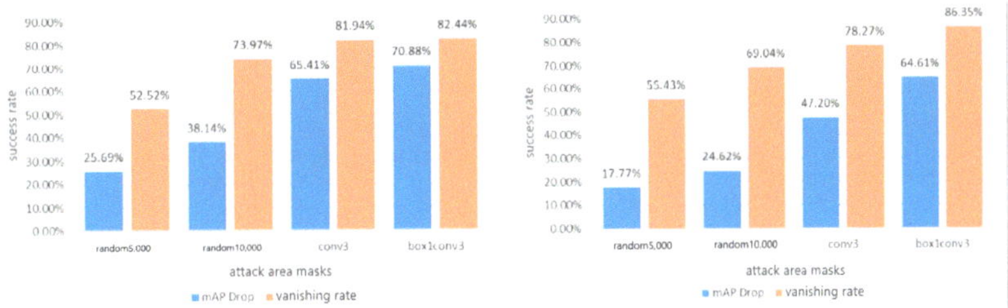

(**a**) (**b**)

Figure 6. Comparison of attack effects based on different attack area masks. (**a**) Gliding Vertex ; (**b**) ROI-Transformer.

Figure 6a shows the result of attacking the Gliding Vertex model, and Figure 6b shows the result of attacking the ROI-Transformer model. From Figure 6, it can be intuitively seen that the attack effect of the local pixel attack based on $conv3$ mask is better than that of the local pixel attack based on $random10,000$ mask for the Gliding Vertex model and the ROI-Transformer model with less than 1% difference in the attack modification rate. The mAP Drop of the attack is 27.27% and 22.28% higher on the two models, and the vanishing rate is 7.97% and 9.2% higher, respectively. The experimental results effectively demonstrate the effectiveness of the selected sensitive pixel points in enhancing the effect of local pixel attacks.

In addition, it can be learned from Figure 6 that the $box1conv3$ mask constructed according to the attack region mask scheme reduces the attack modification rate in the SPL-C&W attack. In contrast, the attack effect performs the best in several groups of comparison experiments. With less than 2% difference in the attack modification rate, the attack improves the mAP Drop on the two models by 45.19% and 46.84% for the Gliding Vertex model and ROI-Transformer model respectively, and the vanishing rate by 29.92% and 30.92%; compared with the SPL-C&W attack based on the $conv3$ mask, for the Gliding Vertex and ROI-Transformer models, the attack on the two models has a 4.81% and 5.04% lower modification rate, 5.47% and 17.41% higher mAP Drop, and vanishing rate increased by 0.5% and 8.08% respectively. The SPL-C&W attack based on $box1conv3$ mask can achieve more than 80% vanishing rate on two models with less than 3% modification rate only. The experimental results further prove the effectiveness of the selected sensitive pixel points on the local pixel attack effect and verify the superiority of the attack area mask scheme.

4.3. Attack on Remote Sensing Object Models

After verifying the effectiveness of the attack sensitivity mapping algorithm and the constructed attack region mask proposed in this chapter, it is necessary to explore the attack effect of the SPL-C&W attack. Firstly, we analyze the effect of different detection frame expansion parameters $kernel_0$ on the attack effect of SPL-C&W attack. As shown in Figure 7, the changes of mAP Drop and vanishing rate when the detection frame expansion parameter $kernel_0$ takes different values during the construction of the attack area mask for the local pixel attack with two white-box models. Table 1 shows the average modification rate of the attack on the image for different values of $kernel_0$.

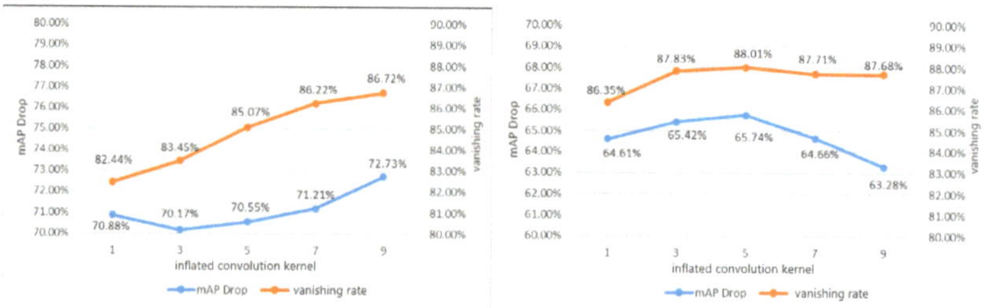

(a) (b)

Figure 7. Comparison of attack effects under different size of $kernel_0$. (**a**) Gliding Vertex; (**b**) ROI-Transformer.

Table 1. Average modification rate of local pixel attack under different $kernel_0$.

Model	1	3	5	7	9
Gliding Vertex	2.82%	2.95%	3.12%	3.24%	3.37%
ROI-Transformer	2.29%	2.41%	2.49%	2.60%	2.72%

After finding the appropriate detection frame mask parameters, it is necessary to analyze whether the local pixel attack implemented by the SPL-C&W algorithm can achieve a good balance between the success rate of the attack and the attack modification pixel overhead with the appropriate parameters. A comparison of the attack effectiveness between the global pixel attack SW-C&W and the local pixel attack SPL-C&W is performed, as shown in Table 2 for the comparison of the attack success rate against the sample in the white-box case. From Table 2, we can learn that the difference between the mAP Drop of the SPL-C&W attack on the two white-box models and the SW-C&W attack is less than 5%. The maximum vanishing rate is reduced by about 11%, but the modification rate can be reduced from the original 100% to less than 4%. The loss of the attack effect brought by the decrease in the number of attack pixels is within the acceptable range.

Table 2. Comparison of global and local pixel attacks on two models.

Model	Attack	mAP Drop	Vanishing Rate	Modification Rate
Gliding Vertex	SW-C&W	76.12%	97.70%	100%
	SPL-C&W	72.73%	86.72%	3.37%
ROI-Transformer	SW-C&W	65.43%	94.74%	100%
	SPL-C&W	65.74%	88.01%	2.49%

As shown in Figures 8 and 9, the comparison of the transferability of the adversarial samples generated by the global pixel attack SW-C&W and the local pixel attack SPL-C&W on the black-box model is shown. From Figures 8 and 9, we can see that the difference between the adversarial samples generated by SW-C&W and SPL-C&W on the two white-box models is less than 0.1% on the local black-box R3Det model, which is related to the fact that the R3Det model itself is easier to break single-stage target detection model; the ROI-Transformer model as a black-box model, the transferability of the adversarial samples generated by SPL-C&W is even improved compared with SW-C&W, the mAP Drop is improved by 3.62%, and the vanishing rate improves by 20.23%; when the Gliding Vertex model is used as a black-box model, the attack of the adversarial samples generated by SPL-C&W attack For the local black-box BBAVectors model, the mAP Drop of the adversarial samples generated by the SPL-C&W algorithm attacking the Gliding Vertex model and the adversarial samples generated by the ROI-Transformer model decreased by 5.34% and 4.06%, respectively. Moreover, 4.06% and the vanishing rate decrease by 4.55% and 0.56%, respectively, and the loss of transferability of the adversarial samples due to the reduction of the number of attack pixels is within the acceptable range.

The experimental results effectively demonstrate that the local pixel attack proposed in this chapter reduces the attack overhead at the expense of a small fraction of the attack success rate and transferability. The average modification rate of the image is reduced by more than 96% relative to the global pixel attack.

(a) (b)

Figure 8. Adversarial Sample Transferability Tests Generated by Attacking the Gliding Vertex. (a) mAP Drop; (b) vanishing rate.

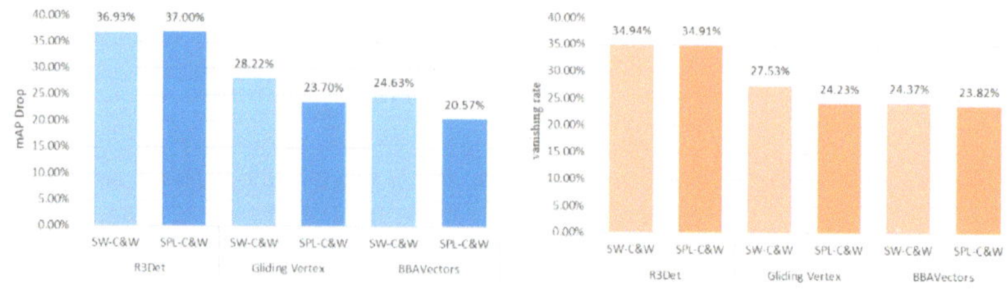

(**a**) (**b**)

Figure 9. Adversarial sample transferability test generated by attacking the ROI-Transformer. (**a**) mAP Drop; (**b**) vanishing rate.

Figures 10 and 11 present the visual detection results of the SPL-C&W attack on the two white-box models obtained for the adversarial samples. The first column of each row shows the visual detection result of the original image on the model, and the second column shows the final generated noise map. The third column shows the visual detection result of the adversarial sample on the model. From Figures 10 and 11, we can see that after applying the vanishing attack on the two white-box models using the SPL-C&W method, the effect of hiding all objects in the image by attacking only some pixels in the image is successfully achieved.

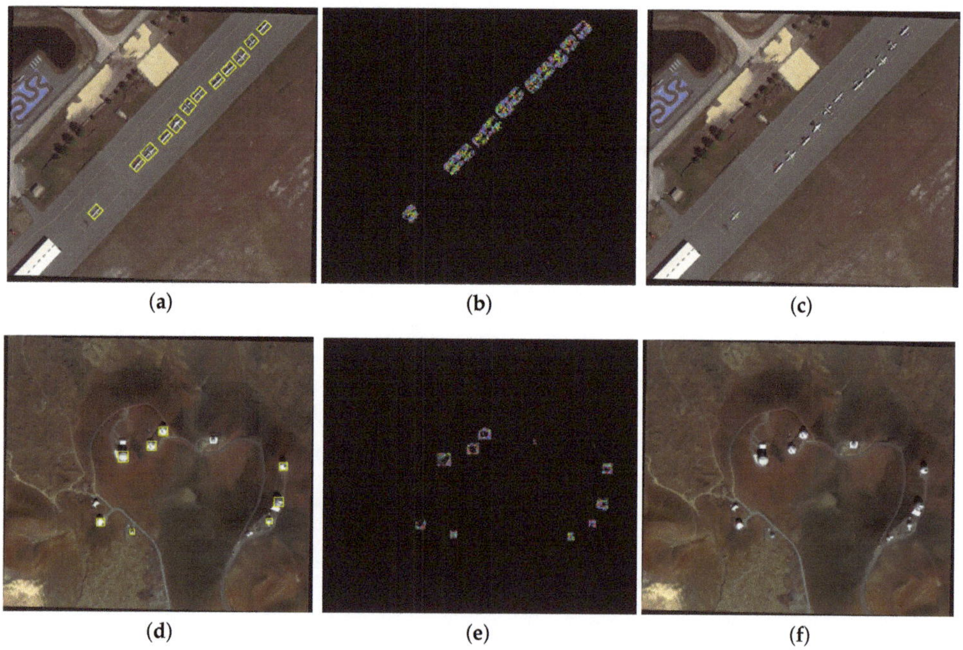

Figure 10. Results visualization for Gliding Vertex model. (**a**) Original image; (**b**) Perturbation image; (**c**) Adversarial image; (**d**) Original image; (**e**) Perturbation image; (**f**) Adversarial image.

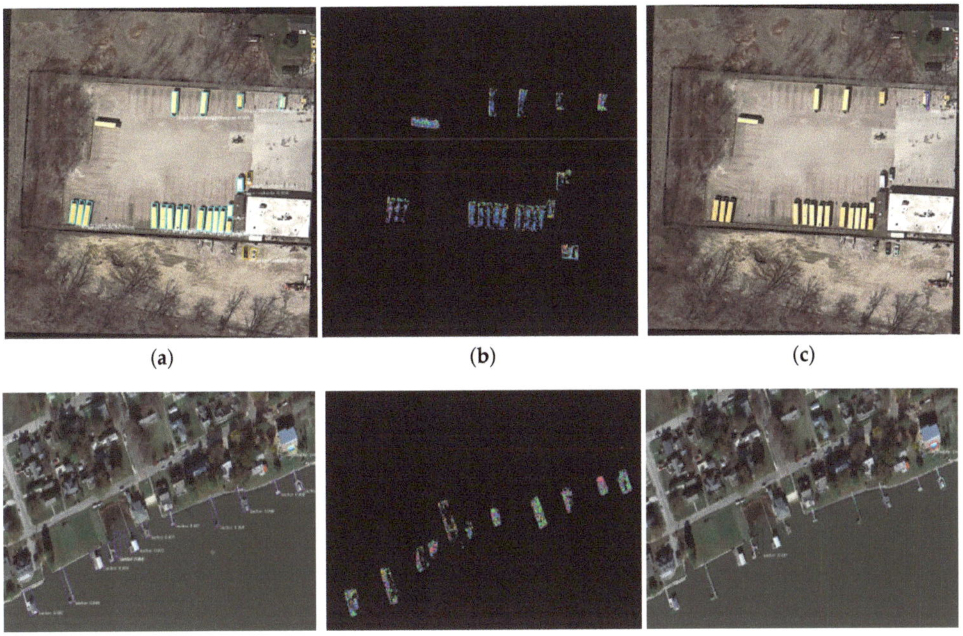

(a) (b) (c)

(d) (c) (f)

Figure 11. Results visualization for ROI-Transformer model. (**a**) Original image; (**b**) Perturbation image; (**c**) Adversarial image; (**d**) Original image; (**e**) Perturbation image; (**f**) Adversarial image.

5. Conclusions

In this work, we propose a local pixel attack method SPL-C&W applicable to remote sensing target detection models and implement the vanishing attack on several remote sensing object detectors. We design an attack adaptation method based on cut blocks' perturbation superposition and successfully adapt a typical adversarial attack algorithm to a remote sensing target detection model. A generalized hot restart perturbation update strategy is used in the algorithm, which can be used in combination with various attack algorithms to effectively solve the perturbation failure problem caused by cutting preprocessing modules. We implement the search for the location of attack-sensitive pixel points in the image by designing an attack sensitivity mapping method. The attack region mask scheme with the detection frame information limits the search range of sensitive pixel points, reducing the overhead of attack modification pixels. The experimental results show the superiority of the adversarial samples generated by our method in terms of attack effect and transferability, laying a solid foundation for the subsequent research on adversarial samples in the field of remote sensing image recognition and providing reference and guidance for the development of more secure and robust remote sensing image recognition models in the future.

Author Contributions: Conceptualization, methodology, L.L.; validation, Z.X. and H.G.; formal analysis, D.Y.; investigation, Z.X.; resources, H.G.; data curation, D.H.; writing—original draft preparation, L.L.; writing—review and editing, Z.X. All authors have read and agreed to the published version of the manuscript.

Funding: This work has been supported by Beijing Science and Technology Program No. Z211100004121009.

Conflicts of Interest: The authors declare no conflict of interest.

References

1. Hu, F.; Xia, G.S.; Hu, J.; Zhang, L. Transferring Deep Convolutional Neural Networks for the Scene Classification of High-Resolution Remote Sensing Imagery. *Remote Sens.* **2015**, *7*, 14680–14707. [CrossRef]
2. Zhang, F.; Du, B.; Zhang, L. Scene Classification via a Gradient Boosting Random Convolutional Network Framework. *IEEE Trans. Geosci. Remote Sens.* **2016**, *54*, 1793–1802. [CrossRef]
3. Chen, Y.; Jiang, H.; Li, C.; Jia, X.; Ghamisi, P. Deep Feature Extraction and Classification of Hyperspectral Images Based on Convolutional Neural Networks. *IEEE Trans. Geosci. Remote Sens.* **2016**, *54*, 6232–6251. [CrossRef]
4. Cheng, G.; Yang, C.; Yao, X.; Guo, L.; Han, J. When Deep Learning Meets Metric Learning: Remote Sensing Image Scene Classification via Learning Discriminative CNNs. *IEEE Trans. Geosci. Remote Sens.* **2018**, *56*, 2811–2821. [CrossRef]
5. Xu, Y.; Fu, M.; Wang, Q.; Wang, Y.; Chen, K.; Xia, G.S.; Bai, X. Gliding Vertex on the Horizontal Bounding Box for Multi-Oriented Object Detection. *IEEE Trans. Pattern Anal. Mach. Intell.* **2021**, *43*, 1452–1459. [CrossRef] [PubMed]
6. Ding, J.; Xue, N.; Long, Y.; Xia, G.S.; Lu, Q. Learning RoI Transformer for Oriented Object Detection in Aerial Images. In Proceedings of the 2019 IEEE/CVF Conference on Computer Vision and Pattern Recognition (CVPR), Long Beach, CA, USA, 15–20 June 2019; pp. 2844–2853. [CrossRef]
7. Chen, S.T.; Cornelius, C.; Martin, J.; Chau, D.H.P. ShapeShifter: Robust Physical Adversarial Attack on Faster R-CNN Object Detector. In Proceedings of the Machine Learning and Knowledge Discovery in Databases, Dublin, Ireland, 10–14 September 2018; Berlingerio, M., Bonchi, F., Gärtner, T., Hurley, N., Ifrim, G., Eds.; Lecture Notes in Computer Science; Springer International Publishing: Cham, Switzerland, 2019; pp. 52–68. [CrossRef]
8. Zhou, B.; Khosla, A.; Lapedriza, A.; Oliva, A.; Torralba, A. Learning Deep Features for Discriminative Localization. In Proceedings of the 2016 IEEE Conference on Computer Vision and Pattern Recognition (CVPR), Las Vegas, NV, USA, 27–30 June 2016; pp. 2921–2929. [CrossRef]
9. Qian, W.; Yang, X.; Peng, S.; Yan, J.; Guo, Y. Learning Modulated Loss for Rotated Object Detection. *Proc. AAAI Conf. Artif. Intell.* **2021**, *35*, 2458–2466. [CrossRef]
10. Simonyan, K.; Vedaldi, A.; Zisserman, A. Deep Inside Convolutional Networks: Visualising Image Classification Models and Saliency Maps. *arXiv* **2014**, arXiv:1312.6034.
11. Goodfellow, I.J.; Shlens, J.; Szegedy, C. Explaining and Harnessing Adversarial Examples. In Proceedings of the ICLR, San Diego, CA, USA, 7–9 May 2015.
12. Madry, A.; Makelov, A.; Schmidt, L.; Tsipras, D.; Vladu, A. Towards Deep Learning Models Resistant to Adversarial Attacks. In Proceedings of the ICLR, Vancouver, BC, Canada, 30 April–3 May 2018.
13. Kurakin, A.; Goodfellow, I.; Bengio, S. Adversarial examples in the physical world. In Proceedings of the ICLR, Toulon, France, 24–26 April 2017.
14. Dong, Y.; Liao, F.; Pang, T.; Su, H.; Zhu, J.; Hu, X.; Li, J. Boosting Adversarial Attacks with Momentum. In Proceedings of the 2018 IEEE/CVF Conference on Computer Vision and Pattern Recognition, Salt Lake City, UT, USA, 18–23 June 2018; pp. 9185–9193. [CrossRef]
15. Carlini, N.; Wagner, D. Towards Evaluating the Robustness of Neural Networks. In Proceedings of the 2017 IEEE Symposium on Security and Privacy (SP), San Jose, CA, USA, 22–24 May 2017; pp. 39–57. [CrossRef]
16. Chen, L.; Zhu, G.; Li, Q.; Li, H. Adversarial Example in Remote Sensing Image Recognition. *arXiv* **2020**, arXiv:1910.13222.
17. Ai, S.; Voundi Koe, A.S.; Huang, T. Adversarial perturbation in remote sensing image recognition. *Appl. Soft Comput.* **2021**, *105*, 107252. [CrossRef]
18. Burnel, J.C.; Fatras, K.; Flamary, R.; Courty, N. Generating Natural Adversarial Remote Sensing Images. *IEEE Trans. Geosci. Remote Sens.* **2022**, *60*, 1–14. [CrossRef]
19. Czaja, W.; Fendley, N.; Pekala, M.; Ratto, C.; Wang, I.J. Adversarial examples in remote sensing. In Proceedings of the 26th ACM SIGSPATIAL International Conference on Advances in Geographic Information Systems, Seattle, WA, USA, 6–9 November 2018; pp. 408–411. [CrossRef]
20. Xu, Y.; Ghamisi, P. Universal Adversarial Examples in Remote Sensing: Methodology and Benchmark. *IEEE Trans. Geosci. Remote Sens.* **2022**, *60*, 1–15. [CrossRef]
21. Den Hollander, R.; Adhikari, A.; Tolios, I.; Van Bekkum, M.; Bal, A.; Hendriks, S.; Kruithof, M.; Gross, D.; Jansen, N.; Perez, G.; et al. Adversarial patch camouflage against aerial detection. In Proceedings of the Artificial Intelligence and Machine Learning in Defense Applications II, Online Only, UK, 21–25 September 2020; p. 11. [CrossRef]
22. Ren, S.; He, K.; Girshick, R.; Sun, J. Faster R-CNN: Towards Real-Time Object Detection with Region Proposal Networks. *IEEE Trans. Pattern Anal. Mach. Intell.* **2017**, *39*, 1137–1149. [CrossRef] [PubMed]
23. Redmon, J.; Divvala, S.; Girshick, R.; Farhadi, A. You Only Look Once: Unified, Real-Time Object Detection. In Proceedings of the 2016 IEEE Conference on Computer Vision and Pattern Recognition (CVPR), Las Vegas, NV, USA, 27–30 June 2016; pp. 779–788. [CrossRef]
24. Xia, G.S.; Bai, X.; Ding, J.; Zhu, Z.; Belongie, S.; Luo, J.; Datcu, M.; Pelillo, M.; Zhang, L. DOTA: A Large-Scale Dataset for Object Detection in Aerial Images. In Proceedings of the 2018 IEEE/CVF Conference on Computer Vision and Pattern Recognition, Salt Lake City, UT, USA, 18–23 June 2018; pp. 3974–3983. [CrossRef]

25. Xie, C.; Wang, J.; Zhang, Z.; Zhou, Y.; Xie, L.; Yuille, A. Adversarial Examples for Semantic Segmentation and Object Detection. In Proceedings of the 2017 IEEE International Conference on Computer Vision (ICCV), Venice, Italy, 22–29 October 2017; pp. 1378–1387. [CrossRef]
26. Yang, X.; Yan, J.; Feng, Z.; He, T. R3Det: Refined Single-Stage Detector with Feature Refinement for Rotating Object. *Proc. AAAI Conf. Artif. Intell.* **2021**, *35*, 3163–3171. [CrossRef]
27. Yi, J.; Wu, P.; Liu, B.; Huang, Q.; Qu, H.; Metaxas, D. Oriented Object Detection in Aerial Images with Box Boundary-Aware Vectors. In Proceedings of the 2021 IEEE Winter Conference on Applications of Computer Vision (WACV), Waikoloa, HI, USA, 3–8 January 2021; pp. 2149–2158. [CrossRef]

electronics

Article

Strong Interference UAV Motion Target Tracking Based on Target Consistency Algorithm

Li Tan [1,2,*], Xiaokai Huang [1], Xinyue Lv [1], Xujie Jiang [1] and He Liu [3]

1 School of Computer Science and Engineering, Beijing Technology and Business University, Beijing 100048, China; huangxk@st.btbu.edu.cn (X.H.); lvxy@nercita.org.cn (X.L.); 2130072019@st.btbu.edu.cn (X.J.)
2 Chongqing Institute of Microelectronics Industry Technology, University of Electronic Science and Technology of China, Chongqing 400031, China
3 Chongqing Academy of Education Science, Chongqing 400015, China; 20221401016@stu.cqu.edu.cn
* Correspondence: tanli@th.btbu.edu.cn

Abstract: In recent years, unmanned aerial vehicle (UAV) image target tracking technology, which obtains motion parameters of moving targets and achieves a behavioral understanding of moving targets by identifying, detecting and tracking moving targets in UAV images, has been widely used in urban safety fields such as accident rescue, traffic monitoring and personnel detection. Due to the problems of complex backgrounds, small scale and a high density of targets, as well as mutual occlusion among targets in UAV images, this leads to inaccurate results of single object tracking (SOT). To solve the problem of tracking target loss caused by inaccurate tracking results, this paper proposes a strong interference motion target tracking method based on the target consistency algorithm for SOT based on an interframe fusion and trajectory confidence mechanism, fusing previous frames for the tracking trajectory correction of current frames, learning again from previous frames to update the model and adjusting the tracking trajectory according to the tracking duration. The experimental results can show that the accuracy of the proposed method in this paper is improved by 6.3% and the accuracy is improved by 2.6% compared with the benchmark method, which is more suitable for applications in the case of background clutter, camera motion and viewpoint change.

Keywords: UAVs; target tracking; interframe fusion; trajectory confidence

check for updates

Citation: Tan, L.; Huang, X.; Lv, X.; Jiang, X.; Liu, H. Strong Interference UAV Motion Target Tracking Based on Target Consistency Algorithm. *Electronics* **2023**, *12*, 1773. https://doi.org/10.3390/electronics12081773

Academic Editor: Mahmut Reyhanoglu

Received: 6 March 2023
Revised: 31 March 2023
Accepted: 5 April 2023
Published: 8 April 2023

1. Introduction

In recent years, unmanned aerial vehicles (UAVs) have developed rapidly. Due to their small size, low cost and high mobility, UAVs are widely used in exploration, rescue, traffic monitoring, personnel detection and other urban safety fields [1]. For special missions such as disaster rescue, urban patrol and anti-terrorist investigation, UAVs are usually used to accomplish tasks due to the complexity of the environment and mission scenarios [2]; thus, they have great potential for application in the field of urban security. Meanwhile, they play an important role in emergency rescue work in several security fields such as emergency mapping, environmental monitoring, earthquake relief, etc., where UAVs play an important role due to their flexibility, remote operation and powerful scalability [3,4].

With the continuous development of computer vision technology, target tracking in complex scenes with UAVs has gradually become a challenging research direction and focus, attracting many experts and scholars to conduct in-depth research and exploration and promoting the rapid development and wide application of UAV target tracking technology on the basis of deep learning [5].

Currently, target tracking methods can be divided into three categories: correlation filter-based target tracking, multi-feature fusion-based target tracking and deep learning method-based target tracking. Among them, the correlation filter-based target tracking method proposes a filtering template for performing operations on candidate target regions. The target position of the current frame is the position of its maximum output response. Correlation filtering-based target tracking methods are suitable for real-time applications, especially on embedded systems with limited computational resources. For example, Qin et al. [6] constructed a target tracking model based on Kalman filtering and the Camshift method of multi-feature fusion, which can effectively improve the tracking effectiveness. Zhang et al. [7] introduced the background information of a target's neighborhood into the similarity measurement between the target and the candidate, proposed a scale estimation mechanism that relies only on the Hellinger distance mean shift process and detected the size estimation to reduce the effect of background clutter.

To address the limitations of single features, researchers have investigated ways to improve the performance of target tracking by fusing different features. The Staple [8] algorithm uses a combination of the global color histogram and histogram of oriented gradient (HOG) methods to describe the target. First, in the global color template, the motion foreground and static background are further computed based on their pre-estimated positions, and then the score of each pixel is obtained to derive the color response map. Then, in the HOG template, the HOG features are extracted from the previously determined target regions, and, thus, the dense response template is obtained. Finally, the scores of the two templates are linearly combined and the location of the target is finally estimated. The spatially regularized discriminative correlation filters (SRDCF) [9] tracking algorithm uses spatially regularized components to address boundary effects, employing regularized weights to penalize the filter coefficients during training and generate a more discriminative model. The temporal regularized correlation filters (STRCF) [10] tracking algorithm introduces temporal regularization into the SRDCF tracking algorithm. The background-aware correlation filters (BACF) [11] tracking algorithm dynamically models the foreground and background of the target using HOG features, while an alternating direction method of multipliers (ADMM) [12] optimization method is designed to solve the filter. The aberrance repressed correlation filters (ARCF) [13] tracking algorithm suppresses the rate of change of the response map that occurs at the time of detection and then suppresses the aberration of the response map in cases such as target occlusion, as a way to improve the tracking accuracy.

The purpose of a target tracking method based on deep learning is to optimize the distance metric between detections. Due to the consideration of a variety of influencing factors that are not beneficial for target tracking, such as the generally low resolution of aerial UAV videos, more interfering targets, and faster viewpoint transformation, Bi et al. [14] proposed a context-based target tracking method for aerial UAV videos. The effect of regression is improved by connecting multiple convolutional layers with a residual module, which can effectively improve the tracking effect of the algorithm. Zha et al. [15] added the semantic space sub-module to the twin network-based model as an adaptation to track the target captured by the UAV in the middle of the temporal space, which can solve the problems of target occlusion and target disappearance and improve the accuracy of target tracking.

In summary, the general step of target tracking is to estimate the trajectory model (including position, the direction of motion, shape, etc.) of the tracked target in each scene of the captured video, and a powerful tracker can then assign consistent markers to the target object in successive scenes. Therefore, visual tracking is an operation designed to locate, detect and define a dynamic configuration of one or more targets in a video sequence from one or more cameras. With the rapid development of UAVs and the rapid increase in video material from aerial UAV photography, single target tracking for aerial UAV video is one of the key problems studied by scholars, which can provide fundamental support for practical applications in related UAV fields.

Therefore, to address the problem of inaccurate target tracking results in aerial UAV video due to complex backgrounds, a high density of small-scale targets and mutual occlusion between targets, this paper proposes a strong interference motion target tracking method based on the target consistency algorithm for UAVs. The main contributions of the method are as follows:

(1) The interframe fusion method is introduced in the model to correct the model's tracking trajectory of the target by fusing the current frame with the previous frames, and to update the model's tracking trajectory by combining the tracking results of the previous frames and learning them again.
(2) The model introduces a trajectory confidence mechanism, which defines the confidence level of the trajectory according to the duration of the tracked trajectory, and corrects and updates the trajectory in multiple directions to ensure the accuracy of the tracking results.
(3) The model optimizes the objective function using the ADMM algorithm and solves the function by iteration to obtain the optimal tracking trajectory.

The remainder of this paper is organized as follows. Section 2 presents the related work. Section 3 details the proposed method. The experiments and results analyses are provided in Section 4 while introducing the selected dataset and evaluation indicators. Finally, conclusions are drawn in Section 5.

2. Related Works

At present, scholars related to target tracking methods for aerial UAV video have conducted in-depth research and exploration, and many excellent results have been achieved; the details of some UAV target tracking algorithms are shown in Table 1. Among them, Liu et al. [16] constructed a target tracker TLD-KCF based on a conditional scale adaptive algorithm for aerial UAV video, and this method improved the tracking capability of quadrotor UAVs in complex outdoor scenes. Li et al. [17] designed a multi-vehicle tracking method for UAVs by combining SOT-based forward position prediction with results from intersection over union tracker (IOUT), which enhanced the detection results of the association phase. Chu et al. [18] used the results of target detection as SOT results and designed a multiple object tracking (MOT) network using multiple target interactions, which had a significant improvement in the performance of the MOT. Since a large number of targets overlap and obscure each other when performing UAV image multi-object tracking, this leads to identity-switch problems between targets and affects the performance of the algorithm. Feng et al. [19] used an SOT tracker and a reidentification network of the siamese region proposal network (SiameseRPN) [20] to extract short-term and long-term cues of targets, respectively. Then, a data association method with switcher-aware classification was used to improve the tracking results of the network while solving the identity-switch problem. However, in this method, the mutual independence of the SOT tracker and data association prevented the modules from collaborating well in the algorithm. For this reason, Zhu et al. [21] proposed a dual matching attention network to integrate single object tracking and data association into a unified framework to deal with intra-class interference and frequent interactions between targets. Wan et al. [22] designed a target tracking method based on sparse representation theory for aerial drone videos to solve the problem of partial occlusion between objects present in aerial drone videos that are used to localize the objects captured by UAVs, which contain pedestrians, vehicles, etc.

Table 1. Details of some UAV target tracking algorithms.

Proposer(s)	Dataset	Description	Characteristic
Liu et al. [16]	VOT 2014	A target tracker TLD-KCF based on a conditional scale adaptive algorithm for aerial UAV video.	Improved tracking capability of quadcopter UAVs in complex outdoor scenarios.
Li et al. [17]	UA-DETRAC	A multi-vehicle tracking method for UAV.	Combining SOT-based forward position prediction with results from IOUT enhances detection results in the association stage.

Table 1. *Cont.*

Proposer(s)	Dataset	Description	Characteristic
Chu et al. [18]	MOT15 MOT16	A CNN-based framework for online MOT.	The MOT network is designed through the interaction of multiple SOT results, so that the performance of MOT is significantly improved.
Feng et al. [19]	MOT16 MOT17	A unified MOT learning framework.	Makes full use of both long-term and short-term cues to deal with the complexities of MOT scenes, and considers potential identity-switch through switcher-aware classification.
Zhu et al. [21]	MOT16 MOT17	An MOT with Dual Matching attention networks.	Integrates the merits of single object tracking and data association methods in a unified framework to handle noisy detections and frequent interactions between targets.
Wan et al. [22]	VOT2015	A target tracking method for aerial UAV video based on sparse representation theory.	Solves the problem of partial occlusion between targets in aerial drone video.
Liu et al. [23]	MDMT	A multi-match authentication network MIA-net for multi-target tracking missions with multiple UAVs.	Solves cross-UAV association problems by constructing cross-UAV target topology relationships through local–global matching algorithms.
Yeom [24]	Practical scenarios	A long-range ground target tracking algorithm for small UAVs.	Selects the most suitable trajectory from multiple trajectories in a dense trajectory environment using nearest neighbor association rules.
Jiang et al. [25]	The 1st Anti-UAV Workshop and Challenge	An improved YOLOv5 UAV detection and tracking algorithm.	High-speed tracking performance by training low-resolution detectors combined with Kalman algorithms.
Lin et al. [26]	VisDrone2019	An improved UAV multi-target tracking model based on FairMOT.	Improves model tracking performance by sorting out temporal correlation structures and separating different functional heads.
Bhagat et al. [27]	Simulation experiments	A DQN-based persistent target tracking model for urban environments.	Enables UAVs to continuously track targets in different environments while avoiding obstacles in the environment.
Yang et al. [28]	ImageNet	A novel framework for hierarchical deep learning task assignments.	Performs tasks that require intensive computing with mobile edge computing servers that are rich in computing resources.
Bi et al. [14]	UAV123	A context-based remote sensing target tracking method for aerial UAV video MDnet.	Introduction of the RA-CACF module into the online tracking phase of the tracking network.
He et al. [29]	Visdrone-mot2020	A method for tracking different classes of multiple targets in different scenarios COFE model	Includes three main modules: multi-class target detection, coarse-class multi-target tracking and fine-grained trajectory refinement.

Liu et al. [23] proposed a multi-matching identity authentication network (MIA-Net) for a multi-target tracking task with multiple UAVs. The MIA-Net effectively solved the cross-UAV association problem by constructing cross-UAV target topology relationships through a local–global matching algorithm, and effectively complemented the obscured targets by taking advantage of multiple UAV viewpoint mapping. Yeom [24] studied ground target tracking algorithms at long distances (up to 1 km) using small UAVs and improved the association between trajectories by selecting the most suitable of multiple trajectories in a dense trajectory environment using nearest neighbor association rules. The detection of moving targets in the algorithm also includes frame-to-frame subtraction and thresholding, morphological operations and false alarm elimination based on object size and shape property, and the target's trajectory is initialized by the difference between the two nearest points in consecutive frames; then, the measurement statistically nearest to the state prediction updates the target's state. Jiang et al. [25] proposed an improved YOLOv5 UAV detection algorithm and tracking method to address the difficulties of poor imaging contrast, complex background and small target scale. The method improved UAV detection probability by adding a detection head and attention module, and achieved high-speed tracking performance by training low-resolution detectors combined with the Kalman algorithm. Lin et al. [26] proposed an improved UAV multi-target tracking model based on FairMOT. The model contains a structure that separates the detection head and the ReID head to reduce the influence between each functional head. In addition, they developed a temporal embedding structure to enhance the characterization capability of the model. By combing the temporal association structure and separating the different functional heads, the performance of the model in UAV tracking tasks is improved.

Bhagat et al. [27] proposed a deep learning technique based on target-tracking DQN networks for persistent target tracking in urban environments. After experiments, it was shown that the algorithm enabled UAVs to persistently track targets in different environments while avoiding obstacles in both the training environment and the unseen environment. Since UAVs are generally severely limited in power supply and have a low computational power to perform tasks requiring intensive computation on their own, this poses a great challenge in terms of computational power, low latency and inference accuracy. Based on the above reasons, Yang et al. [28] proposed a novel hierarchical deep learning task assignment framework in which UAVs are embedded in the lower layers of the pre-trained CNN models, while mobile edge computing servers with abundant computational resources handle the higher layers of the CNN models; the effectiveness of the proposed offloading framework was demonstrated after experimental results. Bi et al. [14] proposed a context-based remote sensing target tracking method MDnet for aerial UAV video. In the network structure, residual connections are applied to fuse multiple convolutions, thus improving the network representation of remote sensing targets. In the pre-training phase, an enhancement strategy of rotating an adversarial autoencoder is used to generate enough negative samples to enhance the ability to distinguish between targets and background interference. In the online tracking phase, the RA-CACF module is introduced into the tracking network for remote sensing target tracking in aerial UAV video applications. He et al. [29] proposed a COFE method model for tracking different classes of multi-targets in different scenarios. The method contains three main modules: multi-class target detection, coarse-class multi-target tracking and fine-grained trajectory refinement.

With the development of UAV target tracking technology, we must at the same time be primarily aware of the risks involved. Especially when UAV target detection technology is applied in the field of urban security, it is important for professionals to be aware of the importance of UAV communication security, to understand possible threats, attacks and countermeasures related to UAV communication. It is also able to secure its communication using technologies such as blockchain technology, machine learning technology, fog computing and software-defined networking to guarantee the security and privacy of relevant data [30]. To deal with attacks and security threats such as jamming, information leakage and spoofing in UAV communication, Ko et al. [31] proposed a secure protocol after studying the security prerequisites of UAV communication protocols as a way to protect the communication between UAVs and between UAVs and ground control stations. The protocol can achieve perfect forward secrecy and non-repudiation, and is believed to have good applications in the field of urban security, where a high level of communication security is required. In summary, the correlation filter-based target tracking method can update the tracker at any time according to the diverse changes of the tracked targets, and it runs faster and is more suitable for target tracking in aerial UAV videos. Existing discriminative correlation filter-based trackers use predefined regularization terms to optimize learning for the target, such as to suppress the learning for the background or to adjust the change rate of the correlation filter. However, the predefined parameters not only require a lot of effort to adjust, but also cannot be adapted to new situations where no rules have been established.

Therefore, the automatic spatio-temporal regularization tracker (AutoTrack) [32] tracking algorithm improves on the STRCF algorithm, which uses the connection of the responses of two adjacent frames as an adaptive spatio-temporal regularization term and uses the global response change to determine its update rate, thus improving the tracking performance. The spatio-temporal regularization term proposed in this algorithm can make full use of local and global response variations to achieve both spatial and temporal regularization, as well as automatic and adaptive hyperparameter optimization, based on the local and global information hidden in the response graph. The algorithm uses response variation to achieve regularization because the information hidden in the response graph is crucial in the detection process, and its quality somehow reflects the similarity between the target appearance model learned in the previous frames and the actual target detected in the current frame. Additionally, the reason why the algorithm utilizes both local and global response changes is that, if only global response map changes are used, then local response changes in the plausibility of different locations in the target image are ignored, and drastic local changes will lead to low plausibility, and vice versa.

Existing target tracking algorithms use a frame-by-frame approach to update the model, which can easily ignore the issue of whether the tracking effect of the current frame is accurate or not and update the tracker blindly, which can lead to tracker learning errors. Therefore, this paper proposes a strong interference motion target tracking method based on the target consistency algorithm for the problem of losing the tracked target due to the inaccurate tracking result of the current frame.

3. Method

3.1. Overall Structure

We propose in this paper a strong interference motion target tracking method based on the target consistency algorithm for aerial UAV video, and the general framework is shown in Figure 1. In the tracking model, the current frame is fused with the previous frame for tracking trajectory correction, and the previous frame is combined to update the model. Secondly, a trajectory confidence mechanism is proposed in the tracking model. The longer a trajectory is tracked, the more reliable this trajectory is, as a way to enhance the accuracy of subsequent tracking. Finally, the objective function is optimized using ADMM, and the problem is decomposed into multiple sub-problems to iteratively solve the problem and finally obtain the global optimal solution.

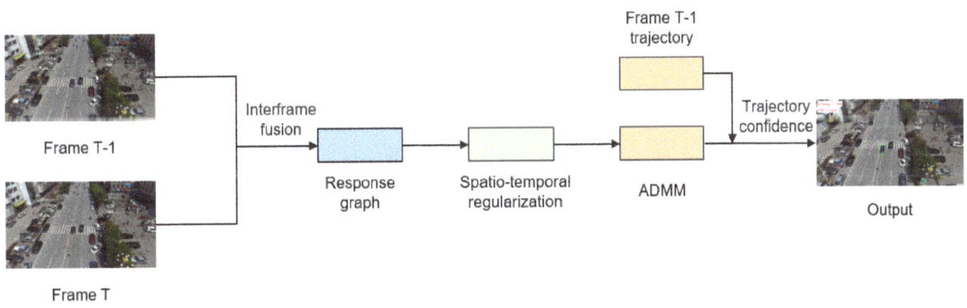

Figure 1. The general framework diagram.

3.2. Interframe Fusion

Since the tracking effect of the AutoTrack algorithm on the target only depends on the response map linkage between adjacent frames, when there is wrong tracking, it will cause the model to lose the effective tracking target information. Therefore, this paper improves the method based on the AutoTrack algorithm to enhance the interframe fusion capability of the model.

The method learns online and updates the relevant parameters automatically, using spatial local response variation as spatial regularization, allowing the filter to focus on learning the plausible places while using global response variation to determine the update rate of the filter and ensure its stability. This method adaptively learns and continuously adjusts the predefined parameters, which also use local as well as global response maps, with local variation indicating local plausibility in the target bounding box and global variation indicating global plausibility in the target bounding box, where severe illumination changes and partial occlusion reduce the plausibility of the appearance, to dynamically adjust the spatial as well as temporal weights so that it is possible to make better use of the local and global information implied in the response map.

When the problem of losing the tracking target due to inaccurate tracking results of the current frame occurs, the method fuses the previous frames on the tracking results of the current frame for tracking trajectory correction, and updates the model by combining the previous frames to learn again to avoid tracker learning errors, thus enhancing the accuracy of subsequent tracking.

3.3. *Trajectory Confidence Mechanism*

To integrate the decomposability of the pairwise ascent method with the excellent convergence properties of the augmented Lagrange multiplier method, an improved form of the optimal alternating direction method of multipliers (ADMM) has been proposed. The aim is to be able to decompose the original function and the augmented function to facilitate parallel optimization under more general assumptions.

The core of the correlation filter-based target tracking problem is the solution of filters. With the advent of advanced algorithms, the models of filters are becoming more and more complex and computationally slow, making the advantage of correlation filtering in terms of computational speed less and less obvious. For example, the AutoTrack algorithm we improved in Section 3.2 uses spatio-temporal regularization to solve the boundary effect, and this measure to solve the boundary effect will make the tracking of correlation filtering face the challenge of real-time. Therefore, introducing the ADMM algorithm in this context can be a good way to divide a large optimization problem into multiple subproblems that can be solved simultaneously in a distributed manner, so that the objective function of the filter can be quickly minimized by iterating over the subproblems to obtain the global optimal solution.

The ADMM algorithm provides a framework for solving optimization problems with linear equation constraints, allowing us to break down the original optimization problem into several relatively well-solved suboptimization problems for iterative solving. This "disassembly" function is the core of the ADMM algorithm. The algorithm takes the following form.

$$\begin{aligned} &\min_{x,z} f(x) + g(z) \\ &s.t. Ax + Bz = c \end{aligned} \tag{1}$$

Here, both $f(x)$ and $g(z)$ are convex functions. At this point, their corresponding augmented Lagrangian functions are:

$$L_\rho(x,z,y) = f(x) + g(z) + y^T(Ax + Bz - c) + \left(\frac{\rho}{2}\right)\|Ax + Bz - c\|_2^2 \tag{2}$$

Additionally, its optimization steps are:

$$\begin{aligned} x^{k+1} &:= \arg\min_x L_\rho\left(x, z^k, y^k\right) \\ z^{k+1} &:= \arg\min L_\rho\left(x^{k+1}, z, y^k\right) \\ y^{k+1} &:= y^k + \rho\left(Ax^{k+1} + Bz^{k+1} - c\right) \end{aligned} \tag{3}$$

This is a combination of the pairwise ascent method and the multiplicative Lagrange multiplier method. Theoretically, the optimization variables can be further split into more blocks, such as x, z, $z_1, \ldots$ If we express the optimal solution of the original problem as:

$$p^* = inf\{f(x) + g(z)|Ax + Bz - c\} \tag{4}$$

then the ADMM algorithm, satisfying the basic assumptions, ensures that:

$$f\left(x^k\right) + g\left(z^k\right) \rightarrow p^* ask \rightarrow \infty \tag{5}$$

This also reflects the convergence of the algorithm, i.e., the final global optimal solution is obtained.

In summary, the trajectory confidence mechanism in this paper refers to the process of fusing the previous frames, which is not just a simple additive relationship, but is adjusted according to the tracking duration during the tracking process. The longer the tracking duration indicates that the tracking is more stable and therefore this trajectory is more credible, the higher the weight occupied by the current frame, as shown in Equation (6). This method performs fusion in a cumulative manner, not only with a particular frame, as a way to solve the tracking problem that is overly dependent on two adjacent frames.

$$S_i = \alpha * S_{i-1} + \beta * R_i \tag{6}$$

where i is the current frame, R_i is the detection position of the current frame, S_i is the correct position of the current frame and α and β are the weighting coefficients.

4. Experiment

4.1. Experimental Environment

The operating system of this experimental platform: Memory 16GB, GPU: NVIDIA GeForce RTX 2060, Graphic memory: 8GB.

4.2. Dataset

This experiment used the VisDrone-SOT [33] UAV image single target tracking dataset. This dataset was collected by the AISKYEYE team at the Lab of Machine Learning and Data Mining, Tianjin University, China. The benchmark dataset consists of 400 video clips formed by 265,228 frames and 10,209 static images captured by various drone-mounted cameras, covering a wide range of aspects including location (taken from 14 different cities separated by thousands of kilometers in China), environment (urban and country), objects and density (sparse and crowded scenes). The dataset was collected in different scenarios and under various weather and lighting conditions. These frames were manually annotated by more than 2.6 million bounding boxes or frequent target points of interest, and contain a total of 10 categories of targets for bus, car, van, truck, awning-tricycle, tricycle, motor, bicycle, pedestrian and people. To better utilize the data, some important attributes are also provided, including aspect ratio change, background clutter, camera motion, full occlusion, illumination variation, low resolution, partial occlusion, scale variation, similar objects, viewpoint change and several other cases. Based on the above, we believe that the dataset contains geographic factors, scene factors, weather and lighting factors and common target types in urban security, and can represent a real urban security environment to some extent.

4.3. Evaluation Metrics

To verify the effectiveness of the proposed method, a comparison is made using precision and success rates.

(1) Precision Plot

The accuracy graph mainly measures the percentage of successful frames of the target rectangular bounding box predicted by the tracker within a given threshold distance, and the distance between the predicted target position and the center point between the actual positions was calculated to obtain the accuracy value. The number of video frames whose distance between the predicted position and the center point of the actual position was smaller than the set threshold varies for different thresholds, and their percentage is different, so a curve can be obtained.

(2) Accuracy Plot

The accuracy rate plot shows the proportion of bounding boxes predicted by the tracker with a coincidence rate score greater than a given threshold. The overlap rate is defined as:

$$OS = \frac{|a \cap b|}{|a \cup b|} \tag{7}$$

where OS is the coincidence score, which takes values from 0 to 1, a is the rectangular bounding box of the target predicted by the tracker, b is the rectangular bounding box of the real position of the target and $|\bullet|$ denotes the number of pixels in the region. A frame is a successful frame if its coincidence score is greater than a given threshold. The accuracy rate is the number of all successful frames as a percentage of the number of all frames.

4.4. Experimental Results and Analysis of Target Tracking Algorithms for UAVs

Since the algorithm proposed in this paper is based on a UAV's target tracking task in the urban security domain, we will validate and analyze the experimental results of the algorithm proposed in this paper and some of the UAV tracking algorithms mentioned in Section 2 on the VisDrone-SOT dataset in this section.

The results in Table 2 show that our proposed algorithm is in the leading position in terms of accuracy compared with other UAV target tracking algorithms at 59.8%. However, in terms of precision, the SO-MOT algorithm [34] is the best at 91.7% and our algorithm is 91.5%, with a difference of 0.2%. This is due to the presence of a strong detector based on Cascade RCNN and an embedding model based on a multi-grain network in the SO-MOT algorithm and the creation of a simple online multi-target tracker. The model initializes some tracklets based on the estimated bounding box in the first frame, and in subsequent frames, associates the bounding box with the existing tracklets based on the distance measured by the embedding features, making it possible to update the appearance features of trackers at each time step to handle appearance changes.

Table 2. Experimental results of target tracking algorithms for UAVs.

Methods	Precision (%)	Accuracy (%)
FairMOT + ReID [26]	90.4	57.8
TF-DQN [27]	88.4	52.6
Mdnet [14]	90.2	54.9
COFE [29]	91.1	58.7
SO-MOT [34]	**91.7**	59.6
Ours	91.5	**59.8**

In summary, we believe that the algorithm proposed in this paper can satisfy a UAV's target tracking task in urban security in terms of precision and accuracy. Although the present algorithm is for single-target tracking, we believe that it can still be improved and applied to multi-target tracking tasks, which will be the next step of our research.

4.5. Visualization of Experimental Results

Figure 2 shows a visualization of the experimental results of the proposed method on the dataset, where the leftmost image is a screenshot of the original video, and the three images on the right are screenshots of the visualization of the algorithm tracking a single target on the original video, where the target labeled by the bounding box is the target we need to track.

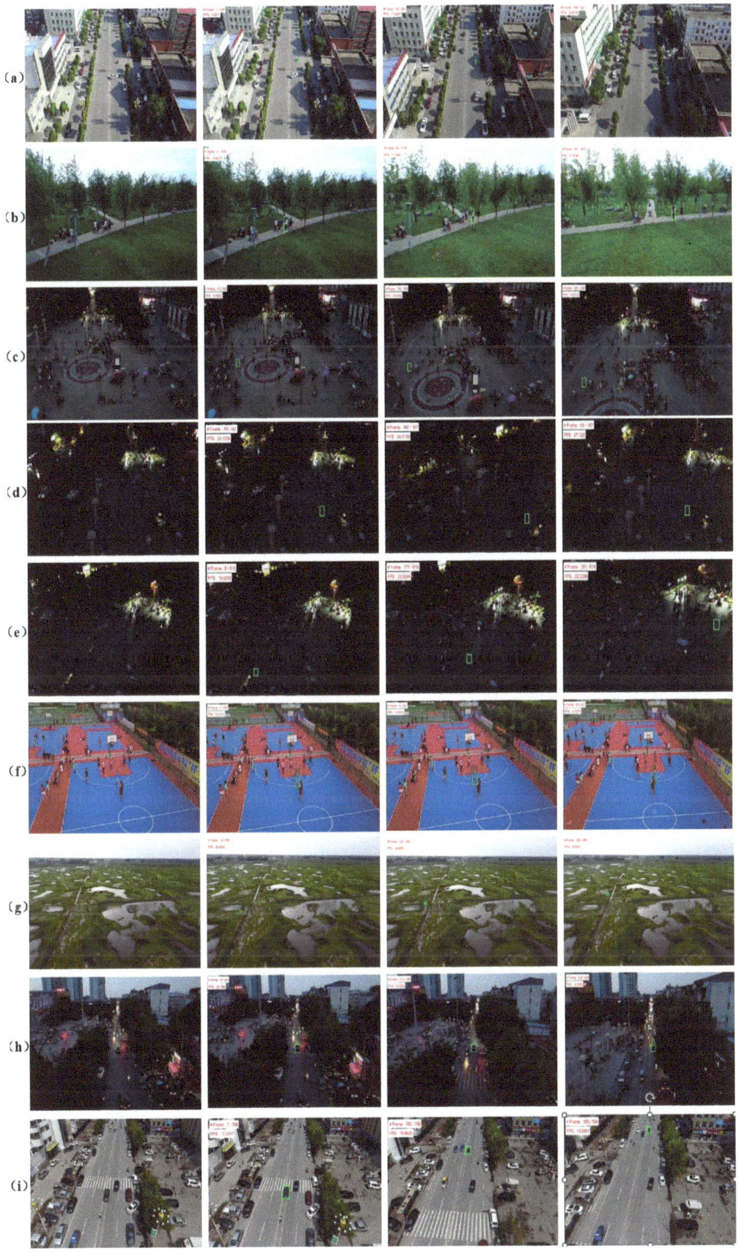

Figure 2. Visualization results of the algorithm under different conditions. The leftmost figure shows the original image in the dataset, and the right three figures show the resultant video frames of the tracking model. (**a**,**i**) shows the tracking effect when the light is sufficient and the targets are small in scale; (**b**,**f**) shows the tracking effect when the light is sufficient and the targets are obscured; (**c**,**h**) shows the tracking effect when the light is insufficient and the targets are dense; (**d**,**e**) shows the tracking effect when it is dark and the targets are small in scale; (**g**) shows the tracking effect when the targets are sparse and too small in scale.

4.6. Analysis of Trajectory Confidence Parameters

For the weight coefficients α and β in Equation (6), α should be less than 0.5, β should be greater than 0.5 and the sum of the weight coefficients should be 1, which means α + β = 1, since the detection position of the current frame should account for a larger percentage. Since the method proposed in this paper is an improvement of the AutoTrack algorithm, we used its experimental results as a benchmark to find the optimal weighting values by comparing the experimental results of α and β of the grid search taking values.

The precision and total precision of the proposed method in various scenarios when the weights α and β were taken as different values are shown in Table 3 and Figure 3. The results of the experiments show that the improved method proposed in this paper does not have the best accuracy in all cases. Among them, in the cases of complete occlusion, illumination change and partial occlusion, the detection precision is higher for the cases of occlusion and the complex environment because the AutoTrack algorithm itself introduces a temporal regularization term to locate similar targets between different video frames. Similarly, the improved method with α = 0.4, β = 0.6 is better in the case of aspect ratio variation and low resolution, because the key information of the target in the previous frames is more helpful for the model to achieve better interframe fusion to track the target correctly in the case of aspect ratio variation and low resolution. The improved method of α = 0.1, β = 0.9 works better when the background is cluttered, the camera is moving and the viewpoint is changing, also because the target position information of the current frame is more important than the previous frame in the above case, which can guarantee the precision better. Finally, according to the results of total precision, it can be seen that the precision of all four weight distributions is higher than that of the original AutoTrack algorithm, among which the precision is highest when α = 0.1, β = 0.9, which is 6.3% better than that of the AutoTrack algorithm.

The accuracy and total accuracy of the proposed method in various scenarios when the weights α and β take different values are also shown in Table 3 and Figure 3. The results of the experiments also show that the improved method proposed in this paper does not have the best accuracy in all cases. Among them, in the cases of aspect ratio change, complete occlusion, illumination change and low resolution, the accuracy of video frame detection in the case of large front-to-back changes of the target and a complex environment will be higher because the AutoTrack algorithm itself has a temporal regularization term. Meanwhile, the improved method of α = 0.2, β = 0.8 works better in the case of proportional change because in this case, the key information of the target in the previous frame needed to be balanced with the target information of the current frame to ensure the detection accuracy of video frames. The improved method of α = 0.1, β =0.9 works better when the background is cluttered, the camera is moving and the viewpoint is changing, again because in this case, the target position information of the current frame was more important than that of the previous frame, which can better guarantee the accuracy. Finally, according to the results of the total accuracy, it can be seen that the accuracy of all four weight distributions is higher than that of the original AutoTrack algorithm, and the accuracy is still the highest when α = 0.1, β = 0.9, which is 2.6% higher than that of the AutoTrack algorithm. Therefore, this paper adopts the improved algorithm with α = 0.1, and β = 0.9 weight distribution.

Table 3. Comparison of precision and accuracy under different weights.

Weights		Aspect Ratio Variation (%)	Background Clutter (%)	Camera Motion (%)	Completely Obscured (%)	Illumination Variation (%)	Low Resolution (%)	Partial Occlusion (%)	Proportional Changes (%)	Similar Objects (%)	Viewpoint Changes (%)	Total (%)
AutoTrack	precision	80.7	78.8	83.5	**88.0**	**94.9**	91.9	**94.0**	92.8	92.8	75.2	85.2
	accuracy	**50.5**	50.6	56.4	**61.3**	**64.9**	**57.9**	65.5	63.4	58.6	48.1	57.2
A = 0.4 B = 0.6	precision	**82.4**	86.7	89.7	87.5	94.5	**94.1**	93.8	92.8	92.8	84.9	90.7
	accuracy	49.9	53.3	58.5	60.5	63.1	57.7	65.4	63.6	59.2	52.5	58.8
A = 0.3 B = 0.7	precision	80.6	81.8	89.8	87.5	89.6	80.0	93.8	92.8	80.9	86.5	87.3
	accuracy	50.2	50.3	58.6	60.5	60.2	50.6	65.4	63.6	52.1	52.5	56.7
A = 0.2 B = 0.8	precision	80.3	87.3	90.1	87.5	94.6	91.9	93.8	92.8	92.8	87.0	91.1
	accuracy	50.3	54.2	59.3	60.8	63.5	57.6	65.5	**63.7**	59.2	53.7	59.5
A = 0.1 B = 0.9	precision	80.0	**87.9**	**90.6**	87.5	94.4	91.9	93.8	92.8	92.8	**87.9**	**91.5**
	accuracy	49.8	**54.7**	**59.6**	60.8	63.2	57.3	65.5	63.5	59.2	**54.6**	**59.8**

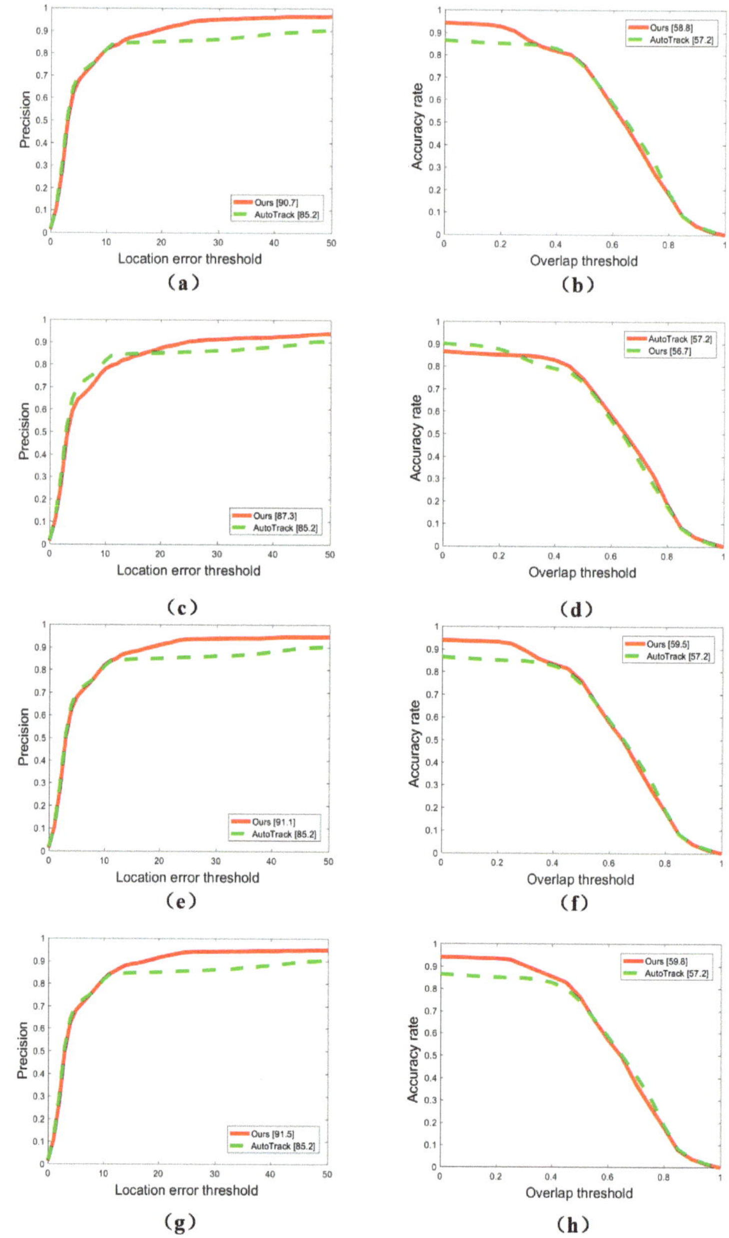

Figure 3. Comparison of total precision and total accuracy under different weights. (**a**) is the precision when $\alpha = 0.4$, $\beta = 0.6$, (**b**) is the accuracy when $\alpha = 0.4$, $\beta = 0.6$, (**c**) is the precision when $\alpha = 0.3$, $\beta = 0.7$, (**d**) is the accuracy when $\alpha = 0.3$, $\beta = 0.7$, (**e**) is the precision when $\alpha = 0.2$, $\beta = 0.8$, (**f**) is the accuracy when $\alpha = 0.2$, $\beta = 0.8$, (**g**) is the precision when $\alpha = 0.1$, $\beta = 0.9$ and (**h**) is the accuracy when $\alpha = 0.1$, $\beta = 0.9$.

4.7. Experiment Results and Analysis of Target Tracking Algorithm Based on Correlation Filtering

To test the effectiveness of the tracking algorithms proposed in this paper, we selected three excellent target tracking algorithms with correlation filter-based performance, Autotrack, Staple and ARCF, mentioned in Sections 1 and 2, and compared them with the algorithm proposed in this paper using the VisDrone-SOT dataset. Among them, Autotrack is the benchmark model of the algorithm proposed in this paper, which achieves both spatial and temporal regularization by making full use of local and global response variations through the spatio-temporal regularization term to achieve target localization. Additionally, Staple, based on the color response map derived from the global color histogram, uses the HOG method to extract the HOG features to obtain the dense response template and linearly combines the scores of the two templates to estimate the target location. In contrast, ARCF suppresses the rate of change of the response map at the time of detection, thus suppressing the distortion of the response map in the case of target occlusion and improving the tracking accuracy. Through experimental comparison with these three methods, the effectiveness of the proposed algorithm in this paper can be verified from three perspectives: the baseline model, the target tracking in complex cases and the target tracking in occlusion cases. The evaluation was performed using One-Pass Evaluation (OPE), which initializes the first frame of the image with the position of the actual labeled target, and the average accuracy and precision were obtained by calculation.

4.7.1. Precision and Accuracy Comparison of Different Correlation Filtering Algorithms

The comparison results of the precision and accuracy of different correlation filtering algorithms for various scenarios are shown in Table 4 and Figure 4.

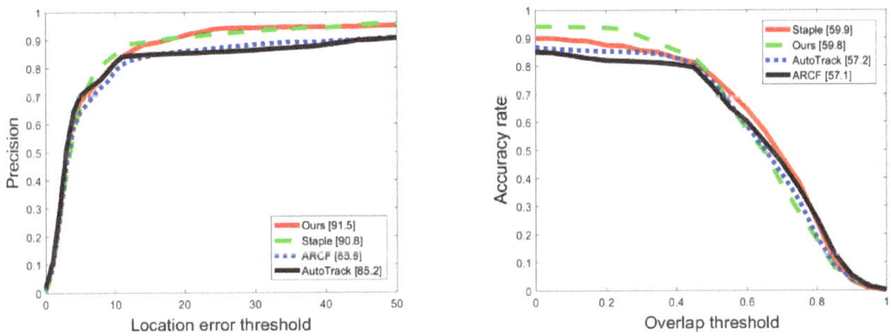

(a) (b)

Figure 4. Comparison of the total precision and total accuracy under different correlation filtering algorithms. (**a**) is the total precision of different algorithms, (**b**) is the total accuracy of different algorithms.

It can be seen that the precision of Staple is higher in the cases of aspect ratio change, camera motion and viewpoint change, because Staple can derive the target location by combining both color response maps and HOG dense response templates, and thus has the best target precision performance for the case of target scale change. Meanwhile, the precision of AutoTrack is higher in cases of complete occlusion, illumination change and partial occlusion, also because it has its spatio-temporal regularization term, which can guarantee the detection precision in the case of target occlusion change. Our proposed algorithm, on the other hand, can still guarantee detection precision in background clutter due to the introduction of the trajectory confidence mechanism. Finally, the comparison of the total precision of different correlation filtering algorithms shows that the precision of the proposed method is as high as 91.5%, which is not only higher than the precision of the AutoTrack algorithm, but also higher than the precision of the Staple and ARCF algorithms. Therefore, the method proposed in this paper is better under the comprehensive consideration of multiple cases.

Table 4. Comparison of the precision and accuracy under different correlation filtering algorithms.

Algorithm		Aspect Ratio Variation (%)	Background Clutter (%)	Camera Motion (%)	Completely Obscured (%)	Illumination Variation (%)	Low Resolution (%)	Partial Occlusion (%)	Proportional Changes (%)	Similar Objects (%)	Viewpoint Changes (%)	Total (%)
AutoTrack	precision	80.7	78.8	83.5	**88.0**	**94.9**	**91.9**	**94.0**	**92.8**	**92.8**	75.2	85.2
	accuracy	50.5	50.6	56.4	61.3	**64.9**	**57.9**	**65.5**	63.4	58.6	48.1	57.2
Staple	precision	**82.5**	86.9	**94.0**	85.0	90.4	79.5	92.5	90.6	78.2	**94.0**	90.8
	accuracy	**53.1**	**57.7**	**62.8**	**62.7**	61.1	42.2	64.6	56.7	47.1	**64.1**	**59.9**
ARCF	precision	66.6	79.9	88.6	62.8	83.4	79.2	81.4	76.0	63.4	84.3	85.9
	accuracy	39.8	49.8	61.2	45.5	54.5	43.9	57.7	53.4	32.5	55.8	57.1
Ours	precision	80.0	**87.9**	90.6	87.5	94.4	**91.9**	93.8	**92.8**	**92.8**	87.9	**91.5**
	accuracy	49.8	54.7	59.6	60.8	63.2	57.3	**65.5**	**63.5**	**59.2**	54.6	59.8

Again, it can be seen that the accuracy of Staple is higher in the cases of aspect ratio change, background clutter, camera motion, complete occlusion and viewpoint change, again because Staple can derive the location of the target from the color response and dense response templates, and thus has the best accuracy for detecting targets in video frames in cases such as target scale change. At the same time, the accuracy of AutoTrack is higher in the case of illumination changes and low resolution, also because it has its spatio-temporal regularization term, which can guarantee detection accuracy in the case of large target changes. Our proposed algorithm, on the other hand, is able to guarantee detection accuracy in the case of scale changes and similar objects due to the introduction of an interframe fusion mechanism. Finally, the comparison of the total accuracy of different correlation filtering algorithms shows that the accuracy of the proposed method in this paper reaches 59.8%, which is higher than the accuracy of AutoTrack and ARCF algorithms and approaches the 59.9% accuracy of Staple. Therefore, the method proposed in this paper still has an excellent performance in a variety of situations.

4.7.2. Robustness Testing of Different Correlation Filtering Algorithms

To verify the robustness of the algorithms, the data set was disrupted in time and space and then evaluated using two evaluation metrics, namely Temporal Robustness Evaluation (TRE) based on disrupted time and Spatial Robustness Evaluation (SRE) based on disrupted space. SRE evaluates whether the algorithm is sensitive to initialization by slightly translating and scaling up or down the real labeled target position to produce an initialized position for target tracking, and finally obtains the average accuracy and precision.

Comparisons of the precision and accuracy of different correlation filtering algorithms under TRE or SRE are shown in Table 5 and Figure 5. In the case of TRE metrics, it can be seen that the precision of ARCF is higher in the case of aspect ratio change, background clutter, camera motion, complete occlusion, partial occlusion and viewpoint change; AutoTrack is more precise in the case of illumination change, low resolution and similar objects; and Staple is more precise in the case of scale change. AutoTrack is more accurate in the case of low resolution and similar objects, and ARCF is more accurate in several other cases. In terms of overall performance, the total precision and total accuracy of the ARCF algorithm under TRE are higher than the other algorithms compared with the total precision and total accuracy, which are both low under OPE. Meanwhile, it can be seen in the case of SRE metrics that AutoTrack has higher precision in cases of aspect ratio change, complete occlusion, partial occlusion, scale change and similar objects, while Staple has higher precision in several other cases. The accuracy of AutoTrack is higher in cases of complete occlusion, partial occlusion, scale change and similar objects, while the accuracy of Staple is higher in cases of aspect ratio change, background clutter, camera motion, illumination change and viewpoint change, and the accuracy of the proposed method in this paper is higher in the case of low resolution. In terms of overall performance, the Staple algorithm has the highest total precision and total accuracy.

In conclusion, after the results of comparison experiments and robustness experiments are evaluated, the method proposed in this paper outperforms AutoTrack in the case of background clutter, camera motion and viewpoint change, the method proposed in this paper has higher precision than other algorithms in the case of background clutter and the method proposed in this paper has higher accuracy than other algorithms in the case of scale change and similar objects. In terms of robustness, the proposed method in this paper is sensitive to the initial position given in the first frame, which will cause a relatively large impact at different positions or frame initials, and is also sensitive to the bounding box given during initialization. Therefore, the generalizability of the algorithm proposed in this paper in detecting both the temporal and spatial aspects of the video needs to be improved by further research. However, at the same time, this algorithm is intended to be applicable to UAV target tracking tasks targeting the urban security field, so a high accuracy and precision in the case of background clutter, camera motion, viewpoint change and similar objects can meet the task requirements well. Additionally, the generalizability of the algorithm for time and spatial location can be compensated to some extent by means of human intervention during the task. Therefore, this method can be well-applied to tracking tasks related to urban security.

Table 5. Comparison of the precision and accuracy of different correlation filtering algorithms under different metrics.

Algorithm	Evaluation Metrics		Aspect Ratio Variation (%)	Background Clutter (%)	Camera Motion (%)	Completely Obscured (%)	Illumination Variation (%)	Low Resolution (%)	Partial Occlusion (%)	Proportional Changes (%)	Similar Objects (%)	Viewpoint Changes (%)	Total (%)
AutoTrack	TRE	precision	71.7	81.9	87.8	78.2	**89.8**	**81.5**	89.1	87.8	**81.9**	85.7	87.3
		accuracy	46.6	54.7	61.1	55.0	62.2	**47.3**	65.2	60.8	**55.2**	60.1	59.3
	SRE	precision	**83.6**	77.7	87.3	**91.3**	90.0	78.3	**95.6**	**95.1**	**81.3**	81.8	84.4
		accuracy	49.2	44.9	55.0	**61.6**	55.9	43.2	**62.5**	**62.7**	**44.5**	49.0	51.8
Staple	TRE	precision	70.5	81.7	88.2	78.2	88.7	79.3	89.1	**88.7**	81.5	86.8	87.2
		accuracy	47.0	56.7	60.8	57.7	61.9	43.9	66.0	55.5	54.9	62.3	59.1
	SRE	precision	81.6	**87.0**	**93.6**	85.5	**90.5**	**80.6**	92.7	91.1	79.9	**93.4**	**90.9**
		accuracy	**49.5**	**54.4**	**59.8**	60.1	**57.6**	40.0	61.8	54.4	44.2	**60.7**	**56.8**
ARCF	TRE	precision	**74.5**	**83.1**	**90.0**	**79.4**	89.6	78.1	**89.7**	88.4	79.1	**89.6**	**88.2**
		accuracy	**50.0**	**57.9**	**64.4**	**60.2**	**64.1**	46.4	**68.4**	**61.8**	54.7	**65.1**	**61.9**
	SRE	precision	66.5	**77.7**	86.9	65.4	83.0	79.6	82.7	77.7	64.9	80.9	84.4
		accuracy	38.4	45.8	57.0	46.6	51.3	40.8	55.5	52.2	31.2	51.7	52.8
Ours	TRE	precision	64.8	78.1	86.1	69.9	85.1	78.0	85.0	82.5	73.0	82.4	84.6
		accuracy	42.2	51.3	59.1	46.7	58.1	45.6	60.8	56.9	49.1	56.4	56.9
	SRE	precision	71.1	72.6	83.0	74.2	85.0	79.0	87.1	83.9	70.9	74.2	80.8
		accuracy	40.7	42.3	52.2	48.7	52.7	**45.4**	56.6	55.2	40.3	44.5	49.9

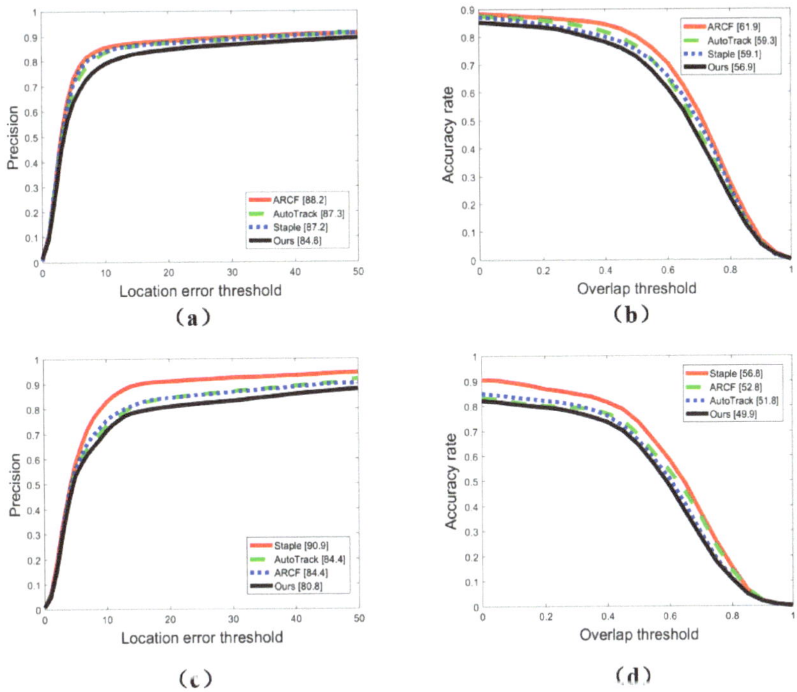

Figure 5. Comparison of the total precision and accuracy of different correlation filtering algorithms under different metrics. (**a**) is the total precision of different correlation filtering algorithms under TRE, (**b**) is the total accuracy of different correlation filtering algorithms under TRE, (**c**) is the total precision of different correlation filtering algorithms under SRE and (**d**) is the total accuracy of different correlation filtering algorithms under SRE.

5. Conclusions

To address the problem of losing the tracked target due to inaccurate tracking results of the current frame, this paper proposes a strong interference motion target tracking method based on the target consistency algorithm. When there is a tracking problem in the current frame, the tracking accuracy of the subsequent tracking is enhanced by combining the previous trajectories to learn again and updating the model according to the trajectory confidence mechanism to avoid tracker learning errors. The experimental results prove that the proposed method of this paper improves 0.2% of the accuracy compared with the current advanced UAV target tracking algorithm SO-MOT on the basis of guaranteed tracking precision, and also improves 6.3% of the total accuracy and 2.6% of the total accuracy compared with the benchmark model AutoTrack, which proves the effectiveness of the method. In particular, the high precision and accuracy in the case of background clutter, camera movement, viewpoint change and similar objects can well-meet the needs of target tracking tasks in aerial UAV video in the field of urban security. In the future, we expect that this method can be better applied in the field of urban security drone inspection to ensure the safety and stability of urban environments.

Author Contributions: Conceptualization: L.T., X.H. and X.L.; methodology: X.H. and X.L.; formal analysis and investigation: X.H. and X.L.; writing—original draft preparation: X.H. and X.L.; writing—review and editing: L.T., X.H., X.L., X.J. and H.L.; supervision: L.T. and H.L. All authors have read and agreed to the published version of the manuscript.

Funding: This research was funded by the Natural Science Foundation of Chongqing (CSTB2022NSCQ-MSX1415).

Data Availability Statement: The dataset used during the current study is available in https://github.com/VisDrone/VisDrone-Dataset (accessed on 11 November 2022).

Acknowledgments: The authors would like to thank the anonymous reviewers for their suggestions.

Conflicts of Interest: The authors declare no conflict of interest.

References

1. Lu, H.; Li, Y.; Mu, S.; Wang, D.; Kim, H. Motor Anomaly Detection for Unmanned Aerial Vehicles using Reinforcement Learning. *IEEE Internet Things J.* **2017**, *5*, 2315–2322. [CrossRef]
2. Zhao, X.; Zhang, Q.; Wang, L.; Xie, F.; Zhang, B. A Special Operation UAV in Urban Space. In *AOPC 2021: Optical Sensing and Imaging Technology*; SPIE: Bellingham, WA, USA, 2021; Volume 12065, pp. 433–442.
3. Xu, Z. Application Research of Tethered UAV Platform in Marine Emergency Communication Network. *J. Web Eng.* **2021**, *20*, 491–511. [CrossRef]
4. Waleed, E.; Arslan, A.; Aliza, M.; Mohamed, I. Energy-Efficient Task Scheduling and Physiological Assessment in Disaster Management using UAV-Assisted Networks. *Comput. Commun.* **2020**, *155*, 150–157.
5. Han, Y.; Liu, H.; Wang, Y.; Liu, C. A Comprehensive Review for Typical Applications Based Upon Unmanned Aerial Vehicle Platform. *IEEE J. Sel. Top. Appl. Earth Obs. Remote Sens.* **2022**, *15*, 9654–9666. [CrossRef]
6. Qin, X.; Wang, T. Visual-based Tracking and Control Algorithm Design for Quadcopter UAV. In Proceedings of the 2019 Chinese Control and Decision Conference (CCDC), Nanchang, China, 3–5 June 2019.
7. Zhang, R.; Sun, S.; Li, Y.; Li, Z.; Tian, K. An Adaptive Scale Estimation Target Tracking Algorithm Based on UAV. In Proceedings of the 2020 International Conference on Robots & Intelligent System (ICRIS), Sanya, China, 7–8 November 2020; pp. 545–551.
8. Bertinetto, L.; Valmadre, J.; Golodetz, S.; Miksik, O.; Torr, P.H. Staple: Complementary Learners for Real-Time Tracking. In Proceedings of the IEEE Conference on Computer Vision and Pattern Recognition, Las Vegas, NV, USA, 27 June–1 July 2016; pp. 1401–1409.
9. Danelljan, M.; Häger, G.; Khan, F.; Felsberg, M. Learning Spatially Regularized Correlation Filters for Visual Tracking. In Proceedings of the IEEE International Conference on Computer Vision, Santiago, Chile, 11–18 December 2015; pp. 4310–4318.
10. Li, F.; Tian, C.; Zuo, W.; Zhang, L.; Yang, M.-H. Learning Spatial-Temporal Regularized Correlation Filters for Visual Tracking. In Proceedings of the IEEE Conference on Computer Vision and Pattern Recognition, Salt Lake City, UT, USA, 18–22 June 2018; pp. 4904–4913.
11. Galoogahi, H.; Fagg, A.; Lucey, S. Learning Background-Aware Correlation Filters for Visual Tracking. In Proceedings of the IEEE International Conference on Computer Vision, Venice, Italy, 22–29 October 2017; pp. 1135–1143.
12. Boyd, S.; Parikh, N.; Chu, E.; Peleato, B.; Eckstein, J. Distributed Optimization and Statistical Learning via the Alternating Direction Method of Multipliers. *Found. Trends Mach. Learn.* **2011**, *3*, 1–122. [CrossRef]
13. Huang, Z.; Fu, C.; Li, Y.; Lin, F.; Lu, P. Learning Aberrance Repressed Correlation Filters for Real-Time UAV Tracking. In Proceedings of the IEEE International Conference on Computer Vision, Seoul, Republic of Korea, 27 October–2 November 2019; pp. 2891–2900.
14. Bi, F.; Lei, M.; Wang, Y. Context-Aware MDNet for Target Tracking in UAV Remote Sensing Videos. *Int. J. Remote Sens.* **2020**, *41*, 3784–3797. [CrossRef]
15. Zha, Y.; Wu, M.; Qiu, Z.; Sun, J.; Zhang, P.; Huang, W. Online Semantic Subspace Learning with Siamese Network for UAV Tracking. *Remote Sens.* **2020**, *12*, 325. [CrossRef]
16. Liu, Y.; Wang, Q.; Hu, H.; He, Y. A Novel Real-Time Moving Target Tracking and Path Planning System for A Quadrotor UAV in Unknown Unstructured Outdoor Scenes. *IEEE Trans. Syst. Man Cybern. Syst.* **2019**, *49*, 2362–2372. [CrossRef]
17. Li, A.; Luo, L.; Tang, S. Real-Time Tracking of Vehicles with Siamese Network and Backward Prediction. In Proceedings of the IEEE ICME, London, UK, 6–10 July 2020; pp. 1–6.
18. Chu, Q.; Ouyang, W.; Li, H.; Wang, X.; Liu, B.; Yu, N. Online Multi-Object Tracking using Cnn-Based Single Object Tracker with Spatial-Temporal Attention Mechanism. In Proceedings of the IEEE International Conference on Computer Vision (ICCV), Venice, Italy, 22–29 October 2017; pp. 4836–4845.
19. Feng, W.; Hu, Z.; Wu, W.; Yan, J.; Ouyang, W. Multi-Object Tracking with Multiple Cues and Switcher-Aware Classification. *arXiv* **2019**, arXiv:1901.06129.
20. Li, B.; Yan, J.; Wu, W.; Zhu, Z.; Hu, X. High-Performance Visual Tracking with Siamese Region Proposal Network. In Proceedings of the IEEE Conference on Computer Vision and Pattern Recognition, Salt Lake City, UT, USA, 18–22 June 2018; pp. 8971–8980.
21. Zhu, J.; Yang, H.; Liu, N.; Kim, M.; Zhang, W.; Yang, M.-H. Online Multi-Object Tracking with Dual Matching Attention Networks. In Proceedings of the European Conference on Computer Vision (ECCV), Munich, Germany, 8–14 September 2018; pp. 366–382.
22. Wan, M.; Gu, G.; Qian, W.; Ren, K.; Maldague, X.; Chen, Q. Unmanned Aerial Vehicle Video-Based Target Tracking Algorithm. *IEEE Internet Things J.* **2019**, *6*, 9689–9706. [CrossRef]
23. Liu, Z.; Shang, Y.; Li, T.; Chen, G.; Wang, Y.; Hu, Q.; Zhu, P. Robust Multi-Drone Multi-Target Tracking to Resolve Target Occlusion: A Benchmark. *IEEE Trans. Multimed.* **2023**, 1–16. [CrossRef]
24. Yeom, S. Long Distance Ground Target Tracking with Aerial Image-to-Position Conversion and Improved Track Association. *Drones* **2022**, *6*, 55. [CrossRef]

25. Jiang, Y.; Jingliang, G.; Yanqing, Z.; Min, W.; Jianwei, W. Detection and Tracking Method of Small-Sized UAV Based on YOLOv5. In Proceedings of the 2022 19th International Computer Conference on Wavelet Active Media Technology and Information Processing (ICCWAMTIP), Chengdu, China, 16–18 December 2022; pp. 1–5.
26. Lin, Y.; Wang, M.; Chen, W.; Gao, W.; Li, L.; Liu, W. Multiple Object Tracking of Drone Videos by A Temporal-Association Network with Separated-Tasks Structure. *Remote Sens.* **2022**, *14*, 3862. [CrossRef]
27. Bhagat, S.; Sujit, P.B. UAV Target Tracking in Urban Environments using Deep Reinforcement Learning. In Proceedings of the 2020 International Conference on Unmanned Aircraft Systems (ICUAS), Athens, Greece, 1–4 September 2020; pp. 694–701.
28. Yang, B.; Cao, X.; Yuen, C.; Qian, L. Offloading Optimization in Edge Computing for Deeplearning-Enabled Target Tracking by Internet of UAVs. *IEEE Internet Things J.* **2020**, *8*, 9878–9893. [CrossRef]
29. Fan, H.; Du, D.; Wen, L.; Zhu, P.; Hu, Q.; Ling, H.; Shah, M.; Pan, J. Visdrone-MOT2020: The Vision Meets Drone Multiple Object Tracking Challenge Results. In Proceedings of the European Conference on Computer Vision, Glasgow, UK, 23–28 August 2020; Springer: Cham, Switzerland, 2020; pp. 713–727.
30. Krichen, M.; Adoni, W.Y.H.; Mihoub, A.; Alzahrani, M.Y.; Nahhal, T. Security Challenges for Drone Communications: Possible Threats, Attacks and Countermeasures. In Proceedings of the 2022 2nd International Conference of Smart Systems and Emerging Technologies, Riyadh, Saudi Arabia, 9–11 May 2022; pp. 184–189.
31. Ko, Y.; Kim, J.; Duguma, D.G.; Astillo, P.V.; You, L.; Pau, G. Drone Secure Communication Protocol for Future Sensitive Applications in Military Zone. *Sensors* **2021**, *21*, 2057. [CrossRef] [PubMed]
32. Li, Y.; Fu, C.; Ding, F.; Huang, Z.; Lu, G. AutoTrack: Towards high-performance visual tracking for UAV with automatic spatio-temporal regularization. In Proceedings of the IEEE Conference on Computer Vision and Pattern Recognition, Seattle, WA, USA, 14–19 June 2020; pp. 11920–11929.
33. Zhu, P.; Wen, L.; Du, D.; Bian, X.; Fan, H.; Hu, Q.; Ling, H. Detection and Tracking Meet Drones Challenge. In *IEEE Transactions on Pattern Analysis and Machine Intelligence*; IEEE: Piscataway, NJ, USA, 2021; Volume 44, pp. 7380–7399.
34. Chen, G.; Wang, W.; He, Z.; Wang, L.; Yuan, Y.; Zhang, D.; Zhang, J.; Zhu, P.; Gool, L.V.; Han, J.; et al. VisDrone-MOT2021: The Vision Meets Drone Multiple Object Tracking Challenge Results. In Proceedings of the IEEE/CVF International Conference on Computer Vision, Montreal, BC, Canada, 11–17 October 2021; pp. 2839–2846.

electronics

MDPI

Article

MalDBA: Detection for Query-Based Malware Black-Box Adversarial Attacks

Zixiao Kong [1], Jingfeng Xue [1], Zhenyan Liu [1,*], Yong Wang [1] and Weijie Han [2]

[1] School of Computer Science and Technology, Beijing Institute of Technology, Beijing 100081, China
[2] School of Space Information, Space Engineering University, Beijing 101416, China
* Correspondence: zhenyanliu@bit.edu.cn

Abstract: The increasing popularity of Industry 4.0 has led to more and more security risks, and malware adversarial attacks emerge in an endless stream, posing great challenges to user data security and privacy protection. In this paper, we investigate the stateful detection method for artificial intelligence deep learning-based malware black-box attacks, i.e., determining the presence of adversarial attacks rather than detecting whether the input samples are malicious or not. To this end, we propose the MalDBA method for experiments on the VirusShare dataset. We find that query-based black-box attacks produce a series of highly similar historical query results (also known as intermediate samples). By comparing the similarity among these intermediate samples and the trend of prediction scores returned by the detector, we can detect the presence of adversarial samples in indexed samples and thus determine whether an adversarial attack has occurred, and then protect user data security and privacy. The experimental results show that the attack detection rate can reach 100%. Compared to similar studies, our method does not require heavy feature extraction tasks or image conversion and can be operated on complete PE files without requiring a strong hardware platform.

Keywords: stateful detection; adversarial defence; artificial intelligence security; privacy protection

Citation: Kong, Z.; Xue, J.; Liu, Z.; Wang, Y.; Han, W. MalDBA: Detection for Query-Based Malware Black-Box Adversarial Attacks. *Electronics* **2023**, *12*, 1751. https://doi.org/10.3390/electronics12071751

Academic Editor: Aryya Gangopadhyay

Received: 27 February 2023
Revised: 26 March 2023
Accepted: 4 April 2023
Published: 6 April 2023

1. Introduction

With the advent of the Industry 4.0 era, security threats have increased dramatically, and the number of malware introduced by attackers is rising every year. The volume of malware threats observed by McAfee Labs averaged 688 threats per minute, an increase of 40 threats per minute (3%) in the first quarter of 2021 [1]. VirusTotal's database had more than one million signed samples that were considered suspicious (with more than 15% anti-viruses detecting them as malicious) from January 2021 to April 2022 [2]. Researchers are constantly looking for effective malware detection and classification methods, and with the popularity of artificial intelligence (AI), they find that deep learning-based malware detection and classification methods work well [3–5]. However, deep learning (DL) models are highly vulnerable to adversarial examples [6,7]. Therefore, analyzing and detecting DL-based malware black-box adversarial attacks is a difficult task for anti-malware researchers. The existing optimal defense methods are stateless detection methods such as adversarial retraining and distillation, which detect whether the input sample is benign or malicious without judging whether there is an adversarial attack [8,9]. Existing malware stateful detection methods are implemented in the feature space, which requires data preprocessing and feature extraction [10,11]. At present, there is no malware stateful detection strategy implemented in the problem space.

Driven by this, we propose the MalDBA(Detection for Query-based Malware Black-box adversarial Attacks) to defend against malware black-box adversarial attacks. The process of MalDBA is as follows: First, malicious datasets are obtained from the VirusShare website [12], benign datasets are collected through crawling, and a malware detection model MalConv is pretrained [13]. Then, two different black-box adversarial attacks are reconstructed [14,15], and the history of query results (also known as the intermediate samples) of these attacks are saved. We can find that the prediction scores of these intermediate samples under MalConv model detection are gradually decreasing (meaning that the original malware tends to become a benign-looking sample after adding perturbations). After that, the similarities of the sample sets saved in the query process are compared using the similarity comparator [16]. We find that these intermediate samples are highly similar to each other and the original malicious file, but not similar to other samples. Thus, we can perform the stateful detection of query-based malware black-box adversarial attacks. When it is found that the samples input to the detector model for querying are similar and the predicted scores returned by these similar samples gradually decrease (from malicious to benign), it is judged that the detector is experiencing adversarial attacks.

We evaluated MalDBA on the downloaded dataset and achieved satisfactory results. In summary, the main contributions in this paper are as follows:

(1) We propose MalDBA to defend against query-based malware black-box attacks, which can help analysts effectively detect the existence of adversarial attacks.

(2) We propose a stateful detection method for black-box adversarial attacks. Most of the previous detection methods for adversarial examples (AEs) are stateless, and the method proposed by us can precisely carry out a supplementary defense. The existing stateful detection methods of malware black-box attacks are based on the feature space level, while our method is based on the complete malicious file (i.e., problem space).

(3) We propose a novel similarity comparator based on the MinHash algorithm to analyze the history of queries (i.e., intermediate samples) received by the malware detector.

(4) MalDBA can be run on ordinary personal workstations and does not require high-performance hardware resources, so it meets the needs of ordinary researchers to deal with a large number of malicious codes.

The structure of the article is as follows: In Section 2, we first introduce the necessary background knowledge and the summary of the related work. Section 3 describes the overall framework of the MalDBA. The experimental details are presented in Section 4. Then evaluate it in Section 5. Section 6 discusses some issues. Finally, we conclude in Section 7.

2. Background and Related Work

The adversarial attack and defense of malware is an iterative and complementary process. In recent years, the research of malware black-box attack and detection has emerged [17–19]. To better introduce the content of this paper, we first outline the research background and related work.

2.1. Background

2.1.1. Query-Based Black-Box Attack

Currently, the black-box adversarial attack can be divided into transfer-based attacks and query-based attacks. Transfer-based attacks generate adversarial examples on local surrogate models and directly use the generated adversarial examples to attack the black-box model. However, the attack performance of transfer-based attacks is usually unsatisfactory due to overfitting the local surrogate models. Query-based attacks approximate the gradient information by queries to the target model to craft adversarial examples. Query-based black-box attack is generally divided into decision-based black-box attack and score-based black-box attacks [20]. The decision-based black-box attack, also known as hard-label black-box adversarial attack, iteratively perturbs the original sample by estimating the gradient or boundary proximity and generating AEs according to some strategies [21]. The score-based black-box attack estimates the gradient of the target model loss function according to the output of the target model for the input samples (i.e., the probability scores of each category), and generates the corresponding adversarial samples [22]. Query-based black-box attack often requires multiple queries to generate a successful AE to achieve optimal attack performance. In this paper, the attack we use is a score-based black-box attack, and the attack scenario is shown in Figure 1.

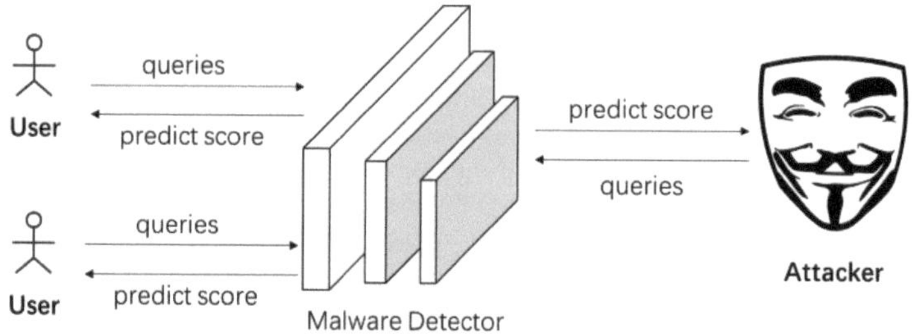

Figure 1. Scenario for score-based malware black-box attacks.

2.1.2. Stateful Detection Method

Stateful detection examines a series of queries submitted by each user to decide whether the user is an attacker [10,23,24]. Given user A and the set of queries he submits, stateful detection checks if an adversarial attack occurred in these queries. Specifically, stateful detection calculates the similarity between queries $q_1, q_2, ..., q_n$ from A. If the similarity exceeds a threshold and the prediction scores returned by the malware detector range from malicious to benign, stateful detection marks A as an adversarial attacker. To calculate the similarity between samples, a similarity comparator is proposed for comparison. In general, the stateful detection method judges whether an adversarial attack has occurred, rather than detecting whether the input samples are malicious.

2.2. Related Work

Research on the detection of adversarial attacks was first proposed in the field of computer vision, including detection methods for model stealing attacks, surrogate model attacks, and evasion attacks [23–27]. Chen et al. [23] proposed a new adversarial sample defense method – stateful detection defense for image black-box attacks. Moreover, they proposed a similarity encoder based on the Euclidean distance metric. Then, they introduce a novel type of attack, query blinding, which is designed to bypass the stateful detection defense. This paper is evaluated using the CIFAR-10 dataset, and the experiments work well. However, this study applies well to image adversarial samples, but is limited to video classification, and does not involve malware detection.

Li et al. [24] designed Blacklight, a defense framework against query-based black-box adversarial attacks. The method uses probabilistic content fingerprint-based query matching to mitigate individual attack queries. They experimentally evaluated Blacklight on multiple datasets and image classification models for eight SOTA black-box attacks, and the experimental results were not only high in detection rate but also fast. Nevertheless, this method cannot defend against surrogate model attacks. If there are not highly similar adversarial examples, Blacklight can be evaded.

For deep neural network models (DNNs), Cohen et al. [26] put forward using Nearest-Neighbours and Influence Functions to detect adversarial samples. The core idea of this algorithm is that there should be a correspondence between the training data and the network classification. That is, for normal images, there is a strong correlation between their nearest neighbors in the DNN embedding space and their most helpful training examples, while adversarial examples are the opposite. They tested the performance of detection in both black-box and white-box attacks. However, this study uses the L_2 distance metric, which is computationally time-consuming and needs to be further improved in the future.

In order to quickly infer the intent of black-box attackers, Pang et al. [27] proposed a new estimation model, AdvMind. This model can reliably identify the query of interest (QOI) and accurately detect the target category of the attack at an early stage for timely remediation. The authors used four datasets and DNNs to perform experiments on the detection of three black-box attacks. However, AdvMind focuses on query-based attacks and is not effective for substitute model attacks.

With the increasing threat of black-box adversarial attacks in the industrial Internet of Things (IIOT), Esmaeili et al. [10] proposed a stateful query analysis strategy for the detection of adversarial scenarios. Their method includes two CNN-based components, namely similarity encoder, and classifier. Moreover, they introduced the Mahalanobis distance metric for the loss function of the detection model, which improved the detection rate. However, their architecture is to process the malware opcode features into greyscale images and use methods in the field of computer vision to classify and generate adversarial images, without generating malicious files. Future research on other distance indicators and data types should also be further developed.

As previous defense methods are static and cannot dynamically adapt to adversarial attacks, Li et al. [11] proposed the first instance-based online machine learning dynamic defense method against black-box attacks. Extensive experiments are conducted on image and malware datasets, and effects significantly outperform existing SOTA defense methods. Nevertheless, DyAdvDefender may need a manual inspection of samples to achieve optimal performance in the real world, and incorrect selection of malware feature sets may lead to defense failure.

Regarding a Windows adversarial attack, Fang et al. [8] proposed an automatic adversarial sample generation model based on reinforcement learning called RLAttackNet, which can successfully bypass the DeepDetectNet malware detection model. They proposed a new method for extracting features of PE files, including the Import Function Feature, General Information Feature, and Bytes Entropy Feature. Retraining the detection model by drawing on the idea of GAN revealed a significant decrease in the success rate of the attack. More attention needs to be paid to hyper-parameter optimization methods in deep learning models in the future.

In addition, unlike previous work, Maiorca et al. [9] presented a survey of PDF malware detection in an adversarial environment. They provide a comprehensive study on PDF pre-processing. Furthermore, they outline adversarial attacks against PDF malware detectors. They have discussed existing mitigating strategies as well as future research directions.

In summary, we can find that there are shortcomings in the existing research results in detecting malware black-box attacks: (1) Most researchers are devoted to the detection of image and PDF adversarial attacks, and the research on stateful detection of malware adversarial attacks is insufficient; (2) The existing stateful detection methods of malware black-box attacks need to extract features from original samples or convert them into images for further processing. Based on this, we propose the MalDBA method for stateful detection research on complete sample files.

3. Overview

3.1. Motivation

Machine learning has great potential in malware analysis, and DL-based malware detectors have been extensively studied, yet the problem remains unsolved. One of the key challenges currently facing malware detection and classification research is the adversarial examples [28]. Without addressing adversarial attacks, proposing malware detectors or classifiers is an endless and unfruitful task lacking substantial scientific advancement. For instance, the DL-based static malware detector proposed in another paper worked well in the evaluation, but malware adversarial samples still sneak through the model [13–15,29]. That is probably why the malware never stops despite the hundreds of detectors being proposed. It is urgent to detect black-box attacks based on the DL malware detector. The stateful detection method has been used in computer vision [11,23,24,27], but it has not been attempted in malware black-box attacks which generate real adversarial samples. Therefore, we designed the MalDBA framework to detect query-based black-box attacks. This article aims to detect the generation of adversarial samples, not to try to detect whether the input files are malicious or benign. When generating an adversarial sample, existing query-based black-box attacks produce a series of highly similar queries (i.e., each query in the set is similar to the previous queries), and the scores returned by the detector gradually change from malicious to benign. Based on this, we propose a defense approach that uses a similarity comparison algorithm to identify such queries and detects black-box attacks against malware detectors through this strategy.

3.2. Overall Framework

MalDBA mainly consists of four steps, namely training the malware detection model, simulating the black-box attack, saving the intermediate samples and prediction scores, and performing adversarial attack detection, as shown in Figure 2.

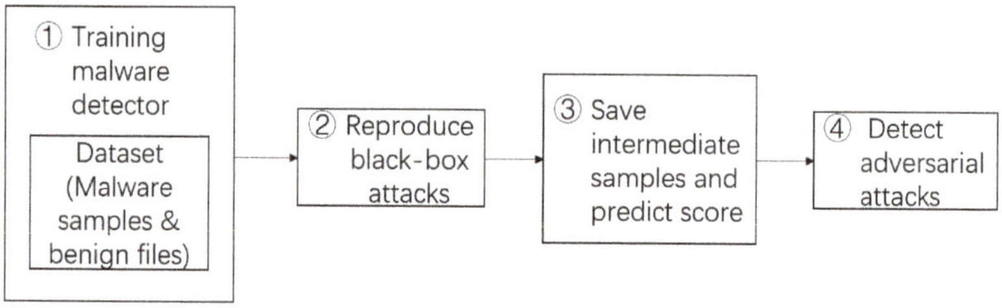

Figure 2. The process of MalDBA.

4. Our Scheme

4.1. Training Malware Detector

The function of this step is to train a mature malware detection model. For the DL-based static malware detector, we choose the MalConv model(as shown in Figure 3), which is not only the current popular malware detection model, but also the target model selected by many malware adversarial attacks [14,15,30–35]. By training the MalConv model, a binary classifier that can distinguish benign samples from malicious samples can be obtained.

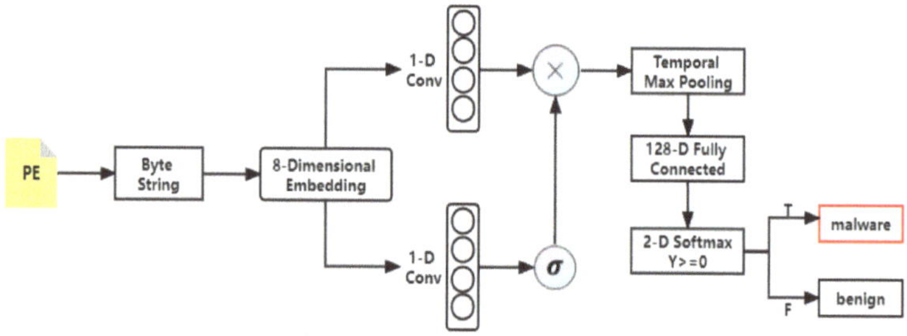

Figure 3. The architecture of MalConv model.

MalConv model is the first convolutional neural network architecture (CNN) addressing the classification problem of extremely long sequences, proposed by Raff et al. [13]. Its input is a PE file and returns a score to judge whether this file is malware or not. The model distinguishes programs based on the byte representation of the input, without extracting any features. If the input file length exceeds 2MB, the file will be truncated to the specified size; otherwise, the file will be padded with the value 0.

4.2. Reproduce Black-Box Attacks

Our work is dedicated to detecting query-based black-box attacks and the function of this module is to reproduce typical query-based black-box attacks. Since malware adversarial attacks were investigated later than image adversarial attacks and most of the AEs are generated on feature vectors or substitute models [28,36–40], there are not many query-based black-box attack methods that can generate real AE files and publish open source codes [14,15,41,42]. We choose two advanced score-based black-box attack frameworks [14,15]. The target detectors of these two attacks are both MalConv models, we reproduce them through open-source code and compare the attack success rate. The process of generating adversarial samples is roughly illustrated in Figure 4.

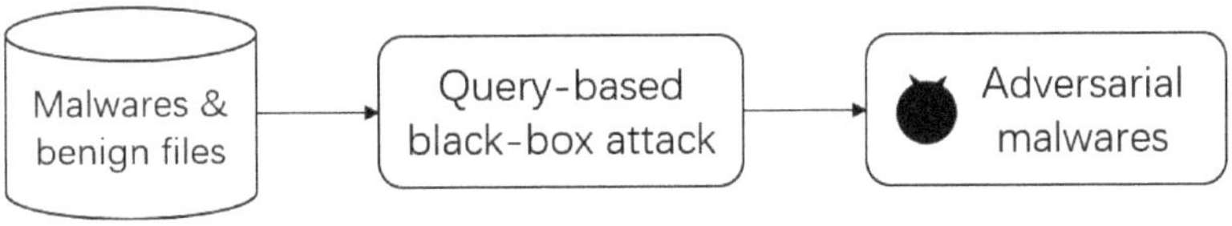

Figure 4. The process of generating adversarial examples.

4.3. *Save the Intermediate Samples*

Figure 5 shows the process of saving the historical query results of the black-box attack. The historical queries (i.e., intermediate samples), as well as the prediction scores returned from the detector in the process of generating adversarial sample queries, are saved in preparation for the next step.

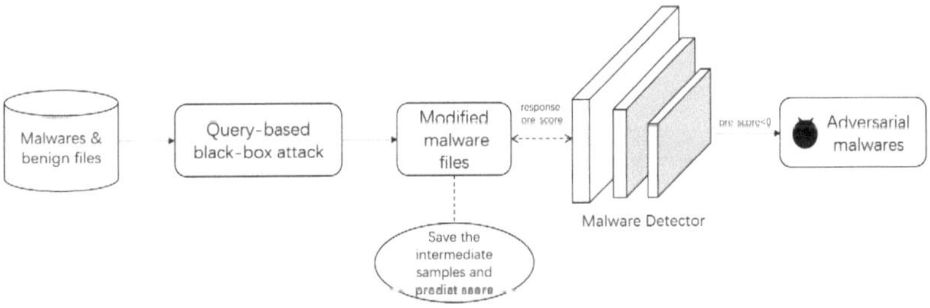

Figure 5. The process of saving the history queries.

4.4. *Detect the Adversarial Attacks*

Algorithm 1 sketches the procedure of MalDBA. Different numbers of benign and malicious samples are randomly selected with the intermediate samples saved above to form the indexed sample sets of different sizes. Then use the similarity comparator based on the Minhash algorithm to compare the similarity and judge whether the scores returned by MalConv gradually decrease, so as to determine whether there is an adversarial attack and achieve the purpose of defense. The process of detection is shown in Figure 6.

Algorithm 1: The procedure of MalDBA

Initialization: indexed samples set K, query_set $(q_1, \ldots, q_n)$, *predict_score* S, similarity comparator H. $(q_i \in K)$
Output: Whether adversarial attacks exist in the K (Ture or False)
for c in K **do**
  $L_c = new\ List\ ()$
  $L_c \leftarrow Obtain\ the\ index\ set\ of\ samples\ similar\ to\ c\ through\ H$
end for
if $(q_1, \ldots, q_n)$ *in the same L and* $(S_{q_1}, \ldots, S_{q_n})$ *decline* **then**
return True

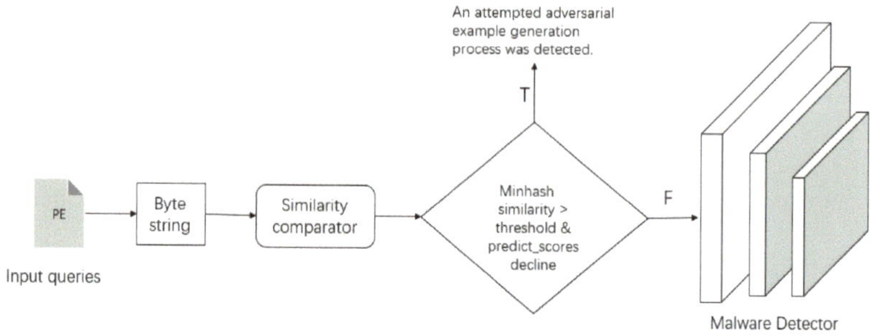

Figure 6. The process of detection.

5. Evaluation

5.1. Experimental Setup

We implemented MalDBA in Python. The experimental environment is configured as follows: (1) Lenovo ThinkStation, Intel®Core ™ i7-6700U CPU @3.40GHz × 16.0 GB RAM, and an Nvidia GeForce GTX 1070 (2) 64bit Windows 10 operation system, (3) Pycharm Professional Edition with Anaconda plugin 2020.

5.1.1. Dataset

The experimental data in this paper includes malware samples and benign files, among which malicious samples are from VirusShare corpus [12], and benign PE files are extracted from Windows 10 system files and different software companies. Since the input file size of the GAMMA model cannot exceed 1MB, we filtered the dataset (samples larger than 1MB are only a minority). Table 1 and Figure 7 illustrates the distribution of the dataset.

Table 1. The Dataset.

Dataset	Benign Files	Malicious Files	Total
Num	5309	3720	9029

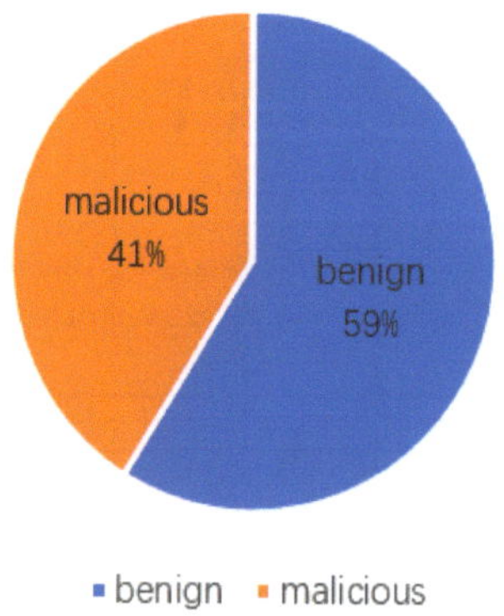

Figure 7. The distribution of a dataset.

5.1.2. Black-Box Attack Methods

Two typical query-based malware black-box attacks are selected for experimentation during our evaluation (as shown in Table 2).

Table 2. Query-based malware black-box attacks.

Black-Box Attack	Method
MalRNN [14]	MalRNN automatically generates adversarial examples to attack DL-based static malware detectors in the way of language modeling. Using the Seq2Seq RNN Language Model to generate benign looking byte sequences successfully eludes anti-malware engines.
GAMMA [15]	GAMMA is a malware adversarial attack method based on optimized genetic algorithm. It extracts benign contents which are easy to evade the DL-based static malware detector and injects them into the end of malicious samples or the newly-created sections (i.e., Padding and Section-Injection attacks)

5.2. Experimental Results and Discussion

In this section, we experimentally evaluate the detection effectiveness of MalDBA. Firstly, we evaluate the MalConv malware detector model selected using the original dataset. Secondly, the selected black-box attack algorithm is applied to the dataset and target detector, and then our proposed MalDBA method is used to detect the black-box attacks and evaluate the attack success rate of the attacks without and with the defense. After that, the relationship between the average response time (ART) and attack detection rate (ADR) with the number of indexed samples (K) on attacks is discussed. Finally, we compare the MalDBA with similar studies.

5.2.1. The Experimental Results of Malware Detector

We chose MalConv, a popular DL-based static malware detection model, which is used as the target model for many malware adversarial attacks [14,15,30–35]. We reproduced the model using the Python programming language. The dataset is divided according to the ratio of training set: validation set: test set = 6:2:2. We conduct the experiments on randomly partitioned datasets and the results are shown in Table 3. The accuracy of the test set is 95.03%, which is not far from the experimental results of the original paper [13].

Table 3. Performance of MalConv model.

Detector \ Metrics	Test_Loss	Test_Accuracy	Train_Loss	Train_Accuracy
MalConv	0.1380	95.03%	0.0862	96.32%

5.2.2. The Detection Results with Different Black-Box Attack Methods

In this section, we replicate the MalRNN and GAMMA black-box attack frameworks, using Attack Success Rate (ASR) as an evaluation metric. Each experiment is performed three times, and the results are averaged as the final experimental results. As shown in Table 4, the effectiveness of two black-box attacks with no defense and defense with the MalDBA detection method is presented. It can be seen from Table 4 that our defense method can reduce the success rate of the attacks to 0%.

Table 4. Attack success rate (ASR) of attacks.

Attack	Defence	ASR
MalRNN	No defence	88.6%
	MalDBA	0%
GAMMA	No defence	86.3%
	MalDBA	0%

5.2.3. The Relation between the ART and ADR with K on Attacks

We randomly save 20 historical query results of malware and randomly select different numbers of benign and malicious files respectively to form the indexed sample set K. The sizes of K are taken as 30, 70, 320, 520, 770, and 1020, respectively. The relationship between the average response time (ART) and the number of indexed samples (K) for MalRNN and GAMMA attacks are shown in Table 5. The relationship between the ART, attack detection rate (ADR) with K for these two attacks are depicted in Figures 8 and 9 respectively. From the figures, it can be found that the ADR of MalDBA for these two black-box attacks is 100%, and the ADR is independent of K. With increasing K, the ART fluctuates to a certain extent and then gradually stabilizes around 23 s.

Table 5. The relationship between the average response time (ART) and the number of indexed samples (K) on MalRNN and GAMMA.

ART(s) \ K / Attack	30	70	320	520	770	1020
MalRNN	7.11	6.71	18.41	23.20	23.10	22.67
GAMMA	7.20	6.62	18.50	23.11	23.22	22.72

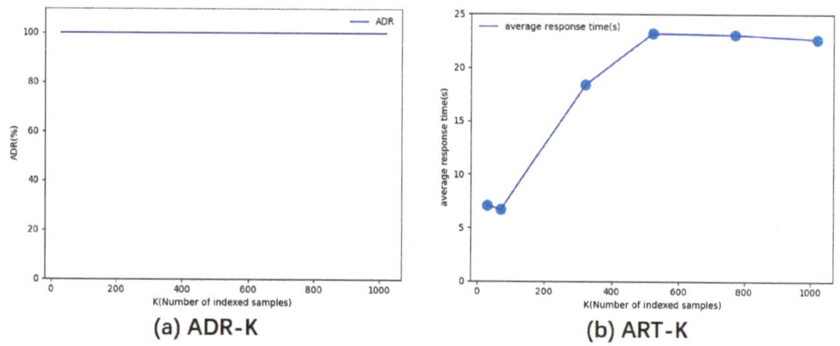

Figure 8. The relation between the attack detection rate (ADR) and average response time (AST) with the number of indexed samples (K) on MalRNN attack.

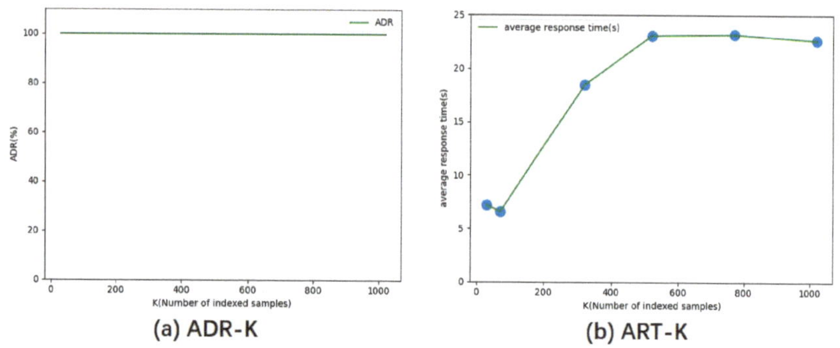

Figure 9. The relation between the attack detection rate (ADR) and average response time (AST) with the number of indexed samples (K) on GAMMA attack.

5.2.4. Comparison with Similar Studies

In this section, we compare MalDBA with similar studies in terms of datasets, target models, experimental setup, the accuracy of the target model, and attack detection rate (ADR). The results of the comparison are shown in Table 6.

Table 6. Comparison with similar studies.

	MalDBA	Esmaeili et al. [10]	Miles Q. Li et al. [11]	Steven Chen et al. [23]	Ren Pang et al. [27]	Huiying Li et al. [24]
Datasets	PE	2-digit hexadecimal bytecode vectors	CIFAR-10, MNIST, PE	CIFAR-10	CIFAR-10, CIFAR-100, ISIC, Mini-VGGface2	MNIST, GTSRB, CIFAR10, ImageNet
Target models	Malconv	CNN	CNN, FNN	ResNet	DNNs	DNN
Experimental setup	A desktop with one Intel®Core ™ i7-6700U CPU, 16.0 GB RAM , and an Nvidia GeForce GTX 1070	-	A server with one Intel®Core ™ i9-9980XE CPU, 128 GB memory, and an Nvidia GeForce RTX 2080 Ti Graphics Card	-	-	Nvidia Titan RTX
Accuracy of target model	95.03%	98%	-	92%	92.44%, 70.47%, 88.17%, 96.17%	-
ADR	100%	93.1%	Extract PE Strings feature: 94.7%	100%	Can reach to 100%	Can reach to 100%

Compared with similar studies, MalDBA has the following advantages: (1) MalDBA references the idea of image stateful detection, but does not need to convert PE files into images (which will lose some important features). (2) MalDBA can directly detect complete malware, skipping the dataset preprocessing, feature extraction, feature selection, and feature fusion stages, saving a lot of time. (3) MalDBA requires a moderate-performance hardware platform, so it has good universality and a high detection rate.

6. Discussion

Our proposed detection method operates on complete files, which inevitably takes some time. Therefore, we put forward an idea: drawing on the knowledge of computer vision, extracting the features of the deep neural network model's middle layer for sample similarity comparisons in order to detect adversarial attacks [43,44]. We adopted three methods to carry out experiments with different numbers of indexed samples (K). The MalConv was chosen for the deep neural network model and the MalRNN framework was selected as the black-box attack model. After extracting the features of the neural network model's middle layer, we adopted L_2 distance, K-means, and Minhash methods to measure the similarity among the indexed samples. Experimental results of different methods with different numbers of index samples are shown in Table 7. From the table, it can be seen that the features of the neural network model's middle layer are not effective for the similarity measure among the samples. The existence of an adversarial attack could not be detected. The reason for this may be that PE samples and images are fundamentally different: The middle layer features of an image under a deep neural network model is an image whose general outline can still be seen, whereas the middle layer features of a malicious or benign sample is a multidimensional array of tensors.

Table 7. The effects of different methods with the number of indexed samples (K) under MalRNN.

Methods \ K	30	200	400
L_2	×	×	×
K-means	×	×	×
Minhash	×	×	×

'×' denotes the features of the neural network model's middle layer are ineffective for the similarity measure among the samples.

7. Limitations and Conclusions

Limitations of MalDBA: (1) The false positive rate of the MalDBA will rise if highly similar malicious samples are fed into the detector for querying (as if there is a similarity among malicious samples of the same family). (2) MalDBA detects historical query sequences generated during the iteration of query-based black-box attacks and cannot defend against non-query-based attacks (e.g., substitute model attacks).

Malware black-box attacks cause security risks to AI and pose a threat to data security as well as privacy, and their defense is a complex issue [18,19]. In this paper, we manage to solve the problem of stateful detection for malware score-based black-box attacks. First, the set of historical query samples generated during the attack is saved. Afterward, similarity comparison is performed on different numbers of indexed samples by a similarity comparator. Finally, the presence or absence of an adversarial attack is detected according to the trend of scores returned by the malware detector. The results show that the detection rate of MalDBA against score-based black-box attacks is 100%, and the detection rate is independent of the number of indexed samples.

In the future, we plan to investigate the following research directions: (1) Study of a general attack strategy for stateful detection defense. (2) Drawing on the similarity encoder proposed in computer vision, consider whether it can be studied by extracting the function call graph or control flow graph of malware and combining it with graph neural networks.

Author Contributions: Conceptualization, Z.L.; Funding acquisition, J.X.; Methodology, Z.K.; Validation, Y.W.; Writing—original draft, W.H. All authors have read and agreed to the published version of the manuscript.

Funding: This work was supported by China Scholarship Council (No. 202106030119), the National Natural Science Foundation of China (No. 62172042), and Major Scientific and Technological Innovation Projects of Shandong Province (2020CXGC010116).

Data Availability Statement: Previously published articles were used to support this study and these prior studies and datasets are cited at relevant places within this article. The link to the datasets is https://virusshare.com/ (accessed on 6 February 2022).

Conflicts of Interest: The authors declare that there is no conflict of interest regarding the publication of this paper.

References

1. Mcafee. *Labs Threats Report*; McAfee: Hong Kong, China, 2021; 24p.
2. VirusTotal. Deception at Scale: How Malware Abuses Trust; VirusTotal: Dublin, Ireland, 2022; 15p.
3. Darem, A.; Abawajy, J.; Makkar, A.; Alhashmi, A.; Alanazi, S. Visualization and deep-learning-based malware variant detection using OpCode-level features. *Future Gener. Comput. Syst.* **2021**, *125*, 314–323. [CrossRef]
4. Sun, G.; Qian, Q. Deep learning and visualization for identifying malware families. *IEEE Trans. Dependable Secur. Comput.* **2018**, *18*, 283–295. [CrossRef]
5. Huang, X.; Ma, L.; Yang, W.; Zhong, Y. A method for windows malware detection based on deep learning. *J. Signal Process. Syst.* **2021**, *93*, 265–273. [CrossRef]
6. Akhtar, N.; Mian, A. Threat of adversarial attacks on deep learning in computer vision: A survey. *IEEE Access* **2018**, *6*, 14410–14430. [CrossRef]
7. Szegedy, C.; Zaremba, W.; Sutskever, I.; Bruna, J.; Erhan, D.; Goodfellow, I.; Fergus, R. Intriguing properties of neural networks. *arXiv* **2013**, arXiv:1312.6199.
8. Fang, Y.; Zeng, Y.; Li, B.; Liu, L.; Zhang, L. DeepDetectNet vs RLAttackNet: An Adversarial Method to Improve Deep Learning-Based Static Malware Detection Model. *PLoS ONE* **2020**, *15*, e0231626. [CrossRef]
9. Maiorca, D.; Biggio, B.; Giacinto, G. Towards Adversarial Malware Detection: Lessons Learned from PDF-based Attacks. *ACM Comput. Surv.* **2020**, *52*, 1–36.
10. Esmaeili, B.; Azmoodeh, A.; Dehghantanha, A.; Zolfaghari, B.; Karimipour, H.; Hammoudeh, M. IIoT Deep Malware Threat Hunting: From Adversarial Example Detection to Adversarial Scenario Detection. *IEEE Trans. Ind. Inform.* **2022**, *18*, 8477–8486. [CrossRef]
11. Li, M.Q.; Fung, B.C.; Charland, P. DyAdvDefender: An instance-based online machine learning model for perturbation-trial-based black-box adversarial defense. *Inf. Sci.* **2022**, *601*, 357–373. [CrossRef]
12. Available online: https://virusshare.com/ (accessed on 6 February 2022).
13. Raff, E.; Barker, J.; Sylvester, J.; Brandon, R.; Catanzaro, B.; Nicholas, C.K. Malware detection by eating a whole exe. In Proceedings of the Workshops at the Thirty-Second AAAI Conference on Artificial Intelligence, New Orleans, LA, USA, 2–7 February 2018.
14. Ebrahimi, M.; Zhang, N.; Hu, J.; Raza, M.T.; Chen, H. Binary Black-box Evasion Attacks Against Deep Learning-based Static Malware Detectors with Adversarial Byte-Level Language Model. In Proceedings of the 2021, AAAI Workshop on Robust, Secure and Efficient Machine Learning (RSEML), Vancouver, BC, Canada, 2–9 February 2021.

15. Demetrio, L.; Biggio, B.; Lagorio, G.; Roli, F.; Armando, A. Functionality-preserving black-box optimization of adversarial windows malware. *IEEE Trans. Inf. Forensics Secur.* **2021**, *16*, 3469–3478. [CrossRef]
16. Wu, W.; Li, B.; Chen, L.; Gao, J.; Zhang, C. A review for weighted minhash algorithms. *IEEE Trans. Knowl. Data Eng.* **2020**, *34*, 2553–2573. [CrossRef]
17. Podschwadt, R.; Takabi, H. On effectiveness of adversarial examples and defenses for malware classification. In *International Conference on Security and Privacy in Communication Systems*; Springer: Cham, Switzerland, 2019; pp. 380–393.
18. Li, D.; Li, Q. Adversarial deep ensemble: Evasion attacks and defenses for malware detection. *IEEE Trans. Inf. Forensics Secur.* **2020**, *15*, 3886–3900. [CrossRef]
19. Huang, Y.; Verma, U.; Fralick, C.; Infantec-Lopez, G.; Kumar, B.; Woodward, C. Malware evasion attack and defense. In Proceedings of the 2019 49th Annual IEEE/IFIP International Conference on Dependable Systems and Networks Workshops (DSN-W), Portland, OR, USA, 24–27 June 2019; pp. 34–38.
20. Li, H.; Xu, X.; Zhang, X.; Yang, S.; Li, B. Qeba: Query-efficient boundary-based blackbox attack. In Proceedings of the IEEE/CVF Conference on Computer Vision and Pattern Recognition, Seattle, WA, USA, 13–19 June 2020; pp. 1221–1230.
21. Brendel, W.; Rauber, J.; Bethge, M. Decision-based adversarial attacks: Reliable attacks against black-box machine learning models. *arXiv* **2017**, arXiv:1712.04248.
22. Yoon, J.; Hwang, S.J.; Lee, J. Adversarial purification with score-based generative models. In Proceedings of the International Conference on Machine Learning, PMLR, Virtual, 18–24 July 2021; pp. 12062–12072.
23. Chen, S.; Carlini, N.; Wagner, D. Stateful detection of black-box adversarial attacks. In Proceedings of the 1st ACM Workshop on Security and Privacy on Artificial Intelligence, Virtual Event, 13 November 2020; pp. 30–39.
24. Li, H.; Shan, S.; Wenger, E.; Zhang, J.; Zheng, H.; Zhao, B.Y. Blacklight: Scalable defense for neural networks against query-based black-box attacks. *arXiv* **2022**, arXiv:2006.14042.
25. Juuti, M.; Szyller, S.; Marchal, S.; Asokan, N. PRADA: Protecting against DNN model stealing attacks. In Proceedings of the 2019 IEEE European Symposium on Security and Privacy (EuroS&P), Stockholm, Sweden, 17–19 June 2019; pp. 512–527.
26. Cohen, G.; Sapiro, G.; Giryes, R. Detecting adversarial samples using influence functions and nearest neighbors. In Proceedings of the IEEE/CVF Conference on Computer Vision and Pattern Recognition, Seattle, WA, USA, 13–19 June 2020; pp. 14453–14462.
27. Pang, R.; Zhang, X.; Ji, S.; Luo, X.; Wang, T. AdvMind: Inferring adversary intent of black-box attacks. In Proceedings of the 26th ACM SIGKDD International Conference on Knowledge Discovery & Data Mining, Virtual, 6–10 July 2020; pp. 1899–1907.
28. Al-Dujaili, A.; Huang, A.; Hemberg, E.; O'Reilly, U.M. Adversarial deep learning for robust detection of binary encoded malware. In Proceedings of the 2018 IEEE Security and Privacy Workshops (SPW), San Francisco, CA, USA, 24 May 2018; pp. 76–82.
29. Castro, R.L.; Schmitt, C.; Dreo, G. Aimed: Evolving malware with genetic programming to evade detection. In Proceedings of the 2019 18th IEEE International Conference On Trust, Security and Privacy in Computing and Communications/13th IEEE International Conference On Big Data Science and Engineering (TrustCom/BigDataSE), Rotorua, New Zealand, 5–8 August 2019; pp. 240–247.
30. Luca, D.; Biggio, B.; Giovanni, L.; Roli, F.; Alessandro, A. Explaining vulnerabilities of deep learning to adversarial malware binaries. In Proceedings of the 3rd Italian Conference on Cyber Security, ITASEC 2019, Pisa, Italy, 12 February 2019; Volume 2315.
31. Kolosnjaji, B.; Demontis, A.; Biggio, B.; Maiorca, D.; Giacinto, G.; Eckert, C.; Roli, F. Adversarial malware binaries: Evading deep learning for malware detection in executables. In Proceedings of the 2018 26th European Signal Processing Conference (EUSIPCO), Rome, Italy, 3–7 September 2018; pp. 533–537.
32. Mosli, R.; Slota, T.J.; Pan, Y. Creating Adversarial Malware Examples Through Guided Metamorphic Changes. In Proceedings of the 2021 IEEE International Symposium on Technologies for Homeland Security (HST), Boston, MA, USA, 8–9 November 2021; pp. 1–7. [CrossRef]
33. Quertier, T.; Marais, B.; Morucci, S.; Fournel, B. MERLIN—Malware Evasion with Reinforcement LearnINg. *arXiv* **2022**, arXiv:2203.129802022.
34. Dasgupta, P.; Osman, Z. A Comparison of State-of-the-Art Techniques for Generating Adversarial Malware Binaries. *arXiv* **2021**, arXiv:2111.11487.
35. Burr, J.; Xu, S. Improving Adversarial Attacks Against Executable Raw Byte Classifiers. In Proceedings of the IEEE INFOCOM 2021—IEEE Conference on Computer Communications Workshops (INFOCOM WKSHPS), Vancouver, BC, Canada, 10–13 May 2021; pp. 1–2. [CrossRef]
36. Li, X.; Nie, Y.; Wang, Z.; Kuang, X.; Qiu, K.; Qian, C.; Zhao, G. BMOP: Bidirectional Universal Adversarial Learning for Binary OpCode Features. *Wirel. Commun. Mob. Comput.* **2020**, *2020*, 8876632. [CrossRef]
37. Rosenberg, I.; Shabtai, A.; Rokach, L.; Elovici, Y. Generic black-box end-to-end attack against state of the art API call based malware classifiers. In *International Symposium on Research in Attacks, Intrusions, and Defenses*; Springer: Cham, Switzerland, 2018; pp. 490–510.
38. Grosse, K.; Papernot, N.; Manoharan, P.; Backes, M.; McDaniel, P. Adversarial perturbations against deep neural networks for malware classification. *arXiv* **2016**, arXiv:1606.04435.
39. Yuan, X.; He, P.; Zhu, Q.; Li, X. Adversarial examples: Attacks and defenses for deep learning. *IEEE Trans. Neural Netw. Learn. Syst.* **2019**, *30*, 2805–2824. [CrossRef]
40. Hu, W.; Tan, Y. Generating adversarial malware examples for black-box attacks based on GAN. *arXiv* **2017**, arXiv:1702.05983.

41. Yuste, J.; Pardo, E.G.; Tapiador, J. Optimization of code caves in malware binaries to evade machine learning detectors. *Comput. Secur.* **2022**, *116*, 102643. [CrossRef]
42. Demetrio, L.; Coull, S.E.; Biggio, B.; Lagorio, G.; Armando, A.; Roli, F. Adversarial exemples: A survey and experimental evaluation of practical attacks on machine learning for windows malware detection. *ACM Trans. Priv. Secur. (TOPS)* **2021**, *24*, 1–31. [CrossRef]
43. Sünderhauf, N.; Dayoub, F.; Shirazi, S.; Upcroft, B.; Milford, M. On the Performance of ConvNet Features for Place Recognition. In Proceedings of the 2015 IEEE/RSJ International Conference on Intelligent Robots and Systems (IROS), Hamburg, Germany, 28 September–2 October 2015.
44. Qiao, Y.; Cappelle, C.; Ruichek, Y.; Yang, T. ConvNet and LSH-based visual localization using localized sequence matching. *Sensors* **2019**, *19*, 2439. [CrossRef] [PubMed]

electronics

Article

NACDA: Naming-Based Access Control and Decentralized Authorization for Secure Many-to-Many Data Sharing

Minghui Li [1], Jingfeng Xue [1], Yong Wang [1,*], Rui Ma [1] and Wei Huo [2,3]

1 School of Computer Science and Technology, Beijing Institute of Technology, Beijing 100081, China
2 Institute of Information Engineering, Chinese Academy of Sciences, Beijing 100081, China
3 School of Cyber Security, University of Chinese Academy of Sciences, Beijing 100081, China
* Correspondence: wangyong@bit.edu.cn

Abstract: The rapid development of wearable technology has facilitated the collection and sharing of health data, allowing patients to benefit from caretakers and medical research. However, these personal health data often contain sensitive information and it is typically not known in advance with whom the information will be shared. Therefore, messages must be encrypted and shared while adhering to the decoupled communication model. This paper presents NACDA, a secure many-to-many data-sharing service on the Named Data Network (NDN). NACDA uses Identity-Based Encryption with Wildcard Key Derivation (WKD-IBE) to allow naming-based access control, enabling data subjects to share data securely and flexibly regardless of the data processor. In addition, NACDA supplements a decentralized authorization mechanism with blockchain to ensure data subjects' data ownership and enforce access policies. We developed an NDN-based prototype and performed a security analysis to demonstrate NACDA's feasibility.

Keywords: NDN; access control; authorization; data sharing

Citation: Li, M.; Xue, J.; Wang, Y.; Ma, R.; Huo, W. NACDA: Naming-Based Access Control and Decentralized Authorization for Secure Many-to-Many Data Sharing. *Electronics* **2023**, *12*, 1651. https://doi.org/10.3390/electronics12071651

Academic Editor: Djamel Djenouri

Received: 7 February 2023
Revised: 24 March 2023
Accepted: 28 March 2023
Published: 31 March 2023

1. Introduction

In recent years, with the development of communication technology, wearable devices have rapidly developed in the healthcare domain. This trend promotes users sharing medical and health data with multiple hospitals or research institutions to enable disease diagnosis and health analysis [1,2]. Thus, the relationship between the user and the institution is a complex many-to-many communication rather than a one-to-one communication. In addition, medical and health data often contain a large amount of private information that, if leaked, would seriously threaten the security of users' personal property. Therefore, secure healthcare data sharing in many-to-many communication scenarios is crucial.

Secure sharing in many-to-many communications requires data subjects (i.e., the owner of data) to securely, selectively, and flexibly grant access to data processors (i.e., someone who wants to access data). Ideally, it provides the four following features: (i) decoupling data subjects and data processors: data subjects that classify and publish data to storage servers, and data processors that request or subscribe to specific data types; (ii) data confidentiality and integrity: encryption primitives are independent of the data processor, and encryption operations are relatively efficient and can be verifiable; (iii) fine-grained access control: data subjects limit what data types to share and who can access which time range of the data; (iv) decentralized management: data subjects are free from dependence on trusted intermediaries, such as resource management and access authorization, avoiding the problems of transparency and single point of failure.

Most current many-to-many communication systems rely on TCP/IP. However, TCP/IP does not directly support many-to-many communication but requires the implementation of complex logic at the application layer [3]. We implement the four above features by utilizing the functionalities provided by NDN, a data-centric network architecture [4]. In NDN, the data receivers drive communication by hierarchical names and fetch cryptographic data from intermediate caches by intelligent forwarding strategies. On top of NDN, several access control schemes have been proposed to enable secure data sharing in NDN, such as role-based access control (RBAC) and attribute-based encryption (ABE) [5]. However, these schemes rely on the role or attributes of the data receivers, and users may not know which institutions they will share in advance. With the publish–subscribe paradigm in NDN, a more appropriate encryption idea is to encrypt the based on the data's properties.

This paper leverages WKD-IBE [6] in NDN. WKD-IBE is a public key encryption scheme that enhances the concept of hierarchical identity-based encryption (HIBE) [7] by allowing more general key delegation patterns. We take NDN's hierarchical naming as a pattern of WKD-IBE to implement naming-based access control. In addition, access control and authorization need to be designed together to enable a complete data-sharing process. We further introduce blockchain technology [8] as a trusted intermediary to address the trust risk of centralized data retrieval and authorization services in NDN. In brief, we build a secure many-to-many data-sharing framework called NACDA with naming-based access control and decentralized authorization. The NACDA's contributions are as follows.

- A naming-based access control model is proposed based on WKD-IBE, which ensures data confidentiality and integrity as well as fine-grained access control for many-to-many communications in NDN.
- To effectively and securely share resources, we introduce a decentralized authorization mechanism, which allows data subjects to manage the data and access policies. Furthermore, this mechanism grants permissions in a transparent and auditable manner.
- We evaluate the prototype of NACDA and analyze its security.

The remainder of this paper is organized into seven sections. Section 2 describes the background and related work. Section 3 describes NACDA at a high level, including design concepts and architecture. Section 4 presents a name-based access control model that encrypts the data for fine-grained access control in NDN. Section 5 offers a decentralized authorization mechanism that manages data and policies for trusted authorization with the blockchain. Section 6 implements and evaluates the prototype. Finally, Section 7 concludes and discusses this paper.

2. Background and Related Work

This section introduces the related work of access control in NDN and blockchain-based authorization.

2.1. Access Control in NDN

NDN communication consists of two types of packets: an interest packet and data packet, as shown in Figure 1. A processor sends an interest packet, specifying the name of the desired data, and then obtains a data packet containing the data's content if the storage or route node owns the data. Therefore, NDN drives communication based on the content name and decouples the content from its original location. This phenomenon leads to a loss of control over the content, which causes challenges in achieving effective access control mechanisms [9]. The existing solutions are as follows.

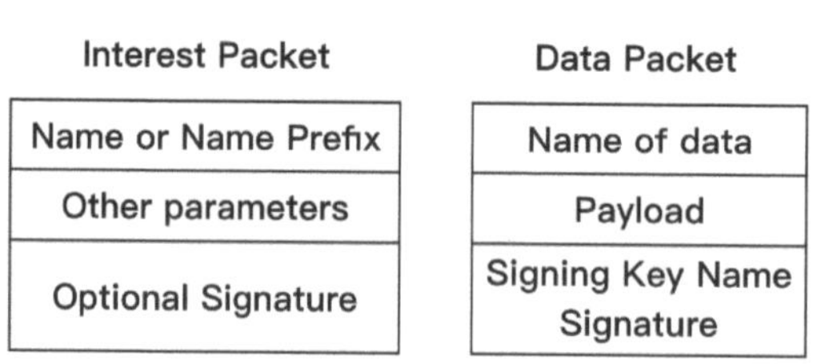

Figure 1. Two packets in NDN.

Zhang et al. [10] proposed a well-designed naming convention that facilitates explicitly communicating access policies and efficiently assigning access control keys. In this work, the data subject generates a production credential named a key encryption key (KEK) and a consumption credential named a key decryption key (KDK) related to the data naming. The data producer obtains the KEK and uses it to encrypt the content key (CK), and the authorized processor will obtain the corresponding KDK and decrypt the data. Fan et al. [11] extended [10] to support spatio-temporal policies by adding location information to the KEK and KDK names. However, in fine-grained data access control cases, the data subject needs to generate, manage and transmit many KEKs and KDKs, resulting in high resource consumption.

Feng et al. [5] propose a decentralized CP-ABE scheme. The publisher creates an access policy and encrypts the data according to the policy, the current time, and the time the router caches the data. However, having full knowledge of the processor attributes in advance in large-scale publish/subscribe systems is not practical, and the solution also requires publishers to be available at all times.

Fotiou et al. [12] used HIBE to build name-based security mechanisms for content distribution. The content owner utilizes the Namecoin blockchain to deliver the system parameters. A subscriber then obtains system parameters to verify a digital signature over the item, no matter the providing endpoint. However, it has limitations in hierarchical key derivation, a helpful function of data sharing in NDN.

Table 1 compares NACDA with other name-based access control research regarding key features. Our work focuses on many-to-many data-sharing service with efficiently fine-grained access control.

Table 1. Comparison of NACDA With Other Name-based Access Control.

Related Research	Name-Based Security	Multiple Naming Granularity	Keys Distribution Flexibility	Decoupling and Namespace Delegation	Namespace Granting Simplicity
[10]	Y	N	N	N	N
[11]	Y	Y	N	N	N
[5]	Y	Y	Y	N	N
[12]	Y	Y	Y	Y	N
Our work	Y	Y	Y	Y	Y

2.2. Blockchain-Based Authorization

While a content-based access control scheme is appropriate in NDN, this scheme cannot be directly associated with data processors. Therefore, it requires additional authorization mechanisms to complement the secure sharing process. The authorization mechanism based on trusted third parties may have the problems of a single point of failure and a non-transparent authorization process. In contrast, blockchain technology is a new decentralized infrastructure and distributed computing paradigm. It has the properties of decentralization, persistency, and auditability, which make the authorization process more secure and credible. The current solutions are presented below.

Ouadda et al. [13] store access policies in blockchain transactions. They use authorization tokens to represent unspent transaction output (UTXO), which can be passed from one peer to another via transactions, thus enabling authorization management. However, its decision-making process counts on a centralized authorization entity, which still suffers from a single point of failure.

Truong et al. [14] proposed a resource access control scheme based on smart contracts, which consists of two ledgers: the 3A_ledger, which is responsible for storing resource summaries and access policies, and the log_ledger, which records authorization tokens. Afterwards, resource servers can query the authorization records in the log_ledger to verify whether the data processors' requests are legitimate. This work implements the

OAuth2 standard [15] authorization process but does not further consider data security and fine-grained access control.

Our research combines a content encryption-based access control scheme with a smart contract-based authorization mechanism to achieve a complete secure sharing process in NDN.

3. NACDA's Overview

This section describes NACDA in a nutshell and its architecture.

3.1. NACDA in a Nutshell

NACDA is a decentralized access control system that enables data subjects to securely, selectively, and granularly share their data with data processors in a scenario of many-to-many communication. NACDA is designed to use namespaces as the basis for data search, data encryption, and access control, as shown in Figure 2. First, NDN uses hierarchical semantic names to identify content, and the resulting namespace is used for NDN data requests (Section 4.2). Second, since fine-grained data sharing is based on fine-grained data encryption, the namespace naturally serves as the basis for fine-grained encryption. That is, the leaf nodes of the namespace serve as the minimum granularity of data encryption (Section 4.3). Thirdly, the data subject sets the namespace's node associated with the access policy (Section 5.1) and then denotes the sub-namespace right to a data processor as an access token (Section 5.2). Finally, since fine-grained data encryption generates many keys, there may be problems with key management and distribution. Therefore, we have adopted an access control approach based on hierarchical encryption, where authorized data processors obtain the decryption keys corresponding to the namespace's nonleaf nodes, and then derive all decryption keys for that sub-namespace themselves (Section 4.3).

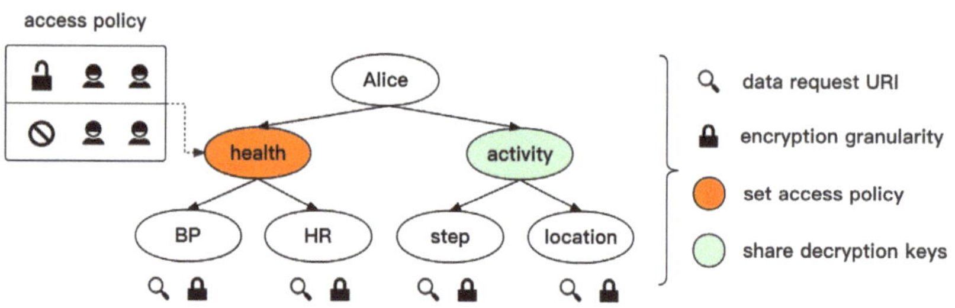

Figure 2. NACDA's design concept.

Note that we covered the terms authorization and access control, which are relatively easy to confuse. Authorization is the specification of access policies, and access control is the enforcement of access policies [16]. In the above paragraph, we discuss the specification of access control policies and their mappings to access tokens, which we summarize as a decentralized authorization mechanism (Section 5). The remaining parts are summarized as a name-based access control model (Section 4).

3.2. Architecture

Figure 3 shows the architecture of NACDA, and Table 2 explains the entities and components involved. It is essential to note that data sharing should comply with GDPR's requirements when EU citizens are involved, so we define the entities referring to GDPR [14,17].

The name-based access control model takes namespaces as the basis for data encryption, as shown in the upper part of Figure 3. First of all, the data subject initializes the namespace, which contains a hierarchy of resources and time, and grants sub-namespace to the IoT devices (Step 1). Furthermore, IoT devices generate and encrypt data in the related namespace (Step 2). The encryption process allows different resources to be encrypted at different times using unique encryption parameters and does not require generating and managing extensive encryption keys. Then, the encrypted data are packaged and published on the NDN (Step 3). NDN uses an in-network cache mechanism so that each node in the transmission path can cache the content and quickly respond to the corresponding request. Additionally, the authorized data processor requests data from the NDN (Step 8) and can decrypt the data with the corresponding decryption keys (Steps 10–12).

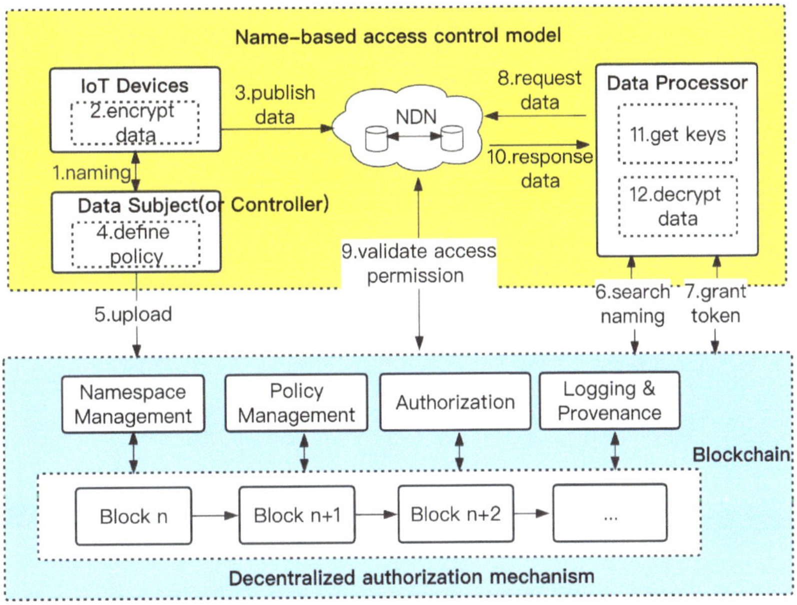

Figure 3. NACDA architecture.

Table 2. Notation of entries in NACDA architecture.

Notation	Description	Function
IoT devices	Devices for producing data	Producing, encrypting, and uploading data
Data subject	The owner of data	The management of names, spaces, access policies, and decryption keys
Data controller	Someone or an institution who manages personal data	Assuring the rights of data subjects
Data processor	Someone who wants to access data	Requesting access rights, decryption keys, and decrypting data
NDN	Internet architecture	Storing, caching, and forwarding data
Blockchain	Decentralized servers	Storing namespaces, access policies, and granting access rights

The name-based access control module ensures data confidentiality. However, it does not adequately consider how to authorize data processors (including verifying identity, managing access policies, and granting access rights). Therefore, the blockchain is introduced to implement a decentralized authorization mechanism, which acts as an agent to handle authorization requests from data processors in a unified manner, as illustrated in the lower part of Figure 3. The data subject uploads the namespace and the corresponding access policy to the blockchain (Steps 4–5). Then, the data processor requests the blockchain to obtain the exact name of the packets and access token (Steps 6–7). When a data processor requests data, the NDN's node that caches the data will validate access permission again based on the blockchain's authorization log and choose to allow or deny the data access request (Step 9).

4. Name-Based Access Control Model

The objectives of the name-based access control model can be summarized as follows: (i) data encryption: using the namespace as the basis for the fine-grained and effective encryption primitives. (ii) access control: a data processor can get succinct keys for an access scope grant. Given all the above, the critical point is that NDN naturally organizes the data into hierarchies, resulting in a namespace that could act as the encryption parameter of the lightweight encryption algorithm WKD-IBE. Furthermore, a WKD-IBE's decryption key related to a namespace can derive all keys of its sub-namespace but not for the parent namespace (Section 4.1). The detailed workflow of the name-based access control module is shown in Figure 4, which is further broken down into name-based encryption (Section 4.2) and fine-grained access control (Section 4.3).

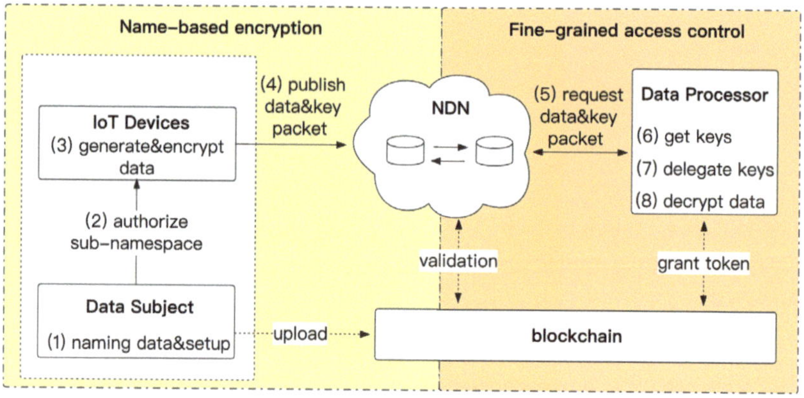

Figure 4. Name-based access control model.

4.1. Generic WKD-IBE

Algorithms

WKD-IBE normally generates a secret key based on an identity string template where wildcards can replace elements. Then, this secret key can derive keys for other identity string vectors that match the above template. Although the original WKD-IBE scheme focuses on the user's identity information as a template, it can also abstract other details as a template. For example, Kumar et al. [18] proposed that in a system where resources have hierarchical structures, a user has a key with the resource prefix a/b/*, i.e., a/b/* is encoded as a string template and * denotes a wildcard, then it can derive keys with resources a/b/c, a/b/d, etc.

WKD-IBE consists of four operations: **Setup**, **KeyDer**, **Enc**, and **Dec**. They are described as follows [18]:

- **Setup**$(1^{\ell}) \rightarrow Params, MasterKey$. This operation outputs public parameters (Params) and master secret key (MasterKey).
- **KeyDer**$(Params, Key_{Pattern_A}, Pattern_B) \rightarrow Key_{Pattern_B}$. This operation derives a key for $Pattern_B$, where $Key_{Pattern_A}$ is $MasterKey$ or $Pattern_A$ matches $Pattern_B$.
- **Enc**$(Params, Pattern, m) \rightarrow Ciphertext_{Pattern,m}$. This operation receives a ciphertext encrypted by $Params$ and $Pattern$.

- **Dec**$(Key_{Pattern_A}, Ciphertext_{Pattern,m}) \rightarrow m$. This operation receives a ciphertext encrypted by $Params$ and $Pattern$. Then, it obtains a plain text message m with the help of $Key_{Pattern}$.

  WKD-IBE can also be used to sign data to verify its integrity. It is illustrated as follows:
- **Sign**$(Params, Key_{Pattern_m}, m) \rightarrow S$. This operation uses $Key_{Pattern_m}$ to sign a message m and output the signature S.
- **Verify**$(S, Params, Pattern_m, m) \rightarrow \top or \bot$. This operation uses the $Pattern_m$ and the message m to verify the signature S. The output $\top$ indicates a successful verification and the output $\bot$ indicates a failed one.

4.2. Name-Based Encryption

The named-based encryption part includes the following steps: the data subject initializes the namespace and WKD-IBE (Section 4.2.1), then grants the IoT devices the right to generate data under the sub-namespace (Section 4.2.2). Finally, the IoT devices generate, encrypt, and publish the data (Section 4.2.3).

4.2.1. Initialization

NDN names resources with hierarchically structured names similar to URI, which group data with similar attributes in the same namespace. This naming way reflects the relationship between different data blocks and facilitates the management and sharing of resources. The data subject and the processor can agree to express a standard namespace structure. Taking the health scenario as an example, the data subject Alice uses the health app to collect her health data and activity data, dividing the corresponding namespace into two sub-namespaces: alice/health and alice/activity, where health data are further divided into blood pressure and heart rate data, corresponding to the sub-namespace: alice/health/BP and alice/health/HR, as shown in Figure 5. Once the resource hierarchy is determined, the resources can be further divided according to the set temporal granularity, i.e., a temporal hierarchy is added to the hierarchy of resources. For example, layers 4–6 in Figure 5 divide the resources by year, month, and day, and the namespace corresponding to the blood pressure data generated by Alice on 12 December 2020 are called alice/health/BP/2020/12/12. The granularity of the namespace division determines the granularity of the subsequent data encryption and sharing.

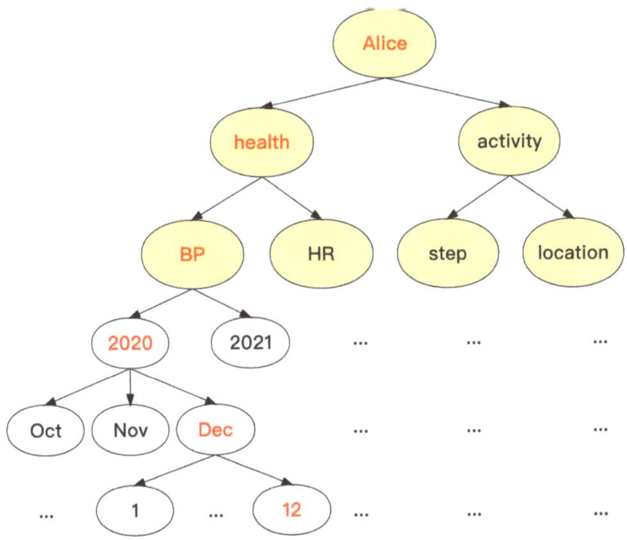

Figure 5. Alice's namespace.

After defining the NDN's namespace, the data subject initiates WKD-IBE, which takes the depth of the namespace as input parameters and outputs the public parameters and the master key. This step is represented as follows.

- **Setup**$\left(1^{\ell}\right)$: select $g, g_2, g_3, h_1, \ldots, h_\ell, h_s \xleftarrow{\$} \mathbb{G}$, $\alpha \xleftarrow{\$} \mathbb{Z}_p$ and let $g_1 = g^{\alpha}$. Then, the output: $Params = (g, g_1, g_2, g_3, h_1, \ldots, h_\ell, h_s)$ and $MasterKey = g_2^{\alpha}$. $\mathbb{G}$ is a bilinear group if the group action in $\mathbb{G}$ can be efficiently computed and there exists both a group $\mathbb{G}_1$ and an efficiently computable bilinear map e: $\mathbb{G} \times \mathbb{G} \to \mathbb{G}_1$.

This datum subject performs this step (or the authority trusted by the data subject) and keeps *MasterKey* secret. *Params* can be stored publicly, which data processors use subsequently, so we can use blockchain to disseminate *Params*, i.e., holding them along with the namespace in the data subject's blockchain account.

Subsequently, the data subject has two aspects of work. One is to grant the right to generate data under the sub-namespace to the IoT devices, and the other is to distribute the decryption keys of an authorized sub-namespace for the data processors. Both of these tasks rely on the key derivation step. Note that we can distinguish encryption and sign by adjusting *Params* and *MasterKey* [19].

- **KeyDer**$(Params, K, Pattern)$: when K is *MasterKey*, let $K = g_2^{\alpha}$, and $r \xleftarrow{\$} \mathbb{Z}_p$. The private key for the *Pattern* of sub-namespace is:

$$\left(g_2^{\alpha} \cdot \left(g_3 \cdot \prod_{(i,a_i)\in \text{fixed}(Pattern)} h_i^{a_i} \right)^r,\ g^r,\ \left\{ \left(j, h_j^r\right) \right\}_{j\in \text{free}(Pattern)} \right).$$

when K is not *MasterKey*, then parse K as (k_0, k_1, B), $B = \{(i, b_i)\}$. Let $t \xleftarrow{\$} \mathbb{Z}_p$. The private key for S is:

$$\left(k_0 \cdot \left(g_3 \cdot \prod_{(i,a_i)\in \text{fixed}(Pattern)} h_i^{a_i} \right)^t \cdot \prod_{\substack{(i,a_i)\in \text{fixed}(Pattern) \\ (i,b_i)\in B}} b_i^{a_i},\ g^t \cdot k_1,\ \left\{ \left(j, h_j^t \cdot b_j\right) \right\}_{j\in \text{free}(Pattern)} \right).$$

The *KeyDer* step considers the case where K is *MasterKey* or not. Generally, the data subject depends on *MasterKey* derivation because these have the right to their entire namespace. The case where K is not *MasterKey*, on the other hand, is typically when the IoT devices or data processors obtain the derived key and handle their own sub-namespace.

4.2.2. Sub-Namespace Authorization

The security of the NDN is built into the data themselves, which requires that each packet be signed. The digital signature's legitimacy ensures the integrity and authentication of the message, preventing it from being tampered with or forged.

Specifically, the data subject grants the producer permission to produce data under its sub-namespace. These permission keys could use an out-of-band channel (e.g., Bluetooth low energy) to exchange between the subject and devices. Then, the devices obtain the keys, generate data, and sign the hash of the data, which is subsequently published to the NDN along with the data packet. The data processor then obtains the data packet and verifies its origin and integrity. The above process is summarized in two steps.

- **Sign**$(Params, Key_{Pattern_m}, Hash_m) \rightarrow S$: Parse the key K as (k_0, k_1, B), $(s, b_s) \in B$. $Hash_m$ is the hash value of message m whose pattern is $Pattern_m$, and $Key_{Pattern_m}$ is the corresponding sign key. Select $t \xleftarrow{\$} \mathbb{Z}_p$ and output the signature S:

$$\left(k_0 \cdot \left(g_3 \cdot h_s^{Hash_m} \cdot \prod_{(i,a_i) \in \text{fixed}(Pattern_m)} h_i^{a_i}\right)^t \cdot b_s^{Hash_m},\quad g^t \cdot k_1\right)$$

- **Verify**$(Params, S, Pattern_m, Hash_m) \rightarrow \top or \bot$: parse the signature S as (s_0, s_1). Check:

$$e(s_0, g) \stackrel{?}{=} e(g_1, g_2) \cdot e\left(g_3 \cdot h_s^{Hash_m} \cdot \prod_{(i,a_i) \in f\text{fixed}(Pattern_m)} h_i^{a_i},\quad s_1\right)$$

The *Sign* function is usually combined with the *KeyDer* function (usually when K is not MasterKey) since the sub-namespace obtained by the IoT device is often not a specific sub-namespace. In addition, the data processor verifies the received S to check whether the signature is correct. If the device is authorized, then the hash value can verify the integrity of the data. We use an example to further illustrate the process. Data subject Alice derives the signing key $Key_{alice/health}$ for sub-namespace alice/health and sends it to her device. When Alice produces plaintext data m under alice/health/BP/2020/12/12, she calculates the $Hash_m$ and signs it, i.e., **KeyDer**$(Params, Key_{alice/health}, Pattern_{alice/health/BP/2020/12/12}) \rightarrow Key_{alice/health/BP/2020/12/12}$, then **Sign**$(Params, Pattern_{alice/health/BP/2020/12/12}, Hash_m) \rightarrow S$. The data processor obtains the signature S and uses $Pattern_{alice/health/BP/2020/12/12}$ to verify the origin and integrity of the m.

4.2.3. Data Encryption

IoT devices generate the data, encrypt them according to WKD-IBE, and publish them to the NDN. Given that IoT devices are usually low-power and have a large amount of data, a hybrid encryption scheme combining WKD-IBE and symmetric encryption is suitable. In detail, the data devices encrypt the plaintext data using a symmetric key and invoke WKD-IBE to encrypt the symmetric key based on the temporal granularity of the namespace. The next encryption round will flip the symmetric key and modify the WKD-IBE encryption parameter. The process is brief in the following step.

- **Enc**$(Params, Pattern_m, K_m) \rightarrow CT_{K_m}$: K_m is the symmetric key of message m, then selects $s \xleftarrow{\$} \mathbb{Z}_p$ and outputs CT_{K_m}:

$$\left(e(g_1, g_2)^s \cdot K_m,\quad g^s,\quad \left(g_3 \cdot \prod_{(i,a_i) \in \text{fixed}(Pattern_m)} h_i^{a_i}\right)^s\right).$$

To further explain the process, we consider an instance of datum m generated under alice/health/BP/2020/12/12. The IoT devices use the AES algorithm to sample a symmetric key K_m to encrypt m. The corresponding generated ciphertext CT_m, together with the signature information in Section 4.2.2, are packaged and published to the NDN. Meanwhile, as another data packet, K_m is encrypted to generate the key ciphertext CT_{K_m}. Note that the minimum time granularity of alice/health/BP/2020/12/12 is in days, so the data producer flips the symmetric key and invokes WKD-IBE to encrypt it once a day. The finer temporal hierarchy brings in the finer encryption's granularity, which benefits flexible data sharing. However, this may cause resource waste, so a balance between granularity and consumption is best based on practical cases.

4.3. *Fine-Grained Access Control*

The fine-grained access control consists of the following steps: the authorized data processor sends an interest packet to the NDN and requests decryption keys within its authorization from the key server (Section 4.3.1). The data processor then obtains the decryption keys and decrypts the data (Section 4.3.2). Note that this subsection assumes that the data processor has already obtained an access token (Section 5).

4.3.1. Decryption Keys Delegation

When requesting data from the NDN, an authorized data processor first retrieves the ciphertext packet, which usually contains the corresponding key packet name so that the data processor can continue to request key packets. In addition, NDN's node will verify the data processor's access token by the blockchain's authorization log before returning the data, which could intercept data requests from attackers or those with expired authorization tokens.

The data processor also needs to request the decryption keys within the scope of the access token. We previously mentioned in Section 4.2.1 that data subjects distribute decryption keys for data users. However, it would be stressful for the data subject to generate and distribute all decryption keys in advance, so we generate them when the authorized data processor triggers the request. In addition, the single point of failure and performance problems may occur if the only data subject is the only key server responding to a decryption key request.

Considering the derivation nature of WKD-IBE's keys, the data processor with privileges and the data subject can act together as a key server. When a user requests authorization from the blockchain, the blockchain acts as an authorization server to determine that the user is legitimate and returns the token along with other processors that can derive the decryption key. After receiving the token, the user requests one of the processors to obtain the decryption key (the token supports obtaining the decryption key only once, and decryption keys could be encrypted with the user's public key), decrypt the data, and verify it against the signature.

4.3.2. Data Decrypt

After obtaining the two packets and the decryption keys, the data processor first decrypts the symmetric key from the key packet and then decrypts the plaintext data using the symmetric key. The operation is succinct in the step below.

- $\mathbf{Dec}(Key_{Pattern_m}, CT_{K_m}) \rightarrow K_m$: Parse the $Key_{Pattern}$ as (k_0, k_1, B), and the ciphertext CT_{K_m} as (X, Y, Z). Output K_m:

$$X \cdot e(k_1, Z) \cdot e(Y, k_0)^{-1}$$

The *Dec* function also depends on the *KeyDer* function to obtain the decryption keys of specific sub-namespace. For example, Bob achieved $Key_{alice/health}$ and then $\mathbf{KeyDer}(Params, Key_{alice/health}, Pattern_{alice/health/BP/2020/12/12}) \rightarrow Key_{alice/health/BP/2020/12/12}$. He used the key to decrypt the symmetric key of alice/health/BP/2020/12/12.

5. Decentralized Authorization Mechanism

The decentralized authorization mechanism consists of two parts: (i) content management: the data subject publishes the namespace and access policy, and the data processor retrieves the relevant content; (ii) decentralized authorization: the data processor is granted an access token according to the access policy. We utilize smart contracts to manage the content and automate the authorization operations for those two parts. As shown in Figure 6, there are three smart contracts: the namespace smart contract, the policy smart contract, and the decentralized authorization smart contract. Moreover, all user operations are recorded in the ledgers for auditing at any time.

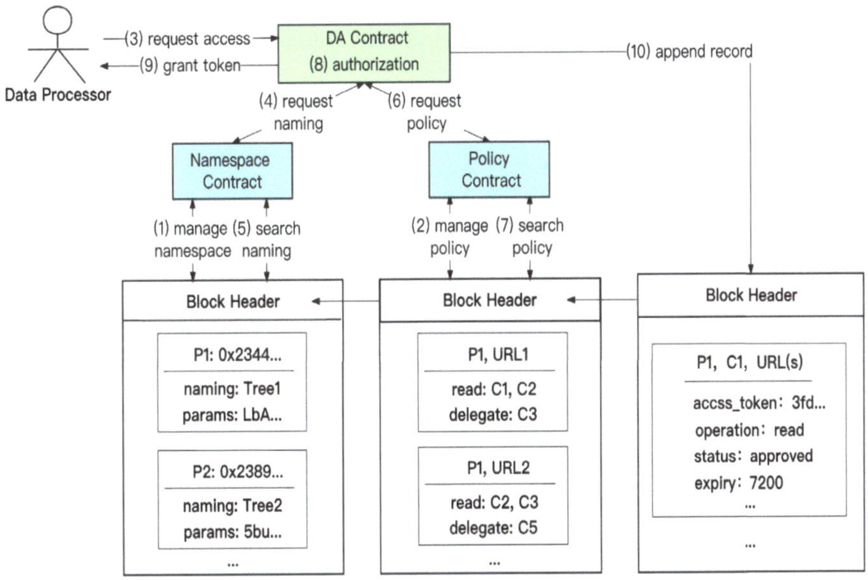

Figure 6. Decentralized Authorization Mechanism.

5.1. Content Management

When a data processor requests dynamically generated data in the NDN, the data are usually retrieved based on the part of the data name. For instance, the data processor sends an interest packet with the name alice/health/BP to retrieve a data packet with the name alice/health/BP/2020/12/12 if it exists and then requests the actual packet. This retrieval process may send multiple interest packets to obtain the datum's exact name, resulting in more invalid interest packets and inefficient retrieval in the NDN. It is desirable to have a retrieval mechanism to confirm the data name before sending interest packets. Centralized retrieval mechanisms run the risk of a single point of failure. Blockchain, as a decentralized and trusted intermediary, can be used to establish a transparent and reliable named retrieval mechanism. Hence, the data subject publishes the namespace on the blockchain, and the data processor queries to efficiently obtain the exact name of the data (Section 5.1.1). Furthermore, the data subject can further update the access policy based on the namespace, allowing the owner to take ownership of its data and share them selectively and flexibly (Section 5.1.2).

5.1.1. Naming Management

The namespace contract implements naming management, which contains creating and updating namespaces by data subjects and retrieving naming by data processors. The first ledger in Figure 6 shows the structure of the content.

Initially, the data subject registers credentials based on a uniquely named prefix identifier, representing the ability to create and update smart contracts. In addition, the namespace uses a dictionary tree as a storage structure, which is query-efficient. The data subject also stores the hash of static resources and the public parameters of WKD-IBE on the namespace, which assists the data processor in validating and decrypting the data. When a data processor retrieves a naming, the contract checks whether the naming format is standardized and retrieves the dictionary tree. If the naming is already fully named, returning exists. Otherwise, it uses naming as a prefix to search for the relevant specific name and returns the set of names (other restricted parameters can be added, such as the rightmost child, which improves the retrieval efficiency). Overall, data processors can reduce the number of invalid interest packets in the NDN by confirming the specific name before sending the interest packet. Algorithm 1 illustrates the naming retrieval process.

Algorithm 1: Naming Retrieval.

Input: pk_{DP}, pk_{DS}, $name_{pre}$
Output: result
Initialization: pk_{DS}'s namespace trees T_1, T_2...
if pk_{DP} *and* pk_{DS} **then**
  if pk_{DS} *exist a tree* T_i *prefix with* $name_{pre}$ **then**
    $result \leftarrow GetState(pk_{DS}).SearchUrls(T_i, name_{pre})$
  else
    $result \leftarrow$ *no such prefix here*
  end
else
  $result \leftarrow$ *no such user here*
end
return *result*

5.1.2. Policy Management

Policy management is implemented in the policy contract, which contains the creation and updating of the policy by data subjects and the retrieval of the policy by data processors. The second ledger in Figure 6 shows the structure of the content.

When a data subject creates an access policy, nodes in the namespace are bound to different access control lists (ACLs) to enable fine-grained access. We can set the ACL to the same level node of the namespace. For example, the data subject Alice uniformly sets her authorization granularity to the fifth level of the namespace, i.e., to authorize access to data by month. This approach improves the efficiency of policy retrieval but limits the minimum sharing granularity. We can also set the ACL to any node of the namespace, which increases the retrieval time but allows flexibility in setting sharing granularity. Algorithm 2 illustrates the policy update process. In addition, there are two types of data-operation abilities for data processors. The authorized data processor can only read the data or further delegate keys to other data processors.

Algorithm 2: Policy update.

Input: pk_{DS}, pk_{DP}, T_i, *URLs*, *Permissions*
Output: result
Initialization: pk_{DS}'s namespace trees T_1, T_2..., some nodes associated with an ACL
if pk_{DP} *and* pk_{DS} **then**
  if pk_{DS} *exist a tree* T_i **then**
    $pu \leftarrow GetState(pk_{DS}).SearchUrls(T_i, URLs)$
    $result \leftarrow PutState(pk_{DS}, UpdatePolicy(pu, pk_{DP}, Permissions))$
  else
    $result \leftarrow$ *no such tree here*
  end
else
  $result \leftarrow$ *no such user here*
end
return *result*

Naming and policies need to be regularly maintained and updated. For the case of data subjects cleaning up outdated data, leading to updates to the namespace. In addition, some malicious users need to be removed from the policy as soon as they are discovered. The data subject must periodically check its namespace and policy whilst the data processors of the relevant updates are notified.

5.2. Decentralized Authorization

The smart contract for decentralized authorization checks the access policy after receiving the request from the data processor. Then, it returns the result and records it in the log ledger. The third ledger in Figure 6 shows the structure of the content.

When a data processor requests read or delegated rights to the resources, the decentralized authorization contract determines the naming's legitimacy based on the naming contract, and whether the processor is in the access policy based on the policy contract. If the conditions are met, the authorization contract returns an access token for the data processor. Algorithm 3 illustrates the decentralized authorization process. The access token consists of the token header and the token payload, where the token header contains the token ID and the token type. The token ID is a (pseudo) random and unique string, and the token type indicates it is a read or delegated operation. The payload contains specific authorization information, including the grantor (data subject), the grantee (data processor), the scope of the authorization, the authorization time, and the expiration. Moreover, decentralized authorization smart contracts confirm the access token, i.e., whether the data processor requests keys or content, the corresponding node will recheck the token to verify its validity.

Algorithm 3: Decentralized authorization.

Input: pk_{DS}, pk_{DP}, $URLs$, $Permissions$
Output: result

Initialization: **if** pk_{DP} *and* pk_{DS} **then**
    if *URLs exist* **then**
        if pk_{DP} *has Permissions for URLs according to ACL* **then**
            $token \leftarrow (pk_{DS}, pk_{DP}, URLs, Permissions, random, Time_{issue}, Time_{expiry}, update_{count})$
            PutState(pk_{DS}, $UpdateAccess(pk_{DP}, token_{enc})$)
            $result \leftarrow token_{enc}$
        else
            $result \leftarrow$ *no permission*
        end
    else
        $result \leftarrow$ *no such resource here*
    end
else
    $result \leftarrow$ *no such user here*
end
return *result*

6. Implementation and Evaluation

This section describes the experiment environment and evaluates the experimental results.

6.1. Experimental Environment

In this section, we implement the NACDA prototype based on the above design ideas. The name-based access control model was developed in C++ and used the Named Data Networking Forwarding Daemon (NFD) [20] to route and forward NDN packets. The decentralized authorization mechanism built the blockchain environment with the Hyperledger Fabric (HLF) [21] platform. The HLF is a consortium blockchain [22] that allows authenticated and authorized nodes to join the network, resulting in higher levels of security. Therefore, HLF is designed for enterprise environments and is more suitable for this paper's many-to-many data-sharing usage scenario. All of the above were evaluated in a macOS Monterey 12.6 operating system configured with a 2 GHz quad-core Intel Core i5, 16 GiB RAM.

6.2. Experimental Results

The goal of the decentralized authorization mechanism is that the data subject publishes the namespace and access policy information on the blockchain, and the data processor retrieves the relevant content and obtains an access token. The detailed experimental design is as follows: (i) The HLF platform consists of two peer organizations, Org1 and Org2, each with two Peers, Peer0, and Peer1. It also configures a single-node Raft ordering service. All HLF participants are issued certificates by the built-in fabric certificate authority (CA). (ii) We measured the performance of the authorization mechanism using Caliper [23], an evaluation tool developed for the Hyperledger Foundation. (iii) The mechanism consists of three smart contracts and two ledgers. Namespace and policy information are stored in one ledger, and the access token is stored in another to facilitate the subsequent token verification operations.

Figures 7 and 8 shows the evaluated results of the decentralized authorization mechanism. Figure 7 interprets the performance results for the query ledger (query naming and policy). Figure 7a sets the Caliper to submit 2000 transactions per round. By varying the transaction's rate controller from 100TPS to 1000TPS, it can be seen that the throughput leveled off after a period of increase, but the latency kept trending upwards. Figure 7b sets the transaction's rate controller to 750 TPS for each round. By varying the number of transactions submitted from 1000 to 10,000, the maintained throughput remained at approximately 700 TPS, with the success rate of transactions at a high level. Figure 7 illustrates that, when the transaction's rate controller reaches approximately 700 TPS, an increase in the transaction throughput is blocked, i.e., the local system processing bottleneck is reached. Figure 8 shows the performance results for the updated ledger (update authorization token). The combination of Figure 8a,b demonstrates that the maximum processing capacity of the system is of approximately 150TPS. Accordingly, comparing Figures 7 and 8, it is evident that the performance of the query ledger is much higher than that of the updated ledger because the query ledger operation involves the interaction with only one peer node. On the contrary, the updated ledger operation involves multiple participants (peer endorser, orderer, committer peer) and multiple stages [15].

In the naming-based access control model, the device encrypts and publishes data packets based on the resource namespace. The data processor sends interest packets to achieve encrypted data and decryption keys and decrypts data according to the derived keys. We assume that all data packets the data processor requests can be returned, and the obtained decryption key can decrypt all relevant data. Furthermore, the calculated time of the data producer includes the total time from generating the data to publishing them, and the data processor's total time includes requesting the data to decrypt them.

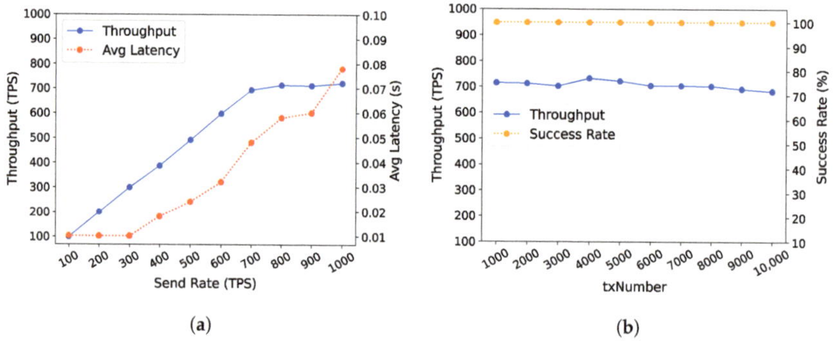

Figure 7. Performance of READ from HLF's ledgers. (**a**) Performance of Different Send Rates with a TxNumber Equal to 2000. (**b**) Performance of Different TxNumber with a Send Rate Equal to 750.

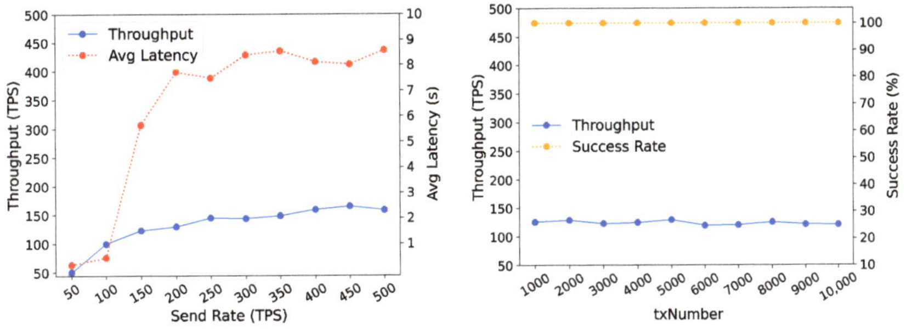

(**a**) (**b**)

Figure 8. Performance of WRITE to HLF's ledgers. (**a**) Performance of Different Send Rates with a TxNumber Equal to 2000. (**b**) Performance of Different TxNumber with a Send Rate Equal to 150.

Figure 9 shows the time of publishing/receiving data with different packet sizes and numbers with the namespace depth equal to 10. In Figure 9a,b, the different size packets merged multiple data points ranging from 1 KB to 6 KB (up to 8 KB per packet). The results show that the time spent on encryption, decryption, signing, and verification accounts for relatively little of the total time. The remaining time includes packet and communication time in NDN, spending a relatively large amount of time. In addition, as the packet size increases, there is a slight increase in the time spent in each phase. In Figure 9c,d, we fix the packet size to 4 KB to verify the effect of namespace depth on the published and received data. The results show that the time spent in each phase increases as the number of packets increases, where the majority of time is still spent in the NDN.

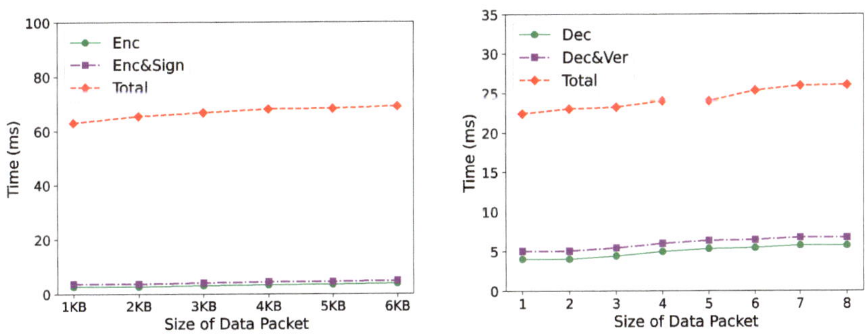

(**a**) Publishing with Different Packet Sizes. (**b**) Receiving with Different Packet Sizes.

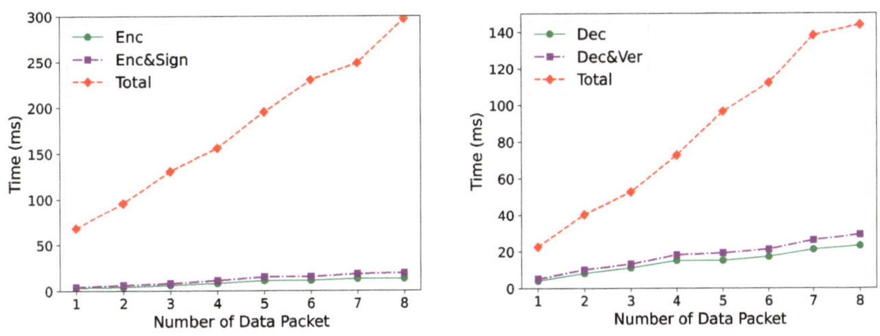

(**c**) Publishing with Different Packet Numbers. (**d**) Receiving with Different Packet Numbers.

Figure 9. Performance of Publishing/Receiving a Message with Different Packet sizes and Numbers.

Figure 10 assesses the relationship between the latency time and packet numbers with different namespace depths. The results of Figure 10a indicate that as the packet numbers increase, a different namespace depth does not have much effect on the publishing time. In contrast, Figure 10b shows that time spent by data processors significantly increases with higher namespace depths. This is because, when the device encrypts data, the namespace's length has little effect on the encryption operation. Instead, the data processor needs to derive multiple keys when deeper in the namespace's length.

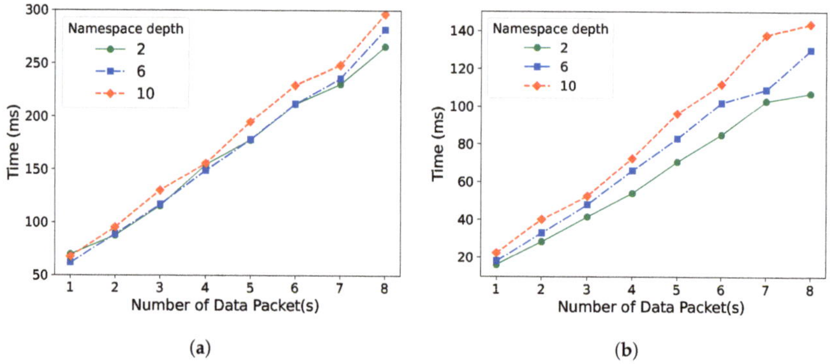

Figure 10. Performance of Publishing/Receiving a Message with Different Namespace Depths and Packet Numbers. (**a**) Publishing with Different Namespace Levels and Packet Numbers. (**b**) Receiving with Different Namespace Levels and Packet Numbers.

Subsequently, we compare NACDA to NAC-ABE [24], which uses ABE in NDN, as shown in Figure 11. Since our method considers a data-centric encryption approach, the user attributes and attribute policies in NAC-ABE are converted into data-centric representation. Take the two sub-namespaces /alice/health/BP and /alice/health/HR as examples. In data encryption, both NACDA and NAC-ABE use "1-alice, 2-health, 3-BP" and "1-alice, 2-health, 3-HR" as encryption parameters. When distributing decryption keys, NACDA only needs to share the key for /alice/health/*. In contrast, NAC-ABE needs to share the key for the policies "(1-alice AND 2-health AND 3-BP) or (1-alice AND 2-health AND 3-HR)". Thus, our method only needs to distribute a smaller size key, which is an advantage, especially when the namespace depth is large. As for decryption, NACDA has one more key derivation step than NAC-ABE. However, we can learn from Figure 9 that the operation in NDN takes more time than data encryption- and decryption-related steps. Thus, reducing the key size can further reduce the time spent on packaging and communication in the NDN, which further reduces the overhead of decryption.

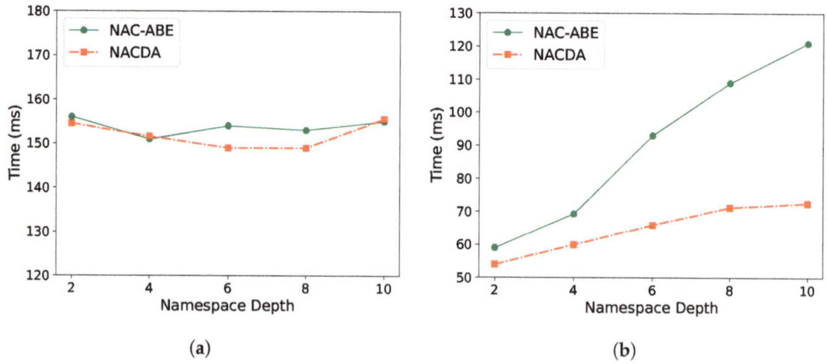

Figure 11. Publishing/Receiving Comparison with Different Namespace Depths: (**a**) Publishing Comparison with Different Namespace Depths; (**b**) Receiving Comparison with Different Namespace Depths.

6.3. Security Analysis

In this section, we analyze the security of our method. We focus on privacy protection and access control in NDN, which includes four security objectives: (i) data security: data security is built into the data themselves and is not dependent on the recipient. (ii) data integrity: the data need to prove their origin; they cannot be altered once created; and (iv) access control: only authorized data processors can access the data. Next, we analyze the objectives and the corresponding attacks in theory and practice. Note that the attacks associated with routing in NDN networks are beyond our scope.

6.3.1. Data Security

NDN relies on WKD-IBE for data security. The WKD-IBE scheme is IND-sWKID-CAP security, described as follows.

Theorem 1. *A WKD-IBE scheme is indistinguishable under a selective-identity, chosen-plaintext attack, i.e., IND-sWKID-CAP secure (Indistinguishability against Selective-Identity with Wildcard Key, Chosen-Plaintext Attack), if and only if for all probabilistic polynomial-time attacker $\mathcal{A}$ whose advantage of winning the following game interacting with challenger C is negligible for the security parameter k [6].*

Initialization. Give the depth of the namespace ℓ and security parameter k, C run Setup to generate the public parameters Params and the master key MasterKey, and then $\mathcal{A}$ obtains Params from the blockchain.

Query1. $\mathcal{A}$ asks C for the keys of its sub-namespace. In the ith query, $\mathcal{A}$ adaptively selects a sub-namespace s. C runs KeyDer to generate sk_s and sends it to $\mathcal{A}$.

Challenge. $\mathcal{A}$ chooses two messages, m_0 and m_1, with the same length and sends them to C. Then, C chooses a random bit $b \in \{0,1\}$, encrypts m_b under the pattern p, runs $Enc(Params, p, m_b)$, and sends the generated ciphertexts to $\mathcal{A}$.

Query2. $\mathcal{A}$ can continue to query like Query 1.

Guess. $\mathcal{A}$ outputs guess b'. if $b = b'$, $\mathcal{A}$ wins the game. The advantage of $\mathcal{A}$ is $\left|\Pr[b = b'] - \frac{1}{2}\right|$.

Analysis. Based on the IND-sWKID-CAP security guarantee, we analyze data security in NDN. In *Initialization*, each data subject initializes *MasterKey* and *Params*, respectively, and *MasterKey* remains private while *Params* is propagated by the blockchain, avoiding single-point-failure attack. In the data encryption phase, IoT devices only encrypt the data but cannot access decryption keys. The decryption keys are also not shared with storage services, intermediate nodes, or authorization services. Then, an A *Query* step is performed by $\mathcal{A}$, and we divide it into two cases. The first case assumes that $\mathcal{A}$ is a non-authorized user. $\mathcal{A}$ will request the authorization service to obtain an access token before requesting the decryption keys. However, $\mathcal{A}$ is not qualified to obtain that token and, thus, not eligible to request the decryption keys. The second case assumes that $\mathcal{A}$ is a user authorized by a data subject. $\mathcal{A}$ obtains an access token and requests the decryption key. Additionally, $\mathcal{A}$ wants to obtain decryption keys outside the authorized scope. However, the token for the keys only supports *Query* once, and does not perform continuous querying. Thus, attacker $\mathcal{A}$ does not have the opportunity to perform an ongoing *Query*, so it is challenging to perform a successful *Guess*.

Accordingly, our method guarantees data confidentiality in the NDN and can block constant attempts by attackers. Furthermore, even if the key of the sub-namespace is compromised, the data storage node will validate the data access token to check whether it is an authorized user. Taking a further step back, even if both the key access token and the data access token are compromised, the attacker can only access data in that sub-namespace scope within the token's validity time.

6.3.2. Data Integrity

The integrity guarantees can be formalized using a game similar to Theorem 1. We do not repeat the description here.

Analysis. Our method is based on WKD-IBE to guarantee data integrity. The data subject allocates to each IoT device a signing key certificate associated with the authorized sub-namespace. Then, the devices put their signing key name into each NDN's packet before publishing. The data processor can verify the signature, which prevents the message from being tampered with or forged. Therefore, the authentication mechanism of each packet prevents the malicious tampering of the message by man-in-the-middle attacks.

6.3.3. Access Control

The standard blockchain threat model assumes that the blockchain network is secure if an adversary cannot control a large percentage of nodes.

Analysis. NDNs are named after content and need to add access control to the content to establish a relationship with authorized consumers. Our approach is based on the blockchain to provide a decentralized authorization service. The decentralized nature of the blockchain ensures that an adversary cannot compromise the blockchain network to make unauthorized changes to the ledger. In addition, if the authorized token is compromised during transmission, a secondary verification mechanism can reconfirm it to prevent compromise, which alleviates token impersonation attacks.

7. Conclusions and Future Work

This paper introduces NACDA, a decentralized access control framework based on NDN. It enables data subjects to share their data autonomously and securely in a many-to-many communication scenario. Specifically, the named-based access control model provides encryption and access control schemes that decouple data subjects and processors, enabling secure, flexible, and selective data sharing. The decentralized authorization mechanism solves the problem of a single point of failure for NDN data retrieval and authorization services, allowing data subjects to customize access policies. Our experimental results and security analysis indicate the feasibility and applicability of NACDA in many-to-many communication scenarios.

There are two aspects to be improved. Firstly, NDN's naming concerns data semantics and access control. An attacker may infer sensitive information about a user by monitoring the user's requests. Therefore, the main challenge for naming is maintaining name privacy while ensuring the routability and decodability. Secondly, blockchain immutability provides the ability to audit authorization records to verify users' compliance with GDPR. However, there exists conflict between the immutability of recorded transactions and the GDPR's 'right to be forgotten'. The above-mentioned decodability can be a way to mitigate that conflict since the 'right to be forgotten' is associated with the ability to decode a namespace on the ledger.

Author Contributions: Conceptualization, M.L. and Y.W.; Methodology, M.L. and Y.W.; Software, M.L.; Validation, M.L. and Y.W.; Investigation, M.L.; Data curation, M.L.; Writing—original draft, M.L.; Writing—review & editing, J.X. and Y.W.; Visualization, M.L.; Supervision, J.X., Y.W., R.M. and W.H.; Project administration, J.X. and Y.W.; Funding acquisition, J.X. All authors have read and agreed to the published version of the manuscript.

Funding: This work was supported by the National Key Research & Development Program of China (No. 2020YFC2006204), the National Natural Science Foundation of China (No. 62172042), and the Opening Foundation of Key Laboratory of Network Evaluation Technology, CAS under Grant KFKT2022-008.

Data Availability Statement: Not applicable.

Conflicts of Interest: The authors declare no conflict of interest.

References

1. Sim, I. Mobile devices and health. *N. Engl. J. Med.* **2019**, *381*, 956–968. [CrossRef] [PubMed]
2. Lu, L.; Zhang, J.; Xie, Y.; Gao, F.; Xu, S.; Wu, X.; Ye, Z. Wearable health devices in health care: Narrative systematic review. *JMIR Mhealth Uhealth* **2020**, *8*, e18907. [CrossRef] [PubMed]

3. Singh, M.; Rajan, M.; Shivraj, V.; Balamuralidhar, P. Secure MQTT for Internet of Things (IoT). In Proceedings of the 2015 Fifth International Conference on Communication Systems and Network Technologies, Gwalior, India, 4–6 April 2015.
4. Zhang, L.; Afanasyev, A.; Burke, J.; Jacobson, V.; Claffy, K.; Crowley, P.; Papadopoulos, C.; Wang, L.; Zhang, B. Named Data Networking. *ACM SIGCOMM Comp. Commun. Rev.* **2014**, *44*, 66–73. [CrossRef]
5. Feng, T.; Guo, J. A New Access Control System Based on CP-ABE in Named Data Networking. *Int. J. Netw. Secur.* **2018**, *20*, 710–720.
6. Abdalla, M.; Kiltz, E.; Neven, G. Generalized Key Delegation for Hierarchical Identity-Based Encryption. In Proceedings of the Computer Security – ESORICS 2007, Dresden, Germany, 24–26 September 2007.
7. Horwitz, J.; Lynn, B. Towards Hierarchical Identity-Based Encryption. In *Advances in Cryptology—EUROCRYPT 2002*; Springer: Berlin/Heidelberg, Germany, 2002.
8. Zheng, Z.; Xie, S.; Dai, H.N.; Chen, X.; Wang, H. Blockchain Challenges and Opportunities: A Survey. *Int. J. Web Grid Serv.* **2018**, *14*, 352–375. [CrossRef]
9. Nour, B.; Khelifi, H.; Hussain, R.; Mastorakis, S.; Moungla, H. Access control mechanisms in named data networks: A comprehensive survey. *ACM Comput. Surv.* **2021**, *54*, 1–35. [CrossRef]
10. Zhang, Z.; Yu, Y.; Afanasyev, A.; Burke, J.; Zhang, L. NAC: Name-Based Access Control in Named Data Networking. In Proceedings of the 4th ACM Conference on Information-Centric Networking (ICN' 17), Berlin, Germany, 26 September 2017.
11. Fan, L.; Yu, Y.; Wang, L. Secure Sharing of Spatio-Temporal Data through Name-based Access Control. In Proceedings of the IEEE INFOCOM 2021—IEEE Conference on Computer Communications Workshops (INFOCOM WKSHPS), Vancouver, BC, Canada, 10–13 May 2021.
12. Fotiou, N.; Polyzos, G. C. Decentralized name-based security for content distribution using blockchains. In Proceedings of the 2016 IEEE Conference on Computer Communications Workshops (INFOCOM WKSHPS), San Francisco, CA, USA, 10–14 April 2016.
13. Ouaddah, A.; Abou Elkalam, A.; Ait Ouahman, A. FairAccess: A New Blockchain-based Access Control Framework for the Internet of Things. *Secur. Commun. Netw.* **2016**, *9*, 5943–5964. [CrossRef]
14. Truong, N.B.; Sun, K.; Lee, G.M.; Guo, Y. GDPR-Compliant Personal Data Management: A Blockchain-Based Solution. *IEEE Trans. Inf. Forensic Secur.* **2020**, *15*, 1746–1761. [CrossRef]
15. Foschini, L.; Gavagna, A.; Martuscelli, G.; Montanari, R. Hyperledger Fabric Blockchain: Chaincode Performance Analysis. In Proceedings of the ICC 2020—2020 IEEE International Conference on Communications (ICC), Dublin, Ireland, 7–11 June 2020.
16. Jøsang, A. A Consistent Definition of Authorization. In Proceedings of the Security and Trust Management, Oslo, Norway, 14–15 September 2017.
17. Chhetri, T. R.; Kurteva, A.; DeLong, R. J.; Hilscher, R.; Korte, K.; Fensel, A. Data Protection by Design Tool for Automated GDPR Compliance Verification Based on Semantically Modeled Informed Consent. *Sensors* **2022**, *22*, 2763. [CrossRef] [PubMed]
18. Kumar, S.; Hu, Y.; Andersen, M.P.; Popa, R.A.; Culler, D.E. JEDI: Many-to-many end-to-end encryption and key delegation for IoT. In Proceedings of the 28th USENIX Conference on Security Symposium (SEC'19), Santa Clara, CA, USA, 14 August 2019.
19. Kumar, S.; Hu, Y.; Andersen, M.P.; Popa, R.A.; Culler, D. JEDI: Many-to-Many End-to-End Encryption and Key Delegation for IoT. *arXiv* **2019**, arXiv:1905.13369v2.
20. NFD: Named Data Networking Forwarding Daemon. Available online: https://named-data.net/doc/NFD/current/ (accessed on 6 February 2023).
21. Hyperledger Fabric. Available online: https://github.com/hyperledger/fabric (accessed on 6 February 2023).
22. Androulaki, E.; Barger, A.; Bortnikov, V.; Cachin, C.; Christidis, K.; De Caro, A.; Enyeart, D.; Ferris, C.; Laventman, G.; Manevich, Y.; et al. Hyperledger Fabric: A Distributed Operating System for Permissioned Blockchains. In Proceedings of the Thirteenth EuroSys Conference (EuroSys '18), Porto, Portugal, 23 April 2018.
23. Hyperledger Caliper. Available online: https://hyperledger.github.io/caliper/ (accessed on 6 February 2023).
24. NAC-ABE. Available online: https://github.com/UCLA-IRL/NAC-ABE (accessed on 6 February 2023).

electronics

Article

Boosting Adversarial Attacks with Nadam Optimizer

Qikun Zhang [1], Yuzhi Zhang [1,*], Yanling Shao [2], Mengqi Liu [1], Jianyong Li [1], Junling Yuan [1] and Ruifang Wang [1]

[1] School of Computer and Communication Engineering, Zhengzhou University of Light Industry, Zhengzhou 450002, China
[2] School of Computer and Software, Nanyang Institute of Technology, Nanyang 473000, China
* Correspondence: 332107040587@email.zzuli.edu.cn

Abstract: Deep neural networks are extremely vulnerable to attacks and threats from adversarial examples. These adversarial examples deliberately crafted by attackers can easily fool classification models by adding imperceptibly tiny perturbations on clean images. This brings a great challenge to image security for deep learning. Therefore, studying and designing attack algorithms for generating adversarial examples is essential for building robust models. Moreover, adversarial examples are transferable in that they can mislead multiple different classifiers across models. This makes black-box attacks feasible for practical applications. However, most attack methods have low success rates and weak transferability against black-box models. This is because they often overfit the model during the production of adversarial examples. To address this issue, we propose a Nadam iterative fast gradient method (NAI-FGM), which combines an improved Nadam optimizer with gradient-based iterative attacks. Specifically, we introduce the look-ahead momentum vector and the adaptive learning rate component based on the Momentum Iterative Fast Gradient Sign Method (MI-FGSM). The look-ahead momentum vector is dedicated to making the loss function converge faster and get rid of the poor local maximum. Additionally, the adaptive learning rate component is used to help the adversarial example to converge to a better extreme point by obtaining adaptive update directions according to the current parameters. Furthermore, we also carry out different input transformations to further enhance the attack performance before using NAI-FGM for attack. Finally, we consider attacking the ensemble model. Extensive experiments show that the NAI-FGM has stronger transferability and black-box attack capability than advanced momentum-based iterative attacks. In particular, when using the adversarial examples produced by way of ensemble attack to test the adversarially trained models, the NAI-FGM improves the success rate by 8% to 11% over the other attack methods. Last but not least, the NAI-DI-TI-SI-FGM combined with the input transformation achieves a success rate of 91.3% on average.

Keywords: adversarial examples; black-box attacks; transferability; deep neural networks

Citation: Zhang, Q.; Zhang, Y.; Shao, Y.; Liu, M.; Li, J.; Yuan, J.; Wang, R. Boosting Adversarial Attacks with Nadam Optimizer. *Electronics* **2023**, *12*, 1464. https://doi.org/10.3390/electronics12061464

Academic Editors: Wojciech Mazurczyk and Djamel Djenouri

Received: 7 February 2023
Revised: 7 March 2023
Accepted: 17 March 2023
Published: 20 March 2023

1. Introduction

Currently, deep learning as the core technology of artificial intelligence is widely applied in various scenarios in life. In particular, deep neural networks (DNNs) show strong advantages in improving the performance of various visual tasks, including image classification [1,2], natural language processing [3], autonomous driving [4] and medical diagnosis [5], and in some areas, even surpass human processing power. However, DNNs show great vulnerability to threats and attacks from adversarial examples [6]. These adversarial examples deliberately crafted by attackers can make the network model misclassify by adding imperceptibly tiny perturbations on clean images. This brings a great challenge to image security for deep learning. Therefore, studying and designing attack algorithms for generating adversarial examples is essential for building robust models. It can also help us to better test and evaluate the security of these models [7–9].

We can classify the attack methods into white-box and black-box attacks based on whether all relevant information of the model can be successfully accessed during the attack. In the white-box situation, the attacker has a sufficient amount of details of the target model. In contrast, in the black-box situation, the attacker only obtains the inputs and outputs to the model. Gradient-based attacks [8,10,11] are extensively used in white-box situations due to their simplicity and speed. This method produces perturbations in the gradient direction of the image about the loss function by maximizing the loss.

In real-world scenarios, attackers are often faced with black-box situations where they cannot access the details of the model. As a result, black-box attacks are often more challenging to implement, but more practical. The most commonly used black-box attacks are transfer-based methods [12–20], with the idea that the adversarial examples produced in a certain model setting may also be adversarial for other models. Liu et al. [21] refer to this property of adversarial examples as transferability. Therefore, we can take full advantage of the transferability property to perform black-box attacks.

To this end, different kinds of strategies have been proposed to boost transfer-based attacks. On the one hand, some works focused on better optimization algorithms for gradient computation [13–16]. On the other hand, other works concentrate on input transformations to perform data augmentation [17,18]. In addition, Dong et al. [13] considered simultaneously attacking ensembles of models to perform model augmentation, while Lin et al. [14] proposed to derive multiple models from the source model for model augmentation. In this paper, we focus on a better optimization algorithm.

However, there are still some problems with the current study. (1) Most of the attacks are less effective and have lower success rates in the black-box situation. (2) The adversarial examples produced by transfer-based attacks normally overfit the training model easily, and usually fall into a poor local extremum. This leads to weaker transferability.

In order to better optimize and solve the above issues, we propose the Nadam Iterative Fast Gradient Method (NAI-FGM), which combines an improved Nadam optimizer with gradient-based iterative attacks. Specifically, we introduce the look-ahead momentum vector and the adaptive learning rate component based on the Momentum Iterative Fast Gradient Sign Method (MI-FGSM) [13]. The look-ahead momentum vector is dedicated to making the loss function converge faster and get rid of the poor local maximum. Additionally, the adaptive learning rate component is used to help the adversarial example to converge to a better extreme point by obtaining adaptive update directions according to the current parameters. We validate the NAI-FGM through a large number of experiments and compare it with advanced attacks. Experimental results show that the NAI-FGM has stronger transferability and black-box attack capability than advanced attacks. The adversarial examples produced by several momentum-based iterative attacks are shown in Figure 1.

The contributions of this paper are as follows:

- Inspired by the idea of the Nesterov-accelerated Adaptive Moment Estimation (Nadam) [22] optimization algorithm, we apply the modified Nadam optimizer for adversarial example generation in each iteration. Based on the MI-FGSM, the look-ahead momentum vector and adaptive learning rate component are introduced. The proposed method can update the direction adaptively according to the current gradient information, optimize the convergence process, and enhance gradient-based adversarial attack transferability.
- We further improve the attack transferability by naturally combining advanced data augmentation methods with the proposed NAI-FGM.
- We apply the strategy of ensemble attack to NAI-FGM to produce higher success rates of the black-box attack.

Figure 1. Raw images and adversarial examples after attack by MI-FGSM [13], NI-FGSM [14], and the proposed NAI-FGM on Inc-v3 [23].

2. Related Work

2.1. Adversarial Attacks

Existing attack methods can be broadly classified into white-box attacks and black-box attacks. Figure 2 briefly depicts the principles and differences between the various kinds of attacks. White-box attacks are further subdivided into gradient-based attacks [8,10,11] and optimization-based attacks [6,7]. Optimization-based attacks can produce visually better adversarial examples than gradient-based attacks, but they can also consume greater time costs. Black-box attacks can also be further classified into transfer-based attacks [12–19], score-based attacks [24,25], and decision-based attacks [26]. In contrast to transfer-based attacks, both score-based and decision-based attacks involve massive accesses and queries to the neural network, which is harder to implement in practical scenarios. Therefore, we focus our research around transfer-based attacks. Transfer-based attacks usually occur in two steps. First, a white-box attack is employed under an alternative model to generate adversarial examples. Afterwards, these examples are transferred to the target model for the attack. This white-box attack is typically referred to as gradient-based attacks, as they are relatively efficient and easy to implement. Here, we mainly review the work related to transfer-based attacks.

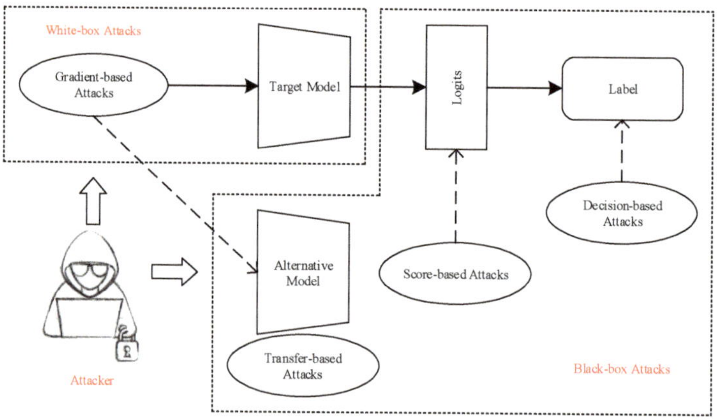

Figure 2. Principles and differences of various types of adversarial attacks.

Dong et al. [13] applied the momentum idea to the Iterative Fast Gradient Sign Method (I-FGSM) [11]. Additionally, they also considered simultaneous attacks on multiple models to enhance attack performance. Lin et al. [14] proposed the Nesterov Iterative Fast Gradient Sign Method (NI-FGSM), which combined Nesterov's accelerated gradient with I-FGSM. The Diverse Input Method (DIM) [17] resizes and pads the input images with a certain probability of transformation. The Translation-Invariant Method (TIM) [18] adopts a translation operation for the input image. The Scale-Invariant Method (SIM) [14] applies a set of scaling transformations to the image. Yin et al. [16] proposed the Adam Iterative Fast Gradient Method (AI-FGM), which uses the Adam optimizer [27] to optimize the gradient calculation. Wu et al. [20] proposed the Adversarial Transformation-Enhanced Transfer Attack (ATTA), which uses blurring and coloring transformations on input images and trains an adversarial transformation network to produce adversarial examples. Wang et al. [15] optimize the adversarial perturbation by variance adjustment strategy. Wang et al. [28] proposed a spatial momentum attack to accumulate the contextual gradients of different regions within the image. Huang et al. [12] superimpose feature information with variances on the images before iterative attacks. Additionally, double sampling variance aggregation is used to optimize the image gradient. Wang et al. [19] designed an affiliated network to capture the potential spatial information of images. Additionally, an edge detection algorithm was combined to find out the minimum effective perturbation region.

However, the transferability of the adversarial examples generated by most existing transfer-based attacks remains poor. The underlying reason is that these adversarial examples tend to overfit the alternative models and usually fall into poor local optima during the generation process. For this reason, we apply a better optimizer to the generation algorithm of adversarial examples. The gradient direction is more rationally computed and optimized so that the adversarial examples converge to a better local optimum during the generation process. The final effect of mitigating the overfitting phenomenon of the adversarial examples and improving the transferability of the attacks is achieved.

2.2. *Adversarial Defenses*

To improve the robustness of DNNs, several advanced defense methods have been proposed. We can roughly summarize these methods into three categories.

Adversarial Training: Adversarial training is widely regarded by academia as the most powerful defense strategy against attacks. This method trains clean examples and adversarial examples in the same model [6,8,10,29]. Tram'er et al. [9] involved adversarial examples from multiple other models in the local model for training, in terms of augmenting the training dataset. This is referred to as ensemble adversarial training.

Input Preprocessing: Input preprocessing aims to alleviate the impact of perturbations on the model by transforming the inputs. Xie et al. [30] used two randomization operations, that is, random resizing of the image and random padding around the image. Guo et al. [31] adopted conversion techniques, such as total variance minimization and image stitching for input images. Liu et al. [32] developed a compression framework of JPEG to improve defense efficiency and reduce marginal accuracy.

Adversarial Examples Detection: Adversarial examples detection includes inconsistency judgments by differences between adversarial examples and normal examples or training additional detectors to detect adversarial examples. Xu et al. [33] adopted a feature compression strategy that combines images corresponding to different feature vectors into one sample, reducing the attacker's search space. Pang et al. [34] used a minimization reverse cross-entropy and threshold strategy as a detector for adversarial examples. Ma et al. [35] designed a technique to extract the invariants of DNNs to detect adversarial examples by analyzing the internal structure of DNNs under different attacks.

3. Methodology

Let x denote a clean example, and y denote its real label. Additionally, f denotes a trained deep neural network classifier that correctly classifies x as y. The attacker generates the adversarial example $x^{adv} = x + \delta$ by adding perturbation δ to x, thus causing f to misclassify. The perturbation δ is obtained in most cases by maximizing the cross-entropy loss function $J(x, y; \theta)$, where θ denotes the parameter of f. For the perturbation δ, we use the L_∞ norm to restrict its size, that is, $||x^{adv} - x||_\infty \leq \epsilon$, ϵ denotes the maximum perturbation value.

Let f_1 and f_2 denote two different deep neural network classifiers, and their corresponding network parameters are, respectively, θ_1 and θ_2. Both of them can correctly classify clean example x as label y. In the black-box situation, only θ_1 is known and θ_2 is unknown. The goal of transfer-based attacks is to produce an adversarial example x^{adv} under f_1 by applying its transferability; f_1 and f_2 can simultaneously classify the clean example x incorrectly, that is, satisfy $f_1(x^{adv}) \neq y$ and $f_2(x^{adv}) \neq y$.

3.1. Gradient-Based Attacks

Since our algorithm is based on MI-FGSM for research and improvement, we briefly introduce MI-FGSM and its related attack methods here.

FGSM [10] is a one-step attack and the first gradient-based method. The updated equation is:

$$x^{adv} = x + \epsilon \cdot sign(\bigtriangledown_x J(x, y; \theta)) \tag{1}$$

where ϵ is the factor regulating the size of the perturbation, $\bigtriangledown_x J(\cdot)$ is the gradient of $J(\cdot)$ about x, and $sign(\cdot)$ is the sign function to make δ meet the L_∞ norm bound.

I-FGSM [11] subdivides the one-step perturbation computation process in FGSM into T steps and restricts the image pixels to the effective area by a clipping operation. The updated equation is:

$$x_0^{adv} = x,\ x_{t+1}^{adv} = Clip_x^{\epsilon}\{x_t^{adv} + \alpha \cdot sign(\bigtriangledown_x J(x_t^{adv}, y; \theta))\} \tag{2}$$

where T is the total number of iterations, $\alpha = \epsilon / T$ is the step size, and $Clip_x^{\epsilon}\{\cdot\}$ serves to constrain adversarial examples x_t^{adv} in the ϵ neighborhood of x.

MI-FGSM [13] introduces the idea of momentum based on I-FGSM, which significantly improves the transferability. The updated equation is:

$$\begin{aligned} g_{t+1} &= \mu \cdot g_t + \frac{\bigtriangledown_x J(x_t^{adv}, y; \theta)}{|| \bigtriangledown_x J(x_t^{adv}, y; \theta)||_1} \\ x_{t+1}^{adv} &= Clip_x^{\epsilon}\{x_t^{adv} + \alpha \cdot sign(g_{t+1})\} \end{aligned} \tag{3}$$

where g_t is the gradient sum accumulated over t iterations, $g_0 = 0$ and μ is the decay factor of the momentum term g_t.

NI-FGSM [14] applies Nesterov's accelerated gradient [36] to I-FGSM, and substitutes to x_t^{adv} in Equation (3) with $x_t^{adv} + \alpha \cdot \mu \cdot g_t$ to further enhance the transferability.

DIM [17] adopts random resizing and padding transformations to images with a certain probability before the start of each iteration, from the perspective of data augmentation to enhance adversarial attacks transferability.

TIM [18] applies translation operations to images to generate adversarial examples. Specifically, TIM uses a Gaussian kernel matrix to convolve the gradients of untranslated images instead of computing the gradients of translating different pixel images, further improving the transferability.

SIM [14] considers model augmentation to improve transferability and exploits the scale-invariant property of DNNs to calculate gradients on the scale copies of the input images.

3.2. Motivation

FGSM is the earliest gradient-based attack with low time cost but a low success rate. I-FGSM subdivides the one-step perturbation calculation process in FGSM into multiple steps to improve attack efficiency. However, I-FGSM are often easy to overfit to the local maximum, so the transferability is weak. MI-FGSM introduces momentum terms into

I-FGSM, which helps adversarial examples to escape from the poor local maximum and stabilize the updating direction. NI-FGSM adopts NAG into I-FGSM to make use of its looking-ahead property to modify the previously accumulated gradient and further improve the transferability.

Momentum and NAG are two algorithms for optimizing gradient descent that can significantly enhance the effect of deep learning models. MI-FGSM and NI-FGSM after combining the advantages of Momentum and NAG, respectively, help the adversarial examples to obtain better transferability. Therefore, we suppose that other gradient descent optimization algorithms can also be applied to attacks to improve their performance.

In this work, we consider applying the modified Nadam optimizer to gradient-based iterative attacks to optimize the gradient calculation.

3.3. Nadam Iterative Fast Gradient Method

Nadam, proposed by Dozat [22], is an advanced gradient descent optimization algorithm, which improves the convergence speed and quality of the DNNs. Nadam is a modification of the Adam [27]. Nadam naturally combines Nesterov's accelerated gradient (NAG) [36] and Adam and modifies the momentum component of Adam while retaining the adaptive learning rate component.

To improve the transferability of adversarial examples, we propose the NAI-FGM (Nadam Iterative Fast Gradient Method), which combines an improved Nadam optimizer with gradient-based iterative attacks. Specifically, we introduce the look-ahead momentum vector and the adaptive learning rate component based on MI-FGSM. Figure 3 describes the attack idea of NAI-FGM. First, we input the pre-processed clean image into the network to obtain the gradient. Then, we process the gradients with the NAI-FGM algorithm to produce adversarial perturbations. Finally, the input images are superimposed with the perturbations to generate adversarial examples after multiple iterations.

Specifically, different from the momentum in MI-FGSM, the momentum in NAI-FGSM accumulates both the gradient and the square of the gradient during the iteration, which helps the loss function converge quickly on the small gradient dimension. At the same time, we directly applied the look-ahead momentum vector to replace applying the momentum step twice to update the gradient and parameter separately in NI-FGSM, which helped us get rid of the poor local maximum more quickly. The adaptive learning rate component uses the gradually decreasing step size, which is helpful to obtain the adaptive updating direction, so as to converge to a better extreme point.

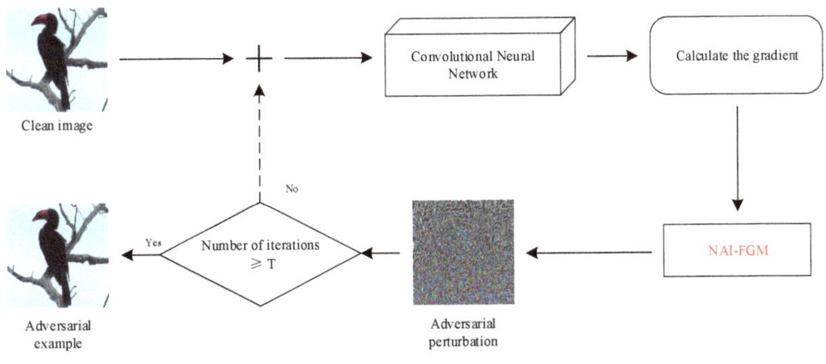

Figure 3. Principle of the attack based on the NAI-FGM algorithm.

The Nadam iterative fast gradient method (NAI-FGM) is summarized in Algorithm 1. Specifically, we first initialize the clean example x as an adversarial example x_0^{adv} and input x_t^{adv} into the classifier f at the first t iteration to obtain the gradient $\nabla_x J(x_t^{adv}, y; \theta)$, then normalize it by its L_1 distance, defined in Equation (5). The term m_t denotes the first momentum used to accumulate the sum of the gradients of t iterations, defined in

Equation (6). The term n_t denotes the second momentum used to accumulate the sum of squares of gradients for t iterations, defined in Equation (7). The terms μ_1 and μ_2 denote the decay factors of m_t and n_t, respectively. The look-ahead momentum vector is $\mu_1 \cdot m_{t+1} + (1 - \mu_1) \cdot g_t$. The terms $m_t^{'}$ and $n_t^{'}$ compute the bias-corrected first and second momentums, defined in Equations (8) and (9), respectively. The updated equation of an adversarial example x_t^{adv} is defined in Equation (10), where ξ is the denominator stability factor to make sure the denominator is not equal to zero. The adaptive learning rate component is $1/\sqrt{n_{t+1}^{'} + \xi}$.

Existing works typically use the sign function to compute the direction of the gradient such that the adversarial perturbation satisfies the limitation of the L_∞ norm. However, our method adaptively updates and calculates the gradient direction. Therefore, we constrain the perturbation within the L_2 norm bound, defined in Equation (10).

3.4. Attacking Ensemble of Models

The attack performance of NAI-FGM can be further enhanced by attacking the ensemble of models. Liu et al. [21] shows that if an adversarial example can fool different network models at the same time, it can also attack other models to a large extent. We adopt the logits ensemble attack strategy in the literature [13], that is, we simultaneously attack several different networks that fuse logit activations together. Specifically, the logits fusion equation for attacking an ensemble of K models is as follows:

$$l(x) = \sum_{k=1}^{K} \omega_k L_k(x) \quad (4)$$

where $l_k(x)$ are the logits output of the k-th model, ω_k is the ensemble weight with $\omega_k \geq 0$ and $\sum_{k=1}^{K} \omega_k = 1$.

Algorithm 1 NAI-FGM

Input: A classifier f with loss function J; a clean example x and ground-truth label y;
Input: Perturbation size ϵ; maximum iterations T; the dimension of the input image N;
Input: Nadam decay factors μ_1 and μ_2; a denominator stability factor ξ.
Output: An adversarial example x^{adv} with $||x^{adv} - x||_\infty \leq \epsilon$.

$\alpha = \epsilon \cdot \sqrt{N}/T$
$m_0 = 0; n_0 = 0; g_0 = 0; x_0^{adv} = x$
for $t = 0$ to $T - 1$ **do**
  obtain the gradient $\nabla_x J(x_t^{adv}, y; \theta)$
  $g_t = \frac{\nabla_x J(x_t^{adv}, y; \theta)}{||\nabla_x J(x_t^{adv}, y; \theta)||_1}$ (5)
  $m_{t+1} = \mu_1 \cdot m_t + (1 - \mu_1) \cdot g_t$ (6)
  $n_{t+1} = \mu_2 \cdot n_t + (1 - \mu_2) \cdot g_t^2$ (7)
  $m_{t+1}^{'} = \frac{\mu_1 \cdot m_{t+1} + (1 - \mu_1) \cdot g_t}{1 - \mu_1^{t+1}}$ (8)
  $n_{t+1}^{'} = \frac{\mu_2 \cdot n_{t+1}}{1 - \mu_2^{t+1}}$ (9)
  $x_{t+1}^{adv} = Clip_x^{\epsilon}\{x_t^{adv} + \alpha \cdot (\frac{m_{t+1}^{'}}{\sqrt{n_{t+1}^{'} + \xi}} / ||\frac{m_{t+1}^{'}}{\sqrt{n_{t+1}^{'} + \xi}}||_2)\}$ (10)
end for
return $x^{adv} = x_T^{adv}$

3.5. Differences from Existing Advanced Attacks

In Table 1, we compare the proposed NAI-FGM with various advanced gradient-based attacks according to the features of different algorithms. The meanings of all the features in the table are mentioned in Section 3.3. Here we can clearly draw the difference between

NAI-FGM and any attack algorithm in the table. For example, compared with AI-FGM, we add a look-ahead momentum vector to optimize the gradient calculation and adopt a constant step size to add perturbation to the image. For another example, we introduce the second momentum and adaptive learning rate component on the basis of NI-FGSM, and replace the limit of L_∞ on adversarial perturbation with L_2.

Table 1. The differences between gradient-based attacks.

Feature	FGSM	I-FGSM	MI-FGSM	NI-FGSM	AI-FGM	NAI-FGM
The one-step attack	Yes					
The iterative attack		Yes	Yes	Yes	Yes	Yes
The momentum/The first momentum				Yes	Yes	Yes
The second momentum					Yes	Yes
The look-ahead momentum vector				Yes		Yes
The adaptive learning rate component					Yes	Yes
The constant step size	Yes	Yes	Yes	Yes		Yes
The variable step size					Yes	
L_∞ norm	Yes	Yes	Yes	Yes		
L_2 norm					Yes	Yes

Table 2 provides a distinction between the current state-of-the-art attacks with input transformations. Each attack in the table has a different input transformation method. In particular, ATTA is quite different from the input transformation methods of other attacks. ATTA first trains an additional adversarial transformation network to destroy the perturbation, and then makes the generated adversarial examples resistant to this transformation, thus enhancing the transferability of the adversarial examples.

Table 2. The difference between attacks with input transformations.

Feature	DIM	TIM	SIM	ATTA
Transformation method of input image	Resizing and padding	Translation	Scaling	Blurring and coloring

4. Experiments

We conduct relevant experiments for NAI-FGM and compare it with some advanced attacks. In Section 4.1, the detailed experimental setup is described. In Section 4.2, we show the experimental results of attacking a single network model using gradient-based methods and combined data and model enhancement methods respectively. In Section 4.3, we provide experimental results of attacking an ensemble of models using several momentum-based iterative methods. Finally, we investigate the influence of NAI-FGM on the attack effect under different hyperparameter settings in Section 4.4. Additionally, we give suggestions for the values of the relevant parameters involved in the attack based on the experimental findings.

4.1. Experimental Setup

Dataset. We use 1000 images from the ImageNet dataset [37], which are randomly selected from different categories. Almost all images are able to be correctly classified by the networks we tested. Before using this dataset, these images are preprocessed to a size of 299 × 299 × 3.

Models. We consider testing the proposed attack method on seven networks, including normally trained models—Inception-v3 (Inc-v3) [23], Inception-v4 (Inc-v4), Inception-Resnet-v2 (IncRes-v2) [38] and Resnet-v2-101 (Res-101) [2], and adversarially trained models—Inc-v3ens3, Inc-v3ens4 and IncRes-v2ens [9].

Hyper-parameters. We set the maximum perturbation $\epsilon = 16$ of each pixel, total iteration number $T = 10$, step size $\alpha = \epsilon/T$ and decay factor $\mu = 1.0$ [13]. We set the transformation probability $p = 0.5$ of input images for DIM [17] and the size of the Gaussian kernel matrix to 7×7 for TIM [18]. For SIM [14], we set up five scale copies. For NAI-FGM, the denominator stability factor is set to $\xi = 10^{-8}$, the Nadam decay factors $\mu_1 = 0.99$ and $\mu_2 = 0.999$ [16]. Additionally, the dimension N of the input image is set to $299 \times 299 \times 3$, step size $\alpha = \epsilon \cdot \sqrt{N}/T$.

4.2. Attack a Single Model

4.2.1. Comparison with Advanced Gradient-Based Attacks

First, we compare and test the attack performance of FGSM, I-FGSM, MI-FGSM and NAI-FGM on seven models. The experimental results are presented in Table 3, where * indicate the white-box attacks and the data in bold indicates the highest success rates of four attack algorithms for testing the same model. We use the four network models in the first column to produce adversarial examples by four attacks mentioned above. The seven network models in the first row are used for testing transferable effects of these adversarial examples. The attack success rate is used as an assessment indicator for the transferable effect of the adversarial example. Here, the attack success rate means the percentage of the number of adversarial images that can cause the test model to misclassify to the total number of adversarial images generated by each attack. In addition, in the last two columns of the table, we evaluate and calculate the time complexity of various attack algorithms and the generation time of each adversarial example.

Table 3. The success rates (%) of NAI-FGM compared to advanced gradient-based attacks when attacking a single model. * indicates the white-box attacks.

Model	Attack	Inc-v3	Inc-v4	IncRes-v2	Res-101	Inc-v3ens3	Inc-v3ens4	IncRes-v2ens	Time Complexity	The Generation Time (s) of an Adversarial Example
Inc-v3	FGSM	67.7 *	26.4	25.7	24.7	10.2	10.1	4.8	O(1)	0.3
	I-FGSM	**100.0** *	22.2	19.4	15.4	5.8	5.4	3.1	O(n)	2.3
	MI-FGSM	**100.0** *	44.7	41.6	35.4	14.6	12.4	6.2	O(n)	3.5
	NAI-FGM	**100.0** *	**47.5**	**44.6**	**36.1**	**16.7**	**14.3**	**8.6**	O(n)	2.2
Inc-v4	FGSM	27.9	52.5 *	23.0	23.3	9.9	9.8	5.6	O(1)	0.4
	I-FGSM	31.6	99.9 *	21.8	20.9	5.6	6.6	4.1	O(n)	4.2
	MI-FGSM	55.2	99.7 *	46.1	41.1	16.5	15.0	7.7	O(n)	6.9
	NAI-FGM	**60.4**	**100.0** *	**49.6**	**43.1**	**19.7**	**18.7**	**9.7**	O(n)	4.1
IncRes-v2	FGSM	27.3	20.2	42.3 *	24.5	9.9	9.5	5.8	O(1)	0.5
	I-FGSM	32.5	26.2	98.1 *	21.1	7.7	6.6	4.9	O(n)	4.7
	MI-FGSM	60.1	51.4	98.0 *	**45.2**	21.8	16.8	11.6	O(n)	7.8
	NAI-FGM	**61.7**	**52.0**	**98.5** *	45.1	**27.0**	**20.5**	**15.6**	O(n)	4.9
Res-101	FGSM	36.7	31.4	30.4	78.5 *	15.1	13.6	7.2	O(1)	0.5
	I-FGSM	31.4	25.3	23.5	99.8 *	9.0	8.7	5.4	O(n)	5.0
	MI-FGSM	57.7	51.5	48.8	99.3 *	25.0	21.2	12.9	O(n)	8.1
	NAI-FGM	**59.2**	**54.2**	**49.7**	**99.9** *	**27.9**	**26.1**	**17.0**	O(n)	5.1

We can observe that the success rate of all the other three iterative attacks in the white-box setting is almost 100% except the one-step attack FGSM. This indicates that iterative attacks have a significant advantage over one-step attacks. Meanwhile, I-FGSM show the worst results among the six black-box tests in comparison to the other attacks. Therefore, in subsequent experiments, we only compare with momentum-based attacks. And in the black-box situation, NAI-FGM has the highest success rate among these four attack methods. For example, NAI-FGM achieved a 100% white-box success rate when attacking Inc-v3, which is the same effect as I-FGSM and MI-FGSM. In addition, the success rate of NAI-FGM is 60.4% and 18.7% when the adversarial examples produced on Inc-v4 are transferred to Inc-v3 and Inc-v3ens4. Nevertheless, the success rate of MI-FGSM with good transferability is 55.2% and 15.0%, respectively, which fully demonstrates the advantage of NAI-FGM in improving attack transferability.

Moreover, from the time complexity point of view, the time complexity of iterative attacks is $O(1)$, while that of single-step attacks is $O(n)$. This indicates that iterative attacks consume more time. Meanwhile, the time to generate an adversarial example for NAI-FGM under Res-101 is 5.1 s, compared to 8.1 s for MI-FGSM and 5.0 s for I-FGSM. This shows that NAI-FGM only needs to spend approximately the same time as I-FGSM to obtain better effects than MI-FGSM.

4.2.2. Comparison with Momentum-Based Iterative Attacks with Input Transformations

The work of DIM, TIM and SIM shows that integrating the ideas of data augmentation and model augmentation into gradient-based adversarial attacks can significantly improve the transferability. Therefore, we combine NAI-FGM and two other momentum-based iterative attacks (MI-FGSM, NI-FGSM) with the above mentioned enhancement methods, called NAI-DI-TI-SI-FGM, MI-DI-TI-SI-FGSM and NI-DI-TI-SI-FGSM. We use these three methods to attack a single model and compare the success rates.

From Table 4 we can observe that NAI-DI-TI-SI-FGM has significantly higher success rates in testing the three adversarially trained networks. Specially, the success rate of NAI-DI-TI-SI-FGM outperforms NI-DI-TI-SI-FGSM against adversarially trained models by 5–15%, and the average success rate of NAI-DI-TI-SI-FGM increased by more than 5% of MI-DI-TI-SI-FGSM. As described in Table 2, the integrated methods enable the attack to be transferred more effectively.

Table 4. Comparison of the success rates (%) of attacking a single model by three momentum-based iterative attacks with input transformations. * indicates the white-box attacks.

Model	Attack	Inc-v3	Inc-v4	IncRes-v2	Res-101	Inc-v3ens3	Inc-v3ens4	IncRes-v2ens	Time Complexity	The Generation Time (s) of an Adversarial Example
Inc-v3	MI-DI-TI-SI-FGSM	**99.5** *	85.0	80.5	76.0	65.1	62.5	47.5	$O(n^2)$	10.5
	NI-DI-TI-SI-FGSM	**99.5** *	84.3	81.0	77.2	60.1	56.6	40.1	$O(n^2)$	10.5
	NAI-DI-TI-SI-FGM	**99.5** *	**87.0**	**81.3**	76.4	**70.4**	**70.0**	**51.6**	$O(n^2)$	10.5
Inc-v4	MI-DI-TI-SI-FGSM	86.2	98.8 *	82.6	77.1	70.0	67.5	56.7	$O(n^2)$	19.8
	NI-DI-TI-SI-FGSM	87.1	**99.6** *	83.7	77.5	66.5	62.8	50.0	$O(n^2)$	19.8
	NAI-DI-TI-SI-FGM	**87.8**	98.6 *	**83.8**	**78.7**	**75.9**	**70.4**	**60.9**	$O(n^2)$	20.0
IncRes-v2	MI-DI-TI-SI-FGSM	88.7	86.4	98.4 *	83.9	78.6	74.5	72.6	$O(n^2)$	21.7
	NI-DI-TI-SI-FGSM	89.6	88.5	**99.5** *	83.1	73.0	67.6	63.5	$O(n^2)$	22.0
	NAI-DI-TI-SI-FGM	**90.1**	**88.6**	98.5 *	**85.4**	**82.7**	**79.3**	**78.0**	$O(n^2)$	22.0
Res-101	MI-DI-TI-SI-FGSM	85.5	81.7	84.3	98.9 *	75.8	71.7	62.1	$O(n^2)$	22.8
	NI-DI-TI-SI-FGSM	85.7	**84.0**	**85.0**	**99.6** *	72.9	67.8	57.3	$O(n^2)$	22.4
	NAI-DI-TI-SI-FGM	**86.4**	83.5	84.6	98.9 *	**80.4**	**76.8**	**69.4**	$O(n^2)$	22.5

4.3. *Attack an Ensemble of Models*

Furthermore, we also implement ensemble attacks on multiple network models simultaneously with NAI-FGM and NAI-DI-TI-SI-FGM, respectively. Specifically, we attack the ensemble of Inc-v3, Inc-v4, IncRes-v2, and Res-101, and each model is set to the same ensemble weights, that is, $\omega_k = 1/4$. It is worth noting that we set up 2 scale copies of the SIM for the time cost.

From Table 5 we can observe that the success rates of NAI-FGM in attacking the three adversarially trained models can improve MI-FGSM by more than 8% and NI-FGSM by more than 11%. In addition, NAI-DI-TI-SI-FGM obtains 88.9–93.0% attack success rates on all three adversarially training models. However, MI-DI-TI-SI-FGSM and NI-DI-TI-SI-FGSM only obtained the corresponding 81.2–88.5% and 83.0–91.7% attack success rates, respectively, further demonstrating the advantage of NAI-DI-TI-SI-FGM. Meanwhile, the proposed method can still maintain similar white-box success rates as the two other momentum-based iterative attacks.

Table 5. Comparison of the success rates (%) of various advanced momentum-based iterative attacks when attacking an ensemble of models. The bolded data indicates the highest success rate for the same type of attack.

Attack	Inc-v3	Inc-v4	IncRes-v2	Res-101	Inc-v3ens3	Inc-v3ens4	IncRes-v2ens	Time Complexity	The Generation Time (s) of an Adversarial Example
MI-FGSM	99.9	99.6	99.3	99.0	47.8	43.2	28.0	O(n)	14.6
NI-FGSM	**100.0**	99.9	**99.9**	**100.0**	46.1	40.6	25.9	O(n)	14.8
NAI-FGM	**100.0**	**100.0**	99.5	**100.0**	**57.4**	**52.1**	**36.1**	O(n)	14.8
MI-DI-TI-SI-FGSM	99.6	99.4	99.0	99.4	88.5	87.4	81.2	O(n^2)	30.4
NI-DI-TI-SI-FGSM	**100.0**	**99.9**	**99.8**	**100.0**	91.7	88.4	83.0	O(n^2)	30.9
NAI-DI-TI-SI-FGM	99.9	**99.9**	**99.8**	99.9	**93.0**	**92.0**	**88.9**	O(n^2)	31.2

4.4. Study on Hyperparameters

Decay factors μ_1 and μ_2. First, we study the effects of the decay factors μ_1 and μ_2 on the attack performance. We produce adversarial examples on Inc-v3 and test them on Inc-v3, Inc-v4 and Inc-v3ens4. These three models are chosen because they represent a white-box attack, an attack against an undefended model and an attack against a defended model, respectively. This makes our study more adequate and experimental findings more general. Figure 4 shows the attack effect of NAI-FGM with different decay factor settings. In the experiment, μ_1 and μ_2 are set to the same value and the size varies from 0.1 to 0.9 in step of 0.1. From the Figure 4, we can observe that the success rate of the white-box model remains at 100% as μ_1 and μ_2 increase, and the success rates of the two black-box models as a whole are increasing.

From this, we can draw a preliminary conclusion that the size of the decay factor is irrelevant to the effectiveness of the white-box attack. Meanwhile, as the gradual grow of the value of the decay factor, the effect of the black-box attack improve accordingly. Also, since we first set the values of the two decay factors in the interval $[0.1, 0.9]$, then we should continue to explore in the interval with values $[0.9, 1)$. Here, values of the two decay factors cannot be set to 0, 1 or other range of values due to the limitation of our algorithm.

To further study the optimal values of the two decay factors on the attack performance, we choose different combinations of values for μ_1 and μ_2 in the interval of $[0.9, 1)$ to test the success rate of NAI-FGM. From Table 6 we can observe that the maximum values of the success rate of each model of the attack fall in the interval of $\mu_1 \in (0.99, 0.999)$. Additionally, we conjecture that the sensitivity of different models to the decay factors μ_1 and μ_2 may be different, but the optimal value of μ_1 should be in the interval of $(0.99, 1)$ and the optimal value of μ_2 should be in the interval of $(0.9, 1)$. Therefore, we can select and set the optimal value of the decay factor according to the specific attack target. In this experiment, we set the values of μ_1 and μ_2 to 0.99 and 0.999, respectively.

Size of perturbation ϵ. Second, we study the effect of the ϵ on the attack performance. Figure 5 demonstrates the effect of NAI-FGM attack at different sizes of perturbation. In this experiment, the size of perturbation ϵ varies from 0 to 20 in step of 2. From the Figure 5, we can clearly see that the success rate of the white-box model of NAI-FGM can reach 100% very quickly. Additionally, The effectiveness of the attack under the six black-box models tested improves with increasing of ϵ.

However, the larger the perturbation value, the worse the visual effect of the antagonistic example produced by the attack will be. Ultimately, we propose to set the perturbation size of NAI-FGM to $\epsilon = 16$.

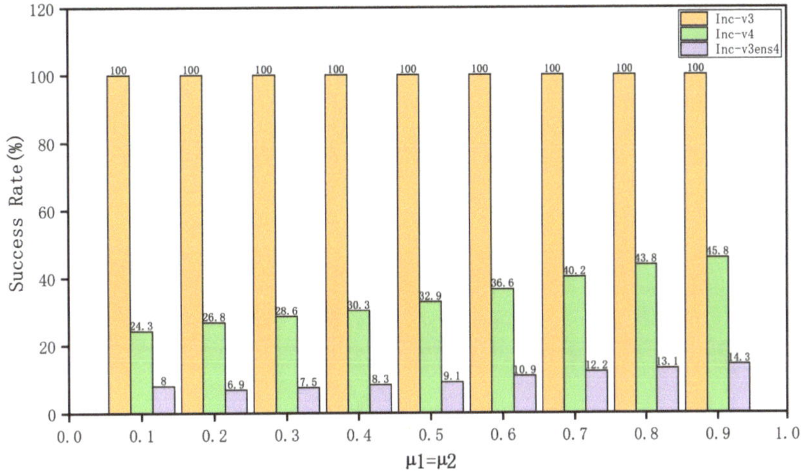

Figure 4. Attack success rates (%) of NAI-FGM on three networks using adversarial examples produced on Inc-v3 with different decay factors.

Table 6. Attack success rates (%) of NAI-FGM on seven networks using adversarial examples produced on Inc-v3 with different combinations of decay factors. The data marked with * indicate the highest success rate on each black-box model, and the bolded data indicate the success rate that is in the largest integer interval in each model.

μ_1 & μ_2	Inc-v3	Inc-v4	IncRes-v2	Res-101	Inc-v3ens3	Inc-v3ens4	IncRes-v2ens
0.9 & 0.9	**100.0**	45.8	42.1	35.2	15.9	**14.3**	**8.0**
0.9 & 0.99	**100.0**	45.4	41.2	35.8	15.9	**14.0**	7.0
0.9 & 0.999	**100.0**	44.3	42.8	35.2	15.3	**14.2**	7.9
0.99 & 0.9	**100.0**	**47.4**	**44.9** *	**37.9** *	**17.1**	13.7	8.5
0.99 & 0.99	**100.0**	**47.6**	**44.4**	36.6	16.8	**14.3**	**8.5**
0.99 & 0.999	**100.0**	**47.5**	**44.6**	36.1	16.7	**14.3**	**8.6** *
0.999 & 0.9	**100.0**	**47.7** *	**44.4**	**37.1**	**17.1**	**14.6** *	7.7
0.999 & 0.99	**100.0**	46.2	**44.2**	36.8	**17.4** *	**14.5**	7.6
0.999 & 0.999	**100.0**	46.6	**44.9** *	**37.4**	**17.4** *	**14.1**	**8.2**

Total iteration number T. Finally, we study the effect of the T on the attack performance against three adversarially trained black-box models. Figure 6 shows the effect of three momentum-based iterative attacks (NAI-FGM, MI-FGSM and NI-FGSM) with different iteration number. In this experiment, T varies from 2 to 16 in step of 2. We use adversarial examples produced on Inc-v3 to attack Inc-v3ens3, Inc-v3ens4 and IncRes-v2ens models. From figure (a), (b) and (c), we can observe that the overall success rates of NAI-FGM outperform MI-FGSM and NI-FGSM for different black-box model settings and different iteration number settings. Because the points on the red line representing the success rate of the NAI-FGM are above the blue and green line points. From another perspective, NAI-FGM requires only fewer iterations to can obtain similar success rates as other two attacks. This indicates that NAI-FGM requires less time cost when the success rates are the same. For example, when attacking the Inc-v3ens3, NAI-FGM achieves a success rate of about 15% in only 4 iterations, while MI-FGSM requires 10 iterations, which fully shows the advantages of NAI-FGM.

In addition, Figure 6 presents that the attack success rate curve of NAI-FGM under different iteration number settings undergoes a slight oscillation. However, with T increases, the attack effect is getting better in the overall. Therefore, we can derive that the greater the number of iterations, the better the attack effect, but the corresponding time cost will also increase. Ultimately, we propose to set the number of iterations of NAI-FGM to $T = 10$.

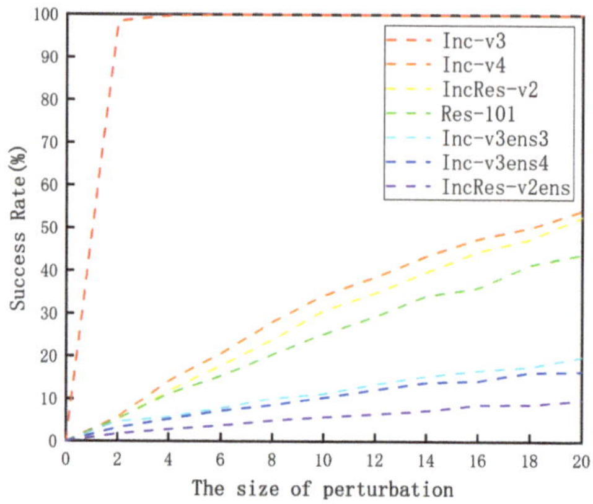

Figure 5. Attack success rates (%) of NAI-FGM on seven networks with Inc-v3 as the origin model with different sizes of perturbation.

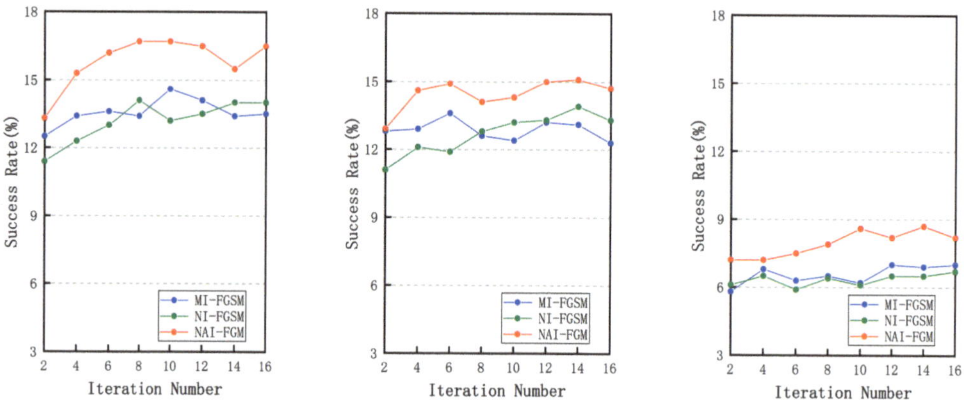

(**a**) Inc-v3ens3 (**b**) Inc-v3ens4 (**c**) IncRes-v2ens

Figure 6. Attack success rates (%) of NAI-FGM, MI-FGSM and NI-FGSM on three adversarially trained networks with Inc-v3 as the origin model with different number of iterations.

5. Discussion

We design a new adversarial example generation algorithm: NAI-FGM. First, a look-ahead momentum component is added to MI-FGSM, which speeds up the convergence of the loss function and gets rid of the poorer local maxima. Secondly, we introduce an adaptive learning rate component to obtain an adaptive update direction based on the current gradient information and converge to a better local extreme point. After extensive experimental validation, our approach mitigates the overfitting effect of the adversarial examples produced in the current attack methods and enhances the transferability of them to some extent.

However, our method still has some shortcomings. For example, without combining input transformation and integration, our black-box attack success rate is only about 50% for the undefended model. Additionally, our attack success rate is still less than 30% for the model with defense. This indicates that the transfer-based attacks still need to be improved. We conjecture that it may be due to the fact that our study only produces adversarial examples relied on the information of the current gradient, and does not consider the gradient information of multiple samples in different time states. This is an important reason why the attack is less effective under black-box testing and it is something that will be investigated in our next work.

In future research, we will also consider linking adversarial attacks to IoT-related technologies. In particular, in the field of communication, the attack efficiency is quite sensitive to the latency of data processing. How to trade-off and choose between time cost, complexity of training alternative models and attack algorithm performance is the issue we have to focus on.

6. Conclusions

In this work, we propose the Nadam iterative fast gradient method (NAI-FGM) to boost adversarial attacks from the perspective of improving the transferability of adversarial examples. Although our attack is based on MI-FGSM with improvements, there are still some differences. First, the momentum term of MI-FGSM accumulates only the sum of the gradients during the iteration. While the first momentum term of NAI-FGM is used to accumulate the gradient sums, the second momentum term gathers the sum of squares of the gradients. Meanwhile, the second momentum term constitutes the adaptive learning rate component, which is used to help the adversarial example to converge to a better extreme point by obtaining adaptive update directions according to the current parameters. Second, we introduce the look-ahead momentum vector, which is dedicated to make the loss function converge faster and get rid of the poor local maximum. Thirdly, we use L_2 norm instead of L_∞ norm to calculate the direction of change of the current gradient, with the aim of matching our algorithm to obtain adaptive update directions.

Experimental results indicate that NAI-FGM realizes obviously higher attack success rates in the black-box case and obtains similar success rates against the white-box models compared to traditional momentum-based iterative attack methods. In particular, when using the adversarial examples produced by way of ensemble attack to test the adversarially trained models, the NAI-FGM improves the success rate by 8% to 11% over the other attack methods on attacking ensemble models. Last but not least, the NAI-DI-TI-SI-FGM combined with the input transformation achieves a high success rate of 91.3% on average. This poses higher requirements and greater challenges to the security of DNNs. Therefore, it is urgent and necessary to study and design models with better performance and higher robustness.

Author Contributions: Conceptualization, Q.Z. and Y.Z.; methodology, Y.Z.; software, Q.Z.; validation, Y.Z. and M.L.; formal analysis, Y.S.; resources, Q.Z.; writing—original draft preparation, Y.Z.; writing—review and editing, J.L. and J.Y.; visualization, M.L.; supervision, Y.S. and R.W.; project administration, Q.Z.; funding acquisition, Q.Z. All authors have read and agreed to the published version of the manuscript.

Funding: This work is supported by National Natural Science Foundation of China under Grant (No. 61971380), and the key technologies R&D Program of Henan Province (No. 222102210025), and the Key scientific research project plans of higher education institutions in Henan Province (Nos. 23A520012, 22A520047, 21zx014).

Data Availability Statement: Not applicable.

Conflicts of Interest: The authors declare no conflict of interest.

References

1. Krizhevsky, A.; Sutskever, I.; Hinton, G.E. Imagenet classification with deep convolutional neural networks. *Commun. ACM* **2017**, *60*, 84–90. [CrossRef]
2. He, K.; Zhang, X.; Ren, S.; Sun, J. Deep residual learning for image recognition. In Proceedings of the IEEE Conference on Computer Vision and Pattern Recognition, Las Vegas, NV, USA, 27–30 June 2016; pp. 770–778.
3. Vaswani, A.; Shazeer, N.; Parmar, N.; Uszkoreit, J.; Jones, L.; Gomez, A.N.; Kaiser, L.; Polosukhin, I. Attention is all you need. *arXiv* **2017**, arXiv:1706.03762.

4. Chen, C.; Seff, A.; Kornhauser, A.; Xiao, J. Deepdriving: Learning affordance for direct perception in autonomous driving. In Proceedings of the 2015 IEEE International Conference on Computer Vision (ICCV), Santiago, Chile, 7–13 December 2015; pp. 2722–2730.
5. Liao, Y.; Vakanski, A.; Xian, M. A deep learning framework for assessing physical rehabilitation exercises. *IEEE Trans. Neural Syst. Rehabil. Eng.* **2020**, *28*, 468–477. [CrossRef] [PubMed]
6. Szegedy, C.; Zaremba, W.; Sutskever, I.; Bruna, J.; Erhan, D.; Goodfellow, I.; Fergus, R. Intriguing properties of neural networks. *arXiv* **2013**, arXiv:1312.6199.
7. Carlini, N.; Wagner, D. Towards evaluating the robustness of neural networks. In Proceedings of the 2017 IEEE Symposium on Security and Privacy (SP), San Jose, CA, USA, 22–26 May 2017; pp. 39–57.
8. Madry, A.; Makelov, A.; Schmidt, L.; Tsipras, D.; Vladu, A. Towards deep learning models resistant to adversarial attacks. *arXiv* **2017**, arXiv:1706.06083.
9. Tramèr, F.; Kurakin, A.; Papernot, N.; Goodfellow, I.; Boneh, D.; McDaniel, P. Ensemble adversarial training: Attacks and defenses. *arXiv* **2017**, arXiv:1705.07204.
10. Goodfellow, I.J.; Shlens, J.; Szegedy, C. Explaining and harnessing adversarial examples. *arXiv* **2014**, arXiv:1412.6572.
11. Kurakin, A.; Goodfellow, I.J.; Bengio, S. Adversarial examples in the physical world. In *Artificial Intelligence Safety and Security*; Chapman and Hall/CRC: Boca Raton, FL, USA, 2018; pp. 99–112.
12. Huang, Y.; Chen, Y.; Wang, X.; Yang, J.; Wang, Q. Promoting Adversarial Transferability via Dual-Sampling Variance Aggregation and Feature-Heterogeneity Attacks. *Electronics* **2023**, *12*, 767. [CrossRef]
13. Dong, Y.; Liao, F.; Pang, T.; Su, H.; Zhu, J.; Hu, X.; Li, J. Boosting adversarial attacks with momentum. In Proceedings of the 2018 IEEE/CVF Conference on Computer Vision and Pattern Recognition, Salt Lake City, UT, USA, 18–23 June 2018; pp. 9185–9193.
14. Lin, J.; Song, C.; He, K.; Wang, L.; Hopcroft, J.E. Nesterov accelerated gradient and scale invariance for adversarial attacks. *arXiv* **2019**, arXiv:1908.06281.
15. Wang, X.; He, K. Enhancing the transferability of adversarial attacks through variance tuning. In Proceedings of the IEEE/CVF Conference on Computer Vision and Pattern Recognition, Nashville, TN, USA, 20–25 June 2021; pp. 1924–1933.
16. Yin, H.; Zhang, H.; Wang, J.; Dou, R. Boosting adversarial attacks on neural networks with better optimizer. *Secur. Commun. Netw.* **2021**, *2021*, 9983309. [CrossRef]
17. Xie, C.; Zhang, Z.; Zhou, Y.; Bai, S.; Wang, J.; Ren, Z.; Yuille, A.L. Improving transferability of adversarial examples with input diversity. In Proceedings of the IEEE/CVF Conference on Computer Vision and Pattern Recognition, Long Beach, CA, USA, 15–20 June 2019; pp. 2730–2739.
18. Dong, Y.; Pang, T.; Su, H.; Zhu, J. Evading defenses to transferable adversarial examples by translation-invariant attacks. In Proceedings of the IEEE/CVF Conference on Computer Vision and Pattern Recognition, Long Beach, CA, USA, 15–20 June 2019; pp. 4312–4321.
19. Wang, H.; Zhu, C.; Cao, Y.; Zhuang, Y.; Li, J.; Chen, X. ADSAttack: An Adversarial Attack Algorithm via Searching Adversarial Distribution in Latent Space. *Electronics* **2023**, *12*, 816. [CrossRef]
20. Wu, W.; Su, Y.; Lyu, M.R.; King, I. Improving the Transferability of Adversarial Samples with Adversarial Transformations. In Proceedings of the 2021 IEEE/CVF Conference on Computer Vision and Pattern Recognition (CVPR), Nashville, TN, USA, 20–25 June 2021.
21. Liu, Y.; Chen, X.; Liu, C.; Song, D. Delving into transferable adversarial examples and black-box attacks. *arXiv* **2016**, arXiv:1611.02770.
22. Dozat, T. Incorporating Nesterov Momentum into Adam. Available online: https://openreview.net/forum?id=OM0jvwB8jIp57ZJjtNEZ (accessed on 7 February 2023).
23. Szegedy, C.; Vanhoucke, V.; Ioffe, S.; Shlens, J.; Wojna, Z. Rethinking the inception architecture for computer vision. In Proceedings of the IEEE Conference on Computer Vision and Pattern Recognition, Las Vegas, NV, USA, 27–30 June 2016; pp. 2818–2826.
24. Chen, P.Y.; Zhang, H.; Sharma, Y.; Yi, J.; Hsieh, C.J. Zoo: Zeroth order optimization based black-box attacks to deep neural networks without training substitute models. *arXiv* **2017**, arXiv:1708.03999.
25. Su, J.; Vargas, D.V.; Kouichi, S. One pixel attack for fooling deep neural networks. *IEEE Trans. Evol. Comput.* **2017**, *23*, 828–841. [CrossRef]
26. Brendel, W.; Rauber, J.; Bethge, M. Decision-based adversarial attacks: Reliable attacks against black-box machine learning models. *arXiv* **2017**, arXiv:1712.04248.
27. Kingma, D.P.; Ba, J. Adam: A method for stochastic optimization. *arXiv* **2014**, arXiv:1412.6980.
28. Wang, G.; Yan, H.; Wei, X. Enhancing transferability of adversarial examples with spatial momentum. In *Pattern Recognition and Computer Vision, 5th Chinese Conference, PRCV 2022, Shenzhen, China, 4–7 November 2022, Proceedings, Part I*; Springer International Publishing: Cham, Switzerland, 2022; pp. 593–604.
29. Kurakin, A.; Goodfellow, I.; Bengio, S. Adversarial machine learning at scale. *arXiv* **2016**, arXiv:1611.01236.
30. Xie, C.; Wang, J.; Zhang, Z.; Ren, Z.; Yuille, A. Mitigating adversarial effects through randomization. *arXiv* **2017**, arXiv:1711.01991.
31. Guo, C.; Rana, M.; Cisse, M.; Van Der Maaten, L. Countering adversarial images using input transformations. *arXiv* **2017**, arXiv:1711.00117.

32. Liu, Z.; Liu, Q.; Liu, T.; Xu, N.; Lin, X.; Wang, Y.; Wen, W. Feature distillation: Dnn-oriented jpeg compression against adversarial examples. In Proceedings of the 2019 IEEE/CVF Conference on Computer Vision and Pattern Recognition (CVPR), Long Beach, CA, USA, 15–20 June 2019; pp. 860–868.
33. Xu, W.; Evans, D.; Qi, Y. Feature squeezing: Detecting adversarial examples in deep neural networks. *arXiv* **2017**, arXiv:1704.01155.
34. Pang, T.; Du, C.; Dong, Y.; Zhu, J. Towards robust detection of adversarial examples. *arXiv* **2018**, arXiv:1706.00633.
35. Ma, S.; Liu, Y. Nic: Detecting adversarial samples with neural network invariant checking. In Proceedings of the 26th Network and Distributed System Security Symposium (NDSS 2019), San Diego, CA, USA, 24–27 February 2019 .
36. Nesterov, Y. A method for unconstrained convex minimization problem with the rate of convergence O $(1/k\hat{2})$. *Dokl. AN USSR Proc. USSR Acad. Sci.* **1983**, *269*, 543–547.
37. Russakovsky, O.; Deng, J.; Su, H.; Krause, J.; Satheesh, S.; Ma, S.; Huang, Z.; Karpathy, A.; Khosla, A.; Bernstein, M.; et al. Imagenet large scale visual recognition challenge. *Int. J. Comput. Vis.* **2015**, *115*, 211–252. [CrossRef]
38. Szegedy, C.; Ioffe, S.; Vanhoucke, V.; Alemi, A.A. Inception-v4, inception-resnet and the impact of residual connections on learning. In Proceedings of the Thirty-First AAAI Conference on Artificial Intelligence, San Francisco, CA, USA, 4–9 February 2017 .

electronics

MDPI

Article

A Coverless Audio Steganography Based on Generative Adversarial Networks

Jing Li, Kaixi Wang * and Xiaozhu Jia

College of Computer Science and Technology, Qingdao University, Qingdao 266071, China
* Correspondence: kxwang@qdu.edu.cn

Abstract: Traditional audio steganography by cover modification causes changes to the cover features during the embedding of a secret, which is easy to detect with emerging neural-network steganalysis tools. To address the problem, this paper proposes a coverless audio-steganography model to conceal a secret audio. In this method, the stego-audio is directly synthesized by our model, which is based on the WaveGAN framework. An extractor is meticulously designed to reconstruct the secret audio, and it contains resolution blocks to learn the different resolution features. The method does not perform any modification to an existing or generated cover, and as far as we know, this is the first directly generated stego-audio. The experimental results also show that it is difficult for the current steganalysis methods to detect the existence of a secret in the stego-audio generated by our method because there is no cover audio. The MOS metric indicates that the generated stego-audio has high audio quality. The steganography capacity can be measured from two perspectives, one is that it can reach 50% of the stego-audio from the simple size perspective, the other is that 22–37 bits can be hidden in a two-second stego-audio from the semantic. In addition, we prove using spectrum diagrams in different forms that the extractor can reconstruct the secret audio successfully on hearing, which guarantees complete semantic transmission. Finally, the experiment of noise impacts on the stego-audio transmission shows that the extractor can still completely reconstruct the semantics of the secret audios, which indicates that the proposed method has good robustness.

Keywords: audio steganography; coverless steganography; GAN; covert communication; information hiding

Citation: Li, J.; Wang, K.; Jia, X. A Coverless Audio Steganography Based on Generative Adversarial Networks. *Electronics* **2023**, *12*, 1253. https://doi.org/10.3390/electronics12051253

Academic Editors: Krzysztof Szczypiorski and Xiao Yu

Received: 22 December 2022
Revised: 12 February 2023
Accepted: 28 February 2023
Published: 5 March 2023

1. Introduction

The many rapidly developed internet technologies make our lives more convenient. However, in some cases, there is a strong demand for a private secure transmission that can prevent a message from being disclosed. Information hiding is an important technology to protect private information. Currently, information hiding technology has been developed into two branches: digital steganography and digital watermarking technology [1]. The former is mainly used for covert communication, and the latter is mainly used for copyright protection. Steganography is an art and science that hides a secret in one or more covers and then the stego-objects are transmitted in public channels without being noticed.

At present, the digital covers for steganography include texts, images, audios, videos, and network traffic. With the prevalence of social networks supporting short audio files [2] and the popularization of VoIP services [3], audio has become a popular media. This prevalence is one feature of the best covers. Our hearing system is not very sensitive, and audio files have large redundancy. Therefore, audio has become a main cover for digital steganography. Traditional audio steganography mainly utilizes the redundancy of audio to embed a secret [4]. This kind of embedding generally performs some modifications to the cover, which, in turn, leads to changes to the cover features.

A third party can detect the existence of a secret in such a stego-audio by analyzing the changes to the statistical features. More importantly, with the emergence of various new detection tools, especially those based on the neural networks and deep-learning technologies, the detection accuracy has become very high [5]. Table 1 shows the detection accuracy of different steganalysis methods based on deep-learning technologies for the traditional steganography methods by cover modification with the difference embedding rates. The high detection accuracy shows that the traditional audio steganography by cover modification has lost its utility. Compared to steganography by cover modification, steganography by cover generation aims to generate a natural cover to cope with the detection issues caused by cover modification.

Generative Adversarial Networks (GANs) [6] are an important technology to realize steganography by cover generation, and they have been applied in audio covers. Ref. [7] first proposed audio steganography based on adversarial examples to modify an existing audio cover. Ref. [8] encoded the cover audio and the secret audio to generate a stego-audio automatically based on a GAN. Ref. [9] proposed a framework based on a GAN to achieve optimal embedding for audio steganography in the temporal domain. Ref. [10] employed LSBM steganography to embed a secret into a generated cover with high security.

In [11], the secret audio and cover audio were preprocessed using the time-domain zero-padding method and then input into the encoder to generate the stego-audio, which improved the security greatly. Ref. [12] proposed end-to-end audio steganography, and the encoder encoded the secret message into the audio cover. However, the encoder generated a modified vector of the audio sample value instead of stego-audio, which greatly reduced the distortion caused by message embedding.

Although these previous works utilized GANs for audio steganography, they performed modifications on an existing or generated cover, and a third party can still detect the existence of a secret in the stego-audio by analyzing the changes to the statistical features of the generated cover. As far as we know, there are currently no steganography methods that directly generate a stego-audio without a cover-audio.

Table 1. The detection accuracy of different steganalysis methods based on deep learning under the different embedding rates.

Steganalysis Methods	Steganography Methods	Embedding Rates	Accuracy
Spec-ResNet [13]	LSB-EE [4]	0.1	0.9151
		0.2	0.946
		0.3	0.9608
		0.5	0.9724
LARxNet [5]	SIGN [14]	0.1	0.9427
		0.2	0.9665
		0.3	0.9854
		0.5	0.9912
WASDN [15]	MIN [16]	0.1	0.9357
		0.2	0.9572
		0.3	0.9643
		0.5	0.9881
MultiSpecNet [17]	LSB-EE [4]	0.1	0.9433
		0.2	0.957
		0.3	0.9675
		0.5	0.9796

In this paper, a coverless audio steganography that does not perform any modification to an existing or generated cover is proposed. Herein, being coverless does not mean that there is no media to carry a secret, instead, it means that there is not any embedding operation on the existing or generated cover [18].

Consequently, the stego-audio is directly generated without a cover in this work. Therefore, the proposed method only needs to transmit the stego-audio. For attackers, there is no cover to refer to. This application scenario has better security than the traditional audio steganography by cover modification. The main contributions of this paper are summarized as follows:

(1) A coverless audio-steganography model is proposed based on the general audio synthesis framework WaveGAN [19] to directly synthesize a stego-audio instead of modifying an existing or generated audio to generate a stego-audio. A post-processing layer is replenished in the original WaveGAN generator to improve the quality of the generated stego-audio. The loss metrics indicate that the improved model has good convergence performance. Furthermore, extensive experiments show that this steganography method has high security and undetectability. Some previous works have utilized GAN for audio steganography; however, those works either modified an existing audio or perform certain changes on a generated one. As far as we know, our method is the first directly generated stego-audio.
(2) As an essential part of a steganography method, an extractor is carefully designed to reconstruct the secret audio from the stego-audio. This consists of five resolution blocks, which are composed with a residual network structure to learn the acoustic features of different frequency bands on the audio spectrum, and this can effectively reduce feature loss. The experimental results show that this extractor can guarantee the complete transmission of a secret audio in both auditory and semantic aspects.
(3) The proposed method does not perform any embedding operation on the existing or generated audio cover, and the distributions of the sample value of the stego-audio and real audio are the same, which can fundamentally resist detection from steganalysis tools.

The rest of this paper is organized as follows. The relevant literature is summarized and analyzed in Section 2. Section 3 describes the details of the proposed method. Our experiments and analyses are presented in Section 4 to verify the performance. Finally, our conclusions are given in Section 5.

2. Related Work

Traditional audio steganography can be implemented in three domains: the time domain, transform domain, and compression domain [20]. In the time domain, the most common is Least Significant Bit (LSB) steganography [21], whose basic idea is to replace the least significant bit in audio sample values with a secret bit. Other typical audio steganography methods in this domain include echo steganography [22], which utilizes the masking effect of the human auditory system; spread spectrum steganography [23], in which, a narrow band information signal is expanded over a wide frequency range; and Quantized Index Modulation steganography (QIM), which treats a secret message as a quantization index [24].

The transform domains used for audio steganography methods include discrete Fourier transform (DFT) [25], discrete cosine transform (DCT) [26] and discrete wavelet transform (DWT) [27]. With the development of audio compression technologies, audio encoded in a compressed way has become popular and, thus, has become a suitable cover option. Furthermore, this kind of steganography can be categorized into three approaches [28]: one is to embed a secret into an audio cover to obtain a stego-audio and then compress it, another is to directly embed a secret into a compressed audio cover, and the last is to decompress the compressed cover and embed a secret and then recompress it to obtain a stego-audio.

GANs [6] were, first, applied to natural language processing [29], computer vision [30], and other fields and are gradually being employed in the information hiding field. Until now, most steganography methods based on GANs took images as covers. Furthermore, coverless image steganography based on GANs is becoming a research hotspot and has also achieved some fruitful research findings. In 2017, Volkhonskiy et al. [31] opened up a new space for a GAN in information hiding fields and proposed a DCGAN based image steganography model, which consists of three parts: a generator (G), a discriminator (D), and a steganalyzer (S).

Ref. [32] proposed an adaptive steganography method based on a GAN by learning the embedding cost for image steganography, and this outperformed hand-crafted steganography algorithms for the first time in all kinds of steganographic performance. Furthermore, ref. [18] encoded a secret into a cover image using GAN to generate a stego-image. The stego-image is visually indistinguishable from its corresponding cover image. Although a stego-image is generated in this method, the cover is modified. Furthermore, the steganalysis methods can still detect the existence of a secret in the generated stego-image by analyzing the changes to the statistical features.

Ref. [33] first realized coverless information hiding based on a GAN, where the stego-image was directly generated by replacing the class labels of the input data with a secret as a driver, and then the secret was extracted from the stego-image by the discriminator. Herein, as mentioned above, 'coverless' does not mean that there is no media to carry a secret; instead, it means that it does not perform any embedding operation on an existing cover.

Ref. [34] also proposed a coverless image information hiding method, which employed the Wasserstein Generative Adversarial Network (WGAN) and was driven by a secret image to generate a stego-image directly without performing any modification to either the existing cover or a generated cover. In 2021, a cryptographic coverless information hiding method [35] was proposed, which utilized a generative model to transmit a secret image between two different image domains. Aiming at the problem of face privacy leakage in social robots, ref. [36] proposed a visual face privacy protection method. Based on the above knowledge, it can be seen that GANs have been well applied in image covers.

Due to the great achievements of GANs regarding images, they have been gradually applied to audio media, such as audio synthesis [37], speech enhancement [38], and speech emotion [39]. In 2019, a general audio synthesis framework based on DCGAN, named WaveGAN [19], was proposed. WaveGAN is the first attempt to employ a GAN to synthesize raw waveform audio in an unsupervised way. Its main work is to flatten a two-dimensional DCGAN into a one-dimensional model due to the different structures of images and audios.

This contribution provided a new idea for generative audio steganography. In addition, the existing generative audio steganography still needs a cover, which might be an existing cover or a generated cover, and this still relies on the security and robustness of the algorithm as in the traditional methods. Therefore, in order to fundamentally resist the detection of the steganography analysis tools, this paper proposes audio steganography based on WaveGAN that directly generates a stego-audio driven by a secret audio without any modification.

3. The Coverless Audio Steganography Framework

In this section, a coverless audio steganography method is proposed based on WaveGAN, which directly generates a stego-audio when a secret audio is input. In addition, the reconstruction module is designed to reconstruct the secret message from the stego-audio. In order to describe the proposed method more clearly, the relevant symbols in this paper are summarized in Table 2.

Table 2. The meanings of the main symbols used in this paper.

Symbol	The Meaning
R, S	Real dataset, Secret dataset
θ	Network parameters
r, s	Real audio, Secret audio
D, G, E	Discriminator, Generator, Extractor
B	Batch size
M, N	The number of rows and columns in an audio 2-D array
MD	The matrix of the MFCC distance
C	The number of correctly recognized audios
T	Total number of tested audios
X_{spec}, Y_{spec}	The matrix obtained by short-time Fourier transform of the secret audio and the reconstructed secret audio
X, Y	The norm matrixes, representing the norms of each elements in X_{spec} and Y_{spec}, respectively.
D_{fake}	The probability of misattribution that the discriminator regards the input stego-audio from the generator as a real audio
D_{real}	The probability that the discriminator regards the input real audio from the real dataset as a real audio
D_{fake}^{valid}	The probability of misattribution that the discriminator regards the input stego-audio from the generator as a real audio in the validation procedure
D_{real}^{valid}	The probability that the discriminator regards the input real audio from the validation dataset as a real audio
gp	The clipped gradient norm in the training dataset
gp^{valid}	The clipped gradient norm in the validation dataset

3.1. The Proposed Method

A complete steganography algorithm includes the process of hiding a secret and extracting a secret. Similarly, a complete coverless steganography algorithm also includes the generation module of the stego-audio and the extraction module of the secret messages. Therefore, the proposed model is divided into two subsections: the generation module and the reconstruction module. The entire model is illustrated in Figure 1. Furthermore, each module is introduced in detail from two perspectives: the function perspective and its network architecture perspective.

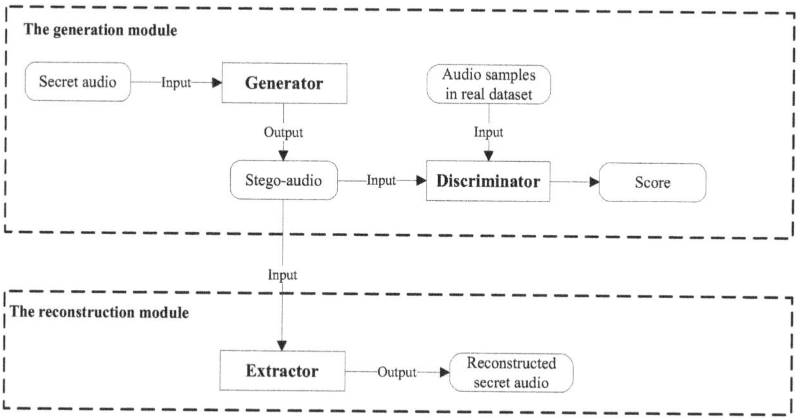

Figure 1. The model of the proposed steganography.

3.1.1. The Generation Module

In this paper, the stego-audios are expected to be generated directly. Therefore, the audio synthesis model WaveGAN is applied to the generation module, which consists of a generator and a discriminator, to generate stego-audios. However, it was improved as follows: First, instead of a noise being fed into the WaveGAN, a secret audio is input into the generator. Second, a post-processing layer is added after the generator. Consequently, the secret audio will be transformed into a stego-audio in our model.

At the same time, for the sake of security, an essential demand is that the feature distribution and the auditory characteristics of the stego-audio should be the same as the audios in the real dataset. In order to meet the above security requirements, the discriminator is used to guide the training of the generator to generate a more authentic stego-audio. When the stego-audio or real audio is input to the discriminator, the discriminant score will be obtained. Specifically, the stego-audio is input to the discriminator to output the probability D_{fake}, and the real audio is input to output the probability D_{real}. These two probabilities will be used to calculate the loss functions to optimize this model.

The design principle of the generation module is essentially audio generation, and the audio synthesis model WaveGAN is employed as the basis of the generation module to realize the generative steganography. The generator is composed of two parts: the core part and the post-processing part. The core part and the discriminator are based on the WaveGAN as shown in Figure 2. Since the audio signal is sequential, the WaveGAN model employs 1D convolution (Conv1d) to extract sequential features. The core part of the generator consists of a linear layer, five groups of transposed convolutions and their activation functions.

After the secret audio is input to the generator, the secret audio will be input to the post-processing part after passing through the core part to obtain the final stego-audio. The structure of the discriminator is in the opposite state to the core part of the generator. The discriminator is composed of five groups of Conv1d, a linear layer and the activation function between them. The discriminator introduces the phase shuffle operation after each activation function. The reason why phase shuffle is introduced is that the transposed convolution in the generator gives the generated stego-audio strong periodic information. Furthermore, the kind of periodic information makes the discriminator judge the authenticity of the stego-audio only through periodicity.

Consequently, the discriminator will not work well, and the generator cannot generate high-quality stego-audio. In order to solve the above problem, a phase-shuffling operation is added between each Conv1d to randomly change the phase of the audio, which can remove the periodic noise effect. Consequently, the discriminator can judge more accurately, and the audio generated by the generator sounds more realistic.

In this work, WaveGAN is used to directly generate stego-audio and realize coverless audio steganography. However, for the security of the steganography algorithm, it is necessary to guarantee the audio quality of the stego-audio first. Therefore, on the basis of using WaveGAN as the generation module, a post-processing layer is replenished to reduce the noise and improve the quality of the generated stego-audio. The post-processing part is supplied after the core part of the network structure in the generation module. Furthermore, it is composed of a Conv1d layer. Subsequent ablation experiment in Section 4.4 show that the post-processing layer effectively improves the audio quality of the generated stego-audio.

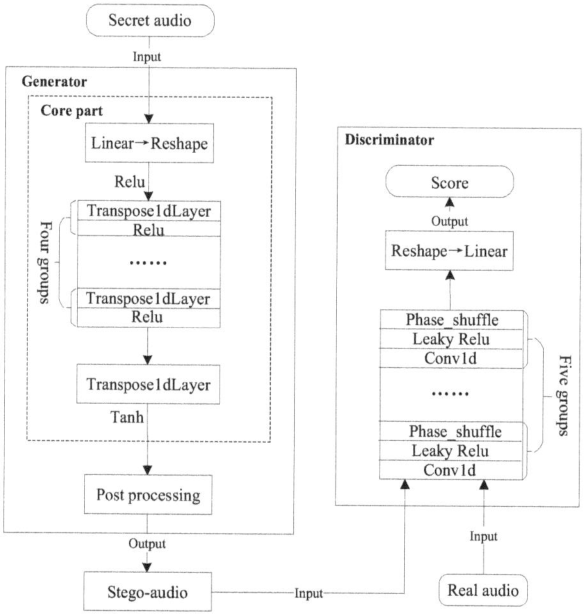

Figure 2. The generator and discriminator structure.

3.1.2. The Reconstruction Module

The reconstruction module is carefully designed as an extractor denoted as E. Its design principle is that the receiver directly inputs the stego-audios into the extractor to reconstruct the secret audios. In the scenario considered in this work, the receiver does not have prior knowledge of the original secret audio. Therefore, in the beginning, the reconstruction module should be trained until the reconstruction module can effectively reconstruct the complete secret audio. The sender and receiver share the trained model. After receiving the stego-audio, the receiver inputs it into the trained reconstruction module to obtain the secret audio. Therefore, unlike the traditional steganography, the proposed method does not need an extra secret key. In other words, for the steganography framework proposed in this paper, the received stego-audio itself is the key.

Its network structure is illustrated in Figure 3. The generated stego-audios are input into the extractor. This network includes five groups of convolution neural networks and a full connection layer. Each group consists of a Conv1d operation and a resolution block. The resolution block is a residual network structure consisting of four Dilated Conv1d layers and four Conv1d layers. The Dilated Conv1d in the resolution block can provide the different receptive fields. In addition, a residual network structure is used in the resolution block to learn the acoustic features of different frequency bands on the audio spectrum, which effectively reduces feature loss during training. Finally, a feature transformation is performed through the fully connected layer to obtain the final reconstructed secret audio.

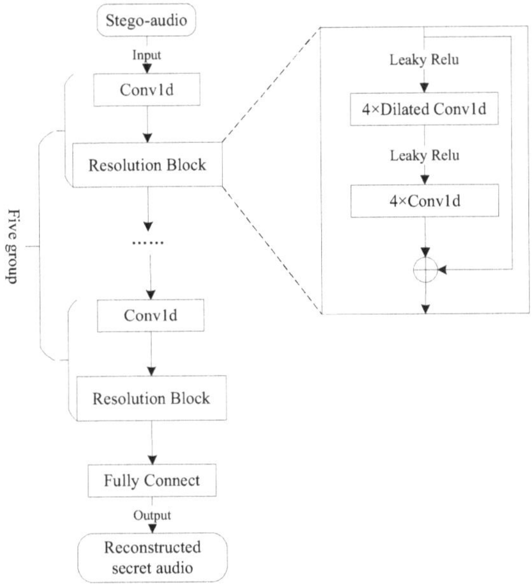

Figure 3. The extractor structure.

3.2. The Loss Function

In this paper, two types of loss functions are defined. One is only involved in backpropagation to guide the training; and the other is used to verify the results without participating in the backpropagation. Among them, four loss functions are defined to guide the model training, including L_D^{train}, D_{wass}^{train}, L_G, and L_{array}.

The first two loss functions (namely, L_D^{train} and D_{wass}^{train}) improve the discriminator to judge accurately; L_G guides the generator to generate more realistic stego-audios; and L_{array} ensures that the reconstructed secret audios by the extractor are less loss and more sound. At the same time, four loss functions are defined to verify the results—namely, L_D^{valid}, D_{wass}^{valid}, L_{mag}, and L_{sc}. L_D^{valid} and D_{wass}^{valid} are used to verify the distinctive ability of the discriminator, and L_{mag} and L_{sc} are employed to verify the reconstruction ability of the extractor. The above loss functions are described as follows in the module that they are located in.

In the generation module, the generator and the discriminator are trained iteratively. The generator is optimized by minimizing D_{fake} to make the generated stego-audio increasingly realistic, and its loss function is shown below:

$$L_G = -\left(D_{fake}\right) \tag{1}$$

For the discriminator, the generated stego-audio and the audio samples from the real dataset are fed at the same time. The same loss indicators as used in the WaveGAN are employed to optimize the discriminator, including D_{wass}^{train} and L_D^{train}, and they are calculated as follows:

$$L_D^{train} = D_{fake} - D_{real} + gp \tag{2}$$

$$D_{wass}^{train} = D_{real} - D_{fake} \tag{3}$$

The former minimizes the distribution difference between the generated stego-audio and the samples from the real dataset by minimizing the Wasserstein distance; the latter replaces the weight clipping in [40] and adds the gradient penalty [41] to strengthen the constraints to successfully train the model.

At the same time, the discriminator, as a steganalyzer, determines whether the input data is real audio or stego-audio, that is to say, the discriminator is used to determine whether the input data contains the secret or not. After the continuous optimization on the generator and the discriminator, the statistic features of the generated stego-audio are near to the real ones to such an extent that the steganalyzer cannot determine whether the input audio contains a secret.

In order to prevent the overfitting phenomenon, the following loss function is given to verify the distinctive ability of the discriminator

$$L_D^{valid} = D_{fake}^{valid} - D_{real}^{valid} + gp^{valid} \tag{4}$$

$$D_{wass}^{valid} = D_{real}^{valid} - D_{fake}^{valid} \tag{5}$$

During the training, after a batch of secret audios are fed into the generator, stego-audios are synthesized. In the reconstruction module, the stego-audios are fed into the extractor to reconstruct the secret audios. Every original secret audio has one corresponding reconstructed secret audio. Herein, the first extractor loss L_{array} is defined as the function (6), and it is used to optimize the extractor in the gradient back propagation.

$$L_{array} = \frac{1}{B \times M \times N} \sum_{b=1}^{B} \sum_{i=1}^{M} \sum_{j=1}^{N} |s_{ij} - E_{ij}(G(s))| \tag{6}$$

Herein, the secret audio and the reconstructed secret audio are represented in the form of multi-dimension arrays, and M and N represent the number of rows and columns of the array, respectively. M is the frame of the audio, N is the channel of the audio, and B is the batch size. s_{ij} represents the sampling value of the jth channel in the ith frame in the original secret audio; $E_{ij}(G(s))$ represents the element in the reconstructed secret audio extracted by the extractor E.

To further verify the integrity of the reconstructed secret audio, the following two loss indicators are defined, namely, L_{mag} and L_{sc}. The former is to evaluate the differences in amplitude, and the latter is to evaluate the differences in the frequency domain. In addition, they are only verification indicators and do not participate in the gradient back propagation.

$$X = ||X_{spec}|| \tag{7}$$

$$Y = ||Y_{spec}|| \tag{8}$$

$$L_{mag} = \frac{1}{B} \sum_{b=1}^{B} \left| \log_e^{Y_b} - \log_e^{X_b} \right| \tag{9}$$

where X_{spec} and Y_{spec} represent the matrix obtained by short-time Fourier transform of the secret audio and the reconstructed secret audio, respectively. X and Y are the norm matrix, whose values are the norms of the corresponding elements in X_{spec} and Y_{spec}, respectively.

$$L_{sc} = \sum_{b=1}^{B} \frac{\sqrt{\sum_i \sum_j \left(Y_{b,i,j} - X_{b,i,j}\right)^2}}{\sqrt{\sum_i \sum_j \left(Y_{b,i,j}\right)^2}} \tag{10}$$

where $X_{b,i,j}$ is the element in X. Concretely, $X_{b,i,j}$ represents the value of the element whose time is i and frequency is j in the bth audio. Similarly, $Y_{b,i,j}$ represents an element in Y.

The whole training process is shown in the following pseudocode marked as Algorithm 1.

Algorithm 1 The training process of the proposed model.

Initialize the real dataset R and the secret dataset S, Batch size B;
Initialize the generator net G with random θ_g;
Initialize the discriminator net D with random θ_d;
Initialize the extractor net E with random θ_e;
for each training iteration **do**
    Sample a batch of real data (denoted as r) from R;
    Sample a batch of secret data (denoted as s^d) from S;
    Obtain fake audio $G(s^d)$ by inputting s^d to *Generator*;
    Obtain D_{fake} by inputting fake audio $G(s^d)$ to *Discriminator*;
    Update *Discriminator* parameters θ_d by minimizing:
        $\tilde{V} = \frac{1}{B}\sum_{i=1}^{B} \log D(r_i) + \frac{1}{B}\sum_{i=1}^{B} \log(1 - D(fake_i))$,
        $\theta_d \leftarrow \theta_d + \eta \nabla \tilde{V}(\theta_d)$
    Sample another batch of secret data (denoted as s^g) from S;
    Update *Generator* parameters θ_g by minimizing:
        $\tilde{V} = \frac{1}{B}\sum_{i=1}^{B} \log\left(1 - D\left(G\left(s_i^g\right)\right)\right)$,
        $\theta_g \leftarrow \theta_g + \eta \nabla \tilde{V}(\theta_g)$
    Freeze *Generator* parameters θ_g and *Discriminator* parameters θ_d;
    Sample another batch of secret data (denoted as s^c) from S;
    Update *extractor* parameters θ_e by minimizing:
        $L_{array} = \frac{1}{B \times M \times N} \sum_{b=1}^{B} \sum_{i=1}^{M} \sum_{j=1}^{N} |s_{ij}^e - E_{ij}(G(s^e))|$
        $\theta_e \leftarrow \theta_e + \eta \nabla L_{array}(\theta_e)$
end for

4. The Experiments and Analysis

In this section, extensive experiments are presented to verify the effectiveness of our method. The proposed method was implemented using PyTorch1.18.0 and trained on NVIDIA RTX2080 Ti GPUs, with a total of 500 training epochs. The parameter settings of the proposed method is shown in Table 3.

Table 3. Parameter settings.

Generator	Value	Discriminator	Value	Extractor	Value
TransposeConv1d Layer	5	Conv1d Layer	5	Conv1d Layer	5
Upsample Factor	4	PhaseShuffle Layer	4	Resolution Block	5
Stride	1	PhaseShuffle Factor	0.2	Dilated Conv1d Layer	4
Learning Rate	1×10^{-4}	Learning Rate	1×10^{-4}	Learning Rate	1×10^{-4}

Two kinds of datasets are required to train our model: the secret audios and the real dataset. The SC09 dataset was taken as the secret audios. The SC09 dataset is a subset of the Speech Commands Dataset [42], which contains 0∼9 monophonic voice commands of various male and female voices, and the duration of each voice command is one second. The sampling rate of the SC09 dataset was degraded from 16,000 to 8000.

A subset [43] of the Xeno Canto [44] bird sound dataset was modified as the real dataset, which contains 88 kinds of bird songs. In order to save computing resources, the modifications were performed as follows: (1) convert the original flac files into wav files; (2) crop them into two-second bird sound audios and filter out the cropped blank audios; and (3) modify the original sampling rate from 44,100 to 8000.

A total of 800 secret audios and 1600 real audios were randomly chosen for training in the whole experiment. Additionally, the training dataset, test dataset, and validation dataset are split into an 80:10:10 ratio.

4.1. Model Performance

The loss function used in the training process of the model is mentioned above, and the experimental results are shown in Figures 4 and 5. Figure 4 shows the changes in various loss indicators for the generator and the discriminator. Figure 5 displays the changes in various loss indicators for the extractor. It can be seen from the above two figures that, with the increase of the training epochs, the values of each loss indicator tend to be stable. This shows that the model can converge well. On the premise of the convergence performance, analysis was performed on the steganography performance and the reconstructed secret audios.

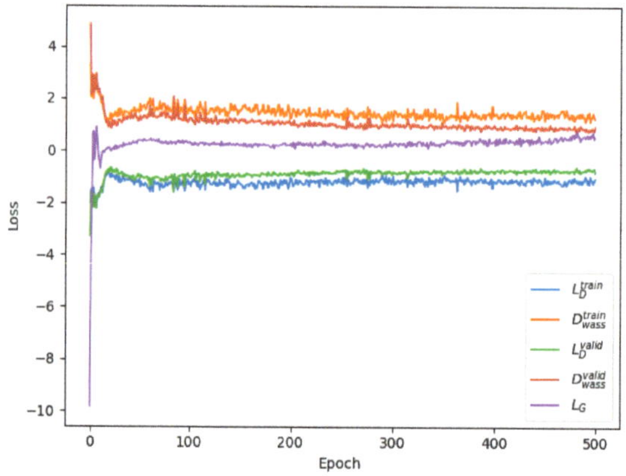

Figure 4. The changes of the loss indicators for the generator and discriminator.

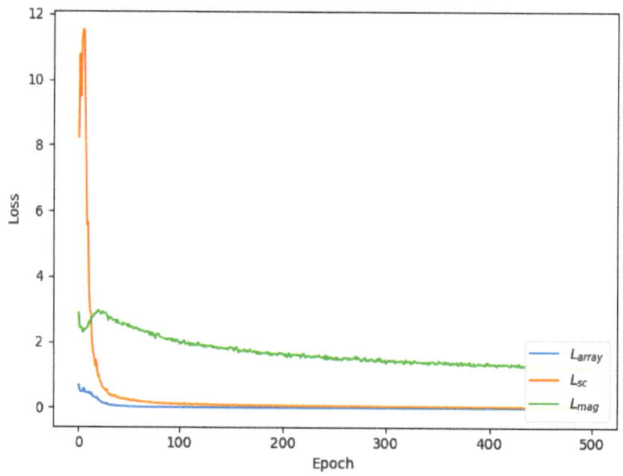

Figure 5. The changes of the loss indicators for the extractor.

4.2. Analysis on the Steganography Performance

4.2.1. The Steganographic Capacity

Steganographic capacity refers to the maximum number of bits that can hide secret messages in a digital cover under the precondition that it cannot be detected. In the proposed coverless steganography method, a two-second stego-audio is generated by the generator driven by a one-second secret audio. Furthermore, different from the previous steganography, the form of the secret in the proposed method is audio. In this section, the steganographic capacity of this method is calculated from the following two perspectives: one is a general method from the size perspective; the other is calculated from the semantic perspective.

From the first perspective, two-second stego-audio is generated directly driven by one-second secret audio, and the ratio of their time lengths between the secret audio and the generated stego-audio can be used to calculate the steganographic capacity. In the proposed method, the read secret audio is fed into the generator in the form of an array, and the stego-audio is also generated in the form of an array.

The ratio between the length of the secret audio array and the length of the generated stego-audio array can also be used to indirectly measure its steganographic capacity. After experimental measurement, the length of the secret audio array to be hidden is 8192, and the length of the generated stego-audio array is 16,384. Consequently, from this perspective, the ratio of the above two methods is 50%. As a result, the proposed method has a high capacity according to this measure indicator.

Although the secret message is transmitted in the form of audio, what is transmitted in essence is the semantic content in the secret audio. From the second perspective, the semantic content in the secret audio should be extracted, and its bit-length is calculated as its steganographic capacity. In this experiment, the duration of each secret audio is one-second, and the semantic content is the speech command of 0∼9. The semantic content that needs to be transmitted is uncertain. Thus, we need to calculate the semantic content that can be generally transmitted in one second. This is expressed in letters in English and similar languages or in alternate characters or digits in other languages.

The following takes secret messages in English as an example. The number of letters can be an indicator of the steganography capacity. It is found that the average speaking speed of British English reaches 198 words per minute [45]. Average word lengths were computed in the range of 6.665∼11.14 [46]. According to ASCII or UTF-8 encoding rules, an English letter is equal to 8 bits. Therefore, it can be concluded that the words that can be speech per minute occupy an average of about 1320∼2206 bits. As a result, it can be calculated that 22∼37 bits of semantic content can be transmitted in a one-second audio.

4.2.2. The Audio Quality

In the proposed method, the stego-audio is generated directly. It must be ensured that the generated stego-audios are acoustically indistinguishable from the natural audios. Therefore, a subjective indicator, MOS (Mean Opinion Score) [47], was chosen to measure the quality of the generated stego-audio. It adopts five levels to evaluate the quality of the tested speech. Thirty listeners were selected to rate the generated stego-audio. Before that, each listener was required to listen to a series of audio samples from the real dataset to ensure that they have the same standard as much as possible.

Ten stego-audios were selected randomly for the experiment. Each listener listened to the ten audios and gave a score. Thus, each stego-audio received 30 scores from 30 different listeners. Finally, the average score of each stego-audio was calculated in turn, and these are listed in Table 4. This shows that the generated stego-audio had high quality and low distortion. The average MOS of the above stego-audios was further calculated as 4.15, indicating that it is not easy for third parties to detect the existence of the secret message.

Table 4. The average MOS of ten randomly selected stego-audios generated by this model with a post-processing layer.

The Stego-Audios	1	2	3	4	5	6	7	8	9	10
The average MOS	4.13	4.09	4.17	4.09	4.21	4.12	4.25	4.14	4.01	4.30

4.2.3. The Authenticity in Statistical Characteristics

In order to prevent third parties from detecting the presence of the secret message, it is necessary to ensure not only the speech quality of the generated stego-audio but also its authenticity compared with the real audio. Therefore, in this section, two different methods were meticulously designed to verify the authenticity of the generated stego-audio in terms of the statistical characteristics.

Kernel Density Estimation

The GAN makes it impossible to find the real audio in the real dataset corresponding to a given stego-audio. That is to say, there is no one-to-one relationship between a stego-audio and a real audio. Kernel Density Estimation (KDE) is usually used to estimate the unknown density function in the probability theory, which is one nonparametric test method. The distribution of the sample data itself can be seen intuitively through the kernel density estimation diagram. Therefore, KDE is employed to calculate the distribution of the generated stego-audios and real audios.

To calculate their sample value distribution, ten audios were randomly selected from the generated stego-audios and real audios, respectively. The statistical results are shown in Figures 6 and 7. It can be seen in the figures that the generated stego-audios and real audios have very similar distributions. Therefore, the conclusion can be drawn that the generated stego-audios and the real audios have the same statistical distribution.

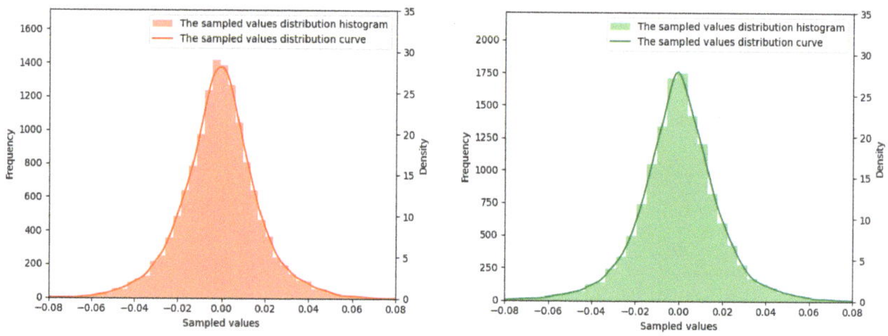

Figure 6. The sample value distribution comparison. On the left is the distribution curve and histogram of the sample values in the real audios, where the x-axis represents random variables, the left y-axis represents the frequency, and the right y-axis represents the density which is calculated as multiplying the frequency by the group distance. The same is true on the right for the stego-audios.

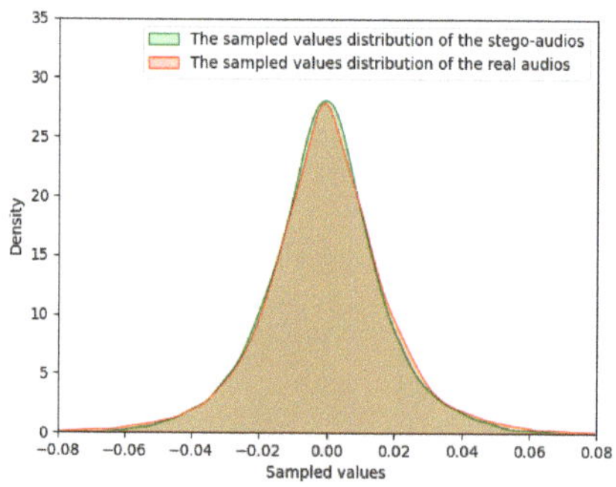

Figure 7. The distributions of the stego-audios and real audio samples.

The Euclidean Distances between the MFCCs

The human auditory system is a special nonlinear system, and its sensitivity to different frequency signals is different from these. The nonlinear representation of the MFCC (Mel Frequency Cepstrum Coefficient) can well reflect the specific features of audio. The Euclidean distance between the MFCCs of the two audios can reflect the difference between them.

Furthermore, the Euclidean distance between the MFCCs of the generated stego-audio and its most similar audio in the real dataset can reflect the authenticity of the generated stego-audio. Therefore, the nearest neighbor in the training dataset for each generated stego-audio was found, and the Euclidean distances between the MFCCs were calculated. In order to verify the effectiveness of the nearest neighbor in the training dataset, the nearest neighbor in the test dataset for each generated stego-audio was found again, and the Euclidean distances between the MFCCs were calculated.

Then, we compared the Euclidean distances between the MFCCs of each generated stego-audio with its nearest neighbors in the training dataset and test dataset to verify the authenticity of the generated stego-audios. The experimental steps are briefly described as follows:

(1) Calculate the Euclidean distances between the MFCCs of each stego-audio and all real audio samples in the training dataset in turn, denoted as MD^{train}, which is a matrix of size $m * n$. m and n denote the number of stego-audios and real audio samples in the training dataset, respectively. Each element $MD_{ij}^{train}(i \in \{1, ..., m\}, j \in \{1, ..., n\})$ of the matrix represents the Euclidean distance between the MFCCs of the ith stego-audio and the jth real audio sample in the training dataset. Find the minimum value of each row in the matrix MD^{train}, denoted as MD_{min}^{train}, which is a matrix of size $m * 1$. This step is illustrated in Figure 8. Consequently, we find the most similar audio samples for each stego-audio from the training dataset. In other words, the nearest neighbors from the training dataset for each stego-audio are found.

(2) Calculate the Euclidean distances between the MFCCs of each stego-audio and all real audio samples in the test dataset, denoted as MD^{test}, which is a matrix of size $m * t$. t is the number of audio samples in the test dataset. Each element $MD_{ij}^{test}(i \in \{1, \ldots, m\}, j \in \{1, \ldots, t\})$ of the matrix represents the Euclidean distance between the MFCCs of the ith stego-audio and the jth real audio sample in the test dataset. Find the minimum value of each row in the matrix MD^{test}, marked as MD_{min}^{test}, which is a matrix of size $m * 1$. This step is illustrated in Figure 9. Therefore, we find the most similar audio samples for each stego-audio from the test dataset. In other words, the nearest neighbors from the test dataset for each stego-audio are found.

(3) Compare the values of the corresponding elements in the MD_{min}^{train} and MD_{min}^{test}.

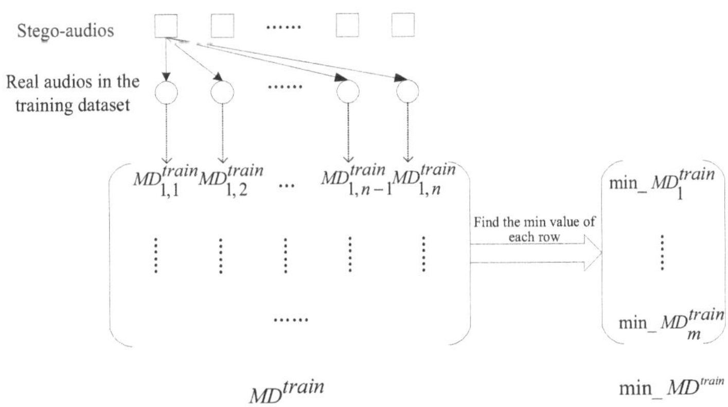

Figure 8. Illustration of Step (1).

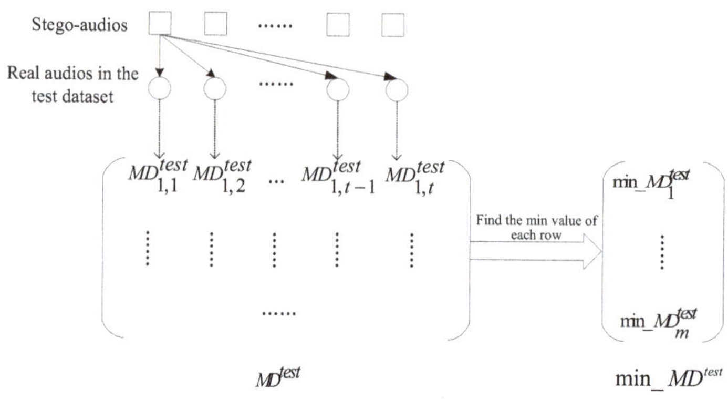

Figure 9. Illustration of Step (2).

As shown in Figure 10, the green and red curves represent the MD^{train}_{min} and MD^{test}_{min}, respectively. Furthermore, the different values between their corresponding elements in MD^{train}_{min} and MD^{test}_{min} are shown in the blue curve of Figure 10. It can be seen from Figure 10 that the Euclidean distances between the MFCCs of each stego-audio and its nearest neighbor in the training dataset are basically the same as the Euclidean distances between the MFCCs of its nearest neighbor in the test dataset. The different values of their Euclidean distances between the MFCCs are very small.

This shows that the generated stego-audios have great similarity with the real audios. Consequently, the generated stego-audio is very real, and it is not easy for a third party to detect the existence of a secret by detecting the particularity of the generated stego-audio. In addition, the similarity of the distances between the MFCCs of the stego-audio and the nearest neighbors in the training dataset and test dataset can also indicate that there is no overfitting in this model.

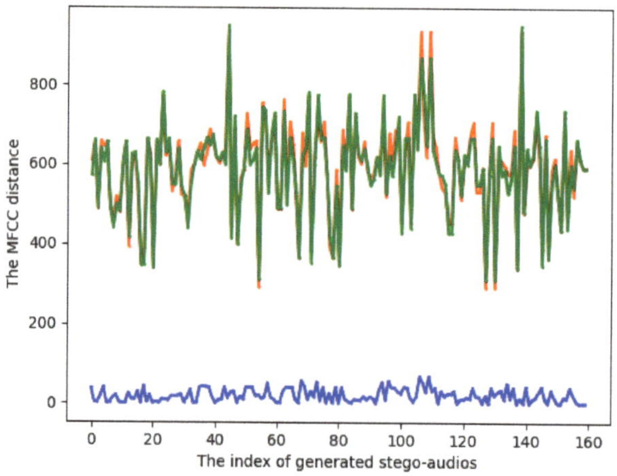

Figure 10. The Euclidean distances between the MFCCs of each stego-audio and the nearest neighbor in the training dataset as well as its nearest neighbor in the test dataset.

4.2.4. Steganalysis

To verify that the proposed method is fundamentally resistant to detection by existing steganalysis methods, we used the trained steganalysis methods Chen-Net [48] and Lin-Net [49] to directly detect the generated stego-audios. Furthermore, we compared the accuracy with three different audio steganographies: The traditional steganography method [50] refers to a modified audio steganography that embeds a secret in the cover.

The method based on generating a cover [10] refers to audio steganography that embeds a secret in the generated cover. The proposed method refers to audio steganography that directly generates the stego-audio. As shown in Table 5, the accuracy of the method based on generating the cover is significantly lower than the traditional method, and the trained steganalysis methods fail to detect this proposed method. Therefore, our method is fundamentally resistant to detection by steganalysis methods.

Table 5. The accuracy of steganalysis detection with the different steganography algorithms under different embedding rates.

Steganography Methods	Steganalysis Methods	Embedding Rates			
		0.1	**0.2**	**0.3**	**0.5**
Traditional method	Chen-Net	50.00	56.95	63.28	69.77
	Lin-Net	57.34	64.06	67.93	74.13
Based on generating a cover	Chen-Net	48.14	51.29	57.34	61.25
	Lin-Net	49.03	52.33	59.43	64.39
The proposed method	Chen-Net	50.00	50.00	50.00	50.00
	Lin-Net	50.00	50.00	50.00	50.00

4.3. Analysis on the Reconstructed Secret Audio

4.3.1. On the Auditory

In the proposed algorithm, the type of secret messages is audio, and the secret is reconstructed by neural networks, which might make the reconstructed secret audios distorted. This distortion may affect the transmission of secret audios on the audio. Therefore, this distortion can be measured by comparing the difference between the secret audios to be hidden and the reconstructed secret audios. In this section, two methods are used to compare the differences between them. One is to employ the various loss indicators of the extractor. The other is to use various spectrograms to visually compare differences.

In the process of model training, the secret audio to be hidden and the reconstructed secret audio were guaranteed to have a one-to-one correspondence. Therefore, the differences between them are compared by calculating the L_{array}, which can reflect the distortion degree of the reconstructed secret audios in the time domain. In addition, based on the above information, L_{mag} can reflect the differences between the secret audio and the reconstructed secret audio in amplitude, and L_{sc} can reflect their differences in the frequency spectrum. Figure 5 shows that, with the increase of training epochs, these three loss values are all close to 0. This indicates that the difference between them becomes very little. It can be stated that the extractor successfully reconstructs the secret audio with little distortion. Due to the large redundancy of the audio, it is verified that the secret audios can be transmitted completely through audio.

In order to further observe the differences between them, different forms of spectrograms are used for comparison. Figures 11–13 show the comparison results of two groups of secret audio and reconstructed secret audio, respectively. Furthermore, in Figures 11–13, the upper and lower lines are a group of secret audios and the reconstructed secret audios, respectively. It can be seen from Figures 11–13 that there is a small gap between them. Furthermore, this gap is caused by the subtle noise of the reconstructed secret audios. As audios have some redundancy, the secret audios can still be transmitted integrally on audio.

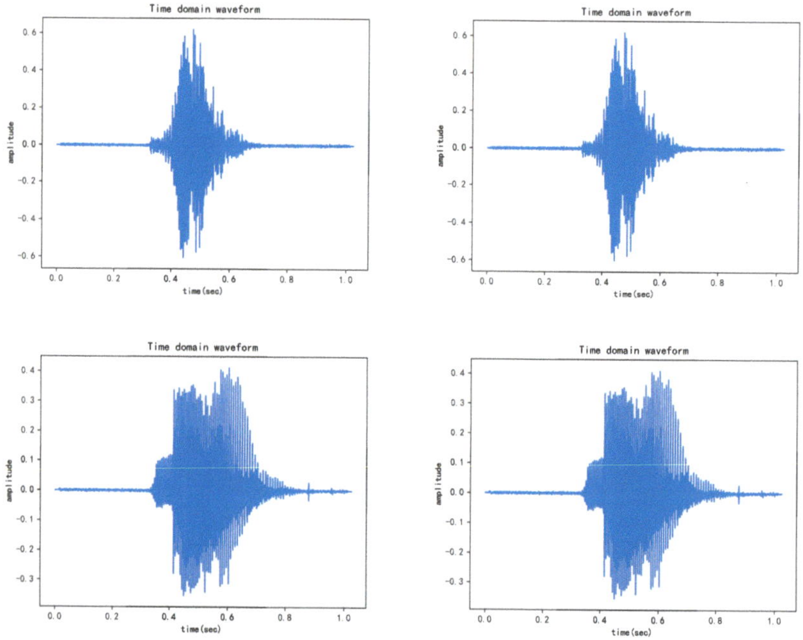

Figure 11. The time-domain waveform. The left column is the time-domain waveform of the secret audios, and the right column is the time-domain waveform of the reconstructed secret audios.

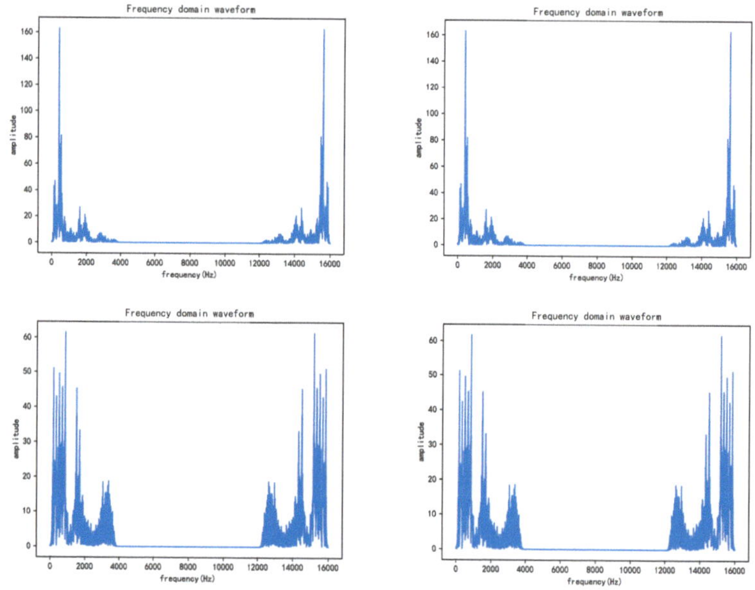

Figure 12. The frequency-domain waveform. The left column is the frequency-domain waveform of the secret audios, and the right column is the frequency-domain waveform of the reconstructed secret audios.

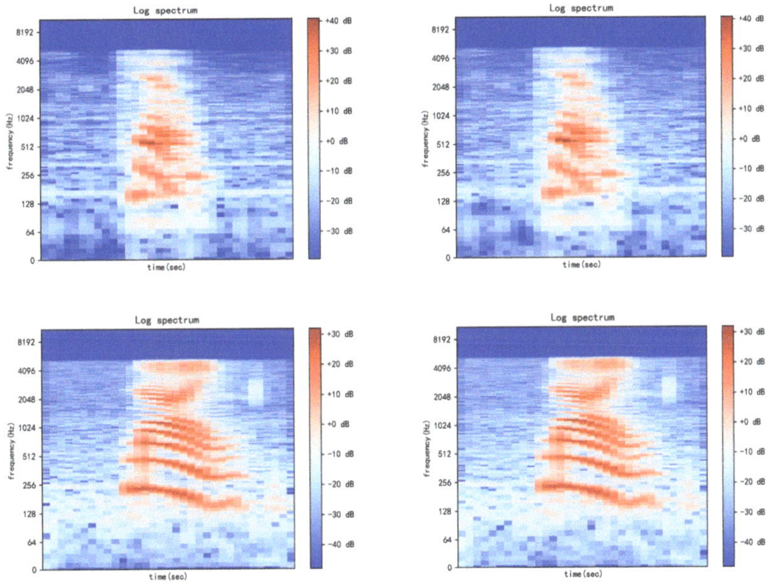

Figure 13. The log spectrogram. The left column is the log spectrogram of the secret audios, and the right column is log spectrogram of the reconstructed secret audios.

4.3.2. On the Semantics

In essence, the ultimate goal of reconstructing the secret audios is to recover their complete secret semantics. As mentioned above, the reconstructed secret audios have some slight distortion, which likely affects the complete semantic transmission of a secret. In this section, we verify that this method guarantees the semantic transmission of the secret audios. These experiments are conducted from the following two perspectives: One is to use the STOI (Short Time Objective Intelligibility) indicator to test the degree that the reconstructed secret audios can be fully understood. Another is to use speech recognition methods to test the probability that the semantics in the reconstructed secret audios can be correctly recognized.

STOI is one of the important indicators to measure speech intelligibility. A word in a speech signal can only be understood or not. From this perspective, it can be considered that the intelligibility is binary; thus, the value range of STOI is quantified between 0 and 1. STOI represents whether a word can be understood correctly, and a value of 1 indicates that the speech can be fully understood [51].

Since the audios have some redundancy, the reconstructed secret audios are allowed to be distorted; however, it is necessary to ensure that the receivers can understand them. Accordingly, the STOI indicator was chosen to verify the integrity of the reconstructed secret audios. In this experiment, twenty-four reconstructed secret audios were randomly selected to detect their STOI values, and the results are shown in Table 6. The calculations show that the average STOI was 0.9887, indicating that the reconstructed secret audios can be understood well and completely transmitted with semantics.

Table 6. The STOI values of the reconstructed secret audios.

Number	1	2	3	4	5	6	7	8
STOI	0.9993	0.9495	0.9990	0.9885	0.9860	0.9948	0.9972	0.9554
Number	9	10	11	12	13	14	15	16
STOI	0.9642	0.9745	0.9990	0.9981	0.9999	0.9991	0.9994	0.9983
Number	17	18	19	20	21	22	23	24
STOI	0.9998	0.9841	0.9457	0.9996	0.9995	0.9992	0.9999	0.9979

From the second perspective, the speech recognition method was used to detect the specific semantic information of the reconstructed secret audios. In this experiment, sixty-four reconstructed secret audios were randomly selected, and speech recognition was performed on them. Two speech recognition tools were chosen: Speech Recognition-PocketSphinx [52] and Google Cloud Speech API [53]. The speech recognition accuracy rate is defined as the following formula. Table 7 shows the accuracy rate of the secret audio using the above speech recognition tools. Table 7 explains that the semantic information of all the reconstructed secret audios was correctly identified. As a result, the proposed method realized the complete semantic transmission of the secret messages.

$$Accuracy = \frac{C}{T} \times 100\% \tag{11}$$

where C is the number of correctly recognized audios and T is the total number of detected audios.

Table 7. The speech recognition accuracy under different speech recognition APIs.

Speech Recognition Tools	Accuracy
Speech Recognition-PocketSphinx	100%
Google Cloud Speech API	100%

4.4. Ablation Experiment

A post-processing layer was added to solve the noise problem in the generated stego-audios in this model. Therefore, it was necessary that ablation experiments were conducted to demonstrate the effectiveness. The speech quality of the generated stego-audio was tested using the same method as in Section 4.2.2 when the post-processing layer was not added. The ten stego-audios generated by this model without the post-processing layer were selected randomly for the experiment. The average MOS values of these ten stego-audios are listed in Table 8.

Compared with Table 4, it can be seen that the average MOS of the generated stego-audios with a post-processing layer had better voice quality. In addition, the average MOS of all the stego-audios without a post-processing layer was calculated as 3.52, and the average MOS of all the stego-audios with a post-processing layer was calculated as 4.15 as shown in Table 9. Apparently, the post-processing layer effectively solved the noise problem and improved the speech quality.

Table 8. The average MOS of ten randomly selected stego-audios generated by this model without a post-processing layer.

The Stego-Audios	1	2	3	4	5	6	7	8	9	10
Their average MOS	3.70	3.51	3.65	3.54	3.38	3.49	3.47	3.42	3.43	3.56

Table 9. The MOS ablation experiment for a post-processing layer.

The Post-Processing Layer	Yes	No
MOS	4.15	3.52

4.5. Robustness Experiment

The stego-audio may be jammed during transmission in the public channel; thus, the received audio may contain some extra noises, which might lead to the reconstruction failure of a secret audio. Therefore, it is necessary to evaluate the robustness of the proposed model. The experimental settings were as follows. Thirty-two stego-audios were randomly selected for the robustness testing. Every stego-audio with superposed noises of 5, 10, 15, and 20 db was sent to the extractor, respectively, and 128 audios were reconstructed.

We performed speech recognition on these 128 reconstructed secret audios using the same speech recognition methods as in Section 4.3.2. The speech recognition accuracy rate defined in Equation (11) was also employed here. The experimental results are shown in Table 10. It can be seen in the table that additional noises added to stego-audios did not affect the reconstruction of the secret audios. In other words, even if a stego-audio is jammed to some extent, the receiver can still completely recover the meaning of the secret audio. Thus, the result states that the proposed method has good robustness.

Table 10. The speech recognition accuracy.

Speech Recognition Method	Accuracy				
	0 db	5 db	10 db	15 db	20 db
Speech Recognition-PocketSphinx	100%	100%	100%	100%	100%
Google Cloud Speech API	100%	100%	100%	100%	100%

5. Summary

In this paper, we proposed a new coverless audio steganography method. This is the first work that directly generates stego-audio in audio steganography. The covert communication of the proposed method demonstrated good reliability and security. Experimental and theoretical analysis shows that this proposed method not only has high security and undetectability but also guarantees the complete semantic transmission of secret audio even in the case of distortion.

However, there are still some shortcomings. First, this work considered an idealized scenario in which the sender shares the network model with the receiver, and this premise is a great challenge in reality. In addition, the generation module and the reconstruction module need prior knowledge of the secret audio. If a new secret audio is given, the proposed method needs be further trained on the original basis. Therefore, in future work, we plan to propose a model-free audio steganography framework that can achieve audio steganography from both the time and frequency domains.

Author Contributions: Conceptualization, J.L. and K.W.; methodology, J.L. and K.W.; software, J.L.; validation, J.L. and K.W.; investigation, J.L.; data curation, J.L.; writing—original draft preparation, J.L.; writing—review and editing, K.W.; supervision, K.W. and X.J.; project administration, K.W. and X.J. All authors have read and agreed to the published version of the manuscript.

Funding: This paper is supported by the Public Sector Support Project of Science and Technology Plan of Shinan District, Qingdao City (Grant No. 2022-2-025-XX).

Conflicts of Interest: The authors declare no conflict of interest.

References

1. Xiao, B.; Huang, Y.; Tang, S. An approach to information hiding in low bit-rate speech stream. In Proceedings of the IEEE GLOBECOM 2008—2008 IEEE Global Telecommunications Conference, New Orleans, LA, USA, 30 November–4 December 2008; IEEE: New York, NY, USA, 2008; pp. 1–5.
2. Wang, T.; Wang, K. Information hiding method based on short video classification and duration. *J. Qingdao Univ. Nat. Sci. Ed.* **2021**, *34*, 6.
3. Hu, Y.; Huang, Y.; Yang, Z.; Huang, Y. Detection of heterogeneous parallel steganography for low bit-rate VoIP speech streams. *Neurocomputing* **2021**, *419*, 70–79. [CrossRef]
4. Wang, Y.; Guo, L.; Wei, Y.; Wang, C. A steganography method for aac audio based on escape sequences. In Proceedings of the 2010 International Conference on Multimedia Information Networking and Security, Nanjing, China, 4–6 November 2010; IEEE: New York, NY, USA, 2010; pp. 841–845.
5. Wei, Z.; Wang, K. Lightweight AAC Audio Steganalysis Model Based on ResNeXt. *Wirel. Commun. Mob. Comput.* **2022**, *2022*, 9074771. [CrossRef]
6. Goodfellow, I.; Pouget-Abadie, J.; Mirza, M.; Xu, B.; Warde-Farley, D.; Ozair, S.; Courville, A.; Bengio, Y. Generative adversarial nets. *arXiv* **2014**, arXiv:1406.2661.
7. Wu, J.; Chen, B.; Luo, W.; Fang, Y. Audio steganography based on iterative adversarial attacks against convolutional neural networks. *IEEE Trans. Inf. Forensics Secur.* **2020**, *15*, 2282–2294. [CrossRef]
8. Ye, D.; Jiang, S.; Huang, J. Heard more than heard: An audio steganography method based on gan. *arXiv* **2019**, arXiv:1907.04986.
9. Yang, J.; Zheng, H.; Kang, X.; Shi, Y.Q. Approaching optimal embedding in audio steganography with GAN. In Proceedings of the ICASSP 2020—2020 IEEE International Conference on Acoustics, Speech and Signal Processing (ICASSP), Barcelona, Spain, 4–8 May 2020; IEEE: New York, NY, USA, 2020; pp. 2827–2831.
10. Chen, L.; Wang, R.; Yan, D.; Wang, J. Learning to generate steganographic cover for audio steganography using gan. *IEEE Access* **2021**, *9*, 88098–88107. [CrossRef]
11. Yue, F.; Zhu, H.; Su, Z.; Zhang, G. An Adaptive Audio Steganography Using BN Optimizing SNGAN. *Chin. J. Comput.* **2022**, *45*, 427–440.
12. Wang, J.; Wang, R.; Dong, L.; Yan, D. Robust, Imperceptible and End-to-End Audio Steganography Based on CNN. In Proceedings of the Security and Privacy in Digital Economy: First International Conference, SPDE 2020, Quzhou, China, 30 October–1 November 2020; Springer: Berlin/Heidelberg, Germany, 2020; pp. 427–442.
13. Ren, Y.; Liu, D.; Xiong, Q.; Fu, J.; Wang, L. Spec-resnet: A general audio steganalysis scheme based on deep residual network of spectrogram. *arXiv* **2019**, arXiv:1901.06838.
14. Zhu, J.; Wang, R.; Yan, D. The sign bits of huffman codeword-based steganography for aac audio. In Proceedings of the 2010 International Conference on Multimedia Technology, Ningbo, China, 29–31 October 2010; IEEE: New York, NY, USA, 2010; pp. 1–4.
15. Wang, Y.; Yang, K.; Yi, X.; Zhao, X.; Xu, Z. CNN-based steganalysis of MP3 steganography in the entropy code domain. In Proceedings of the Proceedings of the sixth ACM Workshop on Information Hiding and Multimedia Security, Innsbruck, Austria, 20–22 June 2018; pp. 55–65.
16. Wang, Y.J.; Guo, L.; Wang, C.P. Steganography method for advanced audio coding. *J. Chin. Comput. Syst.* **2011**, *32*, 1465–1468.
17. Ren, Y.; Liu, D.; Liu, C.; Xiong, Q.; Fu, J.; Wang, L. A Universal Audio Steganalysis Scheme based on Multiscale Spectrograms and DeepResNet. *IEEE Trans. Dependable Secur. Comput.* **2022**, *20*, 665–679. [CrossRef]
18. Qin, J.; Wang, J.; Tan, Y.; Huang, H.; Xiang, X.; He, Z. Coverless Image Steganography Based on Generative Adversarial Network. *Mathematics* **2020**, *8*, 1394. [CrossRef]
19. Donahue, C.; McAuley, J.; Puckette, M. Adversarial audio synthesis. *arXiv* **2018**, arXiv:1802.04208.
20. Wang, Y. Research on the Mechanism and Key Technology of Audio Steganalysis. Ph.D. Thesis, University of Science and Technology of China, Hefei, Anhui, 2011.
21. Balgurgi, P.P.; Jagtap, S.K. Audio steganography used for secure data transmission. In *Proceedings of the International Conference on Advances in Computing*; Springer: Berlin/Heidelberg, Germany, 2013; pp. 699–706.
22. Erfani, Y.; Siahpoush, S. Robust audio watermarking using improved TS echo hiding. *Digit. Signal Process.* **2009**, *19*, 809–814. [CrossRef]
23. Dutta, H.; Das, R.K.; Nandi, S.; Prasanna, S.M. An overview of digital audio steganography. *IETE Tech. Rev.* **2020**, *37*, 632–650. [CrossRef]
24. Sun, X.; Wang, K.; Li, S. Audio steganography with less modification to the optimal matching CNV-QIM path with the minimal hamming distance expected value to a secret. *Multimed. Syst.* **2021**, *27*, 341–352. [CrossRef]
25. Gang, L.; Akansu, A.N.; Ramkumar, M. MP3 resistant oblivious steganography. In Proceedings of the 2001 IEEE International Conference on Acoustics, Speech, and Signal Processing, Salt Lake City, UT, USA, 7–11 May 2001; Proceedings (Cat. No. 01CH37221); IEEE: New York, NY, USA, 2001; Volume 3, pp. 1365–1368.
26. Ma, Y.; Han, J. Audio watermarking in the DCT domain: Embedding strategies and algorithms. *Acta Electron. Sin.* **2006**, *34*, 1260–1264.
27. Sheikhan, M.; Asadollahi, K.; Shahnazi, R. Improvement of embedding capacity and quality of DWT-based audio steganography systems. *World Appl. Sci. J.* **2011**, *13*, 507–516.

28. Ru, X. Research on Audio Steganography and Analysis Technology. PhD Thesis, Zhejiang University, Hangzhou, China, 2006.
29. Yu, L.; Zhang, W.; Wang, J.; Yu, Y. Seqgan: Sequence generative adversarial nets with policy gradient. In Proceedings of the AAAI Conference on Artificial Intelligence, San Francisco, CA, USA 4–9 February 2017; Volume 31.
30. Chen, J.; Zhang, Z.; Xie, X.; Li, Y.; Xu, T.; Ma, K.; Zheng, Y. Beyond Mutual Information: Generative Adversarial Network for Domain Adaptation Using Information Bottleneck Constraint. *IEEE Trans. Med. Imaging* **2021**, *41*, 595–607. [CrossRef]
31. Volkhonskiy, D.; Nazarov, I.; Burnaev, E. Steganographic generative adversarial networks. In Proceedings of the Twelfth International Conference on Machine Vision (ICMV 2019), Amsterdam, Netherlands, 16–18 November 2019; SPIE: Washington, DC, USA, 2020; Volume 11433, pp. 991–1005.
32. Yang, J.; Ruan, D.; Huang, J.; Kang, X.; Shi, Y.Q. An embedding cost learning framework using GAN. *IEEE Trans. Inf. Forensics Secur.* **2019**, *15*, 839–851. [CrossRef]
33. Liu, M.m.; Zhang, M.q.; Liu, J.; Zhang, Y.n.; Ke, Y. Coverless information hiding based on generative adversarial networks. *arXiv* **2017**, arXiv:1712.06951.
34. Duan, X.; Song, H. Coverless information hiding based on generative model. *arXiv* **2018**, arXiv:1802.03528.
35. Li, Q.; Wang, X.; Wang, X.; Ma, B.; Wang, C.; Shi, Y. An encrypted coverless information hiding method based on generative models. *Inf. Sci.* **2021**, *553*, 19–30. [CrossRef]
36. Lin, J.; Li, Y.; Yang, G. FPGAN: Face de-identification method with generative adversarial networks for social robots. *Neural Netw.* **2021**, *133*, 132–147. [CrossRef]
37. Kim, J.H.; Lee, S.H.; Lee, J.H.; Lee, S.W. Fre-GAN: Adversarial frequency-consistent audio synthesis. *arXiv* **2021**, arXiv:2106.02297.
38. Li, Y.; Sun, M.; Zhang, X. Perception-guided generative adversarial network for end-to-end speech enhancement. *Appl. Soft Comput.* **2022**, *128*, 109446. [CrossRef]
39. Sahu, S.; Gupta, R.; Espy-Wilson, C. Modeling Feature Representations for Affective Speech Using Generative Adversarial Networks. *IEEE Trans. Affect. Comput.* **2022**, *13*, 1098–1110. [CrossRef]
40. Arjovsky, M.; Chintala, S.; Bottou, L. Wasserstein GAN. *arXiv* **2017**, arXiv:1701.07875v3.
41. Gulrajani, I.; Ahmed, F.; Arjovsky, M.; Dumoulin, V.; Courville, A.C. Improved training of wasserstein gans. *arXiv* **2017**, arXiv:1704.00028.
42. Warden, P. Speech commands: A dataset for limited-vocabulary speech recognition. *arXiv* **2018**, arXiv:1804.03209.
43. Tatman, R. British Birdsong Dataset. Available online: https://www.kaggle.com/rtatman (accessed on 25 November 2022).
44. Xeno, C. Speech Commands Zero Through Nine (SC09) Dataset. Available online: https://xeno-canto.org/ (accessed on 23 November 2022).
45. Li, W. British English-Speaking Speed 2020. *Acad. J. Humanit. Soc. Sci.* **2021**, *4*, 93–100. [CrossRef]
46. Rajput, N.K.; Ahuja, B.; Riyal, M.K. Alphabet usage pattern, word lengths, and sparsity in seven Indo-European languages. *Digit. Scholarsh. Humanit.* **2020**, *35*, 727–736. [CrossRef]
47. Viswanathan, M.; Viswanathan, M. Measuring speech quality for text-to-speech systems: Development and assessment of a modified mean opinion score (MOS) scale. *Comput. Speech Lang.* **2005**, *19*, 55–83. [CrossRef]
48. Chen, B.; Luo, W.; Li, H. Audio steganalysis with convolutional neural network. In Proceedings of the fifth ACM Workshop on Information Hiding and Multimedia Security, Philadelphia, PA, USA, 20–22 June 2017; pp. 85–90.
49. Lin, Y.; Wang, R.; Yan, D.; Dong, L.; Zhang, X. Audio steganalysis with improved convolutional neural network. In Proceedings of the ACM Workshop on Information Hiding and Multimedia Security, Paris, France, 3–5 July 2019; pp. 210–215.
50. Mielikainen, J. LSB matching revisited. *IEEE Signal Process. Lett.* **2006**, *13*, 285–287. [CrossRef]
51. Taal, C.H.; Hendriks, R.C.; Heusdens, R.; Jensen, J. An algorithm for intelligibility prediction of time–frequency weighted noisy speech. *IEEE Trans. Audio Speech Lang. Process.* **2011**, *19*, 2125–2136. [CrossRef]
52. CMU. Speech Recognition-PocketSphinx. Available online: https://github.com/cmusphinx/pocketsphinx (accessed on 13 July 2022).
53. Google. Google Cloud Speech API. Available online: https://cloud.google.com/speech-to-text/docs/ (accessed on 13 July 2022).

electronics

MDPI

Article

Conditional Generative Adversarial Network for Monocular Image Depth Map Prediction

Shengang Hao [1], Li Zhang [2,*], Kefan Qiu [1] and Zheng Zhang [1]

1 School of Computer Science, Beijing Institute of Technology, Beijing 100081, China
2 School of Media Engineering, Communication University of Zhejiang, Hangzhou 310018, China
* Correspondence: nythhsg@163.com; Tel.: +86-178-1661-5955

Abstract: Deep map prediction plays a crucial role in comprehending the three-dimensional structure of a scene, which is essential for enabling mobile robots to navigate autonomously and avoid obstacles in complex environments. However, most existing depth estimation algorithms based on deep neural networks rely heavily on specific datasets, resulting in poor resistance to model interference. To address this issue, this paper proposes and implements an optimized monocular image depth estimation algorithm based on conditional generative adversarial networks. The goal is to overcome the limitations of insufficient training data diversity and overly blurred depth estimation contours in current monocular image depth estimation algorithms based on generative adversarial networks. The proposed algorithm employs an enhanced conditional generative adversarial network model with a generator that adopts a network structure similar to UNet and a novel feature upsampling module. The discriminator uses a multi-layer patchGAN conditional discriminator and incorporates the original depth map as input to effectively utilize prior knowledge. The loss function combines the least squares loss function and the L1 loss function. Compared to traditional depth estimation algorithms, the proposed optimization algorithm can effectively restore image contour information and enhance the visualization capability of depth prediction maps. Experimental results demonstrate that our method can expedite the convergence of the model on NYU-V2 and Make3D datasets, and generate predicted depth maps that contain more details and clearer object contours.

Keywords: autonomous mobile robot; conditional generative adversarial network; depth map prediction; intelligent manufacturing

check for updates

Citation: Hao, S.; Zhang, L.; Qiu, K.; Zhang, Z. Conditional Generative Adversarial Network for Monocular Image Depth Map Prediction. *Electronics* **2023**, *12*, 1189. https://doi.org/10.3390/electronics12051189

Academic Editor: Mehdi Sookhak

Received: 19 January 2023
Revised: 6 February 2023
Accepted: 25 February 2023
Published: 1 March 2023

1. Introduction

Today, intelligent logistics has become an essential component of the promotion of "intelligent manufacturing". It is extensively used in production line assembly for discrete manufacturing industries and material access in enterprise warehouse rooms. Intelligent warehousing, a result of warehouse automation, can be achieved through various automation and interconnection technologies that work together to enhance the production efficiency of the production line and the distribution efficiency of the warehouse, minimize labor, and reduce errors.

In intelligent logistics and warehousing, Automated Guided Vehicles (AGVs) [1] and Autonomous Mobile Robots (AMRs) [2] play vital roles in handling materials such as raw materials, tools, products, and accessories. Unlike AGVs, which require preset guidance devices and simple programming instructions, AMRs can carry out more complex operations and processing and provide greater flexibility. They can realize more intelligent navigation functions such as map construction and autonomous obstacle avoidance, making them the best choice for realizing intelligent logistics and warehousing.

As the environmental complexity increases in intelligent manufacturing enterprises, two-dimensional maps are no longer sufficient for mobile robots' environmental perception.

Three-dimensional maps can provide more comprehensive environmental information and are a current research hotspot in the field of mobile robot map construction [3].

The depth map is a common way of expressing 3D scene information, where the value of each pixel in the map represents the distance between the corresponding point of the object and the collector in the scene. Image depth prediction, widely used in autonomous driving, robot obstacle avoidance, 3D map reconstruction, and object detection [4], is a classic problem in computer vision research. When using two or more cameras to predict the depth of the same object., the method is called binocular or binocular image depth prediction. The method of monocular image depth prediction only requires obtaining a large quantity of depth information from a single camera, which is low-cost and more widespread, and increasingly a current research focus in the field of computer vision.

With the rapid development of deep learning, much progress has been made in solving classical problems in computer vision. Deep learning has played an essential role in addressing computer vision tasks such as object recognition, object tracking, and image segmentation, resulting in significant improvements in efficiency and accuracy. The first monocular image depth prediction method that utilized a convolutional neural network was proposed by Eigen et al. [5] in 2014. Their approach, which employed an AlexNet-based network structure, consisted of two scales: one to capture global information and the other to capture local information. The global information capture was partly based on AlexNet. This method achieved promising results on both the NYU Depth and KITTI datasets. Since then, several monocular image deep models based on convolutional neural networks have been proposed, resulting in a range of outcomes [6–8]. Although existing models have shown effectiveness on standard public datasets, they rely too heavily on specific datasets and are vulnerable to security attacks.

In practical applications, recognized objects can vary greatly in shape, and the lighting of the environment can change. Intelligent warehousing scenarios pose particular challenges due to highly stacked objects, and the diverse shapes and sizes of goods, which can make it difficult for intelligent vehicles to accurately estimate depth information. Moreover, deep neural networks themselves are prone to security issues and can be vulnerable to security attacks.

To improve the robustness and generalization ability of the deep estimation algorithm, and to mitigate potential security threats, this article proposes an optimization algorithm for monocular image depth estimation, based on conditional generative adversarial networks.

The contributions to this article are as follows:

First, we present the conditional generative adversarial network (cGAN) structure as the fundamental framework for the monocular depth estimation algorithm. The cGAN can generate more realistic synthetic data, which increases the amount of available training data. The model uses conditional variables, such as the depth map and original image, as prior knowledge to enhance the accuracy of generated depth maps and the discrimination ability of the discriminator. Moreover, the cGAN training improves the learning of the mapping between input images and depth images, thereby enhancing the robustness of the system.

Second, we introduce a novel feature upsampling module in the generator that improves the resolution of the feature map. This is achieved by incorporating new deconvolution layers into the existing upsampling module, thereby improving the accuracy of the generated depth maps. We also use an improved loss function that combines the L1 norm loss with the least squares loss function. This resolves the issues of difficult convergence and mode collapse commonly encountered in generative adversarial networks. The improved loss function guides the model to generate more accurate depth maps.

The rest of this article is arranged as follows: Section 2 provides a brief overview of the current state-of-the-art in monocular image deep estimation methods, as well as adversarial generative networks based on convolutional neural networks. Section 3 delves into the key techniques and algorithmic framework design. Section 4 presents the implementation results and their analysis. Finally, in Section 5, we draw conclusions from the results and discuss the next work.

2. Related Work

2.1. Deep Estimation Methods for Monocular Images Based on Deep Learning

The monocular image deep prediction methods based on deep learning can be broadly classified into three categories: supervised learning, unsupervised learning, and semi-supervised learning. Supervised learning, which involves training a model on labeled data, was pioneered by Eigen et al. in 2014 [5] and 2015 [6]. They used convolutional neural networks, including AlexNet and VGGNet-16, to estimate monocular image depth. In 2014, the author used AlexNet [5] as the fundamental model to produce an initial global depth map. To refine the depth map, a local fine network structure was used in conjunction with the original image information, which yielded favorable results at that time. However, due to the limited expressiveness of the AlexNet network, the depth prediction results were not satisfactory. Shortly after, in 2015, Eigen et al. [6] improved this work by incorporating deeper and more multi-scale convolutional neural networks. The authors employed VGGNet-16 for feature extraction and depth prediction, leading to better performance on standard datasets. Laina et al. [7] proposed a fully convolutional neural network structure based on deep residual networks to address the issue of excessive network parameters in monocular depth prediction. To enhance the depth prediction results, they introduced an up-projection module and utilized back-pooling to increase the depth map resolution.

Monocular image depth prediction is a complex task that involves calculating the depth value for each pixel in an image. Typically, this is treated as a high-dimensional regression problem where the model estimates the difference between the predicted depth value and the actual depth value, which is then used as the basis for the loss function. However, a more efficient approach is to transform the problem into a classification problem by dividing depth values into intervals and grouping pixels into corresponding bins, similar to a histogram. Cao et al. [8] applied this technique to extract features using deep residual networks, which were then fused using fully connected conditional random fields. The resulting model was trained using cross-entropy loss in the classification model. Liu et al. [9] used isolated conditional random fields for monocular image depth prediction. SENet-154 [10] introduced a new Squeeze-and-Excitation (SE) network module, which can adaptively learn the correlations between feature channels, thereby enhancing the network's representation and generalization capabilities. Meanwhile, the DenseDepth algorithm [11] proposed a transfer learning-based method that fine-tunes pre-trained models from large datasets like ImageNet for depth estimation. To further enhance the robustness and precision of depth estimation, the AdaBins algorithm [12] presents an adaptive depth estimation technique that adjusts the depth range in different scenarios and employs a novel loss function. Finally, the GLPDepth [13] algorithm proposes a novel Vertical CutDepth depth estimation method that leverages vertical information in-depth images to improve accuracy and efficiency. The authors also suggest a global-local path network architecture that captures both global and local information in scenes, leading to more accurate depth estimation.

In the field of unsupervised and semi-supervised learning, several researchers have proposed innovative methods to improve the accuracy and robustness of depth prediction and camera motion estimation. Godard et al. [14] utilized left-right view consistency for unsupervised depth prediction, which improved robustness by leveraging parallax and optimizing performance. Kuznietsov et al. [15] proposed a semi-supervised approach that utilizes sparse deep images as labels to achieve better performance. Mahjourian et al. [3] proposed an end-to-end learning approach that uses view synthesis as a supervised signal, resulting in a video sequence-based unsupervised learning framework for monocular image depth and camera motion estimation. Bian et al. [16] leveraged geometric consistency constraints to achieve scale consistency between adjacent frames and used this to detect and remove dynamic objects and masked regions. This approach outperforms previous algorithms trained on binocular video. Casser et al. [17] proposed a model that takes RGB image sequences as input and is supplemented by a pre-computed instance segmentation mask. Bhutani et al. [18] proposed a Bayesian inference-based method for monocular image depth estimation and confidence prediction. This method estimates the posterior distribution of each pixel's depth and confidence through a combination of a neural network that estimates the prior distribution of pixel depth and a noise model, and the pixel values of the input image. Almalioglu et al. [19] proposed a monocular visual odometry (VO) and depth estimation algorithm based on depth learning. This method trains an unsupervised monocular VO and depth estimation model using geometric constraints from binocular vision, allowing for motion estimation and scene depth estimation even in extreme environments. The method introduces a new "Persistent" loss function which enables the network to learn persistent estimation of optical flow and scene depth, while reverse depth estimation and optical flow prediction increase the loss function's robustness. The method also employs a pyramid depth network, designed to extract depth information from various scale feature maps, resulting in more accurate and robust depth estimation.

Although the results may not always be outstanding, these methods and their practical applications are still worth exploring.

2.2. *Current Status of Generative Adversarial Networks*

In 2014, Ian J. Goodfellow [20] introduced Generative Adversarial Networks (GANs), which consist of a generator and a discriminator. The generator takes a high-dimensional noise vector as input and generates data that is fed into the discriminator. The discriminator then determines whether the input is a real sample or a fake sample generated by the generator. GANs use an unsupervised learning approach and reach an equilibrium point through a two-player game. at which point the generator can produce data that the discriminator cannot effectively distinguish as fake.

However, early GANs faced issues with training stability and the lack of control over the output. To address these problems, researchers introduced conditional GANs (cGANs) [21] in 2014, which incorporate additional conditional information during training to ensure the generator produces specific content. Despite these efforts, GANs are still challenging to train. The literature proposes various modifications to improve training stability, including Deep Convolutional Generative Adversarial Networks (DCGANs [22]), least squares loss functions (LSGANs [23]), Wasserstein loss functions (WGANs [24]), gradient normalization (WGAN-up [25]), and proportional control (BEGAN [26]).

In the context of monocular image depth prediction, GANs can partially solve the problem of over-smooth or under-detailed depth prediction. By training a GAN to measure the similarity between the predicted depth graph and the original depth label, the visualization of the depth estimate can be improved. Lsola et al. [27] propose a general model based on conditional GANs to solve image-to-image translation problems, including the monocular image depth prediction problem.

3. Methods

Similar to the conditional generative adversarial network structure proposed in the literature [27], we utilize an enhanced conditional generator and conditional discriminator for our GAN model. Specifically, we incorporate a generator structure based on deep residual networks, which includes a new up-sampling module (labeled as Up-Decon). Our discriminator classifier structure is based on the conditional patchGAN classifier introduced in literature [27], but with modifications to the loss function to enhance the performance of the generative adversarial networks.

3.1. *Network Structure*

The original GAN structure generates images by processing random noise through a neural network, which can lead to uncontrolled output content. To overcome this limitation, additional constraints must be imposed on the original GAN. This paper proposes an optimized conditional GAN (op-cGAN) for monocular image depth estimation, which is a visual task performed at the image-to-image level. The specific model structure is depicted in Figure 1. The generator (G) takes the original image (x), the depth map (y), and random noise (z) as inputs, and outputs the predicted depth map (y′). The discriminator (D) takes the original image (x) and depth map as inputs and determines whether the depth map is from the training dataset (y) or generated by the generator (y′). A "fake" output from the discriminator indicates that the depth map is generated; while a "real" output indicates that the depth map is from the training dataset. By including the original image (x) as a constraint, the discriminator has access to additional priori knowledge, resulting in a more accurate and detailed depth map generation.

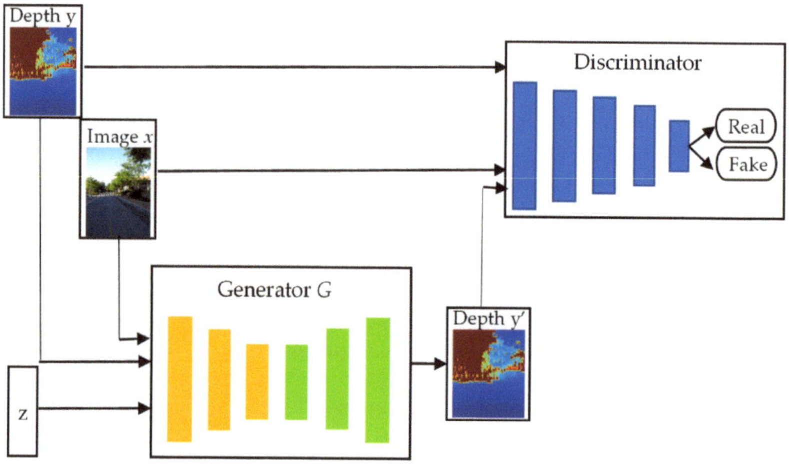

Figure 1. Network Structure of op-cGAN.

3.2. Generator

The generator section of the model follows an encoder-decoder structure, where the encoder extracts features and the decoder transforms these features into the final output. As shown in Figure 2, the generator employs a network structure based on deep residuals. The feature extraction process is aligned with the ResNet And begins with a stride-convolution and max-pooling to reduce the input image's resolution and minimize the number of parameters. The feature map then passes through four ResBlock, which reduces the feature map's resolution by half after each ResBlock while doubling the number of feature map layers. This process results in a feature map resolution that is 1/32 of the input resolution.

After extracting the upper feature map, a 1×1 convolutional kernel integrates the features. Next, the feature map passes through four Up-Decon modules, each consisting of three parts. The first part is a convolutional layer, followed by a concatenation layer that directly concatenates features of the same resolution extracted from the previous feature extraction stage. Lastly, a deconvolution layer is used to increase the feature map's resolution. The convolutional layer uses a 1×1 kernel to integrate cross-channel information and adjust the number of feature map channels. The concatenation layer uses concatenation or bitwise addition to combine the features and the deconvolution layer uses a 4×4 kernel with a stride of 2 and padding of 1 to double the feature map's resolution. After the Up-Decon modules, the feature map is processed by two convolutional modules to generate a depth prediction map with half the input resolution. Each pixel in the depth prediction map represents a predicted depth value in meters and is stored as a 32-bit floating-point number.

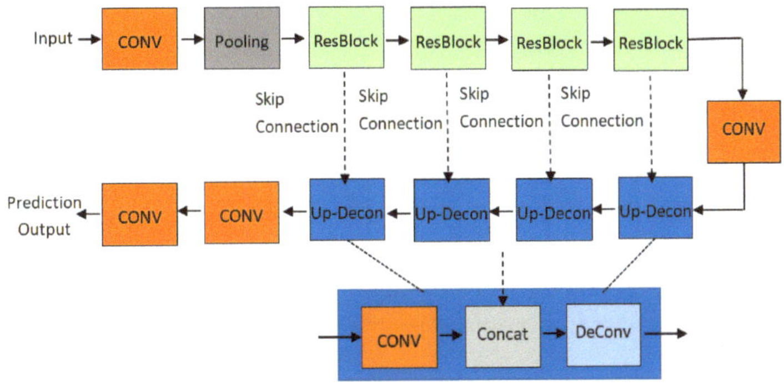

Figure 2. Network Structure of Generator.

3.3. Discriminator

To extract local image information, we adopt a conditional patchGAN discriminator, similar to the one proposed in reference [27]. As shown in Figure 3, the discriminator comprises a 5-layer full convolution network, which takes a concatenation of the depth map and the original image as input, without the sigmoid function on the last layer, since we use the least square function for loss calculation in this work. The original image serves as a conditional vector to guide the discriminator's classification. During training, the predicted depth map and the original image are concatenated as the negative samples, while the depth map from the training dataset and the original image are the positive samples. PatchGAN partitions the image into multiple patches and computes the classification results for each patch, thus treating the image as a Markov random field and assuming the independence of pixels across different patches. The final output of the discriminator is obtained by averaging the output of each patch. The loss function is calculated using convolution, enabling the use of smaller block sizes.

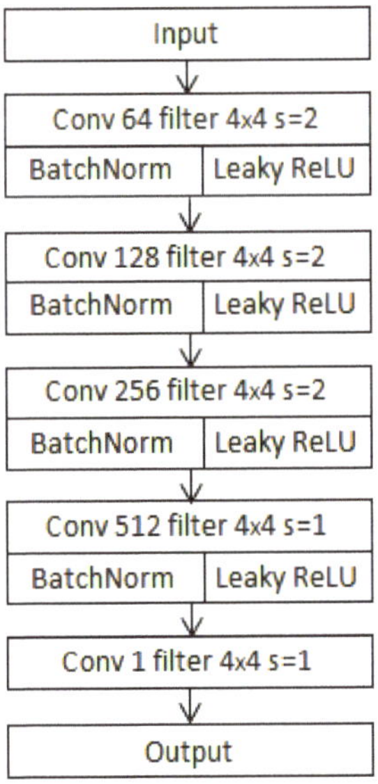

Figure 3. The structure of discriminator.

3.4. Loss Function

The loss function of traditional GAN is:

$$\min_G \max_D V_{GAN}(D,G) = \mathbb{E}_{x\sim p_{data}(x)}[logD(x)] + \mathbb{E}_{z\sim p_z(z)}[log(1-D(G(z)))] \quad (1)$$

in which G is a generator, D is a discriminator, z is a noise variable sampled from a normalized or Gaussian distribution, $p_{data}(x)$ represents the probability distribution of real data x, and $p_z(z)$ represents the probability distribution of z, $\mathbb{E}_{x\sim p_{data}(x)}$ is the expectation value of x and $\mathbb{E}_{z\sim p_{data}(z)}$ is the expectation value of z. The goal is to train G to generate samples that are indistinguishable from real data, while D tries to correctly distinguish between real and fake samples. However, a major issue with traditional GAN training is that as D gets better, the gradient signal that G receives becomes weaker, which leads to poor sample quality. To address this problem, LSGAN (Least Squares GAN) [23] replaces the binary classification objective of D with a least squares regression objective, which removes the sigmoid activation function from its final layer. This change has two main benefits: (1) LSGAN assigns a penalty to samples based on their distance from the decision boundary, which ensures that G generates samples that are closer to the boundary, and (2) LSGAN generates stronger gradients for samples that are far from the boundary, which mitigates the gradient vanishing problem in traditional GAN. The optimal loss functions proposed in this paper are as follows:

$$\min_D V_{LSGAN}(D) = \frac{1}{2}\mathbb{E}_{x\sim p_{data}(x)}\left[(D(x)-1)^2\right] + \frac{1}{2}\mathbb{E}_{z\sim p_z(z)}\left[(D(G(z)))^2\right] \quad (2)$$

$$\min_G V_{LSGAN}(G) = \frac{1}{2}\mathbb{E}_{z\sim p_z(z)}\left[(D(G(z))-1)^2\right] \quad (3)$$

According to reference [21], experiments have shown that adding the L1 loss function to the original loss function during the training of adversarial networks can lead to the generation of more realistic images. The L1 loss function is defined as follows:

$$\mathcal{L}_{L1}(G) = \mathbb{E}_{x,y,z}[\,||y - G\,(x,y,z)\,||_1\,] \quad (4)$$

in which y refers to the depth map from the training datasets that correspond to the real image x. As a result, the final loss function used in this paper can be expressed as follows:

$$\min_D V_{cGAN}(D) = \frac{1}{2}\mathbb{E}_{x,y}\left[(D(x,y)-1)^2\right] + \frac{1}{2}\mathbb{E}_{x,z}\left[(D(x,G(x,y,z)))^2\right] \quad (5)$$

$$\min_G V_{cGAN}(G) = \frac{1}{2}\mathbb{E}_{x,z}\left[(D(x,G(x,y,z))-1)^2\right] + \lambda\mathcal{L}_{L1}(G) \quad (6)$$

4. Experimental Results and Analysis

This section describes the experimental process and results of the monocular image depth prediction algorithm proposed in this study, which is based on op-cGAN.

4.1. Experimental Design

To take into account the complex and unique convergence process of cGAN training, we conducted our experiments in two stages. In the first stage, we compared our op-cGAN algorithm with several monocular image depth prediction algorithms based on classical deep learning models. This is because cGANs are generative models, and the generator in a cGAN can be trained to generate the predicted depth map y′ from an observed image x and a random noise vector z. In the second stage, we compared the monocular image depth prediction algorithm based on op-cGAN with the one based on the original cGAN. We evaluated the performance of these algorithms from both quantitative and qualitative perspectives. To conduct a comprehensive evaluation, we used two datasets: NYU-V2 for indoor scenes and Make3D for indoor and outdoor scenes. We utilized industry-standard valuation metrics to assess the effectiveness of depth prediction from different viewpoints. Assuming that y_i is the actual depth value, $y_i{}^*$ is the predicted depth value, and T represents the number of effective pixels, the evaluation metrics are described as follows:

$$\begin{aligned}
\text{Absolute Relative Difference(rel)} &= \frac{1}{|T|}\sum_{y\in T}|y-y^*|/y^* \\
\text{Root Mean Squared Error(rmse)} &= \sqrt{\frac{1}{|T|}\sum_{y\in T}\left\|y-y^*\right\|^2} \\
\text{Root Mean Squared Log-Error(rmse(log))} &= \sqrt{\frac{1}{|T|}\sum_{y\in T}\left\|\log y-\log y^*\right\|^2} \\
\text{Mean }\log 10\text{ Error}: &\ \frac{1}{|T|}\sum_{y\in T}|\log_{10}(y)-\log_{10}(y^*)|
\end{aligned} \tag{7}$$

4.2. Training Method of Model

Unlike the general deep learning network model, cGAN has its own training method. Algorithm 1 shows the pseudo-code for the training procedure of monocular image depth prediction based on the op-cGAN.

Algorithm 1: Pseudo-code of monocular image depth prediction based on the cGAN

For the number of training iterations, do:
For k steps do:
- sample minibatch of m images $\{x^{(1)}, \ldots, x^{(m)}\}$ and corresponding depths images $\{y^{(1)}, \ldots, y^{(m)}\}$
- sample minibatch of m noise images $\{z^{(1)}, \ldots, z^{(m)}\}$
- update discriminator by descending its stochastic gradient when fixed generator gradient: $\min_D V_{cGAN}(D)$

End for
- sample minibatch of m images $\{x^{(1)}, \ldots, x^{(m)}\}$ and corresponding depths images $\{y^{(1)}, \ldots, y^{(m)}\}$
- sample minibatch of m noise images $\{z^{(1)}, \ldots, z^{(m)}\}$
- update generator by descending its stochastic gradient when fixed discriminator: $\min_G V_{cGAN}(G)$

End for

Training a neural network from scratch can be extremely challenging. Therefore, to achieve better results, the academic community usually relies on pre-trained network models. In this study, we pre-trained our model on ImageNet. Pre-training on ImageNet offers two benefits: (1) it speeds up the training process as the pre-trained model has learned feature extraction methods on millions of training examples, and fine-tuning is sufficient to achieve better results on small datasets; (2) it improves the results on the training set, as deep networks are challenging to train, and the millions of training examples on ImageNet can enhance the network's expressive power. In our experiment, we set the K value to 1 because the generator's main body is pre-trained with ResNet-50, which provides it with a strong feature extraction ability.

Furthermore, Batch normalization is highly effective in aiding the flow of gradients flow within the network and reducing the impact of parameter initial values on the training process. This allows for a higher learning rate during training and also helps to regularize the model, reducing the need for Dropout operations. The formula for batch normalization is as follows:

$$\hat{x}^{(k)} = \frac{x^{(k)} - E\left[x^{(k)}\right]}{\sqrt{Var\left[x^{(k)}\right]}} \tag{8}$$

where $x^{(k)}$ represents the output of each layer's linear activation function. Batch Normalization is applied to this output by subtracting the mean and standard deviation of the minibatch it belongs to. This normalization transforms $\hat{x}^{(k)}$ into a normal distribution with mean 0 and variance 1, effectively solving the "internal covariate shift" problem. However, this transformation can reduce the expressive power of the network. To address this issue, the authors of [28] introduced two learnable parameters, scale, and shift, to each layer's output. With the addition of these two parameters, the original normalization method is modified into $y^{(k)} = r^{(k)}\,\hat{x}^{(k)} + \beta^{(k)}$, in which $r^{(k)}$ and $\beta^{(k)}$ has a size equal to the original batch size.

However, a drawback of this approach is that during inference, when there is only an input instance (i.e., batch size of 1), the statistics used for normalization become meaningless. To address this, practical deep-learning frameworks do not use batch normalization during inference. During training, the batch mean and variance are computed in the same way, but additional variables that are independent of batch size are retained to calculate the global mean and variance. During inference, batch normalization uses the global mean and variance that was calculated during training.

4.3. Experimental Results and Conclusions

4.3.1. NYU-V2 Dataset

We demonstrate the efficacy of our proposed algorithm using the NYU-V2 dataset, which is one of the largest indoor depth datasets worldwide. The NYU-V2 dataset consists of video sequences captured by Microsoft's Kinect camera. The dataset is divided into groups of continuous frames containing image and depth information, with some images being manually annotated with pixel categories. The dataset includes:

1. 1449 densely annotated aligned image-depth pairs;
2. Data from 464 new scenes across 3 cities;
3. 407,024 unannotated frames.

We sampled around 5000 data pairs evenly from the original dataset, with a pixel resolution of 480 × 640. As the dataset was collected over an extended period, there are many invalid pixels in the surroundings with a depth value of less than 0. To mitigate the impact of these invalid pixels, we excluded them during data processing by determining the average range of invalid pixels in all images and subtracting it from the corresponding training pairs in the original dataset. We then downsampled the data to 224 × 256, and to increase the training data diversity and avoid overfitting, we employed two data augmentation methods:

1. Random noise addition: Add some noise to each random vector during each training epoch, where the noise is sampled from a Gaussian distribution with a mean of 0 and a variance of 1.
2. Conditional vector addition: Use room type, indoor furniture, lighting, and other information vectors as conditional inputs to the generator to generate realistic images.

Each training data pair was augmented with one of these methods, resulting in a final set of 150,000 training pairs.

In the first stage of the experiments, we evaluated the performance of our op-cGAN-based monocular depth estimation model in comparison with established models such as AlexNet [5], VGGNet [6], ResNet [7], DORN [29], and the SOTA algorithm PixelFormer [30]. We carried out quantitative and qualitative assessments, and Table 1 shows the quantitative results. All evaluation metrics in this paper are sourced from the original papers. The generator named ResNet-Up-Decon in our op-cGAN model used the following parameters:

the learning rate r was set to 0.01, the optimization algorithm used was momentum = 0.9, the model was trained for 10 epochs, and the loss function is L1.

Table 1. Comparison of the proposed approach against other methods on the NYU-V2 dataset.

NYU V2	REL	RMSE	RMSE (log)	δ<1.25	δ<1.25^2	δ<1.25^3
Eigen et al. [5]	0.215	0.907	0.285	0.611	0.887	0.971
Eigen and Fergus [6]	0.158	0.641	0.214	0.769	0.95	0.988
Laina et al. [7]	0.127	0.573	0.195	0.811	0.953	0.988
DORN [29]	0.115	0.509	-	0.828	0.964	0.992
PixelFormer [30]	0.090	0.322	-	0.929	0.992	0.998
ours	0.115	0.492	0.167	0.878	0.972	0.992

Our proposed method outperforms all previous algorithms except for the latest algorithm PixelFormer, as measured by all metrics. While literature [5,6] use AlexNET and VGGNet as the model backbone, our method, which benefits from ResNet's stronger network representation, far exceeds the methods presented in these two papers in terms of results. Additionally, our method produces depth estimation images with higher resolution. It is worth mentioning that compared to [7], which also uses pre-trained ResNET-50 as the model backbone, our proposed method achieves a decrease of 0.11 in the rel metric, 0.081 in the rmse metric, and 0.28 in the rmse(log) metric. Most importantly, our method increases by 0.067 on the metric $\delta < 1.25$, which means that 5% more pixels fall within this range of estimated depth values than in [7]. This demonstrates the effectiveness of our proposed method and the improved depth estimation prediction resolution module. Compared with the DORN algorithm [29], which uses the spacing-increasing discretization (SID) strategy, our method still outperforms it in the rmse, log10, $\delta < 1.25$, and $\delta < 1.25^2$ metrics.

The latest algorithm, PixelFormer [30], uses an improved attention module (Skip Attention Module) and Bin Center Predictor (BCP) module. Based on the experimental results of the original paper, PixelFormer outperforms the proposed algorithm across all metrics. As the actual training data used by our algorithm is not exactly the same as the standard NYU-V2 dataset, the absolute difference in evaluation metrics between the two algorithms has little reference value. Nonetheless, PixelFormer still exhibited superior performance. In future work, we will integrate the Skip Attention Module and Bin Center Predictor module into the conditional generative adversarial network framework, and compare it to PixelFormer to explore the impact of the conditional generative adversarial network framework on depth estimation algorithms.

Figure 4 displays the visual results of two depth prediction algorithms based on the VGGNet [6] and ResNet model [7], both implemented by the authors and with model parameters provided in the published parameter files. The visualization shows that the method proposed in [6] can generate relatively good depth map estimations. However, the limited expressive power of the VGGNeT model used for feature extraction, results in many predicted depth values being significantly different from the actual values. Finally, our proposed method not only achieves more accurate depth estimation results, but also resolves the issue of overly smooth depth estimations to a certain extent.

In the second stage of the experiment, we compared the performance of the standalone generator model proposed in this paper with the op-cGAN model as a whole.

During the training of the standalone generator model, we used the momentum optimization algorithm with momentum set to 0.9, a batch size of 8, and an L1 loss function. The learning rate was set to 0.01, and we did not use a learning rate decrease method. The model was trained for 10 epochs, and the best-performing model on the test set was selected from the 10 trained models.

The cGAN training is different from traditional deep learning networks. After numerous experiments, we obtained a set of relatively good training parameters. The generator's learning rate was set to 0.0001, and we used the Adam optimization algorithm. In the loss function, we set the λ value to 10. For the discriminator, we set the learning rate to 5×10^{-4}, the batch size to 8, and used the Adam optimization algorithm.

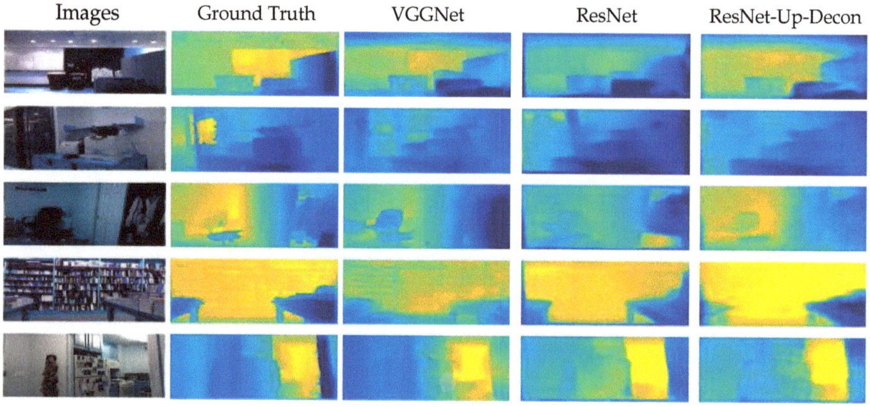

Figure 4. Experimental results on the NYU-V2 dataset of monocular image depth prediction algorithms based on different models.

Figures 5–7 show the experimental results of the two models under different evaluation metrics and training epochs.

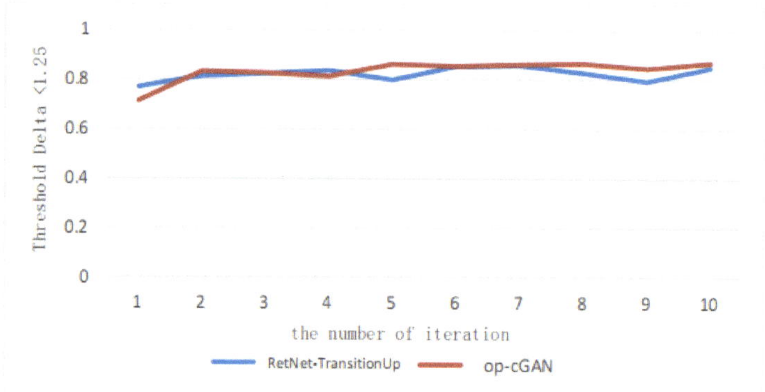

Figure 5. Experimental results of $\delta < 1.25$ for the two different models in each training iteration on the NYU-V2 dataset.

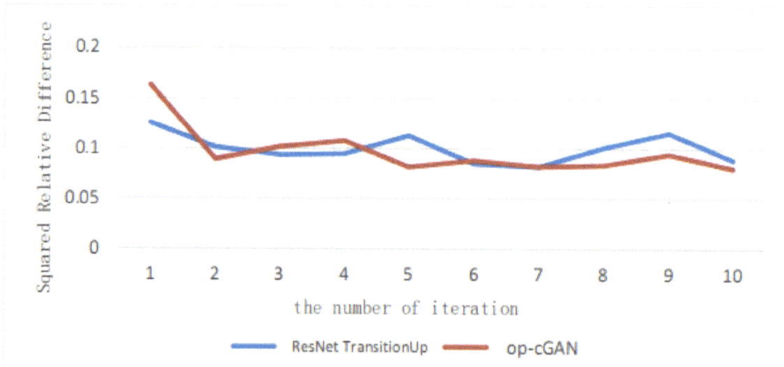

Figure 6. Experimental results of squared relative difference for the two different models in each training iteration on the NYU-V2 dataset.

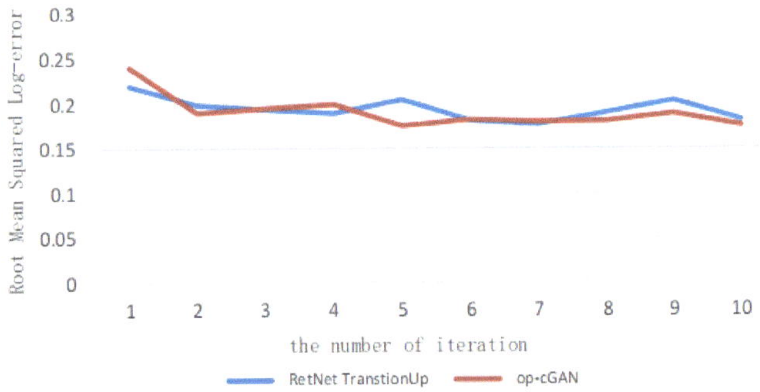

Figure 7. Experimental results of root mean squared log error for the two different models in each training epoch on the NYU-V2 dataset.

Figure 5 depicts the models' performance under different training epochs with a particular evaluation metric $\delta < 1.25$. The op-cGAN model significantly outperformed the standalone generator model after the first epoch and gradually improved in the following epochs. Moreover, the op-cGAN model exhibited greater stability and minimal fluctuations. After ten epochs, the op-cGAN model achieved a depth error value of 0.85, indicating that over 85% of the pixels' depth estimation values were smaller than the actual depth value. These results demonstrated the effectiveness of the op-cGAN model.

Figures 6 and 7 show the performance of the op-cGAN model compared to the standalone generator model in the evaluation metrics rmse and rmse (log) under different training epochs. The figures indicate that the op-cGAN model has a faster convergence rate and higher stability in these two evaluation metrics and outperformed the generator model significantly after the 5th epoch.

As this paper aims to address the issue of blurry depth maps generated by existing monocular image depth prediction algorithms, the visualization results are crucial. We saved the depth map visualization results to a file, adding a "0" as a separator between each depth map. Figure 8 shows selected depth estimation results from the test set, including the ground truth of the depth map, the depth map generated by the standalone generator, and that generated by the op-cGAN model from left to right. The visualization results indicate that the op-cGAN model generates clearer and more accurate depth maps, as demonstrated by the clear display of the windows in the first image's ground truth, object contours in the second image's ground truth, and the door and window in the third image's ground truth. These results confirm the effectiveness of our proposed op-cGAN model.

4.3.2. Make3D Dataset

Next, we will evaluate the performance of different depth estimation algorithms on the Make3D dataset. This dataset contains depth maps of indoor and outdoor scenes obtained from LIDAR scans. The official split includes 400 aligned image-depth pairs for training and 134 images for testing. Due to the age of this dataset, the resolution of the depth map is only 305×55, while the resolution of the images is 1704×2272. Therefore, during preprocessing, we first adjust the resolution of all training data to 256×192 using bilinear interpolation to serve as input to the model. Furthermore, because 400 image-depth pairs are insufficient for training a neural network, we use the following offline data enhancement methods to expand the training dataset.

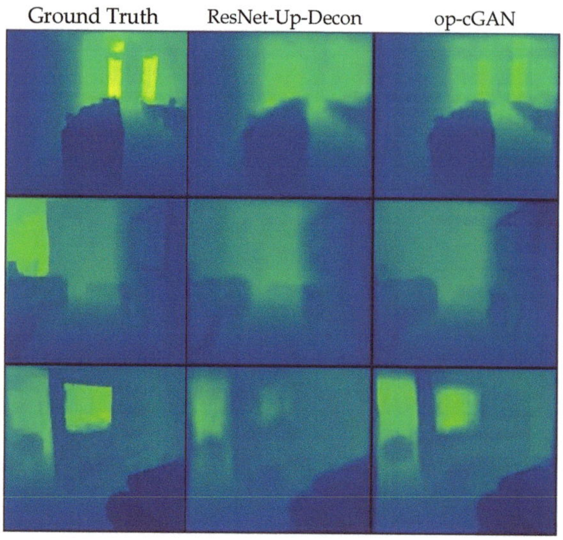

Figure 8. Comparison of visualization effects of different models on NYU-V2 dataset.

1. Scaling: the Input and target images are scaled with the corresponding depth data divided by s ∈ [1, 1.5].
2. Rotation: the input and target images are rotated by r ∈ [−5, 5] degrees.
3. Color adjustment: the Input image is multiplied by a random RGB value c ∈ [0.8, 1.2].
4. Flips: the Input and target images are horizontally flipped with a 0.5 probability
5. Adding conditional vector: information vectors such as city or rural, lighting, and roads can be added as conditional vectors to the generator to generate realistic images.

Specifically, we applied the first four data enhancement methods to each of the original 400 training pairs to generate new training data pairs, which we repeated 10 times. Finally, one of the conditional information from the 5th method is chosen to obtain 50 K training data pairs.

In the first stage of the experiment, we compare the performance of the depth estimation algorithms based on the DCNN model and CRF model [31,32], ResNet model [7], and the generator in the op-cGAN model proposed in this paper, from both quantitative and visual perspectives. Because there are limited evaluations on this dataset, we used results reported in the literature for the quantitative comparison. For the visual results, we could not access the authors' visualization results, so we only present the results of the generator in the op-cGAN model proposed in this paper.

During training, we used the L1 loss function and momentum optimization algorithm with a value of 0.9. The generator was trained for 40 epochs, with the learning rate halved every 20 epochs. The quantitative results are shown in Table 2, where we observed that the proposed method in this paper has improved in all evaluation metrics except for the rmse metric, which is lower than the method proposed in [7]. The reason could be that the dataset is too small and of low quality, making it difficult to train such a large network.

Table 2. Comparison results of different algorithms in the Make3D dataset.

Make 3D	REL	RMSE	Log10
Li et al. [31]	0.335	9.39	0.137
Liu et al. [32]	0.278	7.19	0.092
Laina et al. [7]	0.223	4.89	0.089
ResNet-Up-Decon	0.214	6.99	0.083

The visual results are shown in Figure 9, from which we can see that the proposed method can predict the contours of the depth map well and has no scale prediction error, validating the effectiveness of our method. Due to the limitation of the original training set, the resolution of the image in the training dataset is much higher than that of the depth images, leading to many mismatches.

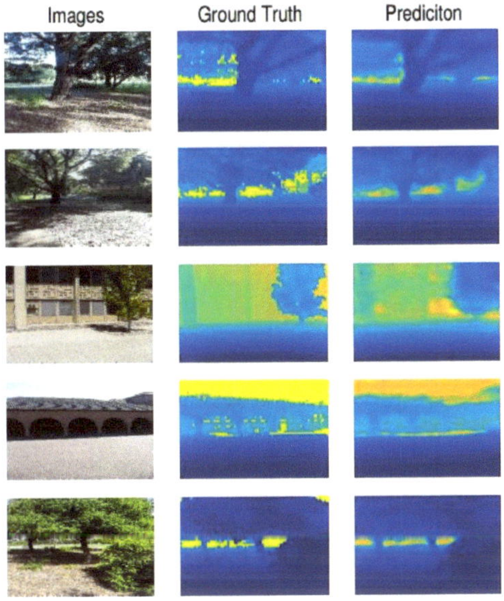

Figure 9. Visualization of Depth Prediction on Make3D.

In the second stage of the experiment, we compared the performance of a generator in the op-cGAN model with the full op-cGAN model for monocular depth estimation.

During the experiment, we trained the ResNet-Up-Decon model on the Make3D dataset, with all hyperparameters the same as those used for the NYU-V2 dataset, except for the number of training epochs, which was set to 20. Similarly, for the full op-cGAN model, we used the same hyperparameters as those used for NYU-V2, except for the number of training epochs, which was also set to 20.

Figures 10 and 11 display the experimental results of these two models under different training iterations. Specifically, Figure 10 presents the performance of the absolute relative difference metric for different training epochs. It can be observed that the depth estimation algorithm based on the cGAN model is superior to the ResNET-Up-Decon model in terms of stability and convergence speed. The former achieved a very low error rate in the first epoch and continued to reduce the error in subsequent epochs.

Figure 11 shows the performance of the log10 error evaluation metric across different training epochs. Invalid values (represented by 0) are caused by negative predicted depth values, which result in an invalid log10 error. The ResNet-Up-Decon model displays fewer invalid values than the op-cGAN model, indicating greater stability. Regarding the error values, the op-cGAN model has low errors, thus providing some validation of the proposed algorithm's effectiveness.

Figure 12 presents the visual results of the two models. For a fair comparison, all final depth values were scaled to the same scale. Values closer to the original depth pixel values are indicative of more accurate results. The op-cGAN model proposed in this paper performs better at recovering contour information from the images, which was attributed to the use of original images in the discriminator's input and the high pixel quality of the original images in the Make3D dataset, leading to the deep neural network learning the details of the original images.

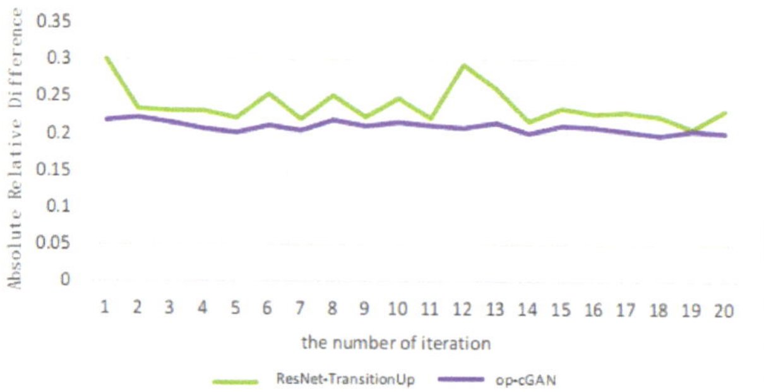

Figure 10. Experimental results of absolute relative difference for the two different models in each training iteration on the Make3D dataset.

Figure 11. Experimental results of log10 error for the two different models in each training iteration on the Make3D dataset.

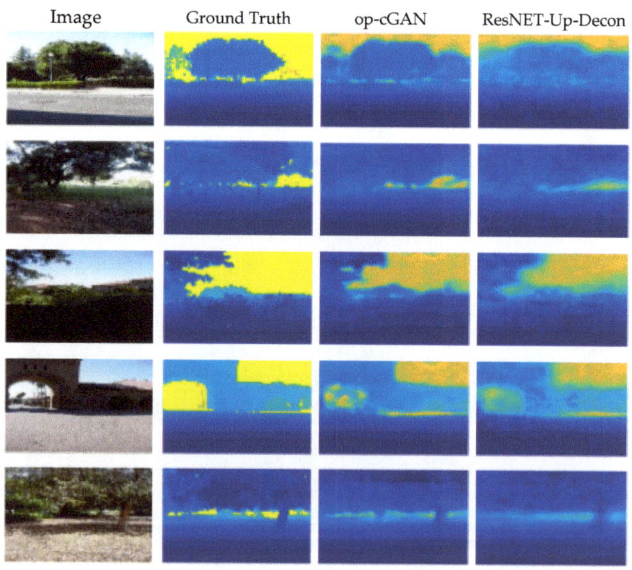

Figure 12. Visualization Comparison of depth prediction on Make3D dataset.

5. Limitation

The limitations of our approach primarily consist of two aspects:

1. The primary drawback of using GANs is that they can be challenging to train. Despite the implementation of various empirical tricks to improve efficiency (such as using batch normalization in our proposed method), GANs remain difficult to train.
2. Compared with the latest monocular image depth estimation algorithms, the performance of our algorithm is not outstanding enough, possibly because we have not optimized the generator structure optimization well, especially since the attention module has not been added. Experiments have shown that the attention mechanism can significantly improve the accuracy and detail extraction of image depth estimation.

6. Conclusions

Mobile robot plays an important role in the intelligent logistics and intelligent warehousing applications of the smart manufacturing industry. 3D map reconstruction is a core problem, which can help mobile robots achieve autonomous cruising and automatic obstacle avoidance in a complex environment. Monocular depth prediction is a fundamental method for understanding the 3D map's geometric information. This paper proposed an improved monocular image depth prediction method based on a conditional generative adversarial network to address the problem of insufficient diversity of training data and of overly blurry depth maps in monocular image depth prediction. Our method employed an improved monocular image depth estimation model based on depth residual networks as the generator of the conditional GAN, with a 5-layer patchGAN network as the discriminator. We combined the LSGAN loss function with the L1 loss function for the generator's loss function. Experimental results indicated that our proposed method can accelerate the convergence on the small Make3D dataset and can achieve a more optimized model on the larger NYN-V2 dataset, despite slower initial convergence. The visualization results show that our method can recover images with more detailed and clearer contours.

Although our proposed monocular depth estimation methods based on cGANs face difficulties in GAN network training and do not have the best performance on the evaluation metrics compared to the latest algorithm PixelFormer, their strong anti-interference with training sample and good model stability make these drawbacks acceptable. In the future, we will integrate the Skip Attention Module and Bin Center Predictor module into the conditional generative adversarial network framework, and compare it to PixelFormer again to explore the impact of the conditional generative adversarial network framework on depth estimation algorithms.

Author Contributions: Methodology, Investigation, Writing—original draft, S.H.; Writing—review & editing, L.Z.; software, validation, K.Q.; software, visualization, Z.Z. All authors have read and agreed to the published version of the manuscript.

Funding: This research was funded by the National Key Research and Development Program of China, grant number 2018YFB1701402, and the National Natural Science Foundation of China, grant numbers U1936218 and 62072037.

Institutional Review Board Statement: Not applicable.

Informed Consent Statement: Not applicable.

Data Availability Statement: Publicly available datasets were analyzed in this study. NYU-V2 data can be found here: [https://cs.nyu.edu/~silberman/datasets/nyu_depth_v2.html, accessed on 17 October 2022] and Make 3D data presented in this study are openly available in [Make3D] at [doi: 10.1109/TPAMI.2008.132].

Conflicts of Interest: The authors declare no conflict of interest. The funders had no role in the design of the study; in the collection, analyses, or interpretation of data; in the writing of the manuscript; or in the decision to publish the results.

References

1. Babic, B.; Miljkovic, Z.; Vukovic, N.; Antic, V. Towards Implementation and Autonomous Navigation of an Intelligent Automated Guided Vehicle in Material Handing Systems. *IJST-T Mech Eng.* **2012**, *36*, 25–40.
2. Jensen, L.K.; Kristensen, B.B.; Demazeau, Y. FLIP: Prototyping multi-robot systems. *Robot Auton. Syst.* **2005**, *53*, 230–243. [CrossRef]
3. Mahjourian, R.; Wicke, M.; Angelova, A. Unsupervised learning of depth and ego-motion from monocular video using 3D geometric constraints. In Proceedings of the IEEE Conference on Computer Vision and Pattern Recognition, Salt Lake City, UT, USA, 18–22 June 2018.
4. Chen, K.; Li, J.; Lin, W.; See, J.; Wang, J.; Duan, L.; Chen, Z.; He, C.; Zou, J. Towards accurate one-stage object detection with AP-loss. In Proceedings of the IEEE Conference on Computer Vision and Pattern Recognition, Los Angeles, CA, USA, 15–21 June 2019.
5. Eigen, D.; Puhrsch, C.; Fergus, R. Depth map prediction from a single image using a multiscale deep network. In Proceedings of the International Conference on Neural Information Processing Systems, Montreal, Canada, 8–13 December 2014.
6. Eigen, D.; Fergus, R. Predicting depth, surface normals and semantic labels with a common multi-scale convolutional architecture. In Proceedings of the IEEE International Conference on Computer Vision, Santiago, Chile, 7–13 December 2015.
7. Laina, I.; Rupprecht, C.; Belagiannis, V.; Tombari, F.; Navab, N. Deeper Depth Prediction with Fully Convolutional Residual Networks. In Proceedings of the 2016 Fourth International Conference on 3D Vision (3DV), Stanford, CA, USA, 25–28 October 2016.
8. Cao, Y.; Wu, Z.; Shen, C. Estimating Depth from Monocular Images as Classification Using Deep Fully Convolutional Residual Networks. *IEEE Trans. Circuits Syst. Video Technol.* **2017**, *28*, 3174–3182. [CrossRef]
9. Liu, M.; Salzmann, M.; He, X. Discrete-Continuous Depth Estimation from a Single Image. In Proceedings of the IEEE Conference on Computer Vision and Pattern Recognition, Columbus, OH, USA, 23–28 June 2014.
10. Hu, J.; Ozay, M.; Zhang, Y.; Okatani, T. Revisiting Single Image Depth Estimation: Toward Higher Resolution Maps with Accurate Object Boundaries. In Proceedings of the 2019 IEEE Winter Conference on Applications of Computer Vision (WACV), Waikoloa, HI, USA, 7–11 January 2019.
11. Alhashim, I.; Wonka, P. High Quality Monocular Depth Estimation via Transfer Learning. In Proceedings of the IEEE Conference on Computer Vision and Pattern Recognition, Long Beach, CA, USA, 15–20 June 2019.
12. Bhat, S.F.; Alhashim, I.; Wonka, P. AdaBins: Depth Estimation Using Adaptive Bins. In Proceedings of the IEEE/CVF Conference on Computer Vision and Pattern Recognition (CVPR), Nashville, TN, USA, 20–25 June 2021.
13. Kim, D.; Ka, W.; Ahn, P.; Joo, D.; Chun, S.; Kim, J. Global-Local Path Networks for Monocular 13. Depth Estimation with Vertical CutDepth. In Proceedings of the IEEE Conference on Computer Vision and Pattern Recognition, New Orleans, LA, USA, 19–23 June 2022.
14. Godard, C.; Mac Aodha, O.; Brostow, G.J. Unsupervised monocular depth estimation with left-right consistency. In Proceedings of the IEEE Conference on Computer Vision and Pattern Recognition, Honolulu, HI, USA, 21–26 July 2017.
15. Kuznietsov, Y.; Stuckler, J.; Leibe, B. Semi-supervised deep learning for monocular depth map prediction. In Proceedings of the IEEE Conference on Computer Vision and Pattern Recognition, Honolulu, HI, USA, 21–26 July 2017.
16. Bian, J.; Li, Z.; Wang, N.; Zhan, H.; Shen, C.; Cheng, M.M.; Reid, I. Unsupervised scale-consistent depth and ego-motion learning from monocular video. In Proceedings of the Advances in Neural Information Processing Systems, Vancouver, BC, Canada, 8–14 December 2019.
17. Casser, V.; Pirk, S.; Mahjourian, R.; Angelova, A. Depth prediction without the sensors: Leveraging structure for unsupervised learning from monocular videos. In Proceedings of the AAAI Conference on Artificial Intelligence, Waikoloa, HI, USA, 27 January–1 February 2019.
18. Bhutani, V.; Vankadari, M.; Jha, O.; Majumder, A.; Kumar, S.; Dutta, S. Unsupervised Depth and Confidence Prediction from Monocular Images using Bayesian Inference. In Proceedings of the 2020 IEEE/RSJ International Conference on Intelligent Robots and Systems (IROS), Las Vegas, NV, USA, 24 October 2020–24 January 2021.
19. Almalioglu, Y.; Saputra, M.R.U.; Gusmão, P.P.B.d.; Markham, A.; Trigoni, N. GANVO: Unsupervised Deep Monocular Visual Odometry and Depth Estimation with Generative Adversarial Networks. In Proceedings of the 2019 International Conference on Robotics and Automation (ICRA), Montreal, QC, Canada, 20–24 May 2019.
20. Goodfellow, I.J.; Pouget-Abadie, J.; Mirza, M.; Xu, B.; Warde-Farley, D.; Ozair, S.; Courville, A.; Bengio, Y. Generative Adversarial Nets. In Proceedings of the International Conference on Neural Information Processing Systems, Montreal, QC, Canada, 8–13 December 2014.
21. Mirza, M.; Osindero, S. Conditional Generative Adversarial Nets. *arXiv* **2014**, arXiv:1411.1784.
22. Radford, A.; Metz, L.; Chintala, S. Unsupervised representation learning with deep convolutional generative adversarial networks. In Proceedings of the 33th International Conference on Machine Learning, San Juan, PR, USA, 2–4 May 2016.
23. Mao, X.; Li, Q.; Xie, H.; Lau, R.Y.; Wang, Z.; Paul Smolley, S. Least Squares Generative Adversarial Networks. In Proceedings of the 2017 IEEE International Conference on Computer Vision (ICCV), Venice, Italy, 22–29 October 2017.
24. Arjovsky, M.; Chintala, S.; Bottou, L. Wasserstein Generative Adversarial Networks. In Proceedings of the 34th International Conference on Machine Learning, Sydney, Australia, 6–11 August 2017.
25. Gulrajani, I.; Ahmed, F.; Arjovsky, M.; Dumoulin, V.; Courville, A.C. Improved Training of Wasserstein GANs. In Proceedings of the Advances in Neural Information Processing Systems, Long Beach, CA, USA, 4–9 December 2017.

26. Berthelot, D.; Schumm, T.; Metz, L. BEGAN: Boundary Equilibrium Generative Adversarial Networks. *arXiv* **2017**, arXiv:1703.10717.
27. Lsola, P.; Zhu, J.Y.; Zhou, T.; Efros, A.A. Image-to-Image Translation with Conditional Adversarial Networks. In Proceedings of the 2017 IEEE Conference on Computer Vision and Pattern Recognition, Honolulu, HI, USA, 21–26 July 2017.
28. Ioffe, S.; Szegedy, C. Batch Normalization: Accelerating Deep Network Training by Reducing Internal Covariate Shift. In Proceedings of the International Conference on International Conference on Machine Learning, Lile, France, 6–11 July 2015.
29. Fu, H.; Gong, M.M.; Wang, C.H.; Batmanghelich, K.; Tao, D. Deep Ordinal Regression Network for Monocular Depth Estimation. In Proceedings of the IEEE Conference on Computer Vision and Pattern Recognition (CVPR), Salt Lake, UT, USA, 18–22 June 2018.
30. Agarwal, A.; Arora, C. Attention Attention Everywhere: Monocular Depth Prediction With Skip Attention. In Proceedings of the IEEE/CVF Winter Conference on Applications of Computer Vision (WACV), Waikoloa, HI, USA, 1–7 January 2023.
31. Li, B.; Shen, C.; Dai, Y.; Van Den Hengel, A.; He, M. Depth and surface normal estimation from monocular images using regressionon deep features and hierarchical crfs. In Proceedings of the IEEE Conference on Computer Vision and Pattern Recognition, Boston, MA, USA, 7–12 June 2015.
32. Liu, F.; Shen, C.; Lin, G. Deep convolutional neural fields for depth estimation from a single image. In Proceedings of the 2015 IEEE Conference on Computer Vision and Pattern Recognition, Boston, MA, USA, 7–12 June 2015.

electronics

MDPI

Article

High Performance Network Intrusion Detection System Using Two-Stage LSTM and Incremental Created Hybrid Features

Jonghoo Han and Wooguil Pak *

Department of Information and Communication Engineering, Yeungnam University, Gyeongsan 38541, Republic of Korea
* Correspondence: wooguilpak@yu.ac.kr; Tel.: +82-53-810-3092

Abstract: Currently, most network intrusion detection systems (NIDSs) use information about an entire session to detect intrusion, which has the fatal disadvantage of delaying detection. To solve this problem, studies have been proposed to detect intrusions using only some packets belonging to the session but have limited effectiveness in increasing the detection performance compared to conventional methods. In addition, space complexity is high because all packets used for classification must be stored. Therefore, we propose a novel NIDS that requires low memory storage space and exhibits high detection performance without detection delay. The proposed method does not need to store packets for the current session and uses only some packets, as in conventional methods, but achieves very high detection performance. Through experiments, it was confirmed that the proposed NIDS uses only a small memory of 25.8% on average compared to existing NIDSs by minimizing memory consumption for feature creation, while its intrusion detection performance is equal to or higher than those of existing ones. As a result, this method is expected to significantly help increase network safety by overcoming the disadvantages of machine-learning-based NIDSs using existing sessions and packets.

Keywords: hybrid feature; network intrusion detection; session feature; packet feature; two-stage LSTM

Citation: Han, J.; Pak, W. High Performance Network Intrusion Detection System Using Two-Stage LSTM and Incremental Created Hybrid Features. *Electronics* **2023**, *12*, 956. https://doi.org/10.3390/electronics12040956

Academic Editors: Yu-an Tan, Qikun Zhang, Yuanzhang Li and Xiao Yu

Received: 19 January 2023
Revised: 13 February 2023
Accepted: 13 February 2023
Published: 15 February 2023

1. Introduction

Currently, a network intrusion detection system (NIDS) manages traffic by dividing it into logical groups called sessions. Therefore, it should collect the necessary information by creating state information for the current active session and monitoring traffic [1–5], implying that an NIDS with finite computing and memory resources has a limited number of simultaneous sessions that can be handled. Owing to the steadily increasing size of networks and the increasing amount of network traffic, the number of sessions that an NIDS has to handle is also increasing [6].

Accurately distinguishing between network intrusion and normal sessions requires much information about the session. To date, many NIDSs have stored the entire traffic belonging to the session, used it to analyze the total traffic sent and received after the session ended, extracted its statistical characteristics, and used them to distinguish intrusion from normal sessions [1–4]. However, collecting all traffic during a session's lifetime requires excessive storage space. Instead of collecting traffic, it can collect only a portion of the packet, such as the packet header, and create features for the session; however, using storage space in proportion to the number of packets remains a problem.

An NIDS using session characteristics requires a high storage space and also has the disadvantage of detecting intrusions only after the session is terminated. To solve these problems, a new type of NIDS that collects only session initial packets and uses them for detection has been proposed [5], where, instead of collecting traffic, it can collect only a portion of the packet, such as the packet header, and create features for the session. However, this approach still uses storage space in proportion to the number of packets.

To solve the problem of existing NIDSs, the proposed method directly inputs the received packet data to the classifier without collecting the packet data and stores the output through it. In addition, when the next session packet is received, the previously stored output and received new packet are input back to the classifier; therefore, partial classification is performed every time a packet is received. Further, whenever a new session packet is received, several state values for the session are updated, and a feature set of the machine-learning (ML) model is finally created using these values. In addition, instead of using all packets for each session, intrusion detection is performed before session termination because only some packets are used at the beginning of the session, as in the conventional method.

Therefore, this study makes the following contributions.

- 002D presents an NIDS model that progressively classifies using an ML model every time a packet is received.
- Suggests a hybrid feature creation method that uses packet and session data simultaneously.
- Proposes an NIDS capable of fast intrusion detection while maintaining high detection performance using partial packet data instead of entire session packets.

The remainder of this study is organized as follows. Section 2 briefly summarizes the related research work. Section 3 describes the proposed NIDS, while Section 4 compares and analyzes the performance of the proposed system with that of the latest competing work. Finally, Section 5 presents the conclusions of the study.

2. Existing Work

2.1. Session-Based NIDS

A machine learning-based NIDS (ML NIDS) converts received traffic into features and classifies them to detect network intrusions. At this time, an ML-NIDS is classified according to how the received traffic is converted into features. Traffic is divided into sessions and monitored, and its nature (intrusion or normal traffic) is determined. Therefore, to convert traffic into features, it is divided into a specific session, and then features for the session are created using traffic belonging to the session [7–13]. A session is a concept that exists in the Transmission Control Protocol (TCP), but the User Datagram Protocol (UDP) and Internet Control Message Protocol (ICMP) also extend the concept of TCP to define sessions. The method primarily used at this time classifies traffic with a key of five tuples: same source IP address, destination IP address, source port, destination port, and protocol. Packets with the same five tuples are considered to belong to the same session, but UDP does not have a packet indicating the end of the session. Therefore, if the packet inter-arrival time (IAT) of two adjacent packets exceeds a certain value (i.e., maximum IAT), the existing session is considered to be terminated. Subsequent packets are considered to belong to another session. In ICMP, a session can be defined as four tuples using the source IP address, destination IP address, type, and protocol fields, rather than five tuples. For this protocol, the end of the session is also defined using the IAT of the adjacent packets.

Thus, when defining the start and end of a session with the value of the IAT, it should be noted that even in TCP, a retransmitted packet may be received during session termination or a timeout may occur owing to packet loss [14]. Ultimately, the maximum IAT for a session in an NIDS should be set to a sufficiently large value to handle these situations. If the maximum IAT is set, packets whose IATs exceed this value are not processed as packets belonging to the existing session, even if they belong to the existing session. Instead, they are treated as packets belonging to a completely new session with the same five tuples. Therefore, the maximum IAT must be carefully assigned. It is assigned a value of 30 to 180 s, although it varies depending on the type of NIDS [15].

Although the maximum IAT is an important value for distinguishing between sessions, it can negatively affect the NIDS detection of intrusions because a delay equal to the maximum IAT necessarily occurs between the times when a session is terminated and when the NIDS determines that the session is terminated. Nevertheless, traffic is classified as a unit of session because NIDS requires tremendous hardware performance to determine whether an intrusion has occurred for every individual packet received. A packet processing performance of up to 30 million packets per second must be supported to process 10 Gbps ethernet traffic without loss, implying that the NIDS must perform deep learning ML classification 30 million times per second, which is difficult to support even with dedicated hardware accelerators. Network traffic should be classified in any unit, i.e., single packet or session, and determining intrusion for each session is the most realistic implementation approach in current hardware technology.

2.2. Session Features

In this section, converting the traffic of each session into an ML input when the network traffic is divided into sessions is explained. The most common approach in existing studies is to extract multiple characteristics for a single session through statistical analysis of session traffic. This method extracts simple characteristics, such as the total data amount of session traffic and the total number of packets of session traffic, as well as those that require total traffic, such as the average value of the IAT or standard deviation. An example of a session feature is presented in Table 1 [9–13].

We call the session information obtained in this manner a session feature. An NIDS using the session feature must collect the entire traffic of each session until it is terminated. Therefore, an NIDS using session features collects intra-session traffic, analyzes session traffic after session termination, creates session features, and uses them to detect intrusions, as shown in Figure 1.

At this time, to detect session termination, the user must wait for the maximum IAT after the actual session termination. Therefore, if a network intrusion occurs, it is detected only after the maximum IAT has elapsed after the actual session termination [10–20]. Therefore, session-based NIDSs have the major disadvantage of long delays in detecting intrusions. Additionally, because the session feature is created using the total traffic per session, a considerable amount of traffic must be stored. Storage space may be saved by only storing packet headers, instead of storing raw packets or storing only some information necessary to create features. However, this process also requires storage space proportional to the number of packets belonging to the session. In addition, an NIDS using session features must decide in advance which characteristics of the session to use as features. These decisions are determined by the designer, with the performance of an NIDS significantly affected by the type of feature selected. Furthermore, when a new attack emerges, existing features may be insufficient to detect it. In this case, a new feature must be designed, posing a considerable burden on NIDS developers. Table 2 lists the strengths and weaknesses of session-based NIDS.

Table 1. ISCXIDS 2012 feature list showing 'act': active, 'avg': average, 'blk': block, 'bwd': backward, 'byts': bytes, 'cnt': count, 'CWR': congestion window reduced flag, 'dst': destination, 'ECE': explicit congestion notification for echo flag, 'fwd': forward, 'IAT': inter-arrival-time, 'init': initial, 'len': length, 'pkt': packet, 'PSH': push flag, 'RST': reset flag, 'seg': segment, 'src': source, 'std': standard deviation, 'tot': total, 'URG': urgent flag, 'var': variance, 'win': window.

No.	Name	No.	Name	No.	Name	No.	Name	No.	Name
1	Src IP	18	Bwd Pkt Len Max	35	Bwd IAT Std	52	SYN Flag Cnt	69	Subflow Fwd Pkts
2	Src Port	19	Bwd Pkt Len Min	36	Bwd IAT Max	53	RST Flag Cnt	70	Subflow Fwd Byts
3	Dst IP	20	Bwd Pkt Len Mean	37	Bwd IAT Min	54	PSH Flag Cnt	71	Subflow Bwd Pkts
4	Dst Port	21	Bwd Pkt Len Std	38	Fwd PSH Flags	55	ACK Flag Cnt	72	Subflow Bwd Byts
5	Protocol_HOPOPT	22	Flow Byts/s	39	Bwd PSH Flags	56	URG Flag Cnt	73	Init Fwd Win Byts
6	Protocol_TCP	23	Flow Pkts/s	40	Fwd URG Flags	57	CWE Flag Count	74	Init Bwd Win Byts
7	Protocol_UDP	24	Flow IAT Mean	41	Bwd URG Flags	58	ECE Flag Cnt	75	Fwd Act Data Pkts
8	Timestamp	25	Flow IAT Std	42	Fwd Header Len	59	Down/Up Ratio	76	Fwd Seg Size Min
9	Flow Duration	26	Flow IAT Max	43	Bwd Header Len	60	Pkt Size Avg	77	Active Mean
10	Tot Fwd Pkts	27	Flow IAT Min	44	Fwd Pkts/s	61	Fwd Seg Size Avg	78	Active Std
11	Tot Bwd Pkts	28	Fwd IAT Tot	45	Bwd Pkts/s	62	Bwd Seg Size Avg	79	Active Max
12	TotLen Fwd Pkts	29	Fwd IAT Mean	46	Pkt Len Min	63	Fwd Byts/b Avg	80	Active Min
13	TotLen Bwd Pkts	30	Fwd IAT Std	47	Pkt Len Max	64	Fwd Pkts/b Avg	81	Idle Mean
14	Fwd Pkt Len Max	31	Fwd IAT Max	48	Pkt Len Mean	65	Fwd Blk Rate Avg	82	Idle Std
15	Fwd Pkt Len Min	32	Fwd IAT Min	49	Pkt Len Std	66	Bwd Byts/b Avg	83	Idle Max
16	Fwd Pkt Len Mean	33	Bwd IAT Tot	50	Pkt Len Var	67	Bwd Pkts/b Avg	84	Idle Min
17	Fwd Pkt Len Std	34	Bwd IAT Mean	51	FIN Flag Cnt	68	Bwd Blk Rate Avg	85	Label

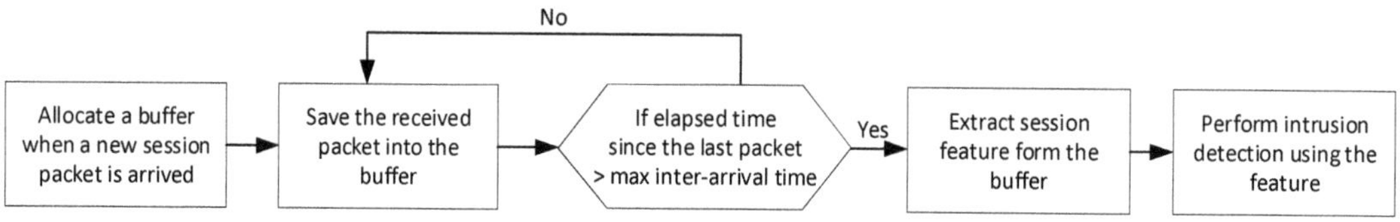

Figure 1. Typical procedure of the session-feature-based-NIDS to process the session.

Table 2. Advantages and disadvantages of session-feature-based NIDS.

Advantages	▪ Intrusion detection is performed at every session termination instead of every received packet, reducing computational overhead required for detection. ▪ Robust against loss of some packets.
Disadvantages	▪ Huge memory requirement to store received packets per session. ▪ The NIDS developer must select and design the feature type. ▪ When a new attack emerges, it is likely that a new feature type will have to be designed. ▪ Detection delay occurs due to waiting for the maximum inter-arrival time to recognize session termination. ▪ Vulnerable to NIDS detection bypass attacks through repetitive transmission of packets by an attacker to change important session feature values.

2.3. Packet Features

Although the session feature has excellent advantages, it also has many fatal disadvantages, necessitating studies for its improvement. Among them, the most effective alternative involves using the traffic belonging to the session as a feature [5]. Using raw packet data directly as a feature fundamentally avoids determining the type of session feature in advance. As the ML model automatically determines the most effective characteristics for existing attacks, it is sufficient to train the model again with the updated dataset when the session data for a new type of intrusion are added. However, because raw packet data are used as a feature, the packet itself must be stored, placing a heavy burden on the storage space per session. Thus, only part of the packet is stored, with only some of the session's initial packets used instead of all the packets. Let us call the features directly transformed from raw packet data packet features. The packet feature uses some session packets, but the actual detection performance is comparable to that of the existing session-feature-based NIDS. In addition, unlike the session feature, maximum IAT need not be used because there is no need to wait until the session ends. Therefore, the NIDS can rapidly detect an intrusion after it has occurred, which is the most important characteristic of the packet-feature-based method; thus, the packet-feature-based NIDS is advantageous in securing networks.

As mentioned earlier, session features and packet features have different characteristics because the methods of creating features are completely different. Considering session and packet features can complement each other's disadvantages, research on a new type of feature that further strengthens the advantages of the two features and improves the disadvantages is continuously required.

However, in the field of NIDS, there is no research to apply both features at the same time. In order to apply both feature types simultaneously, there are problems to be solved. First, the memory usage required for feature creation can increase significantly. Currently, even NIDS using only session features or packet features requires high memory usage, so it is technically very difficult to create both features at the same time. In addition to this, we need a machine learning model that can apply both features together. While all packets belonging to each session are required to create a session feature, only some packets at the beginning of a session are used to create a packet feature. Therefore, a new NIDS design is needed to combine the advantages of both methods rather than simply using them. Table 3 lists the strengths and weaknesses of packet-based NIDS.

Table 3. Advantages and disadvantages of packet-feature-based NIDS.

Advantages	▪ When a new attack emerges, it can automatically create features to detect the new attack, eliminating the need for NIDS developer intervention. ▪ Intrusion detection is possible before session termination. ▪ When it handles long sessions, there is no detection delay due to the maximum inter-arrival time for end-of-session recognition. ▪ It supports deep packet inspection. ▪ Detection rate is very high.
Disadvantages	▪ High memory requirement to store some packet data per session. ▪ Patterns located in packet payloads that are not used as features cannot be detected.

3. Materials and Methods

3.1. Motivation

According to previous studies on NIDS, session and packet features have significantly different characteristics, which can considerably improve detection performance through synergistic effects if they can be used together. However, the amount of information to be stored and maintained increases excessively when both feature types are used simultaneously. In addition, the detection delay may intensify as the time required for packet feature processing is added to the delay required for detection caused by using session features. However, if this problem can be resolved, the intrusion detection performance of the NIDS can be dramatically improved by comprehensively using session and packet features.

The significant data needed to create a feature requires a correspondingly large storage space. Packet feature-based NIDS collects sequentially received packets for each session up to a predetermined size and then inputs them to an ML model for classification. Therefore, past packets must be stored until sufficient packet data are gathered. Hence, creating an ML model where a packet-feature-based NIDS performs classification tasks incrementally every time packets are received and only stores intermediate classification results of small size and does not store packet data will significantly reduce the storage space required for NIDS.

The session-feature-based NIDS stores all packet data or packet headers for all packets in the session and analyzes them after the session is completed to determine their statistical characteristics, resulting in a high storage burden and long delay to confirm session termination, as explained above. Here, re-examining the characteristics of packet-feature-based NIDS indicates that some data from sessions can be used to achieve sufficiently high detection rates; thus, session features obtained from some initial session packets are likely to contain sufficient information. In addition, it is possible to fundamentally solve the delay problem of waiting for the maximum IAT until the end of a session. However, assuming that NIDS has improved to generate session features with only some initial session packets, the same storage space as the existing NIDS will be eventually used if all those packets still need to be stored; thus, storage space issues will remain unresolved again. Therefore, a new approach to creating session features that can address these constraints is urgently needed.

As session features primarily use statistical values that reflect the entire session, packets need not be stored if each session feature can be represented as a recurrent expression. With this approach, packet data can be discarded immediately after updating the existing session feature value every time a packet is received. Therefore, if both ideas can be implemented, the overhead for storing packet data can be fundamentally solved, even if the NIDS uses packet and session features simultaneously.

The proposed approach presents solutions to the two questions presented in the aforementioned motivation: 'Can classification be performed each time a packet is received?' and 'Can session features be generated in a recurrent manner?' Each solution is described in detail.

3.2. Incremental Classification Using Packet Data

In a typical deep learning model with fixed input shapes, it is not possible to perform a gradual classification of the sessions to which the received packets belong each time they are received [21,22]. However, deep learning models, such as recurrent neural network (RNN), gated recurrent unit (GRU), and long short-term memory (LSTM), address these constraints by generating cycles between nodes [23–26]. Thus, the deep learning model of the proposed NIDS performs classification with the LSTM classifier for every packet received, stores the results, and uses this result and newly received packets as LSTM inputs to progressively continue the classification for the session. Therefore, the required storage space can be significantly reduced because the packet data itself need not be stored and only the output result of the corresponding cell of the LSTM needs to be stored. Figure 2 shows a block diagram of the LSTM used in the proposed scheme for the incremental classification of sessions. When the proposed NIDS receives the first packet (i.e., Packet 1) of the session, it inputs packet 1 to the first cell (i.e., Cell 1) of the LSTM classifier. Afterwards, the hidden states and cell states of cell 1 are temporarily stored in the buffer until the next packet of the session (i.e., Packet 2) is received. When NIDS receives Packet 2, it inputs the values stored in the buffer and Packet 2 into Cell 2 to proceed with the next classification process, and the hidden states and cell states of Cell 2 are stored in the buffer again. In this way, classification of one session is gradually progressed, and the output value of the last cell (i.e., Packet N) is used as a feature to classify the session.

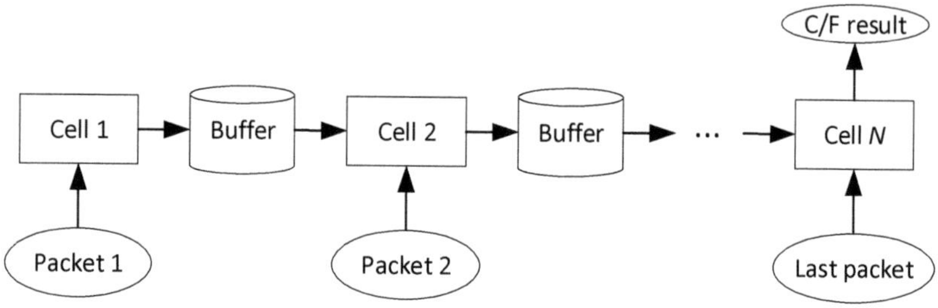

Figure 2. Proposed incremental classification for a session using LSTM.

3.3. Recurrent Session Feature Generation

For the feature set presented in ISCXIDS2012, the importance of each feature was measured using a random forest, and 15 features, including the top 10 features, were selected and analyzed to determine whether they could be expressed recursively. According to the analysis results shown in Table 4, although some states for feature generation need to be added, the features and state values for the current packet can be recurrently calculated through the features and state values for the previous packet. Using this approach, instead of collecting all packets and then creating session features, we update the state and features online as each packet is received and create the features shown in Table 1 when needed, eliminating the need to store any packets.

Table 4. Recurrently creating selected features without storing any packet data. Fifteen features are created recursively using seven states in addition to fifteen features. For example, for the Flow Duration feature, 'old Flow Duration + new Flow IAT' implies that a new Flow Duration value can be obtained by adding the updated Flow IAT value to the previous Flow Duration, when a new packet belonging to the current session is received.

Label	Type	Recurrent Expression
Last Flow Timestamp	State	current packet timestamp
Flow IAT	State	new Last Flow Timestamp—old Last Flow Timestamp
Fwd Last Timestamp	State	new current packet timestamp if the current packet is sent forwards
Bwd Last Timestamp	State	new current packet timestamp if the current packet is sent backwards
Fwd IAT	State	new Last Flow Timestamp—old Fwd Last Timestamp if the current packet is sent forwards
Flow IAT^2 Mean	State	(old Flow IAT^2 Mean $\times$ old Tot Pkts + new Flow IAT^2)/new Tot Pkts
Pkt Len^2 Mean	State	((old Tot Fwd Pkts + old Tot Bwd Pkts) $\times$ old Pkt Len^2 Mean + packet size^2)/(new Tot Fwd Pkts + new Tot Bwd Pkts)
Flow Duration	Feature	old Flow Duration + new Flow IAT
Tot Fwd Pkts	Feature	old Tot Fwd Pkts + 1 if the current packet is sent forwards
Tot Bwd Pkts	Feature	old Tot Bwd Pkts + 1 if the current packet is sent backwards
Flow IAT Mean	Feature	(old Flow IAT Mean $\times$ old Tot Pkts + new Flow IAT)/new Tot Pkts
TotLen Fwd Pkts	Feature	old TotLen Fwd Pkts + the packet size if the current packet is sent forwards
TotLen Bwd Pkts	Feature	old TotLen Bwd Pkts + the packet size if the current packet is sent backwards
Pkt Len Mean	Feature	(new TotLen Fwd Pkts + new TotLen Bwd Pkts)/(new Tot Fwd Pkts + new Tot Bwd Pkts)
Flow IAT Std	Feature	sqrt(new Flow IAT^2 Mean − new Flow IAT Mean^2)
Fwd Pkts/s	Feature	new Tot Fwd Pkts/(new Flow Duration − (new Last Flow Timestamp − new Fwd Last Timestamp)
Flow Pkts/s	Feature	(new Tot Fwd Pkts + new Tot Bwd Pkts)/new Flow Duration
Fwd IAT Mean	Feature	(old Fwd IAT Mean $\times$ old Tot Fwd Pkts + new Fwd IAT)/new Tot Fwd Pkts if current packet is sent forwards
Pkt Len Std	Feature	sqrt(new Pkt Len^2 Mean − new Pkt Len Mean^2)
Bwd Pkts/s	Feature	new Tot Bwd Pkts/(new Flow Duration − (new Last Flow Timestamp − new Fwd Last Timestamp)
Flow IAT Mean	Feature	(old Flow IAT Mean $\times$ old Tot Pkts + new Flow IAT)/new Tot Pkts
Flow IAT Max	Feature	max(old Flow IAT, new Flow IAT)

3.4. System Architecture

Essentially, the packet-feature-based NIDS uses only a few packets at the beginning of the session. Therefore, to use both the packet and session features, a session feature must be created using only the packets used by the packet-feature-based NIDS. If the number of packets used to create a packet feature and session feature is different, using more packets will eventually become a bottleneck in the feature creation speed.

Owing to varying packet sizes, even one packet cannot be classified by deep learning models, such as convolution neural network (CNN) and deep neural network (DNN), which can only process fixed input sizes. Therefore, a classifier consisting of a two-stage LSTM is required. The first-stage LSTM classifies packets of various sizes and inputs the result to a specific cell of the second-stage LSTM, enabling the second-stage LSTM classifier to classify sessions of various lengths.

Simultaneously, packets processed by LSTM update some features and state the values necessary for creating the rest of the session features. For the packet input to the last LSTM cell, after updating the features and states, the session features for the session to which the current packet belongs are created. The generated session features are concatenated with the output of the two-stage LSTM and passed as input to the DNN to detect intrusion.

Figure 3 shows the overall architecture of the proposed NIDS. When packets belonging to a session are sequentially received, NIDS updates states and some feature values used to create session features. When the NIDS receives the M-th packet, the states and features are used to generate session features after updating, and the created session features are input to the DNN. At the same time, the received packet is divided into equal sizes as shown in Figure 3, and each partial packet is sequentially input to the first stage LSTM to create a packet feature to be used in the second stage LSTM. The generated packet feature is input to each cell of the second stage LSTM, and after the packet feature for the M-th packet is input, the output of cell M is input to another feature of the DNN. Now, the DNN determines whether the session is malicious by combining the two input features as inputs and using them for classification.

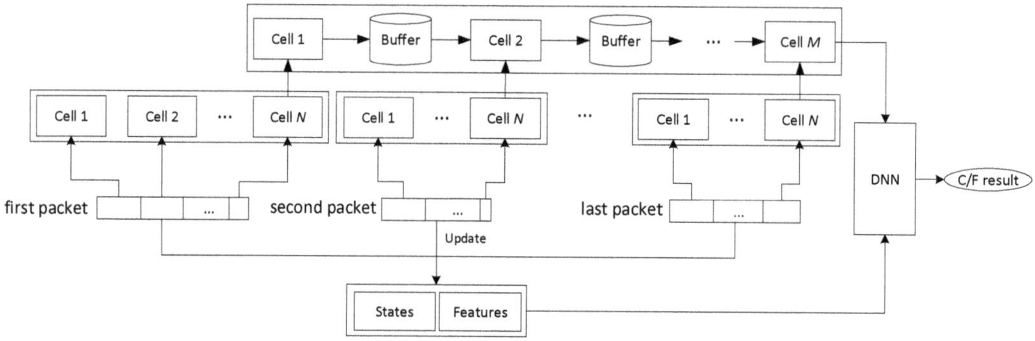

Figure 3. Proposed system architecture composed of two-stage LSTM and DNN.

4. Results

To accurately analyze the performance of the proposed scheme, we compared it with various existing deep-learning-based NIDS. In particular, the ISCXIDS2012 and CIC-IDS2017 datasets were used to verify the performance in various environments [9,10]; the characteristics of these datasets are listed in Tables 5 and 6, respectively. The fields dependent on a specific session, such as the source IP, destination IP, and source port, were removed from the packet data and session features to accurately train the ML models. In addition, representative deep learning algorithms, such as DNN, CNN, and HAST-I, were selected for comparison. Parameter settings for each algorithm are shown in Table 7. For performance analysis, we compared the performance of the proposed method and other algorithms by measuring the accuracy, precision, recall, F1-score, and confusion matrix. Each definition of metric is as follows:

- $\text{accuracy} = \dfrac{TP + TN}{TP + FP + FN + TN}$
- $\text{precision} = \dfrac{TP}{TP + FP}$
- $\text{recall} = \dfrac{TP}{TP + FN}$
- $\text{F1} - \text{score} = \dfrac{2 \cdot \text{recall} \cdot \text{precision}}{\text{recall} + \text{precision}}$

where, TP, TN, FP, and FN represent the true positive, true negative, false positive, and false negative, respectively. We also compared the proposed method and other NIDSs in terms of memory requirement and detection speed.

Table 5. Details of the ISCXIDS2012 dataset.

Number of features	81	
Number of classes	5	
Number of sessions	78,878	
Number of sessions for each class	Normal	22,382
	DDoS	21,702
	BruteForceSSH	18,145
	HTTPDoS	9487
	Infiltration	7162

Table 6. Details of the CIC-IDS2017 dataset.

Number of features	81	
Number of classes	11	
Number of sessions	123,236	
Number of sessions for each class	Benign	27,234
	DDoS	24,860
	DoS Hulk	20,419
	DoS GoldenEye	15,305
	PortScan	6459
	FTP-Patator	6267
	SSH-Patator	6029
	DoS slowloris	5256
	DoS Slowhttptest	4630
	Bot	3546
	Web Attack Brute Force	3231

Table 7. Parameter configuration for each NIDS.

Type	Parameter	Value
Proposed	Packet LSTM Unit	512, 256
	Session LSTM Unit	1024
	Session Unit	256, 128, 16
	Session Drop Out	0.1, 0.1, 0.1
	Activation	ReLU
CNN	Conv Unit	3, 3, 3, 3
	Kernel size	3, 3, 3, 3
	Unit	512, 256, 128
	Activation	ReLU
DNN	Unit	1024, 768, 512, 256, 128
	Density	0.5
	Activation	ReLU
HAST-I	Conv_unit	32, 64
	Kernel size	5, 5
	Pooling size	3, 3
	Unit	1024
	Activation	ReLU

4.1. Memory Requirement

Table 8 shows the memory size required to store the packet data used to create the feature. In the existing session-feature-based NIDS, the size of memory required to store packets for generating features is proportional to the average session length. On the other hand, the existing packet-feature-based NIDS uses some data for an initial fixed number of packets, so the required memory size is smaller than that of the session-feature-based

NIDS. The proposed NIDS minimizes the required memory area even though both feature types are used simultaneously. First, instead of using packet data to create session features, all features are created using only 17 states and some session features. Therefore, the proposed method always uses the same memory to create session features regardless of the session length. In addition, when generating packet features, only the current packet is used instead of several packets received so far, so only a fixed size of memory is used regardless of the session length. From Table 8, the existing session-based NIDS consumes 21,066 and 5791 bytes per session on average for the ISCXIDS2012 and the CIC-IDS2017, respectively. This means that the sessions in the ISCXIDS2012 are longer than the sessions in the CIC-IDS2017 and therefore use more memory. On the other hand, packet-feature-based NIDS requires 418 bytes per session in the CIC-IDS2017 instead of 357 bytes per session in the ISCXIDS2012. From this result, we find that ISCXIDS2012 contains more sessions, or six packets shorter than the CIC-IDS2017.

Table 8. Average memory size in bytes for storing the packet data needed to create the feature. Assume that only initial six packets are used for each session and only 100 bytes of each packet are used to create packet-based features.

Dataset	Session-Feature-Based	Packet-Feature-Based	Proposed
ISCXIDS2012	21,066	357	296 (196 + 100)
CIC-IDS2017	5791	418	296 (196 + 100)

The proposed NIDS creates two types of features simultaneously, using 196 bytes of memory per session for session features and only 100 bytes of memory per session for packet features. Therefore, since a total of 296 bytes of memory is used per session, the proposed NIDS consumes less memory than the existing session-based NIDS or packet-based NIDS, even though both features are used simultaneously. Above all, it is also a great advantage that the size of memory required per session is always fixed. It is advantageous for system design, such as being able to accurately calculate the memory required for the number of concurrent sessions that can be supported.

4.2. Detection Speed

Table 9 shows the number of packets required for intrusion detection per session between the existing session-feature-based NIDS and the proposed NIDS, where a smaller number of packets means faster detection speed. Although the number of packets required for detection varies depending on the dataset used, it shows that the proposed method uses a very small number of packets compared to the existing session-feature-based NIDS. In general, packet-feature-based NIDS is advantageous in increasing intrusion detection speed because it uses only some initial session packets. However, it should be noted that the proposed NIDS uses session features in addition to packet features. From Table 9, it is confirmed that the detection speed of the proposed NIDS can be greatly improved, unlike the existing session-feature-based NIDS, even though the proposed method uses the same session features to session-feature-based NIDSs. Due to the synergistic effect of packet and session features, the proposed NIDS can reduce the number of required packets effectively, increasing detection speed.

Table 9. The average number of packets required to detect an intrusion per session.

Dataset	Session-Feature-Based	Proposed
ISCXIDS2012	32.92	3.6
CIC-IDS2017	9.04	4.1

4.3. Intrusion Detection Accuracy

Figure 4 shows the intrusion detection rates of each algorithm for the datasets mentioned. As shown in the figure, the proposed scheme has the highest detection rate compared with the existing NIDS. In particular, it is noteworthy that the proposed NIDS has the highest performance for all metrics, i.e., accuracy, precision, recall, and F1-score, among all the comparison algorithms. Considering that the proposed method detects intrusion without packet storage, in contrast to the existing methods that require a large memory size to store many packets to create features, the high detection accuracy of the proposed NIDS proves that it effectively mitigates the disadvantages of existing NIDSs while maintaining high detection accuracy.

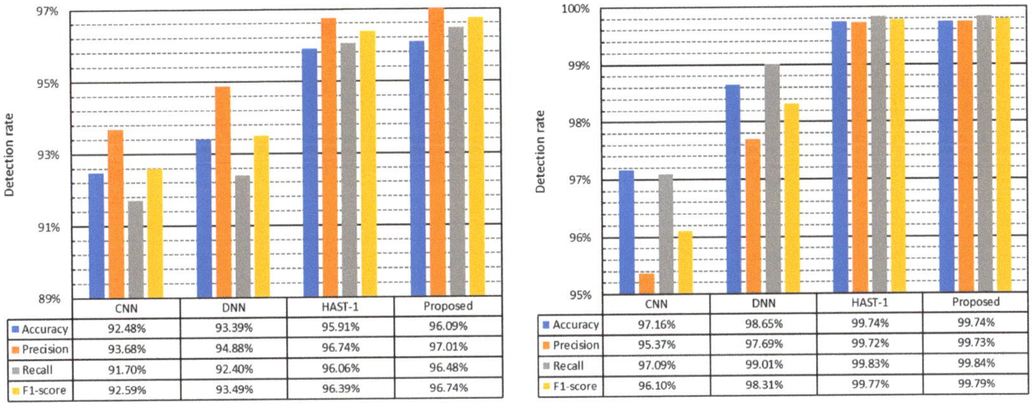

(a)	CNN	DNN	HAST-1	Proposed
Accuracy	92.48%	93.39%	95.91%	96.09%
Precision	93.68%	94.88%	96.74%	97.01%
Recall	91.70%	92.40%	96.06%	96.48%
F1-score	92.59%	93.49%	96.39%	96.74%

(b)	CNN	DNN	HAST-1	Proposed
Accuracy	97.16%	98.65%	99.74%	99.74%
Precision	95.37%	97.69%	99.72%	99.73%
Recall	97.09%	99.01%	99.83%	99.84%
F1-score	96.10%	98.31%	99.77%	99.79%

(**a**) (**b**)

Figure 4. Comparison of intrusion detection rates for each NIDS using each dataset. (**a**) ISCXIDS2012; (**b**) CIC-IDS2017.

4.4. Confusion Matrix

Figures 5 and 6 show the confusion matrices for each algorithm for the two datasets. The confusion matrix is advantageous for analyzing detailed performance because it can analyze the performance of individual classes. When using ISCXIDS2012, the proposed method has a slightly lower detection rate for distributed denial-of-service (DDoS) than HAST-I but exhibits the highest performance for the other classes.

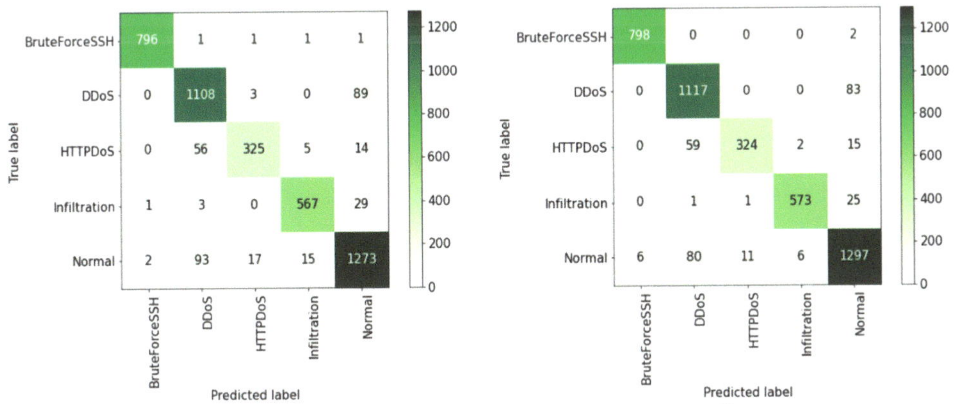

(**a**) (**b**)

Figure 5. *Cont.*

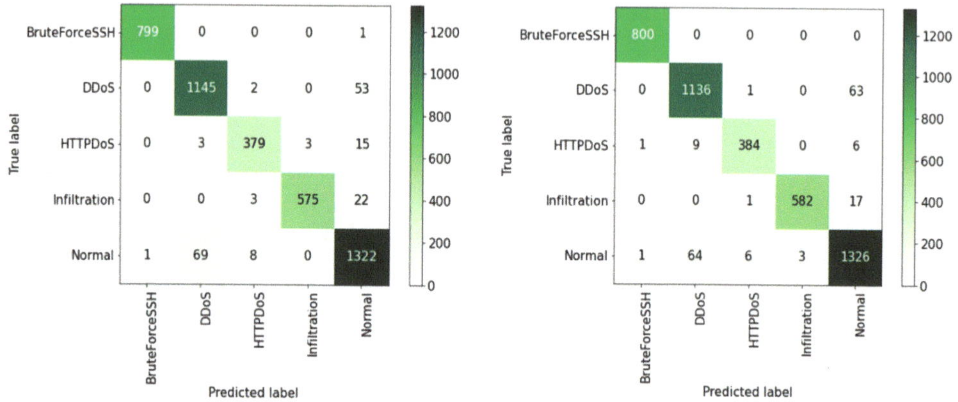

(c) (d)

Figure 5. Confusion matrix for each NIDS using ISCXIDS2012. (**a**) CNN; (**b**) DNN; (**c**) HAST-I; (**d**) Proposed.

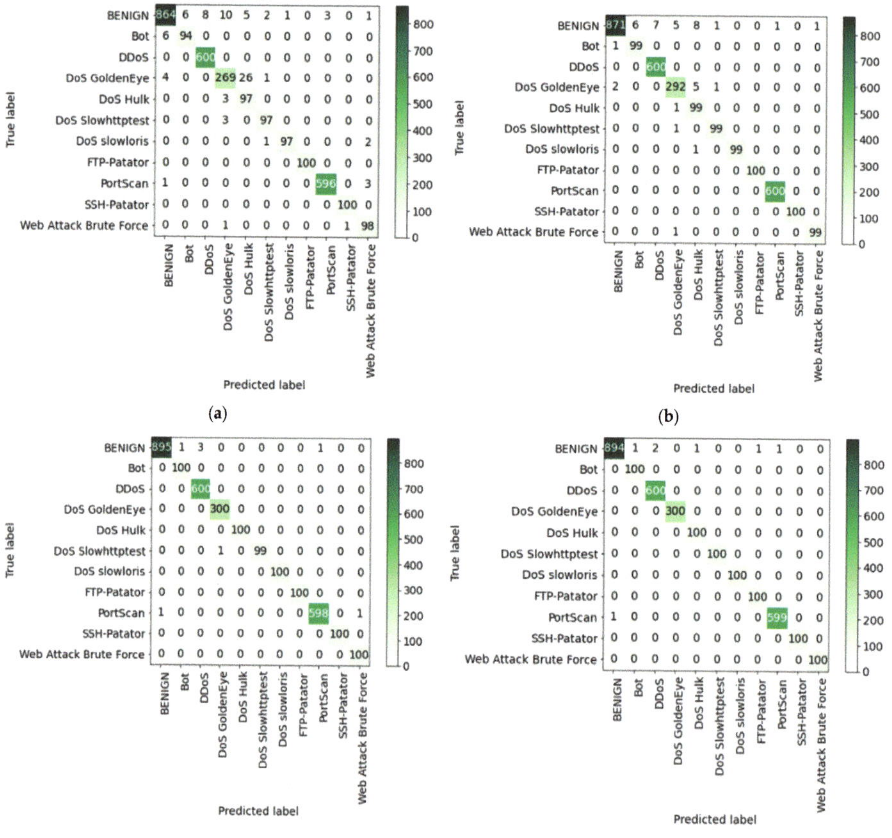

Figure 6. Confusion matrix for each NIDS using CIC-IDS2017. (**a**) CNN; (**b**) DNN; (**c**) HAST-I; (**d**) Proposed.

As shown in Figure 5, the DDoS class shows the lowest detection rate regardless of algorithm type. The reason is that DDoS attacks use many zombie PCs to attack one target with multiple sessions, so the characteristics are very different from other classes. Most NIDS today detect attacks based only on information about a single session, making them vulnerable to DDoS attacks that use multiple sessions. In this case, the additional use of characteristics for multiple sessions is helpful for detection.

In contrast, CIC-IDS2017 exhibits almost the same performance as HAST-I as shown in Figure 6. Therefore, these two confusion matrices confirm that the proposed NIDS has a high detection rate for the entire dataset but can also significantly improve the detection rate for individual classes.

CIC-IDS2017 has fewer noises than other datasets including the ISCXIDS2012. Therefore, compared to the ISCXIDS2012, the classification accuracy is higher regardless of the machine learning algorithm, so the margin for improving the accuracy is very small. Nevertheless, it shows that the proposed method is superior in that the proposed NIDS improves F1-scores by 3.67% points and 1.46% points, respectively, compared to DNN and CNN models. Since performance differences are evident for each classification model, it also shows that the CIC-IDS2017 is sufficient to be used for performance comparison.

5. Conclusions

The proposed NIDS does not need to store the received packets for feature creation; therefore, in contrast to the existing ML-based As, the amount of memory consumed for processing each active session is minimal. Because the same memory can support a greater number of concurrent sessions than other NIDS, the insufficient NIDS processing capacity owing to the recent increase in network traffic can be significantly improved. Above all, it is a significant advantage that the intrusion detection performance can be improved compared to the existing NIDS, despite the small memory footprint. As network attacks diversify and zero-day attacks become frequent in an environment where the amount of network traffic increases drastically, NIDS faces technically significant challenges in simultaneously improving processing capacity, speed, and detection accuracy. Hence, the proposed NIDS is expected to significantly aid in solving these problems.

As the proposed NIDS operates optimally when packets within a session are received in order, the amount of memory used for sorting increases when there are many out-of-order packets. The proposed NIDS is designed under the assumption that session packets are received without loss. However, some packets may be lost in real networks. It is expected that packet loss causes a negative impact on intrusion detection performance. The weaknesses of the proposed NIDS will be addressed through future research, and we expect that the proposed NIDS will be fully applied to an actual network.

Author Contributions: J.H. and W.P. wrote the paper and conducted the research. All authors have read and agreed to the published version of the manuscript.

Funding: This work was supported by the National Research Foundation of Korea (NRF) NRF2022R1A2C1011774.

Institutional Review Board Statement: Not applicable.

Informed Consent Statement: Not applicable.

Data Availability Statement: The datasets utilized in this paper are ISCXIDS2012 dataset (https://www.unb.ca/cic/datasets/ids.html (accessed on 1 February 2023) and CIC-IDS2017 dataset (https://www.unb.ca/cic/datasets/ids-2017.html (accessed on 1 February 2023).

Conflicts of Interest: The authors declare no conflict of interest.

References

1. Kruegel, C.; Toth, T. Using decision trees to improve signature-based intrusion detection. In Proceedings of the 2003 International Workshop on Recent Advances in Intrusion Detection, Pittsburgh, PA, USA, 8–10 September 2003; pp. 173–191. [CrossRef]
2. Wu, S.X.; Banzhaf, W. The use of computational intelligence in intrusion detection systems: A review. *Appl. Soft Comput.* **2010**, *10*, 1–35. [CrossRef]
3. Ektefa, M.; Memar, S.; Sidi, F.; Affendey, L.S. Intrusion detection using data mining techniques. In Proceedings of the 2010 Information Retrieval & Knowledge Management (CAMP), Selangor, Malaysia, 16–18 May 2010; pp. 200–203. [CrossRef]
4. Bilge, L.; Dumitras, T. Before we knew it: An empirical study of zero-day attacks in the real world. In Proceedings of the 2012 ACM Conference on Computer and Communications Security, Raleigh, NC, USA, 16–18 October 2012; pp. 833–844. [CrossRef]
5. Wang, W.; Sheng, Y.; Wang, J.; Zeng, X.; Ye, X.; Huang, Y.; Zhu, M. HAST-IDS: Learning hierarchical spatial-temporal features using deep neural networks to improve intrusion detection. *IEEE Access* **2017**, *6*, 1792–1806. [CrossRef]
6. Cisco. Cisco Annual Internet Report (2018–2023). White Paper, 2017–2022. Available online: https://www.cisco.com/c/en/us/solutions/collateral/executive-perspectives/annual-internet-report/white-paper-c11-741490.html (accessed on 15 January 2023).
7. Li, L.; Yu, Y.; Bai, S.; Hou, Y.; Chen, X. An Effective Two-Step Intrusion Detection Approach Based on Binary Classification and k-NN. *IEEE Access* **2017**, *6*, 12060–12073. [CrossRef]
8. Tavallaee, M.; Bagheri, E.; Lu, W.; Ghorbani, A. A Detailed Analysis of the KDD CUP 99 Data Set. In Proceedings of the 2009 IEEE Symposium on Computational Intelligence for Security and Defense Applications (CISDA), Ottawa, ON, Canada, 8–10 July 2009. [CrossRef]
9. Shiravi, A.; Shiravi, H.; Tavallaee, M.; Ghorbani, A.A. Toward developing a systematic approach to generate benchmark datasets for intrusion detection. *Comput. Secur.* **2012**, *31*, 357–374. [CrossRef]
10. Sharafaldin, I.; Lashkari, A.H.; Ghorbani, A.A. Toward Generating a New Intrusion Detection Dataset and Intrusion Traffic Characterization. In Proceedings of the 2018 4th International Conference on Information Systems Security and Privacy (ICISSP), Madeira, Portugal, 22–24 January 2018. [CrossRef]
11. Soheily-Khah, S.; Marteau, P.; Béchet, N. Intrusion Detection in Network Systems Through Hybrid Supervised and Unsupervised Machine Learning Process: A Case Study on the ISCX Dataset. In Proceedings of the 1st International Conference on Data Intelligence and Security (ICDIS), South Padre Island, TX, USA, 8–10 April 2018; pp. 219–226. [CrossRef]
12. Chen, C.; Xu, X.; Wang, G.; Yang, L. Network intrusion detection model based on neural network feature extraction and PSO-SVM. In Proceedings of the 7th International Conference on Intelligent Computing and Signal Processing (ICSP), Xi'an, China, 15–17 April 2022. [CrossRef]
13. Jiawei, D.; Kai, Y.; Zhentao, H.; Lingjie, H.; Lei, H.; Haixia, Y. Research on Intrusion Detection Algorithm Based on Optimized CNN-LSTM. In Proceedings of the International Conference on Networking and Network Applications (NaNA), Urumqi, China, 18–21 August 2022. [CrossRef]
14. Eddy, W. Transmission Control Protocol (TCP). Available online: https://www.rfc-editor.org/info/rfc9293 (accessed on 15 January 2023).
15. Samsung Secui. BlueMax NXG. Available online: https://www.secui.com/en/network/bluemaxngf (accessed on 15 January 2023).
16. Sharafaldin, I.; Lashkari, A.H.; Hakak, S.; Ghorbani, A.A. Developing Realistic Distributed Denial of Service (DDoS) Attack Dataset and Taxonomy. In Proceedings of the IEEE 53rd International Carnahan Conference on Security Technology, Chennai, India, 1–3 October 2019. [CrossRef]
17. Lashkari, A.H.; Draper-Gil, G.; Mamun, M.; Ghorbani, A.A. Characterization of Tor Traffic Using Time Based Features. In Proceedings of the 2017 3rd International Conference on Information System Security and Privacy, SCITEPRESS, Porto, Portugal, 19–21 February 2017. [CrossRef]
18. Drapper-Gil, G.; Lashkari, A.H.; Mamun, M.; Ghorbani, A.A. Characterization of Encrypted and VPN Traffic Using Time-Related Features. In Proceedings of the 2016 2nd International Conference on Information Systems Security and Privacy (ICISSP 2016), Rome, Italy, 19–21 February 2016; pp. 407–414. [CrossRef]
19. Sahu, S.; Mehtre, B.M. Network intrusion detection system using J48 Decision Tree. In Proceedings of the 2015 International Conference on Advances in Computing, Communications and Informatics (ICACCI), Kochi, India, 10–13 August 2015; pp. 2023–2026. [CrossRef]
20. Description of Kyoto University Benchmark Data. Available online: https://www.takakura.com/Kyoto_data/BenchmarkData-Description-v5.pdf (accessed on 13 January 2023).
21. Gu, J.; Zhu, M.; Zhou, Z.; Zhang, F.; Lin, Z.; Zhang, Q.; Breternitz, M. Implementation and evaluation of deep neural networks (DNN) on mainstream heterogeneous systems. In Proceedings of the 2014 5th Asia-Pacific Workshop on Systems (APSys '14), Beijing, China, 25–26 June 2014; pp. 1–7. [CrossRef]
22. Valueva, M.V.; Nagornov, N.N.; Lyakhov, P.A.; Valuev, G.V.; Chervyakov, N.I. Application of the residue number system to reduce hardware costs of the convolutional neural network implementation. *Math. Comput. Simul.* **2020**, *177*, 232–243. [CrossRef]
23. Rumelhart, D.E.; Hinton, G.E.; Williams, R.J. *Learning Internal Representations by Error Propagation*; Tech. rep. ICS 8504; Institute for Cognitive Science, University of California: San Diego, CA, USA, 1985.
24. Cho, K.; van Merrienboer, B.; Bahdanau, D.; Bengio, Y. On the Properties of Neural Machine Translation: Encoder-Decoder Approaches. In Proceedings of the 2014 8th Workshop on Syntax, Semantics and Structure in Statistical Translation, Doha, Qatar, 24 October 2014. [CrossRef]

25. Fawcett, T. An Introduction to ROC Analysis. *Pattern Recognit. Lett.* **2006**, *27*, 861–874. [CrossRef]
26. Hochreiter, S.; Schmidhuber, J. Long short-term memory. *Neural Comput.* **1997**, *9*, 1735–1780. [CrossRef] [PubMed]

MDPI
St. Alban-Anlage 66
4052 Basel
Switzerland
www.mdpi.com

Electronics Editorial Office
E-mail: electronics@mdpi.com
www.mdpi.com/journal/electronics

www.ingramcontent.com/pod-product-compliance
Lightning Source LLC
Chambersburg PA
CBHW041430210926
51850CB00013B/3395